Investigations

Explorations

Microeconomics

Microeconomics

EARL L. GRINOLS
University of Illinois at Urbana-Champaign

Houghton Mifflin Company ▼ **Boston** ▼ **Toronto**
Geneva, Illinois   Palo Alto   Princeton, New Jersey

Sponsoring Editor: Denise Clinton
Basic Book Editor: Karla Paschkis
Senior Project Editor: Jean Andon
Production/Design Coordinator: Caroline Ryan
Senior Manufacturing Coordinator: Priscilla Bailey
Marketing Manager: Mike Ginley

Cover design by: Beth Santos

Printed in the U.S.A.

Library of Congress Catalog Card Number: 93-78635

ISBN Number: 0-395-53998-6

123456789-DH-96 95 94 93

This book is dedicated to my parents, Earl L. and Betty Wolfe Grinols, and to the memory of their American forebears all the way back to Plymouth Rock, who provided me with the desire to pass on their values and to help educate a new generation.

Contents

▼

Preface

▼

Microeconomics is ultimately based on a few broad principles. More than transmitting a fixed body of material—however comprehensive—we recognize that, as instructors, our primary task is to give students a different way of thinking and looking at the world. As practicing economists, we have seen the profession's clear progress in recent years in its ability to illuminate the forces governing imperfect competition, to better tackle issues of asymmetric information, to provide new perspectives on the relation between property rights and the existence of markets, to explain modern rationales for and against government-backed strategic industrial policy, to analyze demand revelation principles—the list goes on.

Today's microeconomics students should be able to reap the benefits of this progress. An intermediate microeconomics textbook, being in many ways a gateway, should help students appreciate the value of economic principles in an up-to-date context, prepare them for what they will learn later, and, most of all, equip them with the best of today's thinking so that they may independently apply and extend their understanding to economic questions they will subsequently encounter.

This book is designed to help meet as many of these objectives as possible in a one-term course offered to the economics or business student. It contains many innovations to better reflect modern approaches and emphases, yet retains the essential structure and character of the established microeconomics curriculum.

Early in the writing process, I identified a number of areas where available texts did not seem to keep pace with contemporary approaches or emphases, and for which better treatment would help both instructors and students. This text's integrated coverage of information issues, its treatment of the firm manager's decisions in imperfectly competitive markets, its discussions of open economy issues, and its modern Coasian approach to externalities and public goods all reflect my goal of showing current thinking in the context of the core topics of microeconomics. I think a glance at the table of contents shows the extent to which the text has achieved this goal.

Content and Organization

A prominent feature of the book is its unified, coherent coverage. Treating topics within the framework of a standard outline at the place where the material logically fits allows a 16-chapter organization that better fits the typical college term. Covering newer topics where they are most relevant also makes more sense from the student's point of view, and imparts greater sophistication about evaluating the models the text presents. Students appreciate seeing how newer models can handle material that older ones can't. For example, the book treats asymmetric information in Chapters 2, 5, 6, 8, 11, 13, 14, and 15. This recognizes that information can be asymmetric with respect to quantity, quality, or price, and implies different market effects depending on different institutional contexts. I find that most students readily accept that information is not perfect and seem to take comfort in seeing models that take this into account.

Decision Making Focus. Another distinguishing feature of the text is its integrated decision making focus. This is a small, but I think important, adjustment to the market structure focus that frequently seems natural to the experienced economist but appears obscure—or worse, out of touch—to the student. Most students readily accept the constrained optimization paradigm. Further, many will become involved in business. Certainly all will be consumers, investors, and decision makers. The book's topical coverage thus emerges from the question, ''In this circumstance, what would this firm (or household, consumer, investor, manager, etc.) do?'' Since the circumstances in which the firm makes its decisions vary with market type, this approach complements the market structure focus but clarifies it for first-time learners.

Part III, for example, takes the student through quantity, pricing, and other decisions that a firm manager would make in perfectly competitive, monopolistic, monopolistically competitive, and oligopolistic markets. Discussions of firm decisions about pricing with market power—such as bundling, non-linear pricing strategies, and market segmentation—further enhance the core coverage, as does Chapter 9's modern treatment of monopolistic competition. A spatial approach, as used there, is sorely needed to explain why product diversification, advertising, and creation of niche products are all natural outcomes of competition for the modern imperfectly competitive firm.

Special note should be made of Chapter 10. This chapter introduces game theory in its rudimentary form, then carefully ties it to the type of competition that oligopolistic firms face. Using case studies, the chapter discusses different oligopoly solutions, Nash equilibria, credibility, and other aspects of strategic behavior. There is no need to teach oligopolistic equilibrium and game solutions in separate chapters or as separate concepts. Students learn the material once, and the numerous applications show its immediacy and relevance.

The decision making focus also determines the location of Chapter 5 on factor supply and Chapter 11 on factor demand. Naturally providing the material in two chapters allows more in-depth treatment of the important labor supply decision as distinct from the firm's derived demand, and enables more complete coverage of a number of institutional features of labor markets.

International Trade. The text emphasizes international trade issues, both in the comparative statics questions covered in the chapters and in the Investigations that close each part. To give just two examples, Chapter 2 covers the effects of an import quota in addition to discussing price ceilings and price floors, while Chapter 10 discusses strategic trade policy from the point of view of national advantage when government is considered a player with first mover advantage.

Welfare Economics. I consider welfare economics to be the capstone of a course in microeconomics. In spite of my best efforts teaching microeconomics over the past 15 years, I found many students unable to distinguish between the conditions for efficiency that apply in any economy and the specific demonstrations of efficiency in market economies. Since understanding efficiency requires appreciating this distinction, Chapter 12 examines the conceptual issues surrounding efficiency in any economy, while Chapter 13 looks at efficiency in perfectly competitive market economies. This feature has been well received, both by reviewers and by my own students. Chapter 14, dealing with externalities and public goods, follows naturally from the discussions in Chapters 12 and 13.

Special Features

Innovations in content and organization require a text that is simple to learn and teach from. To that end, *Microeconomics* uses a fully integrated pedagogical system designed for flexibility and ease of use.

Applications and Investigations. Applications help a text drive home its point and make each concept the student's own. To understand why it is in AT&T's interest to advertise and protect its market share regardless of how much its rivals MCI and Sprint advertise is to understand dominant strategies in a memorable way. This book has two to five shorter Applications within each chapter and a pair of longer, in-depth Investigations that close each part. The Applications and Investigations examine a wide variety of topics, ranging from funding day care to price wars among pizza franchises to taxes on greenhouse gases. Readers will recognize both classic topics and topics that are still in the news. The goal is student involvement: Applications demonstrate just-taught principles, provide examples, show relevance, and, by being topical, aid retention. Investigations show students how economists approach more detailed issues, providing a window into how microeconomics applies to the policy issues of today.

Explorations. In addition to the Applications and Investigations, each chapter includes one or two Explorations. These extend beyond core coverage to provide additional depth to the material. Many of these Explorations look at information topics, while others give insight into issues to which the theory applies but which might not be dealt with otherwise, such as labor supply decisions in two-income households. Applications and Explorations are clearly identified with icons and distinctive headings.

Active Reading Guides and in-text definitions. Active Reading Guides and in-text definitions are designed with the student in mind. Each chapter opens with a list of the Active Reading Guides, which also appear in the page margins near the material to which they refer. They point out key concepts to students, direct them to tasks they should be able to perform, and provide a review guide for later reference. In-text definitions highlight and introduce key terms, sharpening their meaning at the time when the student needs to see them most.

Summaries. Each chapter includes a concise summary of key concepts, coordinated with the Active Reading Guides. After reading the summary item, the student can easily find the relevant chapter coverage and use the Active Reading Guide there to test his or her understanding of the material.

As should be evident, the book's pedagogical system was designed to encourage students to interact with the subject. Anything that increases student involvement and helps students achieve their learning objectives makes their lives—and that of the instructor—more rewarding. That's what a good textbook is all about.

Course Designs

I think most instructors will be pleased with how easily the book fits into standard course designs. After a brief introduction and review of markets and comparative statics, the book moves to consumer theory, producer theory, and welfare economics (including externalities and public goods), in that order. Intertemporal issues and risk can then be covered if time permits, or inserted in the sequence where desired. For a course that emphasizes the firm, instructors can limit consumer theory or treat it later in the term, and cover Part III earlier in the course. Instructors who want to cover optimality and efficiency sooner have the option of moving right from Chapter 7 on perfectly competitive markets or from Chapter 8 on monopoly to Chapters 12 and 13 on optimality and efficiency. They can then return to imperfect competition if they wish, or go on to externalities, public goods, and market failure in Chapter 14. The flowchart in the To the Student preface shows these alternative sequences. Instructors should have little difficulty adapting the book to their needs.

Ancillaries

The Instructor's Resource Manual with Test Items, written by the author, with Test Items by Kent Hargis of the University of Illinois, includes for each chapter a summary of key concepts, teaching tips, representative lecture outlines, and answers to the text's Review Questions and Numerical and Graphing Exercises. Selected chapters include complete derivations for some models that the text presents in brief form. The Instructor's Resource Manual includes over 800 test items, which are also available on disk. Adoptors of the text can request the Instructor's Resource Manual and disk from the publisher. The Study Guide, by Elizabeth Sawyer Kelly of the University of Wisconsin, Madison, includes chapter reviews keyed to the Active Reading Guides, concept reviews, and a comprehensive variety of multiple choice items and problems.

Acknowledgments

As any author knows, the completion of a book is due to the help and work of many people. In my case, I first would like to acknowledge my wife Anne, who read drafts, made editorial suggestions, and provided support throughout. My four children, Shelly, Kimberly, Lindsay, and Daniel, deserve thanks for their patience when their father seemed to be so preoccupied.

The book would not be what it is without the keen input of both Denise Clinton, Sponsoring Editor, and Karla Paschkis, Basic Book Editor. Denise helped provide the foundation and impetus to begin the project, focused and sharpened the original conception of the book, and monitored its progress as part of the development team. Karla provided excellent and adroit editorial input, evaluating reviews and helping to devise strategies for providing what instructors wanted. Other members of the development team that deserve thanks include Greg Tobin and Sue Warne. Jean Andon, Senior Project Editor, ably saw the manuscript through production. Houghton Mifflin Company promised that it would provide only the finest developmental input and staff, and has more than lived up to its promise.

Finally, I would like to thank the reviewers, unknown to me at the time, who provided the text with a manifest reality check to see if it was on track. I hope that many of them will recognize changes prompted by their excellent suggestions. Their names are listed below.

Neil O. Alper, Northeastern University
Ashraf Afifi, Ferris State University
K. L. Bauge, Augustana College
Swati Bhatt, New York University, Stern School of Business
Eric Bond, Pennsylvania State University
Bradley M. Braun, University of Central Florida
Charles A. Capone, Jr., Baylor University
William T. Carlisle, University of Utah
Joni S. Charles, Southwest Texas State University
Joyce Cooper, Boston University
Mark Cronshaw, University of Colorado, Boulder
Carl Davidson, Michigan State University
Robert T. Deacon, University of California, Santa Barbara
Mark Dynarski, Mathematica Policy Research
Maxim Engers, University of Virginia
James Fain, Oklahoma State University
Ann I. Fraedrich, Marquette University
Simon Hakim, Temple University
Paul M. Hayashi, University of Texas at Arlington
Peter H. Huang, Tulane University
Sharon G. Levin, University of Missouri, St. Louis
Scott Masten, University of Michigan, School of Business Administration
David E. Mills, University of Virginia

W. Douglas Morgan, University of California, Santa Barbara
Kevin J. Murphy, Oakland University
Michael A. Murphy, Tufts University
David Neumark, University of Pennsylvania
Kenneth Ng, California State University—Northridge
Carol Rankin, Xavier University
David C. Rose, University of Missouri, St. Louis
Joshua Rosenbloom, University of Kansas
Jonathan Sandy, University of San Diego
F. M. Scherer, John F. Kennedy School of Government
John F. Scoggins, University of Florida
Helen Tauchen, University of North Carolina, Chapel Hill
Paul Thistle, Western Michigan University
Stephen Turnbull, Ohio State University
Thomas G. Watkins, Eastern Kentucky University
Donald C. Wellington, University of Cincinnati
Lawrence White, New York University Stern School of Business
Ben Yu, California State University—Northridge
Joseph Zeigler, University of Arkansas
Mark Zupan, University of Southern California

I owe special thanks to the text's dedicated accuracy reviewers: Bradley M. Braun, University of Central Florida; William T. Carlisle, University of Utah; Kent Hargis, University of Illinois at Urbana-Champaign; and Elizabeth Sawyer Kelly, University of Wisconsin, Madison.

To the Student

▼

Microeconomics can be divided into five main subjects, connected to one another in the overall economy:

1. Demand and supply in a single market;
2. Decisions of the consumer (what to buy and what to sell);
3. Decisions of the firm manager (the production process, what quantity to sell and at what price, what pricing strategy to employ, choice of product variety, R&D expenditures, and advertising);
4. How to evaluate the efficiency of a market system in generating welfare for its members;
5. The effects of risk and time on the decisions firms and consumers make.

There is a great deal of overlap and commonality in the tools used to analyze each of these topics. This book is designed to take you through microeconomics in a way that allows you to see the forest as well as the trees.

 ## Preview

The accompanying figure displays the five subject areas listed above as groupings of chapters in the book. Each individual chapter is set off in relation to the other chapters and subject flow of the book. The path from demand and supply to the consumer to the producer (under conditions of perfect or imperfect competition) to market efficiency relates succinctly the topography of the forest. To help remember the trees in each part, the book provides a number of learning and reviewing tools.

 ## How to Use This Book

Researchers in critical thinking and learning theory have found that the human mind does not learn the way some buildings appear to be built: by placing one brick on top of another, adding bricks one at a time until the structure is complete. Rather, the human mind learns fastest and best the way skyscrapers are built: by putting up an overall superstructure or frame first, than filling in the gaps until the building is complete. The importance of having a framework in place cannot be overemphasized.

This book is designed to help you first build your framework for each chapter, and then fill it in. Ultimately, the responsibility for learning rests with you, the student, but if you use the tools provided to become an active reader of each chapter, you should find your understanding rising, and your enjoyment rising with it. Here is how to use this book.

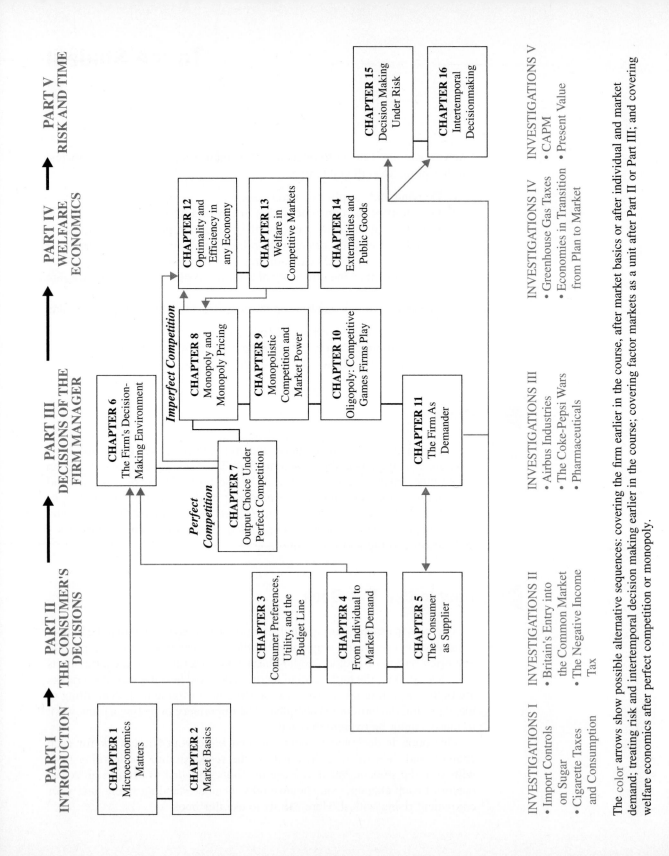

PART I
INTRODUCTION

CHAPTER 1
Microeconomics Matters

CHAPTER 2
Market Basics

PART II
THE CONSUMER'S DECISIONS

CHAPTER 3
Consumer Preferences, Utility, and the Budget Line

CHAPTER 4
From Individual to Market Demand

CHAPTER 5
The Consumer as Supplier

PART III
DECISIONS OF THE FIRM MANAGER

CHAPTER 6
The Firm's Decision-Making Environment

Perfect Competition

CHAPTER 7
Output Choice Under Perfect Competition

Imperfect Competition

CHAPTER 8
Monopoly and Monopoly Pricing

CHAPTER 9
Monopolistic Competition and Market Power

CHAPTER 10
Oligopoly: Competitive Games Firms Play

CHAPTER 11
The Firm As Demander

PART IV
WELFARE ECONOMICS

CHAPTER 12
Optimality and Efficiency in any Economy

CHAPTER 13
Welfare in Competitive Markets

CHAPTER 14
Externalities and Public Goods

PART V
RISK AND TIME

CHAPTER 15
Decision Making Under Risk

CHAPTER 16
Intertemporal Decisionmaking

INVESTIGATIONS I
• Import Controls on Sugar
• Cigarette Taxes and Consumption

INVESTIGATIONS II
• Britain's Entry into the Common Market
• The Negative Income Tax

INVESTIGATIONS III
• Airbus Industries
• The Coke-Pepsi Wars
• Pharmaceuticals

INVESTIGATIONS IV
• Greenhouse Gas Taxes
• Economies in Transition from Plan to Market

INVESTIGATIONS V
• CAPM
• Present Value

The color arrows show possible alternative sequences: covering the firm earlier in the course, after market basics or after individual and market demand; treating risk and intertemporal decision making earlier in the course; covering factor markets as a unit after Part II or Part III; and covering welfare economics after perfect competition or monopoly.

Chapter Overviews and End-of-Chapter Summaries. Each chapter opens with an overview. Read this first, then skim the section headings to the end of the chapter. There you will find a concise summary. Read this next to see what is in the chapter. There's no law against reading something at the end of the chapter sooner! You now have a framework for what you are about to learn. Not all terms and ideas will be clear, but you will find yourself remembering the rest of the chapter better as you delve into it in earnest.

Active Reading Guides. Now read the chapter actively. This does not mean you just soak up what floats by as you read. Instead, you answer questions to yourself as you read. To help you read actively, use the Active Reading Guides placed in the margins. These guides consist of questions or tasks you should be able to do after reading the material to which they relate. The Active Reading Guides tell you what you need to learn from each part of the chapter, and let you test yourself just after reading them to make sure you have picked up the information you need.

In-Text Definitions. In-text definitions give you another aid to your reading. They alert you to the fact that a new concept is being introduced and give you an immediate clarification of it. The glossary at the end of the book includes a complete listing of all definitions, cross-referenced to the chapter where they are introduced.

Summary. When you get to the end of the chapter, reread the summary. Each summary paragraph ends with a reference to the Active Reading Guides. Everything should look familiar by now. If not, go back to the corresponding Active Reading Guide to pick up what you need.

End-of-Chapter Questions. The book provides numerous review questions to test your understanding of the concepts. It also provides numerical and graphing exercises to test your ability to apply these concepts to representative problems. Answers to selected questions are provided at the end of the book. I tried to select questions to answer that would be useful to you in learning particular applications.

Reviewing for Exams and Self-Testing. Inevitably the day will come when you need to study the material again for an exam.

1. Use the end-of-chapter summaries and the in-chapter captions for a quick review.
2. Perform a self-test: Cover the chapter text but leave the Active Reading Guides visible. Answer each one without looking at the text.
3. If you can answer the Active Reading Guides without looking, then you are ready to answer questions from the end of the chapter or from the Study Guide.
4. You should now have a good idea of what you understand solidly, as well as where you are on shaky ground. Write up study notes emphasizing these ''shaky'' areas. Study your notes.

5. As a final step, write your own test as if you were the instructor. Then take your own exam.

As you can see, a lot of thought has gone into making the book useful for active learning. After all, I was once a student myself. If you take the active approach that the book is designed for, I predict great success for you. Best wishes.

E.L.G.

PART ONE

INTRODUCTION

This section begins our study by discussing the major themes, tools, and methods of microeconomics. Chapter 1 explains the organization of text material and its significance to the discipline of microeconomics. The chapter also provides the philosophical and organizational framework on which the rest of the course will be laid. Chapter 2 reviews the notion of a market, demand and supply curves, equilibrium, and comparative statics, laying a careful foundation for the treatment of consumer and producer theory in Parts Two and Three.

CHAPTER 1

Microeconomics Matters

This chapter introduces you to the substance of microeconomics. It begins by describing some of the tools and methods that are used in microeconomics, then turns to the basic procedures in applying economic reasoning to the actions of firms and households and to policy evaluation. It ends with a discussion of the extension of core microeconomics to different economic landscapes.

ACTIVE READING GUIDES

After reading this chapter, you should be able to answer the Active Reading Guides listed below. These guides also appear in the page margins, near the material to which they refer.

1. What is the fundamental reason for studying micro-economics?
2. What does microeconomics study?
3. What are the dimensional units of price, quantity, and value?
4. Give an example showing how price, quantity, and value can be read from a graph.
5. What does *comparative statics* mean?
6. Explain what a model is, and give examples of several different types.
7. What is the subject matter of price theory?
8. What are the two components of an optimization problem?
9. Define the general concept of equilibrium. Give an economic example.
10. What is the difference between partial equilibrium analysis and general equilibrium analysis?
11. Explain the distinction between positive economics and normative economics.
12. Why is the method chosen to organize society economically a policy question that involves normative economics?
13. Give examples of extensions of core microeconomics to different circumstances discussed in the text.

1.1 Introduction

Warsaw, August 10, 1990—As the crowds of shoppers promenade up and down Malczewskiego Street clutching brown paper bags bulging with produce, Adam Smith's invisible hand is meting out some rough supply-and-demand economic justice.[1]

Ideally, the Top 40 ought to be a kind of participatory democracy—the music of the moment, as voted through sales and requests, competing in a free market of noise.[2]

When every blessed thing you hold
Is made of silver, or of gold,
*   You long for simple pewter.*
When you have nothing else to wear
But cloth of gold and satins rare,
For cloth of gold you cease to care—
*   Up goes the price of shoddy.[3]*

1. Stephen Engelberg, ''Winning Shoppers' Hearts and Minds,'' *New York Times,* August 11, 1990, p. 4.
2. Jon Pareles, ''Money Talks, Top 40 Listens,'' *New York Times,* September 2, 1990, p. 18H.
3. W. S. Gilbert (1836–1911), quoted in *The Oxford Dictionary of Quotations,* Digital Edition, Fairlawn, NJ: Oxford University Press, 1989.

As the above quotations show, the parlance of economics has seeped into everyday discourse. Articles on Top-40 songs talk about the free market of noise, Adam Smith's invisible hand waves over discussions of Eastern Europe, and poetic verse speaks of the curiosities of price. They are all matters for which microeconomics matters!

▼
1. What is the fundamental reason for studying micro-economics?

It is easy enough to use economists' words, but understanding the ideas those words represent is a more exacting and more exciting task. Why study microeconomics? In the final analysis—after every other thing is known about an economy, including how scarce resources are allocated and prices are formed—the reason we care boils down to being able to answer the question: How does what goes on in the economy matter to people and their welfare? Microeconomics allows us to answer this question far better than we could otherwise. In studying this question, we must define what we mean by welfare and determine how well the economy provides it. Unlike macroeconomics, which is concerned with aggregate statistics such as the Gross Domestic Product, microeconomics looks at the actions of those who truly make the marketplace go: the households and firms whose choices, consciously or not, drive the economy.

To think clearly about microeconomic questions, you need a framework to organize your information. The following sections discuss several themes and techniques that you will encounter repeatedly in your study of micro-economics. The idea that firms and households make choices in their own self-interest, given the available options, is one such theme. The more you learn about microeconomic theory, the better you will understand that these themes order a seemingly random, arcane topic into a pattern. This chapter and future chapters reveal the pattern.

This chapter introduces you to the basic tools and core topics of micro-economics. It briefly highlights how these are applied in the text and extended to a variety of economic landscapes, and it shows you the methods that microeconomists use to apply their theories to the real world. Remember, this is an *introductory* chapter. We will rush past a lot of topics and come back to them in more detail later in the book. For now, I hope you get a sense of the power, applicability, and variety of microeconomics.

1.2 Variables and Tools of Microeconomics

Microeconomics is primarily concerned with explaining economic variables at the household or firm level.

▼
2. What does microeconomics study?

> *Microeconomics is the study of economics from the point of view of markets and the individual decisions of firms and households.*

Often the explained variables fall into one of three types: prices, quantities, or values. As you remember from your course in economic principles, price is the rate at which currency exchanges for a good. The price of milk, for example, might be $2.49 per gallon. If the exchange is one of barter, then price is the quantity of one thing that exchanges for another.

> *A **price** is the per-unit rate at which money is exchanged for a service or a good. For example, $1 per pound might be the price of something sold by weight. In barter, a **barter price** is a per-unit rate at which one thing is exchanged for another. For example, if two cows trade for one horse, the cow price of a horse is two cows per horse.*

Quantity is the amount of something in whatever units are used to measure it, such as gallons for milk or pounds for potatoes.

> *A **quantity** is the amount of a good or service measured in specific numerical units such as its weight, its number, its length, its area, or its volume.*

Values are variables that represent the total worth of something. If we use dollars as the measure, values are numbers expressed in units of dollars. Income, revenues, and profits are often treated as value variables.[4]

> ***Value** is the numerical representation of total worth. For example, the value of 25 objects that sell for a price of $5 per object would be $125.*

In the English language and in microeconomics, the word *cost* refers either to the price paid for something or to the total expenditure for something. Cost is therefore a price variable or a value variable.

Knowing that there are three types of variables to be explained in most economic situations helps make the underlying patterns more apparent. By the end of your course, you will be able to explain such things as how prices are determined in the marketplace, how firms and households choose what quantities of goods to produce and consume, and how these decisions determine firms' revenues and profits and households' incomes.

Although microeconomics is also concerned with such things as consumer welfare or satisfaction, these are not usually the types of things that are directly measurable or quantifiable in the way that you might weigh yourself on a bathroom scale. Prices, quantities, and values, however, usually *can* be observed and measured. Most variables that we discuss, therefore, will fall into one of these categories. Various changes in consumer welfare, for example, are often converted into dollar terms in microeconomic analysis.

Sometimes individual producers or consumers choose variables directly, as when your university plans how many students to admit, IBM lowers its prices to spur buying, or you decide to switch to ''lite'' food products to be more health conscious. At other times, producers or consumers must react to variables that are generated by the market as a whole. For example, General Motors might make smaller cars because of increased competition from abroad, or you might buy a CD player because it now costs less than a tape deck.

---

4. Income, profit, and sales are also often reported as value per unit of time. For example, a firm's annual sales may be reported as $3 million, or its quarterly profit as $750 thousand per quarter.

To evaluate these kinds of choices intelligently, a firm or household has to keep track of many different kinds of prices, quantities, and values. It is therefore worthwhile to spend a little time looking at dimensional units.

Working with Dimensional Units

▼
3. What are the dimensional units of price, quantity, and value?

A *dimensional unit* is a determinate quantity that tells what *type* of measurement (such as length, time, or volume) is being reported. For quantities, the dimensional units are units of the good or service itself: five pounds of sugar, three hours of labor, one dozen machines. Prices, on the other hand, have dimensional units of *dollars per unit of good* ($/unit good); for instance, you exchange $35 per shirt, or you pay $.89 per dozen eggs. Value, the third basic type of variable, has dimensional units of pure dollars.

These three kinds of dimensional units relate to one another very clearly. When a price is multiplied by a quantity of the corresponding good, the result is a value expressed in pure dollars.

$$\underset{\text{Price}}{\frac{\$}{\text{unit good}}} \times \underset{\text{Quantity}}{\text{unit good}} = \underset{\text{Value}}{\$}$$

For example, multiplying $3 per pound times 1 pound gives 3 dollars.

Keeping track of dimensional units can help to keep your economic thinking straight. For example, finding improper dimensional units when you compute with economic data is a hint that you should review your methods. If a price is multiplied by the quantity of a noncorresponding good, for example, the result will have units that are neither a price, a quantity, nor a value—a very good indication that something has not been done right.

As an example of keeping track of dimensional units, consider the following problem. You have arranged to travel by automobile from London to the north of England. Your car rents for £3.4 per hour (a price). Your car gets 25 miles per gallon of gasoline, which costs £2 per gallon (another price). If you travel at 60 miles per hour, and the exchange rate between dollars and British pounds is $1.75 per pound, how many dollars per hour are you spending on gasoline? How many dollars per hour are you spending altogether?

In this problem, there are enough pieces of information to make it worthwhile to use dimensional units to solve the problem and check consistency. Thus, let's arrange the information we have according to dimensional units. At each step we multiply to cancel units that should not appear in the final answer. Since we want our answer in terms of dollars per hour, we cancel any units that aren't dollars or hours. To find the dollars spent for gasoline, start by writing the exchange rate with its dimensional units to the right,

$$\frac{1.75\ \$}{£}.$$

Multiply this rate by the cost of gasoline,

$$\frac{1.75\ \$}{\pounds} \times \frac{2\pounds}{\text{gallon}}.$$

Continue with the remainder of the information and write

$$\frac{1.75\ \$}{\pounds} \times \frac{2\pounds}{\text{gallon}} \times \frac{1\ \text{gallon}}{25\ \text{miles}} \times \frac{60\ \text{miles}}{\text{hour}}.$$

Next, collect numerals and dimensional units together; cancel dimensional units in the numerator and denominator and multiply numerals to get

$$1.75 \times 2 \times \frac{1}{25} \times 60 \left[\frac{\$}{\pounds} \times \frac{\pounds}{\text{gallon}} \times \frac{\text{gallon}}{\text{miles}} \times \frac{\text{miles}}{\text{hour}} \right] =$$

$$8.4 \qquad\qquad\qquad \frac{\$}{\text{hour}}.$$

This is the amount of dollars you spend on gasoline per hour. Since you also spend money on renting the car, your dollar costs include

$$\frac{3.4\ \pounds}{\text{hour}} \times \frac{1.75\ \$}{\pounds} = 3.4 \times 1.75\ \frac{\$}{\text{hour}} = 5.95\ \frac{\$}{\text{hour}}.$$

This shows your rental cost in units of dollars per hour. You can add it to your gas costs to get 14.35 dollars per hour, which we write in the familiar form, $14.35/hour. Five pieces of information have been distilled to the desired one. Further, we are more confident that the information has been used correctly because we have checked dimensional units to see that they cancel to the desired form.

What were the key features in this example? First and foremost, we paid attention to the dimensions of the numbers that we used. There are many ways to manipulate five numbers, but we wanted only one type of number as our result. Second, we separated the dimensional units from the numerical quantities so we could cancel units as needed. Proper cancellation of units performs a check to ensure, for example, that we did not divide when we should have multiplied. Finally, we added numbers together only when they had the same dimensional units: adding 5 apples to 5 apples gives you 10 apples, but adding 5 apples to 5 pigeons does not give you 10 of anything because the things being added are not commensurable. You are invited to play with some examples of your own, even ones with nonsensical units, to test yourself on this simple but important topic.

We now turn to two other tools used in microeconomics: graphing and functions.

Graphing

When trying to analyze an economic situation, you will often find yourself with a great deal of information that you want to simplify so that you can use it. Graphing the data to provide a pictorial representation often accom-

Table 1.1	The Relationship Between Two Variables

Price *($/large pizza)*	*Quantity* *(number of large pizzas sold)*
$ 0.00	500
$ 1.00	475
$ 2.00	450
$ 3.00	425
$ 4.00	400
$ 5.00	375
$ 6.00	350
$ 7.00	325
$ 8.00	300
$ 9.00	275
$10.00	250
$11.00	225
$12.00	200
$13.00	175
$14.00	150
$15.00	125
$16.00	100
$17.00	75
$18.00	50
$19.00	25
$20.00	0

plishes this objective because the visual information shows patterns that can be taken in at a glance. You can also redraw the graph to see the effect of changing variables.

Let's say that you own a local Domino's pizza franchise, and you notice that your sales of large pizzas on Friday nights vary with the price you charge. Table 1.1 shows the prices you charge on the left and the resulting quantities sold (numbers of large pizzas) on the right. The fact that your sales of large pizzas are determined by the price you charge indicates a *functional relationship* between the two variables "price of large pizza," p, and "quantity of large pizzas sold," q. To say that "q is a function of p" means that once p is given, q is determined according to the rule, or function, that relates the two variables.

Although Table 1.1 summarizes the information about the relationship between the price of large pizzas and the quantity you sell, there are simpler ways to arrange the information, such as graphing it. *Graphing* involves plotting variables on a two-dimensional diagram using vertical and horizontal distance to represent the magnitude of the two variables. For example, in Table 1.1 we find that at a price of $1 per large pizza, you sell 475 pizzas.

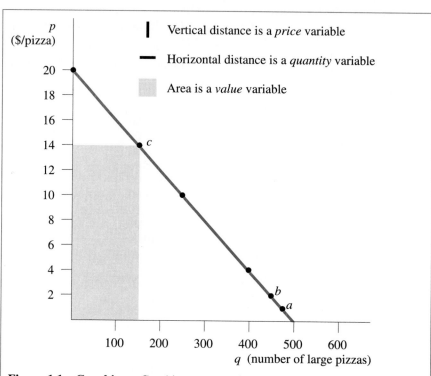

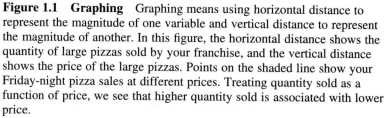

Figure 1.1   Graphing   Graphing means using horizontal distance to represent the magnitude of one variable and vertical distance to represent the magnitude of another. In this figure, the horizontal distance shows the quantity of large pizzas sold by your franchise, and the vertical distance shows the price of the large pizzas. Points on the shaded line show your Friday-night pizza sales at different prices. Treating quantity sold as a function of price, we see that higher quantity sold is associated with lower price.

To show this piece of information on the graph in Figure 1.1, label the horizontal axis as the quantity direction and label the vertical axis as the price direction. Distances in the vertical direction, therefore, represent the price of pizza, and distances in the horizontal direction represent the quantity of pizza. Move *up* one unit on the vertical axis, *to the right* 475 units on the horizontal axis, and plot the resulting point as point *a*. Refer next to Table 1.1 to see that 450 large pizzas are sold when the price is $2 per pizza. Moving up two units (for price) and 450 units to the right (for quantity) results in point *b*. Continuing in this way, we can plot every price and quantity pair in Table 1.1. Figure 1.1 graphs a sample of other points that lie to the northwest of points *a* and *b*.

   Price in this case is sometimes called the *independent variable,* because its value is chosen first, independently of needing to know quantity. Quantity is the *dependent variable,* because its value is chosen second, and it depends on price. Historically, microeconomists have drawn the relationship between price and quantity with the independent variable (price) on the vertical axis rather than the horizontal axis. This reverses the diagram from the standard format used in mathematics, where the independent variable is on the horizontal axis. This book will adhere to the standard practice in economics. Thus, when looking at slopes in diagrams and at their equations, you will have to take into account the different orientation of the diagram.

▼
4. Give an example showing how price, quantity, and value can be read from a graph.

As you graph more points, they begin to reveal a pattern: connecting the points results in the curve in Figure 1.1 passing through the plotted points. Lines representing a relationship between two variables are often called *curves*, even though they are sometimes straight. Using this curve as a reference, you can read from the graph information about the relation between price and quantity sold. For example, if you want to know how many large pizzas sell when the price is $14 per pizza, you move up 14 units in the price direction and then move to the right until you reach the line. This happens at point *c*. Since point *c* lies 150 units to the right in the quantity direction, you find that you sell 150 large pizzas when you charge $14 for a pizza.

In addition to showing the relationship between price and quantity, the graph can also tell us about value. For example, can you see from the graph how many total dollars you would take in each Friday night if you set your price, say, at $14 per large pizza as at point *c*? In this case, the total value in dollars is shown by the shaded area below point *c*. To understand why this shaded area equals the value, remember the dimensional units of price, quantity, and value. To calculate a rectangular area, we multiply its height by its width; therefore, the shaded area on the graph equals price (the vertical dimension) times quantity (the horizontal dimension), or $/pizza × pizzas. The result of this multiplication is pure dollars, the dimensional unit of value.

Functions

Graphing is not the only way to summarize the relationship between two variables, such as the price of pizza and the quantity of pizzas sold. Another way to represent the relationship is to write

$$q = f(p),$$

where the notation is read, "Quantity is a function of price." Using the word *function* simply means that there is some rule you use to go from the price to the quantity.

When one variable is a function of another variable, the rule that describes the relationship can often be written in a mathematical formula that is easier to write than an entire table of numbers and that lends itself to calculations. In the case of Table 1.1, the functional relationship between price and quantity can be written as

$$q = f(p) = 500 - 25p.$$

That is, to get from price to quantity, multiply price by 25 and subtract the result from 500. This is the quantity that will be sold at the price.

If you were to graph the function $f(p) = 500 - 25p$, you would start with a price, say 0, find the corresponding quantity—in this case $500 - (25 \times 0) = 500$—and graph the point as zero units up and 500 units to the right. Since this point is on the horizontal axis, it is called the *horizontal intercept* for the line. Doing this for another price, say 2, would yield the quantity $500 - (25 \times 2) = 450$, which you would plot in the same way. Doing this for all choices of price would lead to the line in Figure 1.1 that we obtained from connecting points plotted from Table 1.1. At price 20 we find that the point is on the vertical axis. Intersection of the line with the vertical axis is called the *vertical intercept,* just as intersection with the horizontal axis is the horizontal intercept. Thus the function compactly contains the same information as the more cumbersome table.

Occasionally in this book we will need to distinguish between different prices and quantities using various notations. In general, we will try to use lower-case letters for prices and quantities except in cases where it is important for the notation to distinguish between variables that are individual numbers (*scalars* in mathematics) and lists of numbers (*vectors* in mathematics). In these few cases, we will use upper-case letters to refer to vectors. For example, p would be a (scalar) price and P would be a vector of prices. Where needed, we will use subscripts to identify variables that apply to individual firms or households and superscripts to identify marketwide distinctions. For example, q_i might be used to refer to the quantity sold by firm i, and q^D might be used to refer to the quantity demanded by the market.

The Method of Comparative Statics

Functions and graphs are practical tools for presenting data more simply, but we can use them to go beyond mere description. Once we have determined what might happen in a particular economic situation, we often want to know how things would *change* if a part of the problem were different. This requires predictive ability. Understanding prices, quantities, and values also means being able to describe how they will change in response to a change in circumstances. The method that economists use to analyze such change in a variable due to a change in circumstance is *comparative statics.*

▼

5. What does *comparative statics* mean?

For example, if James currently buys new cars at the rate of one every four years, how much would this rate increase if cars cost $7,000 each instead of $15,000? Using a model of James's buying habits, we can predict what his purchases would be for each price. The difference between the two is the answer to our question. This method compares the outcome in each of two static situations that differ from one another because another variable (in this instance, the price of cars) is different. The term *statics* refers to a system in balance, at a natural resting place, or in equilibrium. (Equilibrium is discussed later in this chapter and in more detail in Chapter 2.) Comparative statics, therefore, is the comparison of two equilibrium or static positions.

Let's return to the pizza-franchise example to see how graphs and functions can be used in comparative statics. Say there is a sports arena down the street from your franchise. You notice that you sell more pizzas on nights when there is a game or concert at the arena. Likewise, you sell fewer pizzas when the arena is empty. This means that for any given price you must take into account a new variable—call this A for attendance—which also affects quantity. You now write $q = f(p, A)$ to indicate that quantity of pizza sold, q, depends on attendance, A, as well as price, p. To show the relationship between quantity and attendance, you could form another table like Table 1.1 with different columns for each attendance level. Such a table could get quite large, however, since there are a large number of combinations of price and attendance for which you would want to know quantity sold. In this case, therefore, we will use a functional form for $f(p, A)$ to summarize the same information,

$$q = f(p, A) = 350 - 25p + \frac{A}{300}.$$

Using this function, you can find quantity for whatever price and attendance combination you wish. Notice that if arena attendance is 45,000, the quantity of pizzas sold is identical to the original function graphed in Figure 1.1.[5]

This Friday's attendance at the arena was 45,000 fans, and you sold 150 large pizzas at \$14 per pizza. Suppose that you now want to know how many more pizzas to order for next Friday's game, when attendance at the arena will be 90,000 fans. This is a *comparative statics* question, because you want to find out how one variable (quantity) will change when another (arena attendance) rises.

To solve this comparative statics problem graphically, graph the sales you will have for each price when attendance A equals 45,000. This graph, the same one that we did in Figure 1.1, is reproduced as the left-hand line in Figure 1.2. On the same diagram, graph the quantity of pizzas sold at different prices if attendance A equals 90,000. This graphing is done in exactly the same way in which you graphed the original information, except that now you substitute 90,000 for A in the formula. The quantity of pizzas sold is $f(p, 90,000) = 350 - 25p + 90,000/300 = 650 - 25p$. The horizontal intercept for the new line is 650, since $q = 650$ if $p = 0$. We also know that for each dollar of price increase, quantity falls by 25. This rate of change determines the slope of the line. Recalling the economic convention that places price on the vertical axis, we see that the more negative the slope, the steeper the line. Setting $p = \$14$ gives $q = 300$, which is point d in Figure 1.2. By connecting several plotted points, we get the right-hand line in Figure 1.2.

If you fix your price at \$14 per pizza, your quantity sold must lie somewhere on the horizontal line shown at $p = \$14$/pizza. The intersection of the original curve with the horizontal price line occurs at point c, representing 150 pizzas sold. When attendance rises to 90,000, the intersection occurs at point d, corresponding to 300 pizzas. The comparative statics effect of increasing attendance from 45,000 to 90,000, therefore, is to raise pizza sales by 150 pizzas. You should prepare for selling 300 pizzas total.

5. If $A = 45,000$, then $350 - 25p + A/300 = 350 - 25p + 45,000/300 = 500 - 25p$. This is the function graphed in Figure 1.1.

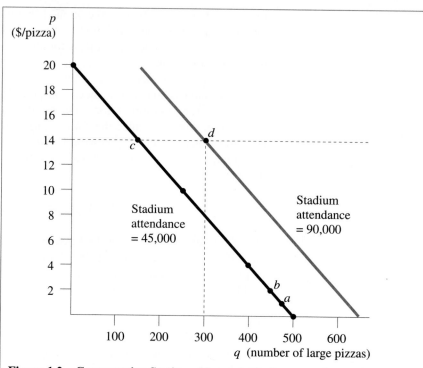

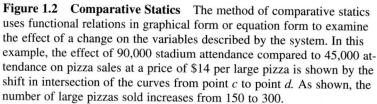

Figure 1.2 Comparative Statics The method of comparative statics uses functional relations in graphical form or equation form to examine the effect of a change on the variables described by the system. In this example, the effect of 90,000 stadium attendance compared to 45,000 attendance on pizza sales at a price of $14 per large pizza is shown by the shift in intersection of the curves from point c to point d. As shown, the number of large pizzas sold increases from 150 to 300.

Mathematically, the comparative statics effect of increasing attendance to 90,000 can be calculated from the original equation simply by comparing the quantity q' when price is $14 per pizza and attendance is 45,000 [the quantity $f(14, 45,000)$] with the quantity q'' when price is $14 per pizza and attendance is 90,000 [the quantity $f(14, 90,000)$]. Peforming the computation, we find that $q' = 150$ and $q'' = 300$. The difference is the comparative statics effect of the attendance increase.

Although this example is simple, it illustrates an important feature about the method of comparative statics: the graphical solution to a comparative statics problem often involves shifting one or more curves to see the effect that this has on the location of the intersection point. The location of the intersection point graphically depicts the level of the variable or variables in which we are interested (in this case it was quantity). Each curve on a graph represents a particular relationship between variables that must be satisfied;

and if two relationships are involved, only a point on both curves—the intersection—satisfies both relationships. In our case, the relationships that had to be satisfied were that the price was $14 per pizza (giving us the horizontal line in Figure 1.2) and that the number of pizzas sold had to be defined by $q = f(p, A)$ (the slanted lines). Later in the book we will use comparative statics methods to consider the effects of taxes and other variables on economic variables such as price, quantity, and tax revenues.

Models and Model Building

▼
6. Explain what a model is, and give examples of several different types.

When an architect plans for the construction of a building on a particular site, he or she will often make a three-dimensional replica or model of the building to help in the visualization of the final structure. In our discussion of pizza sales and stadium attendance, we also made use of a model.

*A **model** is any representation of a larger reality that contains its most important features and can be more easily understood and manipulated than the object under study.*

Today, an architect's model might be a computer simulation instead of a physical, three-dimensional construction. The same is true of microeconomic models. In microeconomics our models will sometimes be contained in a diagram, sometimes in a series of equations, and sometimes in something as simple as a flow chart. In the pizza-sales example above, we modeled the sales both with an equation, $q = f(p, A)$, and with a diagram. By moving curves in the diagram around or by manipulating the equation for pizza sales, we used the model to predict the effect of an increase in arena attendance. In this case, the task we performed was simple enough that the model probably was not vital to our accomplishing what we wanted; but even in this basic case, the model helped simplify the analysis. In more complicated situations, a model often becomes crucial to accomplishing what we want.

Robert Solow, a Nobel Prize–winning economist, has said that a road map on a scale of one to one is useless. For the same reason, a model that is just as complicated as the thing being described is probably not useful. Models, in some essential way, must be simpler than the thing they describe. In the pizza example, we started with a detailed table of numbers. Modeling the same information in a simple formula not only replaced the table, but made it easier to add elements to our analysis and see the effects of a change in them.

Building a model helps in other ways as well: (1) it provides structure to the problem; (2) it helps sort out what is important to getting the answer and what is not; and (3) it makes it easier to check the solution for internal consistency. In the problem of finding out how fast we were spending money in our drive from London to the north of England, arranging the dimensional units as we did was a form of modeling. By making us keep track of cancellation of dimensional units, the model provided structure for checking the consistency of our work and helped ensure that we were using the numbers in the right way.

Since many economic models consist of sets of equations, each one describing the relationship between two or more economic variables (prices, quantities, and so forth), the laws of mathematics help to keep our work correct as we manipulate the equations. The most careful thought, therefore, goes into making the model and selecting the relationships to be put into the equations. Thereafter, the manipulation and comparative statics can be done following the rules of mathematics. As another Nobel Prize–winning economist, Paul Samuelson, said of economic models, *you* don't have to be smart, the mathematics is smart.

Although a model is only as good as the parts that make it, graphical models in economics turn out to be incredibly powerful. In this book most of our models will consist of graphs, because graphs can be manipulated by shifting the locations of curves. To the extent that curves are the diagrammatic representation of equations, these models are equivalent to a system of equations. To paraphrase Paul Samuelson, you don't have to be smart, the diagrams are smart. One purpose of this book, therefore, is to teach you which diagrams to use and why.

1.3 Price Theory

▼

7. What is the subject matter of price theory?

Since price is one of the key variables in microeconomics, it is not surprising that much of microeconomics deals with price theory. Questions in price theory might include the following: Why do some commodities have high prices and others low prices? What determines a worker's wage? Why do prominent entertainers make large salaries while those in other professional occupations often get less?

> **Price theory** *is the study of the workings of the price system, including (1) how prices are determined by the actions of buyers and sellers, and (2) how prices influence the choices and actions of buyers and sellers.*

One of the more famous price theory puzzles is the water-diamond paradox. Why is it that a vital good such as water has a relatively *low* price, while an inessential and less useful object such as a diamond has a *high* price? The paradox is resolved when we realize that a price may or may not reflect the intrinsic usefulness of the item to life as judged by some means other than its value in exchange. In most places in this country, water is plentiful in relation to the minimal needs for life that make it essential. The consumer benefits little from having more water once these needs are met. Thus the willingness to pay for water beyond these needs is small. Diamonds, on the other hand, are relatively rare in relation to the demand for them for decorative and sentimental reasons. Willingness to pay for a diamond is therefore high. Were the situation reversed, and water in scarce supply, water might well have a higher price than diamonds. Market price reflects what is called *marginal valuation* in exchange, meaning the amount that someone is willing to give up for another (marginal) unit. When we use price theory to understand demand, supply, and what a price represents, the "paradox" is not really a paradox.[6]

1.4 Predicting Choices Through Optimization

If firms or households make choices randomly, without regard for self-interest or the costs of one choice relative to another, there is little that we can hope to say about their economic behavior in general. In fact, firms and households seem to choose what they do with an eye to self-interest, given the options that they have available and the relative costs to them of alternative choices. Our description of firms and households is based on this observation. Thus, in the microeconomic analysis of firms and households, we have to consider the nature of the optimization problem that the firm or household faces. *Optimization* is the process or act of choosing the best alternative from a set of possible choices.

Imagine that Helen's dream vacation is to fly to Paris on the Concorde, stay at the Ritz, and dine at three-star restaurants. However, she hasn't been able to save more than $900, and so she can afford only to fly a super-saver, stay at a boarding house, and eat at bistros. Helen's $900 and what it will buy are her *constraint*; a ticket on the Concorde and a dream vacation in Paris are her *objective*. These are the two components of her optimization problem. Seeing that she won't be able to afford her dream vacation, she decides that she would rather go to Paris on a budget than not go at all. Helen ranks her feasible alternatives and chooses the most attractive one. Throughout this book, we will examine just this sort of optimization problem by looking at economic decision makers and describing their objectives and constraints.

Of course, individual consumers aren't the only ones to face optimization problems. A firm's objective might be to maximize its profits.[7] A police department might want to minimize the amount of crime in its precinct given its personnel and budget. A governor might want to fund a jobs program to lessen dependency on the state in the least costly way. All of these decisions can be analyzed in terms of the microeconomic principles we will study in this book. Think of Helen: we described what she wanted to do, how she ranked her alternatives, what was feasible given her constraints, and what she ended up actually doing. In a nutshell, choosing what is "best" from the available alternatives is what optimization is all about.[8]

▼
8. What are the two components of an optimization problem?

---

6. Chapter 2 discusses demand and supply in detail.

7. *Maximization* means making the outcome as favorable as possible given the circumstances in which the firm or household operates.

8. Chapters 3 and 4 discuss rationality and consumer choice, and Chapters 6 through 11 discuss the objectives and choices of firms. Chapters 12 and 13 look at welfare economics to consider what "best" might mean for the economy as a whole.

1.5 Equilibrium

In addition to describing what individual firms and households do, microeconomics is interested in describing their interactions. A grocery store is a good example of interaction between buyers and sellers. The customers decide which goods to buy on the basis of prices, their personal preferences, and the amount of money they have available. The store's manager decides what goods to stock on the shelves, how much space to use to display them, and so on. These choices take place day after day over long periods of time with a certain kind of balance. For example, the grocery store does not continually overstock milk so that large portions of what is put on the shelves spoil each week and must be discarded. Similarly, the manager avoids understocking, which would cause shortages and perhaps anger the shoppers. The store does best when the manager neither overstocks nor understocks. The manager also puts higher prices on those items that the store has a harder time getting and pays more for. This causes consumers to limit their purchases of the higher-priced items, again working in the direction of balancing the supply of grocery items on the shelves with what the consumers demand. An important part of describing the interaction of buyers and sellers in the market for groceries, therefore, is to describe this balance in an effective way. To do this, microeconomics uses the concept of equilibrium.

▼
9. Define the general concept of equilibrium. Give an economic example.

Equilibrium *is a state of balance between opposing or divergent influences.*

In Chapter 2 we will refine the definition of equilibrium as it relates to prices and quantities in a market. For now, we want to focus on the bigger picture of why equilibrium is such an important tool in microeconomics. Let's return to the grocery store and say that we want to describe what goes on there. If our description has the consumers buying more milk each week than the manager stocks the shelves with, it cannot be right. If our description has consumers buying less milk every week than the manager stocks, it suggests that our manager could raise profits by stocking a little less milk each week and saving on spoilage costs. Either way, the absence of balance or equilibrium between the rate of purchases by consumers and the rate at which shelves are stocked suggests that our description is inconsistent or wrong, because the manager's and consumers' actions do not match up sensibly. If the grocery store operates without a balance between purchases and stocking, we also might suspect that eventually something will change to bring the two into line. On the other hand, a grocery store that has balance between its stocking and purchases can more likely sustain that situation without need for change.

We find two important features of equilibrium in this example: (1) equilibrium implies that the choices of households and firms must ''fit together'' in a consistent way; and (2) the choices must represent a ''resting place'' or sustainable position for what is being described. If our description of the grocery store, or whatever we are describing, does not represent an equilibrium, it is often the case that something in our description—for instance, a price or a description of the firm's or household's choice—should be adjusted. Just as optimization is a tool for describing what individual firms or households do, equilibrium is a conceptual tool for describing how their actions interact.

Frequently in microeconomics we will define what it means for a market to be in equilibrium without saying what happens if the market is *out* of equilibrium. Maybe we don't always need to know this. Maybe what we are studying adjusts fast enough that we never get the chance to observe it out of equilibrium. Describing how some entity, such as a grocery store, behaves if it is out of equilibrium is often a separate task from describing how it behaves in equilibrium. In fact, describing the nonequilibrium situation can be very difficult. Generally, there is only one way for a market to be in equilibrium in a given circumstance, but there may be many ways for it to be out of equilibrium.

Partial Equilibrium Versus General Equilibrium

▼
10. What is the difference between partial equilibrium analysis and general equilibrium analysis?

Just as individual firms and households interact in the buying and selling of a single product (say, milk), so the buying and selling of *all* products, from shoes to sealing wax, interact with one another to make up the economy. Let us refer to the buying and selling by firms and households of a given good or service as a *market*.[9] Then, when *all* the markets for *all* the products in an economy are in equilibrium, we call this a *general equilibrium*. To distinguish the analysis of a single product, where equilibrium in only one market is considered, from analysis that considers equilibrium in all markets, we use separate terms.

> *(i)* ***General equilibrium analysis*** *is conducted under the assumption that all markets are in equilibrium. Thus all market variables and the effects of all decisions by firms and households have been accounted for in the analysis, and they are reflected in prices and quantities.*
> *(ii)* ***Partial equilibrium analysis*** *looks at only one market, or a subset of markets, treating some or all of the variables generated in the other markets as fixed. It does not require that all market variables and the effects of all decisions by firms and households be accounted for in the analysis and reflected in the prices and quantities.*

How do you know when partial equilibrium analysis is the appropriate way to approach a problem? Sometimes, requiring general equilibrium would greatly complicate the study without materially affecting the results. For example, in deciding what the effect of a small sales tax will be on purchases of cigarettes, it makes sense to consider what the change will do to the market price of cigarettes. It would not make much difference, though, to note that the income of tobacco firms will decline, reducing the income of shareholders in tobacco companies and thereby reducing the demand for cigarettes because these shareholders will have less money to spend, causing them to buy fewer

---

9. Again, Chapter 2 will give a more formal definition. For now, we will preview in more general terms some of the ideas that we will encounter later.

cigarettes.[10] Although the effect operating through the income of shareholders is present, it is too small to matter. Partial equilibrium analysis in this case would treat the consumer's income as given, ignoring the small income-related effects of the tax.

On the other hand, there are cases where the effects operating through other markets are too imporant to ignore. In these cases general equilibrium analysis is called for. For example, assume that you want to know the employment implications of increased exports of Boeing airplanes to foreign countries. Since increased Boeing employment comes partly from decreased employment in other firms in the economy, an accurate assessment would have to look at the employment effects over all markets. In this case general equilibrium analysis would be more appropriate.

How can you tell whether to use partial equilibrium analysis or general equilibrium analysis? There is no simple rule. It depends on your judgment about whether the answer you get by partial equilibrium analysis is accurate enough for your purposes.

We now leave our preview of the tools of economics and turn to a discussion of the philosophical objectives of microeconomics, the ultimate why's and wherefore's of what we are trying to accomplish.

1.6 Positive Versus Normative Economics

A popular joke about economists goes like this: if you laid all the economists in the world end to end, they couldn't reach a conclusion. Although the message of the joke is probably untrue when it comes to agreeing on matters of economic analysis, there is a germ of truth to it when it comes to agreement on the goals of economic policy. As a social science, economics deals both with *what is,* on which there is often much agreement, and with *what should be,* on which there is often less agreement. In this section we discuss both roles for economics and the relationship of microeconomics to policy.

What Is Versus What Should Be

Refer again momentarily to our earlier example of Helen's trip to Paris. Describing Helen's choice of vacation in terms of an optimization problem allows us to make an important distinction between what Helen *does* and what Helen *should do* to reach some agreed-upon objective. The first type of analysis relates to the action chosen, regardless of whether it is "best" in any sense, and the second relates to what action *should* be chosen because it is best according to some standard. The first is called positive economics, and the second is called normative economics.

---

10. Investigation I.B will take a closer look at the connection between cigarette smoking and taxes.

▼
11. Explain the distinction between positive economics and normative economics.

Positive economics *is the study of what is, how the economic system works, and what economic decision makers do. Positive economics studies existing economic conditions and explains them.*

For example, what is the effect of international trade on the wage rate of union workers? Why does the price of wheat rise when there is a drought? What is the effect of a wage increase on the supply of workers? Why do markets with single sellers charge prices higher than their cost of production? Do interest rates tend to rise when a society is declining in terms of some particular definition of decline? Each of these questions relates to positive economics.

When we compare how the economic system works with a *norm* or standard of operation, however, we do normative economics.

Normative economics *is the study of what should be done in an economic situation. Given an objective and a set of constraints, normative economics asks what action is best to get as close to the objective as possible.*

If a firm is trying to maximize profits, for example, we might ask whether this is indeed the right thing to do. Is the firm's choice to maximize profits the best for the firm's shareholders? Is the free market the best way to meet the material needs of consumers? Is the distribution of income the best that it can be to reflect the relative contributions to output of different workers? These are questions in normative economics.

Normative economics frequently involves making judgments about the effectiveness of policies or actions by firms, households, and government. Implicit in making these judgments is the acceptance of an objective and a listing of the constraints that are present. Disagreement about normative economics questions can occur either because of differences in opinion about what the objectives should be or differences in opinion about the nature of the constraints. For example, you cannot talk about whether the personal income tax is the best way to raise revenue until you describe the alternative taxes that could raise the same revenue (constraints on the types of taxes you can choose from) and until you explain *how* you evaluate the effects of the different alternatives (how they measure up relative to your choice of objectives). If the alternative is a national sales tax on all items and your objective is to collect revenue without encouraging an increase in overall taxes, you might prefer the income tax if you believe the temptation for Congress to raise the level of a national sales tax would be too great to withstand. People listening to your argument might agree that the government should raise taxes in this way, or they might discuss whether your objectives are correct or whether other alternative taxes are feasible.

Since normative economics often requires subjective input regarding economic objectives—and subjective input can vary from person to person—most of the material in this book falls under the classification of positive economics. However, occasionally we will discuss normative questions, as in Chapter 8 when we discuss whether the actions of firms that are sole sellers of their product should be changed in any way, or in Chapters 12 and 13 when we discuss how to measure the effectiveness of an entire economy in providing material well-being to its members. In those cases we will explicitly describe the objectives and constraints that we are using to make normative judgments.

Policy and Welfare

Normative questions frequently arise from a desire to evaluate policy decisions. Should the federal government raise the minimum wage, say, to $500 per hour so that every worker's income would be $100,000 per year? Should the president sign a bill limiting textile and apparel imports? Is a reduction in the marginal tax rate on personal income to 15 percent a good idea for encouraging greater output? Should the government nationalize the airline industry or the health care industry? In each case, the ultimate acceptance or rejection of the policy proposal depends on how it affects the incomes and welfare of individual households. The intelligent evaluation of economic policy, therefore, is closely tied to using the tools of microeconomics. Whether the intervention in the market system is through taxes or subsidies, through changes in the rules for imports, or through direct government provision of certain goods and services paid for by taxes, each has welfare consequences. Grounding in the theory and application of microeconomics allows us to make more informed critiques of policies and proposals.

The need to use microeconomics to evaluate different policy alternatives stems from the pervasive existence of scarcity, which is the smallness of supply in proportion to demand. Concerning economic well-being, it is usually true that whatever one's income and assets, it is possible to imagine being better off with more. However, the fundamental fact of life is that there are limits on how much each of us can have, and this means that policies that alter the production and distribution of goods and services affect different households in different ways.

The largest policy decision of all relates to the overall structure of the society. In practice, there are many ways of organizing a society. A system in which households and firms buy and sell at free market prices is one option, but is it the best? Are there other ways of organizing that would "do better" according to our definition of welfare? How would we measure whether a different organization of society works better? Being able to ask these types of questions and having a framework that allows us to provide answers is one objective of this course.

▼
12. Why is the method chosen to organize society economically a policy question that involves normative economics?

APPLICATION: Dollars and Sense

Self-interest says that if an objective can be accomplished through one of several alternatives, buyers will rationally choose the cheapest alternative.[11] Since price is what buyers pay, however, choosing the right alternative in the

11. Information on rock salt in this section is drawn from David Morris, "A Free Market Demands Accurate Prices," *Building Economic Alternatives,* Fall 1990, p. 4.

broadest sense is possible only if prices accurately reflect the choice's costs to the community. Thus, what you don't know *can* hurt you. Take, for example, the problem of deciding how to prevent car accidents on slippery winter streets in northern states.

In the case of rock salt, the preferred de-icer of northern states, the price to cities and local governments is a penny or two a pound, or about $20 a ton. An alternative like calcium magnesium acetate would cost much more, perhaps $400 a ton. So every year states spread hundreds of thousands of tons of rock salt on roads and highways. Rock salt, however, has costs to the community that are not reflected in its price to government. Rock salt, in addition to being a de-icer, is a corrosive, rusting away cars, bridges, and other metal objects it contacts, and polluting roadside vegetation. The Environmental Protection Agency estimates the corrosion costs of rock salt at 40 cents per pound, and a New York State agency puts the number closer to 80 cents per pound or $1,600 a ton. Thus, with prices inaccurately representing community costs, governments make poor choices that harm citizens. Minnesota, for example, spends $4 million applying 200,000 tons of rock salt to its roads each year instead of using an alternative like calcium magnesium acetate that would cost it about $80 million. The $76 million in government savings, however, results in damages to Minnesota residents and businesses of somewhere between $160 million and $300 million—clearly a bad deal for the state as a whole.

So why don't state and local governments make needed changes? The microeconomics answer, in part, is that they have no incentive to do so. Moreover, if citizens who would benefit from a change try to make their will known through collective action, they often incur more costs than their share of the benefits would be worth. A letter to your representative, for example, costs you time, paper, and a stamp and has little chance of effecting a change. You are probably better off simply paying to wash your car more frequently in the winter and hoping to prevent corrosion in that way. Partly, however, the answer is also one of knowledge. The more people in private life and government become educated to the concept of externalities (the divergence between price and community cost, discussed in Chapter 14), the more likely it is that the problem will be recognized and corrected. ■

EXPLORATION: Extending the Core Theory

We've covered a lot of ground in this chapter. We've reviewed the major tools and techniques of microeconomics—variables and units, the use of graphing, functions, comparative statics, and modeling—and we've discussed the major themes of microeconomics that we will pursue in the rest of our study—optimization, equilibrium, and positive and normative economics. But microeconomics is far broader than just tools, techniques, and themes. Beyond the core coverage, the microeconomics theory you will learn in the remainder of the book can be extended to a variety of other economic landscapes. It is in applications to the ''special cases'' that the core theory quickly bears fruit and the power of the tools you've learned becomes clear. In short, microeconomics is more than just a series of subjects: it is a way of thinking that can be helpful to you for the rest of your life. ■

Symmetric Versus Asymmetric Information

▼
13. Give examples of extensions of core microeconomics to different circumstances discussed in the text.

What are some of these extensions to which the microeconomics way of thinking can be applied? Core microeconomics models usually assume that all players on the economic stage have the same information—in other words, that the information is symmetric. But in the real world this is often not the case. For instance, when a baseball team negotiates with a player, it cannot be sure it knows everything about the player; a pitcher's agent might know that his client has chronic elbow pain, but may not disclose this information. Baseball teams spend a lot of time and money trying to ensure that they have the best information possible, but asymmetric information is the norm in this market. In our study of microeconomics, we will pay more attention to markets with asymmetric information than is customary because there is often such a stark difference in how the market behaves in the presence of asymmetric information as compared to symmetric information. Chapter 2 discusses the effect of asymmetric information on market equilibrium of demand and supply; Chapter 5 discusses asymmetric information as it relates to the supply of work and efforts to obtain college degrees; Chapter 8 considers the effect of asymmetric information on pricing; Chapter 11 discusses asymmetric information with respect to equilibrium in the labor market; and Chapter 15 discusses effects of asymmetric information in insurance markets. As a rule, asymmetric information can affect interactions in many types of markets. Other extensions of core theory apply more specifically to the behavior of firms.

Decisions That Extend Beyond Price and Quantity

As we will see in Part Three, the most important decisions firms face are how much of their product to make and how to go about making it. These decisions help determine everything from the firm's size to the prices it charges to how much machinery it uses. Imagine a small bakery that wants to expand its operations. Right now, it makes a hundred loaves of raisin pumpernickel bread a day completely from scratch, delivers only to restaurants in the town, and charges premium prices. In the hope of selling its bread in supermarkets, it decides to automate the mixing and baking and lower the price of each loaf to make the product more competitive with national brands. These are nuts-and-bolts price and quantity choices, covered in Chapters 6 through 8. But the bakery needs to decide other issues as well. Should the bakery advertise? If so, where would its ads help the most, and how much money should be devoted to ads? Should the firm make other kinds of bread as well? Should it use less expensive ingredients, or would this compromise its distinctive ''gourmet'' image? These types of issues involve extensions of the core microeconomics theory, and we will look at them in Chapter 9.

Game Theory and Imperfect Competition

The assumption that firms take market prices as fixed and behave as if they are unable to influence them by their actions underlies the perfect competition model described in Chapter 7. When a market does not satisfy the requirements of perfect competition, core theory then describes the market in terms of single-seller models (monopoly, covered in Chapter 8), models with many sellers of differentiated products (monopolistic competition, covered in Chapter 9), or models with few sellers (oligopoly, discussed in Chapter 10). Economists have increasingly come to realize, however, that the behavior of firms in imperfectly competitive oligopolistic markets is well described by techniques used in game theory.[12] Because the insights of game theory carry over nicely to a wide range of economic phenomena from how two criminals respond to police interrogation, to explaining why credibility and reputation are important in their own right in imperfect competition, to illuminating why firms can sometimes help themselves by limiting their range of options, Chapter 10 explains imperfect competition and oligopoly using a game theory approach. The chapter also uses game theory to explain the rationales for certain trade policies of national governments, including subsidies for domestic firms. Investigations III then provides case studies of oligopolistic competition and national industrial trade policy.

Private Versus Public Goods

Most of the analyses in this book focus on private goods, such as sandwiches, restaurant meals, shirts, toothbrushes, and motor oil, but there are also ''public'' goods such as national defense, the interstate highway system, Yellowstone Park, and radio broadcasts. Public goods characteristically benefit many in society rather than an individual consumer. Of course, one problem with public goods is that people will try to benefit from them without paying. Economists call this free riding. Public goods also raise the issue of externalities. Externalities arise when a firm's or household's production or consumption of a good directly affects another firm's or household's well-being or production. We encountered an externality earlier when we discussed the costs of rock salt. In another example, some summers ago medical waste began washing up on the New Jersey coastline. Because hospitals in New York City were dumping their waste, many people considered the public beaches unsafe. On those same beaches, it is likely that some visitors were blasting their radios or littering, thus making the beaches unpleasant for others. Both of these cases involve externalities. Chapter 14 considers externalities and the economics of public goods—how to decide how much to produce, how to pay for it—by applying principles learned in the core chapters.

12. The definition of a game is discussed in Chapter 10, but in general games include any interaction between two or more players where the payoff to each player depends on his or her own choices and on the choice of the other players.

Certainty Versus Risk

As mentioned earlier, asymmetric information can significantly affect market behavior. Yet even when everyone is equally well informed, decision making may entail *risk*. Neither the baseball team nor the player's agent we discussed could predict with certainty how well the player would play on the basis of past performance. When an economic agent makes a decision knowing the range of possible good and bad outcomes and their relative probabilities but cannot ensure which outcome will occur, the agent makes a decision with risk. When we decide whether to buy shares of Genentech (a biotechnology firm), Pacific Gas and Electric (a West Coast utility), or Microsoft, we take a risk on how our choice of firm will do. The risks and expected rewards are different in each case. Knowing how to evaluate whether the reward is worth the risk is the type of question considered in Chapter 15. The combination of risk and asymmetric information also leads to two other phenomena discussed in Chapter 15: moral hazard and adverse selection. Moral hazard occurs in insurance markets when the individual buying insurance has the ability to influence the probability of an accident's occurring. Only the insuree knows how careful he or she is being to avoid the need for an insurance payout. Adverse selection occurs when an insurer cannot distinguish buyers of insurance who are bad risks from those who are good risks. The insurer must deal with the problem that a policy it offers may disproprotionately attract customers who are bad risks, thereby giving it an adverse selection of customers.

Intertemporal Decision Making

The great bulk of models covered in this book are one-period models; that is, they do not take account of the passage of time. However, we live in a world in which planning for the future is a large determinant of how we use our resources today. When you borrow money today to invest in a business or buy a car, planning to pay back your loan in the future, you are engaging in *intertemporal* decision making. Saving and investing are a key part of most people's lives at one time or another. Is it wise to carry an unpaid balance on a credit card with an interest rate of 19 percent, or would taking out a small home-equity loan at 10 percent be a better alternative if the up-front cost is $2\frac{1}{2}$ points (the borrowing fee expressed as a percentage of the amount borrowed)? What is the value of a stream of monthly payments of $100 each for three years? These are all questions of intertemporal economics.

Fortunately, the core models can be extended without too much difficulty to deal with issues of time. Consumer theory explains the household's purchases of different types of goods and services, and it can also be used to explain the pattern of the household's purchases across time periods. Since saving and investing change the household's pattern of consumption over time, it follows that consumer theory can be extended to explain borrowing and lending. Chapter 16 discusses the determinants of borrowing and lending, the formation of interest rates (the price of borrowing money), and the use of interest rates in intertemporal planning.

Firms also make intertemporal decisions. Among the most important of these are decisions on how much to invest in research and development (R&D). Questions of balancing costs today against future streams of benefits are central to evaluating the effectiveness of an R&D program. Also part and parcel of the firm's R&D planning is its assessment of the nature of future competition, perfect or imperfect, and of the profits it will make in the expected competitive environment. These subjects, too, are discussed in Chapter 16.

Closed Versus Open Economy

Finally, although traditional microeconomic theory was typically presented as if economies were implicitly closed—in other words, as if they did not trade with foreign nations—this model is becoming less and less valid. One look around a typical mall makes this abundantly clear: many of the cars in the parking lot are Swedish, German, Japanese, or South Korean; most of the appliances on the shelves are imported as well; the clothes in the shops are sewn in the Philippines, India, or Taiwan; and many of the shoes are manufactured in Singapore or Brazil. Changes in trade among European countries are changing the face of the European Economic Community. In North America the U.S.-Canada Free Trade Agreement and the proposed North American Free Trade Area are much in the news and likely to remain prominent well into the next millennium. This book employs closed economy models, but it also makes a point of discussing the application of microeconomics to the open economy whenever appropriate. For example, Chapter 2 discusses applications of demand and supply to trade; Chapters 12 and 13 explicitly include the effect of international trade in discussing country welfare; and material in Chapter 10 on imperfect competition is applied to international markets. Investigations I through IV each begin with an application of microeconomic theory that involves international trade. The topic therefore appears frequently in the book as topics warrant.

There is much to be excited about as you begin your study of microeconomic theory. Since you can have the enjoyment of learning a topic for the first time only once, make the most of it. Once you have learned it, you will have the satisfaction of better understanding commerce and *homo economicus.*

Summary

Active Reading Guide numbers are given in parentheses at the end of each summary item.

1. Much of day-to-day life involves material issues that are important for the welfare of households and firms. Microeconomics studies the economic actions of households and firms at the individual or micro level, explaining their actions in terms of prices, quantities, and value variables. (1, 2)

2. Keeping track of dimensional units helps to organize microeconomic analysis. Other important analysis tools include graphing, which is the two-dimensional plotting of data; the use of functions to summarize the mathematical relationships among variables; the construction of models, which are representations of the thing being studied that are simpler and easier-to-manipulate than the thing itself; and the method of comparative statics, which analyzes the change in variables from one position to another. Comparative statics can also be used to predict the effects of changes on other economic variables. (3, 4, 5, 6)

3. One of the important divisions of microeconomics is price theory, the study of the workings of the price system and the formation of prices. (7)

4. Most economic analyses and applications are grounded in two principles, the first of which is optimization. Household and firm choices can be described as the outcome of optimization problems. Optimization requires knowing the agent's objective and the constraints on the agent's available choices. (8)

5. The second major principle is equilibrium. Equilibrium is a state of balance or rest for a system. In microeconomics, equilibrium is used to describe what it means to have agents' actions consistent with one another in a system that is at rest. Partial equilibrium analysis looks at equilibrium in a single market or a subset of markets; general equilibrium analysis looks at equilibrium in all markets at once. (9, 10)

6. Microeconomic analysis can be either positive or normative. Positive economics describes what is; normative economics sets an objective and attempts to specify what action is best to get as close to the objective as possible. Using microeconomics to evaluate economic policy involves both positive economics, as when the effects of a policy are described, and normative economics, as when a policy prescription is chosen from a list of alternatives. (11, 12)

7. Microeconomics can also be described as a method of thinking. Once the basic principles are learned, they can be extended to many kinds of situations that differ in one or more ways from the circumstances described by the core theory. Important extensions covered in the text include asymmetric information; decisions by firms that do not involve prices or quantities; game theory and imperfect competition; public goods and externalities; decision making under conditions of risk; intertemporal decision making; and the open economy. (13)

Review Questions

*1. When rock salt was bought for road de-icing, its price did not accurately reflect community costs, and so too much was used. If a homeowner buys rock salt to de-ice his driveway, will the price be similarly inaccurate, leading the homeowner to use too much? If so, why? If not, what is different between this case and the public case?

2. If everyone's material desires were fully met, why would price theory be unnecessary as a field of study? (Hint: Why is the price of air zero?)

*3. Discuss the following statement: "Price theory helps explain why diamonds, which aren't necessary for life, have a higher price than water, which is."

* Asterisks are used to denote questions that are answered at the back of the book.

4. Which of the following actions involve optimization?
   a) Deciding to use blue cheese or ranch dressing on your salad
   b) Deciding whether to go to a matinee movie on an off day of the week or to a regular showing on Friday night
   c) Saving money to buy a new car in the future or borrowing to buy a new car now
   d) Choosing which stock to invest your money in

*5. Assuming that consumers optimize in their purchases at a grocery store, describe a kind of purchase that you could predict they would *not* make.

6. Separate and describe the two components of optimizing behavior for (a) an example that is economic in nature, and (b) one that is not.

*7. In each of the following optimization problems, describe the constraint and the objective.
   a) Buying the least expensive gasoline for your automobile
   b) Choosing to buy more lean meat to avoid heart disease
   c) Choosing to sell financial planning services rather than accounting services

8. You are asked to predict production in the minivan market in the coming year. The model you construct says that consumers plan to buy 1.5 million units, and producers plan to produce 2.5 million units. Do you go with the higher number, the lower number, or revise your model? Explain why.

*9. Define *comparative statics* and relate the concept to the use of models.

10. "You can't do comparative statics without a model, however simple." Discuss.

*11. Explain why the following statement is true or false: "Since general equilibrium analysis considers all markets at the same time, there is no reason ever to do partial equilibrium analysis."

12. "If economics is a valid science, there should be no disagreement among economists about whether a national sales tax should be instituted." Discuss with respect to positive and normative issues.

*13. Which is a positive statement?
   a) A tax on clothing will disproportionately harm families with children.
   b) Luxuries should be taxed instead of necessities.
   c) An income tax should be used instead of property taxes.

Numerical and Graphing Exercises

*1. In the strange land of the Zorgs, 3 askorgs trade for 2 goutarks. Money is measured in bolteros. The boltero price of a cuggle is 5. By chemical reaction, mixing one cuggle with water produces 5 askorgs. How many bolteros does a Zorgian need to get 15 goutarks in trade for askorgs that he or she produces with purchased cuggles, if water is free?

2. Samuel Gorton finds that his shop in Massachusetts earns $800 per week while his shop in London earns £800 per month. If the exchange rate is 1.5 dollars per pound, how much do both shops earn together per month? (Assume that there are 4.33 weeks to the month.)

*3. Use the following data to graph and identify the relationship.

x	1	2	3	4	5	6	7	8	9	10
y	−.5	1	2.5	4	5.5	7	8.5	10	11.5	13

4. Graph the following information to find out how many apples and oranges the speaker has.
   a) "I don't know how many apples and oranges I have, but their total originally was 250."
   b) "I started with four times as many oranges as I had apples."
   c) "My present number of apples is 10 percent fewer than what I started with."

*5. Working from the following functions, plot the (x, y) pairs that satisfy each of the relationships. Identify how the change in the function changes the location of the graphed points.

$$y = 4 + x \qquad y/4 - 2x/4 = 1$$
$$y = 8 + x \qquad y/4 + x/4 = 1$$

6. Graph the following relationship, identify it, and write it as a functional relationship between x and y. Which of the forms do you find easiest to remember?

x	1	2	3	4	5	6	7	8	9
y	8.94	8.77	8.49	8.06	7.48	6.71	5.66	4.12	0

*7. Make a mathematical model to describe the following facts:
   a) The amount of money that Kimberly spends on Blowpops (a kind of lollipop with a gum center) is always 20 percent of the allowance she gets from her father.
   b) The price of a Blowpop is $.10.

8. Graph the information in exercise 7, assuming that Kimberly's allowance is $10 per month. Perform comparative statics by shifting curves in your graph to show
   a) how many Blowpops Kimberly buys if her allowance is raised 10 percent.
   b) how many Blowpops Kimberly buys if the price of Blowpops rises to $.15.

*9. Draw a diagram containing the following pieces of information to solve the optimization problem stated below.
   a) Jon can travel in any direction he wants as long as he does not get more than 500 miles from home.
   b) Jon's benefit from travel is proportional to the sum of the number of miles he is east of home plus the number of miles he is north of home.

What is John's constraint, what is his objective, and what should he do to get the greatest benefit from travel?

CHAPTER 2

Market Basics

This chapter introduces demand curves, supply curves, market equilibrium, and elasticity. The chapter shows how to work with demand and supply curves and explains how they interact to determine market prices and quantities. It also discusses mistakes to avoid in using demand and supply curves and describes some of the effects of asymmetric information on the market.

ACTIVE READING GUIDES

After reading this chapter, you should be able to answer the Active Reading Guides listed below. These guides also appear in the page margins, near the material to which they refer.

1. What is a market? Explain the implications of being in a specific market.

2. What is a demand curve? What economic variables influence demand?

3. Explain the difference between a change in quantity demanded and a change in demand.

4. What is a supply curve? What economic variables influence supply?

5. Explain the difference between a change in quantity supplied and a change in supply.

6. What do we mean by market equilibrium?

7. Define *elasticity* and apply its formula to an example.

8. List five economic determinants affecting the price elasticity of demand and supply.

9. What is comparative statics?

10. Show the effects of a shift in demand and a shift in supply on equilibrium price and quantity.

11. Describe the effects of an import quota on the price and quantity of imports.

12. How do the effects of a price floor differ from those of a price ceiling?

13. Explain the difference between symmetric and asymmetric information.

14. List some of the possible effects of asymmetric information on market equilibrium.

A.1. What is meant by stability for a general system?

A.2. How would you test to determine whether a market equilibrium was stable or unstable?

2.1 What Is a Market?

The truth is sometimes strange. Did you know that one-third of the entire crop of California navel oranges is regularly held off the market each year and left to rot, dumped into cattle feed, or sold at much reduced prices to juice plants?[1] This is true even when the crops being held off the market are already grown and therefore cost nothing more to produce at the time of the decision. To understand why it is in orange growers' interests to let already-grown crops rot, we need to understand how demand and supply interact to determine market price. In Chapter 1 we surveyed the tools and subject matter of microeconomics. In this chapter we apply those tools to a review of market demand and supply, allowing us to analyze circumstances like that of the navel oranges.

What is a market? Are buyers and sellers in London and New York in the same market for gold bullion? For delicatessen sandwiches? For cement blocks? The answers would seem to be yes, no, and no, respectively, but why?

▼
1. What is a market? Explain the implications of being in a specific market.

*A **market** is a group of buyers and sellers linked together by trade in the sale or purchase of a particular commodity or service.*

1. Since 1937 federal law has allowed farm groups such as Arizona and California citrus growers and California growers of almonds, peaches, nectarines, plums, spearmint, and filberts to control the flow of produce to market by producers, exempting them from antitrust law that otherwise would prevent such actions.

Price is often a good indicator for determining the extent of a market. Buyers and sellers in New York and London are part of the same market in gold bullion because gold is traded across the Atlantic and the price in both places is the same. On the other hand, the price for delicatessen sandwiches in New York may vary up or down without affecting the price in London. Since the two locations have different prices, and since buyers and sellers in one city do not interact with those in the other, the sandwich markets are separate. Cement blocks likewise have different prices across locations and are not traded overseas because it is cheaper to buy a locally made cement block than to have one shipped across the Atlantic. The blocks may be the same, but price differences separate the two markets. Thus a critical feature for being in the same market is that when price changes for one group of buyers and sellers, price changes for all other buyers and sellers to reflect the new conditions.

In many cases, goods are in separate markets because they are not sufficiently alike. Clearly, ball-point pens and lawn mowers perform different functions and are not in the same market. Wood-laminate tennis rackets and metal tennis rackets, on the other hand, perform the same functions and are more nearly alike, though not identical. In cases like this, the degree of difference between the goods and the way consumers view the goods helps to determine whether the commodities are best considered part of the same market.[2] If the degree of difference is great enough, the commodities trade in separate markets. A microwave oven and a conventional oven both cook food, but their characteristics are so different that the two products would normally be considered distinct.

For our definition of a market to be useful, however, we need not require an identical price for two distinct groups of buyers or sellers in the same market. For example, import tariffs and duties imposed by foreign countries on U.S. exports can cause foreign prices to exceed U.S. prices by the amount of the duty. (When Korea applies $1,000 in duties to the import of a U.S. automobile, the Korean price exceeds the U.S. price by $1,000.) Transportation costs can also make the price of a commodity different to different buyers, even though the commodity trades at a common price when these costs are accounted for. In either case, the commodity is in a single market because it trades at a common price once duties or transport costs have been taken into account, arbitrage[3] is not possible, and a change in the price in one location directly affects price at the other.

We can look at a few more examples to clinch the point. Buyers and sellers in the United States would form a single market in stock market securities (because securities are traded all over the country by telephone at common quoted prices), but could represent many separate markets in, say, fresh fruits

2. Chapters 3 and 4 discuss the degree of similarity between goods in terms of their degree of substitutability for one another.
3. Arbitrage is the simultaneous purchase and sale of a commodity to profit from price discrepancies. Buying a commodity from one seller for $10 and immediately selling it to another buyer for $10.50 is an example of arbitrage.

and vegetables sold at local farm stands. On the other hand, the lumber market encompasses nearly all of the buyers and sellers in the United States. Lumber prices farther from the major lumber-producing areas in the Pacific Northwest and the Southeast tend to be marginally higher because prices rise in relation to transportation costs. Nevertheless, lumber represents a single market because a change in demand or supply that affects price in one location will affect the price of lumber in other locations. In the two weeks after Hurricane Andrew struck South Florida in August 1992, for example, plywood prices jumped 18 percent nationwide.[4]

Now that we know what characterizes a market, we can look at the actions of the market participants themselves. Trade requires both buyers and sellers; we start with buyers.

2.2 Demand Curves

▼
2. What is a demand curve? What economic variables influence demand?

Every January, stores around the country advertise clearance sales on merchandise not sold during the previous Christmas season. This occurs because retailers know that lowering the price of their inventory generally leads to an increase in the number of items sold. By lowering price to sell more, retailers make use of one of the most basic relationships in economics. This relationship—between product price and the quantity that buyers want to purchase—is what we term the market demand curve.

> The **market demand curve** tells us for each price what quantity buyers are willing to buy.

Economists often refer to the *law of demand,* which says that the quantity demanded will generally be greater at a low price than at a high price.[5] Let's talk about blue jeans, for example. At a high price the quantity of jeans demanded will be relatively low, both because there will be fewer active buyers in the market and also because those who are buying jeans will tend to buy fewer pairs. Inactive buyers are ones for whom the market price exceeds their *reservation price,* the highest price at which they would be willing to buy. At a low price, the reverse is likely to happen: more buyers will become active in the market, and those who are already buying will tend to buy more. For both reasons we expect that quantity of jeans demanded will vary *inversely* with the price of jeans. This inverse relationship is the law of demand.

The law of demand implies that demand curves are downward sloping. Figure 2.1 displays a demand curve for blue jeans. When the price is $20 per

4. Mitchell Pacelle, ''Lumber Prices Stay High in Florida But Fall Elsewhere,'' *Wall Street Journal,* September 23, 1992, p. C15.
5. Actually, the law of demand is not a law in the same way that a law of physics is a law, because there are exceptions to it. We will talk about the possibility that buyers want to buy more at a higher price in Chapter 4.

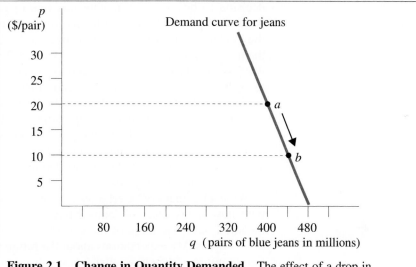

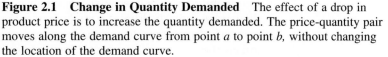

Figure 2.1   Change in Quantity Demanded   The effect of a drop in product price is to increase the quantity demanded. The price-quantity pair moves along the demand curve from point *a* to point *b,* without changing the location of the demand curve.

pair, 400 million pairs are demanded.[6] This is point *a* on the curve. When the price is $10 per pair, 440 million pairs are demanded. This is point *b* on the curve.[7] Because the price of the good itself is one of the variables being plotted, a change in this price leads to a change in the point along the curve. A change in the good's price changes the quantity demanded by moving *along* the curve as we have just done in Figure 2.1.

Although the price of jeans is the most important variable, there are also other things that affect the quantity of blue jeans that consumers want to buy. Let's discuss these next.

Factors That Influence Demand

Other than their price, what things might affect the demand for jeans? The answer partly depends on the alternatives to jeans that are available. For example, I may like jeans because they are rugged and comfortable for casual wear. If there are other types of pants available, like khakis, that could *substitute* for jeans for my purposes, then the price of khakis matters in my

6. Recall that demand and supply curves are drawn with the independent variable (price) on the vertical axis rather than on the horizontal axis, reversing the standard format used in mathematics.
7. Actual sales of men's, women's, and children's jeans in the United States in 1990 totaled 409.2 million pairs at an average price of $17.60 per pair.

decision to buy jeans. Carrying this line of reasoning further, the price of denim jackets could also influence my decision to buy jeans, not because they could be used in place of jeans, but because they could be used *with* them as a complementary good. In Chapters 3 and 4 we will carefully define what we mean by substitutes and complements. For now, all we need to recognize is that the prices of goods that may be used in place of or in conjunction with jeans are likely to matter in my decision to purchase jeans.

Conceivably, the prices of *many* other goods could affect my demand for blue jeans: the price of belts, the price of boots, and even the price of things other than clothes could matter. For now, let's assume that only the prices of khakis (a substitute for jeans) and denim jackets (a complement for jeans) affect my demand for jeans.

What else matters? Certainly my income should have something to do with how many pairs of jeans I buy. For many types of goods, the more income I have, the more of the good I will buy. The same would be true for other buyers. My expectations about the future might also affect my decision. For example, if I believe that jeans will be unavailable next month or that their price will quadruple, I might buy more jeans today. If I consider the demand of everyone in the market, not just myself, the *number* of buyers affects the quantity demanded. Finally, buyers' tastes and preferences affect demand. Fashions change, fads come and go. Demand for jeans may rise just because buyers think they are stylish, and then fall when they go out of style.

Taking note of the other variables that affect the number of blue jeans that consumers want to buy, we write the quantity demanded as

$$q^D = F(p; \overset{-}{p_S}, \overset{+}{p_C}, \overset{-}{I}, \overset{+}{E}, \overset{+}{N}, T),$$

where q^D is the quantity of blue jeans demanded; F stands for a particular functional relationship; p is the price of blue jeans themselves: p_S stands for the price of substitutes to jeans such as khaki pants; p_C stands for the price of complements to jeans such as denim jackets; I is income; E represents expectations about future market conditions for such things as prices; N is the number of buyers in the market; and T stands for buyers' tastes or preferences. Notice the semicolon separating p from the other variables inside the parentheses; we will return to that shortly. The signs over the variables indicate whether an increase raises quantity demanded or lowers it. Thus the effect of a higher price of substitutes in the market is generally to increase the demand for jeans, but the effect of an increase in the price of complements is generally to lower the demand for jeans.

Demographics and Demand. Higher income and a larger number of buyers in the market tend to increase the demand for jeans, as shown by the signs over I and N. But if we consider the quantities demanded for jeans by all buyers, the market demand will also depend on the types of buyers and their frequency in the population: Are they mostly younger or mostly older? Are their tastes mostly of one type or mostly of another type? A population of mostly younger buyers will probably buy more jeans than a population of mostly older buyers, for instance. We will examine factors such as taste that affect demand at the individual household level in Chapter 3. In Chapter 4 we will work up to the market level, discovering how to derive demand functions like the one just discussed. For now, however, we can simply note that other prices, income, expectations, and demographic variables all affect demand. Next, we can explore why price is listed to the left of the semicolon and all the other variables to the right in our equation; this has to do with their different effects on the demand curve.

Demand Versus Quantity Demand

The demand curve displays the quantity of a good demanded at each price. Since variables such as income and the price of other goods also affect demand, we must identify how changes in them affect the demand curve.

Assume as before that khakis are the primary substitute for jeans. If the price of khakis rose from $25 to $150 per pair, this would increase the demand for jeans as consumers satisfied their need for casual pants with relatively cheaper jeans. However, we didn't plot the price of khakis in Figure 2.1, so the effect of the khaki price change on jeans demand cannot be represented by movement along that demand curve. To show the effect of another variable, we need to shift the *location* of the demand curve.

Figure 2.2 redraws the jeans demand curve. Point *a*, as before, shows the demand for jeans when the price is $20 per pair, assuming that the price of

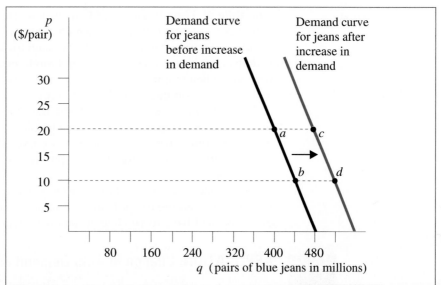

Figure 2.2   Change in Demand   A change in demand shifts the *location* of the demand curve. For each price, the quantity demanded changes. In this example for blue jeans, at a price of $20/pair the quantity demanded shifts from point *a* to point *c,* and at $10/pair the quantity demanded shifts from point *b* to point *d*.

khakis is $25 per pair. When the price of khakis rises to $150 per pair, holding constant the price of jeans, the demand for jeans will shift to point *c*. Thus the quantity demanded changes even though the jeans price is still $20 per pair. A similar shift occurs from point *b* to point *d* if the price of jeans is fixed at $10 per pair. Continuing in this way for all the possible prices of jeans on the vertical axis, we see that the demand curve location has shifted to the right as a result of the increase in the price of the substitute, khaki pants.

▼

3. Explain the difference between a change in quantity demanded and a change in demand.

*(i) A **change in quantity demanded** is a change in the amount consumers want to buy because of a change in the good's own price. This leads to a shift of the price-quantity point* along *the demand curve, which is fixed in location.*
*(ii) A **change in demand** means that the quantity consumers want to buy has changed at each possible price because of a change in other determinants of demand, such as the price of other goods, income, expectations, or taste. This leads to a shift in the location* of the demand curve.

To summarize, a change in a good's own price will move the quantity demanded along the demand curve, as in Figure 2.1. But a change in any other variable affecting demand will change the *location* of the demand curve, because it causes a shift in the price-quantity relationship as in Figure 2.2. That is why, when we write an equation for demand, we put the price of the good itself to the left of the semicolon and all other variables to the right.

The Role of Time in Demand Curves and Demand Analysis. Most problems have a natural time unit in which demand (and supply) is measured. For example, if we are talking about the demand for labor, the usual price measure is dollars per hour. A hamburger stand might measure demand in hamburgers per day. When talking about agricultural crops, the demand and supply over a growing season might be the best unit to use.

Whatever the case being considered, the time frame over which the person making the decision does his or her planning is a reasonable time frame to use in generating the demand or supply curve. The time frame can vary with the problem, and even for a given problem several time frames might be reasonable.

In this book we will rarely need to mention the time frame because we are focusing on learning the principles of microeconomics. In applications, however, you will have to be clear at the outset what the time frame is.

APPLICATION: Change in Auto Demand in 1990

In the months of August, September, and October 1990, gasoline prices rose more than $.35 per gallon at the pump in response to diminished oil supplies caused by the Iraqi invasion of Kuwait, a major world oil supplier. Although Kuwaiti oil made up a small fraction of world supplies, invasion-related uncertainties about oil from other Middle East suppliers, notably Saudi Arabia, caused the price of oil and thus gasoline to rise swiftly. At the same time, Congress was casting about for ways to raise taxes to pay for increased government expenditures. One of the commodities targeted for higher taxes was gasoline. The proposal to increase the federal tax on gasoline from nine cents per gallon to sixteen cents per gallon led consumers to expect even higher gasoline prices to come. Because gasoline is a complementary good to the use of personal automobiles, the price of gasoline is an important determinant of the demand for automobiles.

Increases in fuel prices and plans to raise them further were not lost on car companies or auto analysts. Many auto industry officials changed their forecasts for 1991 sales of automobiles. As one analyst explained, ''There are lots of good reasons not to buy a car now.''[8] In fact, consumers faced with paying more in gasoline costs had several options, including shifting their demand to smaller, more fuel-efficient cars or postponing their purchases of automobiles altogether. As evidence of the change in consumer thinking, subcompact cars and minicars improved their share of the overall new car market by two percentage points in August 1990.[9]

Did these changes in late 1990 reflect a change in *demand* or a change in *quantity demanded*? If you were an auto analyst, what would you look for in the demand curves that are part of the automobile manufacturers' planning process? A clue is that the precipitating event was a change in the price of gasoline, not in the price of cars themselves. This means that at the same price for automobiles, car buyers were demanding a different number of cars, reflecting a *shift in demand*. This shift reduced demand for larger, less fuel-efficient cars, but increased demand for smaller, more fuel-efficient cars. Figure 2.3, which graphs demand for large cars and small cars separately, shows this effect. ■

2.3 Supply Curves

The goods and services consumers buy don't appear out of thin air. They have to be provided and sold by suppliers. We now turn our attention to the other side of the market—supply—and then consider how demand and supply interact.

Factors That Influence Supply

▼
4. What is a supply curve? What economic variables influence supply?

We can begin by defining a supply curve.

*The **supply curve** tells us for each price what quantity suppliers are willing to sell.*

8. ''Taxes Could Give Car Buyers Cold Feet,'' *Wall Street Journal,* October 2, 1990, p. B1.
9. Ibid.

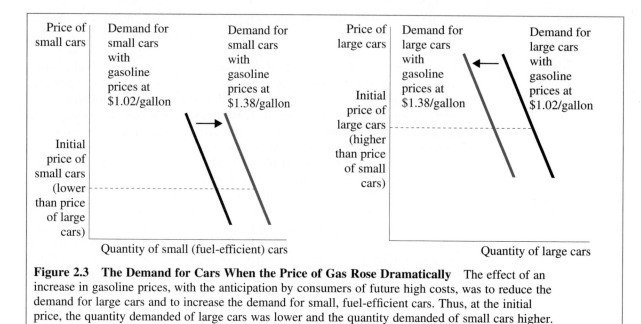

Figure 2.3   The Demand for Cars When the Price of Gas Rose Dramatically   The effect of an increase in gasoline prices, with the anticipation by consumers of future high costs, was to reduce the demand for large cars and to increase the demand for small, fuel-efficient cars. Thus, at the initial price, the quantity demanded of large cars was lower and the quantity demanded of small cars higher.

Supply curves normally slope upward because a higher price of the good makes it more profitable to supply, attracting more suppliers and inducing those already in the market to increase the quantity they want to sell.

In addition to the price of the good itself, however, other factors affect the amount of the good that sellers want to supply. For example, if you own a factory that can produce blue jeans or other types of pants, you are likely to devote more of your production to blue jeans if their price is high in comparison to the price you can get for other pants. Why? Because you will realize higher profits by producing jeans that you can sell at a higher price. On the other hand, if making denim jackets and skirts becomes enormously profitable because the demand for them has risen, you might make more money by devoting all of your factory's resources to making jackets and skirts. If you did that, the quantity of jeans you supplied would drop, even if the price of jeans had not changed.[10]

The prices of raw materials and inputs (components of production needed to produce the finished product) also affect the decision to supply jeans. Higher costs for the plant and equipment, raw materials, and labor used to produce jeans would reduce supply. If buying and maintaining jeans-making

10. In this example, the price of jeans directly influences both the quantity of jeans that buyers want to buy and the quantity of jeans that sellers want to sell. However, the particular set of prices for goods *other* than jeans that matters to the buyer may not be the same set that matters to the seller.

equipment became too expensive, it might not be profitable to produce blue jeans at all.

Finally, the firm's technical knowledge and the efficiency of its production methods affect supply. For example, if improved production methods allowed double the amount of output for the same amount of inputs, the quantity supplied would be twice as great at the same market price.

Summarizing what we have said about the determinants of supply leads to the supply relationship for jeans,

$$q^S = G(\overset{+}{p}; \overset{-}{p_G}, \overset{-}{p_I}, \overset{+}{K}),$$

where q^S is the quantity supplied; G indicates a functional relationship (like the F used earlier); p is the price of jeans themselves; p_G represents the prices of other goods that the supplier could produce; p_I represents the prices of inputs such as raw materials, plant and equipment, and labor; and K stands for technological knowledge. Raising the price of inputs generally leads to a reduction in the quantity that sellers want to sell, as indicated by the negative sign over p_I. An increase in the price of other types of clothing that the supplier of jeans could produce, p_G, would also decrease the supply of jeans because the plant and equipment could earn a better return by producing those other types of clothing. Finally, if technology improved, the quantity of output supplied would be higher at the same price, hence the plus sign over K.

Supply Versus Quantity Supplied

As with demand, a change in the good's own price affects quantity supplied by movement along the supply curve, while a change in variables to the right of the semicolon, such as other prices, changes the location of the supply curve.

▼
5. Explain the difference between a change in quantity supplied and a change in supply.

*(i) A **change in quantity supplied** is a change in the amount suppliers want to sell because of a change in the good's own price. This leads to a shift of the price-quantity point* along *the supply curve, which is fixed in location.*
*(ii) A **change in supply** means that the quantity suppliers want to sell has changed at each possible price because of a change in other determinants of supply, such as the price of material inputs or of other goods. This leads to a shift in the* location *of the supply curve.*

Figure 2.4 shows the supply curve for jeans, using the same axes as were used in Figures 2.1 and 2.2. Part (a) shows that suppliers want to sell 480 million pairs at $20 per pair. If the price is decreased to $10 per pair, the price and quantity point e shifts along the supply curve to point f, indicating that suppliers want to sell only 200 million pairs. *Supply* is unchanged, because the supply curve has not moved, but the *quantity supplied* has changed from 480 million pairs to 200 million pairs.

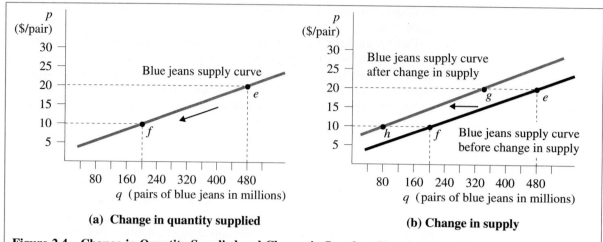

Figure 2.4   Change in Quantity Supplied and Change in Supply   Changing the price of jeans changes the quantity of jeans supplied. The price-quantity pair moves from point e to point f in part (a) in response to a price decrease from $20 per pair to $10 per pair, without changing the location of the supply curve. In contrast, a change in supply shifts the *location* of the supply curve, meaning that at each price the quantity supplied by the market changes. For the decrease in supply in part (b), the quantity supplied shifts from point e to point g at $20 per pair, and at $10 per pair quantity supplied shifts from point f to point h.

An increase in the price of denim fabric, in contrast, leads to a change in supply. Some suppliers with smaller factories, higher distribution costs, and lower profit margins may see their profit margins become negative and take their factories out of jeans production entirely. For other suppliers, only some of their plants may be taken out of jeans production because the largest or most modern plants may still be more profitable in jeans production than in some other activity. The net result of all these suppliers' decisions is that point e shifts to point g in part (b) of Figure 2.4, meaning that at $20 per pair sellers will want to sell 340 million pairs instead of the 480 million that they wanted to sell before production costs increased. Similarly, at $10 per pair, suppliers want to sell only 80 million pairs, and so on. At each price, increasing the production costs reduces the quantity that suppliers want to sell. This is a *change in supply,* because the location of the entire supply curve has shifted.

2.4 Relating Demand and Supply: Market Equilibrium

Although our individual models of demand and supply tell us a lot, we can't really analyze market interactions until we bring buyers and sellers back together. For example, in our earlier application discussing the effect of higher gasoline prices, we found that the *demand* for less fuel-efficient automobiles declined at a fixed price for automobiles. A natural question would be whether this drop in demand would lead to a fall in the price of automobiles because sellers could not sell all of the cars they wanted to at the original price. But if the drop in automobile prices then leads to a change in *quantity demanded,* how do we sort out one effect from the other? To answer requires an understanding of the concept of market equilibrium, which we now consider.

Equating Quantity Demanded and Quantity Supplied

The demand curve and the supply curve tell us for each price what buyers and sellers would like to do. Knowing what buyers and sellers *want to do,* however, does not tell us what they *actually do.* This requires finding a market price and quantity that describe what actually happens in the market; in other words, the price and quantity must make sense for the market as a whole and lead to an outcome consistent with buyers' and sellers' plans. Such a price and quantity represent an equilibrium.

▼
6. What do we mean by market equilibrium?

> *An **equilibrium** in a market is a price* p^* *and a quantity* q^* *such that at price* p^* *the quantity demanded equals the quantity supplied, both of which equal* q^*.

An important implication of equilibrium is that it is a natural balance point or resting place for the market. At the equilibrium price there is no need for either buyers or sellers to adjust what they are doing. Their choices are sustainable. This is not true, say, when sellers want to sell more of the good than buyers want to buy (a condition of *excess supply*), for sellers will find their shelves filling with unsold goods. A market with continual inventory build-up is not in balance because sellers' plans to sell are frustrated. In this case, we would expect price to drop as sellers tried to get rid of unwanted goods. The price would continue to drop until the excess supply was eliminated, implying that when the process ended we would observe a different price than the one from which we started.

Similarly, if there was *excess demand* at a given price, attempts by buyers to acquire the commodity would tend to push up the price. As shelves quickly emptied, sellers would see that they could ask more and that buyers would pay more. Price would rise until the excess demand was eliminated, implying that the price observed in the market at the end of the process would be different from the original price.

At the equilibrium price, however, markets *clear,* meaning that quantity demanded equals quantity supplied, and there is no reason for buyers or sellers to change their plans. All participants can get what they want; plans are consistent with one another, and price and quantity are at rest (that is, not changing in response to excess demand or excess supply). We will return to the issue of the market being at rest in equilibrium when we discuss stability in the appendix to this chapter.

Now that you understand more about demand and supply interactions, can you see why the orange growers mentioned at the start of the chapter would let their crops rot? By reducing supply and artificially creating excess demand, they would drive up the price of oranges. Selling fewer oranges at a high equilibrium price might then earn more for them than selling more oranges at a lower price.

Representing Market Equilibrium

The best way to become familiar with market equilibrium is to find one, and so we return to the demand and supply of jeans that we have been working with throughout the chapter. We can find the equilibrium either graphically or analytically. A graphical approach is often best when you want to take in a lot of information about a market at a glance. An analytical (functional) approach is usually better when you need to calculate a precise number for price or quantity. We start with the graphical representation.

Graphical Representation. Figure 2.5 combines the demand and supply curves from Figures 2.1 and 2.4. Clearly, there is a special point in Figure 2.5: point k, where the demand and the supply curves cross. Point k represents the equilibrium for this market, where the price is $17.50 per pair of jeans. At this price the quantity supplied and the quantity demanded are the same

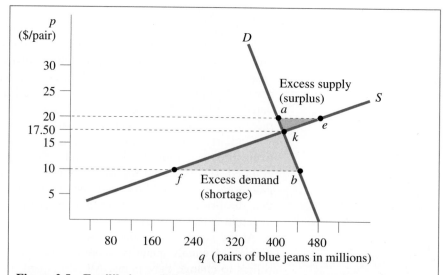

Figure 2.5 Equilibrium Points a, b, e and f are the same points on the demand and supply curves for jeans as in Figures 2.1, 2.2, and 2.4. Equilibrium in the jeans market occurs at point k, where the demand curve crosses the supply curve. This is because at price $17.50 per pair, corresponding to point k, the quantity demanded equals the quantity supplied.

at 410 million pairs. Further, point *k* is on both the demand curve and the supply curve, so both buyers' and sellers' plans are being satisfied.

Other prices do not satisfy these conditions for equilibrium. If the price were higher, say $20, the figure shows that there would be an excess supply of 80 million pairs because the quantity demanded at that price is less than the quantity sellers want to sell. Since sellers' plans to sell are frustrated, this price could not be sustained in the market. Sellers' stocks of unsold goods would build up, putting pressure on prices to fall to eliminate the excess supply. Similarly, at $10 per pair there is an excess demand for goods, showing that consumers want to buy more than the market is providing. Sellers would see an opportunity to sell at a higher price, and this would ultimately lead to higher prices and a larger supply.

Functional Representation. The demand curve for jeans relates the quantity demanded q^D in millions of jeans to the price of jeans *p*,

$$q^D = 480 - 4p.$$

In this representation of the general demand function introduced earlier, $q^D = F(p; p_S, p_C, I, E, N, T)$, we display only the price *p* because all other variables are assumed to be held constant. If price is $20 per pair, for example, quantity demanded is 400 million jeans. This is point *a* in Figure 2.5. Similarly, the supply curve relates the quantity supplied q^S to price *p*,

$$q^S = 28p - 80,$$

where we again display only the price *p* because other variables relating to supply are held constant. Setting quantity demanded equal to quantity supplied implies that

$$480 - 4p = 28p - 80.$$

Solving for price we get $560 = 32p$, which means that $p = $17.50 per pair. At this price, quantity demanded equals quantity supplied equals 410 million pairs, which agrees with the point we found at the intersection of the demand and supply curves. In general, the intersection of any demand curve *F* and supply curve *G* can be found by setting quantity demanded equal to quantity supplied and solving for price. If $q^D = F(p)$ and $q^S = G(p)$, equilibrium price is found by solving $F(p) = G(p)$.

2.5 Elasticity

Quantity demanded and quantity supplied each respond to price changes for the good in question as well as to changes in other prices and variables. Although some curves exhibit a large change in quantity in response to a small change in price, others exhibit very little quantity response to a price change. We need some way to measure and quantify this difference in price sensitivity. This is what *elasticity* does: it measures the responsiveness of one variable to a change in another. Since different types of demand and supply curves react differently to changing market conditions, elasticity helps us predict how markets with different types of demand and supply curves will behave.

Why are elasticity measures so important? The chief reason is that elasticity measures are unit free, and thus give a clear picture of what is going on in the demand for one good as compared to other goods. Statements of the type, "If price rises $1, then the quantity demanded falls by 1 million units," are often not very useful because they are dependent on the units used to measure the quantity. Recall from Chapter 1 the importance of dimensional units. Nowhere is this more crucial than when you compare different markets. Summaries of the effects of a price change on a list of markets would be incredibly difficult to interpret because each market has different dimensional units for output.[11]

This dimensional problem is avoided by focusing on elasticity, which is unit free. Instead of looking at the change in output for a given change in price, we look at the *percentage* change in output for a given *percentage* change in price. Percentage change in output divided by percentage change in price (for a small change) is called a *price elasticity.* Because a percentage change is a number that is independent of any unit of measure, elasticity is a "pure" number. To state the definition formally,

Elasticity is the percentage change in one variable caused by a 1 percent change in another.

▼
7. Define *elasticity* and apply its formula to an example.

The *price elasticity of demand,* for example, is just the percentage change in quantity demanded resulting from a 1 percent change in price. The *price elasticity of supply* is the percentage change in quantity supplied resulting from a 1 percent change in price. *Cross-price elasticities* refer to the effect of a change in the price of one commodity on the quantity of another.

To compute elasticity, we simply take the ratio of percentage changes. If ε is the price elasticity of demand, then

$$\varepsilon = \frac{\%\Delta q^D}{\%\Delta p} = \frac{\Delta q^D/q^D}{\Delta p/p} = \frac{\Delta q^D}{\Delta p}\frac{p}{q^D},$$

where $\%\Delta q^D$ is the percentage change in quantity demanded and $\%\Delta p$ is the percentage change in price.[12] For example, the demand for blue jeans was 410 million pairs when the price was $17.50 per pair. If demand rises to 418.2 million pairs when the price falls to $17.33 per pair, this is a 2 percent increase in quantity demanded (418.2/410 = 1.02) resulting from a 1 percent decrease in price 17.33/17.50 = 0.99). The price elasticity of demand for

---

11. For example, an increase in sales of American-made automobiles of 1 million units per year would be quite significant (such sales are on the order of 7 million units annually), but an increase in the sales of, say, paper clips of 1 million units would not be significant.
12. If x_1 and x_2 are two numbers, their change, $x_2 - x_1$, is written as Δx, using the Greek letter Δ to mean "difference." $\%\Delta x$ for a variable x would then be equal to $\Delta x/x$, where percentages are in decimal form, that is, 50 percent is expressed as 0.5, and so on.

blue jeans therefore is .02/(−.01) = −2. Similarly, if a 1 percent increase in the price of khakis causes a $\frac{1}{2}$ percent increase in the demand for jeans (all else held constant, including the jeans price), then the cross-price elasticity of jeans with respect to the khaki price is (0.5)/1 = 0.5.

Notice that the price elasticity of demand for jeans we first computed was a negative number. This is because demand is downward sloping with respect to its own price: the change in price was negative when the change in quantity was positive. If price had been raised, both signs would have been reversed, and the elasticity would still have been negative. By convention, price elasticities of demand are often reported as positive numbers. This simply involves reversing the sign of the computed number or giving its absolute value. Since it is largely a matter of preference whether one treats elasticities of demand as positive numbers or negative numbers, in this text we will report all elasticities (including demand elasticities and cross-price elasticities) with their natural sign without converting them to positive numbers. A smaller or less responsive price elasticity of demand means one closer to zero. For example, a price elasticity of demand equal to −0.1 means that a 1 percent increase in price causes a 0.1 percent reduction in quantity demanded, a relatively small drop. This demand is much less price responsive (less elastic) than, say, demand for a good for which price elasticity is −10, meaning that a 1 percent increase in price causes a 10 percent drop in quantity demanded.

Example: How can elasticity be useful in market analysis? Assume that you are one of the California orange growers mentioned at the start of the chapter and you want to know how much destroying 1 percent of the California crop will affect the price of oranges, p, and the revenues from orange sales, pq, where q is the quantity of oranges sold. If the price elasticity of demand for oranges is −1, then a 1 percent quantity reduction is associated with a 1 percent increase in price. Higher price exactly counterbalances lower quantity, and revenues stay the same.[13] But if demand is less elastic (ε closer to zero), a larger price change corresponds to a 1 percent change in quantity. In this case, destroying 1 percent of the crop raises price more than 1 percent, so that revenue rises. Thus, if the elasticity of demand for oranges is between −1 and 0, orange growers increase revenues by destroying part of their crop; otherwise, they lose revenue. Do you think the elasticity of demand for oranges is between −1 and zero or not?

Graphically Computing Elasticities

Are there any rules for finding the elasticity of demand and supply by inspection? The answer is yes. Once you get used to the rules, you will find them quite useful in understanding elasticity.

13. Actually, 0.99 × 1.01 = 0.9999, but this is so close to 1 that the difference is negligible.

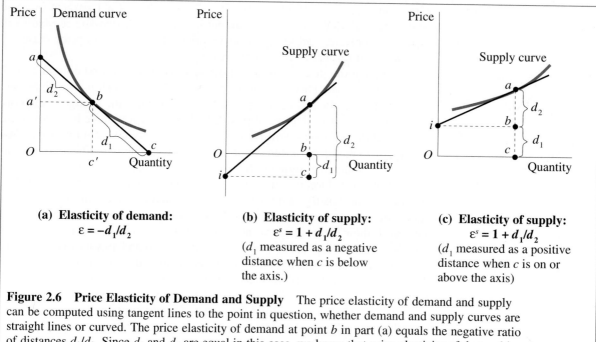

(a) Elasticity of demand:
$$\varepsilon = -d_1/d_2$$

(b) Elasticity of supply:
$$\varepsilon^s = 1 + d_1/d_2$$
(d_1 measured as a negative distance when c is below the axis.)

(c) Elasticity of supply:
$$\varepsilon^s = 1 + d_1/d_2$$
(d_1 measured as a positive distance when c is on or above the axis)

Figure 2.6   Price Elasticity of Demand and Supply   The price elasticity of demand and supply can be computed using tangent lines to the point in question, whether demand and supply curves are straight lines or curved. The price elasticity of demand at point b in part (a) equals the negative ratio of distances d_1/d_2. Since d_1 and d_2 are equal in this case, we know that price elasticity of demand is -1 at point b, so a 1 percent increase in price leads to a 1 percent drop in quantity demanded. The price elasticity of supply equals 1 plus the ratio of distances d_1/d_2, where d_1 is negative if point c is below the axis. In part (b), therefore, the price elasticity of supply at point a is less than 1 and in part (c) it is greater than 1.

Figure 2.6 shows how the price elasticity of demand relates to slope and location of the demand curve. Although up to now we have drawn demand curves as if they were all linear, we now allow for a general curved demand curve. Looking at part (a) of the figure, we can show that the price elasticity of demand equals $-d_1/d_2$, where d_1 and d_2 are the distances from point b to the intersection with the quantity and price axes, respectively. We can see from part (a) that the rate at which q changes with a change in price, $\Delta q^D/\Delta p$, equals the ratio of distances $-c'c/Oa'$. Since p equals distance Oa', and q equals distance Oc', placing these into the formula for price elasticity of demand $\varepsilon = (\Delta q^D/\Delta p)(p/q^D)$ and canceling gives $\varepsilon = -c'c/Oc'$. Since triangle Oac is similar to triangle $c'bc$, however, we have $c'c/bc = (Oc' + c'c)/(ab + bc)$, which implies that $-c'c/Oc = -bc/ab = -d_1/d_2$. Price elasticity of demand can therefore be found by drawing the tangent line to the demand curve at the point in question and finding the ratio of these two distances. If the demand curve is a straight line, it is its own tangent line.

It follows easily from the just derived rule that *a vertical demand curve has zero price elasticity of demand* at every point, and *a horizontal demand curve has negatively infinite price elasticity of demand* at every point. Points on the demand curve for which the two distances are equal are called *unit elastic* because the price elasticity of demand equals −1. Demand that exhibits a larger elasticity (greater price responsiveness) than −1 is called *elastic,* and demand exhibiting a smaller elasticity is called *inelastic.* Horizontal and vertical demand curves are sometimes called *perfectly elastic* and *perfectly inelastic,* respectively.

The *price elasticity of supply* ε^S is computed in the same manner as the price elasticity of demand,

$$\varepsilon^S = \frac{\%\Delta q^S}{\%\Delta p} = \frac{\Delta q^S}{\Delta p} \frac{p}{q^S},$$

where $\%\Delta q^S$ is the percentage change in quantity supplied. Since supply curves are usually upward sloping, the price elasticity of supply is naturally a positive number. The larger the elasticity, the more price-responsive the supply.

Price elasticity of supply is found in parts (b) and (c) of Figure 2.6 by the rule

$$\varepsilon^S = 1 + \frac{d_1}{d_2},$$

where distance d_1 is negative if point c is below the quantity axis and positive otherwise.[14] Thus, to find price elasticity of supply, you start by drawing the tangent line to the point on the supply curve and adding the ratio of the two distances to 1. To remember which distance comes first, note that we are interested in the quantity response to price, and the distance to the quantity axis is the numerator d_1.

From the elasticity rule we see that *a vertical supply curve has zero price elasticity* at every point, *a horizontal curve has infinite price elasticity,* and *any ray from the origin is unit elastic* at every point because the price elasticity of supply is 1. As with demand, supply elasticities greater than 1 are called elastic, and those less than 1 are called inelastic. It is always easy to see if a supply curve is elastic or inelastic at a point by comparing it to the ray from the origin going through the point in question. If it is flatter than the ray it is elastic; if less flat, it is inelastic.

Figure 2.7 presents some different demand and supply curves to show the effect of slope and location on elasticity. As the figure and the above equations show, an increase in quantity for fixed slope and price reduces elasticity (see demand curves 1 and 2 and supply curves 1 and 3), whereas a flattening of the curve for fixed price and quantity makes demand and supply more elastic

---

14. We read from parts (b) and (c) of Figure 2.6 that $\Delta q^D/\Delta p$ equals the ratio of distances ic/d_2 [ib/d_2 in part (c)]; p equals the distance $d_1 + d_2$, where d_1 is treated as a negative number if point c is below the horizontal axis; and q equals the distance ic [ib in part (c)]. Placing these in the formula $\varepsilon^S = (\Delta q^S/\Delta p)(p/q^S)$ gives $\varepsilon = 1 + d_1/d_2$.

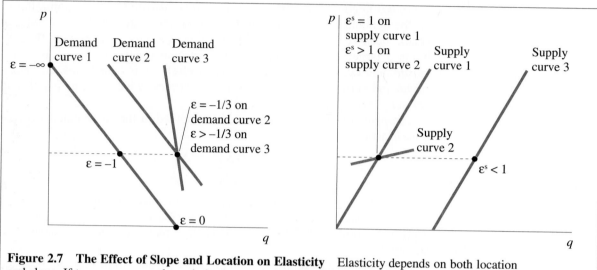

Figure 2.7   The Effect of Slope and Location on Elasticity   Elasticity depends on both location and slope. If two curves pass through the same point, the flatter curve is more elastic (elasticity further from zero). If points on two curves have the same slope and price, the one with the smaller quantity is more elastic. Vertical curves have zero elasticity, and horizontal curves have infinite elasticity (minus infinity for demand curves).

(see demand curves 2 and 3 and supply curves 1 and 2). The difference between slope and elasticity is seen especially in demand curve 1, where slope is the same at all points but elasticity ranges from minus infinity at the price intercept to minus 1 at the midpoint to zero at the quantity intercept. We will turn to some more examples of the use of elasticity after discussing the economic determinants of elasticity.

Determinants of Price Elasticity of Demand and Supply

▼
8. List five economic determinants affecting the price elasticity of demand and supply.

Many factors help explain why some goods have high price elasticities and others have small price elasticities. The degree of *substitutability* of a good with other goods is one of the main determinants of price elasticity of demand. Goods with numerous substitutes are likely to have high elasticities because consumers can easily shift their purchases to a close substitute if price rises. For example, if two types of running shoes are almost identical in their appearance and function, we expect the price elasticity of demand for the first type of shoe to be large because the shoes are close substitutes. A small percentage increase in price would lead to a large percentage reduction in quantity demanded as consumers shifted purchases to the relatively cheaper shoe.[15]

15. We will examine the relationship between consumer preferences and degree of substitutability in Chapter 4.

In general, the more *broadly defined* the good is, the less likely it is to have close substitutes. A single brand of ice cream, for example, has many close substitutes among different brands of ice cream. However, ice cream, broadly defined, has fewer close substitutes in other types of frozen desserts. Taking this logic to its extreme, we can say that food as a whole has *no* close substitutes. Thus the elasticity of demand for food is likely to be lower than the elasticity of demand for ice cream, which in turn is likely to be lower than the elasticity of demand for one brand of ice cream.

The *importance of the item in the budget* of buyers is related to how broadly the good is defined. Other things being equal, we might expect that demand for a good that is a tiny part of buyers' budgets is likely to have lower price elasticity than demand for a good that forms a large part of buyers' budgets. The smaller the good's role in the budget, the more easily buyers can absorb a price increase through small adjustments in their purchases of other goods. For a good which constitutes the entire budget, however, an increase in price forces a reduction in quantity purchased.

Another reason that goods have different price elasticities of demand relates to the *time period* over which the elasticity is measured. Immediately after a price change, buyers accustomed to purchasing given quantities of a good may not have enough time to adjust their purchases, and so price elasticity of demand would be low. Over a longer period of time, however, greater adjustment would be possible, leading to higher price elasticity of demand.

Similar arguments explain why goods have different elasticities of supply. If *production of a good can be easily expanded at constant or near constant costs,* it will have high price elasticity of supply, whereas goods that have rising costs will have low price elasticity of supply. A football player with unique skills or an original Leonardo da Vinci painting cannot be replicated at will, so even if the price paid for such a player or painting is raised a great deal, it is not likely to induce an increase in supply. On the other hand, a manufactured plastic picnic cup costs little to make and can easily be replicated at the same cost. A small increase in market price would therefore induce a large increase in quantity of cups supplied by existing manufacturers and new producers.

The less broadly defined the product and *the larger the market from which it draws its inputs,* the greater the price elasticity of supply will probably be, because conditions are more likely to allow replication at close to constant cost. The supply curve for a particular type of bolt is likely to be more elastic than the supply curve for all kinds of steel nationwide, because the attempt to increase the nation's steel output would drive up costs more than increasing the output of one type of bolt.

Finally, the longer the *time period* over which supply can adjust, the more elastic the supply curve. In a limited time period, it may not be possible to increase supply, at least not without a large increase in cost. Over a longer time period, additional options become available, raising the increase in quantity supplied for a given price increase.

APPLICATION: The Demand for Leaded Gasoline

A variety of environmental taxes have been imposed in Europe in recent years to reduce products and activities that pollute or degrade the environment. One of these products, leaded gasoline, offers us a glimpse into the elasticity of demand for a product that has a close substitute. Since unleaded gasoline can be used to replace leaded gasoline, we expect that an increase in the price of leaded gasoline would have a large impact on the quantity demanded. In fact, this is the case.

A 1990 report by the Commission of the European Communities[16] revealed than an 8 percent tax on leaded gasoline in Britain in 1989 led to an increase in the market share of unleaded gasoline from 4 percent to 30 percent in one year. Assuming that the total quantity of gasoline consumed in Britain did not change substantially in one year, consumption of leaded gasoline went from 96 percent of the market to 70 percent, a change of 26 percentage points. Since this is a large proportionate change, the question arises as to whether it should be measured relative to the starting base (96), ending base (70), or an average of the two (83). Using the average, we find that the percentage change was $(70 - 96)/83 = -.313$ (-31.3 percent). Assuming conservatively that the tax resulted in a full 8 percent change in price to the British consumer of leaded gasoline (that is, the price change amounts to a proportionate shift from 1 to 1.08), the percentage change in price relative to the average base price is $(0.08)/[(1 + 1.08)/2] = 0.0769$ (7.69 percent). Dividing this into the percentage quantity change gives an elasticity of -4.1.

In fact, not all of a sales tax increase is passed on to consumers in the form of higher prices, since some of the tax is borne by suppliers. Because the true price increase to British consumers would therefore be somewhat smaller than 7.69 percent, and because the drop in consumption was measured after only one year's time rather than over a longer period, we can be sure that the true price elasticity of demand for leaded gasoline is larger than -4.1. ∎

2.6 Using Demand and Supply Curves

Chapter 1 briefly discussed the method of comparative statics, which involves comparing the values of economic variables such as price and quantity between two static positions. *Static* refers to bodies or objects in a state of rest or equilibrium. Thus, in economics, *comparative statics* means the comparison of economic variables between two equilibria.

▼
9. What is comparative statics?

> **Comparative statics** *is the comparison of economic variables such as price and quantity between two equilibrium positions.*

16. See "Tax Proposed on Products That Harm Environment," *New York Times,* February 10, 1991, p. 30.

For example, if demand equals supply in the market for packaged sweet rolls at $4.50 per dozen, we might want to know what would happen if demand increased by 20 percent at that price. The original price and quantity would then have to be compared to the price and quantity that would prevail in equilibrium if the demand curve were shifted to the right by the amount representing the specified 20 percent increase in demand. We would solve this problem graphically by drawing the demand and supply curves and noting what happened to their intersection as the demand curve was shifted to the right by the correct amount.

Any variable or event that affects the demand curve, the supply curve, or their relation to one another in equilibrium can lead to a change in equilibrium. From our previous discussion, we know that changes in income, expectations, tastes, or consumer demographics could each have an effect on the equilibrium levels of price and quantity through their effect on the demand curve. Changes in the prices of substitute and complement goods for a particular product and changes in input prices could affect equilibrium by shifting the location of the supply curve. The use of taxes or quantity restrictions such as sales taxes, quotas, price ceilings, or price floors can affect static variables by changing the way demand and supply relate to one another in equilibrium.

To understand how these changes operate, we can work through a number of comparative statics exercises. We will consider the effects of a change in demand, a change in supply, imposition of a quota, imposition of a price ceiling, and imposition of a price floor.

The Effects of a Shift in Demand or Supply

In *The Decline and Fall of the Roman Empire,* historian Edward Gibbon reported that the ancient Roman emperor Aurelian "complained that a pound of silk was sold at Rome for twelve ounces of gold; but the supply increased with the demand, and the price diminished with the supply."[17] We can use our demand and supply model to check this description of economic events that occurred over 1,700 years ago. We expect that an increase in demand would raise both price and quantity bought, while an increase in supply would lower price and raise quantity sold.

Part (a) of Figure 2.8 illustrates the effect of an increase in demand when the supply curve is unchanging. The effect of the increase in demand (the shift to the right of the demand curve labeled D to curve D') is to move equilibrium from point e to point e'. In conjunction with this change, we see that price rises and quantity demanded rises. Since the supply curve has not changed, the two equilibria e and e' both lie on the supply curve labeled S. Supply has not changed, but the *quantity supplied* has gone up.

Part (b) of Figure 2.8 illustrates the case of an increase in supply that is not accompanied by a change in demand. The final supply curve is labeled

▼
10. Show the effects of a shift in demand and a shift in supply on equilibrium price and quantity.

17. Edward Gibbon, *The Decline and Fall of the Roman Empire,* Vol. I, London: Encyclopaedia Britannica, 1952, p. 656.

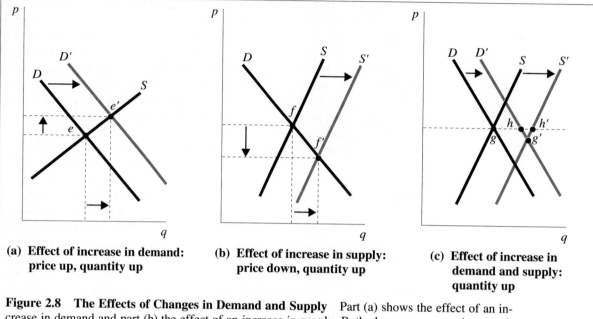

(a) Effect of increase in demand: price up, quantity up

(b) Effect of increase in supply: price down, quantity up

(c) Effect of increase in demand and supply: quantity up

Figure 2.8 The Effects of Changes in Demand and Supply   Part (a) shows the effect of an increase in demand and part (b) the effect of an increase in supply. Both changes cause an increase in equilibrium quantity, but they have different effects on equilibrium price. When *both* demand and supply increase, quantity increases but the price change depends on whether demand or supply has shifted more. In part (c) price falls because the supply curve has shifted more to the right at the original price (from point *g* to *h'*) than has demand (from point *g* to *h*).

S'. Now the equilibrium shifts from point *f* to *f'*, leading to a drop in price and an increase in quantity. Since the demand curve has not changed in this case, both *f* and *f'* lie on the original demand curve *D*.

In the case of Rome's silk market, both demand and supply increased at the same time. Since an increase in demand and an increase in supply both imply greater quantity, such a change should have led to a greater quantity of silk bought and sold in Rome (such, in fact, was the case). Whether the price of silk rose or fell depends on which shift was greater. If the increase in supply was the relatively greater increase, then the price of silk in Rome should have fallen. This is the case shown in part (c) of Figure 2.8.

How do we know which effect was larger? The answer is found by comparing the quantity demanded on the new curve *D'* with the quantity supplied on the new supply curve *S'* at the *original* equilibrium price. These points are marked in Figure 2.8 as points *h* and *h'*. Since *h'* is to the right of *h*, the shift in the supply curve was relatively larger (excess supply was created at the original equilibrium price). To bring demand and supply into equality would require a drop in price.

In summary, the final equilibrium point g' corresponds to a larger quantity in equilibrium, verifying the prediction about quantity. With respect to price, g' corresponds to a lower price than g because the supply increase "won out" over the demand increase. Similarly, you should be able to consider the effects of other changes in demand and supply on price and quantity by seeing how the intersection of demand and supply shifts in response to each change.

Quantity Restrictions: Effects of an Import Quota

▼
11. Describe the effects of an import quota on the price and quantity of imports.

When the quantity of a good consumed domestically at the market price exceeds the domestically supplied quantity, the difference must be made up by a nondomestic source such as imports. Figure 2.9 illustrates demand and supply for a country that imports from the rest of the world. D is the domestic demand, and S is the domestic supply. At price p^*, which is fixed on world markets, the domestic market consumes q^{**} units of the good, q^* of which are produced at home and $(q^{**} - q^*)$ units of which are imported.

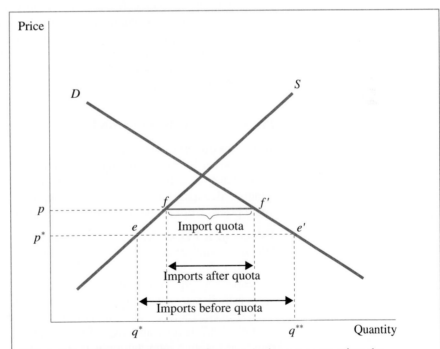

Figure 2.9   Effects of an Import Quota   An import quota raises the domestic price and reduces the domestic quantity consumed. If an import quota is imposed, a price must be found at which the domestic demand exceeds the domestic supply by no more than the quota amount. The quantity consumed domestically is reduced because demanders buy fewer units at the higher price.

What happens to price and quantity if the country imposes an import quota (a limitation on the quantity that can be imported)? For example, in the United States, quotas limit imports of peanuts to approximately seven peanuts per person each year. Fresh cream and milk are embargoed entirely (banned from import), and imports of men's heavy worsted wool suits are capped at 1.2 million, or roughly one imported suit every dozen years for each male manager or professional. Sugar quotas are said to be responsible for roughly doubling the price of sugar and causing large sugar users such as soft-drink manufacturers to shift to corn syrup.[18] Let's use our demand and supply model to check these effects.

Since a quota has dimensional units of quantity, the quota amount is shown as a horizontal distance. To find the equilibrium, we must locate the combination of points in the diagram where the quantity domestic consumers demand exceeds the quantity domestic producers supply by the amount of the quota. At price p, domestic suppliers are willing to provide the quantity corresponding to point f on domestic supply curve S. At this price, which exceeds the original price that prevailed before the quota, foreign producers would be willing to supply more than the quota amount but are permitted to sell only up to the quota. Adding their supply to domestic supply just equals the quantity of domestic demand corresponding to point f' on the domestic demand curve. The quota therefore raises the price consumers pay and reduces the quantity demanded from e' to f'. Since price is higher, consumers have been hurt by the quota. Domestic producers, on the other hand, benefit from a higher selling price, and their quantity supplied rises from point e to point f.

Price Restrictions: Price Ceilings and Price Floors

Just as an import quota is a market intervention that limits quantity, there are other market interventions that limit prices. A *price ceiling* prevents prices from rising to a high enough level to clear the market (that is, to allow quantity demanded to equal quantity supplied); similarly, a *price floor* prevents prices from dropping to a low enough level to clear the market.

Effects of a Price Ceiling. Rent control is an example of a price ceiling. When housing prices rise, municipalities such as New York, Los Angeles, and other cities have sometimes passed local ordinances to prevent the prices of rental housing from going above a certain level. Cambridge, Massachusetts, established rent control in 1970, for example, in response to a perceived "housing emergency" when rents were rising steeply. Rents were rolled back to their 1967 levels, and rules for raising them were strictly defined. The rationale for such intervention is that housing is a necessity and that limiting its price helps renters at the expense of landlords. In practice, rent control

18. The next time you drink a can of soda, check to see whether the sweetener is sugar or corn syrup.

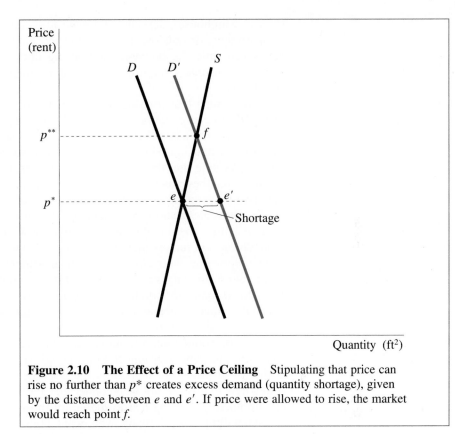

Figure 2.10   The Effect of a Price Ceiling   Stipulating that price can rise no further than p^* creates excess demand (quantity shortage), given by the distance between e and e'. If price were allowed to rise, the market would reach point f.

helps some renters and harms others. It can also lead to black markets,[19] a decrease in housing and housing construction, and costly controls to enforce the ceiling. In Cambridge, rent control deprived many lower-income tenants of affordable housing at the same time that some higher-income tenants benefited from living in rent-controlled apartments for lower rent.[20] Let's use our demand and supply model to examine these effects.

Figure 2.10 presents demand and supply curves for housing, where the quantity of housing is represented in square feet of living space. Demand and supply are drawn as relatively price inelastic, because at any given time the supply of housing stock is fixed, although when housing prices rise, buildings

19. A black market is the buying and selling of goods or services in violation of official regulations. Those who operate black markets for a living are often engaged in other forms of illegal activity.
20. See Gary Chafetz, "Effect of Rent Control Waning," *Boston Globe,* February 18, 1992, pp. 15–16.

such as warehouses, schools, and even fire stations often will be converted to apartments or condos, thus creating more units of housing. Similarly, at any given time the demand for housing does not vary much with price, because consumers require time to adjust their lifestyles to new housing conditions.

Now assume that for various reasons the demand for housing rises from D to D'. Because demand and supply are relatively insensitive to price changes, this has a large effect on price. In the absence of market intervention, the price of housing would rise to p^{**}, corresponding to the equilibrium at point f. Assume that the city council members, believing that housing is an essential that they must try to keep affordable, pass a rent control law freezing the price for housing at level p^*. What is the effect of this price ceiling?[21]

First, it creates a shortage of housing, shown as the excess demand between e and e'. Since there is no way for everyone who wants to rent space to get it, landlords and renters must resort to other ways to allocate rental space. Of course, someone who already has an apartment has an advantage over a newcomer to the city's rental market. For newcomers, ''knowing someone'' starts to become important, and favoritism plays a role in deciding whose demand is met. Whereas a market is anonymous (whoever pays the price receives the product, regardless of the buyer's appearance, personal characteristics, or connections), nonmarket rationing is not anonymous and can sometimes become very unjust. Some people (those fortunate to have housing at the lower price) are helped by the price ceiling at the expense of others (those new to town or not well connected). Paradoxically, price ceilings often end up making housing *less* available for those who need it most.

The willingness of many who want housing to pay a premium for it encourages black marketers to deal in finder's fees, key fees, higher security deposits, and other devices aimed at circumventing the rent control rules. Landlords are often aided and encouraged in this by renters themselves, who may feel fortunate to get whatever apartment they can. Circumvention, of course, leads to the need for greater vigilance in enforcement of the rent control laws, tying up court time or creating greater workloads for judicial bodies set up to administer the laws. The cost of this is borne by the city's taxpayers, many of whom are ironically the very renters whom rent control was supposed to help.

The full effect of the price ceiling becomes evident after the passage of time. As demand continues to rise, supply does not respond because price is kept fixed. The problems of excess demand increase through time, and any incentive to provide new rental units is short-circuited. Moreover, existing rent-controlled units are often poorly maintained or allowed to deteriorate to the point where their owners can take them off the market. This housing

---

21. Before proceeding, you might pause to consider this question: If city legislators really believe that they can make housing affordable just by passing a law, why don't they make it completely affordable by legislating that the price of rental housing be zero?

stock is either lost or replaced with noncontrolled units if local rules permit. Long after those responsible for the rent control legislation have turned their attention to other matters, the housing shortage problems they created will persist.

▼
12. How do the effects of a price floor differ from those of a price ceiling?

Effects of a Price Floor. The effects of a price floor are different from those of a price ceiling. Whereas price ceilings are meant to help the buyer by keeping price low (although, as we have seen, they may not do this for all buyers), a price floor is intended to help the *seller* by keeping price high. The American farm program based on the Agricultural Adjustment Act of 1933 and later amendments is an example of a policy that attempts to raise the price of certain crops by the use of price floors. The method of support most commonly used in the United States is the nonrecourse loan, whereby a farmer receives a loan from the Commodity Credit Corporation that may be repaid by delivering the crop at the support price or, if the market price is higher, by selling the crop and repaying in cash. Price is supported by the government's willingness to accept the crop at the stated price. The government, which now owns the crop, can either store it, destroy it, or give it away. Many other countries, such as Japan and members of the European Economic Community, also employ price supports for agriculture. Agriculture is often a target of price supports because of its historical importance and because farm income often varies greatly with changes in growing conditions. Critics of the farm program have questioned why farmers should receive government dollars when other sectors in the economy facing equally difficult circumstances receive none.

Figure 2.11 shows the effects of a price floor. Instead of equilibrium occurring at point *i* where *D* and *S* intersect, the price floor at p_F creates excess supply. The difference in quantity between point *k* on the supply curve and point *j* on the demand curve shows the excess.

The problems arising from excess supply are different from those of excess demand. Storing commodities is costly and wasteful. Taxpayers end up providing dollars not only to purchase the quantities in excess supply, but also to pay storage costs. Moreover, consumers must pay more for their food. Under the price-support system, the total costs to consumers, in the form of direct purchases as well as taxes to cover government acquisitions, are shown by the larger shaded area in Figure 2.11. Without the price floor, consumers would have paid only the lesser amount represented by the smaller shaded area.

EXPLORATION: Market Effects of Asymmetric Information

As we have just seen, limitations imposed on quantity and price impede the market's ability to deliver goods impersonally from sellers to buyers. The effects change the way markets operate, helping some participants and harm-

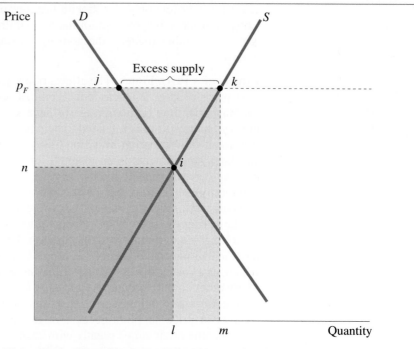

Figure 2.11   The Effect of a Price Floor   If price is artificially kept from dropping below p_F, the result is an excess supply equal to the distance between j and k. If price were allowed to drop, market equilibrium would be reached at point i.

▼

13. Explain the difference between symmetric and asymmetric information.

ing others.[22] Another way in which market function can be impaired is by lack of full information about the product being sold. This can happen when information is *asymmetric*—when sellers, for example, know more about the product than buyers.

So far in this chapter we have been describing markets with symmetric information. A market with *symmetric* information is one in which all buyers and sellers are equally informed about the nature, quality, and description of the commodity being bought and sold. If you buy a package of brand-name cassette tapes, you know what type of tapes you are buying, what their physical characteristics are, and what their usable life is likely to be. There is probably no misrepresentation by the seller about the tapes, nor any misapprehension by you, the buyer, about what you are getting.

22. Later, after we have covered consumer and producer surplus in Chapters 4 and 7, we will be able to explain why market interventions usually harm those who lose more than they help those who gain.

Information and Uncertainty

Rarely is information perfect in an absolute sense. We are often uncertain about a product because our information is incomplete. Yet incomplete information need not imply asymmetric information. There may be intrinsic uncertainty about the product's characteristics or performance. In the cassette-tape market, for example, the quality of any given tape cannot be known with certainty, but the problem is typically handled by noting that the likelihood of getting a nondefective tape is better than, say, 98 percent. The tape quality for each brand becomes part of the description of the product, and both buyer and seller are aware of the situation. A Maxell high-bias tape usually sells for a higher price than a lesser-name house brand. For other types of commodities, uncertainty about how a specific item will perform can sometimes be countered by warranty agreements, the right of the buyer to return the product, and so on.

Asymmetric Information

The cassette-tape example illustrates incomplete information and uncertainty of a type that buyers and sellers can deal with because information is equally available. The situation changes when there is *asymmetric imperfect* information about a product. If either the buyer or the seller knows more about the product, market prices will reflect not only the characteristics and intrinsic worth of the product, but the distribution of information. Asymmetric information can create artificial uncertainty, in the sense that if everyone's information were publicly known, the uncertainty would be absent. It can also cause prices and quantities to react differently than they otherwise would. In some cases, asymmetric information can make a market shut down completely. The following application examines the effects of asymmetric information in the market for used cars. ■

APPLICATION: Used Cars

Have you ever wondered why a new car, once it has been privately owned for even a short time, drops greatly in value? For example, a $16,000 car, once the ownership papers have been written and it has been driven off the dealer's lot, cannot be sold for $16,000 to another buyer even if it has been driven only a few miles. Why? The answer relates to asymmetric information about used cars.

Consider your own decision to buy such a car. Once a car has been used, you cannot be sure why it is for sale. Maybe the owner has discovered a major defect. (Why would someone buy a car and immediately decide to sell it?) Even though the likelihood of a problem with the car is small, the chances are greater that something is amiss. Because your alternative would be to buy the same car from a new car dealer, you would not buy the used car unless its price were substantially lower. You might have a thorough mechanical review made of the car, but since this is costly, it would not be worth your while unless the used car sold for less money. Only if you knew with certainty that the used car and the new car were identical might you consider treating them as equal purchases.

The problem of determining the quality of a used car is also present in comparing two different used cars. Inherently, used cars are a commodity about which the buyer typically knows less than the seller. What is the effect of this asymmetric information on the used car market? We know already that used cars will sell at a substantial discount relative to equivalent new cars. To see what other effects could occur in the market for used cars, let's think through a simple case where there are only two types of used cars: high-quality used cars and low-quality used cars.[23] Very low-quality used cars are commonly referred to as ''lemons.'' A lemon requires more maintenance and delivers less reliable transportation than a high-quality used car.

If everyone knew which used cars were lemons and which were high quality, each type of car would be traded in a separate market since the nature of the two commodities differs. Figure 2.12 shows the demand and supply curves for such separate markets, with low-quality used cars in part (a) and high-quality used cars in part (b). The two markets are related to one another. We would not expect any demand for low-quality cars if their price exceeded the price for high-quality cars, because any potential buyer of a low-quality car could instead buy a high-quality car for less money.

The market supply of low-quality cars is shown by the curve *abc* in part (a). Sellers of low-quality cars in this example provide 1 million cars per year to the market as long as the price they can get is price *a* or higher. That is why the curve is horizontal at price *a* but becomes vertical at point *b*. The demand for low-quality used cars causes the market price to be slightly higher than *a*, and all of the cars offered on the market are sold. Similarly, the supply curve of high-quality cars is indicated by curve *def* in part (b). Sellers of high-quality used cars sell 1 million cars per year as long as the price they receive is higher than price *d*. Buyers of high-quality used cars are willing to pay a higher price, so the demand curve is located higher than the demand curve for low-quality used cars.

As drawn, the market price for high-quality used cars is slightly higher than *d*. Each demand curve is drawn assuming the price for cars in the other market is given. Thus, if the price for low-quality used cars were sufficiently high to be near price *d*, the demand for low-quality used cars would fall to zero.

Now presume that buyers cannot tell whether a used car is high quality or low quality. Sellers of high-quality cars will certainly tell buyers that their cars are of high quality, but how should the buyers respond to this? Will sellers of lemons be honest enough to advertise their cars as such, knowing

---

23. For an original study of the used car market, see George Akerlof, ''The Market for 'Lemons': Quality Uncertainty and the Market Mechanism,'' *Quarterly Journal of Economics,* 84 (1970), pp. 488–500.

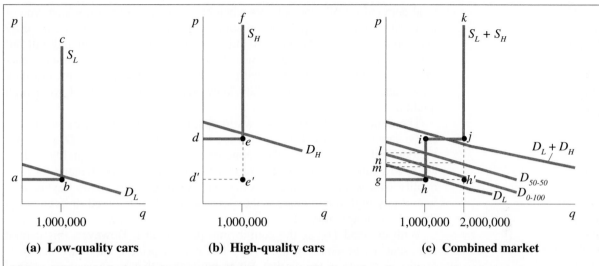

(a) Low-quality cars   **(b) High-quality cars**   **(c) Combined market**

Figure 2.12   Markets and Asymmetric Information   If information about the quality of used cars were equally well known by buyers and sellers, two markets would exist with two separate prices for cars—one for low-quality used cars, shown in part (a), and one for high-quality used cars, shown in part (b). When buyers cannot distinguish used car quality, all cars must be sold in one market at the same price. Part (c) shows the supply curve for the combined market as curve *ghijk*. Demand depends on what mix of cars buyers believe they will get on average when they buy a used car. Though its shape cannot be determined from the curves in parts (a) and (b) directly, we know the demand curve must lie to the right of the demand for low-quality cars alone, D_L, because some former high-quality used car buyers will demand cars in the combined market. Similarly, the curve must be to the left of the combined demand for high and low quality cars, $D_L + D_H$, because some former high-quality used car buyers will leave the combined market and cease buying any used cars when they cannot be sure of getting high quality.

that lemons sell for a lower price? In some cases the seller will be honest, but in all too many cases sellers will jettison their honesty for the prospect of receiving more money. For our example, then, let us assume the worst case, which is that *all* cars are represented to the buyer as high-quality used cars.

▼

14. List some of the possible effects of asymmetric information on market equilibrium.

If all cars appear the same to the buyer, there can be only one market in used cars. Part (c) in Figure 2.12 therefore shows the supply curve for all used cars as the curve containing points *ghijk*. At a price below *g*, no used cars come on the market (owners use them until they are junked). At prices between *g* and the price corresponding to point *i*, only low-quality used cars come on the market. At prices higher than the price corresponding to point *i,* equal numbers of high-quality and low-quality used cars are offered for sale. This gives the supply curve its stepped shape.

On the other side of the market, demand for used cars depends on the proportion of the two types of cars in the market. The lines labeled D_L and $D_L + D_H$ indicate the demand curve for low-quality used cars alone and the total demand for all types of cars when buyers can distinguish which type of used car they are buying.[24] When some cars are of each quality, demand by high-quality used car buyers will shift inward, so that total demand will fall somewhere between these extremes. At a given price, buyers want more cars than they would if they knew with certainty that all were lemons, but they also want fewer cars than if they knew with certainty that all were high quality.

The demand curve $D_{50\text{-}50}$ shows market demand for used cars when half of the cars are high quality and half are low quality. In contrast, $D_{0\text{-}100}$ shows the demand for used cars when none of the cars are of high quality and all are of low quality. This curve is farther to the right than the demand for low-quality cars when there are two markets because some of the buyers who would buy high-quality cars if they were available are forced to buy cars in the only available market.

With demand $D_{50\text{-}50}$, the equilibrium price is at l. However, this cannot represent a true equilibrium. Why? Because at price l, there are no high-quality used cars in the market. When buyers see that *every* used car offered for sale is a lemon, their demand will not be $D_{50\text{-}50}$ but $D_{0\text{-}100}$. Equilibrium price will be m, and at this price buyers expect all used cars to be lemons, which is just what the market supplies.

The effect of asymmetric information in this case is to prevent the sale of high-quality used cars altogether. Because sellers of high-quality used cars cannot prove the worth of their cars to the buyer, they have no choice but to accept price m or not to sell.

It is possible that some sellers of high-quality used cars would be willing to sell for whatever price is offered, simply because they want to buy a new car every few years. If the supply curve of high-quality used cars is identical to that of low-quality used cars, the supply curve would become $d'e'f$ in part (b) of Figure 2.12. The supply curve for cars of all types then becomes $gh'k$ in part (c) of the figure. Now that the demand curve is $D_{50\text{-}50}$, equilibrium price is at n. Buyers expect that they will end up with a lemon half the time, and this is what the market provides. The net result now is that high-quality and low-quality used cars sell for the same price, and the absence of symmetric information makes buyers uncertain about which quality car they are getting.[25] ■

---

24. At each price, the quantity on the total curve in part (c) is the sum of quantities demanded for that price shown by curves D_L and D_H in parts (a) and (b). This leads to a slight kink in the curve in part (c). We'll see why in Chapter 4.

25. As an exercise, you might want to redraw Figure 2.12 using linear, upward-sloping supply curves without corners. Instead of high-quality cars being totally in the market or totally out of the market, you can generate intermediate cases where some high-quality used cars are offered and some are not offered at a particular equilibrium.

2.7 Summing Up Demand, Supply, and Markets

We've covered a lot of ground in this chapter. It is worthwhile to pull together what we have learned. Without a doubt, the main message of the chapter is that demand, supply, and the concept of market equilibrium simplify the study of market price and quantity. Once the differences between a shift in quantity demanded and a shift in demand are understood (as well as their counterparts, a shift in quantity supplied and a shift in supply), it is possible to analyze the effect of virtually any disturbance on market price and quantity. We can use elasticity to measure the degree of responsiveness of demand and supply curves to the price of the product itself, and we can talk about how the increase in the price of one product affects the quantity demanded of another through cross-price elasticity. We can explain how the increase in the price of one product affects the market price of another product through its effect on the demand and supply curves of the other product. Thus, most of the chapter was devoted to explaining demand and supply and giving examples of how to use demand and supply curves in market analysis.

The chapter alerted you to the fact that markets can behave very differently when there are price, quantity, or information restrictions present. For example, when information is imperfect and asymmetric, we found that the market price can differ from what would have occurred if information were equally available to everyone. As we saw in our used-car application, this situation may even result in some goods not being offered for sale. Possibly, markets may shut down entirely. The bottom line is that the market concepts introduced here are some of the most powerful and versatile tools you will learn in your college career.

Summary

Active Reading Guide numbers are given in parentheses at the end of each summary item.

1. A market is a group of buyers and sellers who are linked together by trade with one another in a particular good or service. (1)

2. Demand and supply are ideas for studying a market that simplify the understanding of price formation and the determination of quantities. Demand relates price to what buyers want to purchase. Supply relates price to what sellers want to sell. The demand curve plots the quantity demanded for each price. The supply curve plots the quantity supplied for each price. Normally, demand curves slope downward and supply curves slope upward. (2, 4)

3. A shift of the price-quantity point along the demand or supply curve is a *change in quantity demanded* or *change in quantity supplied,* respectively. Income, the prices of other goods, expectations, the number of buyers in the market, and preferences can all influence the location of the demand curve. Change in location of the demand curve is termed a *change in demand.* The prices of other goods, the prices of factors of production, and technology influence the location of the supply curve. Change in location of the supply curve is termed a *change in supply.* (3, 5)

4. Equilibrium is a price and quantity such that quantity demanded and quantity supplied are equal at the given price. At equilibrium the choices of

buyers and sellers are consistent with each other, and there is no incentive for buyers or sellers to change their current actions. (6).

5. Elasticity is the percentage change in one variable caused by a 1 percent change in another. The price elasticity of demand, measuring the price responsiveness of demand, is computed as the percentage change in quantity demanded divided by the percentage change in price. Similarly, the price elasticity of supply is the percentage change in quantity supplied divided by the percentage change in price. The price elasticities of supply and demand relate to both the slope and the location of the demand and supply curves. Given the same slope, the larger the quantity, the less elastic the curve. Given the same quantity, the flatter the curve, the more elastic the curve. (7)

6. One economic determinant of a high price elasticity of demand is the presence of a close substitute good. In general, the more broadly a good is defined (say, all food), the less likely it is to have close substitutes, and the less broadly it is defined (say, ice cream), the more likely it is to have close substitutes (frozen yogurt). Other determinants of high price elasticity of demand include (a) the good's being a large part of consumers' budgets, and (b) a long period of time over which the quantity response to the price change is measured. High price elasticity of supply, on the other hand, reflects the ability of producers to increase the quantity of output without causing an increase in costs. The more narrowly defined the product and the larger the market from which it draws its inputs, the more

elastic the supply curve is likely to be. As with demand, the longer the time period over which supply response is measured, the greater the price elasticity is likely to be. (8)

7. Comparative statics is the comparison of equilibria. Anything that affects demand, supply, or how they interact with one another has comparative static effects. An increase in demand means that the demand curve has shifted to the right. An increase in demand moves the equilibrium point to the right on the (stationary) supply curve. Similarly, a decrease in demand moves the demand curve to the left and the equilibrium point to the left on the stationary supply curve. An increase in supply means that the supply curve has shifted to the right. An increase in supply moves the equilibrium point to the right on the (stationary) demand curve. Similarly, a decrease in supply moves the supply curve to the left and the equilibrium point to the left on the stationary demand curve. (9)

8. Under normal conditions of downward-sloping demand and upward-sloping supply, an import quota that reduces imports leads to an increase in domestic price. A price ceiling lowers price and leads to excess demand, whereas a price floor raises price and leads to excess supply. (10, 11, 12)

9. Asymmetric information exists when some buyers or sellers are better informed about relevant economic information than others. Asymmetric information can lead to equilibria with different prices and quantities, quality uncertainty about commodities that are traded, or market shutdown. (13, 14)

Review Questions

1. In the winter of 1990, a major freeze hit the state of California. Shortly thereafter, citrus prices rose all over the country. Is this a good indication that the United States forms a unified market for citrus? Elaborate.

*2. A 1991 article in the *Wall Street Journal* described the U.S. government's plans to place stiff

duties on Japanese-made display screens used in portable computers.[26] The article reported that U.S. computer makers were angry, ''saying the action will make it more difficult for them to compete with the Japanese in the growing market for portables.'' Explain this response in terms of the action's effect on the U.S. computer makers' supply curve.

26. ''Computers,'' *Wall Street Journal,* February 11, 1991, pp. B1, B3
* Asterisks are used to denote questions that are answered at the back of the book.

3. Discuss how each of the following would affect the supply of wool jackets.
   a) An increase in the market price of wool jackets
   b) An increase in the price of wool
   c) An increase in the wages for woolen-mill workers

*4. What is wrong with the following statement: ''Demand goes up when price falls.''

5. Find the mistake in the following reasoning: The supply of hogs increased, leading to a fall in the price of pork. The drop in the pork price in turn increased the demand for pork. The increase in demand for pork led to an increase in price, so it is not possible to tell whether the price of pork rose or fell overall.

*6. Do comparative statics to explain why the Iraqi invasion of Kuwait on August 2, 1990, led to an overnight increase in the price of gasoline at the pump, even though no change in world oil supplies had yet occurred. Is this evidence of oil companies and retailers taking advantage of the situation to get higher prices from consumers?

7. In each of the following pairs, which item do you think would have higher price elasticity of demand? Justify your answer in each case.

a) Toothpaste in a 6-ounce tube. All toothpaste.
b) Basic telephone service. Vacation trips to Cancun.
c) Home heating fuel one month after a permanent price increase in January. Home heating fuel five years after a permanent price increase in January.
d) Use of heroin by addicts. Meals eaten at restaurants.

8. Why is slope not a good measure of price responsiveness for demand or supply?

*9. What is the comparative statics analysis to explain why California orange growers regularly destroy part of their crop?

10. What are the differences among imperfect information, asymmetric information, and uncertainty?

*11. In the used car market, would the problems of asymmetric information disappear if every car buyer could tell at a glance whether a car was of high or low quality? Would a car buyer be willing to pay for such information? If so, what might prevent such information from being available?

Numerical and Graphing Exercises

1. The demand curve for a given commodity is given by $q^D/1,500 + p/1,500 = 1$ and the supply curve is given by $q^S = 4p$. Find the equilibrium price and quantity for this market.

*2. In the market for exercise 1, find the excess supply or excess demand if price is 500.

3. Draw a downward-sloping demand curve and an upward-sloping supply curve. How would an increase in demand plus an increase in supply affect price and quantity if, at the original equilibrium price, the changes led to an excess supply?

*4. Gasoline is sold by two gas stations, A and B, that stand opposite each other at the intersection of two roads. Gas station A sells fuel refined from domestic oil, and station B sells identical fuel refined from foreign oil. Domestic and foreign unre-

fined oil have an identical price determined on world markets. Both types of oil cost the same to refine. What would happen to the prices and quantities of gasoline sold at each station if the government put a per-gallon tax only on the sales of fuel produced from foreign oil?

*5. Using the information from exercise 14, draw the demand curve for all gasoline purchased at the intersection. Then draw the demand curve for gasoline for each station separately, assuming a fixed price of gasoline at the other station. (Hint: How does the price of gasoline at one station affect the demand at the other?)

6. Use the demand and supply curves for jeans given earlier in the chapter (Figure 2.5). If the government established a price floor of $p = \$22$ by

buying any jeans not bought by the private sector, how much money would this cost the taxpayers? How much of this total cost would result from higher costs for jeans and how much from other types of costs? Explain.

*7. If your price elasticity of demand is −0.2, how much will your food purchases fall in quantity terms if the price of food goes up 2 percent?

8. Draw linear supply curves having the following price elasticities of supply at the point corresponding to price $10: 0, 0.5, 1, 2, infinity.

9. The supply of housing on a city block near a university campus is fixed at 100 units, whatever the market price is. Demand for housing on this block is given by $q^D = 200 − (20/73)p$, where p is rental dollars per month.
   a) Find the equilibrium monthly rental price per unit.
   b) Demand now increases to $q^D = 230 − (20/73)p$. What is the effect of a price ceiling that keeps price from rising any higher than the original equilibrium price?
   c) Since the quantity of housing is fixed, can a price ceiling cause a housing shortage in this case?

10. Assume that, in the short run, consumers of home heating oil cannot reduce their use at all in response to an increase in price, but that over time they can institute conservation measures that reduce quantity. Analyze the immediate impact of a 25 percent reduction in the supply of home heating oil on price and quantity and compare it to the impact in the long run.

*11. Let domestic demand for cloth be given by $q^D = 350 − 50p$, and domestic supply be given by $q^S = −500 + 200p$.
   a) What are imports of cloth if the world price of cloth is 3?
   b) What is the effect on domestic price and quantity consumed of an import quota that is set to cut imports of cloth by one-half the unrestricted market amount?

*12. Turn-of-the-century developers and resort owners on Key West, Florida, subsidized train tickets to Key West. Use demand and supply curves to explain their motives.

13. Designer handbags are prominently labeled with the name of the designer. Low-quality imitators, however, make handbags that are nearly indistinguishable from the designer bags and label them with imitations of the designer labels. Draw demand and supply curves describing the market for designer handbags and imitations if
   a) Buyers cannot distinguish imitations from designer bags at the time of purchase or at any time during the life of the handbag.
   b) Buyers cannot distinguish imitations from designer bags at the time of purchase, but discover later that imitation bags do not perform satisfactorily. (This discovery occurs too late for the bags to be returned!)
   c) Buyers can distinguish imitations from designer bags at the time of purchase and know that imitation bags will not perform as well as designer bags in the long run.

APPENDIX: Equilibrium and Stability

As we discussed earlier in this chapter, the idea of equilibrium carries with it the implication that the market is at a resting point. That is, at equilibrium the price is neither rising nor falling. If the market is not at rest and thus out of equilibrium, a natural question to ask is whether the market will eventually move to equilibrium. After all, if markets do not move to equilibrium, there is little point in using equilibrium to describe what happens in a market. The concept of market stability helps us address this question.

▼
A.1. What is meant by stability for a general system?

Stability is the property of any system to return to equilibrium, or rest, from a position out of equilibrium. For example, a textbook lying flat on a table is in equilibrium because it is not moving (the force of gravity pulling it toward the center of the earth is exactly counterbalanced by the force of the table preventing it from moving). If I lift one edge of the book one inch above the table, the book is out of equilibrium because from that position it will drop if I let the corner go. The fact that the book will return to its original equilibrium position indicates that the resting position for the book is *stable* for small perturbations of one corner of an inch or less.

If I now manage to balance the book on one corner so that it stays balanced, the book is again in equilibrium. Now, however, if the book is moved by the slightest breath of wind, it will cease being balanced and fall. This equilibrium is *unstable* because the book does not return to the original equilibrium in response to a small perturbation.

A third type of equilibrium is represented by a cylindrical piece of chalk lying on its side on a flat surface. If the chalk is rolled a small distance from its original resting place, it will remain at rest in whatever position it is left. The equilibrium is one of neutral stability because a perturbation results in neither a return to the original equilibrium nor a position different from the perturbed position. Any position is an equilibrium.

▼
A.2. How would you test to determine whether a market equilibrium was stable or unstable?

In markets a similar question of stability arises. To ask whether a market equilibrium is stable or unstable, we need to specify the laws of motion for the market when it is out of equilibrium. In the case of the book or the chalk, the laws of motion were given to us by physics and the laws of gravity so we did not have to think much about them. In the case of a market, however, we need to think about what it means to be *out* of equilibrium.

One definition is that we are out of equilibrium whenever there is a price in the market that is higher or lower than the equilibrium price. If there is excess supply of a commodity, a reasonable ''law of motion'' is that the price of the commodity falls. That is, if there is unsold product, sellers will probably lower the price in an attempt to induce customers to buy the excess. If there is excess demand, the price rises because sellers can sell the product even if the price they charge is higher than what they are currently charging.

The laws of motion that we have just described were suggested by a French economist of the late 1800s and early 1900s, Marie-Esprit-Léon Walras. A system that returns to equilibrium under these laws of motion is called *Walrasian stable* in his honor.[27] Walrasian laws of motion are valid for many markets. Buyers who cannot get the good they want at the going price have an incentive to offer more for the good rather than go without. At the same time, sellers, seeing their stock disappear, have an incentive to raise their prices. The reverse pressures occur when there is excess supply, as sellers see unsold goods piling up and buyers must be induced by lower price to demand a greater quantity of the good.

27. Alfred Marshall, an English economist of the early 1900s, suggested another ''law of motion'': quantity will fall if at that quantity the price on the supply curve is above the price on the demand curve, and quantity will rise if the reverse is true. Other forms of stability depend on other laws of motion. Today, Marshallian stability is less commonly used than Walrasian stability.

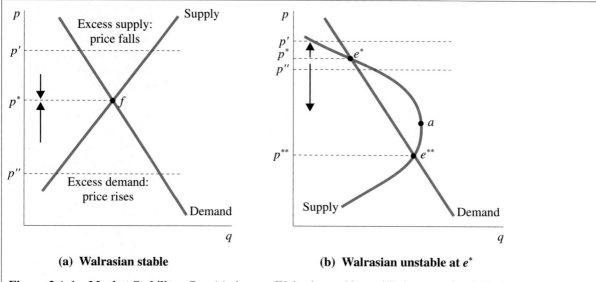

(a) Walrasian stable   **(b) Walrasian unstable at** e^*

Figure 2.A.1   Market Stability   Part (a) shows a Walrasian-stable equilibrium at point f. If price were above the equilibrium level of p^*, as at p', excess supply would occur, driving price back down to the equilibrium level. Similarly, if price were too low, as at p'', excess demand would drive price back up to the equilibrium level. Part (b) shows a Walrasian-unstable equilibrium at point e^*. If price were slightly above equilibrium price p^*, demand would exceed supply, driving price up and farther away from equilibrium price p^*. Similarly, if price were slightly below p^*, supply would exceed demand, driving price down and farther away from p^*.

Under these laws of motion, the market will generally be stable. Part (a) of Figure 2.A.1 illustrates standard market demand and supply curves with equilibrium price given by p^*. If the market is perturbed to another price, say, price p' (higher than the equilibrium price), excess supply at that price (following the Walrasian law of motion) causes the price to fall. Similarly, if the price is perturbed to a price such as p'', which is too low, excess demand induces the price to rise. In either case, the price will continue to move until the original equilibrium at p^* is reached. The market in part (a) of Figure 2.A.1 is therefore Walrasian stable.

*A market equilibrium is **stable** if, under the laws of motion that govern the market when it is out of equilibrium, the market returns to equilibrium when perturbed to a nearby position out of equilibrium.*

Part (b) of Figure 2.A.1 suggests a case where instability can occur. The supply curve has a backward-bending portion above point a.[28] This type of

28. That is, at prices below point a an increase in price leads to an increase in quantity supplied. For prices above point a, an increase in price leads to a decrease in quantity supplied.

supply curve can sometimes be applicable, for example, to labor supply: as the wage rate offered gets higher, it eventually reaches a point where workers earn so much income that they begin to work less in order to have the time to enjoy their income. Enjoying their income, of course, takes leisure time, which must come from fewer work hours. We will look at this phenomenon in Chapter 5.

Points e^* and e^{**} are both equilibria for this market. Point e^* is Walrasian unstable because we see that at a price above p^* there is an excess demand for labor, which would tend to drive the price of labor up, pulling it further away from p^* (remember our laws of motion).[29] If the price instead is perturbed to p'', which is below p^*, the induced excess supply of labor causes the price to fall even further from p^*. Thus, if price is too high it tends to get higher, and if price is too low it tends to get lower. In either case, the price tends to move away from the equilibrium price at e^*. Because e^* is unstable, we would expect never to observe such an equilibrium (just as we virtually never observe books balanced on their corners). Instead, in this market we would expect to see e^{**} as the equilibrium. This is true because e^{**} is Walrasian stable, as you should verify by checking whether there is excess demand or excess supply when the price is slightly above or slightly below p^{**}. ▨

29. Price cannot continue to rise forever. Eventually something must change, stopping the price rise and making the original demand and supply curves no longer relevant to the problem.

INVESTIGATIONS I

A. Import Controls and the U.S. Sugar Market

Aerodynamic engineers cannot tell you how the bumblebee flies, and I cannot tell you how the sugar program functions.

Congressman W. R. Poage, sugar program sponsor[1]

The more I studied the many administrative decisions required to operate the program, the more convinced I became that the sugar program with its quotas and the processes by which those quotas are determined is truly an evil system.

D. Gale Johnson, American Enterprise Institute[2]

Although many Americans could tell you something about the impact of sugar on their diet, most don't have a clue about the massive intervention in the sugar market by the federal government, an intervention that increases manyfold the price of sugar and results in higher prices for the numerous products that contain it. This investigation reviews the nature of sugar market import controls in the United States and shows how demand and supply tools can be used to evaluate their effects.

Sugar in History and Politics

At the time of Edward the Confessor (A.D. 1002–1066) Europeans did not even know of the existence of sugar. By the middle 1600s, however, the nobility were regular users, and by 1900 sugar played such a prominent role in the diet of certain developed countries that it supplied nearly one in five calories consumed.[3] In the 1700s sugar occupied the role in commerce and international trade that steel was to occupy in the 1800s and oil in the 1900s.[4]

Today, sugar is one of the most widely grown agricultural commodities. Approximately 60 percent of the world's sugar comes from sugar cane and 40 percent from sugar beets.[5] Less than one-third of world production, 121

1. Quoted in Scott B. MacDonald and Georges A. Fauriol, ''Introduction,'' *The Politics of the U.S.–Caribbean Basin Sugar Trade,* New York: Praeger, 1991, p. 18.
2. D. Gale Johnson, *The Sugar Program: Large Costs and Small Benefits,* Washington, D.C.: American Enterprise Institute for Public Policy Research, 1974, p. 33.
3. MacDonald and Fauriol, op. cit., p. 1.
4. Ibid.
5. Lloyd Chilvers and Robin Foster, *The International Sugar Market,* Special Report No. 106, London: The Economist Intelligence Unit, Ltd., 1981, p. 3.

million tons in the 1990–1991 crop year, is traded internationally, because of the large consumption at home of most producing countries. Sugar consumption tends to grow with the income of the consuming country, peaking somewhere around 100 to 130 pounds annually per person. The relatively high cost of sugar in the United States has led to the expansion of alternative corn-derived sweeteners such as high-fructose corn syrup. U.S. total consumption of caloric sweeteners per capita in 1990 was a record 136.7 pounds per person, of which sugar accounted for 47 percent, or 63.9 pounds per person. Of the remainder, 71.4 pounds were provided by corn sweeteners. Sugar is big business, and the politics of the sugar program is important not only to U.S. growers, but to the 650 sugar mills in Latin America and nations of the Caribbean Basin such as the Dominican Republic, Haiti, Jamaica, Guyana, Barbados, Belize, and others.[6]

U.S. Intervention in the Sugar Trade

The U.S. government has a long history of involvement in sugar. In 1789, almost as soon as the nation was established, Congress imposed a tariff on sugar imports. Until 1890, when the tariff was temporarily removed before being reinstated in 1894, sugar accounted for almost 20 percent of all duties collected.

In spite of protection of domestic sugar producers, the sugar market has remained a volatile and highly political market. In this century the sugar program dates back to the Franklin Roosevelt administration. In May 1932 sugar prices reached a low of 1 cent per pound after having been considerably higher in previous years (prices peaked at 19 cents per pound in May 1920). In response, the Jones-Costigan Act was passed in 1934, establishing comprehensive government management of the U.S. sugar market. The act set quotas on foreign and domestic producers, established market shares, and provided for payments to domestic producers to maintain higher prices. This remained the basis of U.S. law until 1974, when a 300 percent price increase in one year (sugar prices reached almost 60 cents per pound) weakened support for extension of the program. Interestingly, this was only the third time since 1948 that world sugar prices had exceeded the domestically regulated rates.[7]

The U.S. sugar market was completely free for two years, 1975 and 1976. When world prices returned to more normal levels, however (7.6 cents per pound in December 1976), pressure resumed for government payments to U.S. farmers. In 1977 President Carter instituted price supports at 13.5 cents per pound, and farm legislation in 1981 and 1982 included sugar provisions setting supports at 16.25 cents per pound, raising tariffs to over 4 cents per pound, and setting import quotas. Though President Reagan opposed the sugar provisions and publicly espoused free trade, he found it necessary to compromise in order to get other legislative objectives met.

6. Jose Antonia Cerro, ''The View from Latin America and the Caribbean,'' in MacDonald and Fauriol, op. cit., p. 35.
7. MacDonald and Fauriol, op. cit., p. 18.

To many Americans, the prospect of the government's spending their tax dollars to pay sugar producers, despite the presence of a large federal deficit, was unpalatable. Thus 1985 farm legislation mandated that the sugar program be continued, but "at no cost" to the government. This meant that direct price supports were to be avoided by limiting sugar imports to the point where domestic prices reached target levels. Quotas were assigned to foreign exporting countries and adjusted as needed to meet targets; quotas were also adjusted in light of political considerations such as the Caribbean Basin Initiative, which sought to help developing nations in the Caribbean by giving them greater access to the U.S. market. Paradoxically, the sugar program frequently produced results for foreign countries that were opposite those desired.

Even when the sugar program does not appear as a line item in the government's budget, its costs are still being paid by the U.S. public in the form of higher prices for sugar and substitute corn sweeteners. A Department of Commerce study in 1988 set the total cost of the program at $3.7 billion annually for the period 1982–1985.[8] This works out to more than $39 annually per household or $55 annually per family, a very high cost to pay, considering that sweeteners are only one small item out of the hundreds consumed annually. Imagine the same costs expanded to cover each of the items in a household's entire food budget!

How does the Commerce Department come up with these numbers? We now use our market tools to evaluate the cost of the program to the American public in the late 1980s and early 1990s.

Evaluating the Effects of Import Controls

The main cost of the sugar program is higher prices to consumers. To find the size of these costs, we first need to know the size of the market. U.S. sugar production between 1985 and 1991 varied between 6 and 7 million tons per year, averaging around 6.67 million tons.[9] Consumption, in turn, varied between 8.4 and 9.4 million tons, with the period average just under 9 million tons. Of this, an average 2.3 million tons were imported each year.[10] The average domestic price for sugar was 22 cents per pound (20.34 cents per pound in 1985, rising to 23.35 cents in 1990), whereas world prices were 4 cents per pound in 1985 and 12.5 in 1990, averaging about 8.5 cents.

8. International Trade Aministration, *United States Sugar Policy: An Analysis,* Washington, D.C.: U.S. Department of Commerce, April 1988, p. 5.
9. U.S. Department of Agriculture, *Sugar and Sweeener Situation and Outlook Report,* Washington, D.C.: Economic Research Service, March 1991.
10. In 1990–1991 2.3 million tons of sugar were eligible for first-tier import. Under the post–October 1990 tariff-rate quota system, imports enter under the first-tier duty of 0.625 cents per pound (with zero duty for specified countries and Caribbean Basin Initiative trade partners) until the eligible quantity has been reached. Thereafter, imports are subject to a second-tier duty of 16 cents per pound. A small amount of quota-exempt imports is allowed for domestic processing, if the processed sugar is re-exported within 90 days or transferred to manufacturers of sugar-containing products for export.

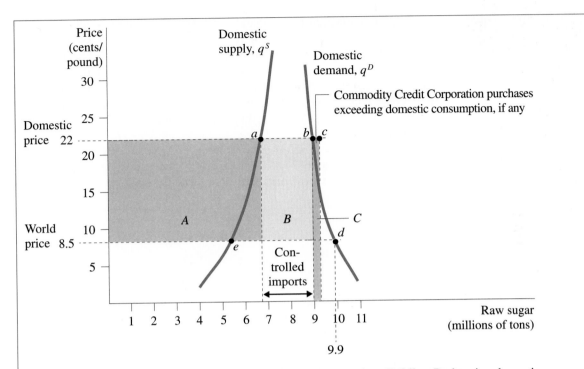

Figure I.1   Cost of Government Sugar Program to the American Public   By keeping domestic sugar prices much higher than the world price, the sugar support program costs the public money equal to area *A* + *B*, or $2.43 billion per year on average. Because quantity demanded would be at *d* at world price, the total cost to the public also includes the area between the demand curve and world price between points *b* and *d*, an additional $0.12 billion/year. If there are government purchases by the Commodity Credit Corporation, there are additional costs equal to government budget outlays for purchase of sugar, area *C*.

Plotting this information gives us the situation portrayed in Figure I.1. Point *a* represents the supply of sugar by U.S. producers and point *b* consumption by the public. The difference between the quantity consumed and the quantity produced domestically is made up by controlled imports.

Maintaining domestic prices at 22 cents per pound benefits high-cost U.S. producers[11] at the expense of consumers, who pay more than the world price of 8.5 cents. Without knowing the shape of the demand curve, however, we cannot be sure what purchases would be at the lower price. Published sources

11. U.S. production and processing costs came to 18.9 cents per pound for the 1987–1988 crop according to U.S. Department of Agriculture, *Sugar: Background for 1990 Farm Legislation,* Washington D.C., 1990, p. 16. Since this was the average cost, some producers had higher and some lower costs.

report the price elasticity of demand for sugar to be quite small, -0.1 for the United States.[12] A demand curve with elasticity -0.1 passing through price 22 and quantity 9 at point b is given by $q^D = 9(p/22)^{-0.1}$. This is plotted at the demand curve between points b and d. The price elasticity of supply, on the other hand, is estimated by a World Bank study to be 0.225.[13] A supply curve with elasticity 0.225 passing through price 22 and quantity 6.67 is given by $q^S = 6.67(p/22)^{0.225}$; this is plotted in Figure I.1 as the domestic supply curve.

The effects of the program can now be explained in terms of areas in Figure I.1. First, the amount of money paid by the public for sugar exceeds what it would be at world prices by the shaded area $A + B$. Making the relevant conversion, this area is

$$\frac{22 - 8.5 \text{ cents}}{\text{lb}} \times \frac{9 \text{ m tons}}{\text{year}} \times \frac{2,000 \text{ lb}}{\text{ton}} \times \frac{0.01 \text{ \$}}{\text{cent}}$$

$$\times \frac{0.001 \text{ b}}{\text{m}} = \frac{\$2.43 \text{ b}}{\text{year}}.$$

However, in addition to the direct higher costs of sugar, the public also consumes less sugar at point b than it would have at point d. This also has costs (rather than use low-priced sugar buyers must shift to higher-priced substitutes), which we can measure as the area between the world price and demand curve between points b and d, \$0.12 billion. This brings the total to \$2.55 billion per year.[14]

Although since 1985 the program has been mandated to operate at ''no cost,'' in 1986 the government price support agency, the Commodity Credit Corporation, created controversy by selling to the People's Republic of China over 168,000 tons of sugar previously acquired at 18 cents per pound for less than 4.75 cents per pound (world price was 6.3 cents per pound before the sale).[15] As indicated earlier, the current program is designed to eliminate such purchases and resales, but if such purchases are made their cost is also borne by the public in the form of taxes. This is shown in Figure I.1 as area C.

Because the difference between world and U.S. price has sometimes been as high as 16.3 cents in the period in question instead of the 13.5 cents we assumed, and because we have considered only the effects of the program on the sugar portion of the sweetener market, we can easily understand the higher

12. Chilvers and Foster, op. cit., p. 42. Most country elasticities reported are higher, in the -0.15 to -0.4 range. However, a smaller price elasticity of demand tends to understate the costs of the sugar program, so we use the smaller figure to be conservative in our estimates.
13. World Bank, *The World Sugar Economy: An Econometric Analysis of Long Term Developments,* World Bank Staff Commodity Working Paper No. 5, Washington, D.C.: World Bank, 1980, p. 34.
14. The reason for including this area in the costs is explained when we cover consumer surplus in Chapter 4. A triangle approximation gives the area as one-half triangle height times length. Since the length of the triangle is one-tenth the distance of rectangle $A + B$, the area is one-twentieth the area of $A + B$ or \$0.12 billion per year.
15. MacDonald and Fauriol, op. cit., p. 19.

figure of $3.7 billion per year calculated by the Commerce Department for the early 1980s. We also were conservative in not using a greater elasticity of demand for our estimate. (On both points, see the suggestions for further investigation at the end of this section.)

Benefits of the Program

Figure I.1 can also be used to describe briefly the distribution of gains in the sugar program. Area *A* is a direct transfer from consumers to sugar farmers (that is, higher prices paid by consumers go directly to farmers). Because domestic farmers produce at higher costs than world suppliers, many domestic sugar producers are kept in the sugar business by the program and would shift to other crops without it. The output of producers who would leave sugar production at the world price corresponds to the quantity associated with the difference between points *a* and *e*. In fact, consistent with the diagram, in 1987–1988 the sugar crop was 24 percent larger than it had been eight years earlier, before the current program began offering its effective subsidies averaging $250,000 per producer.[16] In comparison, other businesses in the United States typically receive negative transfers from the government (that is, they *pay* taxes), and even the heavily subsidized dairy and wheat programs average gifts (unearned transfers) of only $9,000 and $3,500 per producer, respectively. In one case, a single family owning land in Florida has been estimated to make $52 million annually as a result of the U.S. sugar program.[17] Foreign suppliers of sugar fortunate to have quota allotments benefit from the U.S. program by area *B*, less whatever import duties they incur, because they can sell sugar to American buyers at prices that are two to three times the price they could get on the world market. In describing the U.S. sugar program, Congressman Stephen Solarz aptly borrowed from Winston Churchill when he said, ''Never have so few extracted so much from so many.''[18]

Suggestions for Further Investigation. (a) Other estimates of the U.S. elasticity of demand for sugar place it as high as -0.4. Evaluate the cost of the sugar program when the elasticity of demand is -0.4. (b) The corn sweetener market expanded tremendously in the 1980s as a result of the sugar program because liquid corn sweetener such as high-fructose corn syrup is a close substitute for liquid sugar. Another cost of the sugar program is the effect that it has on increasing prices in the substitute corn sweetener market. What information about the corn sweetener demand curve, supply curve, and the relationship between corn sweetener demand and the price of sugar would you need to calculate the price of corn sweetener in the absence of the sugar program? How would you calculate the additional costs of this side effect of the sugar program?

16. Ibid., pp. 25, 28.
17. Ibid.
18. Quoted by MacDonald and Fauriol, op. cit., p. 28.

B. Prices, Taxes, and Cigarette Consumption

In spite of medical research that links cigarette smoking to lung cancer, emphysema, and heart disease, retail sales of cigarettes remain a $39 billion industry in the United States.[19] The costs of smoking are borne not just by those who smoke and those who become sick by it, but by society as a whole in the form of lower output, higher prices, and increased medical costs. A study for the National Bureau of Economic Research concluded that smoking can be reduced with higher prices in spite of the fact that smokers, according to the study's authors, behave in some ways as if they were addicted.[20]

This investigation looks at the effect of taxes on market equilibrium using cigarette smoking as the example. It shows how taxes raise prices to consumers, lower prices to producers, and reduce market quantity. The investigation also shows clearly how the elasticity of demand and supply are functionally related to the market's response.

Prices and Puffs

How much does price matter to smokers' demand? According to the cited study, the answer depends on whether the price change is permanent or temporary and whether smokers have a short or long time to respond to the change. A permanent price increase of 10 percent reduced cigarette consumption by 4 percent in the first year, whereas demand for cigarettes fell 7.5 percent over a five-year period. Taking one year to be the short run, the short-run elasticity of demand for cigarettes, therefore, is an inelastic -0.4, and the long-run price elasticity of demand for cigarettes is -0.75.[21] The fact that the long-run elasticity is larger than the short-run elasticity agrees with what we said in Chapter 2 about the economic determinants of demand elasticity. Other studies, focusing on particular regions, have found greater price elasticities of demand for cigarettes, such as -13.5 in the case of a single state that raises prices.[22] Elasticities for a single state's cigarette demand are greater than for the national demand because many smokers can shift purchases of cigarettes outside the state's tax jurisdiction.

19. Information is from the Tobacco Institute trade group, reported in the *New York Times*, June 12, 1990, pp. D1, D22.

20. Gary Becker, Michael Grossman, and Kevin Murphy, ''An Empirical Analysis of Cigarette Addiction,'' National Bureau of Economic Research Working Paper No. 3322, Cambridge, MA, April 1990. Whether cigarettes have addictive qualities has been debated by scientists.

21. The *long run* in this case is defined as a time period long enough for consumers to adjust fully to the cigarette price change.

22. Daniel Sumner, ''Measures of Monopoly Power: An Application to the Cigarette Industry,'' *Journal of Political Economy*, 89 (October 1981), pp. 1010–1019.

Is a price elasticity of -0.75 big or small? An earlier study of heroin consumption, cited in the same report by the National Bureau of Economic Research, found that a 50 percent increase in heroin prices reduced consumption by 13 percent. This implies a price elasticity of demand for heroin of -0.26. Even though heroin is regarded as one of the most addictive of drugs, demand for it by addicts does show price responsiveness. Cigarette consumption is three times more price responsive.

To Tax and Destroy

How might cigarette use be limited? The United States has long recognized that taxes not only raise money, but tend to restrict the object of taxation. In 1819 Supreme Court Chief Justice John Marshall presided over the case of *McCulloch v. Maryland,* in which important issues of government tax jurisdiction were decided. In the landmark opinion, Marshall stated the subsequently oft-cited principle that "the power to tax involves the power to destroy." This idea, that taxation tends to reduce the amount of the thing being taxed, has been used both as a reason to refrain from taxation and as a reason to engage in taxation. For example, taxing institutions of religion is generally viewed in America as dangerous to the principle of freedom of religion.[23] On the other hand, alcohol, cigarettes, and harmful substances, where not banned outright, are often limited by taxation. The policy question is: How potent are taxes in reducing cigarette use?

Graphical Representation of Tax Effects

Information from the Tobacco Institute reveals that there are 13 major companies supplying cigarettes. In 1990 the average retail price of a pack of cigarettes was $1.61. Suppliers received $1.25, to which an additional 28.8 percent in taxes was added to reach the buyer's price of $1.61.[24] Retail sales totaled $39 billion per year, with 24 billion packs being sold. Total taxes collected were $9.9 billion. Figure I.2 displays this information using linear demand and supply curves.[25] There is a simple graphical technique for showing the effects of the tax on cigarettes. With no tax, the equilibrium would be at point e, where the demand curve and the supply curve intersect. Price would be p^* and quantity q^*.[26] When a tax is imposed on cigarette purchases, the price paid by the buyer rises above the price received by the seller by the

23. Later opinions of the Supreme Court noted that Congress has viewed the religion clauses of the Constitution as authorizing exemption from property taxes and certain other taxes for religious bodies. See, for example, *Walz v. Tax Commission,* 397 U.S. 677 (1970).
24. Federal taxes accounted for $.16 of the buyer's price, and state and municipal taxes accounted for approximately $.20 per pack on average.
25. We assume for this exercise that supply has an elasticity between 2 and infinity. The figure shows the supply curve as if it has a price elasticity of 2, which probably lies below the true figure for an agriculturally based industry of this type. In our analysis we will also consider an infinite elasticity of supply to bracket the true figure on the other extreme.
26. The text intentionally leaves the computation of p^* and q^* as an exercise for you. A hint is given at the end of this investigation.

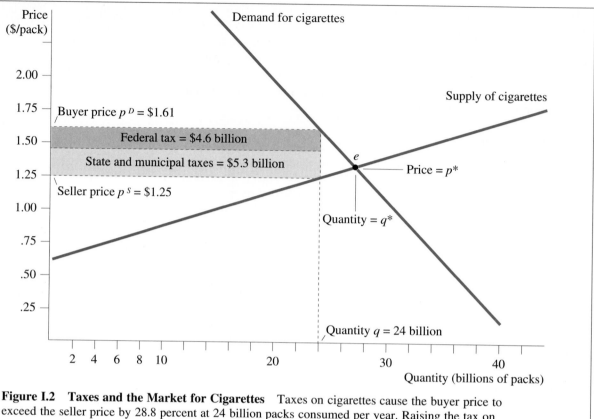

Figure I.2   Taxes and the Market for Cigarettes   Taxes on cigarettes cause the buyer price to exceed the seller price by 28.8 percent at 24 billion packs consumed per year. Raising the tax on cigarettes widens the gap between the buyer price and the seller price, causing the quantity of cigarettes consumed to fall. Assuming a price elasticity of demand of -0.75 and price elasticity of supply of 2 at the quantity of 24 billion packs, increasing the tax rate from 28.8 percent of seller price to 30.8 percent of seller price would reduce the quantity by 0.85 percent or 204 million packs per year.

amount of the tax. Thus *equilibrium in the presence of a tax occurs at a quantity for which the price on the demand curve is higher than the price on the supply curve by the amount of the tax* (in this case, 28.8 percent of the seller price per pack). As the figure also shows, the tax decreases the quantity of cigarettes, and a sufficiently high tax could stop transactions altogether. (Justice Marshall was right.) It might also encourage a black market in cigarettes to avoid tax payment.

Another feature is evident from the geometry of Figure I.2: Leaving point *e* fixed, if the demand curve or the supply curve is steeper (has an elasticity of demand or supply closer to zero), the effect of the tax on quantity is reduced. Thus the effect of the tax is closely linked to the elasticity of both curves.

One way to measure the effectiveness of the tax is to measure the effect on price and quantity if the tax on cigarettes is increased a small amount, say, from 28.8 percent to 30.8 percent, an increase of two percentage points. Since this is a small increase in the tax, we can make use of the elasticity information from the study on cigarettes. To do this, we introduce two simple rules for working with small percentage changes.

Simple Elasticity Algebra

The first rule says that for small changes the percentage change in the multiple of two variables equals the sum of the percentage changes in the individual variables.[27] For example, if $pq = V$, then $\%\Delta V = \%\Delta p + \%\Delta q$, where $\%\Delta$ denotes the percentage change in a variable.[28]

The second rule simply rewrites the definition of elasticity. For example, if y is a function of x, $y = f(x)$, then $\%\Delta y = \varepsilon(\%\Delta x)$ where ε is the elasticity of y with respect to a change in x.

Now apply these rules to relate demand and supply elasticity to the effects of a tax. Writing quantity demanded as a function of the price paid by consumers, $F(p^D)$, and quantity supplied as a function of the price received by sellers, $G(p^S)$, we have quantity supplied equals quantity demanded in equilibrium,

$$q = F(p^D) = G(p^S).$$

From the second rule we have $\%\Delta q = \varepsilon(\%\Delta p^D)$, where ε is the price elasticity of demand, and $\%\Delta q = \varepsilon^S(\%\Delta p^S)$, where ε^S is the price elasticity of supply. Thus

$$\%\Delta q = \varepsilon(\%\Delta p^D) = \varepsilon^S(\%\Delta p^S). \tag{1}$$

Now make use of the first rule. When a tax is present, the buyer price exceeds the seller price by the tax percentage, or $p^D = p^S(1 + t)$, where t is the tax percentage expressed as a decimal. The percentage change in 1 plus the tax would be written as $\%\Delta(1 + t)$,[29] and therefore the first rule gives us

$$\%\Delta p^D = \%\Delta p^S + \%\Delta(1 + t). \tag{2}$$

27. We take small percentage changes to mean changes smaller than 10 percent.
28. Working backwards from the definition for percentage change, simple algebra shows that $\%\Delta p + \%\Delta q + (\%\Delta p)(\%\Delta q) = \%\Delta V$. For $\%\Delta p$, $\%\Delta q < 0.1$, $(\%\Delta p)(\%\Delta q)$ will be an order of magnitude smaller (that is, a smaller number by one decimal place or more) than either $\%\Delta p$ or $\%\Delta q$ and thus can be ignored. This gives the resulting expression in the text.
29. For example, if the tax is 5 percent and we raise it to 7 percent, then $1 + t = 1.05$ before the change and 1.07 after the change. The percentage change in $1 + t$ is $\%\Delta(1 + t)$ $= 0.02/1.05 = 0.019$.

Equations (1) and (2) can easily be solved[30] to find

$$\%\Delta p^S = \left[\frac{\varepsilon}{\varepsilon^S - \varepsilon}\right] [\%\Delta(1 + t)]$$

$$\%\Delta p^D = \left[\frac{\varepsilon^S}{\varepsilon^S - \varepsilon}\right] [\%\Delta(1 + t)]$$

$$\%\Delta q = \left[\frac{\varepsilon\varepsilon^S}{\varepsilon^S - \varepsilon}\right] [\%\Delta(1 + t)].$$

Short-Run, Long-Run, and Single-State Tax Effects

From the elasticities of demand and supply for cigarettes, we can now compute how much change is implied. Since $(1 + t)$ rises from 1.288 to 1.308, the increase in $(1 + t)$ is 1.55 percent. Table I.1 computes the change in price and quantity according to the formulas just given. As noted, the key ingredients are the change in the tax rate and the price elasticities of demand and supply. In part A of the table, we compute the effects of the tax increase under the assumption that the price elasticity of supply is 2. In the short run, the price elasticity of demand is -0.4, so that the price to buyers rises 1.29 percent, or 2.1 cents per pack.[31] Reading across the row, we see that the smaller the price increase to buyers, the larger the price elasticity of demand. For example, if the price elasticity of demand is -13.5, the price to buyers rises only 0.2 percent. The reduction in quantity of cigarette consumption can be read from the second row. In the short run the quantity of cigarettes consumed drops 0.52 percent, or 124 million packs per year.[32] In general, the larger the elasticity of demand and supply, the larger the quantity reduction from a given tax increase.

Part B of the table shows the effect of the tax if the supply curve is perfectly elastic. In each case the price to the buyer rises by the full amount of the tax, 1.55 percent (a 2.5 cent per pack increase). The effect on quantity consumed, as in part A, increases with the elasticity of demand.

In conclusion, since ε^S is a positive number and $(\varepsilon^S - \varepsilon)$ is a larger positive number, we see that the percentage increase in the buyer price is a fraction between zero and 1 of the increase in the tax $\%\Delta(1 + t)$ and that the drop in the seller price makes up the remainder of the fraction. The formula verifies that the larger the elasticity of demand and the smaller the elasticity of supply, the less the tax burden falls on buyers (the less their price rises); and the larger the elasticity of supply and the smaller the elasticity of demand, the less the tax burden falls on sellers (the less their price falls).

---

30. Replace $\%\Delta p^D$ in equation 1 by $\%\Delta p^S + \%\Delta(1 + t)$ and solve for $\%\Delta p^S$. The relationship for $\%\Delta p^D$ follows from noting that $\%\Delta p^D$ equals $\%\Delta p^S + \%\Delta(1 + t)$. The rest follows from $\%\Delta q = \varepsilon(\%\Delta p^D)$.

31. \$1.61 × 0.0129 = \$.021.

32. 0.0052 × 24 billion = 124 million.

Table I.1 Effect of an Increase in the Tax Rate on Cigarettes from 28.8 percent to 30.8 percent

A. Case 1: Price Elasticity of Supply = 2

Elasticity of Demand

	Short Run −0.4	Long Run −0.75	Single-State −13.5
Change in price paid by buyers (% and cents)	1.29% 2.1¢	1.13% 1.8¢	0.20% 0.3¢
Reduction in quantity (% and millions of packs)	−0.52% −124	−0.85% −203	−2.7% −648

B. Case 2: Price Elasticity of Supply = Infinity

Elasticity of Demand

	Short Run −0.4	Long Run −0.75	Single-State −13.5
Change in price paid by buyers (% and cents)	1.55% 2.5¢	1.55% 2.5¢	1.55% 2.5¢
Reduction in quantity (% and million packs)	−0.62% −149	−1.16% −279	−20.93% −5,022

Note: Initially buyer price is $1.61 per pack and quantity is 24 billion packs per year. Thus a 0.62 percent price increase equals 1 cent per pack and a 1 percent quantity reduction equals 240 million packs per year.

Suggestion for Further Investigation. The elasticity rules we have derived apply to small changes. For large changes, the approximations the rules are based on are no longer sufficiently accurate. Assuming linear demand and supply curves that have price elasticities of −0.75 and 2 at the original equilibrium price of $1.61 per pack for buyers, $1.25 per pack for sellers, and 24 billion packs per year, use the facts that demand equals supply, $q = F(p^D) = G(p^S)$, and buyer price exceeds seller price by the tax amount, $p^D = p^S(1 + t)$, to predict the effect of reducing cigarette taxes to *zero* (shown by p^* and q^* in Figure I.2) or of *doubling* the tax rate on cigarettes. (Hint: The line given by $q = q^0(1 - \varepsilon) + \varepsilon(q^0/p^0)p$ passes through the point where price is p^0 and quantity is q^0 and has elasticity equal to ε at that point.)

▼

PART TWO

THE CONSUMER'S DECISIONS

Chapters 3, 4, and 5 delve behind the demand curve. Starting from consumer preferences, the most basic microeconomic feature, these chapters show how to determine the consumer's demand curve by choosing consumption that makes the consumer as well off as possible, given the constraints imposed by the consumer's ability to pay. Combining the demands of all consumers then leads to the market demand curve. In the journey from consumer to market, we carefully dissect the various influences, becoming familiar with the effect that changing each has on consumer and market demand. Chapter 5 applies the same theory of maximization subject to a budget constraint to explain the household's labor supply decision.

▼

CHAPTER 3

Consumer Preferences, Utility, and the Budget Line

In this chapter we model rational consumers who act in their own interest, have preferences that they seek to satisfy, and face constraints on the choices that are possible to them. The chapter begins with a discussion of what it means to be rational, followed by a description of preferences using diagrams and functions. This explains what the consumer would like to do. Then we discuss the constraints or limitations on the alternatives from which the consumer is able to choose. Putting preferences and constraints together allows us to describe what the consumer does in a given situation.

ACTIVE READING GUIDES

After reading this chapter, you should be able to answer the Active Reading Guides listed below. These guides also appear in the page margins, near the material to which they refer.

1. What are the four conditions that we use to define rationality?

2. Explain what an indifference curve is, including how its shape, slope, and orientation reveal consumer preferences.

3. What does the marginal rate of substitution say about how the consumer values additional quantities of goods?

4. Explain what a utility function is and relate it to indifference curves.

5. Distinguish ordinal from cardinal utility and explain why ordinal utility is sufficient to represent preferences.

6. Define marginal utility and relate it to the marginal rate of substitution.

7. Define the choice set and the budget set, explaining how they relate to one another.

8. What two requirements must the consumer's constrained optimization choice satisfy?

9. Explain what tangency is important to the consumer's optimization choice and why.

10. Give the mathematical condition for tangency of the indifference curve and budget line.

11. Give an example in which the consumer's utility-maximizing bundle is not at a tangency and interpret it in terms of the marginal rate of substitution and the price ratio.

A.1. What is the principle of revealed preference?

A.2. Draw a diagram showing the set of bundles for which a given bundle is revealed to be preferred.

A.3. Show how the location and shape of the indifference curve can be deduced from properly chosen repeated observations of consumer choices.

3.1 Consumer Preferences

In the 1980s the Jeep Cherokee four-wheel drive (4WD) became increasingly popular as a family and recreational vehicle, even among urban dwellers and buyers not likely to spend many hours off-road. (Jeep was later bought out and became a division of Chrysler Corporation.) At first, Ford Motor Company had no entry in this increasingly popular market. After several years of consumer surveys, planning, and design, Ford decided to discontinue its Bronco II 4WD and replace it with a larger vehicle. The Ford Explorer entered the market in midyear 1990. Its designers gave it a full six-foot rear bed when back seats were down, a 4.0-liter six-cylinder engine, reclining front seats, a 60–40 split rear seat, and a spare tire stowed underneath the vehicle. The Explorer was an almost immediate success, receiving the 4WD Car of the Year award from *Motor Trend* and *4 Wheeler* magazines and becoming the best-selling car in its class, outstripping the Jeep Cherokee and four or five competing vehicles that entered the market soon afterward. Soon, roughly one in seven vehicles purchased were of this type. How did Ford know that it was time to enter the 4WD market? And once it had decided that the market was profitable, how did it know what features to design into the car?[1] The answers depend on how consumers make choices to spend their money. In

---

1. These kinds of questions relating closely to firm decision making will be addressed in Part Three. Aspects relating closely to consumer choice theory can be discussed in this chapter.

Ford's case, the question concerned cars, but the problem is a more general one. Is there any way to simplify a problem so complex as trying to explain how people buy what they buy to make themselves as happy as possible? This is the basic question of consumer theory that we take up in this chapter.

Having considered demand curves as a tool of market analysis in Chapter 2, we look in this chapter at what lies behind the demand curve. Starting from the basic description of the consumer's wants, our objective is to build upward until we can explain how the consumer decides to buy what he or she buys.

Constructing a Model of Consumer Behavior

To construct a worthwhile model of consumer behavior, we need to make some basic assumptions about how consumers use their income to purchase bundles of goods and services. First, we limit our discussion to *rational* consumers. Rational consumers make the best possible choices in their own interest and behave in reasonable and therefore predictable ways. For example, rational consumers spend all their income. Unused income means that consumers could have spent more money for *something* to make them better off. Not doing so is irrational. (Later, we will consider ''goods'' such as saving, which make this assumption a little more obvious).[2] *Irrational* consumers do not make the best possible choices in their own interest, or else they change their preferences from moment to moment, so discussing their actions is difficult and basically pointless.

Second, we want to explain how consumers choose goods and services. Goods and services are sometimes defined very broadly. For instance, rather than separately studying cake, pasta, meat, beans, and apples, we frequently group them together as one good, food. Goods and services are not just physical products; shelter, air, and music are considered goods and services, too. Even though not all goods are tangible, we still recognize that they can be ''purchased.'' For instance, you can't buy time in a store, but you purchase it by choosing which activities to do; if you want to go to a concert and decide not to finish the mystery you're reading that night, you just ''bought'' three hours. Being able to describe these purchases in terms of consumer preferences and constraints is the purpose of modeling consumer behavior.

Choices consumers make are presented in terms of market *baskets* or *bundles.* Each market basket or bundle is a collection of goods, such as two units of food and three of shelter, or six of shelter and one of food. For purposes of discussion, we assume that market baskets or bundles consist of two goods. This allows us to talk about choices between different goods and also to draw pictures in two dimensions. Of course, we don't live in a world of just two goods, so sometimes our model will graph choices between a

---

2. Savings is a form of expenditure that effectively corresponds to the consumer's provision for purchase of future goods and services. Until Chapter 16, when we consider savings and intertemporal choice, we will use a one-period model, which assumes that all income is spent on current goods and services with no separate category of spending designated for saving.

specific good, such as food, and a composite good, which is all other goods lumped together and considered as one.[3]

To learn about rational consumers, let's start with their preferences.

Axioms of Consumer Preferences

Our rational consumer—let's call him Ernest—has to make choices in a variety of situations. By examining Ernest's choices, we can introduce four axioms of consumer preferences. As simple as they are, these axioms are the building blocks of consumer theory.

As we step in on Ernest, we find that he faces a choice among several bundles. Bundle *a* consists of 4 ski trips and no trips to the Virgin Islands, denoted (4, 0); bundle *b* consists of 2 ski trips and 1 trip to the Virgin Islands (2, 1); and *c* is two trips to the Islands and no skiing (0, 2). Though it is a hard choice, Ernest is able to tell us which bundle he prefers (he thinks two ski trips and one to the Virgin Islands is the best choice). Ernest has just fulfilled the first of our axioms, completeness.

▼
1. What are the four conditions that we use to define rationality?

> *(i) **Completeness:** Given any two alternatives* a *and* b, *the consumer can rank them precisely as meeting one of three possibilities: either* a *is strictly preferred to* b, b *is strictly preferred to* a, *or* a *and* b *are indifferent.*

This axiom, which seems innocuous enough, says that Ernest is able to make up his mind by providing a ranking of any two alternatives we might select. If he is able to make up his mind for some alternatives but not for others, or if he sometimes picks one ranking and sometimes another, there is little that logically can be said about his preferences.[4]

Ernest's ranking also fulfills our second axiom, reflexivity. This almost trivial axiom asserts that any alternative is at least as good as itself.

> *(ii) **Reflexivity:** Given alternative* a, *it is always true that* a *is indifferent to itself.*

---

3. The use of composite goods does not change the theory of consumer behavior or the diagrams we use, as long as the prices of goods making up the composite are fixed relative to one another in the analysis. We will assume this whenever a composite good is being used.
4. Is it conceivable that a consumer ever might *not* be able to make a choice? A poignant example comes from the annals of the ancient Roman emperor Theodosius who, to punish the entire city of Thessalonica for the death of one of his officers in that city, resolved to massacre at a public circus citizens of the town who were invited there by the emperor for that secret purpose. History records that a foreign merchant "offered his own life and all of his wealth to supply the place of *one* of his two sons; but while the father hesitated with equal tenderness, while he was doubtful to choose, and unwilling to condemn, the soldiers determined his suspense," killing both. We can fully understand the inability of the father to satisfy the completeness axiom by making such a terrible choice. This example also underscores why we do not attempt to describe choices in situations like this where the completeness axiom fails to apply. The quotation is from Edward Gibbon, *The Decline and Fall of the Roman Empire,* Chicago: William Benton, 1952, p. 451.

We need this axiom because without it we could reach nonsensical conclusions. For example, if 4 ski trips are indifferent to 2 island trips but 2 island trips are not indifferent to themselves, what does it mean to say that 4 ski trips are indifferent to 2 island trips? Reflexivity prevents this problem and also is needed when we consider chains of comparisons.

Now let's say that Ernest must choose just one of *a, b,* or *c.* Ernest strictly prefers *a* to *b* and *b* to *c,* but also strictly prefers *c* to *a.* No matter what choice he makes, there is always a better pick! How can Ernest choose? Transitivity rules out the possibility of such a dilemma.

> *(iii)* **Transitivity:** *Given three alternatives,* a, b, *and* c, *if the consumer strictly prefers* a *to* b *and* b *to* c, *then the consumer also strictly prefers* a *to* c. *Likewise, if the consumer is indifferent between* a *and* b *and between* b *and* c, *then the consumer is indifferent between* a *and* c.

This axiom also seems noncontroversial in that it rules out the possibility of cycles. For example, given a large list of alternatives (''I would rather build a chicken coop than wash the car''; ''I would rather wash the car than clean my room''; ''I would rather clean my room than eat broccoli''; and so on), there is no ordering with each item strictly preferred to the following one that closes back on itself with the last item strictly preferred to the first. In the above series, for example, I could not rationally say, ''I would rather eat broccoli than build a chicken coop,'' because it would produce a cycle.

Surprisingly, the above three axioms are all we need to define rationality. However, they allow for some kinds of unusual behavior that, while rational, are less interesting for study than more standard behavior. We therefore add one more axiom to limit discussion to the most important cases. Our fourth axiom notes that most consumers could consume far more than the amount available to them without being sated. This is partly because the physical availability of goods is limited in most situations, but more importantly because most of us inevitably want more regardless of how much we currently have. The nonsatiation axiom says that whatever we are doing, there is something else that would be better.

> *(iv)* **Nonsatiation:** *For any bundle* a *there is another bundle* b *that the consumer ranks as strictly preferred to* a.

As we will see later, this axiom (as well as completeness, reflexivity, and transitivity) applies to ''bads'' such as pollution or garbage for which the consumer is better off if there is less of the bad, as well as to goods for which the consumer is better off with more. Usually, however, we will be interested in cases where ''More of any good is always preferred to less.'' In these cases the nonsatiation axiom is satisfied automatically because a larger bundle (one that is bigger or the same with respect to every component) is always preferred to a smaller one.

As we just noted, we could construct a theory of preferences without the nonsatiation axiom. For some of the wealthiest people in history, for example, it may have been the case that having more money to use as they pleased gave them no further ability to enhance their satisfaction, but for most of us that level is far beyond our reach. Thus it makes sense to devote our time to describing the more usual case in which more is preferred to less.

Now that we know what rationality means, converting preferences to graphs and functions gives us a way to work with them. Graphing preferences is the subject of the next section.

3.2 Representing Preferences with Indifference Curves

A graph tells us a lot more about Ernest's preferences than a verbal description, in the same way that a photograph would tell us more about his appearance. We assume that Ernest is rational (his choices satisfy the axioms), but graphing his preferences allows us to explain the differences between his choices and those of another consumer.

Definition of Indifference Curves

Indifference curves are the main component for graphing preferences.

> An ***indifference curve*** *is a collection of bundles that are indifferent to one another in the consumer's preferences.*

▼
2. Explain what an indifference curve is, including how its shape, slope, and orientation reveal consumer preferences.

Strictly speaking, the axioms of consumer preferences do not imply that indifference curves must exist in every case, but the cases where they do not are relatively unusual and need not concern us.[5] For our purposes, we assume that consumers have indifference curves.

What would an indifference curve look like for Ernest? Figure 3.1 starts by plotting points *a, b,* and *c,* which represent the three bundles of trips that Ernest chose from, as well as some other bundles labeled *d, e,* and *f.* In the figure, the axes represent quantities of the two types of trips. To draw the indifference curve containing point *b,* we can first eliminate certain points that are not in the running. We know that the shaded points to the northeast of *b* are strictly preferred because they contain more of both kinds of travel; likewise, the shaded bundles to the southwest of *b* are strictly less preferred than *b* because they contain less of each. It follows that indifferent bundles must lie to the northwest and southeast of *b.* This means that *indifference curves are downward sloping.* To be more specific, however, we have to ask Ernest how he personally ranks points to the northwest and southeast of *b.* In this case, he tells us that points on the curved line through *b* are indifferent to each other.[6] With information from the indifference curve, we can now

5. For those who are interested, the last exercise in this chapter contains an example of a rational consumer who does not have indifference curves.
6. The chapter appendix describes how in principle we could learn the location of Ernest's indifference curve by observing his actions from a judiciously chosen sequence of choices.

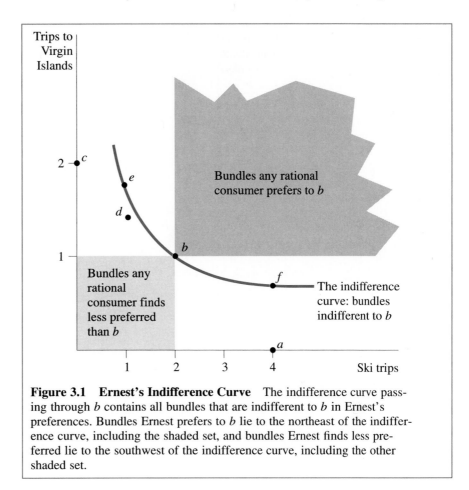

Figure 3.1   Ernest's Indifference Curve   The indifference curve passing through *b* contains all bundles that are indifferent to *b* in Ernest's preferences. Bundles Ernest prefers to *b* lie to the northeast of the indifference curve, including the shaded set, and bundles Ernest finds less preferred lie to the southwest of the indifference curve, including the other shaded set.

say that points *b, e* and *f* are indifferent, that all points above the curve are strictly preferred, and that all points below are strictly less preferred.

The rational consumer tries to reach as high an indifference curve as possible. This observation will be important to us later on as we describe consumer choices.

Properties of Indifference Curves

In drawing Ernest's indifference curve, we used some information that followed from consumer rationality and thus applied to any consumer's indifference curve, as well as information that depended on specific features of Ernest's preferences. We now discuss some of the more important working properties of indifference curves.

Indifference Curves Are Space Filling. Since every bundle can be ranked and provides some level of satisfaction, there is an indifference curve passing through every point. Thus indifference curves are space filling, even though

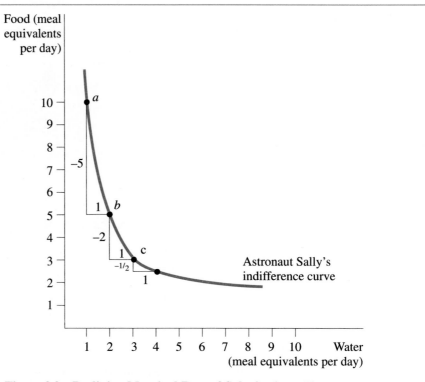

Figure 3.2   Declining Marginal Rate of Substitution   The more water Sally has relative to food, the less food she is willing to give up to gain an additional unit of water. This implies that Sally's indifference curve has a declining marginal rate of substitution of water for food and is therefore convex with respect to the origin.

we may draw only a selection of them at any one time. By looking at each indifference curve, we can see at a glance what points give the same level of satisfaction and what points give different levels of satisfaction.

Indifference Curves Are Convex and Have Declining Marginal Rate of Substitution. The indifference curve in Figure 3.1 was downward sloping because indifferent points had to lie to the northwest or southeast. The *rate* at which the curve declined (its slope), however, depended on Ernest's willingness to trade off one type of good for the other, and its *curvature* depended on how this slope changed along the curve. We now discuss why we drew the indifference curve in Figure 3.1 as convex, meaning it was bowed toward the origin.

Figure 3.2 shows an indifference curve for Sally, an astronaut on an orbital mission. Sally's curve passes through points *a, b,* and *c* for the goods food and water. At point *a* Sally has 10 units of food and 1 unit of water, where

▼

3. What does the marginal rate of substitution say about how the consumer values additional quantities of goods?

units are measured in meal equivalents per day. Since she is short on water at point *a,* but has more than three meals per day worth of food, Sally would be willing to give up 5 units of food in return for 1 additional unit of water, reaching point *b* on the same indifference curve. At point *b,* where she has 5 units of food and 2 units of water, she would be willing to give up 2 units of food for 1 more unit of water, putting her at point *c,* which corresponds to equal units of food and water per day. At this point, Sally would be willing to give up only $\frac{1}{2}$ unit of food for 1 additional unit of water. In other words, the greater Sally's supply of food and the smaller her supply of water, the more food she is willing to give up in exchange for additional water. At any point, the rate at which she would exchange water and food is indicated by the slope of the indifference curve. The curve's slope is negative, but we want to speak of the rate as a positive number; thus we reverse the sign of the indifference curve's slope, producing a rate called the marginal rate of substitution of water for food.

> The **marginal rate of substitution of good x for good y (MRS$_{x,y}$)** *is the maximum amount of good* y *that a consumer would give up to get an additional unit of good* x.

A simple way to remember the marginal rate of substitution of *x* for *y* is to think of it as the consumer's private ''*y*-price of *x*,'' telling us how many *y*'s are needed in exchange for an *x,* just as price tells us how many dollars exchange per unit good. Since the negative of the slope of the indifference curve equals this number, the flatter the indifference curve, the smaller the MRS$_{x,y}$.[7] When Sally had little water, she was willing to give up more food for it than when she had a lot of water relative to food. Along her indifference curve, then, the marginal rate of substitution of water for food declined. *This property of declining marginal rate of substitution implies that indifference curves are convex (that is, bowed toward the origin).* Convexity is a property of indifference curves that makes sense because we would expect that as less of one good is available and more of another, the consumer would be willing to give up increasingly fewer units of the scarce good for units of the abundant one. Diminishing marginal rate of substitution is not necessarily implied by rationality, but it is a property of preferences that is reasonable to expect in most cases, and economists generally take it as an additional property of indifference curves. With the exception of indifference curves that are straight lines, we will assume that indifference curves satisfy the property of diminishing marginal rate of substitution.

Another way to describe declining marginal rate of substitution is to note that convex indifference curves imply that consumers prefer greater variety or balance in their consumption. For example, let's say you equally like French and blue cheese dressing on your salads. In Figure 3.3 French and

---

7. In our discussion we assume that *x* is measured on the horizontal axis and *y* on the vertical. Reversing the order of the goods means that the slopes must be measured with the axes reversed accordingly.

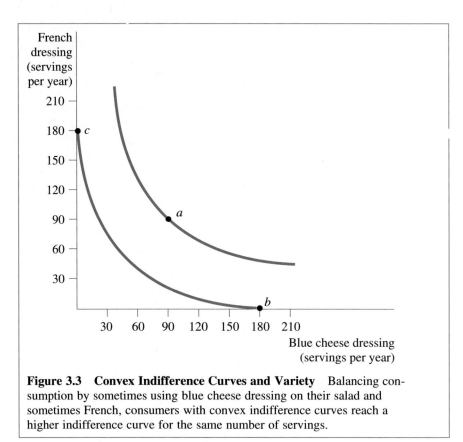

Figure 3.3 Convex Indifference Curves and Variety Balancing consumption by sometimes using blue cheese dressing on their salad and sometimes French, consumers with convex indifference curves reach a higher indifference curve for the same number of servings.

blue cheese are listed as the two types of dressing. If you *always* chose blue cheese, you would be at point *b,* showing that you consume 180 servings of dressing per year (assuming you eat a salad roughly every other day). If you *always* chose French, you would be equally well off at point *c.* However, by sometimes choosing French and sometimes blue cheese (point *a*), you balance your use of dressings and increase the variety of dressings you use. The convexity of indifference curves implies that this places you on a *higher* indifference curve. As we noted before, the consumer wants to attain as high an indifference curve as possible to maximize utility.

Indifference Curves Can Never Cross. Another important property of indifference curves is that they can never cross. Why? Because if they did the axiom of transitivity would imply that all points on the crossing curves are indifferent to one another, contradicting the fact that they represent different indifference curves. Figure 3.4 shows two indifference curves for a consumer that cross at point *b.* Point *c* is preferred to point *a* because point *c* contains more of both goods than point *a.* Point *c* is indifferent to point *b* because they are on the same indifference curve, and point *b* is indifferent to point *a*

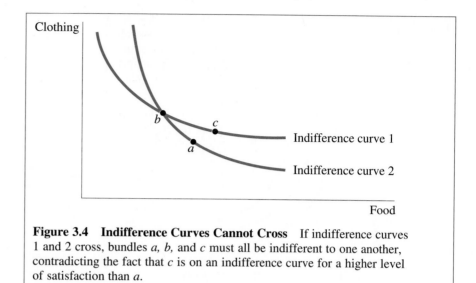

Figure 3.4 Indifference Curves Cannot Cross If indifference curves
1 and 2 cross, bundles *a, b,* and *c* must all be indifferent to one another,
contradicting the fact that *c* is on an indifference curve for a higher level
of satisfaction than *a.*

because they are on the same indifference curve. Thus, by transitivity points
a and *c* are indifferent. However, this contradicts the fact that *c* is strictly
preferred to *a.* Hence, indifference curves cannot cross.

Indifference Curve Orientation Tells About Preferences. The orientation
of the entire family of indifference curves also tells us a great deal. Figure
3.5, for example, shows Charlotte's and Cy's preferences for opera and
basketball. Both Charlotte and Cy like attending opera and basketball games,
because points with more of each imply higher indifference curves. Nevertheless, Cy and Charlotte differ from one another in the relative strength of
their preferences for the two goods. Can you tell which consumer tends to
favor opera and which tends to favor basketball? Using point *a* as a reference,
we see that Charlotte's family of indifference curves look as if they are rotated
more toward the opera axis (their slopes are closer to vertical, indicating a
high marginal rate of substitution of opera for basketball), and Cy's curves
look as if they are rotated more toward the basketball axis (their slopes are
closer to horizontal, meaning a low marginal rate of substitution of opera for
basketball). Since point *a* was chosen arbitrarily, a similar comparison of
indifference curve slopes could be made at other points. Thus, through a
comparison of the amounts of basketball needed to compensate for the loss
of one unit of opera at common points, Charlotte demonstrates relatively
stronger preferences for opera and Cy relatively stronger preferences for
basketball.

Later in the chapter, we will be able to see that if Charlotte and Cy have
the same income and face the same prices for basketball and opera, Charlotte
will buy more opera and less basketball than Cy.

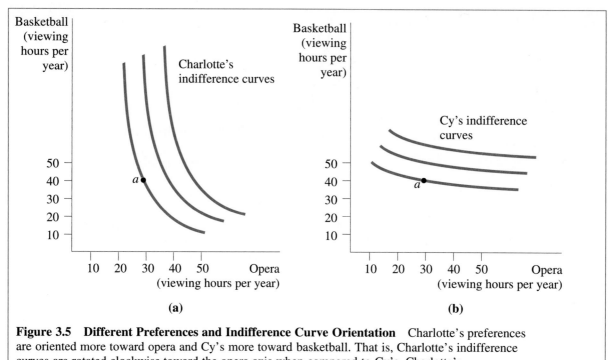

Figure 3.5 Different Preferences and Indifference Curve Orientation   Charlotte's preferences are oriented more toward opera and Cy's more toward basketball. That is, Charlotte's indifference curves are rotated clockwise toward the opera axis when compared to Cy's. Charlotte's $MRS_{opera,basketball}$ thus exceeds Cy's.

Shapes of Indifference Curves Vary for Different Types of Goods. Indifference curves vary in shape depending on the type of good. Just as physicians can be trained to read X-rays to learn about a patient's condition, so we can be trained to learn about preferences from the shape of indifference curves. These shapes may vary both because the goods are fundamentally different in nature and because consumers differ in the ways they rate goods.

Perfect Substitutes Part (a) of Figure 3.6 shows the indifference curves for Peter, who is buying citrus fruits. In this case we assume that Peter cares about the vitamin C content that comes from eating citrus fruit but doesn't care which kind of fruit he eats to get it. Assume on average that a grapefruit is twice as large as a tangerine. Since one grapefruit gives the same amount of fruit as two tangerines, we know that Peter is indifferent between these quantities of the two fruits. Since he substitutes grapefruit and tangerines for one another, what will his indifference curves look like? Drawing a line between the points for one grapefruit on the horizontal axis and two tangerines on the vertical axis shows the combinations that are of equal value to Peter. His indifference curve therefore appears as a straight line with a slope (the rise over the run) of -2. But Peter might consume more than the equivalent

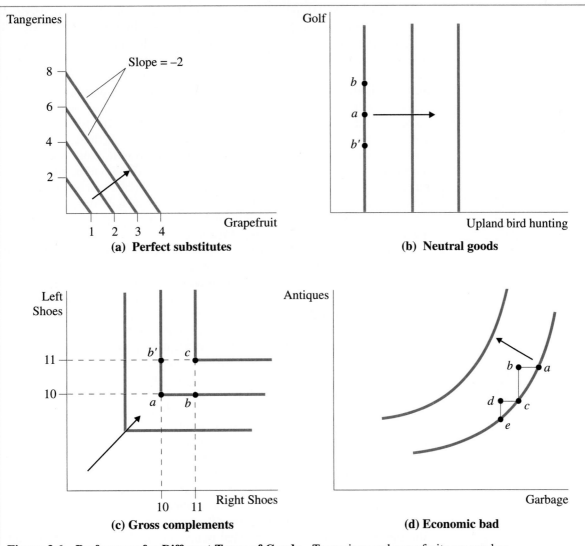

Figure 3.6   Preferences for Different Types of Goods   Tangerines and grapefruits are used as substitutes for each other by the consumer in part (a), whereas right shoes and left shoes are used as complements to one another by the consumer in part (c). Golf does not matter to the consumer's satisfaction in part (b), and garbage is a bad to the consumer in part (d).

of just one grapefruit. He is better off with more fruit, so we can draw parallel indifference curves for more fruit, further from the origin as the arrow indicates (higher indifference curves lie to the northeast). This example shows the shape of indifference curves for goods that the consumer considers *perfect substitutes*.

Neutral Goods The principle that we used to construct Peter's indifference curves for citrus was to start with a given point and find the set of points that were indifferent to it in his preferences. Then we found which way to move to find higher indifference curves. The same principle can be used in part (b) of Figure 3.6. Here we show the preferences of Mike, who enjoys upland bird hunting but is *neutral* toward golf. He neither likes golf nor dislikes it; it just doesn't matter to him either way. Starting at point *a* we ask what other points would give him the same level of satisfaction. If Mike plays more golf, this moves him up to point *b*. However, since golf does not enter his preferences and he does not gain any satisfaction from it, point *b* must be at the same level of satisfaction as point *a*. The same thing will be true if Mike plays less golf, moving to point *b'*. Mike's indifference curves are vertical straight lines. From his point of view, he is better off only if he can move to the right by hunting more, as indicated by the horizontal arrow pointing to higher indifference curves in that direction.

Gross Complements Part (c) in Figure 3.6 shows a different kind of situation, in which Anne is considering shoes. We assume that Anne is able-bodied and thus gets satisfaction from complete pairs of shoes. Left shoes and right shoes *complement* one another. Since Anne needs shoes in equal proportions, what will her indifference curves look like?

We proceed in the same way as before. Point *a* shows Anne's consumption of 10 pairs of shoes. To find points indifferent to *a,* consider the change in Anne's satisfaction if we give her an additional right shoe, moving her to point *b*. Does the extra right shoe make Anne any better off? Since there is no matching left shoe to go with it, the answer is no. Thus, point *b* is on the same indifference curve as point *a*. Similarly, point *b'*, showing consumption with an extra left shoe, is on the same indifference curve. If we give Anne an additional *pair* of shoes, her consumption moves to point *c*. Since she likes shoes, this increases her satisfaction; therefore *c* is on a higher indifference curve. Each indifference curve is L-shaped, with the direction of improvement moving to the northeast as the arrow indicates.[8]

Bads In part (d) of Figure 3.6, the vertical axis shows antiques, which Ralph likes, and the horizontal axis shows garbage, which Ralph dislikes. Starting at an arbitrary point *a,* what points are indifferent to it? If we take some garbage from Ralph, he moves to point *b* and is better off. To find points on the same indifference curve, therefore, we must take away some of his antiques to get him back to his initial level of satisfaction. Taking just the right amount away gets us to point *c,* which is indifferent to point *a*. If we repeat the process by taking away the same amount of garbage, moving to

---

8. If Anne had, say, 27 right shoes and only the left shoes for 17 of them, her level of satisfaction would be the same as if she had 17 pairs of shoes. In general, the usefulness of shoes to Anne is given by the *minimum* of the number of left shoes or right shoes, since this equals the number of pairs of shoes. In Chapter 4 we will discuss complements and substitutes in more detail, distinguishing among complements, substitutes, gross complements, and gross substitutes. Left shoes and right shoes are technically gross complements, but not complements or substitutes.

point *d,* the declining marginal rate of substitution implies that Ralph needs to give up fewer antiques to leave him as well off as he was initially. Thus the amount of antiques that we need to subtract to move from point *d* to *e* is smaller than from *b* to *c.* The curvature of the indifference curve is therefore shown by the indifferent points *a, c,* and *e.* Simultaneously removing garbage and increasing antiques moves Ralph to a higher indifference curve as the arrow illustrates.

We just said that Ralph's level of satisfaction fell as he was given more garbage. Goods that decrease a consumer's satisfaction are often referred to as economic *bads* to distinguish them from economic *goods,* which increase satisfaction. Whether or not something is a good or a bad depends on the specific consumer's preferences and what that consumer's current consumption bundle is.

> An **economic good** is a commodity for which more is preferred to less. An **economic bad** is a commodity for which less is preferred to more.

Although consumer theory handles the possibility of economic bads without difficulty, it is cumbersome to continually allow for the fact that some commodities might be bads. In most cases, it is possible to convert a bad into a good. For instance, we could substitute garbage removal for garbage. In Ralph's case, more garbage removal makes him better off. Thus, unless specifically stated otherwise, we will assume that all commodities are economic goods.

3.3 Representing Preferences with the Utility Function

Indifference curves are not the only way to represent preferences. Another way to describe preferences is through a mathematical function called a utility function. As long as the set of bundles that are strictly preferred or indifferent to any bundle, and the set of bundles that are strictly less preferred or indifferent to any bundle, are closed sets, it is possible to represent the consumer's preferences in terms of a utility function. (Essentially, a set is closed if it contains its own edges.) Utility functions and indifference curves are used together, but often the compact utility function is easier to work with in consumer theory.

Definition of a Utility Function

How do you find a utility function? One way is to proceed as follows. Given that one indifference curve contains bundles that are preferred to bundles in another indifference curve, assign a number to each curve so that the numbers reflect the relative standing of each curve in the consumer's preferences. The level of satisfaction derived from a bundle is called *utility.* If bundle *a* is preferred to bundle *b,* then the utility of bundle *a* is numerically greater than the utility of bundle *b.* If *a* and *b* are indifferent to one another, their utility is the same. The function that assigns a number to each bundle is called the utility function.

▼

4. Explain what a utility function is and relate it to indifference curves.

*A **utility function** assigns a number to each consumption bundle so that if bundle* a *is preferred to bundle* b, *the number for* a *will be greater than the number for* b.

The numbers assigned to consumption bundles are typically referred to as *utils.* A bundle giving 5 utils is preferred to a bundle giving 3 utils, for example. All bundles giving 8 utils are indifferent to one another and therefore form the bundles of an indifference curve. To get a better feel for utility functions, we turn to a discussion of their most important properties.

Cardinal and Ordinal Utility

The first thing to note about utility is that the assigned numbers can be anything we want as long as they correctly represent the relative ranking of bundles. In Figure 3.5, for example, Charlotte's indifference curves could be labeled with numbers 2, 4 and 6. If bundle *a* is on the curve giving 2 utils, we know it is less preferred than a bundle on the curve labeled 4 utils. However, if the numbers we assigned were all doubled, *they would still give the same ordinal ranking of bundles.* Since the utility numbers have meaning for us only because they are ordered with respect to one another, utils are *ordinal* numbers that we distinguish from *cardinal* numbers.

▼

5. Distinguish ordinal from cardinal utility and explain why ordinal utility is sufficient to represent preferences.

Cardinal numbers are numbers whose magnitudes are commensurable in an absolute way. Unlike ordinal numbers, their magnitude relates meaningfully to their relative size. For example, a thermometer on the Kelvin scale measures temperature from absolute zero, so a temperature of 100° K is precisely twice as warm as a temperature of 50° K. On the other hand, a utility of 10 does not mean twice as much happiness as a utility of 5, because the information in utility is only of an ordinal type. What is needed to produce a cardinal number is a natural unit of measurement whose magnitude has absolute meaning. For example, if prices were fixed and you always spent your money to get to the highest possible indifference curve, you could define your utility in terms of the amount of money you spent. This utility measure would have cardinal meaning: a utility of 100 would require exactly twice the income to achieve as a utility of 50, and so on.

For most purposes in microeconomics, it is not necessary to devise a cardinal scale of utility since we care only about comparing utilities.[9] Thus most utility functions are ordinal. Even though we can evaluate them, the numbers that we get have meaning only in comparison to other utility numbers from the same individual. Bearing this in mind, we now turn to a study of the numerical properties of utility functions.

9. We will construct a cardinal measure of utility in Chapter 4 when we discuss the effect of a price change on consumer welfare.

Marginal Utility

Now that we have a utility function that assigns numbers to indifference curves, we can talk about the consumer's welfare (level of satisfaction or well-being) interchangeably with the consumer's utility. A change in the consumer's welfare, therefore, is measured by how much utility rises when additional units of a good are added to the consumer's consumption bundle. The term used to refer to this number is marginal utility.

▼
6. Define marginal utility and relate it to the marginal rate of substitution.

> The **marginal utility of good x (MU_x)** is the increase in utility per additional small amount of good x consumed.

Since utility is an ordinal number, marginal utility is also an ordinal number that changes with whatever scale is used to describe utility. (We will explain how marginal utility is used to construct a cardinal number when we relate it to the marginal rate of substitution.) Figure 3.7 shows an indifference curve containing points a and b, and another containing points a' and b'. At

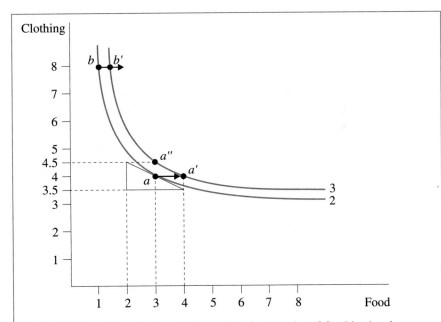

Figure 3.7   Marginal Utility   Increasing the quantity of food by 1 unit at point a increases utility from 2 to 3, whereas at point b utility rises by more than 1 unit for the same increase in food. Increasing the quantity of clothing by one-half unit at point a also increases utility from 2 to 3. Thus the marginal utility of food at point a, MU_{food}, is 1, and at point b it is greater than 1. $MU_{clothing}$ at point a is 2. Taking the ratio of the two marginal utilities, we find that $MRS_{food,clothing} = \frac{1}{2}$, as verified by the triangle showing the slope of the indifference curve at point a, where two units of food compensate for one unit of clothing.

point *a*, increasing food consumption from 3 to 4 causes the consumer's bundle to shift to *a'* and utility to rise from 2 to 3. Since utility rises 1 unit for a 1-unit increase in food, the marginal utility of food is 1 at point *a*. Marginal utility at other points can be computed in the same way. At point *b*, for example, the marginal utility of food is greater than 1 because the same unit increase in food increases utility by more than 1 unit, as indicated by the fact that the arrow showing increase in food of 1 unit lies beyond point *b'*.

Marginal Utility and the Marginal Rate of Substitution

We said previously that the consumer's $MRS_{x,y}$ could be thought of as the consumer's personal *y*-price of *x*. It told us what the value to the consumer of an additional unit of *x* was by showing how much *y* the consumer would be willing to give up for an additional unit of *x*. Marginal utility also tells us something about the value to the consumer of good *x* by indicating how much utility rises with additional units of *x*. It should not be surprising, then, that marginal utility and the marginal rate of substitution are related to one another in a simple but important way. In a sense, the marginal rate of substitution is the cardinal version of marginal utility. To explain the link, let's begin with a story.

Let's say you gave you friend Stephanie a travel bag for her birthday, and she told you her marginal utility from receiving it was 20 billion utils. Does she like the bag a lot or a little? Since utility is an ordinal number, you have no way of knowing except by comparison to some other utility figure Stephanie gives you. Now you learn that on the same day another of Stephanie's friends took her to the latest Stephen Spielberg movie, and she tells you her marginal utility from the movie was 1 billion utils. What would you say now? Dividing the marginal utility of the travel bag by the marginal utility of the movie, you would say that 1 travel bag was worth 20 Stephen Spielberg movies. Apparently, she liked the bag quite a bit. However, there is another way to describe what you just did. By dividing the marginal utilities, you found the rate at which Stephanie would exchange movies for a travel bag while holding her utility constant. *This rate is the marginal rate of substitution of travel bags for movies.* In fact, the connection between marginal utility and the marginal rate of substitution is a general one, which we summarize as follows:

> *The marginal rate of substitution of* **x** *for* **y**, **MRS**$_{x,y}$, *is related to the marginal utility of* x, MU_x, *and the marginal utility of* y, MU_y, *as the ratio*

$$MRS_{x,y} = \frac{MU_x}{MU_y}.$$

We have already seen that the marginal rate of substitution is determined by the slope of the indifference curve and that the declining marginal rate of substitution along an indifference curve implies that indifference curves are convex to the origin. In Figure 3.7 utility increases from 2 to 3 for a $\frac{1}{2}$-unit increase in clothing from point a to point a''. Thus utility rises at a rate of 2 units per unit increase in clothing. Thus $MU_{food}/MU_{clothing} = \frac{1}{2} = MRS_{food,clothing}$ at point a. This marginal rate of substitution is verified by the tangent triangle showing the slope of the indifference curve at point a: that is, 2 units of food (the horizontal distance) must be given up for every unit of clothing (the vertical distance) to stay on the indifference curve.

3.4 Choice Sets and Budget Sets

Up to this point, we've concentrated on what the consumer *would like to do,* as determined by preferences. We know the consumer wants to get to the highest indifference curve possible. Knowing preferences does not tell us what the consumer *will do,* however, because we need to know what choices are feasible. You may want unlimited quantities of many goods, but that would be a poor prediction of what you actually consume. We also need to describe the constraints that limit the consumer from choosing too much. Modeling the consumer's choice problem as a maximization problem subject to these constraints allows us to describe what the consumer does. Such problems are called *constrained optimization problems.*

The Choice Set

▼
7. Define the choice set and the budget set, explaining how they relate to one another.

Let's start with a simple example. Robinson Crusoe must choose between food and shelter. Since he is alone on his desert island, the maximum amounts of food and shelter Robinson can consume are determined by his ability to find or make these things for himself. For each possible combination of food and shelter, there is a limit to what Robinson can provide. This limit is drawn in Figure 3.8 as the bundles contained in the region bounded by the solid line *PP* that is concave with respect to the origin. Curve *PP* is also called a *production possibility frontier* because it shows the frontier of all possible production points.[10] It follows that the shaded bundles in Figure 3.8 determine the set from which Robinson Crusoe is constrained to choose.

> The **choice set** is the set of feasible bundles from which the consumer can choose.

In Robinson's case, we said nothing about markets or buying goods, and in fact we could describe his choices and behavior without using the ideas of prices and markets. However, consumer choices are usually limited by what is affordable. An important element for determining feasible choices when consumers *buy* what they consume is the budget set, a special case of the choice set given by the set of bundles that the consumer is able to afford.

10. We will describe production possibility frontiers in greater detail and make more extensive use of them in Part Four when we discuss the workings of the entire economy.

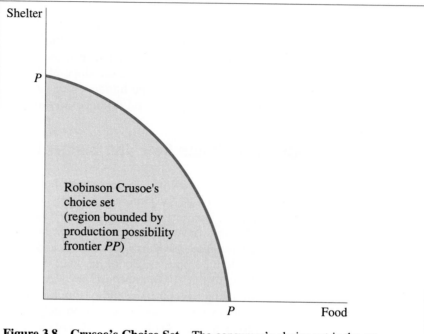

Figure 3.8 Crusoe's Choice Set The consumer's choice set is the set of bundles that the consumer can choose from. Robinson Crusoe's choices are limited by his ability to produce food and shelter for himself.

The Budget Set

Now let's move to a contemporary city and consider the choices of Robert Crusoe, Robinson's great-great-grandson. Robert also needs food and shelter, but he buys them: food at price p_f = $20 per bag and shelter at price p_s = $2.50 per square foot per month. (Robert spends his income on other things, but for the sake of the example we will limit ourselves to these two.) Let I = $2,000 represent Robert's monthly income.[11] If f is the amount of food bought per month, then $20f$ is the amount he spends on food monthly. Likewise, $2.5s$ is the amount of money spent on shelter, where s is the amount of shelter. Since the amount Robert spends equals his income, Robert's budget constraint is given by

$$\$20f + \$2.5s = \$2,000.$$

11. We will discuss the source of the consumer's income later. Usually, the consumer sells labor services in return for wages and this generates income, which is spent on goods. Since for the time being we are limiting ourselves to the discussion of two goods, we do not need to augment the list of goods by the labor services that the consumer sells. In general, labor services would enter into the consumer's utility function, as we will discuss in Chapter 5, but for now we simply take the consumer's available income as given.

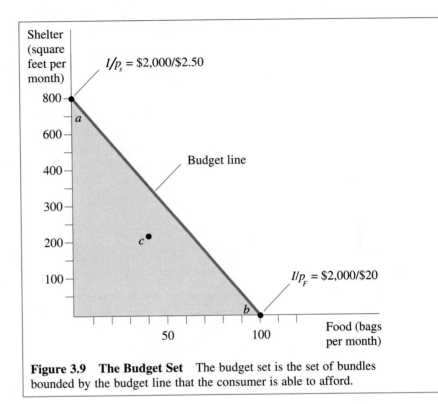

Figure 3.9   The Budget Set   The budget set is the set of bundles bounded by the budget line that the consumer is able to afford.

The shaded area in Figure 3.9 shows the bundles for which Robert spends an amount less than or equal to his income. For example, if Robert spent all of his income on food, he could spend $20f = $2,000 on food and buy $I/p_f = $2,000/($20 per bag) = 100 bags. Similarly, if he spent all of his income on shelter, he could buy $I/p_s = $2,000/($2.50 per square foot) = 800 square feet. Spending part of his money on each good means that he buys some bundle on the budget line connecting points a and b. If he spends less than his full income, he buys at a point below the budget line (for example, point c).

> The **budget set** is the set of bundles bounded by the budget line that the consumer can afford to purchase at market prices. For example, if there are two goods x and y, the budget set is all x and y such that $p_x x + p_y y \leq I$, where I is income.

Since both food and shelter are goods, Robert will always spend all of his income if he is rational. Any bundle such as c that is below the budget line has other bundles to the northeast of it that are affordable. Since these bundles have more of each good, they give higher utility. Thus the consumer does better by buying a bundle that is on the frontier. This implies that the budget constraint is satisfied as an equality by the choice that the consumer makes.

Effect of Price and Income Changes on the Budget Line

Both prices and income determine the orientation and location of the budget line. Figure 3.10 shows some of the effects of price and income changes on Drusilla's budget line. Since she is a college student, she buys only food and books. Part (a) shows that the price of food has gone up while Drusilla's income and the price of books remain unchanged. If Drusilla spent all her income on food, she would be able to buy less of it. The intersection of the budget line with the food axis shifts inward toward the origin. Since the number of books that Drusilla's income could buy is unchanged, the budget

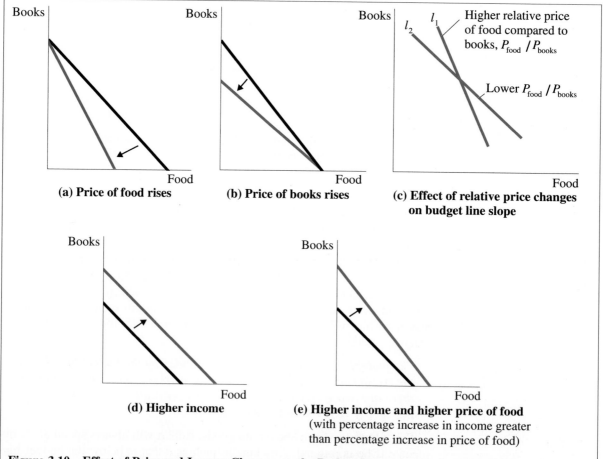

(a) Price of food rises

(b) Price of books rises

(c) Effect of relative price changes on budget line slope

(d) Higher income

(e) Higher income and higher price of food (with percentage increase in income greater than percentage increase in price of food)

Figure 3.10   Effect of Price and Income Changes on the Budget Line   A price increase shifts the corresponding intercept of the budget line toward the origin, whereas a price decrease shifts the budget line outward. The color line shows the final location of each budget line, and the arrows indicate the direction of the shift.

line rotates clockwise, anchored at the original intersection point on the books axis. Part (b) shows the effect of an increase in the price of books. Here the shift is counterclockwise, anchored at the original intersection point on the food axis. In general, the negative of the slope of the budget line equals the ratio of prices of the two goods. For example, part (c) superimposes two budget lines with the same relative final prices as in parts (a) and (b). We can see that line l_1 corresponds to the budget line with the higher price of food relative to clothing because the absolute value of its slope is larger.

If Drusilla's income rises while the prices of food and books stay unchanged, she can buy more of both. This means that the budget line moves outward, as part (d) shows. Finally, if Drusilla's income increases at the same time as the price of either food or books changes, the budget line will rotate as it moves in or out. Part (e) shows a case where Drusilla's income rises at the same time that the price of food goes up or the price of books falls. Her final budget line is steeper, indicating a higher price of food relative to books, but her budget line has shifted outward because her income is higher. Part (e) also shows that Drusilla's income has risen by a greater percentage than the increase in the price of food, because the intercept on the food axis (remember, the intercept is given by income/price) has increased.

3.5 Utility Maximization

By combining the consumer's preferences (represented by the family of indifference curves) and the budget set, we can see how individual consumers decide how much of each type of good to buy. Figure 3.11 shows both ingredients by placing the consumer's indifference curves on the same diagram as the consumer's budget constraint.

Because we assume rationality, there are two things that the consumer's choice must do. First, it must be on the budget line. Second, it must also maximize the consumer's utility. Being on the budget line just means that consumers spend all of their income. Maximizing utility means that they spend it in such a way as to reach the highest possible indifference curve.

In Figure 3.11, each point from *a* through *d* satisfies the first requirement: the consumer's choice is on the budget line. However, point *c* is the only choice that also maximizes utility. It lies on the highest indifference curve (indifference curve $U = 3$) that has a point in common with the budget line. All other points lie either above or below the line or give lower utility. Point *c* therefore maximizes utility subject to the budget constraint and solves the consumer's constrained optimization problem.

Tangency Conditions

The notable feature of bundle *c* in Figure 3.11 is the *tangency* that it represents between the indifference curve and the budget line. The indifference curves through all other points on the budget line *intersect* or *cut* the budget line.

▼
8. What two requirements must the consumer's constrained optimization choice satisfy?

▼
9. Explain what tangency is important to the consumer's optimization choice and why.

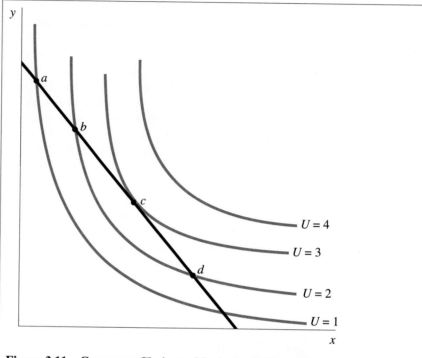

Figure 3.11   Consumer Choice to Maximize Utility   The consumer chooses the bundle that is on the budget line and also on the highest indifference curve that has a point in common with the budget line, in this case bundle *c*.

Tangency between an indifference curve and the budget line occurs where the slope of the indifference curve at a point is identical to the slope of the budget line at the same point.

Tangency implies that the marginal rate of substitution of *x* for *y* is equal to p_x/p_y, the rate at which *x* can be traded for *y* in the market while holding consumer expenditure constant. To see this, note that the market value of a change in *x* is given by $p_x \Delta x$, and the market value of a change in *y* is $p_y \Delta y$. Equating the two values gives us

$$-p_x \Delta x = p_y \Delta y$$

or

$$\frac{-\Delta y}{\Delta x} = -\text{slope of budget line} = \frac{p_x}{p_y}.$$

Since $\text{MRS}_{x,y} = -\text{slope of indifference curve}$, tangency between the indifference curve and the budget line means that

▼
10. Give the mathematical condition for tangency of the indifference curve and budget line.

$$\text{MRS}_{x,y} = \frac{\text{MU}_x}{\text{MU}_y} = \frac{p_x}{p_y}.$$

In essence, the tangency condition says that the consumer maximizes utility when the *value* of an additional unit of x measured in terms of y (this is $\text{MRS}_{x,y}$) equals the *cost* of an additional unit of x measured in terms of y (this is p_x/p_y).

What would happen if $\text{MRS}_{x,y}$ and the price ratio p_x/p_y were unequal? In these cases, the consumer could always raise utility by buying more of one of the goods. Only when the "bang per buck" (utility per dollar spent on the good) is balanced for the two goods, as at a tangency position, would it not raise the consumer's utility to increase spending on either good. For example, assume that the two goods are Reese's Pieces and M&Ms, which we denote by R and M, respectively. You have spent all of your income on the two candies so you are on your budget line, but you find yourself in the position

$$8 = \text{MRS}_{R,M} > \frac{p_R}{p_M} = 1,$$

which is point a in part (a) of Figure 3.12. In this case, we have $p_R = p_M = 1$, $\text{MU}_R = 4$, and $\text{MU}_M = \frac{1}{2}$. By rewriting we see that

$$4 = \frac{\text{MU}_R}{p_R} > \frac{\text{MU}_M}{p_M} = \frac{1}{2},$$

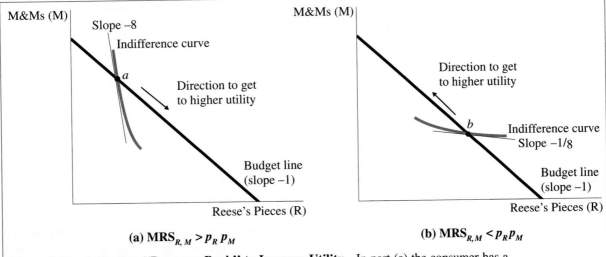

(a) $\text{MRS}_{R,M} > p_R \, p_M$ 　　　　　　　　(b) $\text{MRS}_{R,M} < p_R p_M$

Figure 3.12   Adjusting "Bang per Buck" to Improve Utility   In part (a) the consumer has a higher marginal rate of substitution of Reese's Pieces for M&Ms than the relative price of Reeses' Pieces (i.e., Reese's Pieces' bang per buck, MU_R/p_R, is higher than the bang per buck for M&Ms, MU_M/p_M). To improve utility, the consumer thus shifts purchases on the budget line to buy more Reese's Pieces at the expense of M&Ms. In part (b) the reverse situation occurs. Here the consumer should buy more M&Ms.

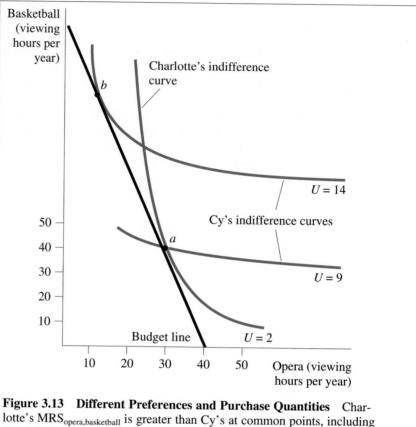

Figure 3.13   Different Preferences and Purchase Quantities   Charlotte's MRS$_{\text{opera,basketball}}$ is greater than Cy's at common points, including Charlotte's choice point a on the budget line. As a result, Cy's utility-maximizing choice for the same budget line lies above Charlotte's at point b.

which says that the utility you gain from spending an additional dollar on Reese's Pieces is eight times more (4 divided by $\frac{1}{2}$ is 8) than the utility you gain from spending an additional dollar on M&Ms. In simpler terms, your "bang per buck" is greater for Reese's Pieces than for M&Ms. You therefore raise your utility by shifting spending out of low-bang-per-buck M&Ms and into higher-bang-per-buck Reese's. This means moving in the direction of the arrow in part (a). Part (b) of Figure 3.12 shows the reverse case where

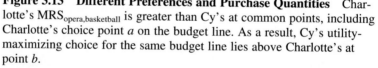

$$\frac{1}{2} = \frac{\text{MU}_R}{p_R} < \frac{\text{MU}_M}{p_M} = 4.$$

Now you improve utility by increasing M and decreasing R.

Preferences and Purchases

Now that we know how the steepness or flatness of the consumer's indifference curve relative to the budget line determines where on the budget line the consumer buys, we can relate the shape and orientation of indifference curves to purchases. In section 3.2 we described Charlotte's family of indifference curves as being oriented more toward the opera axis compared to Cy's, meaning that at common points Charlotte's $MRS_{opera,basketball}$ was higher than Cy's. (Equivalently, Cy's $MRS_{basketball,opera}$ was higher than Charlotte's.) Figure 3.13 shows how this implies that Charlotte will spend more of her money on opera and Cy more on basketball, other things being equal. Given the budget line, Charlotte's choice of consumption is at point *a*, where her indifference curve is tangent to the budget line. We have also drawn Cy's indifference curve passing through point *a*. Since Cy's $MRS_{basketball, opera}$ is higher than Charlotte's, his indifference curve at point *a* is flatter than the budget line, implying that another, higher indifference curve for Cy would be tangent to the budget line at point *b*. Since *b* is to the left of *a*, it follows that Cy will spend more on basketball and Charlotte more on opera when they have the same budget line.

Nontangencies and Corner Solutions

Sometimes the consumer won't be able to find a point of perfect tangency, but the bang-per-buck principle still holds true. Figure 3.14 shows several ways in which the consumer's optimal choice does not lead to a tangency but still maximizes utility.

▼
11. Give an example in which the consumer's utility-maximizing bundle is not at a tangency and interpret it in terms of the marginal rate of substitution and the price ratio.

In part (a) we have reproduced Mike's indifference curves for golf and upland bird hunting from Figure 3.6 and superimposed his budget line for the two activities. There is no hope of tangency anywhere in the picture because none of the indifference curves have the same slope as the budget line. Since Mike does not care about golf and receives utility only from bird hunting, his indifference curves are vertical lines, with higher utility associated with bundles to the right. The point of highest utility on the budget line is at bundle *t*. Not suprisingly, Mike chooses to spend all of his money on hunting and none on golf.

The choice of bundle *t* is called a *corner solution* because the consumer's choice of consumption bundle is at a corner of the budget set. The same rules involving comparison of the marginal rate of substitution with the price ratio for moving to a superior bundle apply, but the consumer is prevented from further movement in the utility-increasing direction by the axis-boundary of the choice set (in this case, the limitation that the consumer cannot consume any smaller quantity of golf).

Evaluating the marginal rate of substitution of hunting for golf at point *t* shows that it is greater than the price ratio. In fact, since the marginal utility of golf is zero, the marginal rate of substitution of hunting for golf is infinite. (Alternatively, the marginal rate of substitution of golf for hunting is zero.)

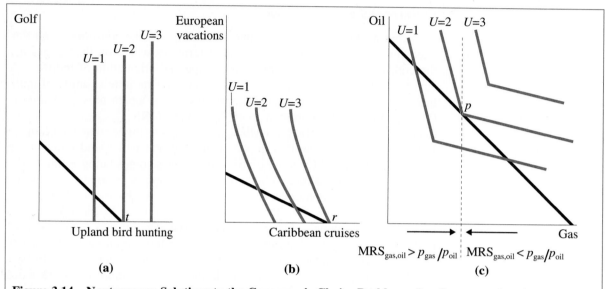

Figure 3.14 Nontangency Solutions to the Consumer's Choice Problem Bundles *t*, *r*, and *p* give the consumer the highest utility, although the indifference curve in each case is not tangent to the budget line. In part (a) the marginal rate of substitution of golf for upland bird hunting is zero; the consumer reduces money spent on golf to zero. In (b), the marginal rate of substitution of European vacations for Caribbean cruises is positive but not great enough to equal the relative price of a European vacation; the consumer vacations only in the Caribbean. In (c), on either side of bundle *p* on the budget line, the marginal rate of substitution of gas for oil compared to the price ratio causes the consumer to increase utility by moving back toward point *p*.

Mike would therefore like to decrease his expenditures on golf and use the money for hunting instead. He can't do this, though, because he has already reduced his golf to zero, and the edge of the budget set prevents any further moves to the right or down.

Part (b) of Figure 3.14 shows a corner solution where the consumer has conventional indifference curves for Caribbean cruises and European vacations. Although the indifference curves exhibit a declining marginal rate of substitution, they still do not lead to a tangency in the middle part of the budget line. Utility is maximized at point *r*, even though the marginal rate of substitution of Caribbean cruises for European vacations is greater than the price of Caribbean cruises relative to European vacations. The interpretation is that even though the consumer likes both types of vacations, the Caribbean vacations are so much cheaper than European vacations that the consumer takes only Caribbean vacations.

Part (c) of the figure shows a third example where the solution is not a tangency. Although this example is technically not a corner solution, since the solution is in the interior of the budget line rather than on the axes, we can understand it by the same principles used for corner solutions. Certain types of small engines, such as those in chain saws or outboard boat motors, often require a mixture of oil and gas for their fuel (mixing is done by the owner). Particular proportions of oil and gas are recommended by the manufacturer, though mixtures with other proportions will work. In our graph the indifference curves for the fuel mixture show a sharp corner at the recommended mix, though not with a 90-degree angle. For an operator purchasing fuel, the point of greatest utility on the budget line is at point p, where the marginal rate of substitution cannot be defined because of the sharp angle of the indifference curve. Although the budget line cannot be strictly tangent to the indifference curve, we see by checking any point on the budget line to the right of p that $MRS_{gas,oil}$ is *less than* the price ratio p_{gas}/p_{oil}. Thus the consumer improves welfare by cutting back on gas and using the money to buy more oil instead. On the left side of p, $MRS_{gas,oil}$ is *greater than* p_{gas}/p_{oil}. To the left of p, then, the consumer gets higher utility by cutting back on oil and using the money to buy gas. The directions of these moves are shown by the arrows on the horizontal axis. Only at p itself is there no utility gain to be had by moving to another point. Though $MRS_{gas,oil}$ is not defined at p, it is too high to the left of p and too low to the right of p. The middle is the only place where the consumer cannot raise utility by moving to a different spot.

APPLICATION: Budget Lines and Government Child Care Policy

Historically, mothers have provided the care for their own children, but social and economic changes have caused increasing numbers of women to enter the labor force in recent years. This has led to an increase in the demand for others to care for young children. Although only 11.5 percent of child care is provided by day care centers,[12] there is no question that day care can be expensive. Costs for one child can easily exceed $4,000 to $5,000 per year. Depending on the type of care and the age and number of the children, a family's costs may run into the $15,000 to $20,000 range.

It has been suggested that a solution to the high cost of child care is for the federal government to become involved in promoting and funding day care services. Other observers have suggested that advocates of federal involvement are not really addressing themselves to the needs of parents and children, but to the desires of the caregiving industry for federal dollars. Can the market analysis of Chapter 2 and the consumer theory of this chapter tell us anything about the problem?

---

12. The majority of day care outside of school hours for children under 15 whose parents are working is provided by the family itself, through care by the parent, a relative, or an unrelated person. See ''Child Day Care Services: An Industry at a Crossroads,'' *Monthly Labor Review,* December 1990, pp. 17–24.

This issue can be examined on several dimensions, including whether child care is a public good that the government legitimately should become involved in providing. By and large, however, day care is like other kinds of services that are bought and sold in private markets.[13] Since expensive automobiles, say, can cost as much as or more than day care and we do not seek to have government provide families with expensive automobiles, the impetus for federal involvement in child day care must come from elsewhere. One obvious possibility is the desire to lessen the perceived disproportionate burden on American families with small children.[14]

From our study of the budget constraint, however, we can ascertain that earmarking money for families to use specifically for child care is not the best way to help the family. Why? Because if the family were given the income instead, it could use the money for child care if it wanted, or use it for something else it deemed more necessary. In comparison to receiving nonearmarked money, the family can only be made worse off with earmarked money.

Figure 3.15 shows budget line l_1 for a representative family that buys child care services (on the horizontal axis) and everything else (on the vertical axis). Tangency of the family's indifference curve with l_1 is at point a, since most of the typical family's budget is not spent on child care. If the family receives an earmarked child care subsidy in the amount G, its budget line shifts to l_2 plus segment cd. The corner in the new budget line at point c occurs because, if the family spent all of its private income on everything else, it could consume exactly G units of child care and its consumption of everything else would be at the level given by point d. Increasing the family's *income* by the child care amount, without earmarking, shifts the budget line to l_2 plus segment ce, without any corner at point c. For the corner at point c not to matter, earmarking must presume that the family would want to spend the additional income entirely on child care. In fact, Figure 3.15 shows that the family would spend *part* of the additional income on child care and *part* on everything else (point b). The best the family can do with earmarking, therefore, is point c, which gives lower utility than point b. Only if point b lies on l_2 to the right of point c is earmarking unharmful relative to unrestricted income.

If limiting family aid to child care lowers the money's usefulness to families, then why has there been industry pressure on Congress for child care earmarking rather than for income to families with children? We turn to the demand and supply theory of Chapter 2.

13. We will study the provision of public goods in Chapter 14. Another argument might be that day care provides positive benefits to more than just the families that use it. Such an argument might be made for education, for example. However, child day care is essentially a caretaking function rather than an educational one.

14. Proposals often involve some form of tax rebate for families with children. To the extent that couples who have no children will be supported in their old age by Social Security transfers from other people's children and will benefit from the existence of a succeeding generation, there is a rationale for parents wtih children to retain more income to pay for child-raising costs.

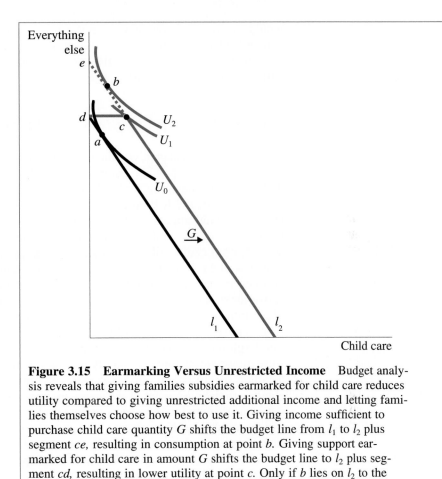

Figure 3.15 Earmarking Versus Unrestricted Income Budget analysis reveals that giving families subsidies earmarked for child care reduces utility compared to giving unrestricted additional income and letting families themselves choose how best to use it. Giving income sufficient to purchase child care quantity G shifts the budget line from l_1 to l_2 plus segment ce, resulting in consumption at point b. Giving support earmarked for child care in amount G shifts the budget line to l_2 plus segment cd, resulting in lower utility at point c. Only if b lies on l_2 to the right of c do the two support methods result in equal utility to the family.

About 60 percent of day care centers today are operated for profit, often as part of a national chain, with 40 percent operated on a nonprofit basis, such as through churches and schools. Industry advocates of government involvement emphasize that the industry needs federal regulations to ensure safety and set standards. By implication, certain types of day care providers would not be federally certified. Although safety is important, we note that similar arguments for federal certification and standard setting could be made for virtually any private good. In this case, by instituting tax-based support for certain types of providers, such as for-profit day care centers, and not certifying others, such as sectarian and home providers of day care, government involvement would (1) increase the number of dollars going to child care providers at the same time that it (2) reduced total supply and (3) directed the flow of dollars more toward for-profit providers. The net effect therefore would be to simultaneously raise the *price* of child care and the *quantity demanded* from certified for-profit institutions. Such a change would work to the advantage of for-profit child care providers but against lower costs of child care to the family. ■

3.6 Summing Up Preferences and Budget Lines

At the start of the chapter, we said that Ford Motor Company used information about consumers' spending habits to help it design its popular Explorer. Now that we know the basic tools of consumer theory, can you see how Ford would apply them? If Ford executives could ascertain the type of buyers the Explorer would appeal to (think of Cy and Charlotte's differently oriented indifference curves and their different purchases given the same budget constraint), Ford could sell more cars by designing into them the features those buyers wanted. In fact, Explorer buyers were found to be about equally split between males and females; 90 percent were married; their family size was above three; and median income was in the $50,000 range. Median age was 41, with more than a third of the buyers college educated. This information reveals a lot about the kind of features that would be attractive to the buyers. The Explorer's six-passenger seating capacity and largest in its class interior were important features for family use, as was the vehicle's car-like ride and handling for drivers of either sex. Storage bins on doors and in other areas, along with the placement of the spare tire under the rear body where it would not interfere with interior space, proved useful for long trips. Exterior styling, which could have been geared in a number of other directions, suggested ruggedness and durability, which also appealed to the class of buyers just described. By predicting the likely demographics of its buyers, and which features were likely to appeal to them, Ford applied basic consumer theory to its styling and promotion decisions. It positioned its 4WD entry in such a way that the group of buyers it targeted would shift their purchases along their budget constraints toward Explorers. The success of the car proved the wisdom of Ford's deliberations.[15]

In terms of the basics of consumer theory, we have learned in this chapter that the preferences of rational consumers can be represented in terms of indifference curves and utility functions. The limitations on their choices can be represented by budget lines and choice sets. When indifference curves and budget lines are combined, the consumer's choice for maximizing utility can be represented as the bundle on the highest indifference curve that can be reached from the budget line. Usually this point is a point of tangency between the indifference curve and the budget line, but sometimes it is not, as when the choice is a corner solution.

---

15. Chapter 9 discusses in greater detail how the firm organizes information about consumer preferences to decide how many and what varieties of goods to offer, including why a firm would seek to position a product to fill a particular market "niche."

In studying indifference curves, utility functions, and budget lines, we also paid special attention to how things changed when preferences were different, when different kinds of goods were being considered, when prices changed, or when income changed. These changes are important, as in the case of Ford Motor Company, because they help us see how the consumer's choices can vary. The next chapter examines these issues in more detail and also shows how consumers' choices of utility-maximizing consumption bundles generate market demand curves.

Summary

Active Reading Guide numbers are given in parentheses at the end of each summary item.

1. Demand theory restricts its attention to the discussion of rational consumers, since there is little point in discussing irrational choices or consumers that act against their own interests. Rationality must be defined. We require rational consumer preferences to be complete, reflexive, transitive, and nonsatiable. (1)

2. In most cases, preferences can be represented by indifference curves. An indifference curve plots the collection of bundles that are indifferent to one another in the consumer's preferences. The axioms of rationality imply that indifference curves are downward sloping, space filling, and cannot cross. The shape, slope, and orientation of indifference curves codify the preferences of consumers. Knowing whether they are flat or curved, tilted or straight, tells us much about consumer preferences. (2)

3. The negative of the slope of the indifference curve equals the marginal rate of substitution of good x for good y, $MRS_{x,y}$. The marginal rate of substitution of good x for good y measures the amount of good y that the consumer would be willing to give up to acquire an additional unit of good x. Since we assume that indifference curves are convex to the origin, $MRS_{x,y}$ declines as one moves to the right along an indifference curve. (3)

4. Utility functions represent preferences and indifference curves mathematically by assigning to every consumption bundle a number whose magnitude indicates the consumer's level of satisfaction measured in utils. Unlike a cardinal function, whose numbers have meaning in terms of their absolute size, utility functions are ordinal. That is, utility numbers have significance only with respect to whether they are larger or smaller than other utility numbers of the same consumer. (4, 5)

5. Marginal utility of good x is the change in consumer utility per small additional amount of x consumed. Marginal utility is related to the marginal rate of substitution by the formula $MRS_{x,y} = MU_x/MU_y$, where MU_x and MU_y are marginal utilities of good x and y, respectively. (6)

6. The choice set is the set of bundles that are feasible for the consumer to choose. The budget set is a special case of the choice set consisting of bundles that the consumer can afford to buy at market prices. The budget set is bounded on the northeast by the budget line, which is the set of bundles that use all of the consumer's income to purchase. (7)

7. A rational consumer chooses the bundle from the choice set that gives highest utility. Nonsatiation implies that the consumer spends all of his or her income, so the bundle must also be on the budget line. (8)

8. Usually, the utility-maximizing bundle is at a point of tangency between the budget line and the indifference curve. Tangency implies that the negative of the slope of the budget line equals the negative of the slope of the indifference curve, or $MRS_{x,y} = p_x/p_y$ for two goods x and y. (9, 10)

9. Sometimes the highest utility bundle occurs at a point of nontangency; even so, the consumer still chooses the bundle giving highest utility of those in the choice set. (11).

Review Questions

*1. In a two-good world, construct an example of bundles chosen by a consumer in different situations that would indicate the consumer is irrational.

2. Economic theory looks at people in terms of a utility function or a family of indifference curves. This seems to imply that happiness depends only on the volume of goods and services that we can consume. Is this a good representation of what motivates people's actions? If not, why would an *economist* focus on it anyway? What would a lawyer's representation focus on? A poet's? A pastor's?

*3. Give an example in which absence of transitive preferences leads to a problem in predicting consumer choice.

*4. People sometimes say that they make choices by "prioritizing" what they do. For example, I might say that my highest priority is devotion to God, followed by family, country, and then myself. Are there ways that people make choices other than by prioritizing? How does prioritizing relate to choosing consumption of competing goods in terms of indifference curves?

5. "One man's garbage is another man's treasure." Assuming greater x_2 raises utility for both men, and x_1 is the commodity spoken of in the quotation, draw the two men's families of indifference curves showing the direction of welfare increase.

6. Give an example in which declining marginal rate of substitution is a plausible assumption.

*7. Give an example in which *increasing* marginal rate of substitution might be a plausible assumption.

8. Shelly's marginal rate of substitution of Clausen pickles (16-ounce jars) for jumbo chocolate chip cookies is 3. If the price ratio of pickles to cookies is 1 and Shelly's MRS is constant, how would Shelly spend her budget of $10 on the two items? How would her choices change if the price ratio were 3.5?

*9. Referring to the example of Robinson Crusoe in the text (section 3.4 and Figure 3.8), in what way do the two rules for consumer choice (to be at a point of tangency and to be on the budget constraint) apply when the constraint bounding the choice set is convex to the origin rather than determined by a budget line?

Numerical and Graphing Exercises

1. Draw indifference curves for the following cases:

a) Both cranberry drink, *x,* and yogurt, *y,* are goods, each measured in 8-ounce units. The consumer is indifferent between 3 *x*'s and 2 *y*'s.

b) Same as above, but the consumer always uses 3 *x*'s in combination with 2 *y*'s.

c) Both gum and lemon drops are goods to two consumers. Consumer I has a higher MRS$_{\text{gum,lemon drops}}$ at any bundle than consumer II.

d) Garden flowers are a good; weeds are a bad. The principle of declining marginal rate of substitution of garden flowers for weeds applies.

e) Bagels are a good; jelly-filled doughnuts are neither a good nor a bad.

*2. A restaurant advertises an "all you can eat" special for $6.00 for its Friday night fish fry. Draw Charlene's Friday night budget set if she spends the $100 in her purse on the two goods "fish fry" and "everything else."

3. Using the budget set from exercise 3, draw Charlene's indifference curves and show (a) under what conditions she will not eat at the restaurant, and (b) under what conditions she does eat at the restaurant. In each case, state her marginal rate of substitution of fish for everthing else relative to the price ratio of the two goods.

*4. Kevin's utility function is of the form, $U = 5X + 2Y$. The price of X is $12 per unit, and the

* Asterisks are used to denote questions that are answered at the back of the book.

price of Y is $3 per unit.
a) What is Kevin's marginal rate of substitution of X for Y?
b) Accurately graph Kevin's indifference curves and his budget constraint, assuming income is $1,200. Find the highest utility bundle on his budget line.

5. A consumer is willing to trade one lobster dinner for two freeze-dried trail meals. She currently consumes one dozen lobster dinners per year and 20 freeze-dried trail meals. The price of lobster dinners is $25.50, and the price of a trail meal is $8.50. Should she decrease her purchases of lobster dinners in order to buy more freeze-dried trail meals or the reverse?

*6. William the Conqueror commands the Norman armies. In battle against the Saxons, the marginal utility to him of another legion of archers (measured in enemy defeated) depends only on how many legions of archers he employs as given in the following table. The marginal utility to him of foot soldiers depends only on the number of legions of foot he has. The cost in men and money of outfitting a legion of foot is the same as outfitting a legion of archers, and he has only enough money and soldiers for 12 legions in his army. Treat the problem as a consumer choice problem with a budget constraint and find what mix his army should be.

7. Ronald likes both jelly beans, B, and white chocolate, C.
a) If Ronald's marginal rate of substitution of jelly beans for white chocolate equals C/B regardless of which indifference curve point (B, C) he is on, how many pounds of jelly beans and white chocolate does Ronald buy if his income is $100 and prices are $p_B = 1.50 per pound, $p_C = 6.00 per pound?
b) If instead Ronald's marginal rate of substitution of jelly beans for white chocolate is 1 when $B > C$, and 10 when $B < C$, how does he spend his money? (Hint: Try drawing a typical indifference curve and Ronald's budget line.)

*8. Show that a consumer with lexicographic preferences has no indifference curves by choosing a bundle and graphing all other bundles that are either strictly better or strictly worse. A *lexicographic ordering* ranks bundles the way a lexicographer (maker of dictionaries) ranks words by alphabetizing them. If two bundles consist of a list of items, the bundle with the larger amount of the first item is preferred. If both bundles have the same amount of the first item, then the bundle with the most of the second item is preferred, and so on down the list until the bundles are ranked or are shown to be the same.

	The Conqueror's Marginal Utility	
Number of Legions	Archers	Foot Soldiers
1	40	25
2	37	24
3	34	23
4	31	22
5	28	21
6	26	20
7	24	19
8	22	18
9	19	17
10	16	16
11	12	15
12	8	14
13	4	13

APPENDIX: Revealed Preference and the Indifference Curve

Our description of demand proceeds from the view that consumers are rational, that they act in their own best interest (they optimize, given their choice set), and that each consumer has some underlying order of preferences represented by a utility function that codifies those preferences.

Utility functions and indifference curves are powerful modeling tools, but aren't ''real'' in the same way that prices facing the consumer, quantities chosen, and income are ''real.'' Can we work backward from observable prices and from quantities the consumer chooses to determine what the underlying preferences must have been?

Revealed Preference

▼

A.1. What is the principle of revealed preference?

If we can observe enough incomes, prices, and quantity choices, and if we know that the consumer always chooses the unique bundle that maximizes utility, the answer is yes. The basic principle we use says that if consumer i chooses bundle a when bundle b was affordable, then bundle a is *directly revealed to be preferred* to bundle b. Ranking of bundles then can be extended to indirect comparisons by transitivity. Let us state this as a formal definition.

If bundle $a = (x_1, x_2)$ *is chosen when bundle* $b = (y_1, y_2)$ *was affordable,*

$$income = p_1x_1 + p_2x_2 \geq p_1y_1 + p_2y_2,$$

then a *is **directly revealed to be preferred** to* b. *Further, if* a *is directly revealed to be preferred to* b, b *is directly revealed to be preferred to* c, *and so on through a chain of bundles to* z, *then by transitivity* a *is **indirectly revealed to be preferred** to* z.

▼

A.2. Draw a diagram showing the set of bundles for which a given bundle is revealed to be preferred.

Figure 3.A.1, which depicts a typical budget set and consumer choice at bundle a, illustrates revealed preference. Bundle a is directly revealed to be preferred to all bundles b in the shaded set. Letting x's refer to the components of bundle a and letting y's refer to components of bundles in the shaded set, we see that b' costs less than a $(p_1x_1 + p_2x_2 > p_1y_1 + p_2y_2)$ and so is affordable. Bundle $b,''$ on the boundary, costing the same as a, is also affordable. Because the consumer chose a, when bundles b were affordable, a is revealed to be preferred to any shaded bundle b.

The Strong Axiom of Revealed Preference

We can now state the critical assumption that allows us to work backward from observed choices to the consumer's preferences.

Strong Axiom of Revealed Preference: Given different bundles a *and* b, *if bundle* a *is directly or indirectly revealed to be preferred to bundle* b, *then bundle* b *can never be directly or indirectly revealed to be preferred to bundle* a.

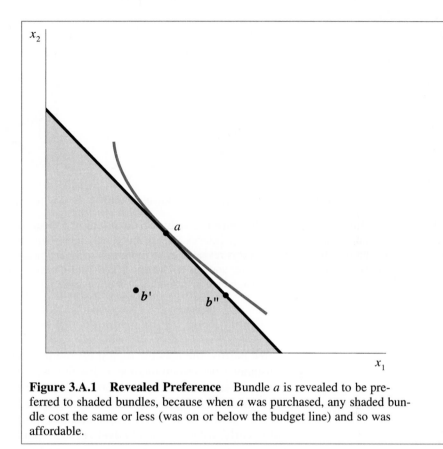

Figure 3.A.1 Revealed Preference Bundle *a* is revealed to be pre-ferred to shaded bundles, because when *a* was purchased, any shaded bun-dle cost the same or less (was on or below the budget line) and so was affordable.

▼
A.3. Show how the location and shape of the indifference curve can be deduced from properly chosen repeated observations of consumer choices.

Since we assume at the outset that we are observing a rational consumer, the definition of revealed preference tells us that the chosen bundles are the best possible given the consumer's budget set. The Strong Axiom of Revealed Preference further ensures that there can be no *chain* of bundles that violates transitivity. Thus, if the consumer can make choices for any income and set of prices, there is no reason, in principle, why the consumer's preference mapping cannot be deduced to any needed degree of accuracy through ap-propriately designed observations of prices, incomes, and choice of quantities.

Figure 3.A.2 shows how the indifference curve can be found by trapping it between increasingly large regions of the quadrant. Part (a) demonstrates the consumer's initial choice at bundle *a*, given the budget line *bc*. According to the Strong Axiom of Revealed Preference, bundles in the shaded region below budget line *bc* cannot be on the indifference curve going through *a*. Similarly, shaded bundles to the northeast of *a* cannot be on the indifference curve because they contain more of both goods and are strictly preferred to *a*. The indifference curve passing through *a* must therefore lie between the two shaded regions.

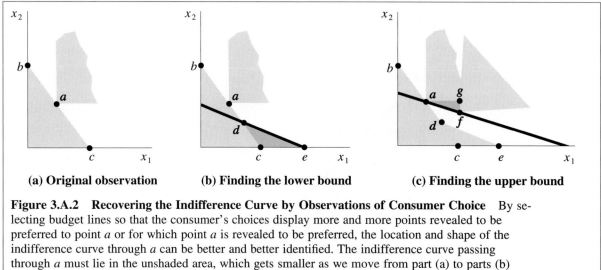

(a) Original observation   **(b) Finding the lower bound**   **(c) Finding the upper bound**

Figure 3.A.2   Recovering the Indifference Curve by Observations of Consumer Choice   By selecting budget lines so that the consumer's choices display more and more points revealed to be
preferred to point a or for which point a is revealed to be preferred, the location and shape of the
indifference curve through a can be better and better identified. The indifference curve passing
through a must lie in the unshaded area, which gets smaller as we move from part (a) to parts (b)
and (c).

We narrow the feasible region for the indifference curve by changing the
consumer's prices and income and seeing what the consumer chooses. In part
(b) we observe the consumer choosing bundle d given the budget line going
through d and e. Lowering the price of good x_1 and reducing the consumer's
income generates a budget line of the type drawn. By reducing income
sufficiently, we generate a budget set such that the consumer chooses a point
(i.e. d), which was previously revealed to be inferior to bundle a. Points in
the triangular region dce are revealed to be inferior to d and can therefore be
added to the shaded region of points that are inferior to a. Continuing by
making other ''cuts'' of this type provides better and better lower bounds of
the feasible region for the indifference curve.

Part (c) of the figure shows how to provide a better upper bound for the
indifference curve. A budget line going through a is selected, and the consumer's choice of f is observed. Since a is on the same budget line, f is
revealed to be preferred to a. Bundles to the northeast of f therefore are also
strictly preferred to a and can be added to the shaded region. Triangle agf
can be added to the shaded region because it is impossible for an indifference
curve exhibiting declining marginal rate of substitution and passing through
both a and a point to the southwest of f to enter the triangle.

Continuing to add to the shaded region by providing better upper bounds
and lower bounds will eventually trap the indifference curve to whatever
degree of accuracy is desired. In principle, repeated observations could provide as near an approximation to the preference mapping as necessary. ▪

CHAPTER 4

From Individual Demand to Market Demand

In this chapter we do four things: We describe how price and income effects work together to produce the overall effect on demand of a price change. We then discover how changes in income and the prices of other goods, both substitutes and complements, affect demand. After introducing the expenditure function to describe the least cost of achieving a particular utility level at a given set of prices, we find how to calculate consumer surplus, a dollar measure of the utility effect of a price change. Finally, we learn how to aggregate individual demand curves to generate market demand. An appendix discusses index numbers as a way to approximate the change in utility and cost of living.

ACTIVE READING GUIDES

After reading this chapter, you should be able to answer the Active Reading Guides listed below. These guides also appear in the page margins near the material to which they refer.

1. Show how to derive the individual's income consumption path and Engel curve.

2. Define normal, inferior and superior goods.

3. What are substitutes and complements? Gross substitutes and gross complements?

4. Relate the degree of substitutability to the curvature of the indifference curve.

5. Show how to derive the individual's price consumption path and demand curve.

6. Show how an income change shifts location of the individual's demand curve.

7. How can the consumer's response to a price change be broken into a substitution (price) effect and an income effect?

8. Define a Giffen good. How is being a Giffen good (a price-related property) linked to normality (an income-related property)?

9. What is income-compensated demand? Graphically relate it to ordinary demand.

10. What is the expenditure function? List its basic properties.

11. Define consumer surplus and show how to find a change in it using the original price and quantity and Δp, Δq.

12. Explain the formula for exact consumer surplus in terms of the expenditure function.

13. How do you derive market demand from individuals' demand?

14. What are three ways of empirically finding market demand?

A.1. Why are indexes used to report changes in prices and quantities?

A.2. How is a price index related to the expenditure function and a quantity index to the utility function?

A.3. Write the formulas for Laspeyres and Paasche price and quantity indexes.

A.4. Give the three fundamental properties of price and quantity indexes.

4.1 How Changes in Price and Income Affect Demand

In Chapter 3 we described how consumers choose what bundles to buy given their preferences and choice sets. In this chapter we examine in more detail how changes in income and prices affect consumers' demand. We use this information both to develop a dollar measure of the effect of a price change on consumer utility and to understand the effects that operate to give us the market demand curve when we aggregate from the individual level to the market level.

Changing Income and Individual Demand

How do market choices respond to variables such as the consumer's income? Let's look at Andrew's purchases of fruit pie, supposing that his income is at different levels and that the other good he consumes is sparkling water.

Part (a) of Figure 4.1 plots Andrew's choices when his income is set at $45, $60, $75, and $90. The price of pie is $6 per pound, and the price of sparkling water is $2 per quart. Starting with the lowest-income budget line closest to the origin and moving outward, we see that Andrew's purchases

▼
1. Show how to derive the individual's income consumption path and Engel curve.

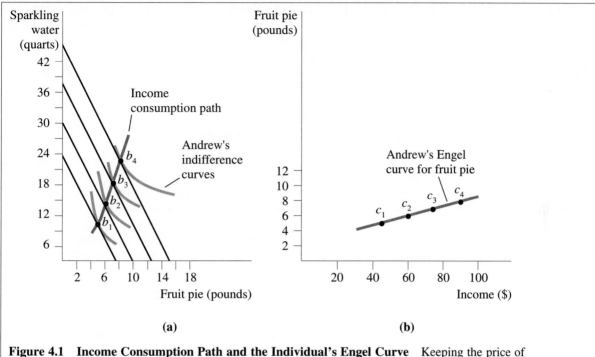

Figure 4.1 Income Consumption Path and the Individual's Engel Curve Keeping the price of sparkling water fixed at $2 per quart and the price of fruit pie fixed at $6 per pound, part (a) shows four budget lines corresponding to income for Andrew of $45, $60, $75, and $90. Andrew's consumption at these incomes is indicated by bundles b_1 through b_4. The income consumption path connects these bundles. In part (b), plotting income and quantity of fruit pie (points c_1 through c_4) and connecting the points gives Andrew's Engel curve for fruit pie.

rise from bundle b_1 to b_4. Each bundle, giving the highest utility among the bundles satisfying Andrew's budget constraint, represents a point of tangency between Andrew's indifference curve and the corresponding budget line. Connecting the bundles together for all such income changes gives us the *income consumption path.* Remember that in drawing Andrew's budget lines, we held the prices of pie and sparkling water fixed.

> *For fixed prices of goods, the **income consumption path** is the collection of bundles that the consumer buys when the consumer's income is set at different levels.*

The income consumption path plots purchases in response to *income* changes. Note that if prices were fixed at a different level, there would be a different income consumption path.

The income consumption path can be used to construct another set of curves, named *Engel curves* after an early economist, Ernst Engel, who worked with these curves. An Engel curve relates purchases of a given good to consumer income. To construct Andrew's Engel curve for fruit pie, let the vertical axis show the amount of pie in each bundle. In this case the quantities are 5, 6, 7, and 8 pounds, respectively. Plotting these in part (b) of Figure 4.1 against the corresponding incomes ($45, $60, $75, and $90) and connecting the points gives us the Engel curve. The figure indicates that demand for pie rises as income rises.[1]

Normal, Inferior, and Superior Goods

Taken as a whole, the consumer's response to increased income must be to spend it on *something*.[2] For individual goods, however, it is possible that purchases could rise or fall as income rises. Normally we expect that the consumer's purchases of particular goods will rise with rising income. When greater income leads to greater consumption of a particular good, we refer to the good as a *normal* good. Calling a good normal does not refer to a property of the good itself; rather, it is a statement about how the good enters into a consumer's preferences at a particular consumption point.

▼

2. Define normal, inferior, and superior goods.

> A ***normal good*** *is one whose quantity demanded rises with income.*

Since prices are held constant when measuring the change, increased quantity is equivalent to increased money spent on the good. Either increased quantity demanded or increased expenditure can therefore be used to define normal goods.

Some goods are not normal, however. If expensive, lean T-bone steaks are your favorite form of meat, then at a high enough income you will buy less hamburger and spend more of your budget on steak. The effect of increased income may therefore be to *reduce* your consumption of hamburger. The reason is that hamburger is intrinsically less desirable to you than T-bone steak. When you can afford to buy less hamburger, you gladly do so. In your preferences, hamburger is an inferior good.

> An ***inferior good*** *is one whose quantity demanded falls with income.*

Note that although we cannot predict whether a particular good is normal or inferior for a given consumer, we do know that at least one good in the consumer's budget must be normal because increased income must be spent on something in our one-period model.

---

1 Unlike demand curves, which place quantity on the horizontal axis, Engel curves historically have been drawn with income on the horizontal axis and quantity on the vertical axis. Since the way the axes are used is immaterial, we will follow historical precedent in each case.

2. Recall that we assume there are only two goods for the time being. This means that forgoing current spending (in other words, saving) is not a viable option. If we did consider savings as a way to increase future goods consumption, then future goods would have to be included in our list of goods. No rational consumer would forgo consumption today if this action did not entail the prospect of spending on goods tomorrow.

Although all goods are either normal or inferior, we can distinguish one final category of good. Engaging in antique collecting might be something of a luxury for you, just as spending time in beautiful scenic wilderness locations scattered around the world might be. All of these things are relatively expensive for you to indulge in, so they form a small portion of your budget expenditure. If your income rose sufficiently, however, not only might you begin to spend more income on these luxuries, but you might also devote a larger *proportion* of your growing budget to them. Goods that consumers treat in this way are called superior goods.

*A good is a **superior good** if the share of the consumer's budget spent on the good rises as income rises.*

By definition, superior goods must be normal goods. Since their *share* of the consumer's budget must rise as income rises, it follows that the percentage increase in expenditure on a superior good must be greater than the percentage increase in income. If income rises 1 percent, spending on a superior good must rise by more than 1 percent. In Chapter 2 we defined elasticity as the percentage change in one variable caused by a 1 percent change in another, and we spoke of price elasticities of supply and demand. Now let's define the *income elasticity of demand* as the percentage change in expenditure per percentage change in income. It follows, then, that normal goods have a positive income elasticity of demand, and *superior goods are normal goods whose income elasticity of demand is greater than 1.*

Analyzing Curves for Normal, Inferior, and Superior Goods

The relationship between normal, inferior, and superior goods can be seen by looking at Figure 4.2. Part (a) shows an income consumption path for hamburger and antiques that generates the Engel curve for hamburger in part (b). Notice that for low levels of income the consumer in this example buys more of both hamburger and antiques as income increases. At point *a* or *b,* then, hamburger is a normal good. But at higher income levels, increasing income causes the consumer to buy less hamburger as the income consumption path shifts toward the antiques axis. Beyond point *c* the consumer treats hamburger as an inferior good.

The share of the budget devoted to antiques or hamburger can be read off the diagram as the proportion of the budget line that lies between the consumption point and the axis for the other good. Point *c,* for example, is midway between the two axes. Since half of the budget line is between the consumption point and the hamburger axis, 50 percent of the budget is devoted to antiques. At point *d,* on the other hand, four-fifths of the budget line lies between the consumption point and the hamburger axis, so 80 percent of the budget is spent on antiques.

In the portion of the income consumption path to the right of point *c,* we know that antiques are a superior good because the consumption point on succeeding budget lines moves to the southeast.

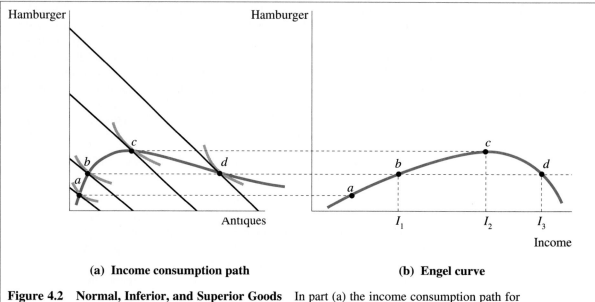

(a) Income consumption path   **(b) Engel curve**

Figure 4.2   Normal, Inferior, and Superior Goods   In part (a) the income consumption path for hamburger and antiques shows that hamburger consumption rises with income until point *c*. Thereafter it falls. This implies a rising Engel curve for hamburger in part (b) up to point *c* and a declining curve to the right of *c*. Because hamburger is an inferior good for incomes higher than I_2, the consumer buys the same quantity of hamburger at income I_3 as at lower income I_1. Antiques consumption rises with income throughout; thus antiques are a normal good. At points like *c* and *d*, antiques are also a superior good because the share of the budget devoted to them rises with income.

Cross-Price Effects, Substitutes, and Complements

Demand for one good also depends on the prices of other goods. In this section, therefore, we consider how the prices of other goods alter demand through cross-price effects.

We can define the *cross-price elasticity of demand* as the percentage change in the quantity demanded for a good caused by a 1 percent change in the price of another. For example, if my quantity demanded of plain cheese pizza increases by 6 percent when the price of pepperoni pizza rises by 2 percent, my cross-price elasticity of demand for plain cheese pizza with respect to the pepperoni pizza price is 3 ($\%\Delta q_{plain}/\%\Delta p_{pepperoni} = 0.06 \div 0.02 = 3$). I increase the purchases of my substitute (plain cheese pizza) when I decrease my purchases of higher-priced pepperoni pizza. This leads us to define a good as a substitute if the following is true.

▼

3. What are substitutes and complements? Gross substitutes and gross complements?

*Good 2 is a **substitute** for good 1 if the cross-price elasticity of demand for good 2 with respect to the price of good 1 is positive when utility is held constant.*

In other words, if the consumer shifts demand out of good 1 (pepperoni) into good 2 (plain) when the price of good 1 rises, then good 2 (plain) is a substitute for good 1. In the definition we also hold utility constant. Why do we do this? The answer is that when the price of pepperoni pizza rises, the consumer's utility falls because the price of something he or she buys has gone up. The higher price makes the consumer poorer, just as a decline in income would make the consumer poorer, and this affects purchases. We will discuss this income-like effect of a price change in detail later, but for now we note that we can eliminate the income effect by adjusting the consumer's income up or down as needed to stay on the same indifference curve. The resulting substitutions in consumption will then be due to pure substitution effects.

Of course, not all goods are substitutes. When you do skin diving, for instance, you need a mask, fins, and a snorkel. If a higher price of skin diving causes you to do less skin diving—say, the cost of travel to Maui or wherever you dive has risen—we expect that you also will buy *less* skin-diving equipment. This is because the mask, fins, and snorkel are used in conjunction with skin diving as complements.

> Good 2 is a **complement** for good 1 if the cross-price elasticity of demand for good 2 with respect to the price of good 1 is negative when utility is held constant.

In other words, if the consumer shifts demand out of both good 1 and good 2 when the price of good 1 rises, good 2 is a complement. Again, holding utility constant just means that the effect being looked at is free of any income effects of the price change.

▼
4. Relate the degree of substitutability to the curvature of the indifference curve.

We can use *preference maps*—graphs of families of indifference curves—to identify different degrees of substitutability. In general, the flatter the indifference curve, the greater the degree of substitutability. Figure 4.3 illustrates three different kinds of preference mappings based on the amount of curvature of the indifference curves. These curves should remind you of the curves for perfect substitutes and gross complements we derived in Figure 3.6. We can see how price affects the consumer's purchases in a condition of constant utility.

Part (a) of Figure 4.3 shows a set of linear indifference curves. These imply *perfect substitutability,* meaning that for a consumer consuming both goods, a vanishingly small increase in price of one of them leads to a large increase in consumption of the other. For example, assume that Daniel views all brands of margarine as identical. When their prices are the same, he sometimes buys one brand, sometimes another. Thus, when prices are the same for both brands of margarine, Daniel maximizes utility regardless of which mix of brands he buys, since any of his choices achieve tangency between his linear indifference curve and his budget line. However, if the price of brand A rises even one cent higher than the price of brand B, Daniel's purchases will shift *entirely* to the cheaper brand.[3]

---

3. The solution to Daniel's consumer problem when one brand is more expensive than the other and the budget line is no longer superimposed on top of the indifference curve becomes a corner solution. Corner solutions were discussed in Chapter 3.

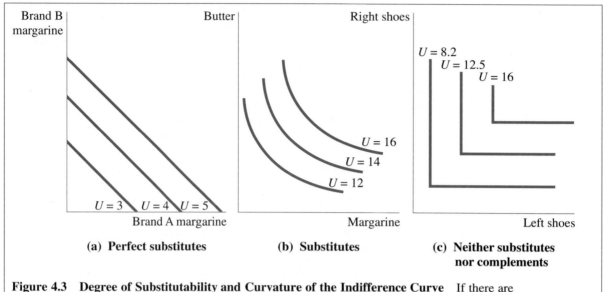

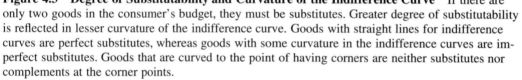

(a) Perfect substitutes   **(b) Substitutes**   **(c) Neither substitutes nor complements**

Figure 4.3   Degree of Substitutability and Curvature of the Indifference Curve   If there are only two goods in the consumer's budget, they must be substitutes. Greater degree of substitutability is reflected in lesser curvature of the indifference curve. Goods with straight lines for indifference curves are perfect substitutes, whereas goods with some curvature in the indifference curves are imperfect substitutes. Goods that are curved to the point of having corners are neither substitutes nor complements at the corner points.

Part (b) of the figure shows a set of convex indifference curves with declining marginal rate of substitution. In this case, butter and margarine must be substitutes, though not perfect substitutes. The effect of increased price of butter (flatter budget lines) would be to increase the consumption of margarine at constant utility. Margarine is a substitute for butter, but the shift to margarine is not complete for a small price change.

Finally, part (c) shows a set of indifference curves with 90-degree corners on a 45-degree line from the origin. Regardless of the relative prices of the two goods—in this case, left shoes and right shoes—the consumer always purchases them in perfect, fixed proportion. For constant utility, an increase in the price of right shoes has no effect on the quantity of left shoes purchased. Thus right shoes are neither complements nor substitutes for left shoes.

Notice that in *none* of the three cases in Figure 4.3 did we find that the two goods were complements. This is because we drew indifference curves between only two goods. If the consumer's budget is spent on just two goods, they cannot be complements because decreasing purchases of one good at constant utility necessarily implies increasing purchases of the other. Thus, the two goods must be substitutes. With three or more goods present, however, increasing the price of one good can lead to an increase or decrease in consumption of the other while holding utility constant.

Two goods can be what are called *gross substitutes* or *gross complements.* The definition of ''gross'' substitutes takes into account the income effects of a price change because it does not require utility to be held constant.

*Good 2 is a **gross substitute** for good 1 if the cross-price elasticity of demand for good 2 with respect to the price of good 1 is positive.*

That is, plain pizza is a gross substitute for pepperoni pizza if the quantity demanded of plain goes up when the price of pepperoni rises.

We can now similarly define gross complements. In Chapter 3 we said that left and right shoes were gross complements because they were purchased in equal proportion. We can now explain this. In part (c) of Figure 4.3 we see (by considering that the consumer buys at the corner point of an indifference curve for any budget constraint) that every time consumption of left shoes rises, so does consumption of right shoes, and vice versa. It follows that any price increase that reduces the consumption of one side of the pair of shoes will also reduce consumption of the other side of the pair.

*Good 2 is a **gross complement** for good 1 if the cross-price elasticity of demand for good 2 with respect to the price of good 1 is negative.*

Note that the property of being a substitute or complement is not an intrinsic feature of the good itself. It is really a description of the consumer's preferences at a particular consumption bundle. What may be a gross substitute for good x for one consumer may be a gross complement for another good for another consumer. It all depends on how the consumer's purchases of x change in response to a change in price of the other good. Even for the same consumer, a good may be a gross substitute for x at certain consumption bundles and income levels, but a gross complement at other consumption bundles or income levels.

To this point we have focused on how income changes and the prices of other goods affect demand. We now take a look at how the price of the good itself (own price) affects demand. Remember that plotting quantity demanded against price of the good gives us the demand curve.

Changing Price and Individual Demand

How do market choices determine the demand curve in response to different prices? Let's return to Andrew's purchases of fruit pie, supposing initially that the price of pie is high. Figure 4.4 shows how lowering the pie price affects his purchases, keeping his income and the price of sparkling water, the other good, constant. We will construct two curves, one of which is the demand curve. Starting in part (a), Andrew's budget line passing through point a_1 is the steepest line, since the price of pie is highest initially at $20 per pound. The amount of pie in bundle a_1 is 2 pounds, read off the diagram as the distance from the origin on the horizontal axis.

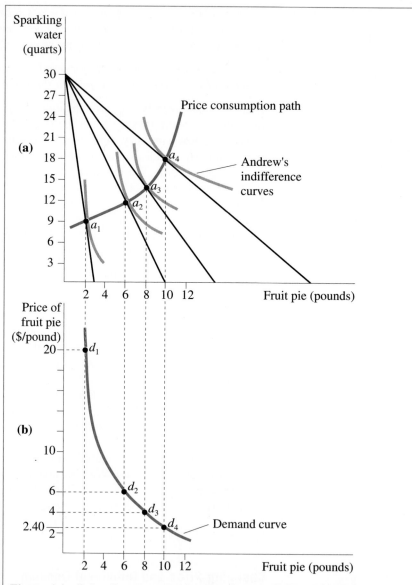

Figure 4.4   Price Consumption Path and the Individual Demand Curve   Lowering the price of pie leads to budget lines further from the origin in part (a) and consumption at points a_1 through a_4 on the price consumption path. Plotting price versus pounds of fruit pie consumed in part (b) gives Andrew's demand curve for fruit pie. Notice that the demand curve slopes downward as the law of demand predicts.

▼

5. Show how to derive the individual's price consumption path and demand curve.

Plotting the combination of $20 for the pie price and 2 pounds for quantity demanded then gives us point d_1 in part (b). Lowering the pie price to $6 per pound rotates the budget line counterclockwise. Andrew now chooses point

a_2 in part (a), which contains 6 pounds of pie. Plotting this at price $6 in part (b) gives us point d_2 on Andrew's demand curve. Lowering the price of pie further to $4 per pound leads to an even flatter budget line in part (a), containing point a_3 with 8 pounds of pie. Plotting this price-quantity pair gives us point d_3. The same procedure is used to find points a_4 and d_4.

Continuing in this fashion, we see that we are finding the points on two curves. The curve in part (a) containing points a_1 through a_4 shows the combination of fruit pie and sparkling water that Andrew consumes for each different price of pie. It is called the price consumption path. This is analogous to the income consumption path we described earlier, but in this case it is the price of the good that varies while income is held constant.

*The **price consumption path** is the collection of bundles showing what the consumer will buy when the price of a good is set at varying levels, with income and prices of other goods held constant.*

From the points on the price consumption path, we found the quantity of fruit pie demanded for each pie price, plotted in part (b). The second curve, which tells us how much pie Andrew will demand at each price, is Andrew's demand curve for pie. Andrew's demand curve is downward sloping, as the law of demand we described in Chapter 2 suggests it should be. Higher prices of pie pull the budget line closer to the vertical axis in part (a) and cause Andrew to buy less pie. To construct Andrew's demand curve for sparkling water, we would have to construct a new price consumption path on which the price of sparkling water changed.

Income Changes and the Demand Curve

▼
6. Show how an income change shifts location of the individual's demand curve.

We have seen how changes in income affect the quantity of pie that Andrew buys at fixed prices, and we know that this depends on whether pie is a normal or inferior good. We also discussed in Chapter 2 how changes in income shift the location of the demand curve. Now let's make use of what we know to see how Andrew's income affects his demand curve for pie.

Part (a) of Figure 4.5 reproduces Andrew's budget lines from Figure 4.4 for income $60 and prices of pie $2.40, $4, and $6 per pound; these are the lines passing through points a_4, a_3, and a_2, respectively. Part (b) shows Andrew's demand for pie when his income is equal to $60 as the right-hand curve. We derived this curve in Figure 4.4. We can now derive the left-hand curve in part (b), which shows what happens when Andrew's income is cut by half to $30. We do so by drawing new budget lines in part (a) corresponding to pie prices of $2.40, $4, and $6 per pound. The decrease in income shifts Andrew's price consumption path to pass through points a_2', a_3', and a_4'. Using these points to plot a new demand curve gives us the curve through points d_2', d_3' and d_4' in part (b). Thus, reducing income has the effect of shifting Andrew's demand curve for pie to the left. For a fixed price of pie, this means that Andrew's quantity demanded is smaller, and pie is therefore a normal good for Andrew. If the demand curve had shifted to the right when Andrew's income went down, pie would be an inferior good.

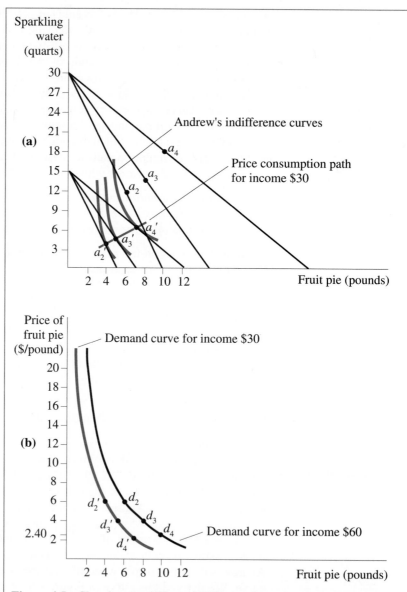

Figure 4.5   Showing the Effect of Different Income on the Demand Curve   When Andrew's income was $60, his price consumption path passed through points a_2, a_3, and a_4 in part (a), as was shown in part (a) of Figure 4.4. Plotting quantity of fruit pie versus price in part (b) led to points d_2, d_3, d_4, and the right-hand demand curve. Lowering Andrew's income to $30 shifts his price consumption path to pass through points a_2', a_3', and a_4', which correspond to the left-hand demand curve in part (b) passing through points d_2', d_3', and d_4'. Thus lower income has shifted Andrew's demand curve for pie to the left.

To summarize, Andrew's demand curve describes how his pie purchases change with price when everything else is constant. His Engel curve, shown in Figure 4.1, describes how his purchases of pie change with income when everything else is constant. We also know how to use the price consumption path to show how the demand curve changes location when income changes.

As we indicated when we defined substitutes and complements, there is a sense in which a price increase works like an income decrease. In the case of pie, a higher price means that Andrew would need to be given some extra income just to allow him to buy what he did before. Distinguishing this income component of a price change turns out to be important for describing how a price increase harms the consumer. Since we now have the tools to deal with this issue, we discuss the separation of income and substitution effects of a price change next. Then, in following sections, we will begin to tackle the interesting question of measuring in dollar terms how much a price increase harms the consumer.

Income and Substitution Effects of a Price Change

If the price of pies rose, Andrew would respond by buying less pie as well as by adjusting his purchases of sparkling water. Part (a) of Figure 4.4, for example, shows that he would end up with less of each good each time the price of pie rose. In this sense, the price increase would be like a drop in purchasing power, much as a drop in income is a drop in purchasing power. For example, if all prices doubled, it would have the same consequences as cutting your income in half. When one price increases, it is a partial step toward that result.

▼

7. How can the consumer's response to a price change be broken into a substitution (price) effect and an income effect?

Consumers actually do two things in response to a price increase. First, they respond to the higher price of a good by tending to decrease purchases of the relatively more expensive good; second, they respond to their lower purchasing power by tending to decrease purchases of all goods. The first of these effects is called the *substitution effect,* and the second is called the *income effect.* For example, at initial budget line T_0T_1 in part (a) of Figure 4.6, Charles buys turtlenecks and oxford shirts in the combination given by bundle a_0. When the price of turtlenecks rises, his budget line rotates clockwise to T_0T_1' and his purchases move to a_2. The total effect of the price change on demand for turtlenecks is measured by the decrease in Charles's turtleneck consumption on the horizontal axis. We want to break that change into the portion due to the substitution effect and the portion due to the income effect.

To find the substitution effect, we want to neutralize any change in purchasing power caused by the price change. To do this, we hold Charles's utility (and thus his real purchasing power) constant at its original level by giving him whatever income is needed to keep him on his original indifference curve when the price of turtlenecks changes. In part (a) of Figure 4.6, this gives Charles a budget line parallel to his final budget line T_0T_1', but just far enough out to be tangent to his *original* indifference curve at point a_1.

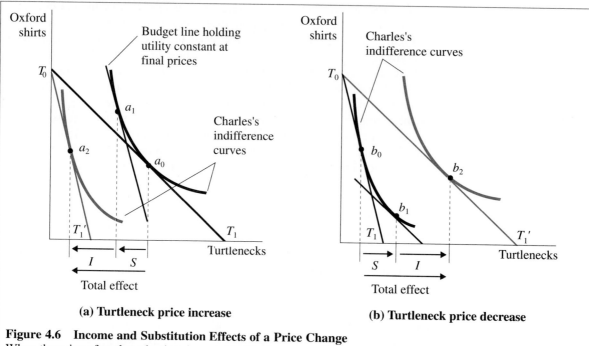

Figure 4.6 Income and Substitution Effects of a Price Change
When the price of turtlenecks rises in part (a), Charles moves from tangency point a_0 to point a_2 on his new budget line T_0T_1'. If we held utility constant when the price increased by giving him enough income to stay on his original indifference curve, Charles would move to a_1. The move from a_0 to a_1 determines the substitution effect for turtlenecks (distance S on the axis), and the shift from a_1 to a_2 determines the income effect (distance I on the axis). Part (b) performs the same exercise for a price decrease, where the shifts from b_0 to b_1 and from b_1 to b_2 determine the substitution and income effects, respectively.

Since Charles would consume at a_1 given such a budget line, the shift from a_0 to a_1 is the substitution effect of the turtleneck price increase. The purchase of turtlenecks changes by amount S on the horizontal axis.

> The **substitution effect** of a price change is the change in quantity purchased when the consumer's utility is fixed at its initial level by an adjustment in income.

Because indifference curves are convex to the origin, the substitution effect always moves consumer purchases in the "expected" direction; that is, purchases rise when the price falls, and purchases fall when the price rises.

To find the income effect, we compare Charles's final budget line and the budget line tangent to the original indifference curve at a_1. (Both budget lines are constructed for final prices.) The change in turtleneck consumption from a_1 to a_2, corresponding to these two budget lines, is I, the income effect.

*The **income effect** of a price change is the change in quantity purchased that would result from holding prices fixed at their final level and adjusting income enough to move the consumer from initial utility to final utility.*

The total effect of the price change is just the sum of the substitution effect and the income effect.

For comparison, part (b) of Figure 4.6 shows the substitution and income effects for a price decrease. There, b_0 is the initial consumption bundle and b_2 the final one. Changing the price while holding utility at its initial level leads to consumption at point b_1 on the original indifference curve. In this case, we have to remove income to keep Charles at his initial utility. Distance S shows the substitution effect of the price decrease for turtlenecks. The income effect, I, is found by shifting the budget line for final prices passing through b_1 (a line parallel to the final budget line and tangent to the initial indifference curve at b_1) out to the final budget line T_0T_1', moving consumption from b_1 to b_2.

A simple way to describe our procedure is that we found the substitution effect by rotating the budget line along the original indifference curve, keeping it tangent until final prices were reached. The difference between the two bundles on the original indifference curve determines the substitution effect. The rotated budget line is then shifted to the final indifference curve to find the income effect.[4]

Are Upward-Sloping Demand Curves Possible?

▼
8. Define a Giffen good. How is being a Giffen good (a price-related property) linked to normality (an income-related property)?

As we have noted, the usual presumption is that demand curves slope downward. The fact that the effect of a price change breaks down into an income effect and a substitution effect, however, suggests the following intriguing possibility: (1) Price goes up, so the consumer buys less of the good because of the substitution effect; (2) the price increase acts like an income decrease, so, since the good is inferior, the income effect causes the consumer to buy more of the good; (3) if the income effect is bigger than the substitution effect, overall demand rises when the price rises! In fact, such a possibility was pointed out over 100 years ago by Sir Robert Giffen, an English economist. To allow for the unlikely case where the demand for a good increases when its price increases, we define the term *Giffen good*.

*A good is defined to be a **Giffen good** if quantity demanded rises when price of the good rises.*

4. Instead of rotating and then shifting the budget line, why don't we shift to the final indifference curve and then rotate? The answer is that for small price changes, the two methods give virtually the same answer. For large changes, however, the substitution and income effects will differ slightly depending on whether we rotate along the initial or final indifference curve. Since it is a difference that does not really matter to us, in this text we will always find the substitution effect by holding utility at the initial level.

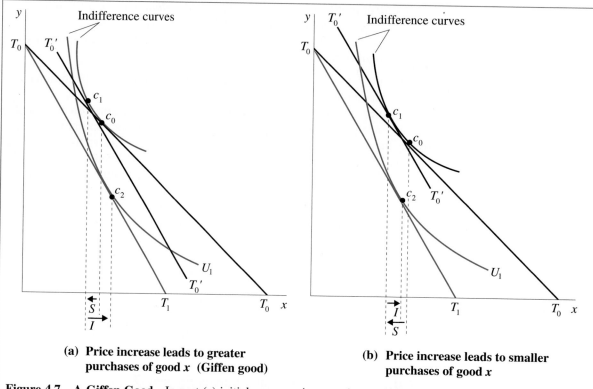

(a) Price increase leads to greater purchases of good *x* (Giffen good)

(b) Price increase leads to smaller purchases of good *x*

Figure 4.7   A Giffen Good   In part (a) initial consumption at point c_0 shifts to final consumption at point c_2 when the budget line shifts inward from T_0T_0 to T_0T_1. Thus consumption of good *x* increases when its price increases, implying that good *x* is a Giffen good. Breaking the price effect into the income effect and the substitution effect reveals that *x* is an inferior good and that the income effect, *I*, is bigger than the substitution effect, *S*. Part (b) shows the same price change for a case where *x* is also inferior, but not inferior enough for the income effect to outweigh the substitution effect. In part (b) good *x* is not a Giffen good.

Giffen observed that Irish peasant diets in the eighteenth century included a large proportion of potatoes and that when the price of potatoes rose, the Irish peasants seemed to buy more, not fewer, potatoes. He explained this puzzling fact by noting that potatoes were an inferior good. When the price of potatoes fell, Irish peasants were able to spend less on this diet staple. This was like an increase in income to the Irish, which they spent on nonpotato items. The net effect, according to Giffen, was that the Irish demand for potatoes fell when the price dropped and rose when the price rose.

The necessary ingredients for potatoes to be a Giffen good are that they are inferior goods, so inferior that the income effect wins out over the substitution effect in consumer purchasing decisions. Figure 4.7 demonstrates the role of the income effect and the substitution effect in the creation of a Giffen good. In part (a) the consumer's initial purchases are at bundle c_0 on budget line T_0T_0. When the price of good x rises, the budget line shifts to T_0T_1 and the consumer's purchases move to c_2. This implies increased purchases of the more expensive good x.

Breaking this shift into its two components, we see that the substitution effect is given by the shift from c_0 to c_1 and the income effect by the shift from c_1 to c_2. Good x is an inferior good, and the income effect is larger than the substitution effect.[5] Part (b) shows the same price change in a case where the good is inferior, but not inferior enough for the income effect to exceed the substitution effect. In part (b), good x is not a Giffen good because quantity demanded falls with the higher price. Figure 4.7 also can be compared to part (a) of Figure 4.6, where turtleneck shirts are a normal good and the substitution effect and income effect both respond to a price increase by reducing consumption of turtlenecks. Of the three cases, only one case—where good x is so inferior that the income effect outweighs the substitution effect—meets the definition of a Giffen good.

Summing up the various terms we have used for goods, we can note that normal, inferior, and superior goods are defined in terms of income and demand, whereas Giffen goods are defined in terms of price and demand. Superior goods must be normal goods, and Giffen goods must be inferior goods.

4.2 Income-Compensated Demand Curves

In the preceding section we talked about the income and substitution effects of a price change, and we found the substitution effect by adjusting the consumer's income to hold utility constant when the price change took place. The amount of this *compensation* to the consumer's income is directly related to the size of the utility consequences of a price change. In the next section we will see how to measure the utility effect of a price change in dollars. To do so, we will need to use the idea of an income-compensated demand curve.

▼
9. What is income-compensated demand? Graphically relate it to ordinary demand.

> ***Income-compensated demand*** *is the demand the consumer would have if income were adjusted in response to every price change to hold utility constant.*

Since holding utility constant is precisely what we did when we found the substitution effect, plotting the income-compensated demand curve along

---

5. Although Giffen goods are theoretically possible, examples are extremely rare. Even the original Giffen choice of potatoes in Ireland has been challenged: if potatoes became scarce in Ireland, thus driving up their price, how could total consumption of potatoes rise? Also, if one takes into account that Irish peasants were suppliers of potatoes, changes in their income would have an effect on their consumption. See G. P. Dyer and C. M. Lindsey, "Robert Giffen and the Irish Potato," *American Economic Review,* March 1984, pp. 188–192.

with the standard demand curve tells us something about the size of the income and substitution effects.[6]

Graphing Demand and Income-Compensated Demand

Figure 4.8 shows the effect of a price decrease on Traci's demand for science fiction books. At the high initial price, Traci's utility is U^0 at point a. When the price of books drops, Traci increases her purchases and her utility rises to U^1 at point b. To lower utility back to U_0, we must take income from Traci, a compensation that reduces her book purchases to point e, assuming that Traci views science fiction as a normal good. Thus the starting point a and point e are on Traci's income-compensated demand curve. Following the same procedure for other prices allows us to create the entire income-compensated demand curve that Figure 4.8 shows passing through point e. The drop in demand from point b to e caused by the income change is the income effect of the price change that we studied in section 4.1. The remainder of the shift is the substitution effect.

If science fiction books were an inferior good, the effect of taking away income would be to *increase* Traci's purchases of books to point e' (remember, purchases rise as income falls for an inferior good). In this case the substitution effect would be the increase in purchases from c to e', and the income effect would be the decrease in purchases from e' to b. The income-compensated demand curve in this case would be the curve that is flatter than the demand curve.

Each time we choose a utility level to keep the consumer's welfare constant, we generate a different income-compensated demand curve. Each point on the demand curve, therefore, has an income-compensated demand curve passing through it, found in the same way that we found the curve through point a.

EXPLORATION: The Expenditure Function and Income Compensation

Adjusting income to hold utility constant after a price change means following a rule for how much income the consumer should have in order to be at the specified utility level. This income rule is called the expenditure function.

> *The **expenditure function**, $e(p_x, p_y; U)$, gives the least amount of money needed to reach utility level* U, *when the prices of buying goods* x *and* y *are* p_x *and* p_y, *respectively.*

10. What is the expenditure function? List its basic properties

6. Another form of income compensation requires adjusting the consumer's income so that buying the original consumption bundle just exhausts income. But we use the compensation notion originally developed by Sir John Hicks, a Nobel Prize winner in economics, because it provides a natural connection between the demand curve and the utility effects of a price change.

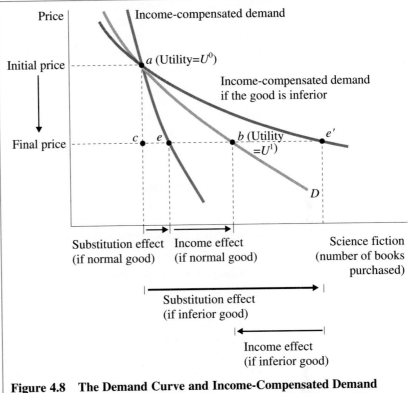

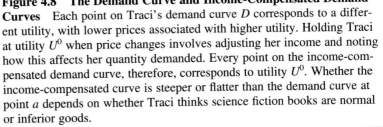

Figure 4.8 **The Demand Curve and Income-Compensated Demand Curves** Each point on Traci's demand curve D corresponds to a different utility, with lower prices associated with higher utility. Holding Traci at utility U^0 when price changes involves adjusting her income and noting how this affects her quantity demanded. Every point on the income-compensated demand curve, therefore, corresponds to utility U^0. Whether the income-compensated curve is steeper or flatter than the demand curve at point a depends on whether Traci thinks science fiction books are normal or inferior goods.

One way to think of the expenditure function is as a ''cost of living'' measure. It is a number that describes how much money it takes to reach a certain standard of living or quality of life, where ''standard of living'' and ''quality of life'' are just other names for utility.

Why introduce the expenditure function? In this book we will use the expenditure function mostly as a shorthand way of describing the cost of the consumer's optimal consumption bundle. By deriving a few simple properties of the expenditure function, we simplify subsequent utility analysis that depends on consumers reaching their utility level at least cost. We know consumers not only want to reach the highest utility, but want to do so at least cost. If they did not, there would exist a cheaper bundle giving the same utility. With the money left over from moving to that cheaper bundle, the consumer could buy additional goods to raise welfare. Reaching utility at least cost means that if the consumer chooses bundle $a^0 = (x^0, y^0)$ to reach utility U^0 when income is I^0 and the list of prices $p^0 = (p_x^0, p_y^0)$, then $U^0 = U(a^0)$ and $I^0 = e(P^0, U^0)$. The last equality just repeats the common-sense observation that there is no way to get the same utility for less if you were doing the best you could before.

There are four important properties of expenditure functions based on this type of simple logic.

1. Expenditure Rises with Price. The first property associated with the cost of reaching a fixed utility is that raising the price of one or more goods will never reduce the cost of achieving that utility. While I may conserve on the use of other goods, there is no way that I can end up using *less* money to reach my original utility level when one good has become more expensive.[7]

2. Expenditure Rises Proportionately If All Prices Rise by the Same Percentage. The second property is that if both prices rise by the same percentage, your expenditure, $e(p_x, p_y; U)$, must go up by that percentage. For example, if everything you buy doubles in price, there is no way for you to adjust purchases to stay at the same level of utility unless your income also doubles. If what you were buying initially minimized the cost of reaching utility U, then buying the same bundle will minimize the cost of reaching utility U after the prices have doubled, and so your expenditure must double as well.

For a simple example, consider a household with utility given by $x^{1/2}y^{1/2}$ that always spends half its income on each good.[8] Since $x = I/(2p_x)$ and $y = I/(2p_y)$, we have $U = I/[2(p_xp_y)^{1/2}]$ or $2(p_xp_y)^{1/2} U = I$. Since expenditure equals income, the expenditure function for the household is $e(p_x, p_y; U) = 2(p_xp_y)^{1/2}U$. Assume for simplicity that $p_x = p_y = U = 1$ initially (expenditure equals 2). Doubling both prices from 1 to 2, keeping U at 1, means that expenditure rises from 2 to $2(2 \times 2)^{1/2}1 = 4$, double its original level.

3. Expenditure Rises with Utility. The third property is that raising U raises the expenditure needed to attain it. This means that $e(p_x, p_y; U)$ strictly increases with the size of U. The expenditure function just derived rises proportionately to U, for example.

---

7. Let oranges be one of the goods that I buy in positive quantity. If buying bundle a, one component of which is oranges, gives me utility U at lower expenditure when the price of oranges is higher, then I could have bought bundle a before the price change and achieved utility U for less money. This contradicts the fact that the original expenditure was the *least* amount needed to reach utility U. (If oranges are a good that I do not buy, then increasing their price has no effect on my cost of reaching utility U.)

8. Maximizing utility subject to budget constraint $p_xx + p_yy = I$ implies that $MU_x/MU_y = p_x/p_y$. For this particular utility function, $MU_x = (y/x)^{1/2}$, $MU_y = (x/y)^{1/2}$, and $MU_x/MU_y = y/x$. Soving $y/x = p_x/p_y$ and the budget constraint gives the demand functions shown in the text.

4. The Change in Expenditure for Small Δp_x Is Approximately $x\Delta p_x$.

The fourth property is that for a small price change, the needed change in $e(p_x, p_y; U)$ is approximately equal to the number of units of the good originally purchased times the change in price,

$$\Delta e = x \times \Delta p_x.$$

For example, if I buy 5 pounds of coffee per month at $3 per pound and the price goes up by 1 cent per pound, I need 5 cents more per month to keep me at my original utility level.[9]

We now make use of this information to discuss the utility value to the consumer of a price change. In the appendix we also make use of the expenditure function to simplify the treatment of index numbers. ■

4.3 Consumer Surplus

Jason wants to buy a navy-style Top Gun leather flight jacket. Before going to the store he decides that he is willing to spend up to $300 for the jacket. Upon arriving at the store, however, he discovers to his pleasant surprise that the price is only $250. If he had had to spend $300, he would have been indifferent between buying the jacket or not. As it is, he didn't have to spend the last $50 and so is better off by this amount. We call this consumer surplus.

▼
11. Define consumer surplus and show how to find a change in it using the original price and quantity and Δp, Δq.

> ***Consumer surplus*** *is the difference between the amount of money the consumer would have been willing to pay for a good and the amount actually paid.*

Relating Consumer Surplus to Indifference Curves and Budget Lines

The size of Jason's consumer surplus clearly depended both on how much he liked flight jackets and how much he paid for them (given by his budget line). To relate consumer surplus to preferences and budget lines, Figure 4.9 considers the case of Marsha, who divides her income between just two things, movies and everything else. Since prices of other goods are constant in this analysis, we treat expenditures on everything else as if they were a composite good with a price of $p_c = \$1$ per unit. The quantity of the composite is then equal to the number of dollars spent on it. We assume Marsha has a monthly income of $2,000 and the price of movies is $p_m = \$7$.

As shown in part (a) of the figure, if the quantity of movies were zero, Marsha's utility would be U^0. But she maximizes utility at point e, corresponding to 4 movies per month, where indifference curve U^1 is tangent to the budget line BB. When Marsha attends 4 movies per month she spends $28 dollars on movies, leaving her with $1,972 to spend on everything else.

---

9. For the household with expenditure function $e(p_x, p_y; U) = 2(p_x p_y)^{1/2}U$, it can be shown that Δe is approximately equal to $(p_y/p_x)^{1/2}U \, \Delta p_x$ for small changes in the price of x. However, from the preceding footnote we know that $p_y/p_x = x/y$ and $U = (xy)^{1/2}$. Substituting for these variables gives us $\Delta e = x\Delta p_x$.

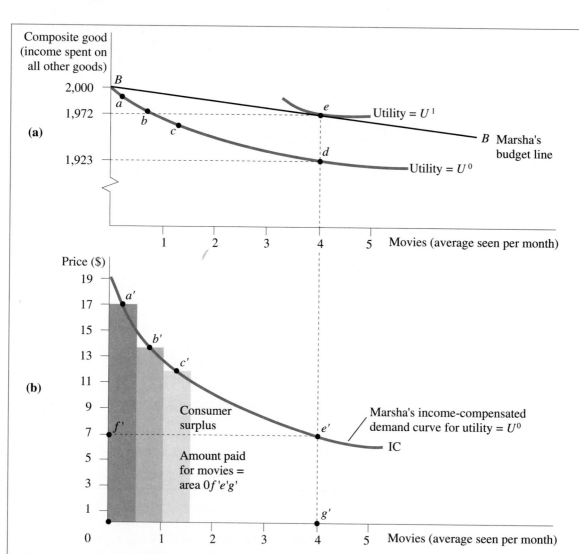

Figure 4.9 Consumer Surplus When Marsha sees four movies per month at point e in part (a) her utility is U^1. If she were restricted to seeing no movies her utility would be U^0. She could pay up to $77 to see four movies (at point d) and still have utility no lower than U^0. Since she pays only $28 for movies, her consumer surplus is $49. In part (b) the most that Marsha could pay and still have utility U^0 is the area under the income-compensated demand curve out to 4 movies. This area is approximated by summing the area of rectangles under points a', b', and c' all the way out to point e'. The amount Marsha actually pays for the 4 movies equals the area of rectangle $0f'e'g'$. Thus consumer surplus equals the area under the income-compensated demand curve and above the price line.

However, as shown by point d, Marsha would have utility U^0 attending 4 movies per month and spending only $1,923 on everything else. Thus she would be willing to give up as much as $2,000 − $1,923 = $77 to attend four movies. She actually spends $28, so her consumer surplus is $49.

Relating Consumer Surplus to the Demand Curve

In practical applications we do not typically have access to the consumer's indifference curves, so creating a graph like part (a) of Figure 4.9 for Marsha would not be possible. We do, however, observe consumers' purchases at different prices, and thus we frequently know something about their demand curves. We can now see how consumer surplus can also be calculated from the income-compensated demand curve. This links consumer surplus to the ordinary demand curve and allows us to compute consumer surplus from observed prices and quantities.

Let's look at Figure 4.9 again. Starting from the intersection of Marsha's indifference curve with the vertical axis, Marsha would be willing to give up income for the first little amount of movie attendance at a rate per movie determined by how fast her indifference curve falls as we move to the right. As discussed in Chapter 3, this rate is the marginal rate of substitution of movies for income, $\text{MRS}_{m,c}$. In this case, $\text{MRS}_{m,c}$ at point a is $17, plotted in part (b) at point a'. In other words, Marsha would be willing to pay $17 per movie to see the first half-movie per month.[10] To find her actual expenditure per month if she sees half a movie per month, we calculate the area of the shaded rectangle under point a', an area that equals $8.50.

Assume now that Marsha has paid $8.50 for the first half-movie. How much more would she be willing to give up to increase movie consumption one-half movie per month more? Since $\text{MRS}_{m,c}$ at point b is $13.50, she would be willing to give $13.50 for the next increment of movies. This is plotted as point b' in part (b). Note also that if we charged $13.50 per movie and adjusted income to keep Marsha's utility at U^0, her budget line would be tangent to U^0 at point b in part (a), and point b would be her utility-maximizing choice. This means that point b' in part (b) is on Marsha's income-compensated demand curve for utility level U^0. Proceeding down indifference curve U^0 in part (a) and plotting the amount Marsha would pay for additional units of movies, we create curve IC in part (b) passing through points a', b', and c'. For each point, the area of the rectangle under the point tells us the amount of money that Marsha would pay for that increment in her movie viewing.

Since IC was found by holding Marsha's utility at U^0, it is the income-compensated demand curve for utility U^0. The area under IC is the total amount of money that Marsha would be willing to pay for consumption of the movies she sees. The money that Marsha actually pays for movies equals

---

10. Actually Marsha would pay somewhat more for the first unit of movies and somewhat less for the later units out to one-half movie. Since we measure only in one-half-movie units, however, we take the average of $8.50 and plot it in the middle of the first one-half-movie range.

the area of the rectangle $0f'e'g'$. *Consumer surplus, therefore, is the area below the income-compensated demand curve and above the price.*

It is this information that allows us to use demand curves to approximate consumer surplus numbers. Because we are interested in the change in consumer surplus in most cases, and the area computed using the demand curve is usually no more than a few percentage points different from the area computed using the income-compensated demand curve, there is little lost if the demand curve is used in place of the income-compensated demand curve. This is the procedure we will use in the following example. After the example, we will also see how exact consumer surplus can be computed using the expenditure function when we relate consumer suplus to the change in utility from a price change.

Approximating the Change in Consumer Surplus

Calculating consumer surplus requires computing an area under the demand curve. This can be done using the formula for the area of a triangle. In the following example, we know just the beginning and ending points on the demand curve. After we discuss market demand curves, we will examine another example in which consumer surplus is computed on the basis of a single point on the demand curve and the demand curve elasticity at that point.

Example: A Household's Consumer Surplus Consider a family that spends 20 percent of its $38,000 annual income on food. We want to know how much it will benefit if the price of food drops by 12 percent. Since the family could spend $0.12 \times 0.2 \times \$38,000 = \$912$ less and still consume as it did originally, it will be better off by at least $912. However, it will want to adjust its purchases to buy more food (now cheaper), and this will generate additional consumer surplus above the $912.

Since we are free to choose the unit we measure food in, let's choose it so the price of food is originally $1 per unit. Figure 4.10 shows the family's initial purchases of food at point a: 7,600 units at price $1 per unit.[11] Reducing the price to $.88 causes the family to purchase 8,636.36 units at point b.

We want to compute the area to the left of the demand curve between prices $1 and $.88. We do this by breaking it up into two parts: the rectangle *acde* and the triangle *abc*. Even though we are not using the exact shape of the demand curve between points a and b, we know that the demand curve passes through both points and so is not likely to be very different from the line connecting a and b. The area of a triangle is one-half its base times its height, or $0.5 \times [(8,636.36 - 7,600)$ units food$] \times (\$.12/\text{unit food}) = \$62.18$; and the area of the rectangle is 7,600 units food $\times \$.12/\text{unit food} = \$912$. Adding the two areas gives us $974.18 as the increase in consumer surplus from the price reduction.[12]

---

11. Recall that the family's income is $38,000 per year. The family demand for food is therefore given by $(0.2) \times \$38,000/p_F$.

12. In this case it can be shown that our approximation differs from the true consumer surplus increase by less than 1.6 percent.

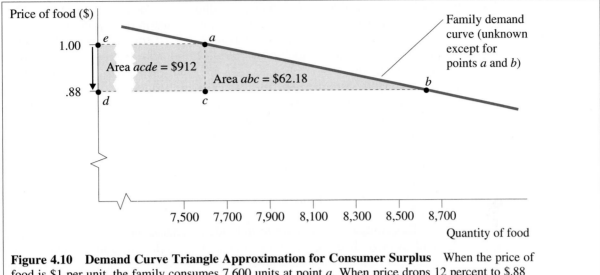

Figure 4.10 Demand Curve Triangle Approximation for Consumer Surplus When the price of food is $1 per unit, the family consumes 7,600 units at point a. When price drops 12 percent to $.88 per unit, the family consumes 8,636.36 units at point b. The increase in consumer surplus is approximately equal to the total shaded area, which equals $974.18.

EXPLORATION: How Do We Know Consumer Surplus Measures Change in Utility?

Let's return now to Jason and his leather flight jacket. We said Jason was willing to pay up to $300.00 for the jacket. If the price were $300.01, then Jason would not buy any jackets and his utility would be U^0, the no-jacket utility level. When price is $250.00, however, he buys one jacket, and he has a consumer surplus of $50.00 and higher utility U^1. In what sense does $50 measure the change in utility $U^1 - U^0$? The answer comes from the expenditure function.

Let $P^0 = (\$300, \$1)$ be the prices for Jason when flight jackets cost $300.00 and $1 is the price of the composite good consisting of everything else. Let $P^1 = (\$250, \$1)$ be the prices when flight jackets cost $250. That is, P^0 and P^1 are the same except that the price of jackets is different. Jason spends all of his income, so we know from the properties of expenditure that $I = e(P^0, U^0) = e(P^1, U^1)$. Jason's consumer surplus is $\$50 = I - e(P^1, U^0)$, since if he paid that much to have prices be P^1, he would be left with $I - [I - e(P^1, U^0)] = e(P^1, U^0)$, which is just enough remaining income to keep him at his original utility. We therefore have the following:

12. Explain the formula for exact consumer surplus in terms of the expenditure function.

$$\text{Consumer surplus} = I - e(P^1, U^0) = e(P^0, U^0) - e(P^1, U^0)$$
$$= e(P^1, U^1) - e(P^1, U^0).$$

We know for given prices that expenditure rises or falls with utility. Thus the difference $[e(P^1, U^1) - e(P^1, U^0)]$ measures in dollars the value to the consumer of an increase in utility from U^0 to U^1 (that is, for fixed prices, it measures the value of the utility change $U^1 - U^0$). However, $[e(P^1, U^1) - e(P^1, U^0)]$ equals $[e(P^0, U^0) - e(P^1, U^0)]$, which is consumer surplus (that is, savings to the consumer from lower prices, staying at fixed utility).

Given this formula, we have several ways to compute consumer surplus. We can approximate it as the area under the demand curve above the price, or we can find it as the difference $e(P^0, U^0) - e(P^1, U^0)$ using the expenditure function. In the latter case, the number is exact and also can be used to find consumer surplus when two or more prices change at the same time. For example, area under the demand curve can no longer be used when prices for Jason change from ($330, $1) to ($250, $.75), but $e(P^0, U^0) - e(P^1, U^0)$ can.

This completes our study of individual demand, how it responds to price and income changes, and how price changes relate to utility. Many of the concepts of individual demand carry over to market demand, which is made up of many individual demands. The sum of individuals' consumer surplus, for example, is approximated by the area under the market demand curve and above price. It is relevant to talk about price, income, and cross-price elasticities of demand for market demand just as it was for individual demand. Next we see how to construct market demand. ▇

4.4 From Individual Demand to Market Demand

By definition, the market demand curve (this is the same curve we studied in Chapter 2) gives the quantity that *all* participants in the market would demand at the stated price. Graphically, this means adding horizontally the demand curves for all the individuals who make up the market. For our purposes this horizontal summation has two significant features. First, the sum of areas under individual demand curves above a given price will be the area under the market demand curve above the same price. Second, different price and income elasticities will affect the shape and location of the market demand curve in much the same way in which they affect individual demand curves.

Deriving Market Demand

▼
13. How do you derive market demand from individuals' demand?

Figure 4.11 displays Annette's demand curve in part (a) and Joel's demand curve in part (b). If Annette and Joel make up the entire market, the market demand curve is the curve given in part (c).

To derive the market demand curve in part (c), start with a price of zero. Note that Annnette demands 2 units of good 1, and Joel demands 1 unit. The market therefore demands 3 units total, which we plot in part (c) on the horizontal axis. At price 1, Annette demands zero units and Joel demands half a unit, so the market demands one-half unit total. Marking this in part

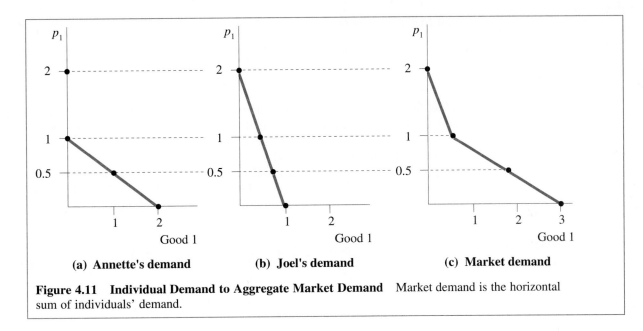

Figure 4.11   Individual Demand to Aggregate Market Demand   Market demand is the horizontal sum of individuals' demand.

(c) gives us a new point on the market demand curve. At prices between 1 and 2, Annette demands no units of good 1, and the entire market demand at these prices equals Joel's demand. At price 2 and above, neither individual is in the market, so the market demand is zero. For prices in between these points, notice that individual demands are linear for the example given; thus we can connect our points linearly in part (c) to find the market curve. Checking at price 0.5 verifies that this procedure works for a representative point. This simple example shows that an increase in market demand comes from increases in purchases by those already making positive purchases, as well as from purchases by new buyers who enter the market because of a price change (purchases from those previously buying zero).

If demand curves are nonlinear, then we need to plot more points to derive the shape of the total market curve. Even when individual curves are linear, the market curve may have kinks like the one at price 1. The kink occurs at that price because at prices below 1 the demand of Annette is suddenly added to the market, changing the slope of the market demand.

Numerical Aggregation of Market Demand

We can also numerically derive the market demand from individual demands. This is necessary in cases where we need to work with an equation rather than a graph. Annette has demand given by

$$q^D_{\text{Annette}} = \begin{cases} 2 - 2p_1 & \text{for } 0 \leq p_1 \leq 1 \\ 0 & \text{for } 1 \leq p_1 \end{cases}$$

and Joel's is given by

$$q^{D}_{\text{Joel}} = \begin{vmatrix} 1 - \dfrac{1}{2}p_1 & \text{for } 0 \le p_1 \le 2 \\ 0 & \text{for } 2 \le p_1 \end{vmatrix}$$

When adding the quantities of different consumers, we must be careful to add formulas that apply for the right price ranges. If we go outside of the relevant price range, the formulas need not be accurate and may give negative demands. Trying to find demand when the price is $90, for example, means noting that both consumers' demand is zero, and we should not use the sum of $(2 - 2p_1) + (1 - \frac{1}{2}p_1) = (2 - 180) + (1 - 45) = -222$. Taking into account the relevant ranges, we add the market demand curve in three segments,

$$D^{\text{market}} = \begin{vmatrix} 3 - \dfrac{5}{2}p_1 & \text{for } 0 \le p_1 \le 1 \\ 1 - \dfrac{1}{2}p_1 & \text{for } 1 \le p_1 \le 2 \\ 0 & \text{for } 2 \le p_1 \end{vmatrix}$$

Comparing demands for various choices for price, such as 0, 0.5, 1, and 2, to the points of Figure 4.11 shows that they are, indeed, the same.

Example: Evaluating Policy Using Consumer Surplus and Market Demand Because market demands are just the horizontal summation of individual demands, a calculation of consumer surplus using the market demand curve gives us the sum of consumer surpluses for all individual consumers making up the market. Since information about the market demand curve is frequently available, this kind of calculation often can be used in policy evaluations, as the following example shows.

Assume that you are the planning engineer for a government that is considering building a highway to a remote region. One benefit of the road is that certain imported consumption goods will be lower in price to the region by 10 percent. These goods, currently transported to the region at great cost, constitute 20 percent of the annual expenditures of the region. The price elasticity of demand for these items is -0.5.[13]

The costs of the project will be paid by the beneficiaries of the project, the citizens of the region. Tax cost is estimated to be 2.5 percent of the region's income annually. Should the road be built?

To answer this question we need to know what the increase in quantity demanded for the consumption goods is likely to be. Since price will drop

---

13. We can presume that you have received this estimate of the price elasticity of demand from a demand study or from already published sources. As we discuss later in the chapter, there are several ways to come by such estimates. Inelastic demand of -0.5 implies that the transported goods are quite important to the inhabitants of the region, because they reduce their consumption of the goods so little in response to a price increase.

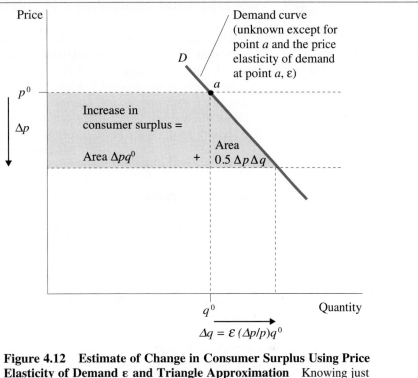

Figure 4.12   Estimate of Change in Consumer Surplus Using Price Elasticity of Demand ε and Triangle Approximation   Knowing just initial price and quantity, it is possible to estimate the size of the quantity response to a given price change using the price elasticity of demand. Consumer surplus is calculated by adding the areas of the shaded rectangle and triangle.

by 10 percent, and price elasticity of demand, **ε**, is −0.5, we expect that quantity will increase by $(\Delta p/p) \times \varepsilon \times q$, or 5 percent.[14] (See Figure 4.12.) Using q^0 to stand for the initial quantity of the consumption good and p^0 for the initial price, the beneficiaries' increase in consumer surplus from the price reduction is given by

$$
\begin{aligned}
\Delta p\, q^0 + 0.5\, \Delta p\, \Delta q &= (0.1p^0)q^0 + 0.5(0.1\, p^0)(0.05q^0) \\
&= [0.1 + (0.5)(0.1)(0.05)]\, p^0 q^0 \\
&= (0.1025)(0.2)\ \text{income} \\
&= .0205\ \text{income.}
\end{aligned}
$$

Since the benefits of the road are only 2.05 percent of income, and the costs are 2.5 percent of income, the road should not be built unless other benefits are found.

14. Recall that $\varepsilon = (\Delta q/q)/(\Delta p/p)$ or $(\Delta q/q) = \varepsilon(\Delta p/p)$.

4.5 Empirical Estimations of Demand

▼
14. What are three ways of empirically finding market demand?

Demand curves and income-compensated demand curves are mental constructs that simplify and explain what goes on in a marketplace. But how does one find a demand curve? They are not "real" in the sense that they can be observed as physical objects can. However, we can infer them from information about prices and quantities.

We usually know the current price of a product and the quantity purchased. This is one point on the demand curve. To know more, we must locate other price-quantity pairs that lie on the same demand curve. There are several ways to get this additional information.

Consumer Surveys

The most direct way of discovering price-quantity pairs is through surveys. For example, assume that your firm sells a particular product that is differentiated from other products. You know the price and your current sales, but you do not know how sales would change if the price were lower. One way to find out might be to hire a survey firm. The survey firm can arrange to question a random sample of buyers about how their purchases would change if the price of your product were lower. Knowing the quantity that would be sold at the lower price gives you a second point on the demand curve, and connecting the two points approximates market demand in the range of prices near the current price and the survey price.

Another way might be to hire the services of demographic specialists who use computerized stores of private and governmentally generated information such as census data and other survey data. If one standard metropolitan statistical area (SMSA) resembles another in its population characteristics, for example, it is reasonable to presume that demand for a product in one SMSA will resemble that in the other. Often, combining survey data with demographic data can produce better demand estimates than either method separately.

Test Marketing

Surveys are not always accurate because buyers sometimes do not truly know how they will behave until actually confronted with different prices. Their responses to the survey may be honestly given, but wrong. To avoid the problems of survey data, moviemakers, for example, sometimes release films in selected cities to see what happens to sales under various conditions. Information about demand from a representative marketing test can then be extrapolated to the entire market. The tests must be carefully designed to hold constant all factors other than those being tested for. For example, if consumers know that the marketing test is to be short-lived—say, a tested price reduction is known to apply only for six months—the consumer response may overstate true market response, since buyers' purchases will be crowded into the "window of opportunity" a lower price offers.

Statistical Estimation

Demand curves also can be estimated through statistical means. If we know that the demand curve has stayed the same over a number of periods, any observed price-quantity pairs must represent different points on the demand curve, and they can be plotted and connected to give the demand curve. When income and prices of other goods change in the sample period, the observed price-quantity pairs will represent changes in quantity demanded caused by these factors, as well as price of the good itself. In this case, demand might be algebraically described as a linear function,

$$q^D = A + Bp_1 + Cp_2 + DI + v,$$

where A through D are constants describing the effect on the quantity demanded of the good's own price, the price of good 2, and income. The term v represents other influences that are of lesser importance, such as random variations in the demographics of buyers, random changes in preferences, and so on, which we believe are zero on average and are unrelated to prices and income. Using observations of (q^D, p_1, p_2, I), regression techniques find values for A, B, C, and D that make the sum of squared differences $(A + Bp_1 + Cp_2 + DI - q^D)^2$ over the observations as small as possible.[15]

Part (a) of Figure 4.13 shows the scatter of price-quantity pairs for different levels of income and different prices of the other good. Curve D approximates demand when income is low, while curves D' and D'' show demand for different levels of p_2 and income.

The functional form chosen for estimating demand can be linear as in part (a) of the figure. However, there is no reason why the form must be limited to a linear one. If a curved demand relationship seems to do a better job of summarizing the observations, a curved form can be substituted. Part (b) shows a demand curve with curvature that seems to fit its scatter of observed prices and quantities better than a linear function would do. This curve illustrates the frequently used log linear demand function, which gets its name because it is a linear relationship between logarithms of the variables. We write the function as

$$\ln q^D = A + B \ln p_1 + C \ln p_2 + D \ln I + v.$$

This form implies that the price elasticity of demand is equal to B, because a small change in the log of a variable equals the percentage change in that variable ($\Delta \ln x = \Delta x/x$). C is the cross-price elasticity of demand, and D is the income elasticity of demand.

By deriving the demand curve and showing how quantity demanded changes with price, income, and the prices of other goods, we have completed our description of the household as consumer. Chapter 3 showed how utility maximization, subject to the budget constraint, led to optimal consumption

---

15. This method, known as ''least squares,'' is described in more detail in any econometrics textbook. See for example, Daniel and Terrel, *Business Statistics,* Boston: Houghton Mifflin, 1992.

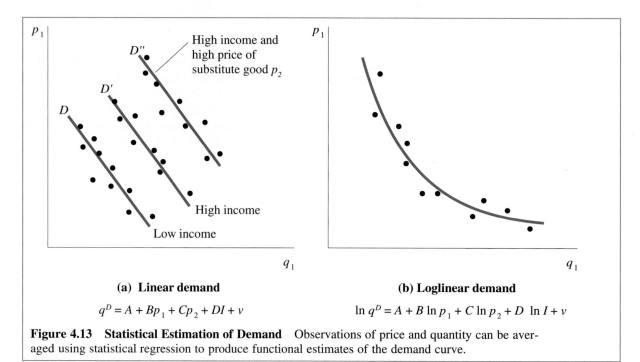

(a) Linear demand

$$q^D = A + Bp_1 + Cp_2 + DI + v$$

(b) Loglinear demand

$$\ln q^D = A + B \ln p_1 + C \ln p_2 + D \ln I + v$$

Figure 4.13   Statistical Estimation of Demand   Observations of price and quantity can be averaged using statistical regression to produce functional estimates of the demand curve.

bundles. This chapter showed how optimal consumption bundles generated the demand curve, as well as responded to price and income changes. Aggregating individual demand curves then generated the market demand curve, the statistical estimation of which we just discussed. In Chapter 5, we wrap up consumer theory by examining household decision making when households act as suppliers of labor and other factors of production.

Summary

Active Reading Guide numbers are given in parentheses at the end of each summary item.

1. By varying income and considering the effect on the consumer's choices, we derive income consumption paths and the individual's Engel curve. The Engel curve plots consumption of the good against income. (1)

2. Goods whose quantity demanded rises with income are called normal goods. Those for which quantity demanded falls when income rises are

called inferior goods, and those whose share of the budget rises when income rises are called superior goods. All superior goods are normal goods. (2)

3. Demand also varies with respect to prices of other goods. If demand for a good rises when the price of another rises and utility is held constant by adjusting income, the good is a substitute for the other good; if it falls it is a complement. In other words, if the cross-price elasticity of demand is positive with utility held constant, the good is a substitute; if the cross-price elasticity is negative

under the same circumstances, the good is a complement. The definitions of ''gross'' substitutes and complements are similar, except that utility is not held constant. A good is a gross substitute for another if its demand rises when the price of the other good rises—that is, if the cross-price elasticity is positive. If this elasticity is negative, the good is a gross complement. The greater the degree of substitutability between the two goods, the flatter the indifference curves. (3, 4)

4. By varying price and considering the effect on the consumer's choices, we derive the price consumption path and the demand curve. Manipulating prices and income in the derivations shows how income changes shift the demand curve. (5, 6)

5. The effect of a price increase on individual demand can be broken into a substitution effect, leading to less consumption of the good, and an income effect, whose effect on consumption can be either positive or negative. (7)

6. A Giffen good is a good whose quantity demanded rises with price. Since the substitution effect works in the direction of smaller demand when price rises, a Giffen good must be sufficiently inferior that the income effect outweighs the substitution effect. (8)

7. The income-compensated demand curve is derived by holding utility constant at a predeter-mined level by adjusting income. It displays changes in demand caused by the pure substitution effect of a price change. The individual demand curve and income-compensated demand curve can be related to one another graphically. (9)

8. The expenditure function is a shorthand way to describe the least cost to the consumer of attaining a specified utility, given the prices that the consumer faces. It rises with utility for fixed prices, and rises with prices for fixed utility. (10)

9. Consumer surplus is the amount of money that a consumer would be willing to pay for a good, less what is actually paid. Consumer surplus is approximated by the area to the left of the demand curve above market price. The exact change in consumer surplus resulting from a price change can be expressed simply in terms of the expenditure function. (11, 12)

10. The market demand curve is found by plotting the sum of all individuals' quantities demanded at each market price. Graphically, this is a horizontal summation of individual demand curves. (13)

11. Market demand can be found empirically through surveys, market tests, and statistical estimation. (14)

Review Questions

*1. Do you think price consumption paths for different income levels could ever cross? How would you show whether they do or not?

2. The price consumption path is to the individual demand curve as the income consumption path is to the Engel curve. Discuss.

*3. Higher-priced, brand-name clothing sells in greater quantity than identical nonbrand clothing. Is this an example of a Giffen good? Why or why not?

4. Show that when there are only two goods, both cannot be inferior.

*5. If there are only two goods, why must they be substitutes?

6. Explain, using the relevant price and cross-price effects, how each of the following groups would view limitation of imports of foreign automobiles:

a) Domestic automobile manufacturers
b) The United Auto Workers
c) American manufacturers of electric motors for automobile window openers
d) American retailers of foreign automobiles
e) Manufacturers of men's socks

*7. Assume that foreign crude oil is a perfect substitute for domestic crude oil. What is the elasticity of demand for domestic crude oil with respect to the price of foreign crude oil?

* Asterisks are used to denote questions that are answered at the back of the book.

8. What happens to the income consumption path if the price of one of the goods is higher?

*9. Is there a utility-increasing direction on the individual demand curve? On the income-compensated demand curve?

10. Let p_0 be the consumer's reservation price, meaning the lowest price which is high enough that the consumer buys no product, and let p_1 be any price lower than this. Is consumer surplus in this case the same as the *change* in consumer surplus that would result from lowering the price from p_0 to p_1?

*11. Exactly what do we mean by horizontal summation of two demand curves? What would vertical summation mean? Relate this to the market demand curve.

Numerical and Graphing Exercises

1. Dawn's demand curve is $q = 200 - 5p$. What is her approximate consumer surplus when price is 20?

*2. A family spends 30 percent of its budget on housing at all housing prices. As a percentage of family income, what is the increase in consumer surplus if the price of housing falls 10 percent?

3. Assume that a family buys only two goods, x and y; it always spends half its income on each good; and its expenditure function is $e(p_x, p_y; U) = 2(p_x p_y)^{1/2} U$. If $p_x = p_y = U = 1$ initially, what is the exact increase in consumer surplus if the price of x falls by 10 percent? Compare this to consumer surplus estimated from the area under the demand curve (use a triangle approximation and two points on the demand curve).

*4. Assume that the price elasticity of demand for foreign apparel is -3; foreign apparel makes up 30 percent of the American market; and all buyers who reduce purchases of foreign apparel because of a price increase shift their quantity one-for-one to domestic apparel. What is the elasticity of demand for domestic apparel with respect to the price of foreign apparel?

5. Given the following information, find the formula for the price consumption path and the Engel curve for good x_1:

$$MU_{x_1} = 0.5/x_1 \qquad MU_{x_2} = 0.5/x_2$$
$$p_1 = 1 \qquad p_2 = 4 \qquad 100 = p_1 x_1 + p_2 x_2.$$

(Hint: Recall the formulas for a tangency and the budget line.)

*6. Use diagrams to determine whether a good can be both a gross complement and a substitute with respect to another. Similarly, determine whether a good can be both a gross substitute and a substitute.

7. Use the budget constraint to prove mathematically that if one good is inferior the other must be superior.

*8. It is discovered that the demand curve and the income-compensated demand curve are identical at the initial price and quantity. Using budget lines and indifference curves, graph the effect of an increase in the price, showing substitution and income effects.

*9. Use a demand curve diagram to show whether the following is possible or not: The income elasticity of demand for automobiles is 3. When real income in the country rises, the demand for automobiles increases, and its price elasticity shifts from -2 to -3.

10. A's demand curve is $100 - 4p$; B's demand curve is $50 - 2p$; and C's demand curve is $25 - p$. All three equations are valid only when they imply positive quantities; when they imply negative quantities, the quantity demanded is zero. Derive the market demand curve graphically and mathematically when these three buyers constitute the market.

*11. This problem is based on the chapter appendix. If food price is 4 percent higher than originally, housing is 1 percent higher, and clothing is 10 percent higher, what is the Laspeyres price index if food comprises 20 percent of the budget, clothing 40 percent, and housing the rest? Is the household better off if its income rose 8 percent over the period? Explain.

APPENDIX: Index Numbers

In this appendix we briefly discuss the construction and interpretation of index numbers. Virtually all readers of this text have encountered indexes at one time or another. Two of the best known indexes are the Consumer Price Index (CPI), reported monthly, and the Gross Domestic Product (GDP), a quantity index of all goods and services produced in the nation, reported quarterly. Though it is not reported on network news, we also frequently consult our own "income index" whenever we check to see if our income this year is higher than it was last year. Why do we use indexes, and what do they signify?

What Do Indexes Measure?

Indexes tell whether something has gone up or down. If we ask whether the price level has risen, however, there are many prices to consider. If all prices rise by 3 percent, we have no problem saying that prices have risen 3 percent, but what do we do if some prices rise at the same time that others fall? A price index constructs a single number that tells us on average whether prices have gone up or down. In calculating such an average, we pay more attention to important prices and count them more heavily than unimportant prices.

▼
A.1. Why are indexes used to report changes in prices and quantities?

A similar statement applies to quantity indexes such as the Gross Domestic Product. If the output of one commodity rises while the output of another falls, we want to be able to say *on average* that output has risen or fallen. This means that the output of important things should be given more weight than the output of less important things. The way the index is constructed accomplishes this weighting.

Consider how we use the Consumer Price Index, the Gross Domestic Product, and income indexes. If I learn that the CPI is 3 percent higher this year than last, I interpret that as saying that my cost of living has risen 3 percent. Then I might compare this percentage to my income index. Let's say I learn that my income is 4 percent higher this year than last. Since my income has risen more than my cost of living, I conclude that I am better off this year than I was last year.

▼
A.2. How is a price index related to the expenditure function and a quantity index to the utility function?

Implicitly, what have I just done? I have said that the CPI represents the amount of money that I would need to reach a certain standard of living, meaning a utility level. This suggests that the CPI, a cost-of-living index, approximates change in the value of the expenditure function, which measures the cost of achieving a given level of utility.

With respect to GDP, we often treat per-capita GDP as a measure of welfare.[16] This is reasonable because an increase in the quantity of goods

16. Of course, using aggregate quantities to infer information about an individual consumer is only an indicative procedure. Separate quantity indexes based on the consumption bundles of each individual would be better, but nearly impossible to accomplish. In using GDP, which refers to output produced within the national borders regardless of ownership, we also ignore the adjustments relating to foreign ownership or claims on domestic output.

and services available to the economy or the individual is a means of achieving higher utility. Such a quantity index therefore approximates utility.

The expenditure function and the utility function, of course, are not the only functions that can be approximated by indexes. In economics, however, where market prices and quantities form the basis for the indexes, these are the functions that we focus on in our discussion. The principles that apply to price and quantity indexes can also be applied to other kinds of indexes.

Price, Quantity, and Income Indexes

Let us begin by giving the definition of a quantity index of apples and oranges. Assume that apples are twice as expensive as oranges. How would we describe total output of fruit, since the dimensional units of the two goods are different? Since we must report a single fruit index, a natural thing to do is to count one unit of apples as equal to two units of oranges. This weights quantity by price. Thus let $Q^0 = $ (apples, oranges) $= (q_1^0, q_2^0)$ be the list of initial quantities, and let $P^0 = (2, 1) = (p_1^0, p_2^0)$ be the initial prices, where upper-case letters refer to a list of prices or quantities and lower-case letters to individual prices and quantities. Multiplying each quantity by its corresponding price converts quantities into common dollar units. Therefore, we measure fruit output as

$$(p_1^0 \times q_1^0) + (p_2^0 \times q_2^0),$$

which we write in simpler notation as

$$P^0 Q^0.$$

▼

A.3. Write the formulas for Laspeyres and Paasche price and quantity indexes.

If Q^1 denotes output in the *final* time period, final total output would be given by $P^0 Q^1$. The *quantity index* is the ratio of total final output to total initial output,

$$L_Q = \frac{P^0 Q^1}{P^0 Q^0}.$$

This index, using *last* year's prices to weight quantities, is called a *Laspeyres quantity index,* after the French economist who developed it. If L_Q is greater than 1, the index has risen, and if L_Q is less than 1, the index has fallen. L_Q is an approximation to the true increase in utility, $e(P^0, U^1)/e(P^0, U^0)$, which measures changes in utility by the change in $e(P^0, U)$ for fixed prices P^0.

The *Paasche quantity index,* named for yet another economist, is

$$P_Q = \frac{P^1 Q^1}{P^1 Q^0}.$$

where the superscript 1 indicates prices from the final period. P_Q is an approximation to the true increase in utility, $e(P^1, U^1)/e(P^1, U^0)$, which measures changes in utility by the change in $e(P^1, U)$ for fixed prices P^1. Comparing the Laspeyres and Paasche indexes shows that they differ by the prices that are used to weight output: Paasche uses final (this year's) prices, and Laspeyres uses initial (last year's) prices.

Just as a quantity index needs to weight the relative importance of different quantities, so a price index needs to weight the relative importance of different prices. If the price of a good constituting half of my budget rises 10 percent, this is a more costly change for me than a 10-percent rise in the price of something that I spend only 1 percent of my budget on.

In the case of two goods, the *share* s_1^0 of my initial income that I spend on good q_1 is $s_1^0 = (p_1^0 \times q_1^0)/I^0$, where I is my total expenditure (given by my income) and superscript 0 indicates that I am using values from the initial period. Using the budget shares from my initial expenditures to weight price changes, my *Laspeyres price index* is

$$s_1^0 \times (p_1^1/p_1^0) + s_2^0 \times (p_2^1/p_2^0),$$

which can be rewritten as

$$
\begin{aligned}
L_P &= (s_1^0/p_1^0) \times p_1^1 + (s_2^0/p_2^0) \times p_2^1 \\
&= (q_1^0/I^0) \times p_1^1 + (q_2^0/I^0) \times p_2^1 \\
&= \frac{q_1^0 \times p_1^1 + q_2^0 \times p_2^1}{I^0} \\
&= \frac{q_1^0 \times p_1^1 + q_2^0 \times p_2^1}{P^0 Q^0} \\
&= \frac{P^1 Q^0}{P^0 Q^0}.
\end{aligned}
$$

In this form the expression looks very much like the quantity indexes we have already described, except that the role of prices and quantities has been reversed. In a price index we compare P^0 to P^1 using quantities Q as weights. The *Paasche price index* is similarly defined using *final* quantities as weights,

$$P_P = \frac{P^1 Q^1}{P^0 Q^1}.$$

The Laspeyres price index approximates the true increase in cost of attaining the initial utility level U^0 when prices change, $e(P^1, U^0)/e(P^0, U^0)$; the Paasche price index approximates the true increase in cost of attaining final utility, $e(P^1, U^1)/e(P^0, U^1)$. You may verify these formulas by using the definition of the expenditure function, $e(P, U)$, discussed earlier in the chapter, as the least cost of attaining utility level U at prices P.

An income index is the ratio of income between two periods, I^1/I^0. Because the expenditure on all goods equals income, we have $I^1 = P^1 Q^1$ and $I^0 = P^0 Q^0$. Thus the income index can also be written as $P^1 Q^1/P^0 Q^0$.

Three Properties of Index Numbers

▼
A.4. Give the three fundamental properties of price and quantity indexes.

As described above, index numbers are used to measure change in utility and the dollar cost of achieving a given utility level. There are three principal properties that link index numbers with utility and prices.

1. Laspeyres Price and Quantity Indexes Overstate the True Values. To show this, use one of the properties of the expenditure function, $e(P^0, U^0) = P^0Q^0$, to write the identities

$$L_P = \frac{P^1Q^0}{P^0Q^0} = \underbrace{\frac{e(P^1, U^0)}{e(P^0, U^0)}}_{\text{Term A}} \times \underbrace{\frac{P^1Q^0}{e(P^1, U^0)}}_{\text{Term B}}$$

and

$$L_Q = \frac{P^0Q^1}{P^0Q^0} = \underbrace{\frac{e(P^0, U^1)}{e(P^0, U^0)}}_{\text{Term A}} \times \underbrace{\frac{P^0Q^1}{e(P^0, U^1)}}_{\text{Term B}}.$$

In each case, Term A is the true change; Term B is a number larger than 1, because the numerator measures the cost of achieving utility by buying a particular bundle and the denominator measures the least cost of achieving that utility. Thus the change shown by the index is larger than the true change.

These equations yield the following immediate property: *If the Laspeyres quantity index, which overstates increase in utility, shows a utility decline, then true utility must have fallen.*

2. Paasche Price and Quantity Indexes Understate the True Values. To show this, use another property of the expenditure function, $e(P^1, U^1) = I^1 = P^1Q^1$, to write the identities

$$P_P = \frac{P^1Q^1}{P^0Q^1} = \underbrace{\frac{e(P^1, U^1)}{e(P^0, U^1)}}_{\text{Term A}} \times \underbrace{\frac{e(P^0, U^1)}{P^0Q^1}}_{\text{Term B}}$$

and

$$P_Q = \frac{P^1Q^1}{P^1Q^0} = \underbrace{\frac{e(P^1, U^1)}{e(P^1, U^0)}}_{\text{Term A}} \times \underbrace{\frac{e(P^1, U^0)}{P^1Q^0}}_{\text{Term B}}.$$

In each case, Term A is the true change; Term B is a number smaller than one, because the deonominator measures the cost of achieving utility by buying a particular bundle and the numerator measures the least cost of achieving that utility.

These equations yield the following immediate property: *If the Paasche quantity index, which understates the increase in utility, shows a utility increase, then true utility must have risen.*

3. Income Index $> L_P$ Implies Utility Up; Income Index $< P_P$ Implies Utility Down. Since the income index equals P^1Q^1/P^0Q^0, if the income index is greater than the Laspeyres price index, then $P^1Q^1/P^0Q^0 > P^1Q^0/P^0Q^0$. Canceling the common denominator, however, this is equivalent to

$P^1Q^1/P^1Q^0 > 1$, which states that the Paasche index is greater than 1. From the previous discussion we know this implies that utility has risen from the initial position to the final position.

Similarly, if the income index is less than Paasche price index, $P^1Q^1/P^0Q^0 < P^1Q^1/P^0Q^1$. Canceling the common numerator, this is equivalent to $P^0Q^1/P^0Q^0 < 1$, which states the Laspeyres quantity index is less than 1. From the previous discussion we know this implies that utility has fallen from the initial position to the final position.

Since the Consumer Price Index is a Laspeyres index (it uses prior-year quantities to weight prices), comparing your income index to the Consumer Price Index is an appropriate way to check for utility increase, assuming that your purchases in the previous period match the pattern used in computing the price index.

Shortcomings of Index Numbers

There are two main shortcomings of index numbers. The first is that the numbers chosen to weight components of the index may not represent the numbers applicable to a given consumer. For example, the Consumer Price Index uses a standardized market basket of goods to weight the component prices of the index. The index works well for an individual whose consumption pattern matches the standardized market basket (and the index properties we have just described would apply), but it would be inaccurate for an individual whose consumption was significantly different.

Even when the weights are appropriate for particular consumers, the second shortcoming of an index is that it is an approximation. This is necessarily the case when a single number is intended to describe, say, the effect of a change on a consumer's welfare without having precise information about that consumer's utility function. Because the index applies to more than one consumer, it necessarily must be accurate for some and not for others. If the index compares two price bundles or two goods bundles that are not too far apart, the approximation is typically quite good, meaning an error of 2 or 3 percent or less. If the bundles compared are further apart, the approximation becomes increasingly poor.

The deviation of the Laspeyres quantity from the actual quantity is given by deviation of the ratio of P^0Q^1 to $e(P^0, U^1)$ from 1. Since $\dfrac{P^0Q^1}{e(P^0, U^1)} - 1 = \dfrac{P^0Q^1 - e(P^0, U^1)}{e(P^0, U^1)}$, Figure 4.A.1 evaluates $P^0Q^1 - e(P^0, U^1)$ in terms of distances between the consumer's budget line and final indifference curve. In the figure we use initial prices to construct three budget lines. The change in welfare is measured by the difference between the budget line tangent to the final indifference curve and the budget line tangent to the initial indifference curve. $P^0Q^1 - e(P^0, U^1)$ is measured by the difference between the

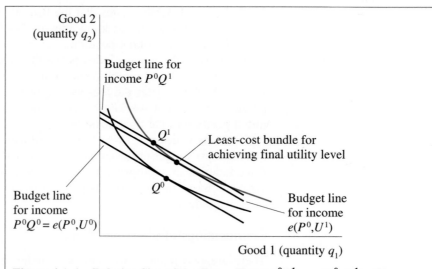

Good 2
(quantity q_2)

Budget line for
income P^0Q^1

Q^1

Least-cost bundle for
achieving final utility level

Q^0

Budget line
for income
$P^0Q^0 = e(P^0,U^0)$

Budget line
for income
$e(P^0,U^1)$

Good 1 (quantity q_1)

Figure 4.A.1   Relative Size of the Error Term $P^0Q^1 - e(P^0, U^1)$ The
difference between the two highest budget lines gives the size of the error.
The difference between the budget line through Q^0 and the least-cost bundle for the final utility level gives the dollar value of the true change in
utility.

budget line through point Q^1 and the budget line tangent to the final indifference curve. Because Q^1 is near a tangent point, the distance between the
two lines will be small, implying a small error. A similar argument applies
to the other error terms, showing that they are small for small changes in the
quantity or price bundle. ■

▼

CHAPTER 5

The Consumer as Supplier

The household is not just a consumer; it is also a supplier of labor services. In juggling its time among work, family, school, church, community, and other uses of leisure (leisure here meaning all nonwork time), the household makes just as critical a decision about its well-being as it does when deciding what mix of goods to buy. In this chapter we turn our attention to the economic decision of the household to supply factors of production to the marketplace: primarily factors such as labor that enter into utility directly, but also factors that do not enter into utility directly, such as physical resources the consumer may own. In short, the chapter examines how utility maximization determines the household's labor choices.

ACTIVE READING GUIDES

After reading this chapter, you should be able to answer the Active Reading Guides listed below. These guides also appear in the page margins, near the material to which they refer.

1. How does the labor supply decision fit our model of utility-maximizing behavior?

2. How do you draw the consumer's budget line, labeling leisure, labor, and consumption?

3. How do you use the consumer choice model to find the consumer's labor supply? How do the income and substitution effects work for labor supply?

4. Derive the consumer's labor supply curve.

5. Explain the cause of a backward-bending supply curve of labor.

6. Construct a market labor supply curve from individual labor supply curves.

7. Construct an example showing the labor supply decision when the budget constraint contains corners. Explain the reason for the shape of the constraint.

8. How is consumer surplus measured for labor supply?

9. What is different in the labor supply model when consuming requires the input of time?

10. Define economic rent. In what way is it related to opportunity cost?

11. Explain why the labor market might exhibit asymmetric information.

12. What is the essential property of a successful job market "signal?"

13. Draw a diagram explaining the decision to supply a factor that does not enter utility directly.

▶ 5.1 Labor and the Consumer's Budget Set

Up to now, we've looked at households only in terms of their roles as demanders of various goods and services. However, consumers also supply labor and other inputs to the production process; these inputs are called *factors of production,* or sometimes simply *factors.* In addition to labor, households may own productive resources such as land, mineral rights, buildings, physical machinery, and intellectual property. Whereas in the past two chapters we mostly treated income as a given, we all know that as consumers we determine our incomes by choosing how much to work and, if we own other resources, how much of them to supply. In this chapter, we will see how households' supply choices in the labor market (and in markets for other factors) fit into our model of utility-maximizing behavior. Although the topic of labor supply decisions may sound new, it's really just another optimization problem of the type we already know. We'll be working with familiar tools in this chapter—budget lines, indifference curves, income and substitution effects—to analyze households' roles as suppliers.

By far the most important factor the household can supply to the market is labor. Households supply labor even though they would prefer leisure, since selling labor earns income that can be spent on goods and services.

> *Labor (or work) is physical or mental activity used in the production of goods or services and performed for a monetary reward such as wages or salary.*

Leisure is defined in relation to labor.

> *Leisure is any time not devoted to supplying labor services.*

▼

1. How does the labor supply decision fit our model of utility-maximizing behavior?

In other words, "leisure" includes all nonmarket activities. It implies not just relaxation, but eating, sleeping, volunteer work, commuting time—any activity not performed in the marketplace for pay.[1] The trade-off between labor and leisure differs from the decision to purchase a good: goods directly raise the consumer's utility, whereas selling labor earns income used to buy more goods. Despite this difference, we can treat the decision to supply labor as a straightforward application of the theory of consumer choice for goods.

The Budget Constraint

Let's consider a representative worker whom we will call Jody. Like other individuals she is endowed with a given allotment of available time. Taking the year as our unit of measure, she has 8,760 available hours per year. If she works full-time, she uses roughly 2,000 hours for work in a typical work year and 6,760 for leisure.[2] Choosing the week as our unit of time, her total available hours would be 168, and her number of leisure and work hours would be 128 and 40, respectively. Regardless of whom we consider, however, everyone would have the same number of available hours. Call this time endowment E.

> The **time endowment** is the total number of hours that the household has available to allocate between work and leisure.

▼

2. How do you draw the consumer's budget line, labeling leisure, labor, and consumption?

If Jody uses her entire endowment working at wage w, her labor income would be wE. If she has nonlabor income I_0 (say, interest from savings or dividends from stocks), her income would be $I_0 + wE$. We will call $I_0 + wE$ her *endowment-time income* to distinguish it from another measure of income that we will consider later. Using any of her time endowment as leisure time L_e would mean that Jody's wage earnings drop by wL_e. In essence, Jody "buys" leisure by giving up potential work earnings. Thinking of Jody's choice this way implies a budget constraint of the form

$$p_C C + wL_e = I_0 + wE.$$

Her purchase of leisure time, wL_e, is shown on the left-hand side, along with her purchase of consumption good C. As we have done in earlier chapters, we think of C as a generic composite good representing purchases of all other goods.

---

1. Economists recognize that much of the true production activity in the economy occurs in the home. Indeed, many goods purchased by households, such as food, lawnmowers, and vacuum cleaners, require the input of household time before the final product of meals, mowed lawns, or clean floors can be consumed. Leisure, therefore, does not necessarily imply pleasurable inactivity or recreation. We make this distinction between labor and leisure to focus our attention on the supply of labor to the marketplace. Once this is done, divisions of the use of time within leisure can also be considered. We will see later in the chapter, for example, how the input of household production time also enters into the household's decision making.
2. Assume 2 weeks per year for vacation. This leaves 50 weeks times 40 hours per week or 2,000 hours in a full-time work year.

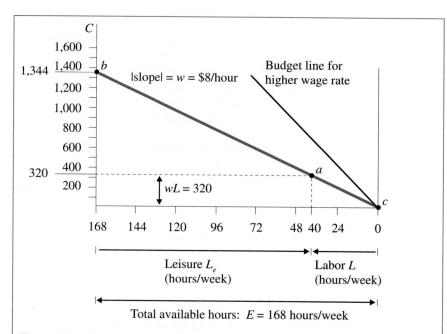

Figure 5.1 Labor-Leisure Trade-off The choice of how much leisure, L_e, to take determines how many labor hours, L, are provided and how much consumption, C, Jody can have. At $8/hour wage, $1,344 would be available for purchasing 1,344 units of C at price $p_C = \$1$ if Jody chose no leisure, and $0 would be available if she chose all leisure. At point a, income is $wL = \$8L$, where $L = 40$ is the number of hours worked per week.

This budget constraint emphasizes the fact that leisure is costly in terms of forgone earnings. Deciding how much leisure to buy is identical to choosing how much labor to supply.

Figure 5.1 shows Jody's budget constraint, assuming that she earns $8 per hour and working is her only source of income. The horizontal axis gives her time endowment E as 168 hours per week. Measuring from the left-hand edge to point a gives the number of hours Jody takes as leisure time, L_e, and measuring the horizontal distance from the right-hand edge gives the number of hours she works, L. L_e plus L equals E. The vertical axis measures her spending on consumption good C where the price for C, p_C, equals $1 per unit. Looking at the figure, you can see that each hour Jody spends in leisure puts her on a lower point on the budget line.

The steepness of the budget line measured from the right shows Jody's wage rate. A higher wage rate implies a steeper line. If the wage rate were zero, the budget line would be a horizontal line at the axis.

Rearranging Jody's budget equation shows that she spends on consumption the amount

$$p_C C = w(E - L_e) + I_0.$$

This form says that Jody's consumption spending equals her wage earnings plus her nonlabor income. Jody's *spendable income,* given by the right-hand side, corresponds to the definition of income used in Chapters 3 and 4, but differs from the endowment-time income mentioned earlier.[3] For example, if Jody has only labor income and decides to work 40 hours per week at a wage of $8 per hour, her spendable income is $320 per week even though her endowment-time income remains $1,344.

The Leisure–Consumption Good Trade-off

Now that we see how leisure and consumption relate to the budget constraint, let's examine how they affect utility. Our starting point is the utility function,

$$U = U(C, L_e),$$

which now includes both the consumption good, C, and leisure, L_e. We assume that the marginal utility for each good, MU_C and MU_{L_e}, is positive.[4] Since leisure time equals $E - L$, utility can also be written

$$U = U(C, E - L).$$

Utility therefore declines with increased labor time, because each additional labor hour decreases leisure by an hour, lowering utility.

Figure 5.2 plots Jody's indifference curves for leisure and consumption. The indifference curves have all of the standard properties that we discussed in Chapter 3. In particular, they do not cross, utility increases with more leisure, and the marginal rate of substitution of leisure for consumption, $MRS_{L_e,C} = MU_{L_e}/MU_C$, declines as one moves to the southeast along an indifference curve. Declining marginal rate of substitution of leisure for consumption means that the less leisure Jody has, the more income she needs to compensate her for any further loss of leisure. In Figure 5.2, Jody requires less payment for loss of leisure at point *a* than at point *b*, for example.

From what we just said about the time endowment and budget constraint, however, we know that changing leisure by one hour means that labor moves one hour in the reverse direction. Also, greater labor hours are directly linked to greater spendable income, which equals consumption. Thus, we can describe the trade-offs between leisure and consumption, between leisure and

---

3. Jody's endowment-time income is $wE = \$1,344$ per week. Her wage earnings are $wL = w(E - L_e)$, an amount that depends on how much she works.

4. It is possible in extreme cases that the consumer has so much free time that additional leisure fails to raise utility. Retired individuals sometimes do volunteer work after retirement just to keep active, for example. In these cases, however, it does not take much work to move to a position where additional labor time would need compensation, indicating that leisure has positive value. We focus, therefore, on the usual case, where the marginal utility of leisure is positive.

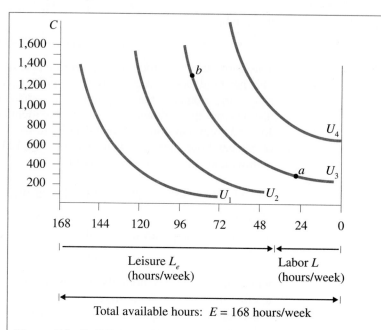

Figure 5.2 Indifference Curves for Leisure and Consumption
Indifference curves for leisure, L_e, and consumption, C, have the standard properties of indifference curves for goods, including declining marginal rate of substitution of leisure for goods. The marginal rate of substitution of leisure for goods is lower at point a than at point b, implying that less consumption is needed to compensate for a small loss in leisure at point a than at point b.

spendable income, and between labor and spendable income in terms of the marginal rate of substitution of leisure for consumption, using the standard utility model that we introduced in Chapter 3.[5]

5.2 The Labor Supply Decision

Figure 5.3 combines the indifference curves with the budget constraint. Jody reaches her highest utility, given her budget, by choosing point a. Writing the usual tangency condition for the purchase of two goods that we learned

---

5. The marginal rate of substitution of leisure for consumption is $\mathrm{MRS}_{L_e C} = \mathrm{MU}_{L_e}/\mathrm{MU}_C$. Since labor goes up one unit for each unit decrease in leisure, $\mathrm{MU}_{L_e} = -\mathrm{MU}_L$. Similarly, since consumption equals spendable income, I, we have $\mathrm{MU}_C = \mathrm{MU}_I$. Thus the marginal rate of substitution of leisure for spendable income equals the marginal rate of substitution of leisure for consumption: $\mathrm{MRS}_{L_e I} = \mathrm{MU}_{L_e}/\mathrm{MU}_I = \mathrm{MU}_{L_e}/\mathrm{MU}_C = \mathrm{MRS}_{L_e C}$. Likewise, the marginal rate of substitution of labor for spendable income equals the negative of the marginal rate of substitution of leisure for consumption:

$$\mathrm{MRS}_{LI} = \frac{\mathrm{MU}_L}{\mathrm{MU}_I} = \frac{-\mathrm{MU}_{L_e}}{\mathrm{MU}_C} = -\mathrm{MRS}_{L_e,C}.$$

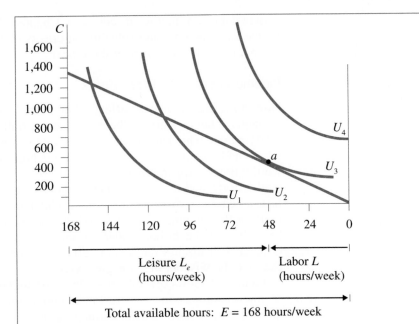

Figure 5.3   The Labor Supply Decision   Jody chooses to maximize her utility by consuming at point *a*. This determines both her consumption of leisure and her labor supply. The more labor she chooses to supply, the greater her spendable income is with which to buy consumption good *C*.

in Chapter 3, we know that at point *a* the marginal utility per dollar to Jody of extra consumption equals the marginal utility per dollar to her of extra leisure,[6]

$$\frac{\text{MU}_C}{p_C} = \frac{\text{MU}_{L_e}}{w}.$$

▼

3. How do you use the consumer choice model to find the consumer's labor supply? How do the income and substitution effects work for labor supply?

If we want to interpret Jody's choice in terms of labor supplied and spendable income, the left-hand side of this tangency condition becomes MU_I, because $C = I$ and the price of the consumption good is 1; the right-hand side becomes $-\text{MU}_L/w$. Substituting and rewriting implies that $-\text{MU}_L/\text{MU}_I = w$. In other words, if Jody is maximizing utility, the rate at which she is willing to trade labor for spendable income must be the same as the wage rate she gets from working. If she needs more than the wage to compensate her for work ($-\text{MU}_L/\text{MU}_I > w$), then she is not being paid enough and her utility can be raised by working less. If $-\text{MU}_L/\text{MU}_I < w$, then the wage is more than she needs to compensate for the utility cost of working, so she could raise utility by working more.

Because the choice to buy leisure—or, equivalently, the choice to supply labor—is based on the same utility maximization subject to the consumer's

6. Recall that for the purchase of two goods the tangency condition is $\text{MU}_1/p_1 = \text{MU}_2/p_2$.

budget constraint that we discussed in Chapters 3 and 4, it is also governed by the same income and substitution effects that govern purchases of consumption goods. We consider these next.

Income Effects and Work Hours

How does higher income affect labor hours? Scottish immigrant Andrew Carnegie, a famous turn-of-the-century industrialist and philanthropist, noted, "The parent who leaves his son enormous wealth generally deadens the talents and energies of the son, and tempts him to lead a less useful and less worthy life."[7] Apparently Carnegie believed that great wealth would hinder work effort,[8] and this would enervate and weaken one's moral character. In fact, he chose to distribute his wealth philanthropically rather than to leave it all for the undoing of his descendants. In today's dollars his giving would be well over 4.8 billion dollars! Using the analysis that we developed in Chapter 4 to discuss the income effect for consumption of goods, we can examine the wisdom of Carnegie's view.

Figure 5.4 shows several budget lines for our consumer, Matthew. Initially Matthew chooses point a on the lowest budget line, where all of his spendable income is derived from labor earnings. Now consider what Matt would do at the same wage rate if his income were higher at every level of work by I_0'. I_0' might represent earnings on past savings, pension income, or a welfare payment from other households via the government. Whatever the source, I_0' is independent of Matt's choices about working.[9] Matt's nonlabor income appears in Figure 5.4 as the vertical distance from the budget line to the horizontal axis, measured above the point of 100 percent leisure.

With higher income, Matt can increase his consumption both of leisure and of the consumption good. Matt's utility-maximizing point when nonlabor income rises to I_0' is point b. Higher income increases Matt's consumption of leisure time, and it reduces his work hours. Tracing Matt's other choices as nonlabor income rises to I_0'' and I_0''' generates the income consumption path connecting points a through d.

In the usual case, we expect that leisure is a normal good. That is the way we have drawn Matt's indifference curves. It is to be expected, then, that as income rises, an individual or household consumes more leisure, which means fewer work hours. Only if leisure were an inferior good would we expect the reverse. Whether leisure is normal or inferior depends on the individual's or household's current consumption of leisure and other goods. If leisure time is scarce, we might reasonably expect additional income to be taken in the form of increased leisure.

---

7. Andrew Carnegie, *Gospel of Wealth*, Cambridge, Mass.: Harvard University Press, 1962, p. 56.

8. As we will see when we consider the effects of asymmetric information on labor supply, work effort can be taken to include the number of *hours* of work as well as the *quality* or *intensity* of work. Although both are important, initially we focus on the economic determinants of the number of hours of work.

9. Economists call income whose level is unchanged by any economic choice that the consumer makes *lump sum* income to emphasize that it is received as a given amount.

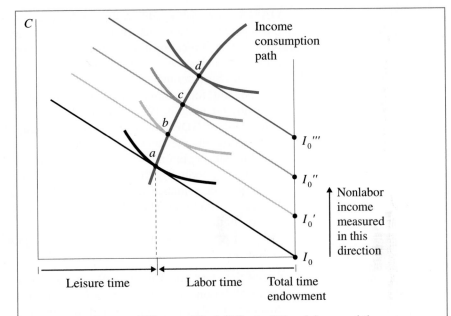

Figure 5.4 Income Effect on Work Effort   When leisure and the consumption good are normal goods, Matt uses some of his higher income from nonlabor sources to consume more consumption good and some to consume more leisure time. Increased leisure implies fewer work hours. For increased income to be associated with increased work hours, the income consumption path would have to point in the northwest direction. Leisure would then be an inferior good.

In Matt's case, Andrew Carnegie's view about the effect of increased income with respect to work is borne out. Thus it is important that we understand what caused the reduction in Matt's work hours and consider whether his case is representative. Evidence on the effect of increased income on work hours appears to bear out the conclusion that leisure is a normal good. Income-maintenance experiments conducted in the United States in the 1970s and 1980s, as well as the wealth of data on various government programs, have shown how welfare and other income-guarantee programs affect work hours, as we see in the following application.

APPLICATION: Income Guarantees and Work Hours

A number of programs in the United States give us a glimpse into the effect of income guarantees on work hours under different circumstances. These include mixtures of welfare and social insurance programs such as Social Security (in particular, the Old Age, Survivors and Disability Insurance, or

OASDI), unemployment insurance, workers' compensation, railroad retirement payments, veterans' pensions, and Medicare in-kind benefits (benefits provided in direct form such as medical care), as well as straight welfare programs such as Aid to Families with Dependent Children (AFDC), Supplemental Security Income (SSI), general assistance, and in-kind benefits such as Medicaid, food stamps, and housing assistance. From about 4.5 percent of GDP in the middle 1960s, such payments have more than doubled as a percentage of GDP to around 10 percent today. In addition, there have been four income-maintenance experiments conducted by the executive branch of government, beginning with the New Jersey and Pennsylvania experiments in 1967 and ending with the Denver and Seattle experiments from 1971 to 1991. Recent evidence from studying the behavior of lottery winners also gives us information. The evidence indicates that higher income reduces labor supply, both in terms of hours of work and in terms of labor force participation.[10] A summary of some of these findings will show us how large these effects are.

Social Security and Retirement. Social Security has been intensely studied for its effect on work and savings for retirement, partly because the program covers virtually every worker and also because Congress has increased the real value of the benefits enormously compared to levels in the 1960s and earlier.

A worker is entitled to Social Security payments upon reaching age 65 if he or she has worked enough years in the system (currently 10 years). At the time of retirement, the value to the worker of the expected future stream of payments depends both on the size of the payments and on the length of life over which the payments are expected. We refer to this as the *present value*. It represents the amount of money that the stream of payments would be worth in the market if they could be sold.[11] Workers have the option of retiring at 62 with smaller payments.

Evidence indicates that the larger the size of the income guarantee, the more likely the recipient is to leave the labor force. For example, if a delay in leaving a job reduces the present value of future Social Security payments by $1,000 in 1977 dollars ($2,400 in 1993 dollars), the probability that an individual will leave rises by 11 percent.[12] For either husbands or wives, eligibility for OASI (the nondisability portion of OASDI) raises the probability of leaving the labor force (retiring) by 12 percent. Increasing the present value of OASI payments by $3,000 in 1980 dollars ($5,333 1993 dollars)

---

10. An individual participates in the labor force if he or she is working or actively seeking work. A drop in the labor force participation rate therefore means that a smaller percentage of the working-age population is working or seeking work.
11. See Investigations V for a discussion of present value.
12. This figure and other data on Social Security are reported in Sheldon Danziger, Robert Haveman, and Robert Plotnick, ''How Income Transfers Affect Work, Savings and the Income Distribution,'' *Journal of Economic Literature,* 19 (September 1981), pp. 975–1029.

increases the probability of acceptance of OASDI at age 62 from 21.2 percent to 23.9 percent. In every case, the income effect is noticeable and negative.[13]

Welfare and Work Effort. AFDC is the prototypical welfare program in the United States. More than 90 percent of recipients are women. In some states AFDC, along with food stamps and Medicaid, provides a larger net income for women with several children than working full-time would do at the federally mandated minimum wage. As we would expect, most studies find that AFDC has a significant negative impact on employment (whether a person works), the number of hours worked, and labor force participation (whether a person is working or actively seeking work).

A number of studies report the elasticity of employment, hours of work, and labor force participation with respect to an increase in the income guarantee.[14] These elasticities imply that a 10 percent increase in the guarantee lowers the employment rate of AFDC recipients somewhere between 7 and 11.1 percent, depending on which study and estimate you use, and reduces the labor force participation rate some 9.4 percent. An increase in the income guarantee of the same size reduces work hours by 9 to 15 percent. One study reported that raising the income guarantee by $1,000 in 1981 dollars ($1,616 in 1993 dollars) reduces annual work hours by 120. Assuming an hourly wage of $4.50 (near minimum wage) implies that the average recipient spends $540, or 33 percent of the $1,616 increase, on additional leisure.

Income-Maintenance Experiments. Income-maintenance experiments, first commissioned in 1967, studied the effect of an income guarantee on families with the head of household between 18 and 58 years of age. Experiments were conducted for populations in New Jersey, Pennsylvania, rural North Carolina and Iowa, Denver, Seattle, and Gary, Indiana.[15] Different grant levels were applied, ranging from half to one-and-a-half times the poverty level. For reference, in 1990 the poverty level for a family of four was at $13,359 annual income.[16] The promise of income support was usually for only 3 years, but lengths of 5 and 20 years were also tried in the Denver experiment.

13. The evidence is complicated by the fact that Social Security has rules about how much income a recipient can earn and still be eligible. On one hand, recipients face the loss of payments if their income rises above the cutoff threshold, implying a high implicit tax on earnings. On the other hand, Social Security recipients pay much less in taxes (because a portion of their payments is tax free) than do younger working individuals with the same household income.

14. Danziger, Haveman, and Plotnick, op. cit., pp. 993–994. The elasticities represent long-run effects.

15. Information on the income-maintenance experiments is taken from Robert Ferber and Werner Z. Hirsch, ''Social Experimentation and Economic Policy: A Survey,'' *Journal of Economic Literature,* 16 (December 1978), pp. 1379–1387.

16. U.S. Department of Commerce, Economic and Statistics Administration, Bureau of the Census. *Poverty in the United States: 1990,* Current Population Reports, Consumer Income Series P-60, No. 175, Washington, D.C.: U.S. Government Printing Office, August 1991, p. 194.

Since the recipients were in their prime working years and the duration of support was so short in most experiments, the effect of the income guarantee on work effort was probably smaller than it would be if the guarantee were permanent or if the recipient were closer to retirement age. In the early years of the Seattle-Denver experiments, the effect was that each $1,000 of income guarantee in 1978 dollars ($2,253 in 1993 dollars) reduced annual work hours by 22 percent for wives, 11 percent for other females, and 5 percent for husbands. Earlier experiments, such as the New Jersey experiment, reported a 7-percent overall reduction in the labor supply with a 3-year income guarantee, and a 20-percent drop in labor force participation by wives.

Hitting the Jackpot and Labor Supply. The final piece of evidence comes neither from welfare and income-guarantee programs nor from experiment. For the last 15 years, the increase in legalized gambling in the form of state lotteries allows us to see the effect on the winners' labor supply. Of those winning a million dollars or more in the lottery, 25 percent quit work.[17] ■

Substitution Effects of a Wage Change

In Chapter 4 we showed that the consumer's purchase of a good declined in response to a price increase when the consumer was held at the initial level of utility by adjusting income. Holding utility constant eliminated any income effect of the price change and left only the substitution effect. In the case of leisure, the price of an additional hour of leisure is the wage rate (the consumer gets leisure by giving up what would have been earned from working). We can find the substitution effect of a wage change for labor hours, therefore, by looking at the substitution effect of a wage increase on leisure.

In Figure 5.5, a higher wage rotates Matt's budget line clockwise. To keep his utility constant, we simultaneously adjust his nonlabor income to keep the new budget line tangent to the original indifference curve. The substitution effect of a wage increase from w_0 to w_0' shifts Matt's choice from point a to point b, reducing his consumption of leisure. Since the substitution effect always causes a decline in purchase of the good whose price has gone up, the substitution effect of a wage increase always works in the direction of reduced leisure and increased work hours.

5.3 The Labor Supply Curve

Now let's see how the income effect and substitution effect combine to give us the individual's labor supply curve. There is some ambiguity to be resolved here. As we've seen, higher wages induce greater work effort through the substitution effect because the pay is better. However, higher pay means

17. Brad Edmondson, "Remaking a Living," *Utne Reader,* July–August 1991, p. 74. Assuming the interest rate is about 2.5 percent higher than the inflation rate, $1 million is roughly equivalent to an income stream of just under $40,000 per year in current purchasing power for 40 years.

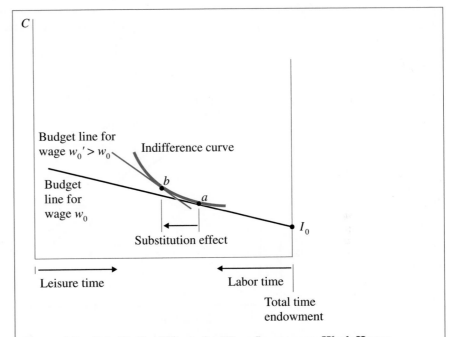

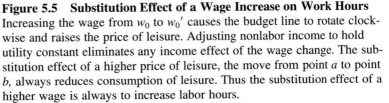

Figure 5.5 Substitution Effect of a Wage Increase on Work Hours
Increasing the wage from w_0 to w_0' causes the budget line to rotate clockwise and raises the price of leisure. Adjusting nonlabor income to hold
utility constant eliminates any income effect of the wage change. The substitution effect of a higher price of leisure, the move from point *a* to point
b, always reduces consumption of leisure. Thus the substitution effect of a
higher wage is always to increase labor hours.

higher income. Through the income effect the consumer may prefer to consume more leisure and thus devote less time to work.

Upward-Sloping Labor Supply Curves

Figure 5.6 illustrates the consumer's choice for a range of wage rates. We
find the number of labor hours corresponding to wage rate w_0 at choice point
a. The labor hours are shown by the horizontal distance from the right-hand
edge to point *a*. When the wage rate is raised to w_1, w_2, and w_3, the consumer's
choice shifts to points *b, c,* and *d,* respectively. Connecting these points gives
us the price consumption path for a wage change, drawn as the line through
points *a* through *d*.

Each wage change can be separated into a substitution effect and an income
effect. For example, to separate the shift from *a* to *b* into the substitution
effect and the income effect, rotate the budget line along the initial indifference curve until its slope matches the slope of the budget line corresponding

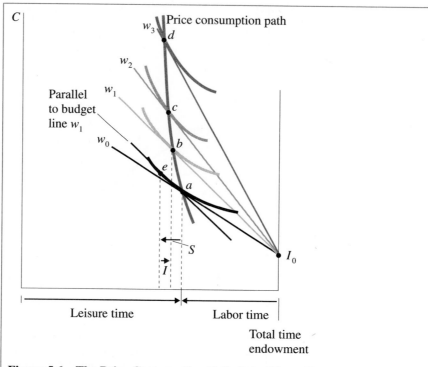

Figure 5.6   The Price Consumption Path for a Wage Change
Raising wages from w_0 to w_1, w_2, and w_3 shifts the budget line clockwise and causes the utility-maximizing point to move from a to b to c to d. Connecting the utility-maximizing points produces the price consumption path, from which the demand curve for leisure and the labor supply curve are derived.

▼
4. Derive the consumer's labor supply curve.

to the higher wage w_1. The shift from point a to point e, where the line tangent to point e has the same slope as the budget line for wage equal to w_1, indicates the substitution effect of the wage increase. The income effect is the shift from point e to point b. This effect causes a partially offsetting decrease in work effort.[18]

Figure 5.7 shows the demand curve for leisure, and hence the supply curve for labor, derived from the price consumption path in Figure 5.6. The procedure follows the same steps for deriving the demand curve discussed in Chapter 4. We lay out each wage rate on the vertical axis in part (a) of Figure 5.7 and plot the number of leisure hours for that wage given by the price consumption path in Figure 5.6. Point a in Figure 5.7 corresponds to point a in Figure 5.6, and so on for the other wage rates. Connecting the wage–leisure hour pairs produces the demand curve for leisure. Since the number

18. In the unlikely case that leisure were an inferior good, the income effect would have led to a further increase in work effort.

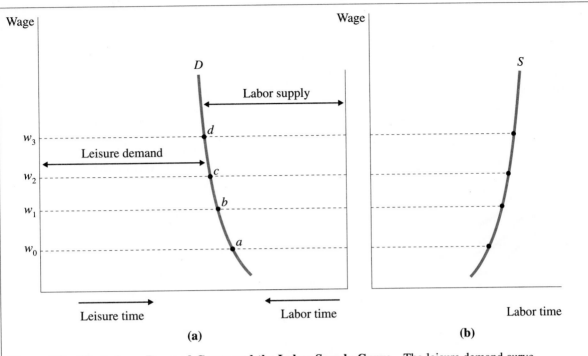

Figure 5.7   The Leisure Demand Curve and the Labor Supply Curve   The leisure demand curve
D in part (a) is determined by the price consumption path generated by the consumer's choice of
leisure hours and consumption of goods. Points *a, b, c,* and *d* correspond to points *a, b, c,* and *d* in
Figure 5.6. Measuring labor hours from the right for each wage rate gives the labor supply curve,
which is plotted in part (b) as curve *S.*

of labor hours supplied is just the time endowment minus leisure ($L = E - L_e$), we find the labor supply curve from the demand curve for leisure by measuring horizontally from the right-hand edge of the diagram the number of labor hours for each wage rate. Viewed from the right-hand edge, the downward-sloping demand curve for leisure becomes an upward-sloping supply curve of labor. Reorienting the supply curve of labor gives us the figure in part (b).

Can Labor Supply Curves Bend Backward?

▼
5. Explain the cause of a back-ward-bending supply curve of labor.

Figure 5.8 shows what is called a ''backward-bending'' labor supply curve. Part (a) shows the choices of the consumer at different wage rates, and part (b) shows the implied labor supply curve. At low wage rates and therefore low income levels, the supply curve slopes upward. However, as the wage rate rises and the consumer's income rises, the labor supply curve becomes vertical at point *c* and eventually bends backward. This is because higher

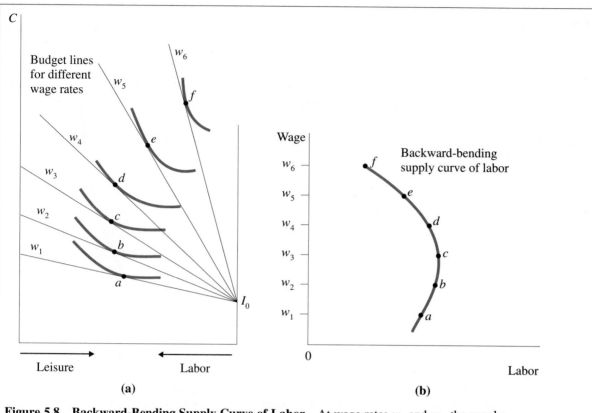

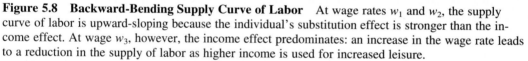

Figure 5.8   Backward-Bending Supply Curve of Labor   At wage rates w_1 and w_2, the supply curve of labor is upward-sloping because the individual's substitution effect is stronger than the income effect. At wage w_3, however, the income effect predominates: an increase in the wage rate leads to a reduction in the supply of labor as higher income is used for increased leisure.

wages lead to higher income, but enjoying this income generally requires leisure time. If leisure is a normal good, which it typically is, then the desire for more leisure time eventually outweighs the desire for more income. When this happens, the income effect dominates the substitution effect.

Evidence on the workweek (presented later in the chapter) shows that the length of the typical workweek has declined with the increase in wage rates. Because the household is a buyer of leisure and simultaneously a seller of the same good (in the form of labor hours), the normality of leisure makes it unsurprising that the supply curve should bend backward for sufficiently high wage rates.

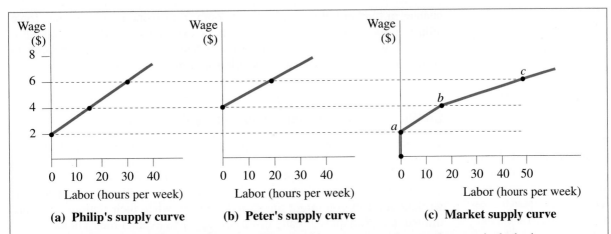

Figure 5.9   Derivation of the Market Labor Supply Curve   The market supply curve is the horizontal summation of individuals' labor supply curves. For each wage, the quantity of labor supplied by each individual is added, and the total is plotted opposite the wage on the market diagram. Connecting the plotted points gives the market supply curve. The kink at point *b* occurs because at wage $4 Peter begins to supply positive amounts of labor, whereas at lower wages only Philip was supplying labor.

From Individual to Market Labor Supply

▼
6. Construct a market labor supply curve from individual labor supply curves.

Given what we learned in Chapter 4 about constructing market demand curves from individual demand, the market supply curve of labor is constructed in the way we would expect: derive the supply curve of labor for every consumer and add the curves horizontally. That is, for each wage rate, find the quantity of labor supplied by each consumer, add these numbers together, and plot the summed quantity of labor. Connecting all such points provides the market supply curve of labor.

Figure 5.9 demonstrates the addition of individual labor supply curves to construct the market labor supply curve. Part (a) shows Philip's labor supply curve, and part (b) shows Peter's labor supply curve. Neither individual supplies any labor at wage rates below $2 per hour: they leave the labor force. Thus the market supply curve in part (c) shows zero labor supply for wage rates less than $2, from the origin to point *a*. At wage $4 per hour, Philip supplies 15 hours per week of labor. Adding this to Peter's supply of zero hours at that wage gives us a total of 15 hours, plotted in part (c) as point *b*. At wage $6 per hour, Philip supplies 30 hours of labor and Peter supplies 20 hours. The total supply of 50 hours is therefore plotted in part (c) as point *c*. Connecting the points in part (c) together gives us the market labor supply curve. In this case, since Philip's and Peter's labor supply curves are linear, the market supply curve is composed of linear segments connecting the origin and points *a, b,* and *c*. From this example we also see that the change in market labor supply results both from workers in the labor force adjusting their hours and from the entry or exit of new workers to the labor force. A worker enters the labor force when the wage is high enough to compensate for the value of the lost leisure time.

Do Workers Control Their Labor Supply Decisions?

▼
7. Construct an example showing the labor supply decision when the budget constraint contains corners. Explain the reason for the shape of the constraint.

The model of consumer labor supply decisions we have developed thus far leaves one crucial question unanswered: do workers really control the number of hours of work they supply at a given wage? The short answer is that (1) as individuals and as a group, workers have more ability to influence their work hours than you might think, and (2) even when their options are more limited, the principles already discussed apply to explain their choices.

On the individual level, workers can opt for jobs that provide the best available match with the type and amount of work they are seeking. For example, different occupations offer different working conditions: seasonal versus year-round work, intensive versus relaxed work, or sustained work versus bursts of activity interspersed with slack periods. Choices also can often be made between full-time and part-time work. The self-employed can control how hard or how much they work, and workers who want to earn more than one job affords can moonlight at a second job. Though individuals at a particular job may not have complete freedom to choose labor hours in a given week, over a longer time period they do have some choice about taking vacations, sick days, and the like.

As a group, workers can establish work norms that relate to their needs. The five-day workweek is an example of a relatively modern innovation of this type. National holidays, though set by government, become accepted or not by the work force at large according to the needs and desires of the workers. Generally, the different features of the work schedule represent a balance between the needs of the worker and those of the firm, such as the requirement that workers be at the work place at the same time (to accomplish the most in their joint activity) or during daylight hours when other firms are open for business. In occupations and industries where different arrangements are feasible, they are accommodated.

Finally, the principles already discussed apply to more complicated work decisions. Part (a) of Figure 5.10 shows the case of an hourly worker, Morgan, who has the choice of not working at all or accepting a job at 40 hours a week at $10 per hour. As drawn, Morgan has a higher utility accepting the job at point a than not working and being limited to less income (I_0). If Morgan could choose how many hours to work at the $10 wage, he would choose to work fewer hours at point b, where his utility would be higher. Rather than exhibiting tangency between his budget constraint and indifference curve, Morgan's acceptance of employment at point a is a corner solution. Even so, we can model his behavior as choosing the point that max-

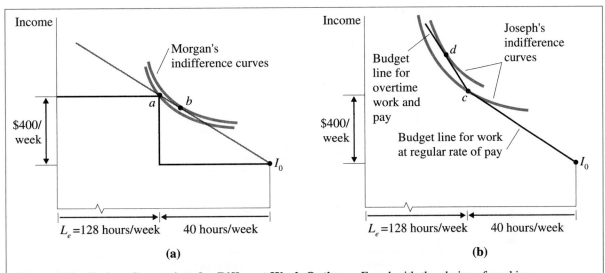

Figure 5.10   Budget Constraints for Different Work Options   Faced with the choice of working 40 hours per week at $10 per hour or not working at all, Morgan in part (a) accepts work at point *a*. If he could choose his number of hours of work, he would prefer to work fewer hours at point *b,* which has higher utility for him. In part (b), Joseph initially chooses to work at point *c*. To induce him to work more hours at point *d,* an overtime wage higher than the base wage is offered for hours per week above 40.

imizes his utility subject to the budget constraint, and we can analyze the situation using the techniques introduced earlier.[19]

Part (b) in Figure 5.10 shows another worker, Joseph, who is given the option of overtime at a higher wage. For example, he may be a member of a union that has negotiated the base wage and hours as part of the union's contract.[20] At the base wage, Joseph chooses point *c,* 40 hours of work per week at the stated wage. As an inducement to work more hours, Joseph is offered a higher wage (overtime) for points to the left of *c.* Joseph has higher utility at point *d* than at point *c* because the steeper budget line compensates him for extra work at a higher rate.

19. For example, the effect of a wage increase can be found by changing his budget constraint to reflect the higher wage and maximizing his utility subject to the new constraint. Income effects can be found by raising his budget constraint at every point by the additional income and observing how Morgan's choice differs. Substitution effects can be found by checking the effect of a wage increase and subtracting the income effect.
20. Negotiations between a union and a firm are discussed in Chapter 11.

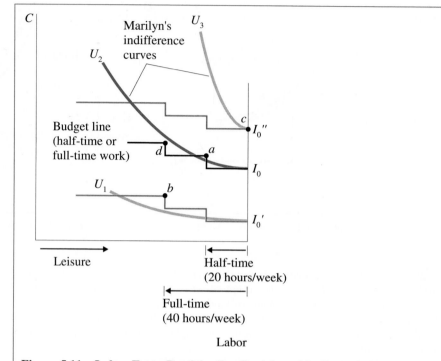

Figure 5.11   Labor Force Participation Decision   Marilyn's decision to enter the labor force depends on her family's other income, the hours of work and pay she has available (half-time or full-time), and the steepness of her indifference curves, which show how valuable her time at home is relative to having more spendable income. When other family income is I_0, she decides to work half-time; when it is I_0', she decides to work full-time; and when it is I_0'', she does not enter the labor force. Flatter indifference curves or higher pay for work would induce her to enter the labor force more readily or to increase her work hours.

EXPLORATION: Labor Supply in Two-Income Households

One of the changing features of the American labor force is the increasing labor force participation rate of women. In 1976, for example, 60 percent of women between the ages of 20 and 44 were in the labor force. By 1988 the equivalent figure had risen to 74 percent. In our final example of labor choice, therefore, we consider the labor force participation decision of Marilyn, whose husband works full-time as a salesman for a lumber supply company. Figure 5.11 shows Marilyn's budget constraint as the sequence of steps starting at I_0 and passing through point a. Marilyn has three options: (1) she can choose not to work, so that she and her family live on her husband's income, I_0; (2) she can accept half-time work at a flat wage, placing her at point *a;* or (3) she can work full-time at 40 hours per week, putting her at point *d.* Marilyn's indifference curves reflect both her preferences and the needs of her household. In this case, since Marilyn's husband earns a good income and the couple has four children, two of whom are under school age, Marilyn's indifference curve starting from I_0 is fairly steep. This indicates that time away from her small children would need to be well compensated to justify her decision to work. The indifference curve starting from I_0'' is even steeper, because higher income for her husband means less necessity for additional income. On the other hand, the curve through I_0' is flatter, because lower earnings by her husband increase the need for family income from other sources.

As the figure shows, Marilyn's best option is to enter the labor force and work part-time at point *a.* If she worked full-time at point *d,* her utility would be lower than her utility from not working, U_2. For comparison, Marilyn's budget lines are also shown for the alternative earnings of her husband, I_0' and I_0''. When her husband's income is lower, it is in her interest to work full-time (point *b*); when it is higher, she exits the labor force at point *c.* The shifts in her optimal choice as her husband's income rises, from point *b* to point *a* to point *c,* show the income effect on Marilyn's labor supply. In general, lower family income from her husband, flatter indifference curves for Marilyn, and/or higher pay for working encourage Marilyn to enter the labor force. For example, if Marilyn had no children, her indifference curves would be flatter than those shown in Figure 5.11, because her utility costs and out-of-pocket costs for not being home (costs such as child care) would be lower. In this case, Marilyn would be more likely to work full-time, even when her husband's income was I_0 or I_0''. A similar analysis could be performed for the labor supply decision of Marilyn's husband, this time taking as given the income Marilyn earned. ■

APPLICATION: The Workweek Then and Now

According to anthropologists, people in preindustrial societies spent 3 to 4 hours per day or about 20 hours per week doing the work necessary for life. Measuring time and work in weekly chunks dates back at least to the time of Moses, around 1500 B.C., with the seventh-day Sabbath honoring God's day of rest after the six days of creation. By the first century B.C., the seven-day week seems to have been adopted throughout the Roman world. Modern comparisons of the amount of work performed per week, however, begin with the Industrial Revolution (1760–1840), which started in England and spread to the rest of the developed world.

Changes in the workweek reflect consumption-leisure preferences at different standards of living and income levels. During the Industrial Revolution, 10- to 12-hour workdays with six workdays per week were the norm. Sunday was generally a day of religious observance. Even with extensive time devoted to work, however, both incomes and standards of living were low. As incomes rose near the end of the Industrial Revolution, it became increasingly common to treat Saturday afternoons as a half holiday. This meant that workers were spending part of their increased income on greater leisure. The half holiday became standard practice in Britain by the 1870s, but did not become common in the United States until the 1920s. According to one account, "Factory owners had little to gain from insisting on a six-day week of workdays of up to twelve hours if on some days so few workers showed up that the factory had to be shut down anyway."[21]

In the United States, the first third of the 20th century saw the workweek move from 60 hours per week to just under 50 hours by the start of the 1930s. In 1914 Henry Ford reduced daily work hours at his plants from 9 to 8. In 1926 he announced that henceforth his factories would close for the entire day on Saturday. At the time, Ford received criticism from other firms such as U.S. Steel and Westinghouse, but the idea was popular with workers.

The Depression years brought with them the notion of job sharing to spread available work around; the workweek dropped to a modern low for the United States of 35 hours. In 1938 the Fair Labor Standards Act mandated a weekly maximum of 40 hours to begin in 1940, and since that time the 8-hour day, 5-day workweek has been the standard in the United States. Adjustment in various places, however, shows that this standard is not immutable. In 1987, for example, German metalworkers struck for and received a 37.5-hour work-week; and many workers in Britain in 1990 won a 37-hour week. Since 1989, the Japanese government has moved from a 6- to a 5-day workweek and has set a national target of 1,800 work hours per year for the average Japanese worker. "Taking holidays was regarded as nearly sinful when Japan was poor," according to Ikuro Takagi, a Japanese professor.[22] The average amount of work per year in Japan in 1989 was 2,088 hours per worker, compared to 1,957 for the United States and 1,646 for France.

There are other ways to take increased income in the form of leisure in addition to reducing the standard workweek and the number of hours in the workday. Ancient Rome, during certain periods of its thousand-year history, is reported to have had 175 public festivals per year; during the Middle Ages Christian Europe's religious holidays also had a regulating effect on work, keeping hours below 2,000 per year. In the United States, our national holidays plus weekends amount to about 115 days off from work per year.[23] Vacations also determine how time is divided between work and leisure. By bargaining agreements, most annual vacations in the United States vary between 2 and 4 weeks. In other countries vacation times are even longer. Finland, France, Spain, and Sweden, for example, set 5 weeks vacation time

21. Witold Rybczynski, "Waiting for the Weekend," *The Atlantic,* August 1991, p. 44. Much of the succeeding history is taken from Rybczynski's account.
22. David E. Sanger, "As Japanese Work Ever Harder to Relax," *New York Times,* July 7, 1991, section 4, p. 2.
23. Holiday observance varies by state, however.

by law, and in many other countries 4 to 6 weeks of vacation are not uncommon by the terms of bargaining agreements.[24]

So what does the typical worker do with all this leisure time? Studies by the Survey Research Center at the University of Maryland[25] divide the week into work, family care (housework, shopping, child care), personal care (sleeping, eating, grooming), and free time. Since the 1960s the average weekly free time has risen from 34 hours to 40 hours for women and to 41 hours for men. Personal care has been roughly constant, accounting for just over 70 hours per week for men and slightly more for women. Family care, on the other hand, has dropped from 40 to 30 hours for women and risen from 11 to 15 hours for men. Work? It has dropped for men from over 45 to just over 40 hours and risen for women from 18 to 25 hours. The most striking differences in free time, however, are for women with preschool children, compared to those with no children. Nonemployed women without children enjoy 48 hours of free time per week, compared to 31 for employed women with preschool children. Employed women with no children enjoy on average 37 hours free time, which is still higher than the free time of nonemployed women with preschool children (36 hours)!

Even though there is evidence of increasing free time, about a third of the population feels rushed, compared to only a quarter of the population who felt that way 25 years ago. Despite this feeling of being rushed, free time spent watching TV has risen tremendously since 1965, today taking about 37 percent of all free time.

Although the trend through history shows that higher income leads to shorter work hours and increased leisure, no single statement accounts for all workers. Some workers take part-time jobs at the same time that others take full-time; and some (more than ever before recorded, fully 5.2 percent of workers in 1989) hold two or more jobs.[26] ■

5.4 Consumer Surplus for Labor Supply

How much better off is the worker when the wage rate rises? Figure 5.12 shows a supply curve of labor, *S,* and two wage rates, w_0 and w_1. Since this diagram is reminiscent of our discussion of consumer surplus in Chapter 4, we would like to say that the household is better off by the shaded area to the left of the supply curve between the two wage rates, area *A.* We can now show that this intuition is correct.

24. ''Reduction of Working Time in Europe.'' *European Industrial Relations Review,* 127 (August 1984), pp. 9–13, reported in Edmondson, op. cit., p. 85.
25. Information from Trish Hall, ''Time on Your Hands? It May Be Increasing,'' *New York Times,* July 3, 1991, p. C1.
26. Rybczynski, op. cit., p. 50.

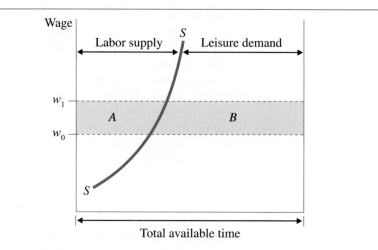

Area A = Net rise in consumer surplus from increased wage rate
Area $A + B$ = Increase in income from increased value of time endowment
Area B = Reduction in consumer surplus from increase in price of leisure

Figure 5.12   Measuring Consumer Surplus for Labor Supply
Increasing the wage rate increases the consumer's endowment-time income at the same time that it reduces consumer surplus in relation to leisure demand. The net effect is measured as the area to the left of the labor supply curve between the beginning and ending wages.

▼
8. How is consumer surplus measured for labor supply?

At each wage rate, measuring from the left of the figure gives labor supply, and measuring from the right gives leisure demand. If the wage rises from w_0 to w_1, the consumer's endowment-time income rises by the sum of areas A and B (wage change times total time endowment). The consumer is better off by this amount of increased income. However, the consumer also buys leisure. Since the wage increase is an increase in the price of leisure, it reduces consumer surplus in relation to leisure demand. As we learned in Chapter 4, this reduction is given by area B. Subtracting area B from the increase in endowment-time income leaves area A as the net effect of the wage increase. The area to the left of the labor supply curve between the two wage rates is the change in consumer surplus caused by the wage change.

EXPLORATION: Time and Household Production

The labor supply model is sometimes criticized because it does not appear to take into account certain features of the household's use of time, such as the fact that consumption may require time as well as income. In essence, the

▼
9. What is different in the labor supply model when consuming requires the input of time?

household buys a market good and adds its own time to produce the final product that the household consumes. A two-week ski vacation is recreation to the household, but to produce it takes skis, space in a ski resort, and *two weeks of time* as inputs. A household that works full-time all year cannot consume the vacation unless it spends two weeks doing so. The criticism that the model does not take time into account, however, is not entirely warranted, because the labor supply model just developed can be quite powerful and useful in describing various labor market phenomena, including time and household production. This section shows that very little adjustment of the basic model is needed to deal with time as an input to consumption.

The effect of household production using time and market goods can be included in our labor supply model as follows. Let t_C be the amount of time needed per unit of the consumption good. This means that the total time endowment divides into *three* distinct uses: L units of labor, L_e units of full leisure (*full leisure* means time devoted neither to working nor to consuming C), and $t_C C$ units of time devoted to consuming C. Thus $E = L + L_e + t_C C$. Since the amount of C that can be bought is given by spendable income, $p_C C = I_0 + wL$, where $p_C = 1$, we use the division of time endowment just given to replace L to get the new budget constraint,

$$(1 + t_C w)C + wL_e = I_0 + wE.$$

Notice that the price of consuming C is now higher than it used to be. Because consuming C is costly in the form of time, the new budget constraint says that the true cost of consuming C is $(1 + t_C w)$: the household pays $1 for good C directly and $t_C w$ in terms of forgone income from time away from work needed to do the consuming.

The main change in the budget constraint is the different price for C. Thus we can analyze the labor supply decision using the new budget constraint in the same manner that we did before. Only two adjustments are needed, (1) to allow for the possibility that taking too much time in full leisure L_e may limit the amount of consumption, and (2) to find how much labor is supplied and time devoted to the consumption. Both can be explained graphically.

To allow for the time involved in consuming C, Figure 5.13 shows the budget constraint starting at point e and going to point g. At point g the budget line has a corner in it, turning downward to point h. The reason for the corner is that for points to the right of g, the amount of full leisure is so high that there is not enough time left to consume all of the C that the household's income can purchase. For example, at point h, the household takes all of its time in leisure, so that no amount of C can be consumed, regardless of how much the household can buy.

Since point g lies to the left of point d, it changes position with the amount of nonlabor income, moving farther to the left on the budget line for higher I_0. For a household with extremely high nonlabor income, point g lies most or all of the way to point e. Such a household is more likely to find its utility-maximizing choice of leisure and C somewhere on the segment gh, meaning

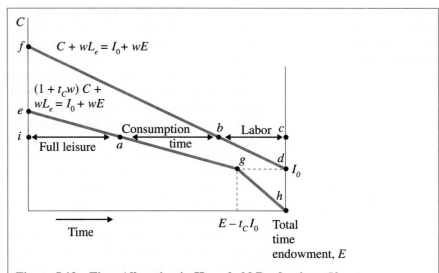

Figure 5.13 Time Allocation in Household Production If consumption of C requires time t_C per unit as an input, the budget constraint shifts from line fd to segments eg and gh, becoming flatter and adding a corner at point g. On segment gh of the budget constraint, there is not enough time to consume as much C as income will buy. The household maximizes utility by choosing a point on eg or gh. Labor time is determined by using line fd to find out how much work is needed to pay for the amount of C bought.

that it has money to buy the consumption good but not enough time to consume it all.[27]

In the usual case, however, we expect that money is the main factor limiting the household's choice, because nonlabor income is low. Such a household maximizes utility by choosing a point on the budget line between points e and g. At point a we measure the amount of full leisure the household chooses as the distance from point i to point a. For each quantity of labor the household supplies (labor is measured from the right-hand edge), the vertical height of line fd shows spendable income. To generate the spendable income to pay for consumption of C at point a, labor must be the distance between points b and c. Thus, time devoted to consumption of C is the remaining distance between points a and b.

Knowing how to draw the budget line and how to find labor supply from Figure 5.13, we could also draw indifference curves on the diagram and analyze the labor supply decision using the methods we have already discussed. ■

27. Increasing the household's wage rate for fixed I_0 leaves point g fixed and moves point e upward. Higher wages cause points e, g, and h to approach colinearity (all three points on the same line), as the time cost $t_C w$ of consuming becomes a greater and greater percentage of the total cost of consuming C.

5.5 Opportunity Costs and Economic Rent

Supplying labor in one type of occupation means that the same time cannot be supplied in another. *Opportunity cost* and *economic rent* are therefore important elements in the labor supply decision as it relates to the overall benefits of providing one type of labor rather than another. The same concepts apply in general to other factors of production. Physical capital and land, for example, are factors of production that households own, and thus households must decide where to use them. If the household rents out land for a parking lot, it gives up the opportunity of building on the same land.

The relationship of opportunity cost and rent to factor supply can best be introduced by an example. Imagine that you are a physician earning $150,000 per year. If you were not a physician, the next best job you could do, say, selling medical supplies, would earn $50,000 per year. Apart from pay, you would be equally satisfied with either job. Your *opportunity cost* of being a physician is the income that you would have earned from the next best alternative. In this case, your opportunity cost of being a physician is $50,000.

> *The **opportunity cost** of supplying a factor for a particular use is the lost benefits of supplying that factor to the next best alternative.*

Opportunity costs can be measured in dollars, as in our example of a physician, but they can also be measured in other things. The opportunity cost of working in an unpleasant factory instead of being self-employed for the same pay, for example, is the lost utility from not doing the more pleasant kind of work.

Economic rent is related to opportunity cost. Economic rent is income you earn from being a physician (or whatever your work is) *above* the minimum necessary to keep you in that line of work. Since you would remain a physician for anything higher than $50,000 per year, $100,000 of your income is economic rent.

> ***Economic rent*** *is payment to a factor above the minimum necessary to keep the factor in the present line of employment.*

Much of what highly paid entertainers and sports stars earn is economic rent because their talent is so specialized. If they had no opportunity to use their special talent, they would have to work at ordinary jobs and earn far less income. Earning economic rent is often associated with the rarity of the thing in demand, because limited supply drives up the market price.[28] Frequently, a thing that earns high economic rent not only is in short supply, but

▼

10. Define economic rent. In what way is it related to opportunity cost?

28. Being the best in one's field usually brings rewards far greater than the difference in skill involved, because winning is often critically important to earnings. For example, if racehorses A and B are identical in every respect except that racehorse A is marginally faster than B, the winnings of horse A are going to be much larger than those of B. In every race where both compete (if the horses run true to form), horse A will come away with the purse. If you were a horse owner, how much would you be willing to pay to own each horse? Contests of this type are called rank-order tournaments. A similar situation exists with respect to the labor market, except that "winning" is defined differently. For lawyers, it might be cases successfully litigated; for scientists, it might be being first with the next computer chip; for athletes,

also cannot be used in any other way. For example, a well-known pitching ace in the National League recently signed a contract for $5.3 million per season.[29] His special pitching skills are useful only in baseball. Nearly all of the $5.3 million, therefore, is economic rent, because his pitching skills would be used only in baseball unless his income fell so low that he decided to leave baseball for some other job.

Those individuals with a unique skill or talent (one in great demand that earns them high economic rent) have it relatively easy in the labor market. Since their talent is so recognizable, they don't have to convince the market of their "hireability." But for most people in the labor market, information plays a crucial role. We will examine this topic in the next section.

▼
11. Explain why the labor market might exhibit asymmetric information.

EXPLORATION: Asymmetric Information in the Labor Market

Up to this point in the chapter, we have implicitly assumed that both buyers and sellers of labor have perfect information: they both know and agree on the type and quality of service being traded, and they can choose a price for labor services based on the quantity and type of service performed. We have also focused our attention on the labor supply decision that takes place in a specific market.

In many cases, however, households can offer their services in several labor markets, and information in those markets is not symmetric. The buyer of labor may not be able to observe the work that is being done, see the amount of care that is being put into completion of the task, or know the quality of the work that is accomplished. If a new hire is being considered, the firm may not know the ability of the applicant to perform the job, and the applicant may not know the nature of the abilities that the job will require.

In this section we look at two ways in which the labor market responds to problems of asymmetric information. In both cases, the seller of labor services knows more than the buyer about the quality or the quantity of work performed and wants to inform the buyer. The labor market has developed mechanisms that help sellers send such signals to the buyers. We will see how this signaling mechanism affects the market for college-educated workers and how it influences competition between workers on the job. Both of these cases differ from the "lemons" model discussed in Chapter 2 because of the sellers' ability to signal buyers.

---

it might be games won or products successfully sold because of endorsements. Some individuals argue that rank-order tournaments explain why corporate business heads are often paid so much in relation to their skills. Being a close second in rank-order tournaments often just doesn't bring the rewards that being first does. As a result, the earnings of the best frequently contain large portions of rent.

29. Leonard Silk, "Economic Scene: Predicting the Pay of Ballplayers," *New York Times,* June 21, 1991, p. D2.

College Degrees as a Market Signal

Young workers entering the labor market have a wide range of job opportunities and alternatives from which to choose. Depending on the alternative chosen, various aspects of the job seeker's personality, abilities, and aptitudes determine his or her success. Employers, by the same token, need people with a variety of specific skills and aptitudes to fill the different jobs they offer. It follows that both job seekers and employers want to identify the individuals with abilities that best match each job. One way prospective employees can prove their suitability is by showing employers successful previous experience in the type of job being offered. Indeed, employers often require experience and references from previous jobs. This provides effective information about job seekers who are already in the labor market. But what does one do for first-time employment?

Without a perfect indicator of ability, the job market needs a *signal* that is *positively correlated* with ability.[30] That is, workers ''sending'' the signal should show higher levels of the ability or aptitude than workers not sending the signal. You are probably able to think of many possible signals. For example, at a job interview it is a good idea to dress appropriately, be courteous, and express yourself well. After all, if you can't do these things for a job interview, employers are likely to think you would not do them on the job. The problem with this signal, however, is that many people are able to dress well, remain courteous at an interview, and speak well. The signal doesn't separate job applicants effectively. *A better signal should be harder to send for those who do not truly have the desired abilities.* Education is a very effective signal.

According to income figures, education, especially college education, matters a great deal to later earnings.[31] Yet not everyone gets a college degree, since doing so is costly in several important ways. First, a college education has considerable up-front costs. Even though it is a good investment, not everyone is able or willing to finance the out-of-pocket costs through family contributions, borrowing, personal earnings, or through working for a scholarship. Second, the opportunity cost of taking four years to complete a degree is high because it postpones earnings. Psychologists have said that the ability to postpone current gratification for future reward is a sign of maturity. For whatever reason, some individuals may be less willing to postpone their earnings than others. Third, getting an education is costly in terms of the

▼
12. What is the essential property of a successful job market "signal?"

30. A good reference on signaling is Michael Spence, *Market Signalling.* Cambridge, MA: Harvard University Press, 1974.
31. In 1991 individuals who had completed one to three years of college had a median income of $26,591. Those with a bachelor's degree had a median income of $36,067, a 35.6 percent increase for just one year's difference (the standard college degree is a four-year degree). Individuals having less than 9th grade education (elementary school) had a median income of $14,736, whereas high school graduates had a median income of $21,546. See U.S. Dept of Commerce, *Money Income of Households, Families, and Persons in the United States: 1991,* Current Population Reports, Consumer Income Series P-60, No. 180, Washington, D.C.: U.S. Government Printing Office, 1992.

mental labor involved. Those with lower motivation or lower ability find this cost more burdensome than those with higher motivation and ability. The net result of these differences in cost is that some people need higher compensation for the investment of getting a college degree than others. A similar argument can be applied to completing high school, although the rewards and costs are on a smaller scale.

Figure 5.14 shows the earnings for different amounts of education as a series of steps.[32] The trade-off in this utility-maximization problem is between income and education. We simplify the problem by considering just three types of workers. For each type of worker, utility increases with income but drops as the amount of education increases (each worker would be happier if he or she could achieve the same income level with less education). Because the costs of acquiring additional education are greatest for the low-motivation/ low-ability workers, they need the greatest compensation in the form of higher income in order to get additional education. Starting from the left, their indifference curves are the steepest and rise the fastest as more education is added. At the other extreme, high-motivation/high ability workers find acquiring a college degree much easier and therefore need less compensation for getting it. Beginning at the left, their indifference curves are relatively flat until schooling includes college; their curves rise steeply only for education beyond college.

As the figure shows, the difference in the intrinsic costs of education for the different types of workers means that each chooses a different amount of education. Low-ability workers end up choosing point *a,* which requires completing only elementary school. Middle-ability workers choose point *b,* requiring high school graduation, while high-ability workers choose point *c,* requiring a college degree. Once a worker's ability is signaled by education level, employers form an expectation about how productive that worker is likely to be. The employer is willing to pay higher salaries for more highly educated workers in the expectation of higher output.

There are two main features necessary for the situation just described to be an effective market mechanism. First, workers of various types must find it in their interest to select *different* amounts of education. In Figure 5.14, for example, if workers have different preferences that are unrelated to ability, those who choose more education will be indistinguishable in ability as a group from those who choose less. Education will no longer effectively signal ability. Likewise, if preferences *are* related to ability but are so similar that all workers choose the same amount of education, education again will cease to be a signal.

Second, in order for the labor market signaling system to work, employers must be willing to pay more for workers with higher education. This means that those with college degrees must have truly higher abilities and higher productivity than those without degrees. Otherwise, there would be no signal and no economic benefit in higher education.

---

32. The incomes refer to the median incomes for 1991 reported in the preceding footnote.

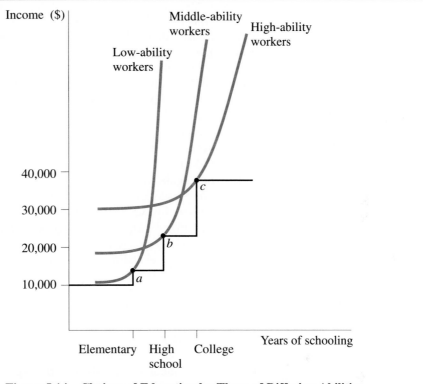

Figure 5.14   Choices of Education by Those of Differing Abilities
The utility cost of education rises fastest for low-motivation/low-ability workers and slowest for high-motivation/high-ability workers. Thus workers with college degrees are the ones in the high-motivation and high-ability group. Whether or not education adds to ability, workers with college degrees will tend to earn a higher market wage because their college degrees signal to employers their greater motivation and ability. The perception that education adds to ability further distinguishes the expected productivity of those with higher degrees from those without them.

Work Effort as a Market Signal

Once the hiring decisions are made, workers and employers are again faced with a signaling problem: how to keep employers informed about the productivity of workers on the job. The labor market deals with this problem in different ways. In the simplest case, the employer may have an inexpensive way to monitor the work being performed, checking it for quantity and quality. A factory operation, for example, might monitor work by having workers punch in and out on a time clock and having a supervisor on the floor during the day to oversee operations. In other cases, workers may be paid at a flat rate for their work and also receive a "piece rate" for output above a specified level. Car salesmen often receive commissions based on how many cars they sell, a measurable number. Likewise, waiters and waitresses typically receive a base salary, but frequently earn most of their income from tips; thus the customer acts as a monitor of the quality of the service performed. In many professions, however, easy measures of individual work quality and quantity aren't available, so other devices must be used.

One way individuals seek to distinguish themselves in their jobs is by working harder to "climb the corporate ladder." Those pressing to get ahead often describe themselves as "forced" by the system to work harder than they would like to gain recognition and advancement. Our second example of signaling deals with work effort as a signal for unobservable productivity. In this context, work effort could mean the number of extra hours worked at the office after closing, the intensity of work, the thoroughness of completing given tasks, membership in a selective company working group—anything that is positively correlated with the worker's output. But why should workers feel forced to work harder than they want? The answer has to do with asymmetric information.

For many types of work, such as that of middle management, employers are unable to attribute specific output to an individual worker, but can observe the group's output and the individual's membership in the group by observing his or her effort level. Since individual output can't be easily monitored, each worker is paid according to the group's average output. Workers who want to earn more income than their current group provides have no recourse except to join another group with higher average output. This "higher" group is identified by effort level. Entering such a higher-paying group requires workers to distinguish themselves from those of lower ability and productivity by expending more effort. Those with lower ability or productivity are unable to keep up the same level of effort as those of high ability and are left in lower-productivity groups—and the higher-ability workers end up expending more effort than they would want to otherwise.

Let's look at a representative case to see how action by workers to place themselves in the "proper" group determines their choice of effort and compensation. In Figure 5.15 the horizontal axis measures effort at levels 0 through 4. The vertical axis measures output (and income). High-productivity workers produce higher output with more effort, as the upper stepped function line illustrates; for low-productivity workers (the lower function line), output also increases with effort, but not so rapidly. Because higher income is utility-increasing and higher effort is utility-reducing, indifference curves in this diagram slope upward. We assume that, because of their abilities, high-productivity workers find it easier to expend more effort than do low-productivity workers. As a consequence, the need for additional income to compensate for increased work effort is lower for high-productivity workers. High-productivity workers' indifference curves are therefore flatter than those of low-productivity workers.

If all workers are low-productivity workers, the firm pays according to that group's output. The lower step function represents the effort-output

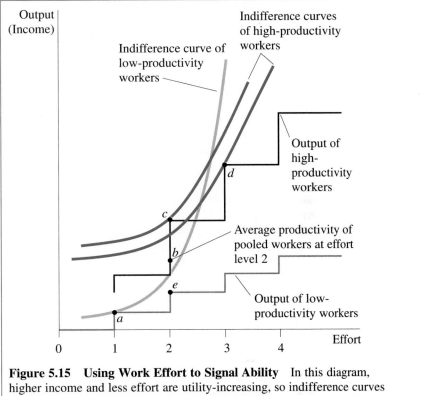

Figure 5.15   Using Work Effort to Signal Ability   In this diagram, higher income and less effort are utility-increasing, so indifference curves slope upward. High-ability workers work harder than is optimal to distinguish themselves from low-ability workers, who would otherwise share equal pay while contributing less output.

schedule for low productivity workers. Given this schedule, effort level 1 at point *a* is the low-productivity workers' optimal choice. On the other hand, if all workers are high-productivity workers, the upper step function shows average output (and therefore income schedule) for high productivity workers. High productivity workers choose effort level 2 at point *c*.

When there are both types of workers and the firm can distinguish between them at a glance, high-productivity workers will be observed to produce more output and supply higher effort than low-productivity workers. Moreover, each group will be paid according to its average output.

Equilibrium and Asymmetric Information

But what happens if employers cannot distinguish between workers? Equilibrium with separate productivity and pay schedules breaks down. In Figure 5.15, starting from the situation where workers were distinguishable, low-productivity workers anticipate that by increasing their effort to level 2 they will be identified as high-productivity workers and paid accordingly (point *c*), even though their contribution to output at level 2 is lower (point *e*). But with all workers working at effort level 2, average output drops to point *b*, and all workers are therefore paid income *b*. The resulting pooling of workers into one group at effort level 2 implies that the output of high-productivity workers is partially used to subsidize the income of low-productivity workers.

Faced with the lower utility of point *b*, high-productivity workers can choose effort level 3. Since low-productivity workers have lower utility at point *d* than at points *a* or *b*, they will not choose effort level 3. Thus the high-productivity workers can distinguish themselves from the low-productivity workers only by working harder than they otherwise would have. When productivity cannot be observed but effort can, high-productivity workers work at level 3, earning income at point *d*. Low-productivity workers work at level 1, earning income at point *a*.[33] In this way, the low- and high-productivity workers are again separated, though workers are working harder and have lower utility than they would if their separate productivities could be observed. ■

5.6 Is Labor the Only Resource Consumers Supply?

We observed earlier that in addition to labor services, consumers sometimes own other factors or resources that they can sell. For example, a household may own an office building whose space can be rented out to insurance firms, dentists, and other small businesses. Unlike the sale of labor time, selling these resources does not necessarily reduce utility directly. In this section, we see how the same model used to explain labor supply decisions that affect utility directly can be applied to nonlabor resource supply decisions.

Let's assume that Lorina owns an office building, and she faces a fixed market price for space. Lorina's supply decision is simple: rent out the entire building at the market price and use the proceeds to purchase other goods that enhance her utility. This is the right response because, if she leaves any part of the building unrented, she has less income and lower utility.[34]

Her decision problem can be seen from Figure 5.16. The horizontal axis measures the total amount of building space, *F*, that Lorina has available. Measuring the amount she supplies to the market from the right-hand edge, her income rises along the budget line drawn from I_0, which represents

▼
13. Draw a diagram explaining the decision to supply a factor that does not enter utility directly.

---

33. Since it is better for all high-productivity workers to move to effort level 3, none are left at effort level 2, and average output at level 2 drops to point *e*, which is less desirable to low-productivity workers than point *a*. They therefore shift back to point *a*.

34. Remember, we said that the resource does not enter utility directly. If it did—if, say, Lorina's family lived in part of the building—her decision would be the same as for labor supply. She would have to decide how much of the total available space to give up, taking into account the reduction in the space available for her family. This is just what we did for labor supply, where the total available was the household's time endowment.

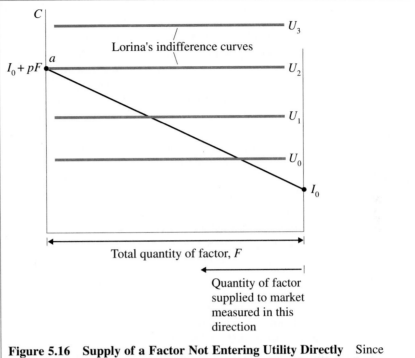

Figure 5.16 Supply of a Factor Not Entering Utility Directly Since the factor (building rental space) does not affect utility directly, Lorina's indifference curves are horizontal lines, showing utility increase for higher consumption of C. I_0 is Lorina's income from other sources. Her budget line rises from I_0 to $I_0 + pF$ as she sells more factor to the market, where F is the total quantity of factor available and p is its market price. Highest utility is reached at point a, where all of the factor is supplied.

Lorina's income from other sources. Lorina's indifference curves are lines U_0 through U_3. Since only C enters utility, her indifference curves are horizontal and rise with higher C. Lorina reaches her highest utility at point a, where she supplies all of her building space to the market.

In closing this chapter, it is interesting to note that by supplying factors other than labor, the household begins to look more like a firm in its decision making. In Lorina's case, for example, we could think of her business as supplying rental space for a profit. We might begin to consider other features of her situation, such as whether the amount of space she rents adds to her costs in any way. Perhaps, for example, she is responsible for cleaning and maintenance, and more rented space means more cleaning and upkeep. We also might want to consider whether Lorina could change the price that she can rent at by offering more or less space to the market. Maybe Lorina would like to rent less space if by so doing she can get a sufficiently higher price for what she does rent, making her rental income greater overall. These are all questions that properly fall under the heading of firm decision making, where profit is the objective. We turn to this next in Chapters 6 through 11.

Summary

Active Reading Guide numbers are given in parentheses at the end of each summary item.

1. The household labor supply decision can be explained as a utility-maximization problem using the same tools that we used to discuss the household's consumption choice. (1)

2. Utility-reducing labor is provided as a means to acquire income, which in turn is spent on utility-increasing goods. If we reinterpret the decision in terms of buying leisure by forgoing the income that could have been earned with that leisure time, the budget constraint becomes a relationship between the amount of money spent on consumption, the amount given up for leisure, and the household's income. (2)

3. Indifference curves between leisure and consumption (where consumption represents the consumer's spending on all other goods) show a declining marginal rate of substitution of leisure for consumption, do not cross, and exhibit positive marginal utility for leisure and consumption. Given the budget constraint and indifference curves, the household's optimization problem becomes a purchasing choice between leisure and consumption, which is resolved by choosing the point on the budget line giving highest utility. The resulting leisure choice and household labor supply are affected by the amount of nonlabor income available and by the wage rate. The income effect leads to a reduction in labor supply because higher income is partly spent on leisure (in the usual case where leisure is a normal good). The substitution effect always leads to greater labor supply for a higher wage because the wage rate is the price of leisure, and increasing the price of leisure while holding utility constant causes the household to buy less leisure. (3)

4. Using the same tools as in earlier chapters, we can draw the consumer's labor supply curve. For upward-sloping labor supply curves, the substitution effect is stronger than the income effect, meaning that the supply of labor rises with increased wages. At higher wage levels, however, it is possible that the income effect is larger than the

substitution effect, with leisure a normal good. In this case, the supply curve of labor becomes backward-bending, because higher wages lower the quantity of labor supplied. (4, 5)

5. The market supply curve of labor is the horizontal summation of the labor supply curves of all households in the market. (6)

6. The basic model of labor supply can be modified in various ways to take into account the specific budget constraints that different workers face. Modifications include workers who must choose between working a set number of hours and not working at all; workers who work different hours at different wages, such as at overtime rates; and workers who take into account the earnings of a spouse in deciding their own labor force activity. As a group, workers exercise control over the standard workday, the standard workweek, the number of holidays taken, and the nature of vacation time. (7)

7. Consumer surplus change for household labor supply resulting from a wage change is calculated as the area to the left of the supply curve of labor between the two wage rates. (8)

8. If the household uses time as an input in the consumption of goods, the model of labor supply is modified by increasing the price of the consumption good to reflect the time cost as well as the direct cost of consuming. The modification takes account of the (unlikely) possibility that the household may be able to purchase more consumption good than it has time to consume. (9)

9. Economic rent is the difference between what a factor is paid and the minimum necessary to induce the factor to be supplied for its present use. The opportunity cost of supplying a factor for a particular use is the amount that the factor could earn in the next best alternative. (10)

10. If information is perfect, factors receive pay based on the quality and quantity of the service they render. If there is asymmetric information so that the quality of a factor cannot be observed directly, the market may respond by creating a signal of quality. To be effective, the signal must be posi-

tively correlated with quality in the population. (11, 12)

11. The supply of a factor that does not enter utility directly is determined by the owner's deci-

sion to maximize the revenue from its sale. This implies selling all of the factor if the market price is fixed. (13)

Review Questions

*1. If leisure is an inferior good, does that mean that the labor supply curve must be upward-sloping? Explain.

2. The term "disutility of labor" is sometimes used in describing the labor supply decision. Using the utility function for leisure and consumption, and the time endowment for leisure and labor, give a definition of the disutility from increasing labor.

*3. What is the effect of each of the following on the worker's choice of labor supply?
   a) A tax of $100 per person per year
   b) A wage tax of one-third of labor earnings

4. In finding the substitution effect of a wage change, is the consumer's utility held fixed by adjusting labor or nonlabor income? Why?

*5. Explain how the income effect is likely to differ if you are:
   a) 64 years old
   b) 28 years old
   c) An unskilled female head of household with a preschool child

   d) A college-educated female head of household with a preschool child
   e) A college-educated male head of household with a wife and children

*6. Assume zero nonlabor income. A worker's marginal rate of substitution of hours of labor per day for income is given by $I/(L - 17.)$. If the wage rate is $10 per hour, how many hours of work per day will the worker supply?

*7. How does the method of constructing the market labor supply curve take into account an increase in labor force participation at higher wages?

8. How does the increase in consumer surplus for labor supply differ from consumer surplus for supply of a factor not entering utility?

9. If the opportunity cost of working at your present job is low, your economic rent will be high. Discuss.

Numerical and Graphing Exercises

*1. Write the household's budget constraint so that only labor hours and consumption appear. Graph the household's labor-consumption problem with labor on the horizontal axis and consumption on the vertical axis. (Hint: What changes in the orientation of the budget line and indifference curves?)

2. What would be the effect on the consumer's income and leisure-labor budget line if the tax rate were zero on earnings up to $5,000, 15 percent on earnings between $5,000 and $15,000, and 25 percent on earnings higher than $15,000? Assume the

worker's hourly wage is $15.

*3. Assume leisure is a normal good, and the income effect is stronger than the substitution effect for a consumer who is at his optimal position on the consumption good–leisure budget line. A tax on labor earnings is imposed. Graphically show whether the worker's before-tax income will rise or fall.

*4. A worker's wage rises 5 percent. What is the worker's consumer surplus increase from labor supply, as a percentage of labor income, if the worker's price elasticity of supply is (a) 0, (b) 0.5, or (c) 2?

* Asterisks are used to denote questions that are answered at the back of the book.

5. Arlene has 8,760 hours per year available to her and can work as much or as little as she wants at $10 per hour. An inheritance provides her an income of $5,000 per year. Compute enough points to derive Arlene's labor supply curve if she always spends two-thirds of her total income (time endowment plus nonlabor income) on leisure.

6. Using the labor supply model in the text, explain the choices of a worker who moonlights at a second job.

*7. Assume that a program for parental leave with half-pay is established at XYZ company. It allows workers to select up to two months' leave each year for a specified list of reasons, such as birth or adoption of a new child. Further, assuming that the leave is paid for by reducing the average wage of all workers at XYZ (the company hires temporary replacements) and that taking the leave is voluntary, draw the relevant budget lines and indifference curves to analyze the effect of the program (including whether leave is taken or not) on a worker with the option of taking parental leave and a worker without parental-leave options. (You may assume that all workers earn the same salary to simplify your answer.)

8. When effort was used as a job signal, high-productivity workers were able to separate themselves from low-productivity workers by finding a level of effort that rewarded them better than a grouping that pooled all workers together. This separation rewarded low-productivity workers less well. Use Figure 5.15 to show a choice of low-productivity preferences that would make this resolution impossible by eliminating equilibria that separated worker types.

INVESTIGATIONS II

A. Britain's Entry into the Common Market

> What are a country's gains from international trade? In the
> case of a single household, we found that consumer surplus
> measured the increase in utility from buying a good at market
> price rather than paying more. Is it possible to measure con-
> sumer surplus for an entire nation? This investigation shows
> that the answer is yes. Furthermore, the principles that apply
> are the same as those that apply to the household. If we are
> willing to say that a dollar's worth of gain to one citizen is
> equally as valuable as a dollar's worth of gain to another,
> then we can compute the national gains from trade by sum-
> ming the gains of all of the nation's citizens.

Price Comparison Shopping and International Trade

Most of us at one time or another have gone to a shopping mall to buy
clothes. We choose which mall to patronize by comparing the prices that we
expect to find at different malls. Moreover, although we normally don't have
to pay an entrance fee, we pay different amounts in the form of travel and
time costs to enter different malls. A similar situation sometimes faces
nations.

Consider the case of Britain's decision to enter the European Common
Market in 1973. The economic question British leaders had to answer at that
time was straightforward: how much was it worth to Britain to become a
member of the Common Market? With a few differences, this is the same
question that consumers face when choosing a shopping mall.[1] There is a
cost for getting to the mall, but the most consumers are willing to give up
for entry is their consumer surplus from being able to buy at the prices
prevailing inside. If these are better than what consumers face outside, they
will be willing to pay an entrance fee. If prices inside are the same as outside,
consumers would not be willing to pay any entrance fee at all. If prices inside
are *worse* than prices outside, then consumers would have to *be paid* to enter
the mall to do their shopping.

---

1. The European Common Market is an association of 12 European nations dedicated to free
trade between member countries and applying a common external tariff structure to trade
with nonmembers. Unlike Saturday-afternoon shopping at a mall, membership in the Common Market was expected to last for a relatively long time, if not be permanent.

In the case of a nation joining an association like the Common Market, the membership fee takes the form of transfers of certain customs duties and taxes to the central authority. The prices that Britain faced after joining were different from its pre-entry prices because of the existence of common tariffs for Common Market members. These kept prices inside the union different from those that prevailed on world markets, because goods coming into union countries from nonmember countries were subject to customs duties. Membership would require Britain to have the same tariffs as all the other countries involved.

Consumer Surplus Revisited

In Chapter 4 we described household consumer surplus as the excess of what the household would be willing to pay for a good over what it actually pays in the marketplace. The change in consumer surplus from being able to buy at a lower price rather than a higher price therefore represented the gain to the consumer from trading at the lower price. A simple formula for measuring the gains from Britain's Common Market membership (trading at the different set of prices) can be constructed in essentially the same way that we constructed it for the household. Applied to a country, this measure is called the *gains from trade*. To understand the formula, consider Figure II.1, where $X^0 = (C^0, F^0)$ is the initial consumption point of the consumer, C is quantity of clothing consumed, F is quantity of food consumed, and X^1 is the final consumption point (in this case drawn on a higher indifference curve). Initial relative prices are represented by the tangent budget line l_1 passing through point X^0. Final prices are given by line l_4, tangent to the curve passing through point X^1. Since budget line l_4 is less steep than l_1, we know that the relative price of clothing is lower in the final position and the price of food relatively higher. We also draw the budget lines l_2 and l_3 using final prices. Our measure of the increase in utility is the difference in income between the budget lines l_2 and l_4, measured by the distance between them. This difference is $P^1 X^1 - e(P^1, U^0)$, where $P^1 X^1$ is shorthand for the sum of values $p_C C^1 + p_F F^1$ for final prices (p_C, p_F). Using the fact that income equals expenditure as discussed in Chapter 4,[2] this difference equals the consumer's income change between the two positions plus consumer surplus, $(I^1 - I^0) + e(P^0, U^0) - e(P^1, U^0)$. The formula for difference in budget lines therefore gives us consumer surplus in the usual case that income is unchanging, but also covers the case where income changes. Returning to the figure, the distance between l_4 and l_2 also can be broken into the distance between l_2 and l_3 plus the distance between l_3 and l_4, so that

$$\text{Gains from trade} = (P^1 X^1 - P^1 X^0) + [P^1 X^0 - e(P^1, U^0)].$$

To derive this gains-from-trade formula, we have used nothing but simple substitution and the properties of the expenditure function. The same figure

---

2. Recall that $e(P^0, U^0) = P^0 X^0 = I^0$ and $e(P^1, U^1) = P^1 X^1 = I^1$ because $P^0 X^0$ and $P^1 X^1$ are the amounts of money spent on all goods in the initial and final situations, respectively.

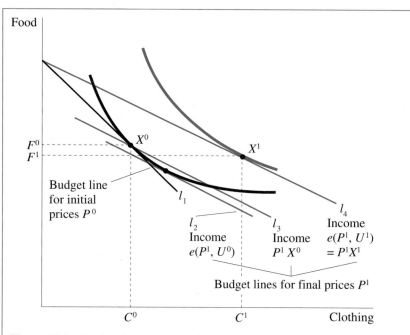

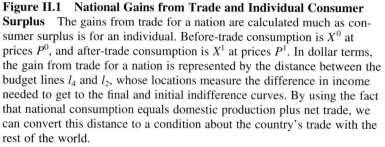

**Figure II.1   National Gains from Trade and Individual Consumer
Surplus**   The gains from trade for a nation are calculated much as consumer surplus is for an individual. Before-trade consumption is X^0 at
prices P^0, and after-trade consumption is X^1 at prices P^1. In dollar terms,
the gain from trade for a nation is represented by the distance between the
budget lines l_4 and l_2, whose locations measure the difference in income
needed to get to the final and initial indifference curves. By using the fact
that national consumption equals domestic production plus net trade, we
can convert this distance to a condition about the country's trade with the
rest of the world.

and formula can be applied to a country engaged in international trade. The
only difference is that in place of two goods, the terms such as P^1X^1 relate
to more than two goods and we must take into account gains for households
in the country.

Gains from Trade: The National Version of Consumer Surplus

Summing the formula derived for an individual over all consumers in the
country gives us $(P^1X^1 - P^1X^0) + [P^1X^0 - \Sigma_i e_i(P^1, U_i^0)]$, where the
quantities now refer to totals for the country and $\Sigma_i e_i(P^1, U_i^0)$ is the sum of
$e_i(P^1, U_i^0)$ over all households i. How does international trade matter to the
country's gains from trade? For a country, total consumption comes from

either domestic production, Y, or from net imports, Z.[3] Thus $X^0 = Y^0 + Z^0$ and $X^1 = Y^1 + Z^1$. Placing these into the formula for X^0 and X^1, we find that a country's gains from trade are

Welfare gains from comparing final trade position to initial trade position $=$
$$P^1(Y^1 - Y^0) + P^1(Z^1 - Z^0) + [P^1X^0 - \Sigma_i e_i(P^1, U_i^0)].$$

| Value of change in domestic production bundle | Value of change in external trade bundle | Non-negative term |

Britain's Entry into the Common Market

Our derivation means that to calculate national gains from trade requires final prices, P^1, the country's production in the initial and final situations, Y^0 and Y^1, and the country's trade, Z^0 and Z^1. Treating 1972, the year before Britain joined the Common Market, as the initial period and treating the years 1973 to 1979 as the final period, we can tabulate the effects as in Table II.1, which uses data from the British Central Statistical Office.[4]

We note several things about Table II.1. First, the value of the change in domestic production, shown in column 5, is always positive. This is what we would expect from theory. Because the producers of the country choose to produce the output that has the highest value at prices P^1, the value of their output, P^1Y^1, is greater than the value of alternative choices of production, including the value of output Y^0, P^1Y^0. Next, the term $[P^1X^0 - \Sigma_i e_i(P^1, U_i^0)]$ $= \Sigma_i [P^1X_i^0 - e_i(P^1, U_i^0)]$ (not shown in the table) is necessarily non-negative, because $P^1X_i^0$ is the cost to the ith household of reaching its initial utility by buying at final prices what it initially bought, and $e_i(P^1, U_i^0)$ is the least cost of getting to initial utility at final prices.

With two of the three terms on the right-hand side of the formula non-negative, it follows that if $P^1(Z^1 - Z^0)$ is positive (that is, $P^1Z^1 > P^1Z^0$), the country *must* gain compared to the initial position.[5] In essence, this is a revealed preference condition for the country, where net imports Z replace consumption X in the condition. From the point of view of world trade, consumption of the country in world markets is its trade Z. If the country chose to purchase Z^1 on world markets when it could have spent less and

---

3. If consumption of the two goods is x_1 and x_2, then $x_1 = y_1 + z_1$ and $x_2 = y_2 + z_2$, where y_1 is domestic production of good 1 and z_1 is net imports of good 1. This means that z_1 is a positive number if imports are positive, and negative if the country is an exporter of good 1. The same is true for good 2. Writing the bundles $X = (x_1, x_2)$, $Y = (y_1, y_2)$, and $Z = (z_1, z_2)$, the two relationships above become $X = Y + Z$.

4. Figures for the term $P^1X^0 - e(P^1, U^0)$ can also be estimated using information about British consumption patterns. We omit discussion of this here, but for the years in question the value of this term averaged about one-third of 1 percent of Britain's Gross Domestic Product.

5. That is, gain in the sense that the gains of those whose utility increases outweigh the losses of those whose utilities fall, when utility change is measured in dollar terms as assumed.

Table II.1 Welfare Effects Following Britain's Entry into the Common Market, 1973–1979

(1) Year	(2) P^1Z^1	(3) P^1Z^0	(4) $P^1(Z^1 - Z^0)$	(5) $P^1(Y^1 - Y^0)$	(6) Sum of Columns 4 and 5	(7) GDP	(8) Column 6 as % of GDP
1973	2,155.50	2,406.80	− 251.30	3,403.00	3,151.70	64,258.00	4.90%
1974	4,760.70	6,149.30	− 1,388.60	2,598.00	1,209.40	74,414.00	1.63%
1975	2,422.00	5,579.70	− 3,157.70	1,824.00	− 1,333.70	93,954.00	− 1.42%
1976	2,038.70	7,466.30	− 5,427.60	3,519.00	− 1,908.60	111,245.00	− 1.72%
1977	− 483.80	8,569.10	− 9,052.90	5,807.00	− 3,245.90	126,111.00	− 2.57%
1978	− 2,031.90	6,645.80	− 8,677.70	10,331.00	1,653.30	144,442.00	1.14%
1979	− 368.20	6,105.90	− 6,474.10	13,565.00	7,090.90	163,647.00	4.33%

purchased Z^0, then the country is better off than it was in the situation when it chose Z^0. Comparing P^1Z^1 to P^1Z^0 is also related to the Paasche index of trade, since at final prices the quantity index of net imports is given by P^1Z^1/P^1Z^0.

The second thing to notice about the British figures is that in the years immediately following 1972, $P^1(Z^1 - Z^0)$ was negative. In other words, Britain's trade opportunities were less helpful to its welfare in those years than before it joined. This was both because the prices Britain faced once inside the Common Market were not as favorable to Britain, and because of the income transfers after membership. Overall, the changes in welfare reported in column (b) for Britain in the years after 1972 are mixed. In three years Britain was worse off than before, and in four years Britain was better off. On average, for the period 1973 to 1979, Britain was better off compared to 1972 by 0.9 percent of its Gross Domestic Product.

The change in welfare for Britain compared to 1972 is not large relative to British income. This is partly attributable to the fact that we are comparing British welfare to a situation in which Britain was *already* trading. If we had made the comparison to an initial situation in which Britain had *no* trade dealings with the rest of the world, the gains from trade would be much larger. In that case, the formula for gains would differ: Z^0 would consist entirely of zeros, since the initial situation was one of no trade.

Studies by economists indicate that, for many nations, the ability to trade with other nations raises national welfare as much as 25 percent. For large nations like the United States, the figure is probably less than 10 or 15 percent. For the tiniest of "nations," a single individual, the ability to trade one's labor services in exchange for goods and services raises utility by many multiples of the income that the individual could achieve in total isolation from others. In this case, obviously, the gains from trade are enormous.

Suggestions for Further Investigation. (a) If you wanted to evaluate the term $[P^1X^0 - \Sigma_i e_i(P^1, U_i^0)]$ in the formula for gains from trade, how might you go about it? (Hint: Recall that it measures the distance between l_2 and l_3

in Figure II.1. If you knew the price changes involved and had knowledge of representative demand, what would this allow you to do?) (b) If in the final situation, but not the original one, the domestic country paid income transfers to another country, how would this change the domestic country's trade Z and the size of its gains from trade? (Hint: $P^1Z^1 = T$, where transfer T is a negative number if the country gives another country income, and PZ is the sum of values of imports less the sum of values of exports of the country in question.)

B. The Effects of a Negative Income Tax

One of the great ironies of public welfare programs is that the act of giving money to low-income households necessarily subsidizes and therefore "rewards" them for being in the low-income state. Straight application of microeconomic principles would say that taxing is the way to discourage an activity and subsidizing it is the way to encourage it. Since there is no way to give money to low-income households without in some way "rewarding" the fact of low earnings, we are left with a fundamental dilemma of trying to devise a welfare program that provides aid without discouraging earnings. This investigation examines the economics of a negative income tax as the basis for a national welfare plan, in order to see why we do not have such a program in spite of its apparent attractiveness.

Of Self-reliance and Social Safety Nets

By far the greatest cause of low income is lack of labor earnings. Roughly seventy-five percent of income in the United States is earned as a reward for labor,[6] and the overwhelming majority of households earn the bulk of their income by labor force participation. A study of American families found that of the 0.7 percent of families that were in poverty each year of the 10-year sample period, 49 percent were unmarried mothers with children, 32 percent were disabled, and 22 percent were elderly females (over the age of 65).[7] In each case, these groups represent individuals who are prevented from working for some reason. Considering that there are probably few elderly unmarried mothers with children, the overlap between these two categories is likely to be small. Even allowing for overlap, the three categories taken together therefore probably account for more than 90 percent of the always-poor group.

6. Compensation of employees amounted to 73.8 percent of national income in 1990, according to *Economic Report of the President, 1992,* Washington, D.C.: U.S. Government Printing Office, 1992, Table B-22.
7. *Five Thousand American Families: Patterns of Economic Progress,* Ann Arbor: Survey Research Center, Institute for Social Research, University of Michigan, 1981, Vol. 9, p. 112.

As of 1990, the poverty level for a family of four stood at $13,359.[8] This means that a family of four earning a total income of less than $13,359 per year is considered to be in poverty. Unskilled labor earns about $5.00 per hour ($10,000 per year), and frequently more, so that two adults, one working full-time and one working half-time at this wage, are capable of providing the poverty level of income. Nevertheless, let us assume that for some reason a family's income is below the poverty level, and we wish to provide it additional income paid for by taxes taken from other working families. We can examine the likely effect of a welfare program by considering two alternatives for a representative family of four: a flat stipend and a negative income tax.

Program 1: Flat Stipend

One approach is simply to give low-income families income equal to the difference between their earnings and the poverty level. Figure II.2 shows us the resulting labor supply decision for a low-income family, an average-income family, and a high-income family. Each family works 2,000 hours per year (50 40-hour weeks) but at a different wage. The low-income family earns less than the poverty amount of $13,359 for a family of four. The family with average income earns $41,000 per year for full-time work, and the high-income family earns more. We assume that the families are identical in their preferences; the only difference among them is that they face different wages and different budget constraints.

The low-income family is below the poverty level by the vertical distance between point a and the horizontal line showing $13,359 per year income. Only if work exceeds point d will the low-income family have income higher than $13,359.

Under the flat-stipend program, a family receives enough money to bring its income to $13,359 regardless of its preprogram earnings. Once the program becomes operational, then, families learn that their income will remain $13,359 even if they earn nothing themselves. For the low-income family, the effective budget constraint becomes the darkened line edf. The optimal economic response of the low income family will be to move to point e, where utility is U_1. In fact, from the diagram we see that any family whose preprogram utility is U_1 or less will find it optimal to cease work and move to point e, including families who were earning more than $13,359 before the program. (If their budget line were drawn tangent to the indifference curve in the figure, it would show U_1 families earning $22,000.) The net result is that the number of families needing assistance will increase, and the cost of the program will rise to the full $13,359 for each family on the program. Because the average-income family and the high-income family

---

8. U.S. Department of Commerce, Economic and Statistics Administration, Bureau of the Census, *Poverty in the United States: 1990,* Current Population Reports, Consumer Income Series P-60, No. 175, Washington, D.C.: U.S. Government Printing Office, August 1991, p. 194.

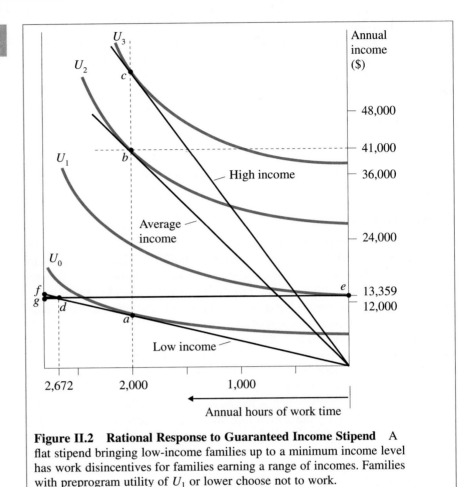

Figure II.2 Rational Response to Guaranteed Income Stipend A flat stipend bringing low-income families up to a minimum income level has work disincentives for families earning a range of incomes. Families with preprogram utility of U_1 or lower choose not to work.

can achieve greater utility by working, the program will not affect them, apart from the taxes that they pay to support the low-income families on the program.

Notice that our analysis did not require that low-income families be any different in their preferences than other families. We have not said that low-income families are unwilling to work. Indeed, they are just as careful to optimize as average- and high-income families. The fact is, however, that being given $13,359 per year with no work gives higher utility to the family on the program than earning the same income with work. A flat-stipend program would be enormously costly to pay for because of the inducement it creates for many families to cease work and depend entirely on the program for their needs.

Program 2: Negative Income Tax

The flat-stipend program had two undesirable features: First, for low-income workers, earnings from labor up to point d in Figure II.2 would not increase family income. Effectively, this is a 100-percent tax on labor earnings for low-income workers! It is unsurprising that rational households respond to the program as we described. Second, the program would be extremely costly to administer, taxing working families heavily to pay for nonworking families. In our next program, therefore, we seek to lower the effective tax rate on labor earnings by giving to each worker a stipend or subsidy amount S, as before, but allowing workers to keep some of their labor earnings.[9] We assume that labor earnings wL are taxed at the rate t, where t is less than 1. Under this program, the after-tax income of the consumer can be written as

$$\text{Program after-tax income} = S + wL - twL.$$

In other words, the household's after-tax income equals the stipend plus labor earnings less taxes. Households receive net payments from the government if $S - twL$ is positive (that is, the households pay a negative income tax), and they pay net taxes if $S - twL$ is negative. In terms of Figure II.2, the effect of the negative income tax is to replace the horizontal line at eg by a sloping line (not drawn, the slope implies greater income for greater work) starting with point e at stipend S.

By reducing the marginal tax rate to t rather than 100 percent, the negative income tax reduces some of the work disincentive for program recipients. The smaller t is, the smaller the work disincentive. Lowering t too much, however, will not generate enough taxes to pay for the program.

A Representative Economy

To examine the feasibility of the negative income tax, we can apply it to a representative economy consisting of 20 families. Assume that these families each have four members, so that we can continue to use $13,359 as the poverty level. Then we can distribute incomes to the families in such a way as to mimic the actual distribution of income for families in the United States.[10]

9. The program is called a negative income tax program because each household starts with a "negative tax" payment of the stipend amount S.
10. Dividing families into quintiles by income, the income of each fifth of the families in the sample matches the income of the corresponding fifth of families in the United States in 1990, with the income of the lowest family in the quintile equaling the cutoff for that quintile among families in the United States. Although individual families move into and out of particular income levels (families just starting out, for example, usually begin at lower income levels than they achieve later), the overall distribution of family incomes is remarkably stable from year to year. The most productive fifth of families earn 44.6 percent of total family income; the second fifth earns 23.7 percent; the third fifth earns 16.5 percent; and the fourth and fifth fifth earn 10.6 and 4.6 percent, respectively. The top 5 percent of families produce 17.9 percent of total family income. Median family income was $34,213 in 1990, and mean family income was $41,506.

In the representative economy in Table II.2, we will be deciding how much to tax some of the families in order to give income to the others and still supply the general tax needs of the government. In 1990 federal expenditures were $1,323 billion, of which $147.3 billion were income security outlays. Since the negative income tax presumably will replace the other income programs, we can assume that the remaining expenditures are $1,175.7 billion. Tax collections in 1990, other than from individual income taxes, were $564.4 billion, meaning that $1,175.7 − $564.4 = $611.3 billion is needed from individual income taxes to cover federal expenditures. In order for the income of our 20 families to equal the income of all households in the United States in 1990, we need to enlarge our figures for the 20-family economy so that they become 86.569 million families. Alternatively, scaling $611.3 billion to the level of 20 families means that the 20 families must provide $141,230 in federal taxes beyond the needs of the income program.

Program Objectives Versus Ability to Pay

So what does the program look like? We start by examining the effect of a $11,070-per-year stipend with the marginal federal tax on earnings set at 28 percent.[11] Since Social Security taxes (the employee's and the employer's contribution combined) are 15.3 percent on income,[12] this implies a combined marginal tax on income of roughly 50 percent, if state, local, and other taxes such as sales taxes are conservatively assumed to be about 7 percent. The true figure could be higher, depending on location. In some states, for example, the marginal income tax rate alone can reach this level, and sales taxes are an additional 5 to 8 percent.

Assuming a perfectly inelastic supply of labor and no work-reducing income effects of the transfer,[13] the progam produces an after-tax income above the poverty level for all our hypothetical families, ranging from $13,364 to $103,735.55, as shown in Table II.2. Notice, however, that setting federal taxes at 28 percent meant that only 8 of the families will be paying federal taxes to support the net payments to the other 12! Moreover, the program as a whole will raise only $48 billion of the $611 billion needed in federal

11. The 1990 federal marginal tax rate on highest incomes was 28 percent.
12. In 1990, income up to $51,300 was subject to Social Security taxes. Of the total 15.3 percent tax, 7.65 percent was paid on the employee's behalf by the employer, and another 7.65 percent was paid by the employee out of his or her wages.
13. Initial tax rates seen by each family are assumed to be 7.65 percent for the employee's half of Social Security tax up to earnings of $51,300, plus 7 percent for other taxes. Federal taxes are assumed to be 0 percent for income up to $14,000, reflecting the approximate standard deduction and personal exemptions for a family of four; 15 percent for income between $14,000 and $48,000; and 28 percent for higher incomes. Under the negative income tax, all federal tax rates become the same. Thus low-income workers receive a stipend but face a higher federal marginal tax rate. The table assumes that moving from, say, 15 percent federal tax rate to 28 percent has no effect on the number of work hours or pretax income, just as the stipend itself is assumed not to lower work hours. This assumption works in the direction of making the program more viable than it would truly be in the face of work disincentive effects.

Table II.2   Effect of Negative Income Tax on 20 Families Representative of the United States in 1990

Family	Preprogram Earnings	Net Income from Federal Program	Other Taxes	Program After-Tax Income
1	$4,000.00	$9,950.00	($586.00)	$13,364.00
2	$8,000.00	$8,830.00	($1,172.00)	$15,658.00
3	$12,000.00	$7,710.00	($1,758.00)	$17,952.00
4	$14,000.00	$7,150.00	($2,051.00)	$19,099.00
5	$16,850.00	$6,352.00	($2,468.53)	$20,733.48
6	$21,000.00	$5,190.00	($3,076.50)	$23,113.50
7	$24,000.00	$4,350.00	($3,516.00)	$24,834.00
8	$26,000.00	$3,790.00	($3,809.00)	$25,981.00
9	$29,500.00	$2,810.00	($4,321.75)	$27,988.25
10	$32,000.00	$2,110.00	($4,688.00)	$29,422.00
11	$36,000.00	$990.00	($5,274.00)	$31,716.00
12	$39,500.00	$10.00	($5,786.75)	$33,723.25
13	$43,000.00	($970.00)	($6,299.50)	$35.730.50
14	$46,000.00	($1,810.00)	($6,739.00)	$37,451.00
15	$51,000.00	($3,210.00)	($7,471.50)	$40,318.50
16	$57,000.00	($4,890.00)	($7,914.45)	$44,195.55
17	$62,750.00	($6,500.00)	($8,316.95)	$47,933.05
18	$70,000.00	($8,530.00)	($8,824.45)	$52,645.55
19	$89,000.00	($13,850.00)	($10,154.45)	$64,995.55
20	$148,600.00	($30,538.00)	($14,326.45)	$103.735.55
Total	$830,200.00	($11,056.00)	($108,554.28)	$710,589.73

	For 20 Families	For Entire Economy (billions)
Federal taxes collected	$232,456.00	$1,006.17
Federal program outlays	($221,400.00)	($958.32)
Net federal taxes	$11,056.00	$47.86
Minimum federal tax needs	$141,230.00	$611.30

Note: Assumptions are as follows: The stipend level is $11,070. The marginal federal tax rate is 28 percent, and the combined Social Security tax rate is 15.3 percent. Other taxes amount to 7 percent, producing a total marginal tax rate of 50.3 percent. For employees, the Social Security tax is applied at the employee rate of 0.0765 up to earnings of $51,300. Further conditions are explained in footnote 13.

revenues. This figure is less than 9 percent of the actual individual income tax revenues for 1990. Clearly the program is too generous to be financed at this level. Either the stipend will have to be reduced or the tax rate on earnings increased, or both.

Table II.3 **Effects of Different Tax Rates and Stipend Amounts on Family Income Tax Revenues**

(a) **After-Tax Annual Family Income of Lowest-Income Family**
(b) **Federal Tax Revenues (Net of Program in Billions of Dollars)**

Stipend Amount		Federal Tax Rate							
		15%	20%	25%	30%	35%	40%	45%	50%
$4,000	(a)	$6,814	$6,614	$6,414	$6,214	$6,014	$5,814	$5,614	$5,414
	(b)	193	372	552	732	911	1091	1271	1450
$6,000	(a)	$8,814	$8,614	$8,414	$8,214	$8,014	$7,814	$7,614	$7,414
	(b)	20	200	437	559	738	918	1098	1277
$8,000	(a)	$10,814	$10,614	$10,414	$10,214	$10,014	$9,814	$9,614	$9,414
	(b)	− 154	26	206	385	565	745	925	1104
$10,000	(a)	$12,814	$12,614	$12,414	$12,214	$12,014	$11,814	$11,614	$11,414
	(b)	− 236	− 147	33	213	392	572	751	931
$12,000	(a)	$14,814	$14,614	$14,414	$14,214	$14,014	$13,814	$13,614	**$13,414**
	(b)	− 500	− 320	− 141	39	219	398	578	**758**

Note: The northeastern region of the table, marked off by the slanted line, contains tax-and-stipend combinations that result in the collection of more than $600 billion in federal taxes. The entries in the bottom section are those that leave the lowest-income family with $13,359 or more in annual after-tax income. The figures in **boldface** show the only combination that satisfies both of these conditions.

Table II.3 shows the effects of changing the marginal federal tax rate and the stipend amount. In each row, the top number gives the income of the lowest-income family, and the bottom number shows the effect on federal revenues. The combinations of stipend and marginal tax rate that keep the lowest family income above the poverty level appear at the bottom of the table, where stipends are high. The combinations of stipend and marginal tax rate that generate enough tax to support the program and the government appear in the right-hand corner of the table marked off with a slanted line. Searching for an overlap of these two regions produces only the lower-right-hand cell, where the stipend is set at $12,000 and the federal tax rate is 50 percent. With federal taxes at 50 percent, Social Security and other taxes raise the total tax rate to over two-thirds of income! We conclude that this is too high a tax rate for us to assume no work disincentive effects, as we have done so far. It is also too high to be acceptable to the American public. We can see, therefore, that either the program cannot keep all families above the poverty line, or taxes must be set at unacceptable levels. There is no way to meet both tax and welfare objectives.

Suggestions for Further Investigation. Our analysis has necessarily been something of a back-of-the envelope calculation. What type of effects might be added? (a) If the data and methodology were made to look even more closely like the American economy, do you think this would make the negative income tax idea more or less feasible? (b) If we somehow taxed the rich more, would this solve our problem? (Hint: If we generously define families with income in the top 5 percent of the population as ''rich'' (a middle-aged college-educated couple, each earning $54,000, for example, would be in this group), how much of annual federal expenditures could be paid for if we taxed 100 percent of their income?)

PART THREE

DECISIONS OF THE FIRM MANAGER

This part examines the optimization decisions of firms. Chapter 6 opens with a discussion of why the firm exists, its decision-making philosophy, and the economic information about production and cost as seen by the firm manager. This material applies to any firm, regardless of what type of market it is in. Depending on whether the market environment is perfectly competitive, monopolistic, monopolistically competitive, or oligopolistic, the firm competes in different ways. Chapters 7–10 cover the different decisions that firms make in these different types of markets, including choice of quantity, price, pricing strategies, advertising, product variety, and strategic competition in markets with few sellers. Chapter 11 closes with the firm's decision about input demand.

CHAPTER 6

▼

The Firm's Decision-Making Environment

Profits, production, and cost—these are concerns of the firm manager. Maximizing profit is the firm's objective; knowing the relationship between input and output is necessary for the firm to compute cost; and cost is needed to compute profit. This chapter begins by investigating the nature of the firm and its profit-maximizing objective. It then introduces the production function and, after clarifying what we mean by economic profits, opportunity costs, and forward-looking decision making, it brings in the cost function. The production function and cost function are the two main tools for summarizing production and cost information. The emphasis in the latter part of the chapter is on tracing the relevant links between inputs and output, and between output and cost. After reading this chapter, you should be familiar with the basic information tools available to the firm for decision making.

ACTIVE READING GUIDES

After reading this chapter, you should be able to answer the Active Reading Guides listed below. These guides also appear in the page margins, near the material to which they refer.

1. How is a firm's profit maximization linked to utility maximization? What impact does asymmetric information have on the firm manager's behavior?

2. Define the production function, total product, marginal product, and average product. Draw curves relating the last three.

3. Explain what causes rising marginal product and what causes diminishing marginal product.

4. Use isoquants to explain the marginal rate of technical substitution, degree of factor substitution, and returns to scale.

5. What is economic profit, and how is it related to opportunity costs and sunk costs?

6. Explain how the principle of cost minimization gets us from output levels to the cost function.

7. Define MC, AC, AVC, and AFC, and draw them in relation to one another and to total cost.

8. Why is there no fixed cost in the long run?

9. Draw a diagram relating short-run and long-run total cost curves, and a diagram relating short-run and long-run average cost curves and marginal cost curves.

10. What are the implications of decreasing, constant, and increasing returns to scale for average cost?

11. What are economies of scope?

6.1 The Firm and Its Objectives

Before you were born, your grandfather started out as a clerk selling hardware to local merchants and individuals. With the help and urging of local bankers, he eventually bought out the store where he worked. Before long, representatives of larger firms whose goods he sold induced him to expand into the selling of specialized pieces of machinery and implements. From his profits he eventually started a peripheral manufacturing operation to make some of the implements that he sold. The manufacturing aspect of the business grew and subsequently became the entire operation. He passed the enterprise on to your father. Under his guidance, the business grew to employ more than a hundred individuals and achieve multiple millions of dollars in annual sales. You are in college studying for your degree (including taking a course in economics) when you learn the sad news that your father has suffered a heart attack, leaving you control of the business. You can get all the raw data that you want about your father's business from the engineers and accountants who work for the firm, but they are looking to you now to know what to provide and how to use it. What do you tell them? Although managing a business is clearly not the same as studying microeconomics, the principles of the firm we consider in this and succeeding chapters provide necessary guidance for understanding the objectives and workings of firms.

Formal theories of the firm mostly start from the premise that firms seek to maximize profit, much as households seek to maximize utility. Implicit in this is the assumption that firms exist as distinct decision-making entities. But why do firms exist at all? We start our study here.

EXPLORATION: Why Do Firms Exist?

At one extreme, we could imagine a society without any decision making or planning by firms. Instead of an engineering firm, consisting of managers, public relations and marketing people, a drafting shop, and field engineers, we could imagine individuals with each of these skills contracting for their respective services as independent consultants. The relations between workers would be governed exclusively by market transactions. At the other extreme, we could imagine a centrally planned economy where, in essence, the entire economy was one great firm directed by the central planner. In this economy the interactions of workers would be governed exclusively by the internal hierarchy of planning within the firm. The more familiar case where different firms exist as separate entities would be in between, with internal operations governed by planning and external relations with other firms and consumers governed by market transactions.

> A ***firm*** *is a business enterprise consisting of one or more individuals working as a decision-making unit to produce goods or services.*

Since commercial undertakings throughout history and in different places and cultures have tended to organize themselves as firms, firms must somehow make it easier to provide the coordination and planning to produce output more efficiently. On the other hand, the events in Russia and Eastern Europe over the last 70 years, underscored by the dramatic changes there in the late 1980s and early 1990s, demonstrate that there are limits to the size of effective planning units. Individuals reap few benefits from economy-wide central planning, and they strive instead for the freedom and responsiveness of a market economy.

Behavioral studies of why firms exist in the sizes and forms that they do are a fascinating part of the subject of industrial organization. Unfortunately, we do not have the space for an in-depth treatment here. Thus, although we recognize that the reason for the firm to exist as a planning unit is an important question in its own right, in this text we will simply take the firm as given and explain its activities using familiar tools relating to its objectives and constraints. ■

Profit Maximization

▼
1. How is a firm's profit maximization linked to utility maximization? What impact does asymmetric information have on the firm manager's behavior?

What do firms want? Theories of the firm generally start from the assumption that firms make choices to maximize profits, where profit is the difference between the firm's revenues and its costs. For example, consider Betty, an entrepreneur who starts a small business. She employs labor and capital to produce business note pads. Although Betty could operate her business in a way that does *not* maximize profits, this would leave her with lower income. We could imagine reasons why Betty might not maximize profits (perhaps she is still learning the note-pad business, or perhaps to her note pads are an art form rather than a moneymaking venture), but a theory based on non-maximization of profits would be open to far more criticisms than one based on profit maximization. In essence, profit maximization derives from the link that *higher income means higher utility for the firm owner.*

Profits, Principal-Agent Relations, and Imperfect Monitoring

Although profit maximization is probably the single best assumption to describe firm objectives, it is not perfect. In previous chapters we emphasized the role that asymmetric information can play in altering the usual assumptions. In this case, too, one reason why firms may not always maximize profits has to do with our old friend, asymmetric information.

In small enterprises, the owner and the manager may be one and the same. The connection between higher profit and higher income is strong, and the incentives of the owner-manager are never subject to information asymmetries because both owner and manager have the same interests and the same information. After all, they are the same person! Most large firms, in contrast, are owned by one group of people and managed by another. A third group may work for the firm, neither owning nor managing it. Moreover, the firm's owners, managers, and workers may have different and conflicting objectives. Situations in which one person (the agent) performs tasks for another (the principal) are referred to as *principal-agent relations.*

Principal-agent relations often involve issues of effectively monitoring the agent's actions and setting up a contract to give the agent incentive to perform in the principal's interests. In Chapter 5 we saw that when individual worker productivity could not be monitored, higher-productivity workers had to expend more effort to distinguish themselves from lower-productivity workers. We now consider how monitoring that involves the owners and managers of a firm relates to profit maximization.

The firm manager often has better information than the owner about the firm's operations, but also has different interests. The owner is probably concerned about the firm's overall profitability, while the manager's interests relate to his or her own income and career advancement. Since it is costly for the owner to monitor the manager's actions directly, the firm owner typically reviews performance on the basis of a list of observable statistics, such as quarterly profits, sales, and other financial data. Whatever the evaluation centers on, however, there is room for the manager to optimize the performance of those statistics at the expense of the owner.

For example, let us say that you are newly appointed to head the Beta Division of XYZ Corporation. Two years from now, you anticipate competing with the managers of the Delta and Gamma divisions for a promotion. The promotion will be based on how each division has performed. How could you win the promotion? One strategy is for you to do whatever you can to make Beta Division's quarterly profits as high as possible in the next two years, even if that means running the long-run health of the division into the ground.[1] You would get the promotion, but someone else would have to pick up the pieces after you had been promoted out of the division. Such strategies are risky but far from unknown. Your success, though, depends on your superiors' information about your division's long-run profitability and health.

Manager's and owners' objectives can differ in other ways. The manager may want to follow a strategy of covering his or her flanks. This negative strategy aims at protecting against criticism. It entails making the kind of decisions that, though dull and unimaginative, are conventional and therefore difficult to criticize. Such decisions also may not maximize profits. In general, it is harder to prove fault by pointing to lost opportunities than it is by pointing to a decision involving a responsible risk that, in the outcome, turned bad.[2]

EXPLORATION: Asymmetric Information, Monitoring, and Incentives

In the case of the information asymmetry between managers and owners, the market has developed a number of monitoring and manager-compensation structures that seek to limit abuse and induce managers to profit maximize. For instance, independent accounting companies regularly audit firms' financial data, and it is a serious matter if the independent auditor cannot certify the company's books. Boards of directors serve a monitoring function when they periodically meet to review the actions of the company's management. These boards, elected by the company's shareholders, typically consist of business leaders and executive officers of other companies.

As an incentive to improve their performance, managers might be offered stock in the company as part of their compensation. Thus, the better the company performs, the higher the manager's reward. End-of-year bonuses serve a similar purpose: the better the company does, the higher the bonus at the end of the year.

Successful firms may be maximizing profits without being directly conscious of it. In most industries, firms that do not maximize profits will have lower returns on the money tied up in their physical plant and equipment than their profit-maximizing competitors. Firms earning higher returns will tend to be rewarded by growing and attracting more financial backing. Over time, the market will tend to consist of profit-maximizing firms as unprofitable firms get weeded out. Also, the market for buying and selling firms works to encourage profit maximization. If managers too obviously do not maximize profits, the firm may be taken over by corporate raiders who seek to earn money by making the firm more efficient, often by reorganizing or replacing

1. For example, a manager who cuts research and development (R&D) expenditures might lower current costs and raise current profits, but the future strength of the company might be jeopardized.
2. Strategies that place great emphasis on avoiding the possibility of anything harmful happening are called minimax strategies in game theory, because they seek to select actions that ''minimize the maximum loss'' that could occur. We will consider strategies of the minimax type in Chapter 10 when we discuss firm competition in markets with few firms.

management. Since managers don't want to be fired in a takeover, they are motivated to maximize profits.

None of these monitoring or incentive devices are perfect. This is partly because business is inherently risky, and even good managers sometimes run into periods of adverse circumstances. It is not always easy to distinguish firms that do not maximize profits from those that do. Nevertheless, the monitoring devices and markets do tend to cause the manager's objectives to coincide more closely with the owners'. All things considered, profit maximization is still the single most reasonable description of the firm's objective. ■

APPLICATION: Executive Sweets

In an article written for *The New Republic,* Michael Kinsley reported that median compensation for 176 U.S. chief executives was $1.7 million in 1990 and that top executives got pay increases averaging 8 to 15 percent over the year.[3] This information contrasts with the fact that America entered a recession in 1990 and that corporate earnings as a whole were down.

Examining this puzzle a little further reveals that, over the past couple of decades, executive pay has increased faster than the economy has grown. Currently, chief executives of large companies earn an average of 70 or 80 times what an average worker does, and the differential has more than doubled in the past 15 years. American executives earn almost twice as much as their counterparts in Canada and Germany (the second- and third-ranking countries for executive pay) and far outpace those in Japan, which is noted for its modest executive pay. This means that a larger portion of the country's output goes to executive pay, but improved company performance does not explain rising executive salaries.

In the United States, top executive compensation is frequently given in stock options, which increase in value with good company performance. The level of compensation is set by the board of directors, who are often chosen for their posts by the same executives whose pay they determine. The size of the compensation, plus the fact that some corporations have retroactively changed top executive stock options to adjust for stock prices that didn't go up as expected, suggests that top executive pay may not be set with an eye to profit maximization. The board-of-directors-based monitoring process may be less than perfectly effective. It can be argued, for example, that the companies would perform just as well, and earn higher profits, if they paid their top executives at a rate more in line with other countries' pay levels and with the history of executive compensation.

But does the above evidence necessarily mean that American executives are overpaid and that firms do not maximize profit? The market conditions in which American executives have to work may have grown harder in recent

3. Michael Kinsley, ''TRB from Washington: Executive Sweets,'' *The New Republic,* April 8, 1991, p. 4.

years, and the demand for the special skills of executives may have increased faster than the supply, for example. In that case, executives would not be overpaid; their higher salaries would be the outcome of demand for their services by profit-maximizing corporations. Even if we grant that American companies do exceed profit-maximizing levels for top executive compensation, however, there may be reasons to think that forces will cause them to return to profit maximizing. One strong inducement to profit maximization is the increasing need over time to compete with foreign and domestic corporations that do not bear equivalent compensation burdens. Also, as Kinsley writes, ''corporations are almost farcically sensitive to bad publicity. Constant harping on bloated executive pay, by the media and by opportunistic politicians, could itself bring some healthy restraint. So would noisier opposition from large institutional shareholders, such as pension funds.''[4] Kinsley's article, and many others that have appeared, can therefore be viewed as part of the monitoring and information process moving corporations back toward profit-maximizing compensation levels. Although this episode may cause us to question whether firms perfectly maximize profit all of the time, it does not rule out profit maximization as the objective to which firms are eventually forced to return. ■

6.2 The Production Function

Let's assume that you accept profit maximization as the objective of the firm. What production information do you need to summarize and construct profit information? You know that profit, the difference between revenue and cost, is calculated by multiplying price times the quantity sold and subtracting cost. Calculating cost, however, requires knowing how much input is needed to produce a given output. This is what the production function tells you.

Summarizing Firm Production Information

The production function summarizes the relationship between inputs and output, given the technical capabilities of the firm. In our discussion of the production function, we will use K and L to stand for the physical quantities of two representative inputs that we will call capital and labor, respectively. Inputs, as we saw in Chapter 5, are also called factors of production. Capital might be measured in numbers of machines, and labor might be measured in hours of labor time. If there are other inputs used, such as electricity, oil, land, skilled labor (as opposed to unskilled labor), buildings, raw materials, and so on, these are included in the list of inputs and measured in their appropriate physical units.

▼
2. Define the production function, total product, marginal product, and average product. Draw curves relating the last three.

*The **production function,** F(K, L), gives the maximum amount of output, q = F(K, L), that can be produced for each bundle of physical inputs, (K, L).*

4. Ibid.

To see how the production function is used, let's consider Alan Austin, the manager of Austin Excavation Company (AEC), a small construction firm that uses backhoes and operator labor to dig foundation sites for buildings. Alan has two backhoes and employs both himself and another operator for 40 hours each week. In the short run, Alan has a fixed number of backhoes at his disposal. If he has to expand the cubic feet of excavating that his firm does per week with only a few hours' notice, he can employ more labor, either by hiring additional operators or by extending the hours he and his employee work, but he cannot change the number of backhoes. In the long run, with more time to arrange for additional backhoes, he would be able to increase the number of backhoes that Austin Excavation uses. The ability to adjust all or only some of the inputs he uses distinguishes Alan's long-run decision making from his short-run decision making. Since the distinction is important and will appear again in this and later chapters, we need to define both terms.

> *(i) The **short run** is a time period in which one or more economic variables are fixed because there is no way to adjust them in the available time.*
> *(ii) The **long run** is a period of time long enough that the firm can change all economic variables.*

With this in mind, we can first look at the information the production function provides in the short run, when Alan's only option is changing the number of labor hours used. We will consider the production function in the long run later in the chapter.

We will see that much of what the firm wants is information on the effects of *changes* or marginal adjustments it makes to variables under its control. *Marginal analysis,* the study of such changes, is important because it implies conditions for profit maximization; it proceeds from the basic requirement that if profit is maximized, a marginal change cannot increase profit further.

Relating Total Product, Marginal Product, and Average Product

Alan has to pay for extra hours of operator time out of the revenues Austin Excavation earns. To know what the firm's revenues will be, however, Alan has to know how many cubic feet of excavating work his firm can produce for a given number of labor hours. The total output that Alan gets from hiring L hours of labor, given the input of backhoes, is called the total product of labor. Total product is simply the output of the firm, and it is given by our equation for the production function, $q = F(K, L)$. Since AEC uses two backhoes, the total product of labor becomes $q = F(2, L)$, where the two backhoes are treated as the firm's capital, K.

> ***Total product of labor*** *is the total output obtained from employing* L *units of labor, holding constant the input of all other factors.*

Alan would also like two other pieces of data. The first is the amount of *extra* output he gets from an *extra* unit of labor, called the marginal product of labor. In other words, if he adds more operators to his crew (or increases the hours they work), what additional output does he get?

> *Marginal product of labor, MP_L, is the* increase *in output for a small unit of increase in labor, holding constant the input of all other factors. This relationship is written as $MP_L = \Delta q/\Delta L$.*

He would also like to know how much excavating his crew does per hour of labor input, an amount that we call his firm's average product. If Austin Excavation excavates 20 foundations over 10 hours of labor time, for example, its average product is 2 foundations per labor hour.

> *Average product of labor, AP_L, is the average output per unit of labor. This relationship is written as $AP_L = q/L$.*

We used labor as the variable unit in our definitions, but similar definitions of total product, marginal product, and average product apply when any other input is the variable. Now let's see what these numbers tell us about Austin Excavation.

Table 6.1 uses Austin Excavation's production function to determine the total product, average product, and marginal product of labor under the assumption that Alan has two backhoes available to him. Column 1 shows the number of 40-hour weeks of labor time, and column 2 lists the amount of excavating in thousands of cubic feet. For example, with 40 hours of labor time (1 week), Austin Excavation can excavate 20 thousand cubic feet. With 2 weeks of labor time, 80 thousand cubic feet can be excavated, and at 3 weeks the amount rises to 210 thousand cubic feet. A more detailed table could be generated by selecting finer divisions of labor time.

Measuring the change in output for a small increment in operator time (1 hour is a small-enough increment) gives us the marginal product of labor figures in column 3. Increasing labor input from 1 week to 1 week plus an hour, for example, increases output by 0.75 thousand cubic feet. In units of marginal output per week, this is 30 thousand cubic feet per week (0.75 thousand cubic feet $\div \frac{1}{40}$ week = 30 thousand cubic feet/week), so column 3 lists the marginal product of labor as 30 thousand cubic feet per week. Other marginal products are shown for weekly intervals. Reading down the column for marginal product reveals that it rises until 2 weeks of labor time are reached (this is full-time work for Alan and his employee) and declines thereafter. At 5 weeks, for example (the equivalent of 5 full-time employees working with Alan's two backhoes), marginal product is negative, meaning that the last labor added *reduced* output a little bit, rather than raising it. Column 4 in Table 6.1 gives the average product as the ratio of output to labor input, column 2 divided by column 1.

Figure 6.1 shows two graphs plotted from the numbers in Table 6.1. The upper graph plots the curve relating total product to labor hours, and the lower graph plots the curves for marginal product and average product versus labor hours. What can we tell from analyzing these curves? First, total product rises as long as marginal product is positive. When marginal product becomes

Table 6.1 Relating Total, Average, and Marginal Product

(1) **Labor** (No. of 40-Hour Weeks)	(2) **Total Product** q (ft^3 × 1,000)	(3) **Marginal Product** **of Labor** MP$_L$ (ft^3/week × 1,000)	(4) **Average Product** **of Labor** AP$_L$ (ft^3/week × 1,000)
0 $\frac{1}{40}$	0 0.125	$0.125/(\frac{1}{40}) = 5$	
1 $1 + \frac{1}{40}$	20 20.75	30	20
2 $2 + \frac{1}{40}$	80 82.75	110	40
3 $3 + \frac{1}{40}$	210 211.75	70	70
4 $4 + \frac{1}{40}$	240 240	0	60
5 $5 + \frac{1}{40}$	200 198.75	−50	40
6 $6 + \frac{1}{40}$	120 117.5	−100	20
7 $7 + \frac{1}{40}$	0 −3	−120	0

Note: Column 3, MP$_L$, is calculated by dividing the *increase* in total product shown by each pair in column 2 by the *increase* in labor shown by the corresponding pair in column 1. Labor increases are shown as small increments of $\frac{1}{40}$ week (1 hour).

negative after just 4 weeks, total product begins to decline. Second, since marginal product measures the *rate of increase* or slope of total product, it is at its highest point when the slope of total product is steepest (this occurs at 2 weeks). Third, for any quantity of output average product is measured by the height of the total product curve divided by labor hours. For example, in the upper graph, the height of point *b* (240 thousand cubic feet) divided by the horizontal distance from the origin (4 weeks) gives the average product of labor at 60 thousand cubic feet of excavation per week. Average product also equals the slope of a ray from the origin to the point in question. This gives us a simple way to find the point of highest average product: find the

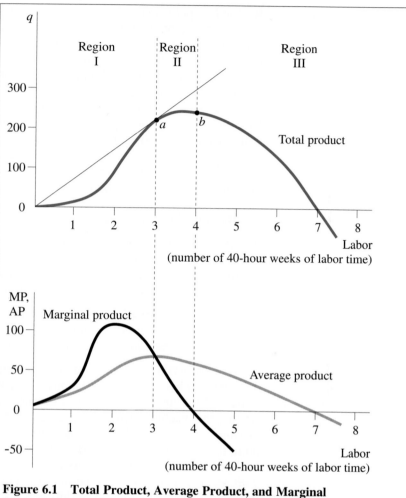

Figure 6.1 Total Product, Average Product, and Marginal Product Total product rises when marginal product is positive and declines when marginal product is negative. Labor would never be used in Region III, where it would cause a reduction in output for additional units hired. Hiring of labor would never stop in Region I, because a 1-percent increase in the amount hired would increase the wages paid by 1 percent but would raise total product by more than 1 percent, since average product is rising in Region I.

point on the total product curve that has a ray from the origin with the highest slope. In Figure 6.1 this is point *a,* which corresponds to 3 weeks of labor time.

Using the point of highest average product and the point where marginal product becomes negative, we can divide the diagram into three regions. In

Region I output is rising and average product is rising. Average product rises when marginal product is above it, falls when marginal product is below it, and neither rises nor falls when the two are the same.[5] In Region II average product is falling but marginal product is still positive. In Region III marginal product is negative and total product is falling.

As we have stated, all of the measures are calculated for a fixed level of the other factors of production, in this case backhoes. If the number of backhoes changes, the average, total, and marginal product of labor curves will also change. Notice that if Austin Excavation used many factors, it could compute total product, marginal product, and average product for any one of them. In addition to the marginal product of labor, we could talk about the marginal product of capital, the marginal product of land, and so on.

Diminishing Marginal Returns

A particularly important property of marginal product is that it diminishes at higher levels of input of the factor. That is, as the input of a particular factor of production is added to the fixed stock of other factors, its impact on output eventually will fall, according to the law of diminishing marginal returns:

> *The law of diminishing marginal returns: As increasing amounts of an input are added to a production process with quantities of other inputs fixed, the marginal product of the factor will eventually fall.*

▼

3. Explain what causes rising marginal product and what causes diminishing marginal product.

What causes different levels of marginal returns? Consider AEC's problem of using backhoes to dig foundations. For a given number of machines, the impact of the first unit of labor is to raise output. The operator begins by starting the machine, getting acquainted with the job that needs to be done, driving to the site, and beginning work. The second unit raises output by more than the first because some of the start-up preparation will not have to be repeated. As more labor hours are added, two workers working together with separate machines may be able to coordinate their work to do better than either of them could do on just one machine. The gains from workers specializing themselves in their tasks allows the extra output from additional labor hours to rise at first. In Figure 6.1 this is the rising portion of the marginal product of labor curve.

With the other inputs fixed, the gains from specialization are eventually exhausted, however. In the case of AEC, this occurs at 2 weeks, with two workers on two backhoes full-time. Hours added beyond this level raise output, but at a diminishing rate. For example, at higher labor input additional workers may have to share machines, leading to a smaller increase in output for the last hour added. Diminishing marginal returns correspond to the declining portion of the marginal product curve in the lower part of Figure

---

5. An average rises when what you are averaging into it is higher than the average. For example, if I am batting .350 and get a hit at my next at-bat, my marginal batting figure is 1.000. This is higher than .350 and so will raise my batting average. Similarly, if my marginal batting is worse than .350, it will drag down my average. If my marginal at-bats have a .350 average, then my overall average does not change.

6.1. Marginal product may also drop to zero. With too many workers, some may have to stand around without a way to be useful, or maybe overtime workers are less productive. For whatever reason, when output no longer rises with additional labor, output has reached its highest absolute level and the marginal product of labor has dropped to zero. In the figure, this happens at 4 weeks. Employing labor beyond this point may even lead to a reduction in output, indicating that marginal product is negative.

Marginal product is particularly important to the question of how much labor Alan wants to use with his two backhoes. He knows that in Region I of Figure 6.1, additional units of labor increase output per worker more than proportionately. That is, going from 1 to 2 weeks (a 100-percent increase in labor) more than doubles output. Going from 2 weeks to 3 (a 50-percent labor increase) raises output by more than 50 percent. As long as the marginal product of the last hour exceeds the average product of the hours before, output per worker rises. In Region II of the figure, hiring more labor increases output less than proportionately. In Region III, more labor actually reduces output.

If product price is fixed and Alan hires labor at a fixed price, the number of workers he hires will be in Region II only, where the average product of labor is declining and marginal product of labor is positive. If it is profitable to hire in Region I, Alan could raise profits by hiring more labor and thus move out of Region I.[6] In Region III Alan would be paying for a factor that had the effect of decreasing his output, so he would never hire at such a point.

Production Information with All Inputs Variable

In the long run, AEC can change its output by changing *all* of its inputs. In Chapter 3 we described utility in terms of the properties of indifference curves. Here we describe the relationship between production and inputs when all inputs are adjustable in terms of an equivalent set of curves called isoquants. The only difference is that we change the terminology to indicate that we are talking about production.

Isoquants. All combinations of inputs producing a fixed output are together called an isoquant, from the prefix *iso* for "same" and *quant* for "quantity". If we fix the quantity of output at the number q_0, say, and ask what combination of inputs can produce this level of output, the answer is that any combination of K and L that satisfies the equation $q_0 = F(K, L)$ will do so.

> An **isoquant** *is the set of input bundles* (K, L) *that produce the same level of output,* q_0*. Mathematically, an isoquant is all combinations of* K *and* L *satisfying the equation* $q_0 = F(K, L)$*, where* F(K, L) *is the production function.*

---

6. Alan's profit is $\pi = pq - wL - rK = (pq/L - w)L - rK = (pAP_L - w)L - rK$, where he spends wL on labor, rK on capital, and $pAP_L - w$ is positive since $\pi > 0$. Holding rK fixed, Alan's profit increases with greater L if pAP_L rises when L rises.

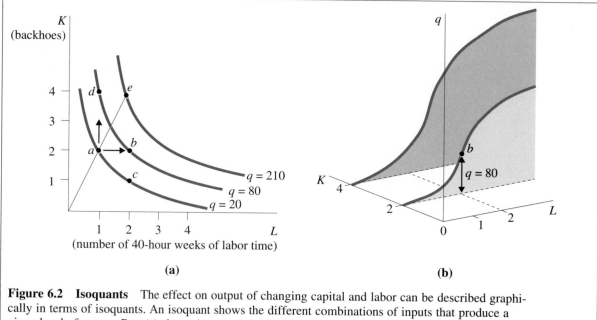

Figure 6.2 Isoquants The effect on output of changing capital and labor can be described graphically in terms of isoquants. An isoquant shows the different combinations of inputs that produce a
given level of output. Part (a) shows isoquants for three output levels. For example, using 2 weeks of
labor with 2 backhoes at point *b* produces the same output (80 units) as using 1 week of labor with 4
backhoes at point *d*. Higher levels of output require larger combinations of inputs. Part (b) three-
dimensionally represents the output level from part (a) as the height of the curve from the *KL* plane.
Point *b* in part (b) is the same as point *b* in part (a).

Part (a) of Figure 6.2 shows a set of isoquants for AEC labeled $q = 20$;
$q = 80$; and $q = 210$. The horizontal axis shows the amount of labor input,
and the vertical axis shows the amount of capital input. Employing 1 week
of labor and 2 backhoes, for example, puts the input bundle at point *a*. These
inputs generate 20 thousand cubic feet of excavation per week, so the isoquant
passing through point *a* is the isoquant labeled $q = 20$.

Isoquants have essentially the same properties as indifference curves, except that they apply to inputs and production instead of consumption goods
and utility. One major difference, though, is that isoquants are cardinal,
whereas indifference curves are ordinal. Isoquants are downward-sloping
because decreasing one input requires increasing the other to keep the quantity
of output from falling. The isoquant through point *a* shows that dropping the
number of machines used from 2 to 1 requires increasing the number of labor
hours to 2 weeks to get back to the isoquant at point *c*, for example.

Isoquants for higher levels of output are further from the origin, signifying
that more inputs are needed to produce more output. Point *e*, for example,
lying to the northeast of point *a*, represents more labor and more capital,
which together produce more output.

Starting from point *a*, increasing labor while holding capital constant
moves us to the right to point *b*, where output is higher according to the

marginal product of labor. The marginal product of labor is represented in Figure 6.2 by how fast higher isoquants are reached as one moves to the right. Similarly, the marginal product of capital is indicated by how fast one reaches higher isoquants when only capital is increased. Capital increases are moves upward in the diagram, such as the move from point *a* to point *d*.

The isoquants in part (a) can be thought of as the contour lines on a topographical map. Higher elevations are higher isoquants. Part (a) is therefore like a hill looked at from above. If we viewed the hill from the side, we would see total product curves, such as the one we drew in Figure 6.1. By combining the two ways of looking at the hill, we get a three-dimensional graph like part (b) of Figure 6.2. For example, fixing the number of backhoes at 2 (shown on the capital axis) and increasing the amount of labor along the labor axis leads to the lower three-dimensional curve. Point *b* in part (b), with 2 weeks of labor and 2 backhoes, corresponds to point *b* in part (a). Higher inputs of capital lead to greater total product of labor, as shown by the larger curve for 4 backhoes.

So far we have been describing how output changes when the input of one factor is increased. How much does one factor have to increase when another is diminished if we want to hold output constant? Our answer should seem familiar, because we have already examined the same question for consumption in terms of the marginal rate of substitution.

▼
4. Use isoquants to explain the marginal rate of technical substitution, degree of factor substitution, and returns to scale.

Marginal Rate of Technical Substitution. Assume that AEC has to use more machines and less labor in production. At what rate does capital replace labor, holding output fixed? To find out, we need the marginal rate of technical substitution. Writing the change in output when both capital and labor are changed gives us $MP_K \Delta K + MP_L \Delta L = \Delta q$, where MP_K is the marginal product of capital, MP_L is the marginal product of labor, and ΔK and ΔL are the changes in capital and labor, respectively. Since we want the change in output, Δq, to be zero, we can solve to find the marginal rate of technical substitution of labor for capital, $MRTS_{L,K}$,

$$-\frac{\Delta K}{\Delta L} = \frac{MP_L}{MP_K} = MRTS_{L,K}.$$

*The **marginal rate of technical substitution of labor for capital**, MRTS_{L,K}, is the rate at which capital must substitute for labor in production to hold output constant.*

Figure 6.3 shows a representative isoquant. If we begin at point *a*, lowering the amount of labor by ΔL requires an increase in capital in the amount ΔK in order to keep us on the isoquant. As with indifference curves and the marginal rate of substitution, for small changes in inputs the marginal rate of technical substitution is the absolute value of the slope of the isoquant at the point of measurement: the line through *a* and *a'* becomes the tangent line at *a* for small changes.

Now that we know the slope of the isoquant corresponds to the marginal rate of technical substitution, we can examine how production considerations affect the slope of the isoquant as we move along it.

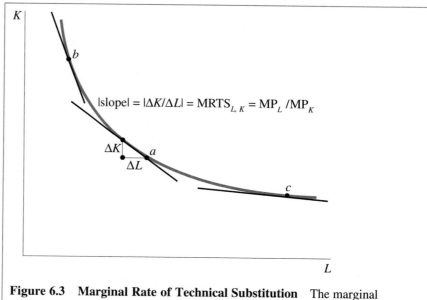

Figure 6.3   Marginal Rate of Technical Substitution   The marginal rate of technical substitution of labor for capital is the amount of capital needed to replace one unit of labor in production, holding output constant. Geometrically, $MRTS_{L,K}$ is the absolute value of the slope of the isoquant. Thus, $MRTS_{L,K}$ is higher at point *b* than at point *a*, and higher at *a* than at point *c*.

Isoquant Curvature and Declining Marginal Rate of Technical Substitution. We have drawn convex isoquants with declining marginal rate of technical substitution for much the same reasons that we drew indifference curves with declining marginal rate of substitution. As fewer and fewer laborers engage in the production process, it is reasonable that they become harder and harder to replace with capital. Thus, at point *b* in Figure 6.3, the $MRTS_{L,K}$ will be higher than at point *a* (the isoquant will get steeper at *b*). The slope of the isoquant might even become infinite—the curve vertical—in which case no amount of capital could compensate for the loss of an additional worker. Similarly, if the production process uses less and less capital, we would expect that it takes more and more labor to make up for the lack of capital. At point *c*, therefore, $MRTS_{L,K}$ is relatively low. In short, the marginal rate of technical substitution of labor for capital falls as the amount of labor grows large relative to capital. This relationship is what makes isoquants convex to the origin.

Degree of Factor Substitution. In the same way that the curvature of indifference curves indicates the degree of substitutability between goods, the curvature of the isoquant indicates the degree of factor substitution. Downward-sloping straight lines, for example, indicate perfect substitutability. To

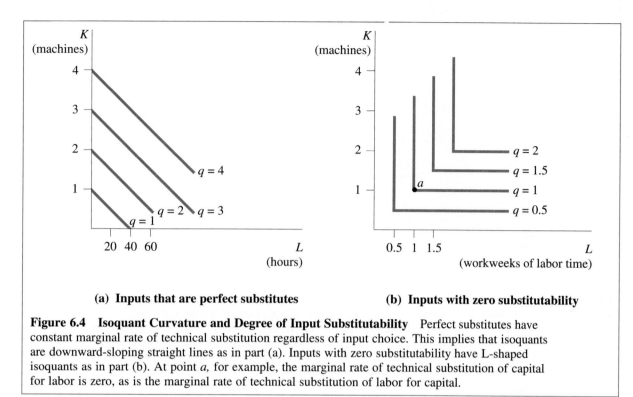

(a) Inputs that are perfect substitutes   **(b) Inputs with zero substitutability**

Figure 6.4   Isoquant Curvature and Degree of Input Substitutability   Perfect substitutes have constant marginal rate of technical substitution regardless of input choice. This implies that isoquants are downward-sloping straight lines as in part (a). Inputs with zero substitutability have L-shaped isoquants as in part (b). At point *a,* for example, the marginal rate of technical substitution of capital for labor is zero, as is the marginal rate of technical substitution of labor for capital.

see why, assume that 1 unit of capital always substitutes for 1 unit of labor. In this case, production would depend only on the sum of capital and labor used, not on the proportion between the two. This indicates perfect substitutability between units of the same input. It follows that perfect substitutability in this case means that the marginal rate of technical substitution is constant and the isoquant is a straight line with slope − 1. However, there is nothing special about replacing a factor for another one-for-one, since we can always make the substitution ratio one-for-one by changing the choice of units for one of the factors. In part (a) of Figure 6.4, for example, 1 unit of capital substitutes for *40 hours* of labor. Equivalently, we could have shown 1 unit of capital substituting for *1 work week* of labor. Any downward-sloping straight-line isoquant, therefore, indicates perfect substitutability.

At the opposite extreme are inputs that cannot substitute for one another at all. Part (b) of Figure 6.4 shows that 1 unit of capital and one unit of labor produce 1 unit of output at point *a.* Since the isoquant is L-shaped at point *a,* no amount of increased capital can substitute for a small reduction in labor, and vice versa. The marginal rate of technical substitution of capital for labor is zero, and the marginal rate of technical substitution of labor for capital is zero. L-shaped isoquants, therefore, imply zero substitutability of factor in-

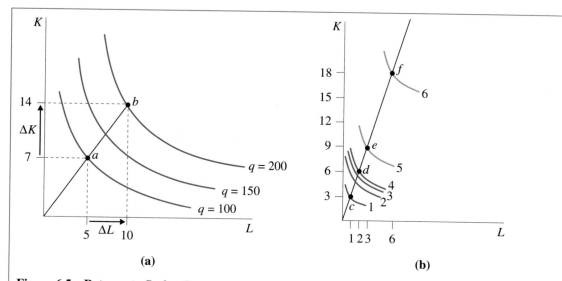

Figure 6.5 Returns to Scale Returns to scale measure the change in output when all factors of production are increased proportionately. If the percentage increase in output matches, exceeds, or falls short of the percentage increase in inputs, the production process exhibits constant, increasing, or decreasing returns to scale, respectively. In part (a) the proportionate spacing of isoquants indicates constant returns to scale. Bunching of isoquants, as from point *c* to point *d* in part (b), indicates increasing returns to scale, whereas isoquants further apart, as from point *e* to point *f*, indicate decreasing returns to scale.

puts. In between perfect substitutability and zero substitutability are isoquants with greater and lesser degrees of curvature. The more the curvature approaches a right angle, the less the degree of substitutability, and vice versa.

Returns to Scale. Figure 6.5 illustrates two sets of isoquants for different production processes. In each part, the ray from the origin shows the direction of input increase if both inputs are increased proportionately. For example, doubling all inputs means doubling the distance from the origin along the ray. We refer to changing all inputs by the same proportion as a change in *scale.* What is the effect on output of a change in scale?

In part (a) we find that doubling inputs leads to a doubling in output. That is, the move from point *a* to point *b* doubles the distance from the origin and also doubles output from 100 to 200. The property of output increasing proportionately to the scale of inputs is called *constant returns to scale,* because the amount of output per bundle of inputs is always constant.

*A production process exhibits **constant returns to scale** if increasing all inputs proportionately increases output in equal proportion.*

Unlike the proportionately spaced isoquants in part (a) of the figure, part (b) has isoquants that bunch closer together or spread out as the distance from the origin along a ray increases. For example, doubling all inputs in the move from point c to point d more than doubles output, but doubling inputs in the move from point e to point f does not come close to doubling output. Production in which output increases more than proportionately to scale is said to exhibit *increasing returns to scale,* and production in which output increases less than proportionately to scale is said to exhibit *decreasing returns to scale.*

> (i) *A production process exhibits* **increasing returns to scale** *if a proportionate increase in all inputs increases output more than proportionately.*

> (ii) *A production process exhibits* **decreasing returns to scale** *if a proportionate increase in all inputs increases output less than proportionately.*

Why might some production processes exhibit constant returns to scale and others exhibit increasing or decreasing returns? One answer is that a larger scale of operation often allows workers and managers to specialize in different tasks. Henry Ford's assembly line, for example, could produce more cars than the same workers and equipment could do if production had to be done one car at a time in separate garages, with each worker designing, machining, assembling, and finishing the cars. On the other hand, large scale can also introduce inefficiencies, often associated with breakdown of coordination and critical information flows.

From a policy perspective, increasing returns to scale seem to imply that large firms are desirable and should be encouraged, because they are able to produce more efficiently than small ones and thus should be able to sell their product at a lower price. Yet, as we will see in Chapters 8 and 9, large firms often have greater market power that would allow them to charge high prices, and so large firms are sometimes broken into smaller, competing firms to encourage lower prices. Alternatively, as in the case of regional electric utilities, large firms may be regulated by government bodies.

Another way to describe the effects of different returns to scale is to graph output against scale. Assuming that we have fixed a particular ratio of inputs (that is, we have limited ourselves to a particular ray from the origin), scale is measured on a graph like Figure 6.5 as the distance from the origin. Plotting scale versus output leads to Figure 6.6. The product-to-scale curve for decreasing returns to scale is concave with respect to the bottom of the graph. For increasing returns to scale, the curve is convex; and for constant returns to scale, it is a ray from the origin.

As an application, let's consider two production functions and determine what types of returns to scale are present. In the first, output equals 15 times the amount of skilled labor plus 5 times the amount of unskilled labor used in production, $q = 15S + 5U$. Multiplying skilled and unskilled labor by

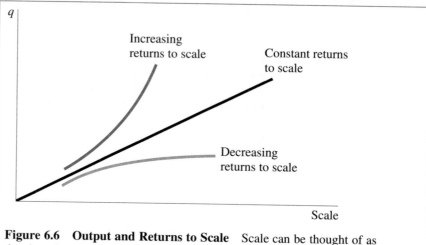

Figure 6.6   Output and Returns to Scale   Scale can be thought of as the size of the firm with rising amounts of all factors. Output, graphed as a function of scale, is a concave curve for decreasing returns to scale and convex for increasing returns to scale. For constant returns to scale, it is a ray from the origin.

two means that the new output q^* becomes $q^* = 15(2S) + 5(2U) = 2(15S + 5U) = 2q$. Production therefore exhibits constant returns to scale, since output doubles. A similar check shows that output rises proportionately for any other multiple of inputs as well. As a second example, consider production given by the Cobb-Douglas production function, $q = AK^\alpha L^\beta$, where A, α, and β are positive constants and K and L are the amounts of capital and labor input. Doubling capital and labor means that output becomes $q^* = A(2K)^\alpha(2L)^\beta = A(2)^\alpha(K)^\alpha(2)^\beta(L)^\beta = 2^{\alpha+\beta}A(K)^\alpha(L)^\beta = 2^{\alpha+\beta}q$. Thus, if $\alpha + \beta$ is equal to one, production exhibits constant returns to scale, because output doubles with a doubling of inputs. However, if $\alpha + \beta$ is greater than one, production exhibits increasing returns to scale (because output more than doubles); and if $\alpha + \beta$ is less than one, production exhibits decreasing returns to scale.

We now know what the production function is and how it determines the various productivity measures: average, marginal, and total product and the effect of scale on output. As previously stated, however, production information is not desired for its own sake but as a way to the firm's costs and, ultimately, profits. As a final piece of the firm's environment, therefore, we need to know the cost information contained in the firm's cost function. Before doing the technical details, let's first take a look at the big picture of what we mean by *economic* profit and costs, what this information means to the firm, and the philosophy of how it is used.

6.3 Economic Profit and Costs

We've talked before about revenue, costs, and profit but have not clarified what we mean by profit in the economic sense. It is the search for *economic profit* that drives firms.

Opportunity Costs and Forward-Looking Decision Making

Just because a firm collects more in revenues than it pays out in costs, it is not necessarily earning economic profit. A firm that owns its own land or machinery, for example, pays only depreciation on the machines and operating costs. Nevertheless, it would be wrong for the firm to treat its land cost as zero or its machine costs as merely depreciation. By using the land and machines itself, the firm is losing the income that it could have had by selling their services to other firms. The forgone income is the true opportunity cost to the firm of using its land and machines. This idea is important enough that we emphasize it with a formal definition.

> The **opportunity cost** of an input is the income that the input could earn in the next best alternative use.

We have already seen in Chapter 5 that opportunity costs are important to the household's decision about where to supply its labor. They are also important to distinguish economic profits used in decision making from accounting (or bookkeeping) profits. Accounting profits do not consider the opportunity costs of resources. Accounting profits are primarily concerned with financial statements, such as income statements and balance sheets, which are associated with describing the past performance of the firm. In contrast, the concept of economic profit is forward-looking, and it aids the firm in making decisions about resource allocation and production.

> **Economic profit** is the difference between total revenue and total cost, where the total cost includes the opportunity costs of inputs.

▼
5. What is economic profit, and how is it related to opportunity costs and sunk costs?

For example, assume that you own fully depreciated carpet-cleaning machines that can be rented out to others for $1,000 per month or can be used in your own commercial carpet-cleaning business. Let $q = 18,000$ be the average amount of carpet that you can clean per month, measured in square feet; also let $p = \$.15$ be the price of cleaning per square foot, $w = \$10/$ hour the wage rate, and $L = 175$ hours your monthly input of labor, all measured when your carpet-cleaning business is doing as well as it can. In evaluating your profits, how should you measure the cost of the machine input?

Assume that you use accounting profit to measure your earnings. Then your revenues are pq and your out-of-pocket costs for labor are wL. Your accounting profit Π is therefore

$$\Pi = pq - wL$$
$$= \frac{\$.15}{ft^2} \frac{18{,}000\ ft^2}{month} - \frac{\$10}{hr} \frac{175\ hr}{month}$$
$$= \frac{\$950}{month}.$$

From the accounting perspective, carpet cleaning looks profitable.

However, in this example, maximizing accounting profit is the wrong thing to do, even when it is positive. If the machine is used in your own carpet-cleaning business, the highest amount you can get from it is $950, but if you rent the machine out to others, the return is $1,000. Renting out the machine is clearly the better thing for you to do.

Now let's see how the computation would change if we measured *economic* profit. Economic profit includes the machine's opportunity costs, which take its potential alternative uses into account. Since the machine could be rented out for $1,000 per month were it not used in production, the rental income is its opportunity cost. The economic profit from production is therefore

$$\Pi = pq - wL - \frac{\$1{,}000}{month}$$
$$= \frac{\$.15}{ft^2} \frac{18{,}000\ ft^2}{month} - \frac{\$10}{hr} \frac{175\ hr}{month}$$
$$- \frac{\$1{,}000}{month}$$
$$= - \frac{\$50}{month}.$$

Even when your business is doing as well as it can, your economic profit is a negative $50 per month, clearly a losing proposition. Calculating the economic profit, therefore, verifies that production should be shut down and the machine rented out for best return to the owner.

Another way to describe this example is to say that the *going return* on machines is $1,000 per month. Only if the earnings from production equal or exceed the going return should production be undertaken. In major corporations, taking the value of goods sold and subtracting the wage bill and the cost of materials and other inputs generates a residual that is available to the owners of the firm (shareholders), who provided the money to buy the plant and equipment that the firm owns. Were shareholders not investing in the corporation, they could have invested their money in other stocks and bonds. The opportunity cost of the shareholders' money being tied up in the firm's assets is therefore the market rate of return on comparable investments. Only if the residual from the firm exceeds the market return on money placed in comparable investments does the corporation earn *economic* profits.

Sunk Costs and Forward-Looking Decision Making

Sunk costs are also significant to the firm's decision making, although for reasons opposite those for opportunity costs. Opportunity costs, though frequently hidden and intangible because they do not represent explicit out-of-pocket expenses, should enter into the firm's optimization decision because they affect economic profit. Sunk costs, on the other hand, are usually tangible and visible out-of-pocket costs that should be ignored in the firm's decision making, because they represent expenses related to past choices and cannot be altered.

> ***Sunk costs*** *are costs that cannot be altered or avoided by current or future decisions of the firm. As such, they are irrelevant to the firm's decision making.*

In other words, if you cannot change something, why take it into account in your planning? However, because sunk costs are often ongoing and tangible, they may be confusing.

For instance, suppose you are considering whether to build a particular plant on a site that needs $1 million of ground preparation. The ground preparation is specific to your plant, and once it is done, the site has no additional value to any other user. The plant itself costs $4 million, for a total outlay of $5 million. Your alternative is to buy an existing plant at a different site for $5.5 million. Until you do the ground preparation, building and ground preparation costs are prospective. The cheaper alternative is therefore to prepare the ground and build.

Now assume that a year has passed; you have paid the $1 million for ground preparation. You see an ad for an existing building for $4.5 million. Should you drop your building plan and buy the $4.5-million plant? The answer is no. The $1 million for ground preparation is a sunk cost that no current decision can retrieve. Continuing to build on the site to get a working plant will cost $4 million. This is cheaper than spending an additional $4.5 million to get a working plant. You may rue the fact that you did not have the $4.5-million choice before you started building (indeed, buying the $4.5-million plant *then* would have been the best choice), but since the $1 million in ground preparation is a sunk cost, there is no point in taking it into account now.

Economic Profit and Rents

A concept related to opportunity costs is economic rent. A firm can sometimes have higher earnings than another firm in the same market because of better management, superior technology, or exclusive rights to an input (such as a patent or land). For example, a grape grower with superior vineyard land on a south slope will have lower costs than a comparable vineyard on a north slope. Yet both vineyards may earn the same economic profit if the quality that makes the south-slope vineyard superior can be transferred to other users of the south-slope land. In that case, we could imagine the south-slope vineyard renting out its land at a higher price than the north-slope vineyard could obtain for its land. The higher opportunity cost of the south-slope land reflects its higher value to other users. When the higher opportunity cost of south-slope land is taken into account, the two vineyards could have the same economic profit.

In Chapter 5 we discussed the economic rent of households as the excess of their earnings over what they could earn in their next best employment. Producers can also earn economic rents.

> **Economic rent** is the difference between what the firm is willing to pay for an input (based on what the input can earn for the firm) and the minimum payment the firm has to make to keep the input in its present use.

For example, assume that the vineyard's south slope allows it to earn $100,000 each year after the opportunity costs of all other inputs are paid. In this case, $100,000 of the vineyard's earnings are economic rent on its land, since it would be willing to pay that much more for the land than it does. Performing the same computation on other inputs shows whether the firm earns rent on them as well.

To summarize what we have learned: (1) Because there may be factors with high value in their current use that the firm pays less for than it would be willing to pay, firm earnings sometimes include rents to the firm's factors; and (2) economic profit is based on opportunity costs, but not on sunk costs, which means that it may differ from accounting profit based on tangible costs and depreciation.

6.4 The Cost Function

With respect to the story at the start of the chapter—the scenario in which you suddenly had to take over your family's business—you should be starting to feel more confident about the nature of the data that a firm uses. You know, though, that you still need more information, your costs. The cost function relates the firm's output to how much it takes for the firm to produce that output at least cost. In this section, therefore, we cover the critical process of converting information about production into information about costs. We begin with the case where the firm uses two inputs, both of which are variable. We will see what happens if one or more inputs are fixed when we discuss short-run costs later in the section.

Isocost Curves

The firm's first job is to find out how much it pays for its inputs. Suppose that capital and labor are the only inputs and that their market prices are r and w, respectively. Then the firm's total cost of hiring K units of capital and L units of labor is

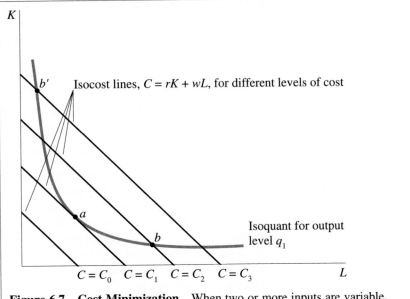

Figure 6.7   Cost Minimization   When two or more inputs are variable, the firm produces its output in the least costly way by finding the lowest isocost line that reaches the desired isoquant. The association of each output level with the corresponding least cost of its production determines the cost function.

$$\text{Total cost} = rK + wL.$$

The total cost equation should look familiar to you because it takes the same form as the consumer's budget constraint, the difference being that it is applied to purchase of inputs rather than purchase of goods. Figure 6.7 shows a representative isoquant for the firm and, superimposed, a number of curves based on the total cost equation called isocost curves (*iso* for ''same,'' and *cost* for ''cost''). An isocost curve gives all combinations of inputs that have the same cost to the firm.

> An **isocost curve** *is all input bundles that have the same cost to the firm. If* L *and* K *are inputs with prices* w *and* r, *respectively, the equation for the isocost curve with cost* C_0 *is* $C_0 = rK + wL$.

As with budget lines, isocost lines further from the origin represent larger amounts of money spent, and isocost lines closer to the origin represent smaller amounts.

Least-Cost Inputs and the Cost Function

We have made progress, but we are still not there yet. What good is the total cost equation if it just provides an obvious accounting truth? To get from isocost lines to the costs that firms really have to pay, we must use the following principle that applies to all firms: whatever output level the firm produces, the manager wants to produce it in the least costly manner. If a firm can produce the same output for less, it can raise its profits. Thus *profit maximization requires cost minimization.* The cost that we want to find is the *lowest cost* of producing each output level. Solving the cost-minimizing optimization problem gives us the cost function.

> The **cost function, C(q),** *relates the level of firm output,* q, *to the lowest total cost of producing it. The equation is written*

$$\text{Total cost} = C(q).$$

▼

6. Explain how the principle of cost minimization gets us from output levels to the cost function.

How does the firm choose the least costly method of producing? Consider the isoquant for output level q_1 drawn in Figure 6.7. Points a, b, and b' all generate q_1 units of output, but at different cost levels. Of all the points on the q_1 isoquant, the least-cost combination of capital and labor is point a. To produce output q_1, therefore, the profit-maximizing firm will use the amounts of capital and labor given by point a. Finding the least-cost input combination for each output level and writing the associated cost in a function gives the firm its total cost function, $C(q)$. $C(q)$ is what the firm actually pays (assuming it is efficiently run!) to produce q units of good. For example, at output level q_1, total cost is C_1. That is, $C_1 = C(q_1)$.

The critical feature of bundle a in Figure 6.7 is the *tangency* between the isocost line and the isoquant. The slope of the isoquant is the negative of the marginal rate of technical substitution of labor for capital. The slope of the isocost line is $-w/r$. We know this because reducing capital by ΔK units means that labor can be increased by ΔL units without changing the cost of inputs if $r\Delta K + w\Delta L = 0$. Solving this for the slope of the isocost line gives us $\Delta K/\Delta L = -w/r$. Setting the two slopes equal means that

$$\frac{w}{r} = \frac{MP_L}{MP_K} = MRTS_{L,K},$$

which can also be written in the form

$$\frac{MP_K}{r} = \frac{MP_L}{w}.$$

The economic meaning of this tangency is as follows. The marginal product of capital has dimensional units equal to output per unit of capital input. The rental rate r has dimensional units of dollars per unit of capital input. Therefore MP_K/r has dimensional units of output per dollar spent on capital, a "bang-per-buck" measure. The equality with MP_L/w means that the bang-per-dollar spent on capital input must equal the bang-per-dollar spent on labor, if output is produced at least cost. If the firm got more output from the last dollar spent on labor than it did from capital, it could take money from capital and use part of it on labor, thereby getting the same output for less money. The tangency condition says that this is impossible.

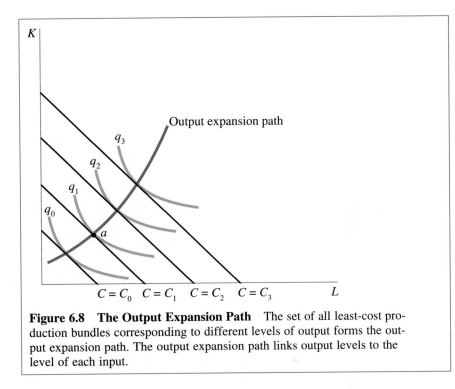

Figure 6.8   The Output Expansion Path   The set of all least-cost production bundles corresponding to different levels of output forms the output expansion path. The output expansion path links output levels to the level of each input.

Output Expansion Paths and the Cost Function

A simple way to describe how to find the cost function is to use the *output expansion path*, a curve analogous to the consumer's income consumption path. The output expansion path is simply the curve whose points are all of the least-cost input bundles corresponding to different levels of output. As with budget lines and indifference curves, least-cost input bundles can occur at corner solutions that are not tangencies; but the possibility of corner solutions does not change the rule that the firm produces whatever level of output it produces at least cost.

> *Given fixed factor prices, the **output expansion path** is the set of least-cost input bundles corresponding to different levels of output.*

Figure 6.8 shows an output expansion path for costs C_0 through C_3. The output expansion path reminds us that the firm makes its economic choices to minimize costs and that these determine the cost function. To find the cost function from the output expansion path, pick an output level on the curve. Find the isocost curve intersecting the point, and assign that cost to the output level. Doing this for any output gives the cost function. Mathematically, the output expansion path determines the cost-minimizing quantities of L and K

for each output level. Call these amounts $L(q)$ and $K(q)$. Total cost is simply the function $C(q) = wL(q) + rK(q)$.

Fixed Inputs and the Cost Function

How does the firm find its total cost if it is not able to adjust one or more of its factors in the short run? In this case, the same principle applies. *Whatever output level the firm produces in the short run, the manager wants to produce it in the least costly manner by adjusting those inputs that are variable.*

In other words, everything applies as before, except that we are not able to adjust some factors that are fixed in the short run. The output expansion path in the short run continues to be the set of least costly combinations of inputs corresponding to different output levels, except that the firm can change only inputs that are variable in the short run. The short-run cost function continues to be the cost of producing each output level on the output expansion path.

To see how this works, assume that you manage Fireyear Company. Fireyear has contracts to lease 25 machines at a rental rate of $r = \$1,000$ per machine per year. One year remains on the leasing contracts. Since changing the quantity of machines is not an option, you are in a short-run situation. Your only other input is labor, hired at the rate of $15 per hour.

Fireyear still wants to produce whatever output it chooses in the least costly way. Figure 6.9 plots Fireyear's isoquants for machines (K) and labor (L). Since 25 machines must be hired in the short run, the firm's input choices lie on the horizontal line starting at $K = 25$. For each output level q, the amount of labor needed to produce it is given by the distance to the right on the labor axis. To produce output $q = 6$, for example, Fireyear needs 22 units of labor. Fireyear's output expansion path is therefore the horizontal line at $K = 25$. Labor for other outputs can be read from the output expansion path.

Fireyear's short-run function is the cost of producing each quantity on the output expansion path. Because Fireyear's capital input is fixed in the short run, daily expenses for machines are fixed at $25 \times \$1,000/250$ or $100 per workday.[7] Daily expenses for labor are $wL(q) = \$15L(q)$, where $L(q)$ is the number of labor hours hired per day for output level q as required by the short-run output expansion path. The short-run cost function is therefore

$$C(q) = rK + wL(q)$$
$$= \$100 + \$15L(q).$$

At $q = 6$, for example, $L(q) = 22$ and short-run total cost is $430. If $q = 0$, $L(q) = 0$ and total cost is $100. For $q = 12$, $L(q) = 32$ and total cost is $580, and so on.

Regardless of whether some or all of the inputs are variable, the firm adjusts whatever inputs it can adjust to produce each output at least cost. This principle determines the output expansion path and thereby the cost function.

---

7. To simplify our calculations, we assume that the work year consists of 50 five-day weeks.

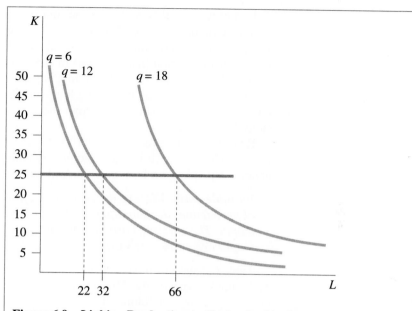

Figure 6.9 Linking Production to Costs In this diagram capital is a fixed factor and labor is the variable factor. The cost of capital is therefore the fixed cost. As output rises, more labor is needed to produce the output. This determines the rising variable cost for labor in Table 6.2.

Now that we know where costs come from, we can explain how managers make the cost function useful. This means graphing some cost curves.

6.5 Cost Curves

Just as it was said that "All roads lead to Rome," so "All cost curves derive from the total cost function." Managers, however, have to pay attention to special components of their costs in addition to the total. In the case of Fireyear, one important consideration was that some costs were fixed in the short run, because 25 machines had to be leased regardless of how much output was produced. The part of total cost that pays for fixed factors regardless of how much output is produced is called *fixed costs.*

> **Fixed costs, FC,** *are the costs to the firm of hiring fixed factors of production, the quantities of which do not change with the quantity of output.*[8]

8. Remember, we noted earlier that fixed costs, and any other costs that the firm uses to determine profit, are opportunity costs of the input in question. Even if a machine does not require out-of-pocket payments because it is company owned, it may nevertheless have opportunity cost.

Earlier we saw that sunk costs are not relevant for firm decisions because they cannot be changed. Fixed costs, however, are invariant only in the short run when they cannot be changed. Since fixed costs are payments for factors of production that are fixed in the short run, they *can* be reduced to zero in the long run. We will see in Chapter 7 that fixed costs therefore are a relevant consideration in making long-run decisions about whether to enter into or remain in production, though they are not relevant to short-run decisions.[9]

Returning to Fireyear, we found that it could control the amount of labor it hired. Costs of such variable factors are called *variable costs* because they change depending on how much output the firm produces.

Variable costs, VC, are the costs to the firm of hiring variable factors of production, the quantities of which change with the quantity of output. The variable costs corresponding to a particular quantity of output are written as *VC*(q).

Table 6.2 shows Fireyear's output, fixed cost, and variable cost in columns 1, 2, and 3, respectively. The sum of columns 2 and 3 equals Fireyear's total cost, $C(q)$ shown in column 4.

The Graphical Relationships Among Costs

Graphing the curves derived from the numbers in Table 6.2 can show us Fireyear's costs at a glance. Part (a) of Figure 6.10 plots Fireyear's fixed and short-run total cost from Table 6.2 for each output level. Since there are fixed costs, all cost curves apply to the short run. The fixed cost curve (FC) is flat because the fixed costs do not change with output. Total cost, however, rises with output, as shown by the curve labeled $C(q)$. Variable costs are indicated by the difference between the curves for total cost and fixed costs. If we drew the variable cost curve, it would have the same shape as the total cost curve, just shifted downward by the amount of the fixed costs. Moreover, the shape of the variable cost curve reflects the shape of the total product of labor curve that we saw in part (b) of Figure 6.2. That is, for small levels of output, variable costs rise steeply because the marginal product of labor is low (total product is rising slowly with additional labor input). At middle levels of output, variable costs rise less steeply because the marginal product of labor is higher (total product is rising faster with additional labor). As the marginal product of labor declines for large levels of output (according to the law of diminishing marginal returns), the variable cost curve begins to rise more steeply again.

Column 5 in Table 6.2 shows marginal cost (MC), which is the increase in cost from production of a small additional output.

---

9. At the risk of abusing terminology, we might say that fixed costs are "sunk" in the short run but not in the long run.

Table 6.2   Knowing Total Cost, $C(q)$, and Fixed Cost, FC, Allows Computation of All Other Costs

(1) q	(2) FC	(3) VC	(4) $C(q)$	(5) MC	(6) AC	(7) AVC	(8) AFC
0	100.00	0.00	100.00				
1	100.00	90.00	190.00	90.00	190.00	90.00	100.00
2	100.00	163.00	263.00	73.00	131.50	81.50	50.00
3	100.00	221.00	321.00	58.00	107.00	73.67	33.33
4	100.00	267.00	367.00	46.00	91.75	66.75	25.00
5	100.00	302.00	402.00	35.00	80.40	60.40	20.00
6	100.00	330.00	430.00	28.00	71.67	55.00	16.67
7	100.00	353.00	453.00	23.00	64.71	50.43	14.29
8	100.00	373.00	473.00	20.00	59.13	46.63	12.50
9	100.00	394.00	494.00	21.00	54.89	43.78	11.11
10	100.00	417.00	517.00	23.00	51.70	41.70	10.00
11	100.00	445.00	545.00	28.00	49.55	40.45	9.09
12	100.00	480.00	580.00	35.00	48.33	40.00	8.33
13	100.00	525.00	625.00	45.00	48.08	40.38	7.69
14	100.00	583.00	683.00	58.00	48.79	41.64	7.14
15	100.00	656.00	756.00	73.00	50.40	43.73	6.67
16	100.00	747.00	847.00	91.00	52.94	46.69	6.25
17	100.00	857.00	957.00	110.00	56.29	50.41	5.88
18	100.00	1,020.00	1,120.00	163.00	62.22	56.67	5.56

▼

7. Define MC, AC, AVC, and AFC, and draw them in relation to one another and to total cost.

Marginal cost, MC, is the increase in cost of production resulting from a small increase in output. In mathematical terms, $MC(q) = \Delta C/\Delta q$.

Another way to think of marginal cost is as the rate at which cost rises for additional output. Since marginal cost is the rate of increase in total cost, it is the slope of the total cost curve.

Figure 6.10 plots marginal cost in part (b). It starts at point a' and declines until point c', the quantity where the slope of the total cost curve is lowest, and rises thereafter. The U-shaped marginal cost curve also reflects the changes in slope of the variable cost curve that we have just noted. The initial steep rise in variable costs occurs for small output levels, where the marginal product of labor is small but rising; correspondingly, the marginal cost curve falls. The subsequent decline in the marginal product of labor, in the region where the law of diminishing returns applies, corresponds to the rising portion of marginal cost.[10]

10. Producing another unit of output requires $1/MP_L$ units of labor, costing w/MP_L. Thus marginal cost is related to marginal product by the relationship $MC = w/MP_L$. It follows that marginal cost falls when marginal product rises, and marginal cost rises when marginal product falls.

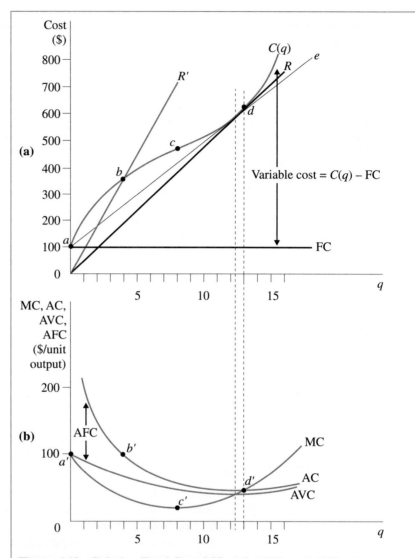

Figure 6.10   Relating Total Cost, MC, AC, AVC, and AFC   In part (a) $C(q)$ is the total cost curve for Fireyear. The fixed cost curve FC is flat because fixed costs do not change. Variable cost is the difference between these two curves. Marginal cost, MC, is the slope of the total cost curve; thus the curve for MC in part (b) reaches its lowest point at point c', corresponding to the point where the slope of the total cost curve is lowest. The curve for average cost, AC, declines as long as marginal cost is below it; it reaches its lowest point where the MC curve cuts across (point d') and rises when MC is above it. Average variable cost, AVC, starts at the same point as MC, reaches its lowest point where MC cuts across, and approaches average cost more closely as quantity rises. Average fixed cost, AFC, is the difference between average cost and average variable cost.

Marginal cost refers to the additional cost of the last unit produced, but it does not tell the firm how much it costs to produce output *on average*. Per-unit cost is given by *average cost*.

> ***Average cost, AC,*** *is the cost of production per unit of output. In mathematical terms AC*(q) = C*(q)/q.*

In Table 6.2, dividing total cost by the quantity produced gives us the average cost in column 6. We plot this average cost in part (b) of Figure 6.10. In general, average cost equals the slope of the ray from the origin to the point on the total cost curve. At point *b* in part (a), for instance, the ray from the origin 0*R'* has a slope given by the height of the line to the point *b* [this distance is $C(q)$] divided by the horizontal distance (this distance is *q*). Average cost reaches its lowest level at point *d*, where the ray from the origin tangent to total cost (ray 0*R*) reaches its lowest slope. In part (b) this is point *d'*, where the marginal cost curve cuts the average cost curve. In other words, average cost declines as output rises until the level of output corresponding to points *d* and *d'*.

For points to the left of *d*, AC, given by the slope of the ray from the origin, gets larger toward the origin until it reaches infinity at point *a*. For example, AC at one unit of output equals the total amount of fixed costs per unit plus the small amount of variable costs at one unit of output, FC/*q* + VC(1)/*q*. This implies that average cost is infinity at zero output levels: even with zero output, fixed costs must still be paid, so FC/*q* approaches infinity as *q* approaches zero.

Average cost is one of the most important costs derived from total cost. Using the fact that total cost equals fixed cost plus variable cost, the simple relationship among average cost, fixed cost, and variable cost is

$$\text{AC}(q) = \frac{C(q)}{q} = \frac{\text{VC} + \text{FC}}{q} = \frac{\text{VC}}{q} + \frac{\text{FC}}{q}.$$

In other words, average cost is the sum of variable cost per unit, VC/*q*, and fixed cost per unit, FC/*q*. Economists call these *average variable cost* and *average fixed cost*, respectively.

> (i) ***Average variable cost, AVC,*** *is the variable cost of production per unit of output. In mathematical terms, AVC*(q) = VC*(q)/q.*

> (ii) ***Average fixed cost, AFC,*** *is the fixed cost of production per unit of output. In mathematical terms, AFC*(q) = FC/q.*

Average variable cost can be found in part (a) of Figure 6.10 from the slope of a ray through the total cost curve in the same way as we found average cost, except that the ray from the origin is replaced by a ray starting at point *a*, where total cost hits the vertical axis at fixed cost FC. As the level of output approaches zero, the slope of the ray approaches the slope of the total cost curve at point *a*. The slope of total cost equals marginal cost. Thus the average variable cost curve in part (b) begins where marginal cost starts, and then declines until the quantity just to the left of point *d* at which the ray from point *a* forms its lowest angle (this is ray *ae*). Average cost curves are just like any other average. An average is brought up by averaging in a number that is above the average, and it is brought down by averaging in a number below the average. It follows that if the extra cost (marginal cost) of the last unit averaged into average cost is *below* the average, average cost must be *falling*. If the marginal cost is *above* the average cost, the average must be *rising*. *If the average is neither rising nor falling, the marginal cost must be the same as the average.*[11] These facts can be checked in Table 6.2, where average variable cost is computed in column 7 by taking variable cost and dividing it by quantity.

One other fact can be gleaned about average variable cost. Since AC = AFC + AVC, it follows that AC − AVC = AFC = FC/q. For large output levels, average fixed cost approaches zero, and the average variable cost curve consequently approaches the average cost curve. In part (b) of Figure 6.10, average fixed cost is the vertical distance between AC and AVC. The figure verifies that the distance falls to zero as output increases.

Relationship Between Short-Run and Long-Run Cost Curves

▼
8. Why is there no fixed cost in the long run?

In the long run, the amounts of *all* factors used by the firm are under the control of the firm manager. For instance, before a new factory is built, a plant calling for any combination of capital and labor can be chosen, and no factor is fixed. The same principles that we learned about graphing cost curves in the short run apply in the long run. As before, all cost curves derive from the total cost curve. Marginal cost and average cost are defined as before. The major difference is that *fixed costs equal zero in the long run.* Thus long-run total cost *is* long-run variable cost, and long-run average cost *is* long-run average variable cost.

Taking a short-run total cost function and setting fixed cost equal to zero in that function does not convert it to the long-run cost function of the firm. Long-run total cost and short-run total cost have to be derived separately, according to which factors are fixed, at what levels they are fixed, and so on, as described in section 6.4. Nevertheless, there is a natural relationship between short-run and long-run cost curves.

▼
9. Draw a diagram relating short-run and long-run total cost curves, and a diagram relating short-run and long-run average cost curves and marginal cost curves.

Let's say that as firm manager you have to decide about building a plant to produce windows for homes. You must decide how big a plant to build, and once it is built you must decide how much labor to hire and how many windows to produce. Nothing has been done yet: you have the option of building no plant, in which case you pay no costs for capital or labor. Since all factors are variable, you are in a long-run planning situation.

You could build a plant designed to produce 10,000 windows per year, 20,000 windows per year, 50,000 windows per year, or a plant of some other size. However, once it is completed, you are committed to the size of plant you have built. Your capital cost becomes fixed, at which point your options

11. Here is a little exercise in the use of averages: Let X be your college's archrival school. Answer this question: How can you take a student from your microeconomics class and send him or her to the corresponding class at X, thereby raising the average IQ of *both* classes?

are limited to how much labor to hire. At that time, you will no longer be in a long-run situation.

What do we mean by a plant of a given size? A little thought tells us that a 50,000-window-per-year plant means a plant designed to produce 50,000 windows each year at lowest average cost. Part (a) of Figure 6.11 shows the

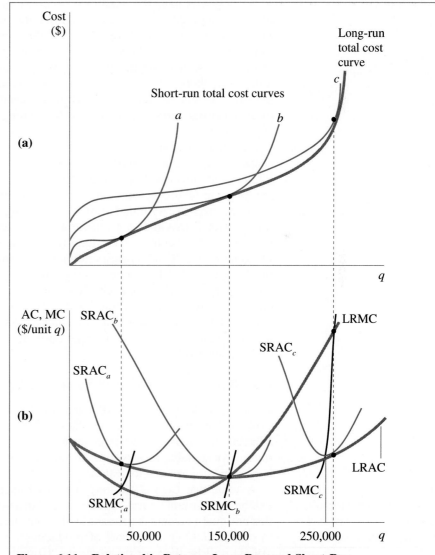

(a)

(b)

Figure 6.11   Relationship Between Long-Run and Short-Run Cost   The long-run total cost curve is the lower envelope of all short-run total cost curves. Long-run average cost and long-run marginal cost are determined from the long-run total cost curve. Because the long-run total cost curve is the lower envelope of short-run total cost curves, the LRAC curve is also the lower envelope of SRAC curves.

cost curves for three plants of different sizes. Curve *a* is the cost curve for a plant that reaches its lowest average cost of production at an output level of 50,000 windows per year. Curves *b* and *c,* respectively, reach the lowest average cost at outputs of 150,000 and 250,000 windows per year. Since each cost curve represents costs for a fixed plant size (fixed capital stock), these are short-run curves. Note that fixed costs increase with plant size.

Because you have the flexibility to choose plant size, your long-run costs of producing a given number of windows are indicated by the lowest cost of the available curves. If there were only three possible plant sizes, the long-run cost would be the lower boundary of the three short-run curves drawn. In most cases, there are likely to be many possible plant sizes, each one with a different short-run cost curve. The lower boundary, or lower *envelope* of the short-run curves (the line consisting for each quantity of the lowest point of all short-run curves), corresponds to the long-run cost curve, as shown in Figure 6.11(a).

Note that the shape of the long-run cost curve cannot be deduced from the shape of any one short-run cost curve. Instead, the locations and shapes of *all* the short-run curves determine the shape of the long-run cost curve. Once the long-run total cost function is known, all derivative long-run curves can be found from it. As noted above, in the long run fixed costs are zero, so long-run total costs and long-run variable costs are identical. Part (b) of Figure 6.11 shows the curves for the long-run average cost (LRAC) and long-run marginal cost (LRMC) corresponding to the long-run total cost curve in part (a). Note that the LRAC curve is the envelope of the short-run average cost curves (SRAC). Also, for each SRAC, the corresponding short-run marginal cost curve (SRMC) cuts average cost at its lowest point, not where the SRAC curve is tangent to long-run average cost.[12] As shown in part (b), curves *a,* *b,* and *c* reach their lowest average costs at 50,000, 150,000, and 250,000 units, respectively.

Long-Run Average Cost and Returns to Scale

Figure 6.11 showed the LRAC curve as U-shaped, although we haven't yet explained what determines the shape of the long-run average cost curve. Whereas the SRAC curve is governed by the law of diminishing marginal returns for variable factors (one or more factors are fixed), the LRAC curve is governed by returns to scale.

▼
10. What are the implications of decreasing, constant, and increasing returns to scale for average cost?

Assume that $C(q)$ is the long-run cost function for a production process exhibiting constant returns to scale. Recall that constant returns to scale means that an equal-percentage increase in all inputs leads to a proportionate increase in output. If $C(1)$ is the cost of producing 1 unit of output, we know that $10C(1)$ will be the cost or producing 10 units of output, because when all

12. Only when the minimum short-run average cost point coincides with the minimum long-run average cost point does short-run marginal cost cut the short-run average cost curve at the point of tangency.

inputs are increased by multiple of 10, output goes up by the same propor-tion.[13] Since this is true for any multiple of output, the cost per unit is the same for any level of production: *average cost is constant for constant-returns-to-scale production.* The LRAC curve for constant returns to scale is a horizontal straight line.

When production exhibits increasing returns to scale, it means that as the scale of operations grows, inputs can be organized and used more efficiently, so that more-than-proportionate increases in output result. To use our earlier example, say you are Henry Ford making cars, a fairly standardized product. Your assembly line of 100 workers can do more than 50 times better than just two workers building cars in a garage. We can now explain why Henry Ford's innovation made cars cheaper and thus available for a wider audience. Imagine how different things would be if Ford hadn't taken advantage of increasing returns to scale in manufacturing!

Let $C(q)$ represent the long-run cost function for cars, exhibiting increasing returns to scale, and let $q' = 1,000\, q$, so that q' is a much larger number of cars than q. We know that multiplying all inputs by 1,000 will increase Ford's output by a proportion *greater* than 1,000. If we want q' output, therefore, it costs less than $1,000C(q)$, since this much money would allow us to produce output greater than $1,000q$. Thus $C(q') < (q'/q)C(q)$, or

$$\frac{C(q')}{q'} < \frac{C(q)}{q}.$$

Hence, average costs fall with output for increasing-returns-to-scale produc-tion.

A similar argument shows that the reverse is true for decreasing returns to scale: *average costs rise with output for decreasing-returns-to-scale produc-tion.*[14] Reasons for the presence of decreasing returns to scale might include the loss of effective coordination in an operation grown too large, the negative effects of slower information flows between parts of the production process, or some other difficulty inherent in large size. For whatever reason, many production processes appear to have an optimal scale of operations above which costs per unit rise.

Figure 6.12 provides a convenient summary of the effects of increasing, constant, and decreasing returns to scale on the long-run cost function. In-creasing returns to scale imply falling average costs, shown in part (a),

13. This shows that the 10 units can be produced *as cheaply per unit* as 1 unit of output. Ten units cannot be produced *more* cheaply than this, because if they could, 1 unit could also be produced more cheaply than $C(1)$ simply by using the 10-unit process at one-tenth the scale.
14. Let q' equal mq, where m is greater than 1. Reducing the inputs used to produce q' units to $1/m$, their original amount produces more than q units of output because of decreasing returns to scale. The cost of producing q units of output must therefore be less than $(1/m)C(q')$. Writing $(1/m)C(q') > C(q)$ and dividing both sides by q says that the average cost of producing q' is greater than the average cost of producing q: average costs rise with output.

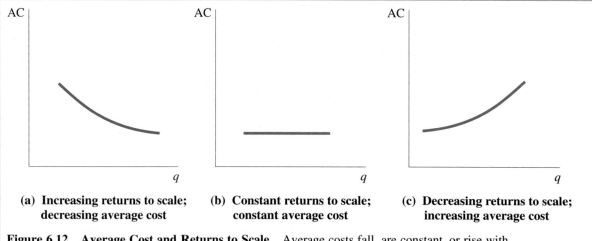

(a) **Increasing returns to scale; decreasing average cost**

(b) **Constant returns to scale; constant average cost**

(c) **Decreasing returns to scale; increasing average cost**

Figure 6.12   Average Cost and Returns to Scale   Average costs fall, are constant, or rise with output depending on whether production exhibits increasing, constant, or decreasing returns to scale. Standard U-shaped cost curves, therefore, exhibit regions of increasing returns, constant returns, and decreasing returns.

whereas decreasing returns to scale imply rising average costs, shown in part (c). The middle graph, part (b), indicates that average costs are constant with constant returns to scale. A U-shaped average cost curve of the type drawn in Figure 6.10 has falling, flat, and rising sections. The falling section corresponds to increasing returns to scale, where larger output allows more efficient use of inputs. The flat section at the bottom of the cost curve corresponds to constant returns to scale, where no particular advantage or disadvantage results from larger size. The rising portion of the curve implies decreasing returns to scale, indicating that the size of operation is beyond the point where costs are at their minimum.

   Some observers contend that any decreasing returns to scale must come from the presence of some factor of production that is unknowingly or implicitly being held constant when all other factors are increased. If not, we could always imagine duplicating the entire globe and everything in it as many times as needed. With identical worlds, output would have to increase in proportion to the increase in all inputs. We would never observe decreasing returns to scale. The fact that some production processes exhibit decreasing returns to scale even though we proportionately increase inputs must therefore mean that some overlooked factor of production is not truly being increased. In this case, decreasing returns to scale are really the result of diminishing marginal product for the inputs that are increased while some other input or inputs are fixed.

Economies of Scope

▼

11. What are economies of scope?

Economists sometimes distinguish another cost-reducing economy called an *economy of scope*. Economies of scope result when it is less costly to combine the production of two or more products than to produce the same quantities of each separately. An example might be a ranching operation that produces meat and hides, or a landscaping service that provides tree trimming and also sells shredded bark and branches for mulch. Another example might be coast-to-coast trucking. Trucking companies generally transport goods both from east to west and from west to east. This is cheaper than transporting goods in only one direction, because trucks that would have to return empty can be used to haul on the return trip. In coast-to-coast trucking, therefore, cost savings result from the shared input. The use of other joint inputs, such as the sharing of management expertise, marketing services, or production facilities, might also explain economies of scope. Sometimes beneficial by-products explain why combining two activities can produce each product at lower cost, as in the ranching and tree-trimming operations. Similarly, apple orchards frequently sell honey because bees help pollinate the apple blossoms, and the availability of apple blossoms aids the gathering of nectar.[15]

The degree of economies of scope is measured by the amount of cost savings from combined production in comparison to separate production. If $C_x(q_x)$ is the cost of producing q_x units of good x, $C_y(q_y)$ is the cost of producing q_y units of good y, and $C(q_x, q_y)$ is the cost of producing the two goods in combination, the savings from economies of scope are written as

$$E_{scope} = \left\{ \frac{[C_x(q_x) + C_y(q_y)]}{C(q_x, q_y)} \right\} - 1.$$

This equation gives us the savings as a decimal proportion of the combined cost. An E_{scope} of 0.2, for example, would mean a savings equal to 20 percent of the cost of producing the two goods in combination.

If there are no interaction effects from combining production, the cost of producing in combination is the same as the cost of producing separately, and the economy of scope measure is zero. On the other hand, if $C(q_x, q_y)$ is less than the cost of separate production, the measure of economies of scope is positive. It is conceivable that combining production of the two goods leads to harmful interactions (imagine trying to supply piano tuning under the same roof as sheet-metal stamping), so that $C(q_x, q_y)$ exceeds the cost of separate production. In this case, the economies of scope measure is negative.

Figure 6.13 displays three-dimensionally a cost function of the form $C(q_x, q_y)$. In part (a) the height of the surface indicates the cost. The front edge of the surface (the cost when no good y is produced) shows the cost of separate production for good x. Cost for good y is shown by the rising edge of the surface corresponding to zero production of good x. The degree of economies of scope is independent of the degree of returns to scale, and vice versa. In this case, total cost for separate production (each good has the same

15. We will discuss the economics of these types of interactions in more detail in Chapter 14.

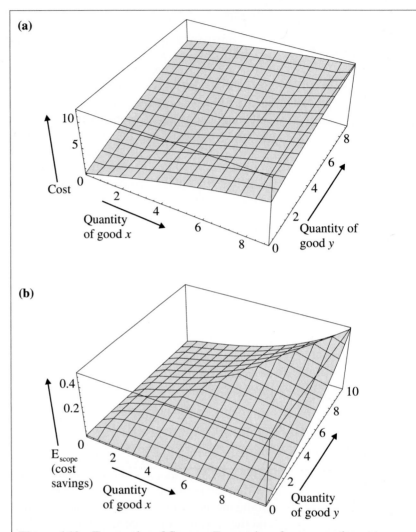

Figure 6.13 Economies of Scope Economies of scope are the cost savings from producing different goods in combination, compared to the cost of producing each separately. Part (a) three-dimensionally shows the cost of producing two goods, where height represents cost. Producing good x in isolation leads to increasing costs along the x-axis. The cost of producing good y is symmetrical to that of x. Producing both x and y together, however, leads to the cost surface, with a crease indicating the presence of cost reductions resulting from economies of scope. Part (b) plots the size of the cost savings from combined production as a decimal proportion. Savings range from zero to nearly 50 percent.

separate production cost) is a ray from the origin, indicating that separate production exhibits constant returns to scale. As can be seen in part (a), the surface dips toward the center. The greater the dip, the greater the economies of scope. Part (b) displays the economies of scope measure, E_{scope}, over the same range of outputs. The height of the surface shows the percentage of cost savings, ranging from zero to nearly 50 percent.

6.6 Summing Up the Firm's Environment

We have come a good way in this chapter toward understanding the world of the firm manager. We know why maximization of economic profit rather than accounting profit is the objective of the firm; how the production function relates inputs to outputs; and, most important, how to get from production data to the cost curve of the firm in the short run and the long run. Faced with the operation of a firm, we have a basic framework within which to gather and organize the necessary information for making further decisions.

By gathering our data so that we know how the firm's choice of quantity produced affects cost and quantity sold, we have simplified the firm manager's problem considerably. The problem becomes one of selecting the quantity of output that maximizes the difference between revenue and cost. This is the subject of Chapter 7.

Summary

Active Reading Guide numbers are given in parentheses at the end of each summary item.

1. The firm exists as a planning and coordinating entity, reducing some of the transaction costs and other frictions of interaction. The primary objective of the firm is to maximize profit, the difference between revenues and costs. The basic rationale for profit maximization is that higher profit implies higher income to the firm's owner or owners, which translates into higher utility. Yet firm managers' interests may differ from those of the firm's owners; the manager may have goals other than maximizing profits. The presence of asymmetric information concerning the manager's actions leads to the need for monitoring by boards of directors and other watchdogs, as well as to the construction of compensation schemes and contractual arrangements to provide incentives for proper management. Profit maximization remains, however, the single most important description of the firm's objectives. (1)

2. To calculate profit, the manager has to know costs, and to know costs requires knowing how inputs relate to output. This information is summarized in the production function, which tells how much output can be produced from a given bundle of inputs. The total product, marginal product, and average product of an input relate, respectively, to total output, additional output per additional unit of an input, and output per unit of the input, when only one factor of production is changed and other factors are fixed. (2)

3. The law of diminishing marginal returns states that, when other factors are held fixed, the marginal product of a factor eventually falls as input increases beyond a certain point. Rising marginal product results from size-related efficiencies, including the gains from specialization. (3)

4. Isoquants graphically describe the information in the production function. The absolute value of their slope equals the marginal rate of technical substitution. The marginal rate of technical substi-

tution, equal to the ratio of marginal products for two inputs, is the rate at which one input can substitute for another in production, holding output constant. The tighter the curvature in the isoquant, the smaller the degree of substitutability between factors. Perfect substitutability corresponds to straight-line isoquants, and zero substitutability corresponds to L-shaped isoquants. Proportionately increasing all inputs is an increase in scale. Equal spacing of isoquants for equal increments in output implies constant returns to scale, whereas increasingly close spacing for equal increments in output implies increasing returns to scale. Increasingly wide spacing of isoquants implies decreasing returns to scale. (4)

5. For the firm to make proper decisions, its profit must be measured the right way—as economic profit. This means including the opportunity costs of inputs, but ignoring sunk costs because they cannot be changed. The opportunity cost of an input is the income that the input could earn for the firm in its next best alternative use. (5)

6. Using the production function to relate factor inputs to output, the firm chooses the least costly combination of inputs to produce each level of output. The set of all least-cost input bundles is the firm's output expansion path. Except for corner solutions, or situations in which only one factor is variable, factor input costs are minimized at the tangency of the isocost line and the isoquant, where the marginal rate of technical substitution of factor a for factor b equals the price of factor a divided by the price of factor b. This tangency indicates that the extra output from each marginal dollar spent on an input should be the same for each input. Relating the least cost of production to each level of output produces the firm's cost function. (6)

7. In the short run, when the input of one or more factors of production is fixed, the cost of hiring fixed factors of production is called fixed cost. Variable costs are the costs of hiring factors whose input level varies with the level of output. The sum of fixed costs plus variable costs equals short-run total cost. From the total cost function, one can derive marginal cost, average cost, average variable cost, and average fixed cost. When marginal cost exceeds average variable cost and average cost, these two curves rise; when marginal cost is below them, these curves fall. (7)

8. In the long run, the firm can choose the inputs of all factors of production, and fixed costs are zero. Long-run total cost curves are the lower envelope of all short-run total cost curves. We derive the long-run average cost curve and long-run marginal cost curve from the long-run total cost curve. Long-run average cost curves are the lower envelope of short-run average cost curves. (8, 9)

9. Average costs rise, fall, or remain flat when production exhibits decreasing, increasing, or constant returns to scale, respectively. Economies of scope describe the cost savings from producing different goods in combination, as compared to producing each good separately. (10, 11)

Review Questions

*1. Firms are sometimes described as "bundles" of related activities or tasks. For example, a firm might have a graphics department, a design department, and a manufacturing division under a single roof. In a large urban market with good communications and transportation, do you think firms would be more or less inclined to offer such specialized activities as stand-alone enterprises? Relate your answer to considerations that might determine how many and what kind of activities a firm carries out under one roof.

*2. List three objectives that you think firms might sometimes pursue other than profit maximization. Are there circumstances in which these might imply profit maximization? (Example: Larger market share might be one such objective.)

3. Give two specific examples in which the objectives of the firm manager might differ from those

* Asterisks are used to denote questions that are answered at the back of the book.

of the owner.

*4. In what way does the cost function already contain the results of optimization?

5. If marginal product is negative, must average product be negative? Does it have to be falling? Explain.

6. Adam Smith, the Scottish founder of the field of economics, in *An Inquiry into the Nature and Causes of the Wealth of Nations* discussed the benefits of specialization in a pin factory. He also advocated free trade, which tends to enlarge the market, allowing larger and more specialized firms. Would the benefits from specialization tend to cause increasing or decreasing returns to scale? Use your answer to discuss how free trade might affect a firm's average costs.

*7. A production function exhibits constant returns to scale, using capital and labor as its inputs. If inputs are increased in increments of the same absolute amount, moving outward on a ray from the origin, does that mean that output will rise by the same absolute amount for each increment?

8. Does average product fall if marginal product

is positive? What about total product? What is true of marginal product if average and total product are rising?

*9. Relate marginal cost to marginal product in the short run when only labor is variable. Use this relationship to explain the effect of the law of diminishing marginal returns on marginal cost.

10. Can you convert a short-run cost function into a long-run cost function by setting fixed costs to zero? Explain.

*11. Is variable cost for output level q equal to the sum of all marginal costs from output zero to output q?

12. Explain why long-run average cost and marginal cost curves start at the same point on the vertical axis, and why marginal cost curves cut the average cost and average variable cost curves at their minimum points.

*13. Average cost curves rise, fall, or are constant with respect to output depending on the nature of returns to scale. Explain why U-shaped cost curves exhibit falling, constant, and rising portions.

Numerical and Graphing Exercises

*1. Draw isoquants for the following production functions:

  a) $q = 3K + 2L$
  b) $q = $ minimum of $(K/3, L/2)$
  c) $q = K^3 L^2$
  d) $q = 3 \log K + 2 \log L$

2. Draw diagrams to construct a firm's cost function when

  a) it has two inputs, one of which is fixed in the short run
  b) it has three inputs, one of which is fixed in the short run

*3. A firm uses land, T, capital, K, and labor, L, to produce output q according to the following production functions. Determine whether production exhibits increasing, decreasing, or constant returns to scale.

  a) $q = T + K + L$
  b) $q = (T + K)^{1/2} + L$
  c) $q = (TK)^{1/2} + L$
  d) $q = (T^{-3} + K^{-3} + L^{-3})^{-1/3}$

4. Assume that capital is fixed in the short run. Find the firm's short-run total cost if production satisfies these equations: $q = K + L$; $w = \$1$ per unit of labor; and $r = \$1$ per unit of capital.

*5. Do exercise 4 assuming that the production function is $q = $ minimum of $(K, L/2)$.

6. What is the long-run cost function in exercise 4?

*7. What is the long-run cost function in exercise 5?

8. Harvey Robertson, Inc., makes a popular brand of motorcycles. In the short run the plant size

is fixed, but output changes as follows, where output is measured in thousands.

Labor Input	Total Output	MP_L	AP_L
0	0	—	—
1		1	1
2	2	1	
3	2.5		
4		0.3	
5			0.6
6	3.1		
7	2.9	−0.2	
8		−0.3	

Fill out the rest of the table. In what region is average product of labor rising? In what regions is it falling or negative? Prove that Robertson is not maximizing profit if it hires less than 2 or more than 6 workers.

CHAPTER 7

Output Choice Under Perfect Competition

The two most important goals of this chapter are to impart an enduring understanding of the nature of perfect competition and to derive the market supply curve from the cost information of perfectly competitive firms. In the preceding chapter we derived the firm's cost curves from its most basic production data. In this chapter we see how the firm uses this information to maximize profits in perfectly competitive markets. From the firm's choices we derive the short-run and long-run supply curves of the firm. To go from firm supply to market supply, we examine the nature of input costs for the industry and the role of perfect competition in driving long-run economic profits to zero. Finally, we revisit the notion of perfectly competitive equilibrium for a better understanding of market adjustments in the short and long run.

ACTIVE READING GUIDES

After reading this chapter, you should be able to answer the Active Reading Guides listed below. These guides also appear in the page margins, near the material to which they refer.

1. What are four conditions for perfect competition? Discuss circumstances in which each might be met.

2. Use graphical representations of profit to justify the firm's profit maximization rule in perfectly competitive markets.

3. How does the $p = MC$ rule apply to the division of output among different plants?

4. Describe how to construct the firm's short-run supply curve.

5. Describe how to construct the firm's long-run supply curve.

6. How are the firm's short-run and long-run costs related?

7. Construct the short-run market supply curve. Explain why it may sometimes differ from the sum of individual firm supply curves.

8. How do you find the long-run market supply curve? List the factors that determine its slope.

9. What is producer surplus? Use the term to describe the benefits to the firm from being able to sell at a higher price?

10. Describe the price, quantity, utility, and producer surplus effects of a tax in perfectly competitive markets.

7.1 The Competitive Market Setting

A little over a decade and a half ago, you and your friend started making personal computers (PCs) in your garage. At that time, large computer manufacturers were still thinking only of mainframes, and you had the PC market to yourself. Although you had to convince consumers to buy PCs, you could pretty much set prices as you thought best, producing as many computers as you could sell. Life was good, and your company, Pear Computers, flourished.

Then the market started to change. Mainframe manufacturers began selling their own personal computer lines. Other small companies sprang up, many of them like Kumquat, Inc., growing phenomenally fast in the enlarging market. Even other countries' firms got into the act. New and more powerful chips were becoming available on a regular basis. Eventually it seemed that almost anyone could begin manufacturing computers with off-the-shelf parts, a little knowledge, and a screwdriver. Consumers were also getting quite sophisticated about PC capabilities. As competition continued to stiffen and the number of your competitors increased, you had less flexibility to set your own prices as before, for fear that some nameless competitor would undercut you with a lower-priced machine of identical capabilities. Now, with many firms manufacturing standardized PCs at known market prices, your competitive concerns are different. You must keep costs as low as possible and choose your quantity to maximize profit, but you no longer have the unique product or the same options that you did at the beginning. Welcome to the world of perfect competition.

Though this hypothetical scenario features PCs,[1] essentially the same elements could have been found in the history of automobiles from the turn of

---

1. Readers may recognize elements of the history of Apple Computer, Compaq, and IBM.

the century to World War II, photocopiers in the 1950s and 1960s, fax machines and cellular phones in the 1980s and 1990s, or any number of other products and markets. Success leads to emulation; emulation leads to standardization and competition; and the limit of competition is what economists call *perfect competition.* Though the production functions and cost curves we derived in Chapter 6 apply to firms in any market, how the firm uses them depends on what type of competition it faces in the market. An important task of this and succeeding chapters is to relate the firm's choices to the nature of market competition.

This chapter discusses the firm's output choice in perfectly competitive markets. Economists reserve a special meaning for perfect competition that differs from what we mean by competition in general. Although advertising, price undercutting, and product differentiation are all elements of market rivalry covered under the general rubric of competition, these are not features of *perfect* competition. Perfectly competitive markets also have desirable efficiency properties that are not always shared by other forms of competition.[2] Thus our first task is to define what we mean by perfect competition.

Conditions for Perfect Competition

▼
1. What are four conditions for perfect competition? Discuss circumstances in which each might be met.

What determines that a high degree of competition is present? Table 7.1 summarizes four conditions that define what we mean by perfect competition. All four are needed for perfect competition. If one or more is violated, competition will not be perfect.[3] We consider each condition in turn.

1. Standardized Product. In perfectly competitive markets, firms sell products that are perfect substitutes for one another to consumers and thus do not compete by differentiating their products. The absence of product differentiation might seem at first to lessen competition rather than heighten it, but the real implication of a standardized product is that the firm is forced to compete directly with the equivalent products of other firms. Some markets, of course, have perfectly homogeneous products, such as chemicals or metals, where the good itself *is* a standardized product. Perfect competition, however, does not require that goods be literally homogeneous, only that consumers view them as equivalent. It is sufficient that Pillsbury's wheat flour is viewed as equivalent to the wheat flour produced by General Mills and other mills, for example, even though they may differ in inessential ways. Needless to say, most markets only approach the limiting case of perfect standardization.

2. Pricetaking. Perfect competition also implies *pricetaking,* meaning that individual firms and households believe their choices have negligible effect on the market price and so take prices as given. Effectively, this means that the firm sees its demand curve as infinitely elastic (a horizontal line) at the

---

2. Chapters 12 and 13 are devoted to the analysis of the efficiency properties of markets, including perfectly competitive markets.
3. In Chapters 8, 9, and 10 we investigate different forms of competition that emerge when one or more of the conditions for perfect competition fail.

Table 7.1   Conditions for Perfect Competition

Condition	Subconditions	Implications
Standardized product	Goods of different firms are perfect substitutes for one another to consumers.	Firms do not compete by offering different types of product
Pricetaking	Individual firms perceive a horizontal demand curve at the market price	Since individual firms and households perceive they cannot influence market price, they take price as given in their decisions
	Individual households perceive a horizontal supply curve at the market price	
	Often associated with large numbers of sellers	
	No strategic behavior; sellers do not consider how their actions might influence the actions of competitors to their own advantage.	
Contestability	Costless entry and exit with absence of sunk costs	The potential for firms to enter or exit the market without cost keeps any one firm from dominating it
	Economic profits reduced to zero in the long run	
Perfect information	Households are informed about the product, its price, its quality, its characteristics, and its availability	Lack of necessary knowledge is not an impediment to firms or consumers
	Firms are informed about potential profit opportunities	

market price, as does the household for its supply curve. Pricetaking by firms is often described as the result of large (even infinitely large) numbers of competing firms, so that any one firm's output is too small to have any effect on market price. After all, a wheat farmer in Kansas is not concerned that planting an additional 50 acres in red winter wheat will cause the market price to drop.

Although the existence of a large number of firms can often produce pricetaking behavior, it is strictly neither necessary nor sufficient for pricetaking. Markets with relatively small numbers of firms (say, 5 to 25) might exhibit pricetaking because the market demand curve is very elastic, so that the firms' effective demand curves are nearly flat despite the small number of firms. Pricetaking might also result from the way the firms compete with one another. On the other hand, a large number of firms could collude with one another to set market price, a situation implying the absence of pricetaking. Lastly, if firms knew that other firms' actions were in some way dependent on their own, they could act strategically. That is, firms could take into account how their choices changed the choices of other firms, thereby affecting price. Pricetaking rules out both collusion and such strategic behavior.[4]

3. Contestability. In addition to standardized product and pricetaking, perfect competition implies that there must be competition *for* the market as well as competition *within* the market. In other words, the market must be *contestable*. A contestable market has costless entry or exit: new firms can enter the market without incurring additional costs beyond those of existing or incumbent firms, and incumbent firms can leave the market without losing part of their investment in unrecoverable sunk costs.[5]

A simple example illustrates both points. Consider a movie firm that wants to enter the market for a new genre of movies. Since entry in this case simply means taking cameras and movie sets and assigning them to the new tasks, there are no costs to the firm beyond the costs of firms already in that genre. Likewise, when the movie firm decides to leave the market, it loses little or nothing by sending its resources elsewhere.

Now consider the same situation with *entry barriers*. Entry barriers can take many forms, such as the time and effort needed to get necessary zoning permits to build a needed plant, the time and costs needed to gather information about market conditions, or the inability to buy some necessary input. In this case, assume that because of technical requirements the movie firm needs to build a totally new set and acquire massive amounts of expensive equipment before it can produce the new movie genre. It will now be at a great disadvantage relative to incumbent firms that do not have equipment costs. By the same token, if the firm needs to exit the market and is unable to sell its structures and equipment for what it paid, it may lose some of the costs that it sank into them. Such a market would not be perfectly contestable.

An important implication of free entry and exit is that firms in perfectly competitive markets may make positive economic profits in the short run, but in the long run economic profits will be zero. That is, as long as positive economic profits can be made as easily by new entrants as by existing firms, new firms have an incentive to enter. New entrants, of course, increase market supply, lower market price, and possibly increase the cost of inputs. The process of entry continues until economic profits are zero and there is no incentive for further entry. For the same reason, firms will continue to leave

4. We will look at these issues in Chapters 8 through 10.
5. The concept of market contestability derives from William J. Baumol, John C. Panzar, and Robert Willig, *Contestable Markets and the Theory of Industry Structure,* New York: Harcourt Brace Jovanovich, 1982.

markets where economic profits are negative until conditions are such that the remaining firms make zero profits.[6]

4. Perfect Information. Lastly, perfect competition requires that firms and consumers have all of the necessary information for their decision making. In a sense, perfect information for consumers is already covered by the requirement of standardized product, since consumers must know the product they are buying, its characteristics relative to the output of competing firms, its price, and so on. A similar condition applies to firms, which must know whether economic profits are positive or negative in order to take advantage of market opportunities and must not face information barriers to entry. Thus perfect competition requires information.

Although few markets completely satisfy the requirements for perfect competition, understanding how firms act in perfectly competitive situations makes it easier to understand how they work in other kinds of markets. Strictly speaking, a firm's choice of output may have some small influence on market price. Nevertheless, the assumption of pricetaking becomes appropriate as the number of firms in a market grows, because each firm's effect on price becomes negligible. Similarly, a firm may make a product which, strictly speaking, is unique. However, there may be extremely close substitutes provided by other firms. As the degree of substitutability rises, the assumption of perfect competition becomes appropriate. Likewise, even though entry is never perfectly free, as the costs associated with entry become small, the perfectly competitive assumption of contestability becomes appropriate. In short, understanding perfectly competitive markets offers a benchmark to which other markets can be compared.

7.2 Profit and the Output Decision

In this section we will see how a perfectly competitive firm uses the cost function discussed in Chapter 6 to maximize profit. In the following sections, we will then relate the firm's choice to its supply curve, the market supply curve, and equilibrium in perfectly competitive markets. The pricetaking firm has two tasks to perform: (1) find the highest profit from positive output, and (2) compare that to the profit from choosing zero output. The firm then does the better of the two. In what follows, we find a simple rule for the firm to use that applies in the long run and in the short run.

---

6. Making zero economic profits does not contradict the fact that firms maximize profits. Recall from Chapter 6 that zero economic profit just means that firms are earning the normal rate of return on their investments after paying for inputs and all factors of production. Firms that did not maximize profit would earn less than the normal return and would find it in their interest to move to greener pastures.

Graphical Representations of Profit and Profit Maximization

Subtracting total cost, $C(q)$, from total revenue, $R(q)$, gives us profit,

$$\Pi = R(q) - C(q).$$

▼

2. Use graphical representations of profit to justify the firm's profit maximization rule in perfectly competitive markets.

Since the perfectly competitive firm takes the price, p, as given, we also know that revenue rises in proportion to output, or $R(q) = pq$. We call this the *revenue function*. Plotting revenue as a function of q produces the ray from the origin in part (a) of Figure 7.1, with slope p. The curved line starting at fixed cost FC is total cost. Since fixed cost is positive, we know the cost curve is short run.

For each quantity in part (a), the firm's profit is the vertical distance between total revenue and total cost. Part (b) plots profit separately. At the highest profit point q^*, the *slope* of the total cost curve must be the same as the *slope* of the total revenue curve. If not, we could adjust quantity a little to the right or left to increase the distance between the two curves in part (a).

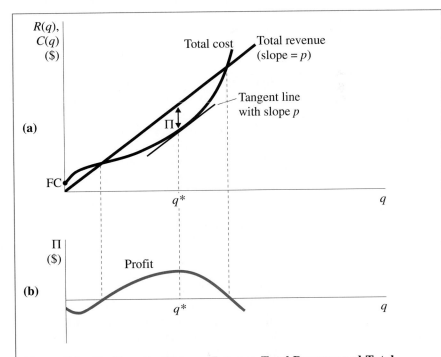

Figure 7.1 Profit as the Distance Between Total Revenue and Total Cost Profit, measured as the vertical distance between revenue and cost in part (a), is plotted separately in part (b). The quantity generating maximum profit occurs where the slope of total revenue, price, is equal to the slope of total cost, MC.

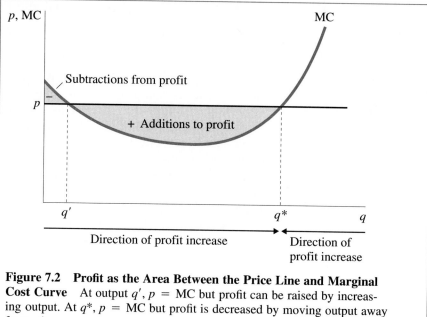

Figure 7.2   Profit as the Area Between the Price Line and Marginal Cost Curve   At output q', $p = $ MC but profit can be raised by increasing output. At q^*, $p = $ MC but profit is decreased by moving output away from q^*.

Since the slope of total revenue is p, and the slope of total cost is marginal cost, the equation $p = $ MC(q) is the necessary condition for profit maximization.

Since the rule depends on price and marginal cost, Figure 7.2 plots both curves to examine it further.[7] Here, we note that marginal cost cuts the horizontal price line at both q' and q^*. When more than one quantity causes price to equal marginal cost, we must choose the quantity that gives highest profit. At q', if we increase the quantity, revenue rises by price p for each additional unit, while cost increases by MC, which is lower than p. Thus, increasing output at q' raises profit, so q' will not give the highest profit. In contrast, a small move from q^* in either direction lowers profit. Thus we see that if profit maximization occurs at positive output, it requires that $p = $ MC and *marginal cost be rising*.[8] Basically, it's easy to see that if it costs an additional $25, say, to produce a unit of output that sells for $15, the firm manager is better off not producing the additional unit. The reverse is true if the unit sells for more than $25. Only if $p = $ MC and the manager cannot do better by moving to more (or fewer) units (MC is rising) is profit maximized.

7. Since the firm is a pricetaker, the horizontal line at price p in Figure 7.2 is also the firm's perceived demand curve.
8. Expressed as a calculus maximization problem, profit is a function of output, $\Pi(q) = pq - C(q)$. For $\Pi(q)$ to be maximized, it must be neither rising nor falling with respect to a change in q. The change in revenue with respect to a change in output is equal to the price,

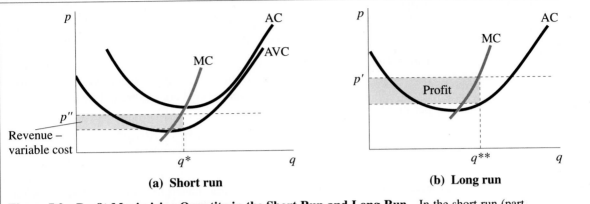

(a) Short run   **(b) Long run**

Figure 7.3 Profit-Maximizing Quantity in the Short Run and Long Run   In the short run (part a), the firm is better off producing q^* as long as profit is above the negative of fixed cost (the loss it would have if it produced no output). This will be true as long as price is above the minimum average variable cost, guaranteeing that revenue minus variable cost is positive. In the long run (part b), however, the firm is better off producing q^{**} as long as profit, equal to the area of the shaded rectangle, is positive. This will be true as long as price is above minimum average cost.

In Figure 7.2, profit is the area between the price line and the marginal cost curve, counting areas where marginal cost is above price as negative. We must also subtract fixed cost from the area shown, but this is unchanging with output. Maximizing profit is therefore equivalent to maximizing the area between the price line and the marginal cost curve. Since the p = MC rule does not depend on fixed costs, it applies to firms in the short run and in the long run. But we still don't know if producing where p = MC gives better profit than not producing at all. For this comparison, considered next, it matters whether fixed costs are positive or zero.

Short Run. Producing zero output in the short run means the firm's losses equal its fixed cost. If we define variable profit per unit as price minus average variable cost, we can write profit as quantity times variable profit per unit, less fixed costs, or

$$\Pi = pq - \text{VC}(q) - \text{FC} = q[p - \text{AVC}(q)] - \text{FC}.$$

Part (a) of Figure 7.3 shows variable profit per unit as the vertical distance between the price line p'' and the average variable cost curve. Multiplying this

---

and the change in costs with respect to a change in output is marginal cost. The condition that the change in profit with respect to a change in output be zero is therefore $d\Pi(q)/dq = p - \text{MC} = 0$, which gives the rule that price equals marginal cost as derived earlier. For a zero change in profits to represent the high point for profits rather than a low point, the second derivative of profits must be pulling profits down if there is any deviation from the profit-maximizing quantity. This condition says that the change in $d\Pi(q)/dq$, which is $-d\text{MC}/dq$, must be negative. That is, marginal cost itself must be rising.

distance by quantity q^* gives the firm's variable profit as the shaded rectangle. As long as price is above minimum average variable cost, this area is positive, $\Pi > -\text{FC}$, meaning that the firm is better off than if it shut down.

Long Run. Long-run fixed costs are zero, so producing nothing means zero profit. The same profit formula continues to apply, except that with zero fixed costs, average variable cost and average cost are identical. Profit is now profit per unit (price minus average cost) times quantity,

$$\Pi = pq - C(q) = q[p - \text{AC}(q)].$$

Part (b) of Figure 7.3 shows profit per unit as the vertical distance between the price line p' and the average cost curve. Multiplying this by quantity q^{**} gives the firm's profit as the area of the shaded rectangle. As long as price is above minimum average cost, this area is positive ($\Pi > 0$) and the firm is better off producing than shutting down. We will discuss the shutdown point in more detail in section 7.3.

The Simple Profit Maximization Rule

We can state what we have learned in a simple rule. Assuming perfect competition (so that firms are pricetakers), we have found that: *Maximum profit occurs at the quantity where price equals marginal cost, subject to the restrictions that (1) marginal cost is rising at the chosen output, and (2) price is above minimum average variable cost. If price is below minimum average variable cost, the firm is better off shutting down.*

Next we note that long-run average variable cost and long-run average cost are the same thing. Thus the same rule applies in the long run as in the short run, except that average cost replaces average variable cost. We will make use of this rule in section 7.3 to derive the supply curve of the firm in the short run and in the long run. At the same time, we will explore further the economics of the rule in terms of the different options open to a firm in the short and long run. First, however, let's take a look at how the price-equals-marginal-cost rule might come into play in an example of firm decision making.

▼
3. How does the $p = \text{MC}$ rule apply to the division of output among different plants?

APPLICATION: The Multiplant Problem

In December 1990 Ralston Purina Company, a maker of pet food and breakfast cereal, announced in its annual report that it was converting a dog-and-cat-food plant in Sparks, Nevada, to make Batman and Teenage Mutant Ninja Turtles breakfast cereals in addition to its traditional Chex line.[9] At the same time, it announced that it was building a cereal factory outside the United States, in Guadalajara, Mexico. Ralston explained that "children's cereals had a record year, with volume up more than 30%" and operating profits on

9. "Ralston Purina Co. Converts Chow Plant to Cereal Facility," *Wall Street Journal,* December 6, 1990, p. B6.

cereals were up substantially. Ralston's report went on to say that "Excellent results were achieved by the Cookie-Crisp, Batman and Teenage Mutant Ninja Turtles brands." We can look at this announcement, and others like it common to the business world, to see how managers make output decisions. As we will find, the issues managers face can be more involved than the models we have discussed so far, but the basic rules still apply.

One notable point is Ralston's response to high operating profits in the breakfast cereal market compared to pet food. Although Ralston already produced breakfast cereal, its plant conversion represented an enlarged presence in the market, confirming the view that profits attract entry. With respect to product homogeneity, Ralston's breakfast cereals are not identical to its competitors' cereals, but the company does produce "knockoff" versions of rival cereals such as Kellogg's Rice Krispies and General Mills' Cheerios. Because of their popularity, some cereals are imitated more frequently and thus have close substitutes. For instance, Post, Kellogg, and General Mills all make raisin bran.

Another issue raised by the Ralston announcement is how best to manage the several plants that produce Ralston cereal. How should the manager allocate production among plants to maximize profit? In this case, Ralston will have a domestic plant in Sparks, Nevada, and a foreign plant in Guadalajara, Mexico. Both plants could produce Batman cereal, but how much should each plant produce? A simple solution would be to split production evenly between plants, but that might not maximize profits. If the Mexican plant could more efficiently produce at low output levels (perhaps it is designed for smaller quantity) and the Nevada plant at high output levels, for example, then Ralston would probably pick the Mexican plant for low-level production, and for high output levels it would choose Nevada. The $p = \text{MC}$ rule gives us the clue to answering this problem.

Let q_N represent Nevada output and q_M Mexico output. Batman cereal from either plant is sold in the unified American and Mexican market, so total revenue is equal to $p(q_N + q_M)$. The cost function for the Nevada plant is $C_N(q_N)$, and for the Mexican plant it is $C_M(q_M)$. Thus profit equals $p(q_N + q_M) - C_N(q_N) - C_M(q_M)$. Raising production by one unit raises revenue by price p. If p is greater than marginal cost for the Nevada plant, producing one more unit there would raise profit by $(p - \text{MC}_N)$. If p is less the MC_N, decreasing production by one unit would increase profit. The same argument applies for the Mexican plant. Thus the production rule for the multiplant manager is: choose production levels q_N and q_M such that

$$p = \text{MC}_N(q_N) = \text{MC}_M(q_M).$$

This tells the manager both the optimal output level and how to divide production between the Mexican and Nevadan plants.[10] Price p fixes the

---

10. The exception would be if the plant with higher marginal cost was already producing zero output. In this case, both marginal costs cannot equal price because it is impossible to shift any further production away from the plant with higher marginal cost.

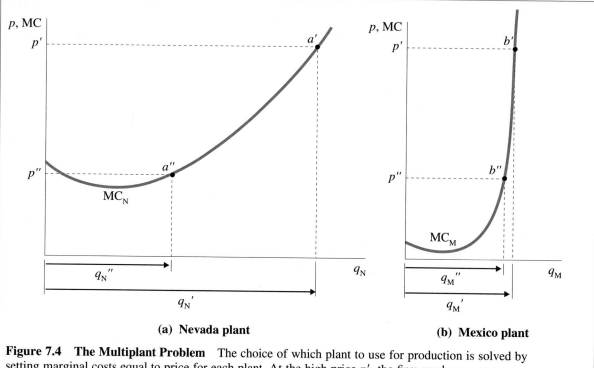

(a) Nevada plant   **(b) Mexico plant**

Figure 7.4   The Multiplant Problem   The choice of which plant to use for production is solved by setting marginal costs equal to price for each plant. At the high price p', the firm produces more output. A large proportion of that output is produced in the Nevada plant, because the marginal cost of production there rises less steeply for larger outputs than the marginal cost for the Mexican plant. At the low price p'', the firm produces less output but concentrates a greater proportion of production in the Mexican plant, which has a low marginal cost of production for low output levels.

output level for each plant, and the sum of those outputs determines total production.

Figure 7.4 shows how to divide total output between plants. The left side measures output on the horizontal axis and marginal cost and price on the vertical axis for the Nevada plant. The right side measures the same variables for the Mexican plant. Choosing quantity in each plant so that price equals marginal cost and dropping a vertical line from the intersection determines output in the two plants. Summing the output of both plants gives total production.

Note that a high price, p', leads to outputs q_N' and q_M', respectively, for the Nevada and Mexican plants. These are larger than the corresponding outputs q_N'' and q_M'' for the lower price p''. For each price, the shapes of the two marginal cost curves determine the optimal division of production between the Nevada and Mexico plants. In this case, a small total output tends to be more equally allocated between plants; but for a higher product price and greater output, more of the output should be produced at the Nevada plant. ■

7.3 The Firm's Short-Run and Long-Run Supply Curves

Most of the work for finding the firm's supply curves has already been done. In this section we simply take note of what we already know.

Short-Run Supply

▼

4. Describe how to construct the firm's short-run supply curve.

Figure 7.5 shows a set of short-run cost curves for a representative firm. Since we assume the firm is a pricetaker, we ask how much quantity the firm produces at each market price, and we collect the answers to form the supply curve. For prices between zero and p_1, the firm suffers losses for any choice of output, because p_1 is strictly below minimum average cost. Further, because price does not cover variable costs, losses from operation would be larger than fixed costs. The firm supplies no output, so the supply curve is the vertical axis for these prices.

For prices between p_1 and p_2, the firm produces on the marginal cost curve where $p = MC$. With price between average cost and average variable cost, the firm suffers losses, but smaller losses than if it produced nothing. Recall that profit can be written as $q[p - AVC(q)] - FC$. If price is above p_1 so that $[p - AVC(q)]$ is positive, profit exceeds $-FC$, the amount the firm would earn if it shut down. The firm does better by producing on its MC curve, so its output corresponds to the section of the marginal cost curve between points a and b.

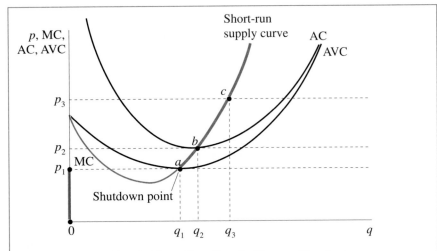

Figure 7.5   The Firm's Short-Run Supply Curve   The short-run supply curve is the marginal cost curve above the point of minimum average variable cost. At prices below minimum average variable cost, supply is zero and the supply curve corresponds to the vertical axis.

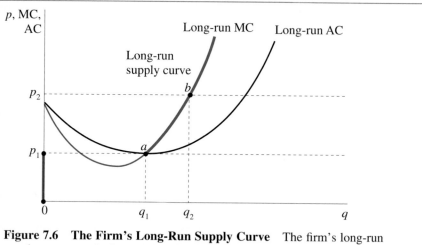

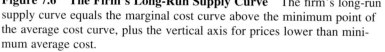

Figure 7.6   The Firm's Long-Run Supply Curve   The firm's long-run supply curve equals the marginal cost curve above the minimum point of the average cost curve, plus the vertical axis for prices lower than minimum average cost.

For prices above p_2 (such as price p_3), the firm makes a positive profit by supplying the quantity on the marginal cost curve. *The firm's supply curve is therefore the marginal cost curve above the minimum average variable cost point, and the vertical axis for prices below minimum average variable cost.* Because of its special role, the minimum point of the average variable cost curve is called the shut down point.

> *The minimum point of the firm's average variable cost curve is called the **shutdown point**, because at prices lower than minimum average variable cost, the firm is better off shutting down operations (producing no output) than producing positive output.*

Even though the firm takes losses for prices between the minimum average cost and the shutdown point, the firm has no choice in the short run but to make the best of a bad situation by continuing production. This is because the firm cannot eliminate fixed costs in the short run. Shutting down would just make losses greater. In the long run, however, no firm will operate with continuing losses. Having derived the firm's short-run supply curve, it is a simple matter to find the firm's long-run supply curve.

Long-Run Supply

▼
5. Describe how to construct the firm's long-run supply curve.

Figure 7.6 shows the firm's long-run marginal and average cost curves.[11] At prices below minimum average cost, the firm clearly will not supply any product, since it would suffer a loss if it did. Since fixed costs are zero in the

11. The shapes of these curves and their relationship to the firm's short-run cost curves were discussed in Chapter 6.

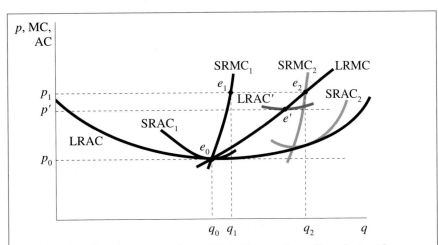

Figure 7.7   The Adjustment from Short-Run to Long-Run Output by the Firm   Starting at point e_0, the firm moves to e_1 in the short run in response to an increase in product price from p_0 to p_1. In the long run, however, the firm has the ability to increase its plant and equipment inputs, shifting its new short-run marginal cost and average cost to $SRMC_2$ and $SRAC_2$, respectively. The firm then moves to point e_2, where the price line again cuts long-run marginal cost and the new short-run marginal cost. This is where the firm remains until market conditions change. At e_2 the firm and other incumbents make positive economic profits. This attracts new entrants, whose increased supply lowers market price or raises the cost of inputs or both. Thus costs may shift to $LRAC'$ and market price to p', so that zero economic profits are restored for firms in the market. The firm's final equilibrium point then becomes e'.

long run, the firm can always do better than a loss by choosing not to produce and earning zero profits. Thus, for any price between zero and p_1, the supply curve is the vertical axis.

At prices above p_1, however, maximum profits are positive for points on the long-run marginal cost curve. Point a is the breakeven point at which price just allows the firm to make zero profits producing q_1. Hence, *the long-run supply curve of the firm is the marginal cost curve above the point of minimum average cost, and the vertical axis for prices below minimum average cost.* Notice that the procedure we used to find the short-run supply curve also applies in the long run if we recognize that long-run average variable cost and long-run average cost are the same curves. The main difference is that the procedure is applied to short-run curves in one case and to long-run curves in the other.

The Relationship Between Short Run and Long Run

The way in which the firm shifts from a short-run supply position to long-run supply can be shown in terms of the relationship between its short-run and long-run cost curves. Figure 7.7 demonstrates the case of a firm that is

▼

6. How are the firm's short-run and long-run costs related?

originally in long-run perfectly competitive equilibrium at point e_0, producing output q_0 at price p_0. The firm's long-run and short-run average cost curves, LRAC and $SRAC_1$, respectively, both pass through point e_0, as do the long-run and short-run marginal cost curves, LRMC and $SRMC_1$, showing that the firm makes zero economic profits. Initially, therefore, the firm has no incentive to exit the market or to change output.

Now assume that price rises to p_1. Since the firm cannot instantly adjust all of its inputs, its initial response must be short run, adjusting those inputs that it can. The firm's first reaction is to move production to e_1 on its short-run marginal cost curve, since this increases profit and it can do so without altering any of its fixed factors. In the long run, however, the firm can do better by adjusting all of its inputs (perhaps this means enlarging its plant and equipment, for example) to get to new short-run average cost $SRAC_2$ and short-run marginal cost $SRMC_2$. In the long run, then, the firm produces quantity q_2 at point e_2, where the short-run and long-run marginal cost curves again cross.

Whereas the *firm* has now returned to long-run equilibrium given market prices, it is now earning positive economic profits (as would other incumbents also). Positive profits would continue to attract new firms to the market, until such time as increases in input prices, reduction in the output price, or both reduced the economic profits of incumbent firms to zero. In the figure this is shown by point e', where a lower final price p' combined with a higher long-run average cost $LRAC'$ reduces the firm's economic profits to zero. Long-run average cost might shift up, for example, as the opportunity cost of using a fixed input rose.[12]

Now that we understand the short- and long-run supply curves of individual firms, we can move up to the level of the market as a whole. We will see how to find market supply curves in both the short run and the long run, and then we will consider producer surplus and equilibrium.

7.4 From Firm Supply to Market Supply

▼
7. Construct the short-run market supply curve. Explain why it may sometimes differ from the sum of individual firm supply curves.

We learned in Chapter 4 to sum individual demand curves horizontally to construct the market demand curve. In the case of the supply curve, this is only part of the process. Other considerations need to be taken into account, such as the entry and exit of firms and the fact that some of the input prices that the individual firm treats as fixed may not be fixed when *all* firms in the market increase their output. We start first with the short run and then consider the long run.

---

12. Of course, there are many ways in which output price, LRMC, and LRAC could change to get back to zero economic profits. This case is only meant to be illustrative.

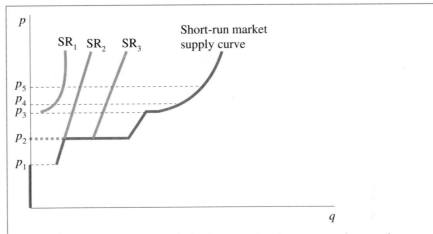

Figure 7.8   Short-Run Market Supply   In the short run, market supply is the horizontal summation of the short-run supply curves of all firms in the market, assuming that increased demand for inputs by the firms does not change input prices. For prices up to p_2 the market supply curve coincides with Firm 2's supply curve because no other firms are producing. It takes a jump at p_2 when Firm 3 begins production, and another jump at p_3 when Firm 1 begins production. Above p_3 the market curve changes with the sum of output of all three curves.

Short-Run Market Supply

The short-run market supply curve shows the amount of output that all firms in the market will supply in the short run at each price. Since entry and exit are not a consideration in the short run, we need to consider only short-run supply curves of firms already engaged in production. We refer to such firms as incumbent firms. Figure 7.8 shows the short-run supply curves for a market with three incumbent firms. Each short-run curve is the individual firm's short-run marginal cost curve above the point of minimum average variable cost. Adding the quantities supplied by all three firms at each market price produces the market supply curve. Notice that the market supply curve takes a jump at each price where a firm's supply curve leaves the vertical axis, and it changes slope according to the rate of increase of all three firms' output.

In many situations, horizontally summing incumbent firms' short-run supply curves is adequate to derive the short-run market supply curve. In other cases, however, the increased demand for inputs when market output goes up leads to an increase in some or all input prices. An increase in the market quantity of laptop computers, for example, could also increase demand for components such as liquid crystal display screens. The higher price for LCD screens would shift the supply curves of individual laptop makers to the left. Then quantity on the market supply curve would be the sum of individual firm quantities adjusted for the new input prices. Higher input prices for larger market size would mean that the market supply curve was less elastic than the sum of the original incumbent supply curves. We will consider the effect of constant, increasing, or decreasing costs when we construct the long-run market supply curve. In the short run, however, we know that firm costs are either constant or increasing, because the suppliers of inputs in the short run must be on *their* own short-run supply curves, which are either constant or upward-sloping.

APPLICATION: The Short-Run Supply of Sugar

Many regions of the world produce sugar; temperate regions use sugar beets, and tropical regions use sugar cane. Once refined, sugar from the two sources is indistinguishable. In the United States, sugar cane is grown in areas such as Florida, Louisiana, and Hawaii. Sugar beets are grown in areas such as Minnesota, North Dakota, and Nebraska. The short-run supply curve of sugar is determined by the costs of existing producers. Land costs, labor costs, and refining costs differ from region to region and country to country. Because sugar production benefits from price supports and subsidies in many regions, including Europe and the United States,[13] we can observe the costs of producers over a wide range of costs.

Table 7.2 uses the fact that zero profit implies marginal cost and minimum average cost are the same to infer marginal cost and quantity data for a selection of major sugar-producing countries. Cuba and the Dominican Republic, producing about 10 percent of the world's sugar at a marginal cost of about 11 cents per pound, are representative of low-cost sugar-producing areas, including other parts of Latin America, Australia, South Africa, and Fiji. The European Community, and certain other countries such as Turkey, can produce sugar from sugar beets for between 13 and 15 cents per pound. Higher-cost producers such as the United States have marginal costs between 17 and 24 cents per pound, depending on location and whether cane or beet sugar is being considered.

Plotting the data in Table 7.2 generates the supply curve of sugar shown in Figure 7.9. At 11 cents per pound, for example, supply consists only of sugar from Cuba and the Dominican Republic. For successively higher prices, the quantities of the other countries are added to produce total supply, as indicated in the right-hand column in Table 7.2. The choppy, steplike appearance of the curve comes from the fact that the data for each country represent an average, with some producers entering production at prices lower than the average and some higher. In Europe, for example, French sugar beet producers have the lowest costs, making them competitive with the lowest-cost cane producers. Using finer data down to the level of individual firms,

---

13. We examined effects of the U.S. sugar program in Investigation I.A.

Table 7.2   World Sugar Supply

| | Selected Major Producers, 1982 | | |
Country	Marginal Cost (cents per pound)	Quantity (millions of tons)	Cumulative Quantity (millions of tons)
United States (beet sugar)	24	3.2	32.9
United States (cane sugar, main-land)	21	2.1	29.7
United States (cane sugar, Hawaii)	17	1	27.6
European Community	13–15	17.1	26.6
Cuba, Dominican Republic	11	9.5	9.5

Sources: U.S. Department of Agriculture, *Agricultural Statistics,* Washington, D.C.: U.S. Government Printing Office, 1984, pp. 82–83; Frederic L. Hoff and Max Lawrence, *Implications of World Sugar Markets, Policies, and Production Costs for U.S. Sugar,* Agricultural Economic Report No. 543, Washington, D.C.: U.S. Department of Agriculture, Economic Research Service, November 1985, Table 9; Scott B. MacDonald and Georges A. Fauriol, "Introduction," *The Politics of the U.S.–Caribbean Basin Sugar Trade,* New York: Praeger, 1991, p. 3.

and obtaining more points on the marginal cost curves of individual suppliers, we could make the approximation in Figure 7.9 look more like the smooth supply curves we are used to. ■

Long-Run Market Supply

▼
8. How do you find the long-run market supply curve? List the factors that determine its slope.

Two new things need to be accounted for when deriving long-run market supply: First, individual firms can adjust all factors of production, including their plant and equipment. Second, new firms can enter the market and incumbent firms can exit. The effect of market size on cost that was relevant in the short run continues to apply in the long run, although in the long run there is the additional possibility that costs could decrease with market output. We divide our discussion according to these costs.

Constant Cost Industries. In constant cost industries, the long-run market supply curve is a horizontal line at market price. Surprisingly, this is true

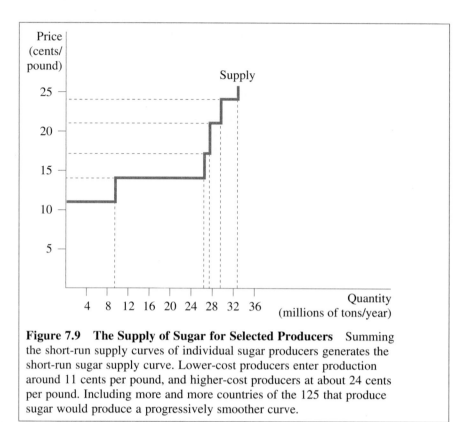

Figure 7.9 The Supply of Sugar for Selected Producers Summing the short-run supply curves of individual sugar producers generates the short-run sugar supply curve. Lower-cost producers enter production around 11 cents per pound, and higher-cost producers at about 24 cents per pound. Including more and more countries of the 125 that produce sugar would produce a progressively smoother curve.

even though every individual firm may have upward-sloping long-run and short-run supply curves! The reason has to do with entry and exit of new firms. *The essential feature of a constant cost industry is that every firm has access to the same technology and faces the same costs.* Zero-profit equilibrium requires that each firm operate at the point of minimum average cost (the same across firms), so market price can never rise above this level or fall below it in the long run. Long-run quantity adjustments take place through the entry and exit of firms and the expansion and contraction of output of firms that have flat average costs at the minimum level.

What kind of an industry might satisfy such conditions? Part (a) of Figure 7.10 draws the cost curves for a representative mail-order catalogue sales firm. Whether it is Spiegel, L. L. Bean, Land's End, J. Crew, Tweeds, Avon, or any of scores of other catalogue favorites that you may use, the inputs to the service of mail-order shopping are basically printing, postal services, merchandise, and clerks and managers to handle the orders. Since prices for printing, postal service, personnel, and merchandise (even in-house merchandise usually competes with close substitutes elsewhere) are set by markets that are much larger than the market in mail-order sales, they are virtually

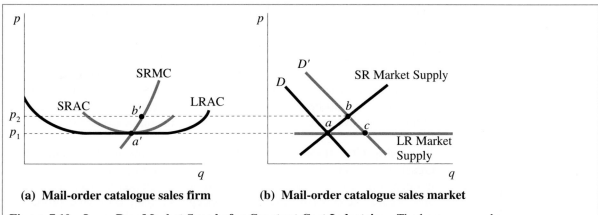

(a) Mail-order catalogue sales firm   **(b) Mail-order catalogue sales market**

Figure 7.10 Long-Run Market Supply for Constant Cost Industries   The long-run supply curve for constant cost industries is a horizontal line because new firms can enter at the same costs as incumbent firms. When demand rises from D to D', causing market price to rise, the individual firm shifts from a' to b'. In the long run, however, positive economic profits (1) attract new entrants that have access to the same LRAC as in part (a), and (2) may cause existing firms to expand to new SRAC curves further to the right. Since input prices are unchanged by larger industry output, entry continues until prices are returned to p_1.

the same for incumbents as well as for potential entrants and are not affected by the size of the mail-order market. In part (a) of the figure, the long-run average cost curve for an individual firm shows a declining portion (firm average costs are smaller once the firm reaches an efficient size), but thereafter exhibits a region where costs are flat. In this case, the firm operates at point a', which is somewhat smaller quantity than the firm could have and still have average costs equal to p_1. Part (b) shows the mail-order catalogue market at initial equilibrium at point a.

To find the market's long-run supply curve, we look at the effect of an increase in demand from D to D'. Equilibrium moves to point b in the short run, raising price to p_2. In the short run, then, the mail-order firm in part (a) increases output to point b', where it begins making positive profits. At this point two things happen. First, since information is perfect in perfectly competitive markets, potential entrants see that they can earn positive profits by entering the mail-order market with the same cost curve as drawn in part (a). From here the story should sound familiar. As discussed earlier, entry continues until price drops and every firm in the market makes zero economic profits. With identical costs, the only price where economic profits are zero is p_1, so in the long run the market moves to point c. The long-run market supply curve is therefore horizontal at price p_1.

There is a second thing that happens, however: the incumbent firm in part (a) may try to expand, too. Because the firm's average cost curve had a flat region, there is room to the right of point a' for the firm to operate at the same costs as p_1. If the firm is successful in the shakedown that occurs when the price drops from p_2 back to p_1, the firm will find itself with larger output than at point a'; if it is unsuccessful, it could find itself smaller. The presence of flat sections of the long-run average cost curve means that it is not possible to predict exactly how large each zero-profit firm will be. Only if the long-run average cost curve has a single minimum point can we say that every surviving firm must be at that scale of operations, because firms that are larger or smaller would have higher, and therefore noncompetitive, costs.

Increasing Cost Industries. To discuss the long-run market supply of increasing cost industries, we take up the case of agriculture, an industry that is interesting both for its policy implications (discussed later in the chapter) and because it helps illustrate the concepts of rent, economic profit, and opportunity costs that are so central to perfect competition.

There was a time in American history when agriculture was probably very nearly a constant cost industry with respect to land. The inputs then were basically the same as they are now—seed, farm implements, water, sun, fertilizer, and labor—but the final ingredient, good land, was in seemingly limitless supply. In the great westward migration, the best land was settled first, followed by the less fertile areas, until all the usable land was settled and the frontier officially was declared closed in 1890. When the quality of land differs across farms, the profitability of farms also differs. Farms in fertile areas pay for the same nonland inputs that farms do in less fertile areas, but the former have larger crops and higher earnings. In spite of this, farming is generally regarded as being close to perfectly competitive.

How are zero economic profits compatible with the higher earnings of some farms? As discussed in Chapter 6, the answer is that some of the higher earnings of farms with the best land represent economic rent on their land. Land that is worth $10,000 per year to the farmer, but which is owned outright and does not depreciate, does not have to be paid for. The difference between what the farmer would be willing to pay and what the farmer does pay is rent. Since the amount for which the land could be rented to another farmer varies with its profitability, $10,000 remains the land's opportunity cost, and the farm's economic profit, properly computed, is zero. For farmers who rent the land they farm (either because it is mortgaged or because they pay the owner to farm on it), the cost of land would not be an opportunity cost, but an actual physical outlay. Their long-run economic profits would also be zero, though the two kinds of farms would show $10,000 and $0 in accounting profit, respectively.

Now, to find the long-run supply curve of an increasing cost industry, consider how the industry responds to a change in demand. Part (a) of Figure 7.11 shows the long-run average cost curve (including the opportunity cost of land) of a farm producing in long-run equilibrium at point a', when price is p_1. Point a in part (b) is also assumed to be on the long-run market supply curve, where market demand D and the sum of incumbent firms' short-run supply curves, SR Market Supply$_1$, cross.

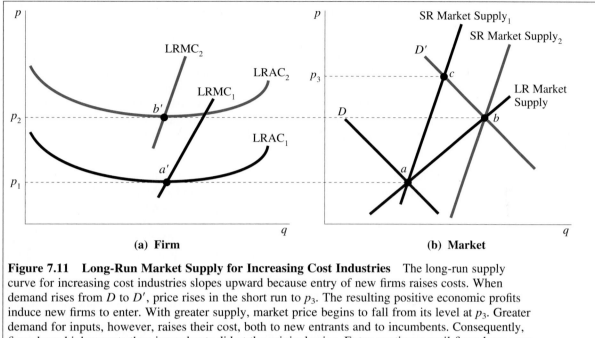

Figure 7.11 Long-Run Market Supply for Increasing Cost Industries The long-run supply curve for increasing cost industries slopes upward because entry of new firms raises costs. When demand rises from D to D', price rises in the short run to p_3. The resulting positive economic profits induce new firms to enter. With greater supply, market price begins to fall from its level at p_3. Greater demand for inputs, however, raises their cost, both to new entrants and to incumbents. Consequently, firms have higher costs than incumbents did at the original price. Entry continues until firms have zero economic profits again at price p_2, and the new short-run market supply curve is SR Market Supply$_2$. The long-run market supply curve passes through points a and b.

Now assume that market demand moves from D to D'. In the short run, price moves to p_3, and incumbent farms earn economic profits. Even if the price of nonland inputs is unchanged, the costs of a farm that owns its own land rise. Why? Because the access to land is now a more valuable asset. Higher prices mean that the earnings potential and therefore the rental value and opportunity cost of land immediately rise. For a farm that rents its land from others, the increase in land costs shows up as an actual outlay.

Returning to Figure 7.11, we can continue a now-familiar story. Higher economic profits encourage incumbents to expand and new entrants to enter farming. Increased market demand for inputs raises their prices. Land that was considered borderline in suitability for farming before may even be brought into production at higher cost. Consequently, the short-run market supply curve shifts to the right to SR Market Supply$_2$, but not as much as it would have if input prices had stayed fixed. The new market equilibrium moves to point b, which corresponds to a price lower than p_3 but higher than p_1. Meanwhile, the higher costs for land and other inputs shift the long-run cost curves of the incumbent firm. Long-run marginal cost shifts to the left, and long-run average cost rises. New long-run equilibrium occurs at point

b', where the firm is again making zero economic profits, producing at its point of minimum average cost.

Even though all farms are again earning zero economic profits, it is interesting to see how they fare. Farms fortunate enough to own the best land earn higher economic rent than before, and firms that own land that is less good also benefit, but to a lesser degree. Farms that rent their land from others find that they are no better off or worse off than before. Their prices are higher, but so are their costs. With all their outlays being actual, their economic and accounting profits are the same before and after the market price rise—zero.

Decreasing Cost Industries. In some cases it is possible that, by being large, an industry can take advantage of methods and techniques that actually *reduce* the costs of inputs and lead to lower prices. Although the short-run market supply curve slopes upward as usual, the long-run market supply curve slopes downward. Consider, for example, the cost of shipping to California. To supply miners at the time of the 1849 Gold Rush, fast clipper ships had to transport goods all the way around Cape Horn and up the west coast of South America. As the quantity of shipping to California increased, however, it became feasible to build railroads and, eventually, the Panama Canal. Neither venture would have been possible unless the quantity of transportation involved was sufficiently great. Since it cost less to transport goods when market quantity was great, the long-run supply curve was downward-sloping.

The benefits to a decreasing cost industry, leading to downward-sloping long-run supply, should be distinguished from the increasing returns to scale that we discussed in Chapter 6. There, the benefits of size accrued to the individual firm. In the case of a decreasing cost industry, the benefits depend on the market quantity. Internally, firms could be experiencing increasing, decreasing, or constant returns to scale, while at the industry level costs decreased with market size. A similar remark applies to constant cost and increasing cost industries.

In the next section, we see how to measure the benefits to a firm of a price change. In the section following that, we apply what we have learned so far to analyze perfectly competitive markets.

7.5 Producer Surplus

9. What is producer surplus? Use the term to describe the benefits to the firm from being able to sell at a higher price.

We learned in Chapter 4 that consumer surplus, measured by the area between the demand curve and market price, can be interpreted as the amount of money by which consumers are better off after having bought the good in question at market price. Equivalently, this is the most the consumers could be made to pay for the right to buy before leaving the market. We can now show that *producer surplus,* meaning the amount of money by which firms are better off by selling their output at market price, can be measured by the area between the supply curve and market price. Equivalently, it is the amount of money the firm earns above the minimum necessary to supply its units of output.

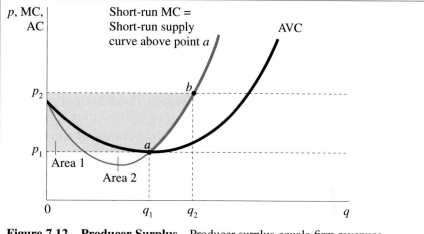

Figure 7.12 Producer Surplus Producer surplus equals firm revenues minus variable costs. It can be measured as the shaded area between the market price and the marginal cost or supply curve.

How much is the firm better off by producing than by producing nothing in an industry? The answer must be the additional profits it gets from being in the industry as compared to leaving the industry. This allows us to make the following definition.

> ***Producer surplus*** *is the economic profit of the firm plus fixed costs, or, equivalently, revenue minus variable costs.*

To see how to compute producer surplus from the firm's short-run supply curve, consider the firm in Figure 7.12, producing at point b for price p_2. As Figure 7.2 demonstrated, the earnings of the firm, if we ignore fixed costs, are just the area between the marginal cost curve and the price line. This area, which equals producer surplus, differs from the shaded area shown in the figure in that the area between marginal cost and the price line includes the portion marked Area 2 but does not include Area 1. However, we know that the sum of all marginal costs from zero to quantity q is equal to the variable cost for producing q. At quantity q_1, corresponding to minimum average variable cost, variable cost is $AVC(q_1)$ times q_1, which is the area of rectangle $0p_1aq_1$. Since this equals the area under the marginal cost curve out to q_1, Area 1 equals Area 2. Thus producer surplus equals the shaded area shown, bounded by the price line and the firm's supply curve. Price minus the marginal cost of producing a unit of output can be thought of as profit on the unit. It follows that producer surplus consists of the sum of profits on the units produced plus any rents the firm earns on its factors of production.

Adding up all of the individual firms' producer surpluses generates producer surplus for the market. Since we know that the area between market price and the supply curve indicates producer surplus, we can measure, for example, the benefit that firms experience from being able to sell at a higher price. The benefit of the higher price would correspond to the increase in this area between the curves. We will make use of this measure when we consider the effects of a tax on perfectly competitive markets in the next section.

7.6 Equilibrium in the Perfectly Competitive Market

In this chapter we have tried to capture the flavor of perfectly competitive markets, both for individual firms and for the market as a whole. In this section we briefly recapitulate the conditions for long-run market equilibrium, after which we apply our skills from Chapter 2 to describe the effects of sales taxes on consumer prices in the constant cost mail order sales market, the effect of price supports on the profit of farmers, and the effect of a sales tax on the size of a decreasing cost industry.

Three Conditions for Perfectly Competitive Long-Run Equilibrium

The driving force in competition is economic profit. Economic profit is important to firms not only because maximizing it implies finding the least-cost production method and total costs, but also because it is an indicator to the firm of whether a particular venture should be started in the first place. In the Ralston Purina example, high profits in the breakfast cereal market led Ralston to convert a dog-and-cat-food plant to make breakfast cereal. Moreover, the existence of economic profits in perfectly competitive markets induces new firms to enter. The following quotation by Andrew Carnegie was originally meant to explain why trusts would be kept in check by competition, even if their aim was to secure monopolies (about which we will have more to say in Chapter 8). It expresses well the ceaseless activity and quest for profit that drive the business world to excel.

> *Capital, ever watchful for an opportunity to make unusual gains, seeks its level by a law of its being, and needs only the opportunity to engage in th[e] highly profitable manufacture. A relative of one of the principal officials or one of the chiefs of a department in the trust, knowing its great profit, gets some friend with capital to build new works in cooperation with him, and the result is that we soon see springing up over the country rival works, each of which has the great giant trust more or less at its mercy. . . . This only whets the appetite of others who see the success of the first innovator, and other works soon spring up. . . . The people may rest assured that neither in one article nor in another is it possible for any trust to exact exorbitant profits without thereby speedily undermining its own foundations.*[14]

14. Andrew Carnegie, ''Popular Illusions About Trusts,'' *The Gospel of Wealth and Other Timely Essays,* ed. Edward C. Kirkland, Cambridge, Mass.: Harvard University Press, 1962, p. 89; originally printed in 1900.

Although Carnegie's words describe competition nearly a century ago, they could have been penned as accurately yesterday. Information, the existence of economic profits ("unusual gains" in Carnegie's words), contestability, and market entry (building "new works") are the elements that still apply. Carnegie did not talk about what the market would be like when competition reached its limiting case, but assuming the other requirements of perfect competition are met, we are able to summarize what we know about the market in terms of three requirements for equilibrium.

The market is in long-run equilibrium when

1. *All firms are maximizing profits* (they are on their short-run supply curves).
2. *Demand equals supply* (the demand curve intersects the short-run market supply curve).
3. *All firms are making zero economic profits* (production is at the minimum point of long-run average cost, meaning that each firm is on its long-run supply curve).

In the short-run adjustment phase, condition 3 might not hold, in which case the market is still experiencing entry or exit.

Market Adjustments in Equilibrium: Three Tax Interventions

▼
10. Describe the price, quantity, utility, and producer surplus effects of a tax in perfectly competitive markets.

Zero economic profits in the long run mean that perfectly competitive markets sometimes behave in ways that seem strange at first, until understood in more depth. In this section we look at market adjustment in response to a sales tax and agricultural price supports. We choose one example from a constant cost industry (catalogue sales), one from an increasing cost industry (agriculture), and one from a decreasing cost industry (satellite delivery services).

Tax Shifting in Constant Cost Industries. Those wanting to raise taxes are fond of phrasing their proposals in ways that sound as if the rich, or business, or some other group, will pay the taxes while the rest of us have only to enjoy the benefits of the program under consideration. Fortunately, most voters are wise enough to recognize that rhetoric needs to be checked against reality. In the case of business taxes, "them" often turns out to be "us."

Figure 7.13 returns us to the catalogue mail-order market to assess the impact of a 7-percent sales tax on catalogue sales. In this case, we assume that the government, in an apparent attempt to spare households an additional tax burden, has mandated that the tax be paid by businesses on the value of their sales. How will the market adjust to this, and who will truly pay the tax?

Since catalogue sales are a constant cost industry, all firms have the same cost curves, shown in part (a) of the figure. Whereas costs were $C(q)$ without the tax, with it they are $C(q) + 0.07pq$, where p denotes the price received by the seller, net of tax.[15] Posttax average cost is therefore $C(q)/q + 0.07p$,

---

15. Price $1.07p$ is paid by buyers, and price p is received by sellers. Thus, if the firm receives $1.07pq$ from buyers, it must pay a tax of $0.07pq$, leaving it with pq net of tax.

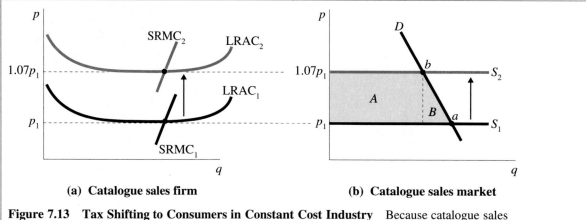

(a) Catalogue sales firm   **(b) Catalogue sales market**

Figure 7.13   Tax Shifting to Consumers in Constant Cost Industry   Because catalogue sales firms have identical costs that are not affected by the size of the catalogue market, a sales tax of 7 percent levied on sales of firms simply raises all firms' marginal and average costs by $0.07p_1$. The after-tax supply curve is higher by $0.07p_1$. Consumers therefore pay all taxes in the form of higher prices, even though nominally the taxes were levied on firms. Consumers lose consumer surplus equal to area $A + B$ in order that government can collect revenue A. Area B is a net loss to society.

which exceeds pretax average cost by $0.07p$. In the first round, then, the average cost curve of all catalogue sales firms rises by $0.07p$. Marginal costs also rise by precisely $0.07p$. This is shown in part (a) as the shift to $SRMC_2$ and $LRAC_2$. In the short run, some firms might respond to the tax by trying to cut costs, but since the curves shown are already at minimum levels there is no room for further cost minimizing. Firms have no choice but to raise prices to $1.07p_1$ or face extinction. In long-run equilibrium, then, firms make zero economic profits once more at prices that are higher by 7 percent.

Part (b) of the figure shows the impact of the tax at the market level. Originally market equilibrium is at point a, with the horizontal supply curve at S_1. Since the average costs of all firms rise by $0.07p_1$, the market supply curve shifts up by the increase in firm minimum average cost to S_2, and market equilibrium moves to point b.

How does the tax affect the participants? First, consumers pay prices that are higher by 7 percent, the amount of the tax, losing consumer surplus equal to area $A + B$. Second, the government collects tax revenue equal to area A.[16] Third, firms make zero economic profits at both the pre-tax and post-tax long-run equilibria. If the tax does not reduce firms' profits, there is a puzzle: why do firms generally ally themselves with consumers in opposition to tax increases? The answer is found in part (b), where we observe the fourth

16. Tax per unit sold is $0.07p_1$ (7 percent of the seller price). Multiplying this by the quantity sold at point b gives the tax as area A.

implication of the tax. The market quantity falls. In the transition to the new long-run equilibrium, therefore, some firms in the market had to exit or shrink in size (assuming a flat portion of the long-run average cost curve). Since no firms want to go out of existence or get smaller, it is in their interest to keep taxes low.

Agricultural Price Supports in an Increasing Cost Industry. Farm employment in 1991 numbered 3.2 million, or just 2.5 percent of the labor force. Judging from the equivalent figures 25 and 50 years ago (3.9 million, or 5.2 percent, and 9.1 million, or 16.3 percent, respectively), it is an industry in serious long-term decline. Judging from the farm sector's ability to produce, however, things have never been better. Indeed, agricultural productivity gains in the United States are one of the major success stories of this century, with crop production per acre more than double what it was just 40 years ago.

Given the conflicting signals in the press and public mind, agricultural policy in the United States presents an interesting application of the perfectly competitive model. How is it that an industry with such tremendous advantages as American agriculture is also one of the most heavily subsidized and supported sectors in the economy? Moreover, how is it that many family farmers will honestly tell you that they are barely getting by?

It is neither for lack of public support nor for absence of support granted over a long enough period of time. Agricultural price supports have been in existence for most of this century and in recent memory have exceeded $\frac{1}{2}$ percent of GDP in total annual amount. (Recall that these payments go to an industry constituting only 2.5 percent of the labor force.) Over the years, support transfers have raised farm income substantially, compared to what it would have been in the absence of farm programs. By this measure, price supports made farm income 39 percent higher in the years 1932 to 1939, 67 percent higher from 1953 to 1963, 85 percent higher from 1959 to 1967, and 25 percent higher for the years 1968 to 1972.[17] Again, from 1982 to 1985, farm income was estimated to be 85 percent higher than it would have been in the free market without the 1981 Farm Bill.[18] Critics of the farm program argue that farmers are harvesting more from the government than from the land. In some counties and regions that approach the size of many states, total federal payments in farm support for the area nearly equal, and in some cases exceed, the area's reported total farm income.[19] Yet net farm income

17. Daryll E. Ray and Earl O. Heady, *Simulated Effects of Alternative Policy and Economic Environment on U.S. Agriculture,* and Frederick James Nelson, *An Economic Analysis of the Impact of Past Farm Programs on Livestock and Crop Prices, Production and Resource Adjustments,* cited in Karl Gertel, *Differing Effects of Farm Commodity Returns on Land Returns and Land Values,* Agricultural Report No. 544, Washington, D.C.: U.S. Department of Agriculture, Economic Research Service, November 1985, p. 3.
18. Daryll Ray, James W. Richardson, and Elton Li, "The 1981 Agriculture and Food Act: Implications for Farm Prices, Incomes and Government Outlays to Farmers," *American Journal of Agricultural Economics,* 64 (December 1982), pp. 957–965, cited in Gertel, op. cit., p. 3.
19. Farm income can be less than federal payments because of various tax write-offs and allowances used in computing farm income for tax purposes.

per capita remains below personal income per capita of the nation as a whole by 16 percent.[20] What is going on here?

We can gain a better understanding of the dynamics of the farm sector if we recall the dynamics of a perfectly competitive industry. This century has witnessed a continual transition in which smaller, less efficient farms have been forced to exit the market because they could not compete effectively. Similar processes were observed in the 1890s and early 1900s, when large department stores forced smaller shops out of business. The process continues today when a Wal-Mart finds a lower-cost way to merchandise and forces out of business some of the franchises and department stores that replaced the mom-and-pop operations of three generations ago.

When a farm goes out of existence, however, its land does not disappear, nor does it typically become idle. More efficient farms, some of them corporate, buy the land and continue farming it. The loss of farms, therefore, is really not a loss, but a transfer from one set of users to another. Federal programs to prevent the ''loss'' of family farms are misguided because they fail to recognize that the elimination of higher-cost producers by lower-cost producers is a phenomenon that continues to be present whether prices are high or low. To see why, refer again to Figure 7.7, where p_0 is the cost to the most efficient producer operating at e_0. In the absence of price supports, market price must move to p_0 in the long run, driving out of business any firms with minimum average costs higher than this. For example, smaller farms with short-run average cost curves to the left of e_0 would have higher costs and economic losses in the long run.

Now assume that market price is raised to p_1 by federal price supports. At first glance, this appears high enough that small farms as well as large can operate at positive profit. However, such a view ignores the nature of perfect competition. Positive economic profits by the most efficient producers induce entry. This tends to increase supply and lower market price, but also bids up the cost of inputs, in particular the price of land. The cost curves of all firms therefore rise in the long run, once again leaving only the most efficient producers with positive economic profits. Less efficient firms suffer losses and continue to exit, in spite of the higher market price!

So who gains from the higher price? In fact, there are gainers, but they are not necessarily farmers. One of the main effects of farm price supports, as we have seen, is to raise the price of farmland. Consider the three crops of wheat, corn, and soybeans, which account for 66 percent of U.S. harvested acreage. For wheat, it is estimated that land prices are double what they would be without price supports; for corn and soybeans, land prices are more than 50 percent higher. Many farmers earning modest incomes during their working years find upon retirement that in land value alone they are more than millionaires.[21] As the population of farm families continues to decline,

---

20. *Economic Report of the President,* Washington, D.C.: U.S. Government Printing Office, February 1992, Table B-93, Table B-30, and Table B-5. Figures are for 1990.
21. Land values have varied greatly in the past 10 to 15 years. Taking corn cropland as an example, prices per acre have been in the $1,500 to $4,000 range.

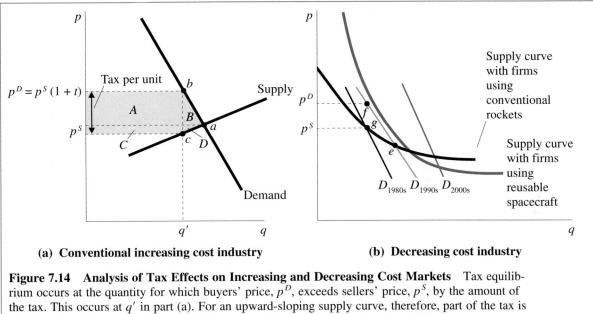

(a) Conventional increasing cost industry   **(b) Decreasing cost industry**

Figure 7.14 **Analysis of Tax Effects on Increasing and Decreasing Cost Markets**   Tax equilibrium occurs at the quantity for which buyers' price, p^D, exceeds sellers' price, p^S, by the amount of the tax. This occurs at q' in part (a). For an upward-sloping supply curve, therefore, part of the tax is paid by buyers and part by sellers. Government receives tax revenue equal to area $A + C$, of which buyers pay A and sellers C. Lost consumer surplus, $A + B$, and lost producer surplus, $C + D$, exceed taxes collected by area $B + D$, which is lost to society. In contrast, in part (b) larger market size allows a transition to newer technology for satellite delivery services. A tax would move the buyer and seller positions to points f and g, both of which have prices higher than the original equilibrium at point e. Consumers end up paying *more* than 100 percent of the taxes collected by government.

however, and more children leave the farm for urban occupations, the heirs of farm estates are less and less likely to be farmers. Others who own farmland, including corporations, absentee landlords, and foreigners, also need not be the same individuals who farm it. Though higher land values create wealth for the fortunate owners (sometimes farmers, sometimes not), they do not stop the competitive process. One thing is certain: higher land values raise the cost of acquiring land for the young individual who would like to start farming, and in that respect they probably *discourage* new family farms.

Tax Effects on Markets with Decreasing Cost and Increasing Cost Industries. We close our discussion of perfectly competitive markets by contrasting the effects of a tax on a decreasing cost industry with the effects on an increasing cost industry. Part (a) of Figure 7.14 shows the demand and supply curves for a perfectly competitive increasing cost industry. Imposition of a sales tax of t percent moves equilibrium from the pretax point, a, to a lower quantity, q', where the price paid by consumers p^D exceeds the price received by sellers p^S by the amount of the tax per unit tp^S. Buyers, therefore, move to point *b* on the demand curve and sellers to point *c* on the supply curve.

With firms initially producing at minimum average cost in long-run equilibrium, how are any able to survive at the lower price p^S? The answer is that lower demand for inputs at q' lowers firms' costs. The most efficient suppliers in the new equilibrium earn zero economic profits, and higher-cost firms exit the market.

In contrast to our example of a constant cost industry, part of the tax in a market with increasing costs is paid by sellers and part by buyers. Lost consumer surplus for the market is the area $A + B$, and lost producer surplus is $C + D$. The taxes collected equal area $A + C$, of which consumers pay A and producers pay C. Area $B + D$ is lost to society. We now contrast this with the case of a decreasing cost industry, where consumers would pay more than the cost of a tax.

To make our example specific, we can look at satellite delivery services. The industry placing communications and weather satellite payloads into orbit is clearly not perfectly competitive, but its infant status and cost structure are ideal for discussing several aspects of a decreasing cost industry. Placing satellites into orbit is an expensive operation, especially if rockets must be used on a one-time basis. Much of the rationale for development of NASA's reusable space shuttles focused on the cost savings possible from reusable spacecraft. Lower costs allow more firms to use shuttle services, and this in turn allows greater cost savings from sharing of such things as launch pads and associated launch, tracking, and retrieval services. In fact, one of the stated goals of the government space program is to establish satellite delivery services as a competitive industry. Already the European Ariadne rockets offer similar services to private firms, and technology makes it feasible for private corporations to operate such a business.

Part (b) of Figure 7.14 shows a downward-sloping supply curve for satellite delivery services. Growing market demand is shown by the increasing demand curves for the 1980s, 1990s, and 2000s. The relevant feature of the figure is that price is higher for small quantities and lower for large quantities. In a decreasing cost industry like this, what would be the effect of a tax? Starting from the equilibrium at point *e,* assume that a tax is imposed. In order for buyer price to exceed seller price by the amount of the tax, equilibrium must move to points *f* and *g* for buyer and seller, respectively. Because *both* of these points are higher than point *e,* the price increase to consumers *exceeds* the amount of the tax, and the price to suppliers also rises. Smaller market size drives up individual launch costs and reduces entry. Consumers, therefore, end up paying the higher cost of the tax plus the higher cost of reduced market size. In the case of satellite delivery systems, smaller market size could also have the effect of delaying or preventing the adoption of technology on which the cost savings depend, in this case the efficient use of re-usable craft.

The example of satellite delivery services brings up another point worth noting about decreasing cost industries. It is tempting to argue that decreasing costs external to the firm should be classified according to whether they result from pure technological improvements or from pure increase in market size. However, lower-cost spacecraft technology cannot be adopted without a sufficiently large industry. Thus, though we may classify (1) increasing returns to scale as a reason for lower costs within the firm for larger firm size, (2) decreasing cost industries as a reason for lower costs within the industry for larger industry size, and (3) technological change as a reason for decreasing costs (sometimes operating across the economy), the distinction in practice among these three sources for decreasing costs is not sharp. Both economic profitability and technical feasibility are needed for a new technology to be developed and adopted, and economic profitability frequently depends on market size.

Summary

Active Reading Guide numbers are given in parentheses at the end of each summary item.

1. This chapter describes perfectly competitive markets and the output decisions of firms operating in them. The four requirements for perfect competition are standardized product, pricetaking behavior by firms and households, market contestability, and perfect information. Standardized product means that consumers consider the output of competing firms as equivalent. Pricetaking means that firms and households treat prices as fixed, independent of their choices. Contestability means that firms have free entry into and exit from the market. Perfect information means that firms are informed about profit opportunities and have the information needed to maximize profit, and that households are informed about prices and products. Although the model of perfect competition is not completely satisfied by most markets, it provides an important benchmark for evaluating other markets. (1)

2. Profit maximization places certain requirements on the perfectly competitive firm's output choice. In particular, for profit to be maximized in the short run, quantity should be chosen such that price equals marginal cost, marginal cost is rising, and price is above minimum average variable cost. Otherwise, the firm is better off shutting down and producing nothing. The conditions are the same in the long run, except that average cost replaces average variable cost. These conditions can be explained in terms of the firm's cost curves, using graphs to find the points where profit is maximized. (2)

3. The rule that marginal costs be equalized across plants under a single firm's control allocates profit-maximizing production among plants. (3)

4. The firm's short-run supply curve consists of the short-run marginal cost curve above the point of minimum average variable cost, plus the vertical axis for prices below minimum average variable cost. (4)

5. The long-run supply curve consists of the firm's long-run marginal cost curve above the point of minimum long-run average cost, plus the vertical axis for prices below minimum average cost. In the short run, the firm may temporarily make positive economic profits or losses in response to market price changes. It increases its plant and equipment to expand production in response to positive profits, and it exits the market in the long run in response to losses. (5, 6)

6. The short-run market supply curve is generally the horizontal sum of individual firms' short-run supply curves. But the short-run market supply curve can differ from the sum of individual firms' short-run supply curves if expansion of market quantity and the associated increased demand for inputs raises the price of inputs, causing individual firms' supply curves to shift to the left. The short-

run market supply curve is then less elastic than the sum of the original firm supply curves because the quantity on the market supply curve is the sum of individual firm quantities based on higher input prices. Input prices cannot decline for an expansion of market quantity in the short run because input suppliers must be on *their* short-run supply curves, which are horizontal or upward-sloping. (7)

7. Long-run market supply must take into account entry and exit of firms. In constant cost industries, the long-run market supply curve is horizontal, because new firms have access to technology with costs identical to those for existing firms and input prices do not change with market size. In increasing cost industries, long-run market supply is upward-sloping, because input prices rise with market quantity. Long-run market supply is downward-sloping for decreasing cost industries. Regardless of industry type, in long-run equilibrium individual firms making up the market produce at their point of minimum long-run average cost at the market price on the long-run market supply curve. (8)

8. Producer surplus equals the firm's economic profit plus fixed costs. Equivalently, it is the firm's revenue minus variable costs. Producer surplus is measured by the area between the supply curve and market price. (9)

9. Equilibrium market price and quantity are determined at the intersection of the market demand and supply curves, where supply is the short-run market supply curve in the short run and the long-run market supply curve in the long run. The effect of a tax on market equilibrium is to shift quantity to a point where buyer price exceeds seller price by the amount of the tax. The smaller quantity in the market in the long run means that some firms must exit, but the firms remaining make zero economic profits. Depending on the elasticities of the demand and supply curves, some or all of the tax—or, in certain cases, an amount even greater than the tax—is shifted to consumers in the form of higher prices. (10)

Review Questions

*1. Contestability implies that economic profits are driven to zero by competition of firms in the market. How might *potential* entry hold profits to zero?

2. On his way through New York City as he was being deported to Sicily, gangster Lucky Luciano was shown what members of the New York Stock Exchange do. His comment was, ''I got into the wrong racket.'' What feature of perfect competition was absent that prevented Lucky from entering the Stock Exchange business instead of the gangster business?

*3. Discuss the following statement: In the short run a firm suffering losses may still produce positive output.

4. Discuss this statement: In the long run the firm's supply curve is more elastic than in the short run. Use cost curves to explain your answer.

*5. Can the long-run market supply curve be horizontal if every firm has an upward-sloping long-run supply curve? Explain.

6. Explain why the absence of any one of the following conditions would violate the requirements for long-run market equilibrium with perfect competition by firms.
  a) All firms in the market are maximizing profits.
  b) No firm believes it can set its output price.
  c) No new entrant could make positive economic profits, and no incumbent firm makes negative economic profits.
  d) The quantity supplied by incumbent firms equals the quantity demanded at market price.

*7. Show that the following definitions of producer surplus are the same:
  a) The earnings of the firm above the minimum

---

* Asterisks are used to denote questions that are answered at the back of the book.

needed to keep the firm in production in the industry in the short run

b) The amount by which the firm is better off by producing and selling its industry output at market price

c) Revenue minus variable cost

d) Profit plus fixed cost

8. If all firms have identical long-run cost curves, does this mean that the market long-run supply curve is horizontal?

*9. Describe conditions for a market in which firms would experience no effect of industry size on the costs of their inputs.

10. Assume that all firms make zero economic profits. Does this mean that the producer surplus is zero if the industry is (a) constant cost, or (b) increasing cost? Explain the differences, if any.

Numerical and Graphing Exercises

*1. A firm has identical variable costs from one year to the next, but its fixed costs continue to rise. Draw the firm's AC, AVC, and MC curves for two successive years on the same diagram.

2. American Glass makes dinner glassware using inputs of glass, forming machines, natural gas (for heating), and labor. Assume that American Glass has already bought its glassmaking machines. What does American Glass's short-run supply curve look like?

*3. Howard Jones makes Christmas candles with the following total costs (quantity in hundreds, cost in hundreds of dollars):

q	C	q	C
0	10	7	73
1	16	8	86
2	23	9	100
3	31	10	115
4	40	11	131
5	50	12	147
6	61		

What quantities will Howard supply if the price is (a) \$7, (b) \$9, (c) \$12, and (d) \$15? What is the lowest price at which Howard makes a positive profit?

4. Average cost is $AC(q) = 45 + (q - 15)^2$.

a) Is this a short-run or a long-run cost function?

b) What is the fixed cost?

c) What is the minimum average cost for this firm?

d) If price is \$20 per unit, how many units will this firm supply?

*5. There are 150 active firms with marginal cost given by $MC(q) = 10 + 3q$, where q is output. The minimum average variable cost is 12. What is the market short-run supply curve?

6. A firm with the production function $q = K^{1/2}L^{1/2}$ has a short-run cost function $C_{SR}(q) = \frac{1}{4}q^2 + 4$ and a long-run cost function $C_{LR}(q) = 2q$, when K is fixed at 4 units in the short run and $w = r = 1$ (where w is wage rate, and r is rental rate on capital). Draw the firm's short-run and long-run supply curves. (Hint: MC for $\frac{1}{4}q^2$ is $\frac{1}{2}q$.)

*7. Use the information in the preceding exercise, assuming that all existing and potential firms are identical. Find the short-run and long-run market supply curves, assuming there are 100 firms in the market initially and industry size does not affect input costs.

8. A firm has two plants, the first of which has marginal cost $MC_1(q) = 2 + 2q$, and the second of which has marginal cost $MC_2(q) = q$. The minimum average variable cost is 5 in each plant. What percentage of output does the firm produce in plant 2 if the price of output is (a) 50, (b) 30, and (c) 10?

*9. In the text example of the Ralston Purina Mexico and Nevada plants, it was assumed that each plant sold its output at the same price. Explain mathematically or draw a diagram showing how applying the $p = MC$ rule to each plant separately would determine the allocation of production between plants if the two plants sold output at different prices.

10. The long-run supply of accounting services uses office space per accountant costing $900 per month and accountant time at $18 per hour. One accountant per unit of office space is the only available combination of space and labor. Choosing a unit of output to measure accountant services, find the long-run cost curve and supply curve for accounting services.

*11. Ice cream street vendors face the following market conditions. Cost is $C(q) = \$430.56q + \$33.33(q - 0.1667)^3 + \$50.15$, where q is numbers of carts of ice cream supplied. Every vendor has the same costs, and the market is contestable.

a) What are the long-run price, quantity, and individual vendor profit if the demand for ice cream on the street is $q^D = 1,500 - p$? How many vendors (i.e. carts) supply the market?

b) In the short run, the number of vendors from part a) is fixed. What is equilibrium price in the short run if demand rises to $q^D = 1,600 - p$?

c) What are the long-run price, quantity, and number of vendors for the demand in part b)?

12. Market demand is given by $q^D = 300 - 2p$. Find the effect of a 3-percent tax on buyer price and seller price for the following cases of increasing, decreasing, and constant cost industries: (a) $q^{S,\ \text{increasing cost}} = -100 + 2p$; (b) $q^{S,\ \text{decreasing cost}} = 1,100 - 10p$; and (c) $p^{S,\ \text{constant cost}} = 100$.

CHAPTER 8
▼

Monopoly and Monopoly Pricing

This chapter discusses the pricing strategies of the firm manager when the firm faces a downward-sloping firm demand curve. We start with the case of a monopolist who can choose a single price and extend to cases where the firm can divide its market into different groups of buyers or select various price schedules for blocks of the good sold. The social costs of monopoly and the nature of regulatory responses are also considered. By the time you finish this chapter, you should better understand some of the prevalent pricing strategies and be able to identify their welfare consequences.

ACTIVE READING GUIDES

After reading this chapter, you should be able to answer the Active Reading Guides listed below. These guides also appear in the page margins, near the material to which they refer.

1. In what sense can monopolies set their own prices?

2. What is marginal revenue (MR)? What does MR < 0 mean?

3. Explain the monopolist's profit maximization rule.

4. Explain the formula for the monopolist's price markup over marginal cost.

5. Show diagrammatically the social costs of monopoly. Explain in your own words why $p > MC$ leads to social costs.

6. Give four strategies that firms with market power can use to capture consumer surplus. What makes each work?

7. Why doesn't a perfectly discriminating monopoly lead to social costs?

8. How might differences in price information and search costs help a monopolist segment its market?

9. Describe five approaches to the regulation of monopoly.

10. What effects do the following taxes or subsidies have on monopoly price and output: (1) production subsidy, (2) franchise tax, and (3) profit tax?

11. Derive the effects of a price ceiling on monopoly output.

12. Name some of the problems of regulation, explaining some of the advantages and difficulties with each of the five regulatory options.

8.1 Monopoly

When Orlando, Florida, resident Melissa Gazaway moved to a new neighborhood, she found that her monthly cable TV bill in the new location was $35.86 for the same 36 basic channels that she had received for $24.32 in her old neighborhood. What made this surprising was that she moved less than two miles, and her new cable TV company was the same as her old one! However, her company had to compete with another supplier in the old neighborhood. In the new neighborhood, there was only one company.[1]

Most of us are familiar with cable TV and so can empathize with Melissa's plight. Her options were two: (1) take it or (2) leave it. Of course, Melissa could always watch broadcast TV even though it was not a perfect substitute for cable. Since no one threatened bodily harm to her if she didn't take cable, we can safely assume that she was better off with cable than without cable if she continued taking it at the higher price. And can we blame her company for selling at the higher price? Why should it sell for less? Yet there are nagging questions that this example brings to the fore. In particular, what explains how the cable company sets its price when there is no competition, and is there any reason to object to the resulting outcome? The remainder of this chapter is essentially devoted to answering these two basic questions.

1. This information was reported in Daniel R. Levine, "Behind the Cable TV Rip-off," *Reader's Digest,* June 1992, pp. 53–57.

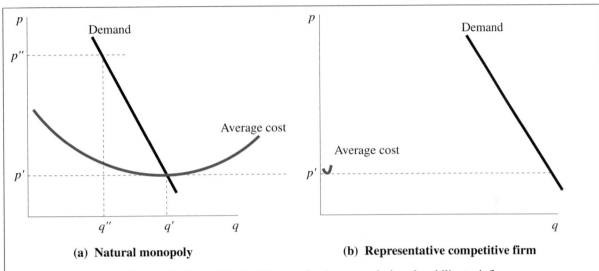

(a) Natural monopoly   **(b) Representative competitive firm**

Figure 8.1   Average Cost Relative to Market Demand   A monopoly has the ability to influence market price, unlike perfectly competitive firms, which are too small relative to the market to have an appreciable influence on market price. In part (a) the decision of the monopolist to cut output from q' to q'' leads to a large increase in price. In part (b) the decision of the competitive firm to shift output to different points on its average cost curve has a negligible effect on market price.

The Origins of Monopoly

The cable company in Melissa's new neighborhood could be considered a monopoly. Economists define a monopoly as a market with a single seller and without competition from substitute goods.

> A ***monopoly*** *is a market for a good without close substitutes that is supplied by a single seller.*

In the range of market types, monopoly represents the opposite extreme from perfect competition. Just as perfect competition describes an ideal case of competition, so monopoly describes the idealization of the absence of competition. Pure monopoly, therefore, requires no more than one seller of the product plus no competition from suppliers of close substitutes. Since most goods have substitutes of one type or another, pure monopolies are rare, and where they do exist they are often short-lived. Our first question, then, concerns how monopolies can arise. Economists identify three main origins for monopoly. We consider each in turn.

1. Natural Monopoly. A situation in which the firm's long-run average cost declines over a large enough range of quantities so that a single firm is profitably able to supply the market at a lower price than a number of smaller firms is called a *natural monopoly*. For example, a single firm operating near or at the minimum point of its long-run average cost curve can sometimes profitably supply all of market demand at a low price. Figure 8.1 shows such a possibility in part (a), where quantity q' at minimum average cost supplies all of quantity demanded at price p'. A firm producing a smaller quantity at the left-hand portion of its average cost curve would have higher average cost and therefore be unable to make a profit unless the price were higher.[2] The expected or natural outcome in such a market (hence the name *natural monopoly*) is that a single large firm will supply the market. A newcomer must face the prospect that the larger firm will simply lower prices to a level where the newcomer's profits become negative, though the larger firm may remain profitable. For comparison, part (b) of the figure shows an average cost curve for a representative firm in a perfectly competitive market.

Electric utilities are a common example of a natural monopoly. Rather than have several competing regional power companies with duplication in equipment and supply lines, it is less costly to have one large company serve the needs of the public. The United States, like most other countries, regulates the prices that utilities charge, a topic we will return to later in the chapter.

2. Government-Granted Monopolies: Patents, Licenses, and Franchises. A second way in which monopoly arises is by government sanction. A visitor to one of our national parks will find that all vending services and canteen items sold in the park are supplied by a single firm. Though many of the souvenir items sold at Glacier or Yellowstone Park are unique reminders of that particular park, snack items and other goods are also supplied by many firms in markets outside the park. In this case, the vendor's park monopoly is granted by the government park service, which prevents competitors from selling on park grounds.

Government also grants monopoly rights to patent holders during the term of the patent. The patentee is legally empowered for a specified number of years (17 in the United States) to control the sale or use of the patented product. For example, a pharmaceutical company can patent a new drug and prevent other companies from making the drug and selling it. The purpose of the patent is to give the patentee enough time to recoup the costs of the invention and earn sufficient economic reward that future invention and innovation will be encouraged. The length and terms of the patent are intended to balance the gains to society from encouraging future inventions against the short-term social losses from limiting use of the invention to the patent holder.[3]

---

2. As discussed in Chapter 6, the declining portion of long-run average cost reflects increasing returns to scale.

3. We look at patents and R & D in Chapter 16 and at the pharmaceutical industry in Investigation III. C.

3. Control over an Essential Input. Andrew Carnegie, the early 1900s steel industrialist whom we quoted in Chapter 7 concerning the competition for economic profits, wrote, "There are only two conditions other than patents which render it possible to maintain a monopoly. These are when the parties absolutely control the raw material out of which the article is produced, or control territory into which rivals can enter only with extreme difficulty."[4] In the case of a raw material, if only one or two locations in the world have the essential input from which a product comes, it is likely that the product will be controlled by the firm that controls the input. Diamonds, for example, come almost exclusively from South African mines controlled by the DeBeers company, a multinational monopoly that deals in the mining, cutting, and distribution of diamonds. Catlinite, from which American Indians make peace pipes, comes from only one site in southwestern Minnesota, access to which is controlled by the Indian tribes. Finally, in the early days of the Standard Oil Company in the late nineteenth century, John D. Rockefeller gained control over oil production and distribution in the United States. He maintained this monopoly position by using his control over regional prices and distribution channels to eliminate or buy out potential entrants and smaller rivals.

For a monopoly to sustain itself, entry of competitors must be carefully prevented. Nothing lasts forever, however. Apart from government-granted monopolies whose livelihoods are determined by the government's actions, monopolistic markets, like markets in general, are eventually challenged by new entrants or close substitute goods. Even if Standard Oil had not been broken up by the U.S. government, for example, later discoveries of oil around the world would have rendered its monopoly difficult to maintain. Markets also can be challenged almost overnight through technological change that provides a substitute good. The Swiss watch industry, though not a monopoly, was altered completely by the introduction of electronic watches in the 1970s. DeBeers today faces competition from producers of synthetic diamonds and other precious stones. Personal observation and the tendency of markets to render pure monopoly short-lived motivated Andrew Carnegie's remark with which we close this section: "Every attempt to monopolize the manufacture of any staple article carries within its bosom the seeds of failure."[5] Before turning to the question of how monopolies set prices, let's take a look at one kind of monopoly that is undergoing change, a monopoly that affects the majority of TV viewers in the United States.

---

4. Andrew Carnegie, "Popular Illusions About Trusts," *The Gospel of Wealth and Other Timely Essays,* ed. Edward C. Kirkland, Cambridge, Mass.: Harvard University Press, 1962, p. 86.
5. Ibid., p. 90.

APPLICATION: Regional Cable TV Monopolies

Providing cable TV services is big business.[6] The United States has more than 56 million subscribers, over 11,000 different cable systems, and cable revenues exceeding $20 billion annually, more than twice as much as the revenues of ABC, CBS, and NBC combined.

Although subscription TV has been around since the start of the 1950s, until the middle 1980s cable was subject to a plethora of regulatory restraints from jurisdictions at the municipal, state, and federal levels, including rate restrictions and programming requirements that limited the industry's growth. Seeking to streamline the regulatory system, Congress passed the Cable Communications Policy Act of 1984. This act transferred oversight of cable rates from cities to the Federal Communications Commission (FCC). The FCC, in turn, deregulated rates for firms operating in a competitive environment, which was interpreted to mean service areas with three or more over-the-air broadcast signals. Since this covered most major markets, cable rates were free to change in most areas when the law went into effect in January 1987. However, the law did not mandate competition *among* cable suppliers, and there was competition among cable systems in only about 65 communities.

The reason for the virtual absence of competition is local government. Through licenses and the granting of exclusive franchises, most communities have been allowed only one supplier. Those opposed to competition argue that cable is a natural monopoly because of its high construction costs, although competition proponents point out that competition has worked where it has been tried and prices have been lower in those markets as a result.

Without competition, what was the response of cable suppliers to deregulation? According to a General Accounting Office study, cable systems raised rates for bare-bones cable service an average of 43 percent after deregulation. Another study found that prices charged by cable suppliers rose 61 percent between 1987 and 1992, more than three times faster than the rate of inflation. In some places the differential has been much greater. In Denver, for example, basic service prices rose 700 percent between 1986 and 1989.

Cable is still a growing industry, and the question of what to do has not been fully resolved. Some argue that a return to rate regulation is the solution; others argue for competition and an end to exclusive government-granted franchises. In October 1992 the federal government enacted Public Law 102-385, which reregulates rates for basic cable service. We will consider cable reregulation in more detail when we take up the question of monopoly regulation later in the chapter. ■

6. The information for this section is taken from L. J. Davis, "Television's Real-Life Cable Baron," *The New York Times Magazine,* Part II: The Business World, December 2, 1990, p. 16; Levine, op. cit.; and "Cable TV Reregulation: Provisions," *Congressional Quarterly Weekly Report,* 50 (1992), pp. 3518–3521.

8.2 Monopoly Pricing with Downward-Sloping Demand

For a market with only one seller, the monopolist's supply *is* the market supply; therefore, any change in the monopolist's output quantity affects market price. In part (a) of Figure 8.1, for example, the monopolist can raise the market price from p' to p'' by reducing quantity from q' to q''. The perfectly competitive firm in part (b), in contrast, could change its quantity over the entire range of its average cost curve and have negligible effect on market price.

Total Revenue in Monopolistic Markets

▼

1. In what sense can monopolies set their own prices?

Monopolies cannot ''choose any price they want'' in the sense of selling a given quantity at the price they choose. But it *is* true that the monopoly can choose a quantity and sell at the price determined by the market demand curve. Since monopolies choose quantity, thus determining the price at which they sell, a monopoly does not have a supply curve as a pricetaking perfectly competitive firm does. How should firm managers use the fact that they can choose any point on the market demand curve by selecting the quantity they sell?

Figure 8.2 works out the total revenue,

$$R = pq,$$

for the demand curve $q^D = 100 - 2p$, where q^D is the quantity demanded and p is price. The upper part of the figure displays the demand curve, and the lower part of the figure displays the total revenue from selling each quantity at the corresponding price on the demand curve. The horizontal axes of the two diagrams are matched so that the same quantities appear in each. From the lower figure it is apparent that the *rate* at which the monopolist's revenues rise changes with quantity. It even reaches a quantity beyond which it starts falling. This is unlike the situation of a competitive firm, whose total revenue curve is a ray from the origin. To monitor how much an increase in quantity sold changes total revenue for a monopoly, we use the marginal revenue curve.

▼

2. What is marginal revenue (MR)? What does MR < 0 mean?

*Given the market demand curve, **marginal revenue** is the amount that total revenue changes per additional unit of good sold.*

Thus, if $R = pq$ is total revenue, marginal revenue is given by $MR = \Delta R/\Delta q$. As long as marginal revenue is positive, increasing the quantity sold raises revenue. If $MR < 0$, increasing quantity sold lowers revenue.

The economics of rising or falling MR relate to the fact that revenue is price times quantity. Increasing quantity means that price is reduced, not only on the last unit sold, but on all previous units. For small changes the percentage change in MR is the sum of percentage changes in price and quantity, $\%\Delta MR = \%\Delta p + \%\Delta q$. Thus, if price falls less than 1 percent when quantity

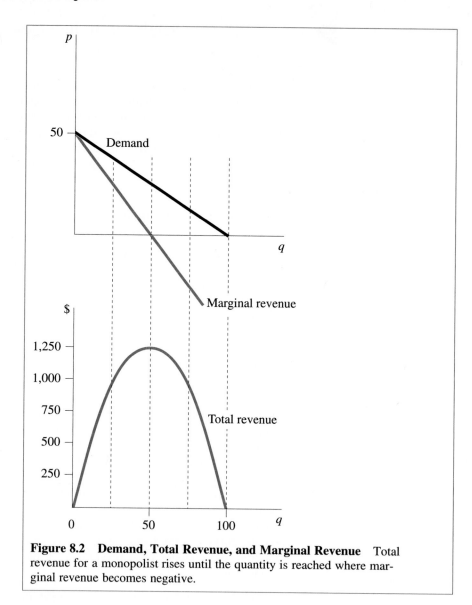

Figure 8.2   Demand, Total Revenue, and Marginal Revenue   Total revenue for a monopolist rises until the quantity is reached where marginal revenue becomes negative.

rises 1 percent, MR will rise; if price falls more than 1 percent, MR will fall. When revenue is maximized, MR neither rises nor falls: $\%\Delta p + \%\Delta q = 0$. This occurs when $\%\Delta q / \%\Delta p = -1$ (the price elasticity of demand is negative 1).

Figure 8.2 shows the line for MR in the upper diagram. It has the same vertical intercept as the demand curve and a horizontal intercept that is one-half the quantity of the demand curve's horizontal intercept. Notice that marginal revenue is zero at 50 units, where total revenue reaches its maximum.

The marginal revenue curve in Figure 8.2 satisfies the general rule for drawing marginal revenue curves given a linear demand curve: Locate the intersections of the demand curve with both axes. Find the point on the horizontal axis that is one-half the distance to the demand curve intercept. Draw the straight line between this point and the demand curve price intercept. The resulting line is the MR curve.[7]

The Choice of Monopoly Price and Quantity

▼
3. Explain the monopolist's profit maximization rule.

Now let's consider a monopolist like Melissa Gazaway's cable TV supplier, who we will assume has the demand curve shown in Figure 8.2. The monopolist has costs that rise with quantity like any other other firm. In this case, let's assume costs are

$$C(q) = 10 + (\tfrac{1}{8})q^2.$$

Given this demand curve and cost function, Figure 8.3 plots the resulting revenue and cost curves, listing under each quantity the financial data such as price, cost, revenue, and profit for that quantity. The upward-sloping ray from the origin is marginal cost, and the downward-sloping curve passing through the horizontal axis at quantity 50 is marginal revenue. Looking just at the profit figures, it is clear that highest profit occurs at the place on the demand curve where quantity is 40 and price is $30. However, there is a simple way to explain why this point is best for the cable supplier.

For quantities below 40, we see that marginal revenue exceeds marginal cost. Increasing quantity therefore raises revenue more than it raises cost, and profits rise. For quantities above 40, marginal cost exceeds marginal revenue. Lowering quantity therefore lowers cost more than it lowers revenue, and profits rise. You should take a few moments to familiarize yourself with the numbers in Figure 8.3 to convince yourself that MR > MC is a signal for the manager to lower price and sell more units, while MR < MC is a signal for the manager to raise price and sell fewer units. This implies that *monopoly profit is maximized at the quantity where marginal revenue equals marginal cost.*

If marginal revenue equals marginal cost at *two* quantities, the manager chooses the one giving higher profit, which will be the quantity where marginal cost cuts marginal revenue from below. Figure 8.4 shows a U-shaped marginal cost curve[8] where marginal revenue equals marginal cost at two

---

7. The same thing can be shown analytically. The formula for an arbitrary linear demand curve can always be written in the form $q/a + p/b = 1$, where q is the quantity demanded and p is price. The quantity denominator a is the quantity intercept (that is if $p = 0$, then $q = a$), and the price intercept is b ($q = 0$ implies $p = b$). Firm revenues pq are given by $R = bq - (b/a)q^2$. For a small change in q, revenues increase at the rate $MR = b - 2(b/a)q$ (this requires calculus). Thus $q/0.5a + MR/b = 1$, which means that marginal revenue has the same price intercept and one-half the quantity intercept as the original demand curve.
8. We discussed the reason for decreasing and increasing portions of marginal cost in Chapter 6.

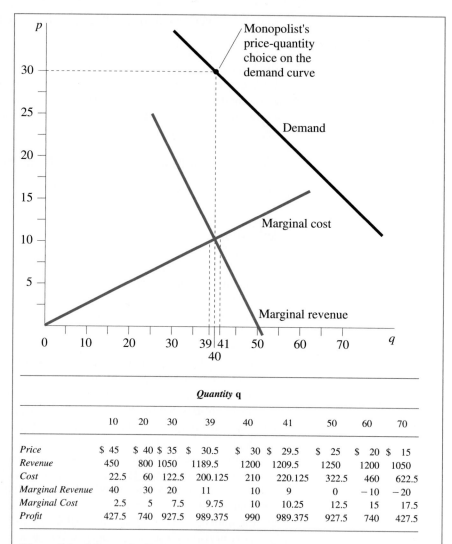

		10	20	30	39	40	41	50	60	70
					Quantity q					
Price		$ 45	$ 40	$ 35	$ 30.5	$ 30	$ 29.5	$ 25	$ 20	$ 15
Revenue		450	800	1050	1189.5	1200	1209.5	1250	1200	1050
Cost		22.5	60	122.5	200.125	210	220.125	322.5	460	622.5
Marginal Revenue		40	30	20	11	10	9	0	−10	−20
Marginal Cost		2.5	5	7.5	9.75	10	10.25	12.5	15	17.5
Profit		427.5	740	927.5	989.375	990	989.375	927.5	740	427.5

Figure 8.3   Monopoly Profit Maximization   The monopolist maximizes profit at the quantity where MR = MC. In the figure this occurs at price $30 and quantity 40. A quantity higher than this raises cost by more than it raises revenue, lowering profit, and a quantity lower than this reduces revenue more than it reduces costs, also lowering profit.

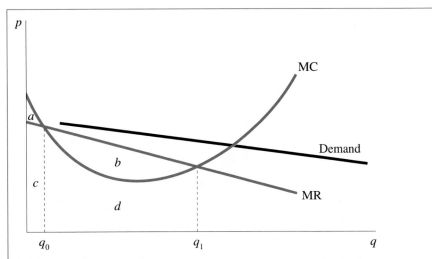

Figure 8.4   MC Cuts MR from Below   The monopolist has higher profit at the quantity for which marginal cost cuts marginal revenue from *below*. At both output q_0 and q_1, marginal revenue equals marginal cost. However, at q_0 marginal cost cuts marginal revenue from above, indicating that output at q_1 gives higher profit. Increasing output from q_0 to q_1 raises revenue by area $b + d$, the sum of all the marginal revenues, while cost increases by area d, the sum of all the marginal costs. Thus profit is higher at q_1 by area b.

quantities. At output q_0 the marginal cost curve cuts the marginal revenue curve from above. Moving quantity to the right of q_0 increases revenue more than it increases costs (that is, MR > MC), which means that profits are higher, so q_0 could not have been profit-maximizing to begin with.[9] In contrast, at q_1, where marginal cost cuts marginal revenue from below, increasing or decreasing quantity lowers profit, so q_1 is the better choice.

We are almost done with our profit-maximizing rule, but not quite. Setting MR = MC where MC cuts MR from below maximizes profit *if the firm produces positive output,* but does the firm do better than it would by not

9. Let us treat the monopolist's choice as a maximization problem in which the monopolist chooses what quantity to sell. Profit is $\Pi(q) = R(q) - C(q)$, where $R(q)$ is revenue and $C(q)$ is cost. At highest profit, (1) the profit is neither rising nor falling for a small change in output, and (2) the change in profit moves downward for a change in output. These imply the first-order and second-order calculus conditions

$$d\Pi/dq = MR(q) - MC(q) = 0$$
$$d[MR(q) - MC(q)]/dq = dMR/dq - dMC/dq < 0.$$

The first condition requires that MR = MC, and the second requires that the slope of MR be smaller than the slope of MC. That is, MC cuts MR from below, as discussed in the text.

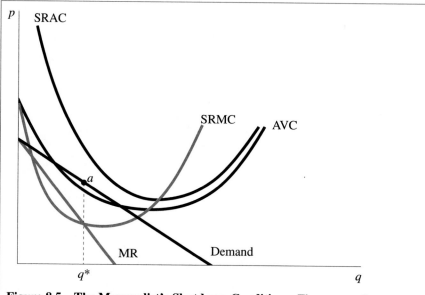

Figure 8.5   The Monopolist's Shutdown Condition   The monopolist makes negative economic profit if price is below average cost for any choice of output, as it is in this diagram. However, the monopolist should shut down in the short run only if price is below AVC for any choice of output. At q^*, short-run marginal cost (SRMC) cuts MR from below and price at a is above AVC. The firm therefore makes smaller losses in the short run by operating at q^* than by shutting down.

producing at all? Just like the perfectly competitive firm in Chapter 7, the monopolist needs to check that price is above average variable cost in the short run. If this is true, then the firm makes higher profits by producing than by shutting down. In the long run, the firm has the ability to change all inputs to improve its profitability. Thus in the long run the firm checks that price is above average cost.[10] Note that, although sunk costs may matter to the monopolist's decision to *enter* the market (since before entry sunk costs are still prospective), once they are paid sunk costs do not matter, since no current decision can affect them.

Figure 8.5 shows how this works out in practice. Because the monopolist can select any point on the demand curve, it will shut down in the short run only if no part of the average variable cost curve lies below the demand

10. Recall that profit can be written as $q(p - \text{AVC}) - \text{FC}$. If the firm shuts down, $q = 0$ and profit equals $-\text{FC}$ (the monopolist makes economic losses equal to FC). However, if price is above AVC for positive quantity, profit exceeds $-\text{FC}$. In the long run, FC = 0 and AVC is the same as AC. Profit then becomes $q(p - \text{AC})$. In the long run, therefore, the firm is better off producing positive output as long as price is above average cost.

curve. Otherwise, it will operate. Point *a,* for example, corresponds to quantity *q**, where short-run marginal cost (SRMC) cuts MR from below. It is therefore the highest profit point for the monopoly firm if it produces. Since price at *a* is above AVC, the firm does better by operating, even though it makes negative economic profit at *q** because the short-run average cost (SRAC) is above the price.

In the long run, the same comparison of curves applies, except that the firm would shut down only if the long-run average cost curve was above the demand curve at all points. If that were true, AC would exceed price no matter what quantity the firm chose, and the monopolist would be better off not producing and making zero economic profit.

In summary, in the short run the monopolist chooses the quantity where marginal cost cuts marginal revenue from below only if price on the demand curve is above AVC. If price is below AVC at this quantity, the firm shuts down. In the long run the firm will operate as long as price is above AC at the quantity where LRMC cuts marginal revenue from below.

Demand Elasticity and Monopoly Pricing

▼
4. Explain the formula for the monopolist's price markup over marginal cost.

Although both perfect competitors and monopolists choose quantity to maximize profit, the monopolist is able to raise price by limiting quantity. We saw in Chapter 7 that the perfect competitor set marginal cost equal to price. Examination of Figure 8.3 or 8.5 shows that price is *above* marginal cost for the monopolist. Do all monopolists choose the same gap between price and marginal cost? To answer, let's re-examine marginal revenue.

When the monopolist increases quantity by one unit, revenue increases by the price at which the unit is sold, *p*. However, by raising quantity the monopolist moves down the demand curve, lowering price. Writing the rate per unit at which price drops as $\Delta p/\Delta q$, we see that the revenue lost on all units sold is $\Delta p/\Delta q$ times quantity *q*. Marginal revenue therefore is

$$\text{MR} = p + \frac{\Delta p}{\Delta q}q = p\left[1 + \frac{\Delta p}{\Delta q}\frac{q}{p}\right].$$

However, $(\Delta q/q)/(\Delta p/p) = \varepsilon$ is the definition of the price elasticity of demand. We therefore find that marginal revenue is related to price according to

$$\text{MR} = p\left(1 + \frac{1}{\varepsilon}\right).$$

Since MR = MC at the profit-maximizing output, we can rearrange terms to relate the gap between price and marginal cost to demand elasticity,

$$\frac{p - \text{MC}}{p} = -\frac{1}{\varepsilon}.$$

This gap between price and marginal cost can be called the monopolist's *price markup.*

Since the price markup rises with the inverse of the elasticity of demand, the measure $-1/\varepsilon$ is frequently also referred to as the *degree of monopoly power*. The less elastic the demand curve is at the profit-maximizing output (the closer ε is to zero), the greater the degree of monopoly power and the greater the markup. For example, assume you know that a monopolist charges $10 for a product for which the cost of producing an additional unit is only $8. Since the $2 gap is one-fifth of the price, you know that the price elasticity of demand is given by $1/5 = -1/\varepsilon$, or $\varepsilon = -5$.

Since price and marginal cost are positive, the degree of monopoly power ranges between zero and one. We are able to learn two interesting facts from the extremes for the degree of monopoly power. First, we notice that the degree of monopoly power is zero for a firm that sets price equal to marginal cost, as a perfectly competitive firm does. The demand curve as seen by such a firm is infinitely elastic at the market price. Thus a perfectly competitive firm can be considered to be a monopolist that happens to have infinitely elastic demand, $\varepsilon = -\infty$, so that MR $= p$. Second, the largest the degree of monopoly power can be is 1. Thus the implied elasticities of demand range from $-\infty$ to -1. Hence, the profit-maximizing monopolist never chooses output for a place on the demand curve where the elasticity of demand is between -1 and 0. Why? Because revenue is falling for elasticities between -1 and 0 (recall the MR formula above for MR < 0). For quantities where demand is inelastic ($-1 < \varepsilon < 0$), the firm can both raise revenue and lower costs by reducing output, and therefore it will leave such a region of demand.

Competition and Monopoly Pricing

By rewriting the formula for MR in the preceding section, we see that profit maximization also implies that

$$p\left(1 + \frac{1}{\varepsilon}\right) = \text{MC}.$$

If we interpret ε as the elasticity of demand for the firm rather than the markets' price elasticity of demand, however, this condition also applies to any firm. This is what we did in the preceding section for the competitive firm, for example, when we said the perfectly competitive firm perceived $\varepsilon = -\infty$. The question is: How do we discover the firm's elasticity of demand in general?

The answer is that no simple rule for determining the firm's elasticity of demand applies in every case. It depends on the nature of competition. For example, a perfectly competitive firm perceives that market price will not change as a result of its quantity choice. In that case, $\varepsilon = -\infty$ and the firm sets $p = \text{MC}$. On the other hand, a pure monopoly with no close substitutes has ε equal to the market demand elasticity. When there are substitutes present, the way the firm's quantity changes with price depends on the way suppliers of competing goods react. This is the usual case for markets where there is a single seller, because most goods have substitute goods available to one degree or another. What the monopolist must do, all things considered, is to decide what the demand curve is for *its* product, and thus decide what quantity it will sell at each price.[11] An application will help us see how this is done.

APPLICATION: The Monopoly Pricing Rule and a New Software Company

David Garver, a mathematics and physics major who finished college in the late 1970s, started his own software company called American Medical Software in 1978.[12] Working nights and weekends while holding another job, he designed a program to handle accounting, receivables, payroll, billing and other such matters in small businesses such as doctors' and dentists' offices. The company grew and was noticed by an older, established company that manufactured printed business forms. Wanting to expand into the computer-form market, the established firm offered to buy out Garver's young company and hire him to work with the software product he had developed. Garver accepted the offer. Being a new product in the relatively new area of personal computers, the business software was the first of its kind and unique in its field. In short, Garver's company and its parent company were a sole seller, facing a downward-sloping demand curve for their product.

This was the situation in December 1986, when David and I met for dinner to discuss national affairs, sports scores, and other matters of import. David mentioned that a competitor had come into the market with a different but related software program, which it would display at the next computer trade fair in Chicago in two months. As is true of many products that begin their lives as pure monopolies, Garver's product was about to face competition from a substitute good and lose its pure monopoly status.

Garver's competitor had set a price for its product of $895, far below his price of $3,500 (which also included a guaranteed service contract for the purchaser). Given the change in demand conditions, David wanted to know what price he should advertise at his booth at the same fair. Being an economist, I was supposed to know things like this, so what did I say? (Before continuing, you might want to consider how you would respond, on the basis of what you have learned to this point in the chapter.)

First, we established that the two software products were sufficiently different that the one with the lower price would not drive the other to zero sales. This meant that treating David's pricing problem as if he were facing a downward-sloping demand curve was still appropriate, although we had to establish what demand curve he now faced. David's current sales were

---

11. Chapters 9 and 10, which study monopolistic competition and oligopoly (markets with few sellers), provide models that explain what determines the firm's demand curve in different situations.

12. Information for this section provided by David Garver; used by permission.

roughly 100 to 110 units per year (107 was our best guess). He expected to be able to maintain sales at this level if he lowered his price to $3,000 per program. (In other words, David's demand curve had shifted to the left as the result of the new entrant.) He also told me that he thought his sales would rise roughly 36 units, to about 143 units per year, if he were to reduce his price by another 10 percent to $2,700.

Assuming that the demand curve is a straight line through the two price-quantity points just described, the slope $\Delta q / \Delta p = -36/300 = -0.12$, and elasticity of demand is $\varepsilon = (\Delta q / \Delta p)p/q = -3.36$ at 107 units and price $3,000. This told us that his marginal revenue, were he to hold price at $3,000 and keep sales at 100 to 110 units, was approximately $p[1 + 1/\varepsilon] = \$3,000[1 - 1/3.36] = \$2,107.14$ per unit. When David told me that his physical cost of supplying an additional unit was approximately $100 to cover the cost of reproducing the software and documentary materials, we knew that MR > MC. *David would raise profit by lowering price and increasing sales.* Assuming that the demand curve continued to fall linearly and marginal costs stayed constant at $100, we expected to maximize profit by lowering price approximately $1,000 and more than doubling sales. In fact, after rechecking our calculations, David ultimately decided to sell the product for $1,995, for which he expected sales of about 228 units per year.

Figure 8.6 displays the information that we discussed. We knew that marginal costs were just the costs of providing the physical product. Although we did not know the exact demand curve, we had enough information about it to help us answer the pricing question. The old demand curve passed through point *a*. We were pretty sure that point *b* was on the new demand curve (107 units at price $3,000), and we had reason to believe that lowering price by 10 percent would increase sales slightly more than one-third. This got us point *c* (143 units at price $2,700). Even if our figures were off a little, it was clear that marginal revenue was far higher than marginal cost according to the new market conditions. Extending the demand curve to point *d*, we found the marginal revenue curve and located where it crossed marginal cost.

After hearing the logic of the marginal-revenue-equals-marginal-cost pricing rule, David knew what to do with the market information and cost data he had. Before our talk, he had not been sure how to proceed. Though he was a highly trained engineer, he had not been exposed to these economic principles, which made immediate sense to him once they were explained. All of our calculations were done on a napkin, we split the dinner check, and I did not charge for my consulting services.[13] Later experience revealed that our estimates had been remarkably good and the predicted increase in sales at the lower price was achieved. ■

---

13. Assuming that David was maximizing profit at the original market position of 107 units at price $3,500, what would that imply about the initial price elasticity of demand?

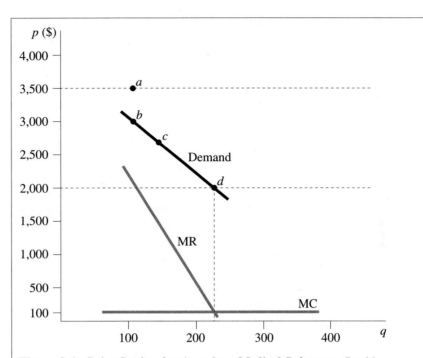

Figure 8.6 Price Setting for American Medical Software David Garver's American Medical Software was originally selling 100 to 110 units per year at a price of $3,500 per unit (point *a*). When another company offered a similar product at a much lower price, David expected to sell roughly the same number of units per year (107) if his price were $3,000. This is point *b* in the figure. We estimated that lowering price by 10 percent would lead to sales of 143 units per year. This is point *c*. Assuming a linear demand curve passing through both points, marginal revenue is the line labeled MR. Setting MR = MC, where David knew MC was $100 per unit, implied that David could maximize profits by choosing a price of around $2,000 and selling 220 to 230 units per year. In fact, he chose a price of $1,995 with expected sales of 228 (point *d*).

8.3 The Social Costs of Monopoly

The material that we have just covered—choosing the point on the demand curve where quantity is such that marginal cost cuts marginal revenue from below and profits are above those from not operating—is pretty much all there is to the basic theory of monopoly. Elaborations on this simple theme, however, are many and interesting. We will cover a number of them in the next section when we discuss ways that monopolists have found to improve their profits beyond the level of the simple theory. Before we turn to that, however, we take up the social-cost implications of monopoly.

Although monopolies are able to select a preferred point on the demand curve, they do not hold a gun to buyers' heads and force them to purchase the product. Even with voluntary purchases, however, there seems to be something wrong with the situation, in that the monopolist takes advantage of the fact that no one else sells the product. In this section we look at some economic reasons for disliking monopoly.

Two Objections to Monopoly

Many people dislike monopoly because its economic profits do not necessarily result from superior product, service, or organization, but from the fact that there is no one else with whom to compete. We might call this the fairness issue.[14] Also, the monopolist may not have to be as careful or solicitous of its clients as a competitive firm, and this, too, is a cause of dislike. The absence of a competitor allows the monopolist to raise price (and lower quantity) to increase its economic profit, whereas in a perfectly competitive market profits are reduced to zero in the long run.

There is a second reason why monopoly may be undesirable, and this reason has strong economic justification. The essence of the objection is based on the fact that monopolists price a product above the marginal cost of providing it. We saw earlier that

$$MR = p\left(1 + \frac{1}{\varepsilon}\right) = MC,$$

which means that $p > MC$. The price a household is willing to pay for a product represents the value to it of the item, whereas marginal cost represents the cost of providing it. An additional unit, therefore, could be provided by charging the household MC and paying this to the monopolist. The household would be better off by $p - MC$, and the monopolist's overall profit would be the same. Thus society as a whole would be better off.

So why doesn't this happen? It doesn't happen because monopolies purposely keep their output low in order to keep price high. They provide units when price is greater than marginal cost, not expanding their output to the point where $p = MC$. This contrasts with competitive markets, where price *equals* marginal cost and potential net gains from producing additional units are impossible.

Figure 8.7 shows a standard monopoly equilibrium. Marginal revenue equals marginal cost at the quantity q_M with corresponding price p_M. If the monopoly were to act as a pricetaking perfect competitor, it would choose to

▼

5. Show diagrammatically the social costs of monopoly. Explain in your own words why $p > MC$ leads to social costs.

14. Sometimes, however, monopoly profits *are* the reward for superior performance and diligence. For example, the 17 years of exclusive use for a new invention granted by American patent law is intended to allow the patentee time to recoup the sunk costs of invention. In some cases, then, dislike of monopoly profit may be more an expression of envy than a position based on an economically sound argument.

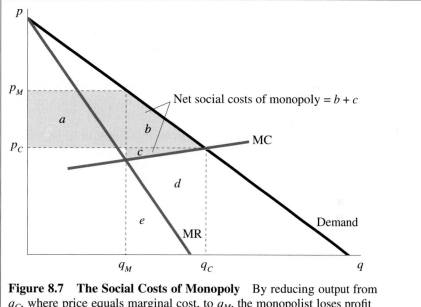

Figure 8.7 **The Social Costs of Monopoly** By reducing output from q_C, where price equals marginal cost, to q_M, the monopolist loses profit equal to area c. However, this is more than made up by the additional revenue area a from selling the q_M units at higher price p_M. The monopolist therefore has a net gain of $a - c$. Consumers, on the other hand, lose consumer surplus equal to areas $a + b$ because of the price rise from p_C to p_M. Overall, then, social costs equal areas $b + c$.

produce where price equals marginal cost, leading to the larger quantity q_C and lower price p_C. By reducing its output from q_C to q_M, the monopoly gives up revenues equal to areas $c + d + e$ but saves the corresponding production costs, areas $d + e$. It then gets to sell q_M units at price p_M rather than at price p_C, and this inceases revenues by area a. The monopoly's net gain therefore equals area $a - c$.

Consumers, on the other hand, lose consumer surplus equal to areas $a + b$ when the monopolist raises price to p_M. The net social effect of monopoly equals the monopolist's gain minus the consumers' loss, $(a - c) - (a + b) = -(b + c)$. Although the monopolist's action transfers money from consumers to the monopolist equal to area a, it also induces a net social loss equal to areas $b + c$.

Why did the social welfare disappear? No consumers were forced to buy goods they did not want, none were forced to pay more than they were willing to pay, and no one's goods were physically destroyed. Instead, *the social cost of monopoly arose because too little of the monopoly good was provided to meet a social need that could have been met cost-effectively.* The lost welfare that could have been provided is the social cost of monopoly. A simple example concerning the provision of commuting services at airports underscores this situation.

APPLICATION: Airport Monopoly and Car Rental Costs

Airports are public monopolies in more than just the provision of runways and regional terminals; they are also monopolies in supplying access to airplane travelers.[15] A company that wants to rent cars to airline passengers must first have access to airline passengers. To buy this access from airports (in the form of a rental counter at the terminal), a rent-a-car company typically pays the airport 10 percent of its gross receipts, costs that are passed along to travelers. Rather than using rent-a-car counters at the airport, however, many passengers are willing to forgo a little convenience for a lower rental price. Such passengers can rent from a company that will pick them up at the curb and shuttle them to its off-airport rental lot.

The cost to the airport of supplying off-airport rental companies with access to airline travelers is almost nothing—just the cost of allowing a limousine or van to drive to the airport curb and pick up passengers. Being a monopoly, however, the airport can charge a price much higher than its costs. In recent years many airports have begun charging off-airport rental companies 8 percent of all rental gross receipts from any customer who rents a car within a short period—say, 48 hours—of arriving at the airport. Off-airport rental companies that refuse to pay may not drive their vans and limos on airport property. Jim Cantwell of Tucson, for example, saw fees rise from $1,400 per year to about $40,000 per year for his Thrifty rental franchise in which he had invested most of his savings. To avert personal bankruptcy, he left the rent-a-car business.

What difference does 8 percent make? In at least one case, it is the difference between bankruptcy and operation of a rental business. For thousands of airline travelers, however, it is the loss of a lower-cost car rental that could have been efficiently provided. The shame is not that airports must charge for access to passengers, but rather that the price they charge is above marginal cost. The result is that too little access to passengers is provided, and a social need that could have been met goes unmet. ■

EXPLORATION: Pricing with Market Power

We have found that a monopolist can increase profit at the expense of lost consumer surplus to buyers. Because of the downward-sloping demand curve, the monopolist can sell a smaller quantity at a higher price, thereby extracting

---

15. See Jonathan Rauch, ''Stop It Hertz: Taking Drivers for a Ride,'' *The New Republic,* April 22, 1991, pp. 19–20.

some of the consumer surplus that buyers otherwise would have had. Naturally, the firm would like to get even more consumer surplus. In this section, we discuss several ways in which a firm with *market power* can do better for itself if it has more options available than just choosing a single price. Market power is the ability to set price above marginal cost.

> *A seller with **market power** is any firm with a downward-sloping firm demand curve that has the ability to set price different from marginal cost.*

Monopolies clearly have market power, because their demand curve is the market demand curve; their market power is measured by the degree of monopoly power, $-1/\varepsilon$, discussed earlier. But other firms that can influence their product prices also exercise varying degrees of market power. We now consider some of their pricing strategies.

Market Segmentation

▼

6. Give four strategies that firms with market power can use to capture consumer surplus. What makes each work?

In the simple monopoly model, the manager had the option of setting just one price for all buyers. If the firm can set *different* prices for *different* buyers, it can raise its profits further. A strategy that discriminates between buyers by segmenting the market into distinct groups is called *market segmentation*. A monopoly that employs market segmentation is often called a *discriminating monopoly*.

> *Market segmentation divides the market into buyer groups that pay different prices for the product.*

How do we know that market segmentation yields higher profit? With two groups of buyers the monopolist's profit is given by

$$\Pi = R_1 + R_2 - C(q_1 + q_2),$$

where R_1 and R_2 are revenues from the two parts of the market, and $C(q_1 + q_2)$ is the cost of producing the total output $(q_1 + q_2)$ that the firm supplies to both parts of the market. Since the firm could always decide to set both prices equal, we know it can do no worse than before, but if the demand curve is different in the two parts of the market it can do better.

The manager's problem is to decide what price to charge each set of buyers—or, what amounts to the same thing, what quantities, q_1 and q_2, to sell to the two segments of the market. Assume that the monopolist has chosen an output for each segment of the market and is considering whether it should raise the quantity (that is, lower the price) to segment 1. If the monopolist lowers price, it gets the marginal revenue from that segment (MR_1), which adds to profit, but it must also pay the marginal cost of producing the extra units. The change in profit is therefore

$$\Delta\Pi = MR_1 - MC.$$

If the change in profit is positive, the discriminating monopolist will expand sales to segment 1 of the market; if the change in profit is negative, it will reduce sales to that segment. Only if $MR_1 = MC$ will the firm stay where it is. Performing the same analysis for the other market segment, we find that the monopolist has highest profits only if

$$MR_1 = MC \quad \text{and} \quad MR_2 = MC.$$

The monopolist therefore chooses prices and quantities in each market segment so that $MR_1 = MR_2 = MC$. This condition is familiar from the rule for the simple monopoly. Since $MR_1 = p_1(1 + 1/\varepsilon_1)$ and $MR_2 = p_2(1 + 1/\varepsilon_2)$, where ε_1 and ε_2 are the price elasticities of demand in the two markets, we see that

$$\frac{p_1(1 + 1/\varepsilon_1)}{p_2(1 + 1/\varepsilon_2)} = 1,$$

or

$$\frac{p_1}{p_2} = \frac{1 + 1/\varepsilon_2}{1 + 1/\varepsilon_1}.$$

Thus the market segment with the *least* elastic demand and highest monopoly power (that is, demand with ε closer to 0 that is less responsive to price change) is charged the higher price.

To see how market segmentation works, let's return to our cable TV example. In Figure 8.3 we found that maximum profit was $990 at quantity 40 and price $30. Now assume that the cable supplier is able to distinguish two types of buyers, those in neighborhood 1 with no other cable supplier and those in neighborhood 2 with a competing cable supplier. Buyers in neighborhood 1 have demand given by

$$q_1 = 100 - 2p \quad \text{for prices between \$50 and \$25}$$
$$q_1 = 50 \quad \quad \quad \text{for all prices below \$25.}$$

This group is willing to pay a high price for cable because it has no alternative cable supplier, but it never wants more than 50 units.

The second group of buyers will buy the product only if the price is $25 or less, according to demand

$$q_2 = 50 - 2p$$

These demands, which sum to the total market demand $q^D = 100 - 2p$ already considered, are displayed in Figure 8.8. If the monopolist continues to charge price $30 to sell 40 units, the only buyers will come from neighborhood 1, who have no cable alternative. However, buyers in neighborhood 2 are willing to pay $25 for the first unit purchased. Assuming the same cost function we defined earlier, the monopolist's marginal cost at 40 units is $10, so if the monopolist could sell to the second group at any price above $10, holding the price and quantity to the first group fixed, its profits would

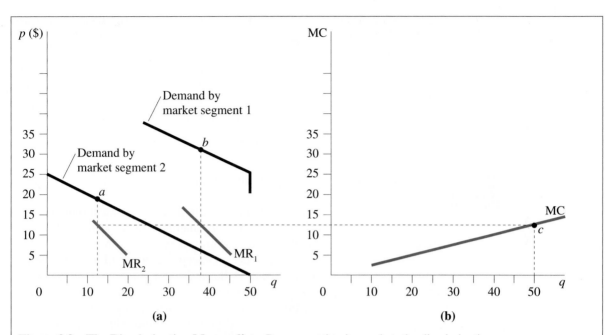

Figure 8.8   The Discriminating Monopolist   By segmenting its market, the discriminating monopolist charges different prices for the same product to different groups of buyers. This allows the
monopolist to raise its profit. In part (a) the demand curves for two groups lead to the two marginal
revenue curves labeled MR_1 and MR_2. The monopolist sets $MR_1 = MR_2 = MC$. With total output at
50 units, part (b) shows that MC is $12.50. Finding the output where $MR = MC = 12.50 for each
market segment shows that segment 1 buyers are sold 37.5 units at price $31.25 (point b), and seg-
ment 2 buyers are sold 12.5 units at price $18.75 (point a).

improve. Of course, increasing output will raise the marginal cost somewhat.
Finding the output level and price for each market segment, such that marginal
revenue in each segment equals marginal revenue in the other, and each
equals marginal cost, implies that the monopolist will sell 37.5 units to
neighborhood 1 buyers at price $31.25 and 12.5 units to neighborhood 2
buyers at price $18.75. Marginal revenue for each segment of the market at
these price levels is $12.50. This equals marginal cost when 50 units are
produced in total, confirming that we have found the monopolist's optimal
position. Computing the monopolist's profit, we have

$$
\begin{aligned}
\Pi &= \quad R^1 \quad + \quad R^2 \quad - \quad C(q) \\
&= \$31.25(37.5) + \$18.75(12.5) - \$5 - (\$0.125)50^2 \\
&= \$1,406.25 - \$317.50 \\
&= \$1,088.75.
\end{aligned}
$$

Market segmentation yields higher profits than charging all buyers the same
price ($1,088.75 > $990). Because the neighborhood with an alternative

cable supplier had more elastic demand at each quantity, the cable supplier had lower monopoly power and charged its residents less. The neighborhood with less elastic demand was charged the higher price.

Market segmentation is a common practice. Only two conditions are required for it to be successful: the seller can distinguish among buyers whose demands differ in some way; and resale of the good or service is not possible.[16] A classic example of price discrimination is the pricing practices of major airlines. ■

APPLICATION: Airline Price Discrimination

"I have to see how many people I can get to give me the most money." said the vice president for ticketing at one of America's major airlines.[17] She did it through a method called *yield management,* based on a computerized system of frequently repricing seats on every upcoming flight until the day of departure. A typical flight from Dallas to New York might have 190 seats. Fifteen seats might have been assigned a value or "yield" of $600 each, another 15 a yield of $400 each, and so on down to, say, $100. Depending on when you, the passenger, booked your ticket and what restrictions you accepted, you could have paid anything from $100 to $600 for your flight.

This particular airline had 2,450 jet departures per day, and each flight averaged 12 different published fares whose availability was constantly changing. All airlines together change fares an astonishing 80,000 times every day. American Airlines, which announced in April 1992 that it was simplifying to a four-fare system, found that it was not as profitable and was back to multiple fares six months later.[18]

Among the many restrictions airlines have devised to segment their buyers into different groups are obligations to: (1) purchase tickets seven days in advance, (2) buy round-trip tickets with no refund or cancellation allowed, (3) travel early in the morning or late in the day, (4) stay over a Saturday night, (5) use tickets by a certain date, and (6) change planes. To consider how just one of these works to segment the market, let's look at the restriction to stay over Saturday night. We might ask: What type of passenger is less likely to want to stay over Saturday night? A reasonable answer would be frequent business travelers, who might scarcely see their families if they were gone for weekends as well as in midweek. Since business travelers are likely to have less elastic demand for air travel than, say, family vacationers, it is

---

16. If resale were possible, buyers who bought the product at a low price could resell their units to buyers who otherwise would buy at a high price. With resale, no buyers would ever buy the product except at a low price from the producer or in the resale market. The monopolist would therefore find itself selling at only one price.

17. Louis Uchitelle, "Off Course," *The New York Times Magazine,* September 1, 1991, p. 25.

18. See James S. Hirsch, "Airlines Wage Fare Battle City by City, Spreading Confusion as Well as Bargains," *Wall Street Journal,* November 13, 1992, pp. B1, B10.

not surprising that the airlines charge higher prices to those who do not stay over Saturday night than to those who do.

Airlines are also notorious for advertising their lowest prices, which are not available for all of the seats on the flights in question.[19] An airline advertising a $318 bargain fare for a flight to Europe, on which other seats might go for $1,944, is usually careful not to say how many seats are available at the lowest price. Spokesmen for the travel industry suggest that such seats probably represent no more than 7 percent of the total, or roughly 20 out of 300 coach seats on a Boeing 747.

The hub system, by which an airline routes its flights to distant locations through a common city (the hub) where transfers and plane changes are made, also seems to be operated partly with an eye to market segmentation. It is not uncommon, for example, to find that 85 percent of traffic into and out of a hub is handled by a single airline. Passengers who begin or end their flights in the hub (often chosen for its population base as well as its geographic location) find themselves forced to pay ticket prices roughly 10 to 15 percent above the norm. Airline industry observers explain that the nonlocals, who merely change planes at the hub, can bargain better and are therefore given better fares. This is exactly what we would predict on the basis of differing elasticity of demand between nonlocals (more elastic) and locals (less elastic). ■

Multipart Pricing

Another way in which monopolists extract more consumer surplus is by *multipart pricing.* Sometimes called *block pricing* or *nonlinear pricing,* multipart pricing occurs when the seller charges a different price for different numbers or blocks of units bought.

> **Multipart pricing** *consists of selling the product in units or blocks so that the buyer pays a different (usually higher) price for earlier blocks than for later blocks.*

For example, a monopolist might charge a high price for the first 10 units bought and a lower price for units after the first 10. Grocery stores practice multipart pricing by charging proportionately lower prices for larger packages. Compare the price for a ''family size'' container of laundry detergent with the price of a smaller container of the same brand.

The difference in packaging costs cannot explain the price disparity, so why do sellers employ multipart pricing? They do so not because they want to give a break to buyers of large quantities, but because they want to collect more consumer surplus from buyers of small quantities. To see the effect of multipart pricing, let's look at Figure 8.9. Stephen's demand for detergent is

19. Nancy Sharkey, ''Bargain Fares, But How Many?'' *New York Times,* March 31, 1991, pp. 3, 5.

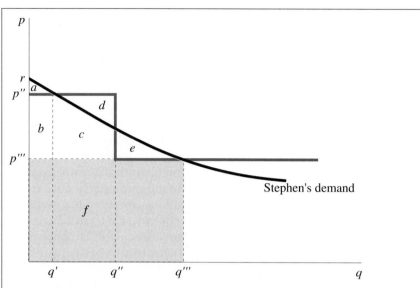

Figure 8.9 Multipart Pricing   The monopolist collects greater revenues for the same number of units sold by charging different prices for
different blocks of units. In the figure, the seller gets revenues equal to
shaded area f if it sells q''' units at price p'''. Stephen retains consumer
surplus equal to areas $a + b + c + e$. However, by pricing the first q''
units at p'' and the remaining units at p''', the multipart pricing firm gets
revenue equal to areas $b + c + d + f$. Stephen retains consumer surplus
equal to area a if he chooses q' units and equal to areas $a - d + e$ if he
chooses q''' units, so he is better off choosing q''' if $a - d + e$ is greater
than a. The firm can make area a zero by setting $p'' \geq r$ and area d equal
to area e, thereby collecting all of Stephen's surplus.

the downward-sloping curve. At single price p''' Stephen demands q''' units
of detergent. The seller receives revenue from the sales equal to area f.
Stephen's consumer surplus is area $a + b + c + e$.

Now consider Stephen's response if the offer is to sell the first q'' units at
price p'' and units after q'' at price p'''. Stephen chooses to buy the quantity
that raises his utility the most by leaving him the greatest consumer surplus.
If he buys q' units he gets consumer surplus equal to area a. If Stephen
purchases q'' units, his consumer surplus will be $a - d$ (in this case negative),
and if he buys q''' units, his surplus will be $a - d + e$. If the seller chooses
prices appropriately, area $a - d + e$ can be made one cent larger than area
a, and area a can be made as small as desired (zero if $p'' \geq r$). The seller thus
sells quantity q''', getting all but one cent of the consumer surplus!

In reality, of course, a seller deals with many buyers who have different
demands. The seller therefore prices according to the *total* demand curve for
the product to collect more of the consumer surplus from all buyers than it
could by charging just a single price.

The Two-Part Tariff

A technique closely related to multipart pricing is the two-part tariff. In this pricing strategy, the buyer pays an up-front entrance fee or membership fee for the right to buy at a flat fee thereafter.

> The **two-part tariff** is a pricing arrangement whereby buyers pay both an entrance fee and usage prices thereafter.

For example, amusement parks often charge an entrance fee and then charge an additional price for each ride inside the park. Utilities sometimes charge a basic monthly service charge coupled with usage fees. Health clubs also typically require an annual membership fee as well as separate fees for lockers, towels, and so on thereafter. In a sense, the entrance fee is the price charged for the first block of zero units, with a lower price charged for subsequent units.

How can this raise the monopolist's profits? In the case of a single buyer, the monopolist can set the entrance fee equal to all of the consumer surplus that the buyer would otherwise receive from buying the good at its stated price. The monopolist then sets the per-unit price at marginal cost, so the buyer pays the cost to the monopolist of supplying the additional units.[20] Figure 8.10 shows the demand curve for a buyer and the firm's marginal cost curve, MC. By setting price equal to p' and charging an entrance fee equal to area a (the buyer's consumer surplus), the firm captures all the consumer surplus.

When the monopolist sells to a large number of buyers with different consumer surpluses and demand curves, the monopolist cannot hope to capture all of each buyer's consumer surplus by charging each buyer the same entrance fee. It can, however, capture some of the consumer surplus that it would not have had otherwise.

Commodity Bundling

Another way in which monopolies can capture more consumer surplus is called *commodity bundling*. Commodity bundling can be used when the monopolist sells two or more goods and cannot price-discriminate.

> **Commodity bundling** is the selling of two or more goods as a package.

When the monopolist charges every buyer the same price, some buyers get the good for less then they would be willing to pay, and others do not buy because the monopolist's price is above their willingness to pay. The *dispersion* of the maximum amount that buyers are willing to pay for the product means that the monopolist cannot choose a single price that precisely

---

20. After the buyer pays the entrance fee, it is a sunk cost and thus does not affect the decision of how many units to buy. Were the monopolist to charge a price higher than marginal cost, the consumer would be willing to buy additional units at a price higher than what it costs the monopolist to supply them. The monopolist could do better by lowering price a little and increasing sales until the price charged equaled marginal cost.

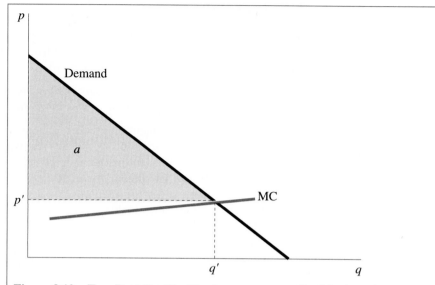

Figure 8.10   Two-Part Tariff   The firm can extract all of the buyer's consumer surplus by setting price at p', determined by the intersection of MC and the buyer's demand curve, and charging an entrance fee equal to area a.

captures all of the consumer surplus. However, if the monopolist sells several different goods, it may be that the dispersion of what buyers are willing to pay for a *bundle* of the goods is less than the dispersion for individual goods in the bundle. The monopolist can then choose a single price for the bundle that better captures consumer surplus.

To understand how this works, consider a simple case of two goods, large drill bits and small drill bits. Many of us have experienced the frustration of going into a hardware store wanting to buy, say, a $\frac{3}{8}$-inch drill bit, only to find that we must buy an entire package of bits to get what we want. Other buyers, wanting to buy only a $\frac{1}{16}$-inch bit, find that they have to buy the entire range as well. There is a method to the packaging. For bits sold separately, there is a maximum price, called the *reservation price,* that each buyer would be willing to pay for each size of drill bit. By plotting reservation prices for bits for all potential buyers in the market, we can compare the results of the monopolist's different pricing strategies.

Figure 8.11 shows how commodity bundling affects 10 buyers of large and small drill bits. Part (a) plots the buyers' reservation prices as points r_1 through r_{10}. For example, buyer 1 would be willing to pay $.75 for large bits and $.20 for small ones (at r_1). Buyer 2 would be willing to pay $.70 for large bits and $.25 for small ones, and so on up to buyer 10, who would be willing to pay $.20 for large and $.75 for small. For large drill bits, the buyers' willingness to pay ranges from $.20 to $.75. The average reservation price is $.515, but by charging this price the seller excludes buyers 6 through 10, who are not willing to pay this much, and charges buyers 1 through 5 less than what they are willing to pay for the good.

No single price does very well at exploiting every buyer's full willingness to pay. The best the monopolist can do by pricing large and small bits separately is to set the price of large bits at $.40, getting revenues of $3.20 on sales to buyers 1 through 8, and set the price of small bits at $.35, getting revenues of $2.45 on sales to buyers 4 through 10, for total revenues of $5.65.

However, part (a) of Figure 8.11 shows the potentially useful fact that the buyers' reservation prices are negatively related to one another. That is, a buyer who is willing to pay more for large bits is willing to pay less for small ones. Thus, the amounts that buyers are willing to pay for the *bundle* of large plus small bits are less dispersed than the amounts buyers will pay for either good separately. In fact, in this example each buyer is willing to pay exactly $.95 for the bundle of two bits!

By bundling large drill bits with small and charging $.95, the monopolist will capture exactly the maximum amount that each buyer is willing to pay for the bundle. Instead of $5.65, the monopolist will have revenues of $9.50. Part (b) of Figure 8.11 shows the price line for drill-bit bundles. Each buyer's reservation price for the bundle lies on the line for bundle price $.95. Since there is no dispersion, selling the bundle at a single price captures every buyer's full consumer surplus.[21]

Commodity bundling often occurs in situations where buyers can put together bundles according to their preferences, choosing from a list or menu of items. Automobile options, for example, are sold item by item or as packages. Restaurants sell items à la carte or bundled as complete meals. Clothing frequently comes "packaged" as combinations or as separates.

The last part in Figure 8.11 explains why some goods may be sold both separately and as part of a bundle. So far we have looked only at how bundling can increase revenue by allowing the monopolist's single price to capture consumer surplus from a less dispersed range of reservation prices. Now we consider the effect of production costs. In part (c) we assume that the marginal costs of producing a large drill bit and a small drill bit are $.225 and $.325, respectively (small bits require more careful machining and different steel). When only the bundled product is available, the buyer spends $.95 for the bundle that costs the monopolist $.55 to make, leaving $.40 profit from each buyer.

However, consider buyer 1 in part (c). This buyer would be willing to pay $.75 for a large bit separately, which is more than $.50 above the $.225 cost

---

21. On the other hand, if the first buyer had been willing to pay, say, $.95 for small bits and $.95 for large ones, the second $.90 for small bits and $.90 for large ones, and so on down to buyer 10, who was willing to pay $.50 for small bits and $.50 for large ones, there would be just as much dispersion in willingness to pay for the bundle as for the goods separately. (In fact, the willingness to pay for the bundle of small plus large bits would range from $1.90 down to $1.) In this case, by selling the bundle of small plus large bits at a single price, the monopolist would do no better than by selling the goods separately.

Figure 8.11   Commodity Bundling   When the monopolist sells several products but cannot price-discriminate, it often can increase profit by bundling its goods. If the dispersion of the buyers' reservation prices is smaller for the bundle than for the individual goods, bundling does a better job of capturing all of each buyer's consumer surplus. In the figure, the reservation prices for large and small drill bits (goods x and y, respectively) are shown by the points labeled r_1 through r_{10}. Buyer 1, for example, would be willing to pay up to $.75 for a large bit and $.20 for a small one, or $.95 for the bundle of both. As shown by comparing parts (a) and (b), the monopolist is better off by bundling than by selling the bits separately. As part (c) shows, bundling in conjunction with selling the goods separately lets the monopolist segment buyers into groups according to what mix of goods they buy. This allows the greatest profit.

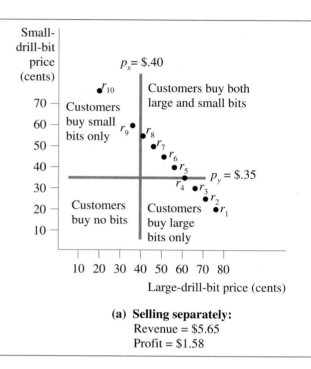

(a) **Selling separately:**
Revenue = $5.65
Profit = $1.58

of producing it. Moreover, this buyer is willing to pay only $.20 for small bits, which is below their $.325 production cost. The monopolist could improve profit if there were some way to sell just large bits to buyer 1 at close to $.75 without having to sell small ones. A similar argument applies to buyer 10, who would be willing to pay $.75 for a small bit alone (profit on the sale of $.425), but only $.20 for a large one (loss on that sale of $.025). The solution is to offer large bits separately at $.74 and small bits separately at $.74. If buyers 1 and 10 buy the bundle, they will retain zero consumer surplus. However, if buyer 1 buys only a large bit, he will retain consumer surplus of $.01 (he was willing to pay $.75 but only had to pay $.74). Similarly, if buyer 10 buys only a small bit, he will retain consumer surplus of $.01. Since the price of buying the two items separately is greater than buying the bundle, consumers 2 through 9 buy the bundle as before. The net result of the mixed pricing is that the monopolist increases profit by $.13 over the bundling scheme.

Any seller that finds it can improve profits by changing its pricing strategy will eventually learn to do so. Pure bundling can increase monopoly profit if the dispersion of reservation prices for the bundle is lower than for selling goods separately. Furthermore, by using bundling together with separate

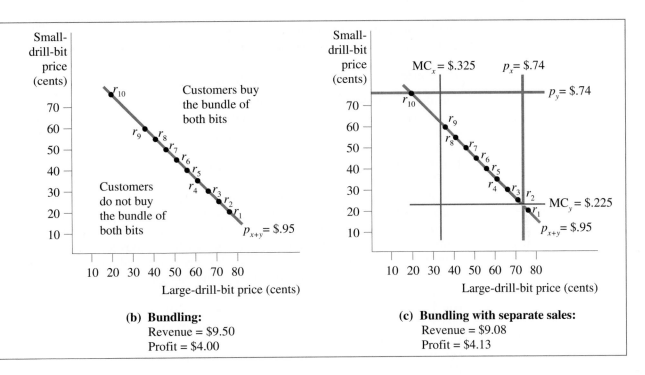

(b) Bundling:
Revenue = $9.50
Profit = $4.00

(c) Bundling with separate sales:
Revenue = $9.08
Profit = $4.13

sales, the monopolist in effect reintroduces market segmentation by causing buyers to select themselves into separate groups depending on what they buy.

As another example, assume that you are an automobile manufacturer. You know that different buyers will pay varying amounts for performance options such as greater engine size and pulling capability, or for comfort features such as automatic transmission, cruise control, interior coverings, and air conditioning. Those who prefer comfort features will not pay as much for performance, whereas those who prefer performance will not pay as much for comfort. A third group of buyers is almost exclusively concerned with performance, for which they will pay significantly more than the usual buyer will pay, and a fourth group is almost exclusively concerned with comfort, for which they will pay considerably more. What does your pricing look like? You want to offer general buyers a package of options that extracts as much from them as they are willing to pay for a combination of comfort and performance, but at the same time you offer performance features and comfort features separately for a high price relative to their cost of provision. This will capture as much surplus as possible from buyers in groups three and four. If a fifth group of buyers is mostly concerned with appearance features, such as exterior trim and upscale wheel covers, you may include special bundles to extract consumer surplus from them as well. In this way, each group will pay as much as possible for just those things that it wants.

The Perfectly Discriminating Monopoly

Our discussion of market segmentation and multipart pricing suggests that by separating the market into more and more distinct groups and charging each group according to a specially designed multipart pricing schedule, the monopolist could combine two types of price discrimination and reap the benefit in increased profits. How far can this process be carried?

The answer can be seen by considering the effect of segmenting the market into individual buyers and charging each one a specially designed multipart price to collect *all* of the consumer surplus from every buyer. The *perfectly discriminating monopoly* simply gives each buyer, *i*, an ultimatum: buy q^i units at price p^i or get nothing. The monopolist then chooses p^i so that the consumer has no consumer surplus from the purchase,[22] and it chooses q^i so that if the monopolist sold another unit to the consumer, the extra revenue the monopolist would get from taking all the consumer surplus would just equal the marginal cost of production. We know that, for each consumer, the value of an additional unit of good, holding utility constant, equals the consumer's marginal rate of substitution MU^i_q/MU^i_C, where C is income the consumer spends on a composite good consisting of everything else, as in Chapter 5. The monopoly therefore sets

$$\frac{MU^1_q}{MU^1_C} = \frac{MU^2_q}{MU^2_C} = \ldots = \frac{MU^i_q}{MU^i_C} = MC.$$

▼

7. Why doesn't a perfectly discriminating monopoly lead to social costs?

An interesting feature of this strategy is that the monopolist ends up producing a quantity at which there are no social costs of the type a simple monopoly creates. There is no need to reduce quantity to raise price, since the perfectly discriminating monopolist already gets all the consumer surplus. Thus the monopolist might as well produce to the point where the last unit sold is sold at a price that just equals marginal cost. Figure 8.12 shows this situation in terms of market demand curve D. The monopolist produces output q^* and collects revenues equal to areas $a + b$. The monopolist could collect extra revenue equal to the height of the demand curve at point q^* by selling another unit. Thus the demand curve becomes the effective marginal revenue curve, which the monopolist cuts from below with the marginal cost curve at q^*.

It is difficult to come up with an example of a perfectly discriminating monopoly because the monopolist must know a great deal about the nature of the buyer's demand for the product. However, some industries may come close. For example, hospitals often require information about a prospective patient's insurance before they will admit the patient. In nonelective procedures, they know that the patient's demand for the medical treatment is not

---

22. Actually, the monopolist leaves the consumer $.01 of consumer surplus, so that the consumer has positive incentive to buy the good at the price p^i.

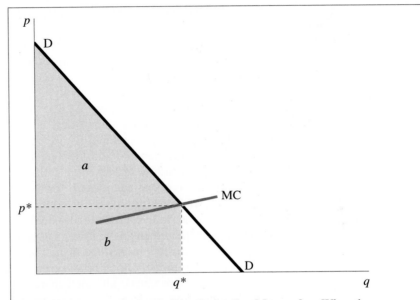

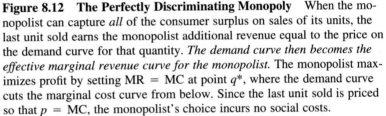

Figure 8.12   The Perfectly Discriminating Monopoly   When the monopolist can capture *all* of the consumer surplus on sales of its units, the last unit sold earns the monopolist additional revenue equal to the price on the demand curve for that quantity. *The demand curve then becomes the effective marginal revenue curve for the monopolist.* The monopolist maximizes profit by setting MR = MC at point q^*, where the demand curve cuts the marginal cost curve from below. Since the last unit sold is priced so that p = MC, the monopolist's choice incurs no social costs.

price-sensitive.[23] Therefore, the hospital knows that it can charge the most that each patient's insurance company is willing to pay and perhaps a little bit extra, which the patient will pay for out of pocket. The better off the patient, the more the "extra" can be. As long as the hospital can conceal the fact that it charges different patients different prices for the same procedure, it can act as a perfectly discriminating monopolist.

Lawyers handling estates are in the same enviable position as hospitals, in that they have perfect information about what the estate is able to pay. Typically in such cases, the fee will be levied as a percantage of the estate being settled. Larger estates thus automatically pay more in legal fees than small ones, even though large estates are not necessarily more time consuming or difficult to settle and, in any case, the settlement fees could be charged on a time-rate basis.

23. How much will a person pay to save his life, for example? If the hospital charges a price so that the person has greater utility from purchasing the treatment than from not purchasing it, the consumer retains consumer surplus and the hospital, in principle, could have charged more.

▼
8. How might differences in price information and search costs help a monopolist segment its market?

EXPLORATION: Asymmetric Information and the Noisy Monopolist

Throughout this book, we have noted ways in which asymmetric information affects markets. In general, information about price, quantity, or quality can be imperfect. In previous chapters, we have looked at cases in which the buyer had imperfect information about quality in the used car market and the labor market. In this section, we see that the monopolist may take advantage of asymmetric information about price.

Assume that you are a retailer whose customers fall into two groups. One group has inelastic demand and high search costs, and the other group has elastic demand and low search costs. In this context, think of search cost as the opportunity costs of each group for the time spent reading ads, making phone calls, and visiting stores for comparison shopping. We will assume that high-income, full-scheduled individuals have high search costs, whereas lower-income individuals have lower search costs.

Travel time matters to customers, and since no other stores are close by, you have a local monopoly on retail services. You face a downward-sloping demand for your products, although there are competing retailers scattered within commuting distance. The low-search-cost group of buyers is well-informed about the prices of products similar to those you sell, because they are price-sensitive and their low search costs make it worth their while to learn what the prices are. The high-search-cost buyers, on the other hand, are poorly informed about prices, and their purchases are less price-sensitive.

Unforturnately, there is no way for you to tell which type of buyer is which. Otherwise, you would price-discriminate. Because of your inability to distinguish between buyer groups, the one price you charge must be relatively low so as not to lose the price-sensitive group of buyers. Is there nothing that you can do to improve this state of affairs?

If we take your buyers' search costs into account, the answer to this question is yes, under certain circumstances. Assume that you make your price "noisy." That is, you choose random periods during the year to hold advertised sales, marking down your merchandise for that limited time and then returning prices to their normal level. What happens? The well-informed buyers tend to bunch their purchases into the period of the sales; because they are price-sensitive, they quickly learn where the best prices are, and they shop wherever price is best. Poorly informed buyers, on the other hand, tend to purchase from you at the same rate whether or not there is a special sale. Lowering your price during sale periods therefore loses revenue from a portion of the poorly informed group who would have paid the higher price, but gains revenue from the well-informed consumers whose purchases increase during the sales.

Depending on the search habits of both groups, the timing of the sales, and the amount of the price reductions, it is possible for you, the retailer, to increase your profits by the strategy of random sales. To take an extreme case, assume that well-informed buyers become *instantly* aware of sales and make their purchases within hours of the start of the sale, but that the other group makes its purchases at a uniform rate throughout the year. A strategy of random sales of short duration would then lose very little revenue from poorly informed buyers, because few of them would happen to buy during the short sale periods, but all of the well-informed buyers would be served at the lower sale price. The net result would be that nearly all of the poorly informed buyers would pay the regular high price and all of the well-informed buyers would pay the lower sale price. You would have effectively segmented your market and raised your profits by charging different prices to different buyers.

As you can tell from the discussion, a full treatment of this sales strategy requires information about how the two groups of buyers differ in their buying habits and search costs. The seller uses this information to infer how the demand of the two groups responds to sales of different magnitudes, durations, and frequencies. Though a treatment in this amount of detail is beyond our scope here, the principle is clear: the monopolist will try to separate buyers according to the information that buyers have about prices, and it will set prices to maximize profits from each group. ■

8.4 Regulation of Monopoly

A direct approach to market regulation would reason as follows: since the market is behaving in a socially harmful way, the government should intervene to correct it. But what form should the correction take? A lawyer might tend to think in terms of passing a law to prevent undesirable behavior, whereas an economist might think in terms of using various taxes to alter prices and induce needed changes. Other disciplines might tend toward different solutions; engineers, for example, might seek to solve social problems through technological improvements.

Direct approaches to market regulation, including monopoly regulation, have come under increasing scrutiny in recent years because of their presumption that "the market is broken, so the government should fix it." In fact, markets are often more self-correcting than we realize, government intervention can cause larger problems than it solves, and we now recognize that government itself has problems that need correcting. In fact, the market can sometimes offer a solution to problems originating in the government. Since intelligent regulation requires an understanding of the available alternatives, we consider five possible approaches.

Approaches to Regulation

▼
9. Describe five approaches to the regulation of monopoly.

The basic problem with monopoly is that lack of competition means the monopolist fails to produce output at the point where price equals marginal cost. As we have seen, setting price above marginal cost allows the monopolist to capture excess consumer surplus and creates a social loss. Five responses to the lack of competition, ordered from the least to the most interventionist, are as follows:

1. Laissez faire
2. Establishing competition
3. Regulating through taxes
4. Direct price control
5. Nationalization

Each has its strong points and its weak points.

Laissez Faire. Laissez fare, or a "hands-off" policy, is the simplest and least costly policy in terms of government resources and tax costs. In many cases it may be the best response to monopoly. First, as we have indicated, a monopoly may be relatively short-lived even without intervention, since it eventually would face competition from other firms or producers of substitute goods. New products and technical innovation are often powerful forces for altering the degree of market power that a monopolist may have.

Second, to the extent that monopolies price-discriminate, the social costs of too little output can be substantially reduced or entirely eliminated. We have already seen that there is no social cost associated with a perfectly discriminating monopolist. Since other forms of price discrimination also capture consumer surplus, it is in the monopolist's interest to have as large a clientele as possible to capture as much consumer surplus as possible. As a result, the problem of producing too little is reduced. Figure 8.13, for example, shows a market demand curve and price schedule for a firm that multipart-prices using just two prices. When the firm sets a single monopoly price, p_M, social costs equal the larger shaded area bounded by the demand curve and marginal cost curve to the right of q_M. This area shrinks considerably when the firm sells q_1 units at multipart price p_1 and $q^* - q_1$ units at multipart price p_2. It is easy to show that a similar shrinkage in social costs over all market segments occurs when the monopolist is able to segment its market. The critical feature is that the monopolist charges a price close to marginal cost for its last unit sold. In the case of airline yield management, for example, it is in the interest of the airlines to fill the last seat before takeoff at any price just above the marginal fuel, beverage, and cleanup costs of having an additional passenger on board.

Third, laissez faire can be the correct policy because many situations that seem to require intervention may not need it at all. Just as there is no sure way to decide how many firms make a market perfectly competitive, there is no sure way to determine how few firms create a market with large social costs. A single seller, for example, may perceive a different demand curve than the market demand curve because of the threat that other firms may enter the market. Keeping price low may be used as a device to discourage entry, thereby preserving a smaller degree of monopoly power for a longer time. If the threat of entry is great enough, the degree of monopoly power exercised may be quite small. In fact, studies trying to measure the extent of

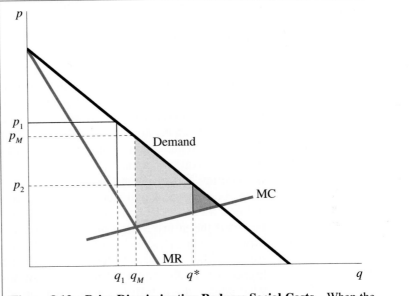

Figure 8.13 Price Discrimination Reduces Social Costs When the firm charges a single monopoly price, p_M, quantity sold is q_M and social costs equal the larger shaded area. When the firm charges multipart prices, selling q_1 units at p_1 and $q^* - q_1$ units at p_2, total quantity rises to q^* and social costs drop substantially to the smaller shaded triangle.

monopoly losses in the economy as a whole typically place the figure at less than 1 percent of national income.[24]

Establishing Competition. Another response to monopoly is to establish competition in the marketplace. In the case of cable TV, for example, some cities have taken steps to license multiple suppliers. They also prohibit anti-competitive pricing practices (such as an established cable company's cutting its rates in one area where a new entrant is present, but not in other areas nearby) and require that all cable suppliers have equal rights to bid for programming. A new cable company, for example, could not be denied the right to bid for various programs offered by program suppliers to existing cable companies. Public Law 102-385, passed in October 1992, also prohibits local franchising authorities from granting exclusive franchises and refusing to award additional competitive licenses.

Government intervention can also serve a preventive role. The Sherman Antitrust Act, passed by Congress in 1890, and the Clayton Antitrust Act, passed in 1914 to strengthen the Sherman Act, are legal tools to regulate anticompetitive behavior by firms. Section I of the Sherman Act prohibits

24. See the discussion in Scherer, F. M. and David Ross, *Industrial Market Structure and Economic Performance,* 3rd ed. Boston, MA: Houghton Mifflin, 1990, pp. 661–667.

conspiracies in restraint of trade, and section II prohibits monopolization and attempts to monopolize.

Antitrust actions are generally regarded as performing a socially useful service when they prevent the formation of monopolies in industries that can naturally sustain competition—that is, industries whose member firms have U-shaped cost curves and outputs that are small relative to market demand. Problems arise, however, when the industry is a natural monopoly, so that preventing a single large firm from dominating the market also prevents cost reductions from economies of scale and downward-sloping average cost. In these cases, regulators are caught between a rock and a hard place: allowing the cost savings of a single firm risks monopoly pricing, and insisting on competition between firms loses the economies of scale.

In some cases, it is better not to break up a natural monopoly. Regional utilities, for example, benefit from substantial economies of scale that would be lost if the utility were replaced by a large number of smaller, competing firms. In such cases, we would expect the market to return eventually to a small number of sellers as lower-cost, larger firms eliminated their smaller, higher-cost rivals. Unfortunately, it is not always known ahead of time to what degree the industry structure will or will not support competition, or whether it would be better off left alone. In one prominent case, the antitrust division of the U.S. Justice Department in 1983 split American Telephone and Telegraph Company (AT&T), which for decades had enjoyed a government-condoned monopoly on telephone service, into regional competing companies. At the same time, it opened long-distance communication services to competition from new entrants. Since that time, there has been some shakeout of companies, and Sprint, MCI, and AT&T are currently competing for most long-distance services. Whether the industry will ultimately sustain three major firms or whether there will be further consolidation remains to be seen.[25]

▼
10. What effects do the following taxes or subsidies have on monopoly price and output: (1) production subsidy, (2) franchise tax, and (3) profit tax?

Regulating Through Taxes. In principle, it is possible to induce the sole seller to produce the socially optimal level of output by offering the monopoly a subsidy for each unit it produces. This will raise the profit of the monopoly, which can then be reduced by simultaneously imposing a profit tax or franchise tax. Here is how this approach works.

Let's say a power company charges its customers 8 cents per kilowatt-hour of electricity. Because electrical power is cheaper if provided by a single producer (as opposed to many firms duplicating generating facilities, power lines, and transformers), the government allows the company to operate without competition but offers, say, a subsidy of 2 cents per kilowatt-hour of electricity sold. This encourages the company to increase its service because it collects from the customers *and* from the government for every kilowatt-hour provided. After total costs are deducted, however, the power company pays tax on its net profits.

25. We will look at these issues again in Chapter 10.

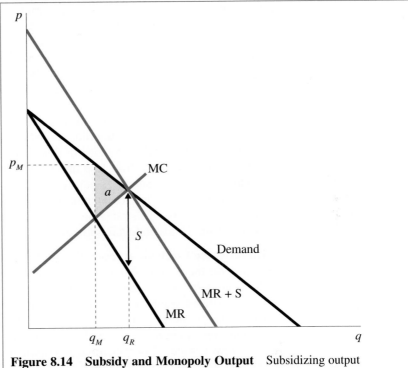

Figure 8.14   Subsidy and Monopoly Output   Subsidizing output moves the monopolist's marginal revenue curve rigidly upward by the subsidy amount S. With the subsidy in place, the monopolist sets MR $+$ S $=$ MC and produces a larger quantity. Because the subsidy equals the gap between MC and MR at the desired regulated quantity q_R, the social costs equal to area a are eliminated.

When the power company receives production subsidy S for each unit of output sold, the monopolist's before-tax profit becomes

$$\Pi(q) = R(q) + Sq - C(q),$$

where $R(q)$ is the monopolist's revenue and $C(q)$ its costs. The subsidy raises marginal revenue by the amount of the subsidy, because every time an additional unit is produced, the firm receives its normal marginal revenue plus the subsidy S. With subsidy S, the firm maximizes profit at the quantity where

$$MR + S = MC.$$

If the government chooses the right subsidy, it causes the firm to select the output level that eliminates the social costs of monopoly.

Figure 8.14 illustrates the effect of a subsidy on monopoly output. Initially the monopolist produces quantity q_M, where marginal revenue equals marginal cost. The social costs of the monopolist's choice equal shaded area a.

To eliminate the social costs, the government would like the monopoly to produce at q_R. It therefore offers the monopolist subsidy S for each unit produced, equal to the difference between MR and MC at quantity q_R. The monopolist's new marginal revenue curve, labeled MR + S, now passes through the marginal cost curve at quantity q_R. The result is that the monopolist produces the socially optimal quantity, eliminating the area of social costs, a.

The side effect of the subsidy is to raise the monopolist's profit. However, if the government charges the monopolist a franchise tax FT (a tax levied as a flat annual fee for the privilege of doing business), the monopolist's profits will be reduced by the franchise tax, though the monopolist will continue to produce the same quantity as before.[26]

A second way to reduce monopoly profit would be to impose a profit tax on the monopolist. This tax would take away a fixed fraction of the monopolist's profit as tax, reducing monopoly profit without changing the output.[27]

▼

11. Derive the effects of a price ceiling on monopoly output.

Direct Price Control. A more direct form of regulation is simply to place a ceiling on the monopolist's price. Before we look at how this would affect the monopolist's price and output decisions, however, consider what we want to achieve: we want the monopolist to *lower* price and *raise* quantity simultaneously. In the case of a competitive market with a horizontal or upward-sloping supply curve, we know that it is not sensible to expect greater quantity for a lower price. However, in a monopolistically supplied market, we will see that lowering price through a price ceiling has a different effect.[28]

Figure 8.15 shows a price ceiling at price p_C, below the monopolist's price p_M. The monopolist can charge price p_C out to q_C units. To sell quantities larger than q_C, the monopolist must charge the price given by the demand curve. The monopolist's effective demand curve is thus the horizontal line segment bc and the section of the market demand curve given by cg. The horizontal section of the demand curve has an infinite elasticity of demand, $\varepsilon = -\infty$. For this section of the demand curve, marginal revenue is given by

$$\text{MR} = p\left(1 + \frac{1}{\varepsilon}\right) = p\left(1 - \frac{1}{\infty}\right) = p.$$

For the section of the demand curve corresponding to segment cg, marginal revenue is shown by the regular marginal revenue curve for the original demand curve. The effective marginal revenue curve therefore consists of

26. The monopolist cannot do anything to alter the franchise tax or shift it to consumers, so its output choice is unchanged. That is, if quantity q^* maximizes profit $R(q) + Sq - C(q)$, then the same q^* also maximizes profit when the fixed fee is paid, $R(q) + Sq - C(q) - FT$. If the monopolist tried to charge a different price to consumers, it would have to produce a different quantity, and this would lower the monopolist's profits.
27. Again, if q^* maximizes $R(q) + Sq - C(q)$, then q^* will also maximize after-tax profit $(1 - t)[R(q) + Sq - C(q)]$, which is just a constant fraction $(1 - t)$ times pretax profit, where t is the profit tax rate between zero and 1.
28. We considered the effect of a price ceiling in a competitive market in Chapter 2.

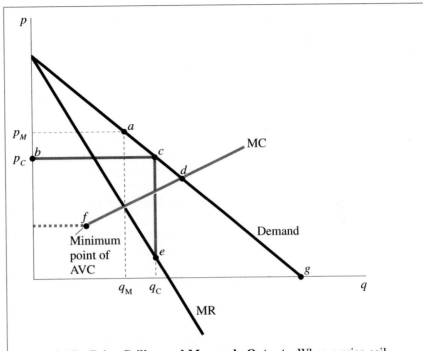

Figure 8.15 Price Ceiling and Monopoly Output When a price ceiling is imposed at price p_C below the monopoly price p_M, the monopolists' effective demand curve becomes bcg. The marginal revenue curve becomes segment bc and MR below point e. The gap in MR is due to the corner in demand at point c. MC then cuts MR at the vertical gap ce, leading to price p_C and quantity q_C.

line segment bc plus MR below point e. The monopolist's response to the price ceiling is to set quantity at q_C, where MC cuts the effective marginal revenue curve in the gap between c and e. The monopolist chooses price p_C because this is the highest price consistent with the demand curve at quantity q_C. Price has gone down and quantity has gone up!

Figure 8.15 also shows that any price ceiling below p_M but higher than the price corresponding to point d causes the monopolist to move down the demand curve from point a to point d. Once the price ceiling falls below d, however, marginal cost intersects the effective demand curve in the horizontal portion. Setting the monopolist's effective marginal revenue equal to marginal cost then implies that the monopolist's choice travels downward from point d to point f on the marginal cost curve. If the price goes below the level of minimum average variable cost at point f, the monopolist shuts down to avoid losing money.

In summary, a price ceiling causes the monopolist's choice to travel down the demand curve from point *a* to point *d,* and then down the marginal cost curve from point *d* to point *f,* as the price ceiling is lowered. Until point *d,* the monopolist simultaneously raises quantity and lowers price; after point *d,* the quantity drops.

If the marginal cost curve is declining over the entire range of output, the price ceiling causes the monopolist to move down the demand curve until the point at which price equals average variable cost. For lower prices, the monopolist shuts down. In the long run, price must equal or exceed average cost for the monopolist to stay in production. Regulation of natural monopolies such as utilities therefore usually sets price where average cost cuts the demand curve. This does not completely eliminate the social costs of monopoly, however. Since average cost is above marginal cost when average cost is falling, the regulated price is above marginal cost and some social costs remain. The only other alternative would be to lower price to the point where MC cuts the demand curve and then subsidize the losses of the firm. However, if the monopoly knows its losses will be subsidized, it has no incentive to minimize costs, a topic to which we will return later.

Nationalization. The most aggressive form of regulation is to nationalize the industry and run it as a government enterprise. Effectively this amounts to telling the industry what quantity to produce and what price to sell it at. If the industry suffers losses, these are covered by tax dollars. Few industries in the United States are nationalized, although the Postal Service might be considered a mixture of private and public, and national defense is government-operated. In foreign countries, industries such as railroads, airlines, mining, and oil have at times been nationalized. Nationalization often results in inefficiencies, including failure by the nationalized firm to produce at least cost. This had led many countries to reprivatize industries that were previously nationalized, in order to force them to deal with their inefficiencies.[29]

We turn now to some of the other common problems of regulation.

Three Problems of Regulation

▼
12. Name some of the problems of regulation, explaining some of the advantages and difficulties with each of the five regulatory options.

Although the problems of industry regulation are too large to cover in depth, it is worthwhile to identify three commonly encountered problems in addition to the ones we have already discussed.

Lack of Information. One problem relates to information. In our examples we have said nothing about how the government *got* the information about market demands and firm costs that it used to regulate monopoly activities. Establishing a government bureaucracy to monitor and gather information is costly, especially if many industries are involved. Further, many of the production and cost figures that the government needs to know must be obtained from the firm itself. Can the government be expected to know demand and

29. We will take up the effects of nationalization and privatization in Investigation IV.B.

production conditions as well as the industry does in order to provide independent checks on what it is told? If not, its regulatory success may be compromised. For example, if the government seeks to limit a utility's price to the level that allows the utility to cover its costs and make zero economic profits, how does the government accurately ascertain what the true costs of the utility are?

X-Inefficiency. If the government chooses to nationalize an industry or regulate it to have a given rate of return, as in the case of natural monopolies, it runs the risk that employees and managers in the industry will no longer have an incentive to run the industry efficiently. After all, if the government is going to control profits and cover losses out of tax dollars, why worry about making costs as low as they could be? On the contrary, regulation often takes the form of allowing the going rate of return—say, 8 percent—on the capital base, so the regulated industry is better off using as much plant and equipment as possible in order to make its capital base large. Overuse of plant and equipment fails to cost minimize. The failure of a firm to cost minimize is called *X-inefficiency,* a phrase coined in the 1960s.[30] In many respects, it is one of the more serious problems of government regulation.

Agency Capture. Finally, we can make a behavioral observation. Government regulatory agencies have often been accused of being ''captured'' by the industries that they were designed to regulate. The agency ends up becoming an advocate for the industry's well-being, a situation that frequently works against the public interest. What the industry would not have been able to accomplish on its own, in terms of restraining competition or competitors, it is able to do with government help. The Civil Aeronautics Board, the regulatory agency for the airlines industry until it was disbanded in the late 1970s, often appeared to *prevent* industry entry and competitive pricing rather than encourage them, because it was concerned about the financial health of the major airlines. Whether it is because government agencies must staff themselves with industry-knowledgeable people who therefore often have industry backgrounds, or because the only lobbyists the agency sees tend to be from the regulated industry rather than from the public, the result is that agencies originally designed to work for the public interest take on an industry point of view.

Capture need not always occur, of course. In many cases overzealous regulators have caused as much damage as underzealous ones. The main point is that government is run by people, just like any other part of the economy, and people in government are as prone to failures as people in the private sector.

---

30. Harvey Leibenstein, ''Allocative Efficiency vs. X-Efficiency,'' *American Economic Review,* June 1966, pp. 392–415.

This ends our brief review of policy responses to monopoly. As we have seen, no single option is perfect in all circumstances. Where a high degree of market segmentation and price discrimination occurs, for example, there may be little social cost, so laissez faire is an acceptable option. This is also true when the industry structure is rapidly undergoing change and competition can be expected to strengthen with time. If competition would be sustainable in the absence of attempts to monopolize the industry, antitrust enforcement seems to be a reasonable response. Where information about costs and market demand is known with a high degree of precision, one might attempt regulation through taxes. Direct price regulation seems the best, albeit imperfect, solution in the case of natural monopolies. And in a few rare cases—probably national defense, the post office, and a few others—a government-run industry may be the only realistic solution.

We began this chapter with a discussion of the effects of lack of competition in the cable TV industry. Remember that Congress deregulated the industry in 1984, removing it from local control. By 1992 it was clear that the needed competition had failed to materialize (virtually none of the nation's 11,000 cable operators faced competition), and the changes were not working in the public's interest. Seven regional Bell companies were pushing to be allowed into the video programming business, a move favored by those who wanted greater competition in the industry as a way to deal with the effects of monopoly. Others favored direct regulation. The bill that was finally passed provides that the Federal Communications Commission (FCC) will regulate the rates for basic cable service (defined as the lowest-priced package, or tier, of cable programs). Cable suppliers can add additional programs to their basic packages, but those rates will also be subject to regulation. Nonbasic cable service is not regulated. Communities that meet standards for effective competition are exempt from rate regulations.[31] The FCC is permitted to adopt formulas "or other mechanisms or procedures" to regulate rates. The bill enjoins the FCC to strive to reduce the administrative costs of the regulations to subscribers, cable operators, franchise authorities, and the commission. (For example, the FCC is supposed to write rules in such a way that the burden of compliance by cable systems with fewer than 1,000 customers will be reduced.) The law also includes provisions for subscribers to file complaints if they are charged too much for cable service outside the basic package, and it offers local franchise authorities some jurisdiction over the industry. Although the bill relies primarily on direct regulation—and therefore is subject to the criticisms of direct regulation we have described—it also promotes competition by prohibiting franchising authorities from granting exclusive franchises or unreasonably refusing to grant additional competitive franchises.

31. Effective competition is defined as areas in which 30 percent of households subscribe to the cable service, areas served by at least two unaffiliated cable operators when either of them reaches 50 percent or more of the market, or areas where 15 percent of households subscribe to a competing supplier.

Summary

Active Reading Guide numbers are given in parentheses at the end of each summary item.

1. A monopoly is a market with a single seller and no close substitute goods. Monopolistic firms can arise (a) as natural monopolies when declining average cost makes a single large firm most efficient, (b) from government patents or licenses, or (c) from exclusive control over an essential input or market area. Monopolies face downward-sloping demand curves as the sole sellers in their markets, and therefore they choose the price and quantity point on the demand curve that maximizes profit. (1)

2. The change in revenue from selling an additional unit of output is called marginal revenue, MR. (2)

3. Profit maximization requires that the monopolist choose a quantity for which MR = MC, marginal cost cuts marginal revenue from below, and the associated price on the demand curve is above average variable cost. Otherwise, the monopolist is better off shutting down in the short run. The same conditions apply in the long run except that long-run average cost replaces average variable cost. (3)

4. Since MR = $p(1 + 1/\varepsilon)$, where ε is the price elasticity of demand, the monopolist's profit maximization rule leads to a convenient formula explaining price markup over marginal cost, $(p - MC)/p = -1/\varepsilon$. If we define market power as the ability to set price above marginal cost, market power rises as elasticity tends to zero. In other words, the less elastic the demand curve is at the monopolist's choice, the greater the firm's market power. Since price minus MC can never be negative, we also find that the monopolist never produces where the elasticity of demand is between -1 and 0 (that is, where MR is negative). (4)

5. Monopolies tend to keep output low, enabling them to charge a price higher than marginal cost. Because they produce where $p > MC$, monopolies create social costs in the form of net losses to the sum of consumer and producer surplus. In contrast, perfectly competitive firms are pricetakers that maximize profit where $p = MC$ and output achieves its optimal level. (5)

6. Whereas a simple monopoly charges a single price to all buyers, a sophisticated monopolist can raise its profits by using one or more of several strategies: (a) The monopolist could segment its market to charge different prices to different groups of buyers. For each group, the monopolist sets marginal revenue equal to marginal cost. (b) Another strategy is multipart pricing, consisting of charging a higher price for the first block of the good and a lower price for later blocks. (c) Another strategy might be to use a two-part tariff, so that the buyer pays an entry fee for the right to purchase and then pays for the product itself at the specified price. These policies work because they allow the monopolist to collect more consumer surplus for the goods sold. (d) Lastly, commodity bundling allows the monopolist to collect more consumer surplus by selling two or more goods together at a bundled price. This strategy applies when there is less dispersion in the prices that consumers are willing to pay for the bundle than in the prices they are willing to pay for individual goods. (6)

7. The limit of the monopolist's ability to collect consumer surplus occurs for a perfectly discriminating monopolist that collects *all* consumer surplus for each buyer. The monopolist collects from each buyer the maximum that buyer would pay, so for the last unit sold the monopolist's MR equals price. Because a perfectly discriminating monopolist sets $p = MR = MC$, there is no associated social loss. (7)

8. A monopolist may be able to use asymmetric information among buyers to segment its market. Random sales allow well-informed buyers to buy at the low sale price, while allowing the firm to sell to less well-informed buyers at the higher regular price. (8)

9. Policies for the regulation of monopoly include (a) laissez faire (allowing the monopoly situation to correct itself); (b) encouraging or establishing competition; (c) applying tax incentives that

encourage socially desirable levels of production; (d) applying direct price control; and (e) nationalizing the monopoly. Tax tools for regulation include production subsidies, franchise taxes, and profit taxes. Production subsidies raise the firm's MR curve by the subsidy and increase firm quantity. Franchise and profit taxes reduce firm profit without affecting quantity. A price ceiling causes the monopolist to move down the demand curve until the point at which MC cuts demand, and then down the MC curve. The monopolist shuts down in the short run if price is below AVC, and in the long run if price is below AC. (9, 10, 11)

10. Problems of government regulation arise because government generally has less information about firm costs and the market than do the firms in the market it is regulating. Firms that are regulated to give them zero economic profit may suffer from X-inefficiency, meaning that they cease to cost minimize. In the case of natural monopolies, regulating to the point where p = MC leads to economic losses for the firm, since declining AC implies that AC is greater than MC. Regulating to the point where AC cuts the demand curve means that some social costs remain (since p > MC) and may provide an incentive for the firm to artificially enlarge its capital base on which its allowed earnings are calculated. Government bureaucracies established to regulate industries also sometimes suffer from "capture" by the industries; they may take on the perspective and objectives of the industry itself instead of the original regulatory objectives. (12)

Review Questions

*1. Can you name an industry that has remained a monopoly for more than 75 years? Explain your answer in terms of the sources of monopoly power.

2. Given price and quantity, does marginal revenue rise or fall with greater elasticity of the demand curve?

*3. Assume that the demand curve is linear. If the monopolist is at its profit maximizing quantity, would it prefer the demand curve to be more or less elastic?

4. If MR = MC but MC cuts MR from above, what would the monopolist do to increase profit?

*5. What is meant by the social costs of monopoly? Does perfect competition have social costs?

6. Three segments of the market have price elasticities of demand at every point on the demand curve of -1.5, -2, and -3, respectively. What will their relative prices be if the product is supplied by a discriminating monopolist?

*7. Provide a verbal proof that market segmentation or multipart pricing *must* leave profits to the monopolist no lower than they would have been under a simple monopoly strategy.

*8. What happens if a monopolist finds that the elasticity of demand equals -0.5 at every point on the demand curve?

9. Construct an example of bundled products, and use the theory of bundling to explain why these products might be bundled. Do the requirements of the theory appear reasonable to you? Explain why or why not.

10. For each of the five approaches to monopoly regulation, give a real-world example and explain why you think the approach is best.

Numerical and Graphing Exercises

1. Draw the appropriate curves to show a monopolist earning positive economic profit. Explain whether the profit will continue in the long run, indicating which curves will be different in the long run, if any. For each of the three sources of mono-

poly, how will competitive firms attempt to enter this market? Summarize the advantages and disadvantages of regulating or nationalizing the monopoly.

*2. Demand is given by $q^D = 1{,}200 - 3p$. Plot

* Asterisks are used to denote questions that are answered at the back of the book.

the demand curve and the marginal revenue curve.

3. Show mathematically why a monopolist always charges a price that is higher than marginal cost.

*4. A monopolist finds that the price elasticity of demand is -2 at every point on the demand curve. If marginal cost is $10/unit, calculate what price the monopolist should charge.

*5. Cable TV has an exclusive franchise to operate in the local community. The city council wants to impose a 5-percent tax on sales of cable, but worries that the tax will be passed on to consumers. Write the formula for the profits of the cable franchise before and after the 5-percent tax. Graphically show the effects of the tax on the cable company's marginal revenue, marginal cost, and the price it charges.

*6. A competitive market has a horizontal supply curve at $p = \$8$. The demand curve is $q^D = 100 - p$. A plan is proposed to impose a specific tax (a tax that is fixed per unit) at a level that will maximize the revenues collected. An opponent of the plan says that this will have the same deleterious effect on consumers as if the government granted a monopoly to one of the firms that supplies the market (this firm has constant marginal costs of $8 per unit). Graphically explain whether this is true or not.

7. Demand is given by $q^D = a - bp$, where a and b are positive constants. Show graphically that marginal revenue is given by the relationship $q^D = (a - b\text{MR})/2$ by using the rule in the text for drawing MR.

*8. Use the rule in exercise 7 to solve the following: If demand is $q^D = 400 - 8p$, and cost is given by $20q$, what is the optimal level of output for the monopolist?

9. A monopolist with constant MC faces demand with constant elasticity of -4. If a tax on quantity of $5 per unit is imposed, how much will the monopolist raise price?

*10. A monopolist has a demand curve given by $q^D = 100 - 2p$ and costs given by $20 + 2q$. What are the monopolist's price and quantity if a 50-percent profit tax is imposed along with a $10-per-

year franchise tax? (You may use the rule in exercise 7 if you wish.)

*11. A foreign monopolist with constant marginal cost c sells its product to the home country. A proposal to impose a specific import duty is put forward by a group that says the duty will collect in tax revenues part of the monopoly profits earned by the foreign firm. Another group argues that the foreign monopolist sells at too high a price already and imposing a tariff will just make the monopolist raise its price higher. Show the effect of the tariff on buyers in the home country, on tax revenues, and on the foreign monopolist. From the home country's perspective, is the tariff a good idea? Why or why not?

12. A monopolist produces output at a marginal cost of $12 per unit. One group of buyers has the demand curve $q^D = 100 - p$, and a second group of buyers has the demand curve $q^D = 72 - 4p$. What price will the monopolist charge each group, and how many units will be sold in total?

*13. When it sells at the same price p_0 throughout the month, a monopolist finds that its demand curve is given by $q^D = 100 - p$. It knows, however, that part of its buyers are well-informed about price. Their demand will vary according to the demand curve $q^D = (60 - p_{\text{sale}}) \sqrt{x}$ when there is a sale (p_{sale} is the sale price, and x is the fraction of the month devoted to the sale) and $(60 - p)(1 - \sqrt{x})$ during the rest of the month at regular price p. The remainder of the buyers, however, check prices only every three months and are therefore uninformed about price. Their demand will stay uniform throughout the month, fixed at the rate per month of $q = 100 - p$ for $100 \geq p \geq 60$, and $q = 40$ for $60 > p$.

a) Find the monopolist's profits if it charges $60 throughout the month and marginal cost is $0 per unit.

b) Assume that the monopolist institutes a sale policy of 50 percent off for fraction $(1 - x)$ of the month. Plot the dollar amount of sales to informed buyers, sales to uninformed buyers, and total sales if the period of discounted prices is $\frac{1}{10}, \frac{2}{10}, \frac{3}{10}, \ldots, \frac{9}{10}, \frac{10}{10}$ of the month, respectively. For what fraction of the month (of those computed) should the monopolist offer price discounts to maximize profits?

▼

CHAPTER 9

Monopolistic Competition and Market Power: Expanding the Monopoly Model

Managers do more than decide quantity and price. In fact, on a day-to-day basis they probably spend more time on decisions that are not related to price or quantity. Many of these decisions have to do with internal operations such as personnel and production methods, but many also involve external planning, such as what products to offer, how much to advertise, and how to relate to competitors. This chapter shows that the same principles we used to study price and quantity can be applied to these decisions. In particular, this chapter considers how many varieties of output to offer, how much to spend on advertising, and issues of cartel participation. Our focus, as in Chapter 8, is on firms that can influence market price.

ACTIVE READING GUIDES

After reading this chapter, you should be able to answer the Active Reading Guides listed below. These guides also appear in the page margins near the material to which they refer.

1. Define monopolistic competition, relating it to the conditions for perfect competition explained in Chapter 7.

2. In monopolistically competitive markets, what conditions does long-run equilibrium imply for the firm?

3. Explain the role of distance and location as they relate to demand in spatial models of monopolistic competition.

4. Summarize the two sources of loss from monopolistic competition. Do monopolistically competitive markets supply too many or too few competing substitute goods?

5. Explain why some types of firm decisions are not relevant to perfectly competitive firms operating in markets with perfect information. Give an example.

6. Explain the steps optimizing firms engage in when they choose the number of varieties to sell.

7. What determines whether a monopoly would produce more or fewer varieties than monopolistically competitive firms, or more or less quantity for each variety, given the number of varieties?

8. How does advertising make markets more competitive, and how might it make markets less competitive?

9. What is the elasticity of demand with respect to advertising, and how is it used in the advertising rule of thumb?

10. Explain how a cartel works, the advantages to a firm of joining a cartel, and the incentives to cheat on the cartel.

9.1 Monopolistic Competition

It's a delectable sunny day in mid-July, with temperatures in the low eighties. You're lying on the beach, half snoozing and so comfortable that you feel as if you never want to move again. No chance of sunburn, since you and your friend already took care of the sunblock. It would be nice, however, to have a cool drink and an ice cream right where you lie. You wonder why getting snacks from the competing beach vendors who are spaced along the beach is so expensive. Given the large quantities that are consumed at this beach each day, shouldn't someone be able to figure a way to provide everything cheaper in bulk? But then you remember that you're *willing* to pay a lot more on a day like this, as long as you don't have to move much to get it. You are beginning to awaken as you think, "What I really want is not just an ice cream and drink, but an ice cream and drink with the characteristic that it be available nearby." Sort of like a unique good. Suddenly you are fully alert as you think with a start: "Say, what kind of market is this, anyway—monopolistic or competitive?"

In this scenario, if you reasoned that the market had elements of competition—in that market entry by vendors didn't seem to be a problem, and the economic profits of any particular vendor were probably zero—you would be right. On the other hand, if you reasoned that the market had elements of monopoly—in that each vendor sold a differentiated product (based primarily on location in this case), and the vendors did not operate at the point of minimum average cost, because average cost would be lower if each vendor sold a larger quantity—you would also be right. This chapter examines markets with elements of *both* monopoly and competition, and it analyzes some of the product and advertising decisions that managers of firms with market power make. By the end of the chapter, we should be at least as comfortable with the mixture of monopoly and competition as we are with the duckbilled platypus, which seemed an equally striking combination of features upon first observation by European scientists in the 1830s.

Nonstandardized Products and Imperfect Competition

As indicated in Chapters 7 and 8, markets that closely resemble the idealizations of perfect competition and pure monopoly are rare. Rather, some form of imperfect competition prevails when one or more of the assumptions of perfect competition or monopoly fail. For example, in most markets products are sufficiently different from those of competitors to be distinguishable, but similar enough that they are substitutes. The perfectly competitive assumption of standardized product therefore fails in varying degrees. Think of different brands of bar soap, household appliances, clothing, automobiles, or almost any other product. In these markets, one firm's sales will not go to zero if its price is a few pennies higher than a competing firm's price, although a higher price may reduce quantity sold and a lower price may increase it.

How does the individual firm respond to this situation? Assume for the moment that we have a firm (call it Bobcraft) producing quantity q^e of fiberglass-hulled boats at price p^e, given by point e in Figure 9.1. Bobcraft's boats differ from those competing firms offer, although similar boats made from different materials and of different designs and sizes are available. Boat prices are not the same, but competitors' prices for comparable models fall within a fairly narrow range. Given a certain amount of brand loyalty among its buyers and the ability to shift some buyers from competing boats by offering a lower price, Bobcraft perceives that its firm demand is given by curve d. From d, Bobcraft calculates the corresponding marginal revenue curve and uses it to set price and quantity.

The description sounds very much like the description of monopoly, with one important exception—how exactly does Bobcraft *know* what its individual demand curve d is, given that it is not related in any simple way to the market demand for all boats? For example, if all the manufacturers were to lower their price 1 percent because Bobcraft lowered its price, boat sales would rise, including Bobcraft's sales. The increase in Bobcraft's quantity sold would be given by points on some other curve, D. We expect that the firm's demand curve d will be more elastic than D, because when Bobcraft lowers its price all other prices will generally *not* be lowered, so the firm will get a net gain of customers from other manufacturers. But even this is not certain unless we know how other firms react or don't react to a change in Bobcraft's price.

There is no simple answer to the question of how the firm determines what its sales will be given its price. The case in which firms react directly to each other's choices is the subject of oligopoly theory, the study of markets with

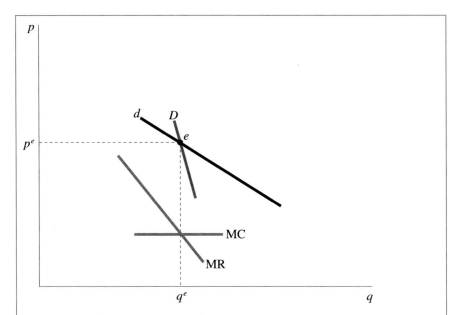

Figure 9.1   The Firm Demand Curve with Competition from Close Substitutes   Bobcraft produces at point *e* corresponding to quantity q^e where MR = MC. Since Bobcraft's boats compete with products that are close substitutes but not perfect substitutes, it can charge a price different from its competitors' without seeing its sales either drop to zero or expand to capture the entire market. Starting at point *e*, if *all* firms in the market reduced their prices by the same percentage, the increase in Bobcraft's quantity sold would be given by points on curve *D*. However, *the firm's* demand curve *d* reflects what happens when Bobcraft lowers its price and other firms do not necessarily lower theirs in lock step. Because Bobcraft's lower price shifts some demand away from competitors and attracts some new buyers, the firm curve *d* is more elastic than *D*.

few sellers (we take this up in Chapter 10). In these cases, there may not even *be* a well-defined firm demand curve, because it may not be certain that other firms react the same way each time an individual firm makes a given choice.

In this chapter, however, we focus on two approaches, based closely on the models of perfect competition and monopoly, that explain how the firm finds its firm demand curve *d* if additional conditions apply. We turn to these next.

The Monopolistic Competition Model

▼
1. Define monopolistic competition, relating it to the conditions for perfect competition explained in Chapter 7.

In our discussion of imperfect competition so far, we have dropped the perfect competition assumption of standardized product, and with it pricetaking, but we have not said anything about contestability of the market or number of competing sellers. A special form of imperfect competition that includes contestability (free entry and exit) is called *monopolistic competition.*

> *A market is characterized by **monopolistic competition** if a large number of firms sell differentiated but highly substitutable products, and there is free entry and exit.*

Since there are a large number of sellers of closely substitutable products in monopolistically competitive markets, *each firm acts as if its choices do not affect the choices competing firms make,* just as in the perfectly competitive market. This resolves the problem in our Bobcraft example of knowing what other firms will do in response to the firm's choice. Close substitutability between products means that each firm sees a downward-sloping demand curve for its product, but one that is highly elastic. Since firms are small, no firm dominates the market. Indeed, models of monopolistic competition frequently assume that all suppliers are identical.

If you and I are monopolistically competitive firms, you may know that I behave just the way you do. But you also know that your actions do not cause my behavior. Thus, if you change your decision, you do not need to worry that I will change mine because of you, even though we may end up responding to market conditions in the same way.

Free entry, on the other hand, means that if monopolistically competitive firms earn positive economic profits, other firms will be attracted to enter the market. Were Miller Lite known to be enormously profitable, we would expect to see Bud Lite, Pabst Lite, Coors Lite, and a host of other replicas springing up until long-run economic profits for light beers were reduced to zero.

▼

2. In monopolistically competitive markets, what conditions does long-run equilibrium imply for the firm?

Figure 9.2 shows the short-run and long-run market positions of a representative monopolistically competitive firm that sells shampoo. In part (a) the firm produces in the short run at point *e* on firm demand curve *d.* When the firm lowers its price, it increases sales to its existing customers and attracts buyers from competing brands. Demand curve *d* with associated marginal revenue MR is therefore more elastic than curve *D,* which shows what the firm's sales would be if all firms in the market lowered their prices by the same percentage. The firm maximizes profit at q^e, where MC cuts MR from below.

Positive economic profits, indicated by the shaded area *a* in part (a) of the figure, attract new firms to enter the shampoo market in the long run. The presence of new firms shifts the firm's demand curve to the left and makes it flatter, as shown in part (b). Entry continues until firms in the market no longer make positive economic profits. Long-run equilibrium therefore occurs where the long-run firm demand curve *d'* is tangent to the firm's long-run average cost curve at *e'*. The firm maximizes profit at *q'*, but the highest profit can be is zero because any other quantity causes price to fall below average cost.

If we assumed identical firms in the shampoo market, the long-run equilibrium of all other shampoo suppliers would look like part (b), and every

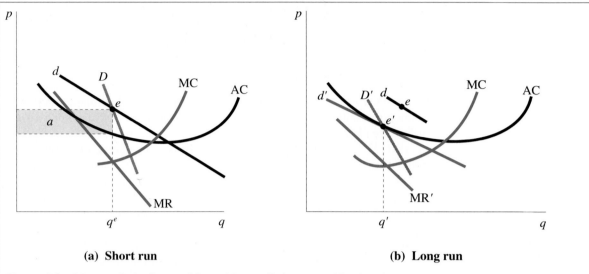

(a) Short run **(b) Long run**

Figure 9.2   Monopolistic Competition   Monopolistic competition involves a downward-sloping demand curve as in monopoly, and zero profits as in perfect competition. In the short run, the firm produces at point *e* on firm demand curve *d*, setting MR = MC and earning positive economic profits equal to area *a*. Positive economic profits attract other firms to enter the market in the long run, shifting the firm's demand curve to the left and making it more elastic at each price. Entry continues until profits are driven to zero at the new equilibrium *e'* on the firm's demand curve *d'*. In each part of the figure, the firm's demand curve is more elastic than the corresponding curve, *D* or *D'*, which show what the firm would sell if *all* firms in the market reduced their prices by the same percentage. This is true because, when the firm alone lowers its price, it attracts some buyers from competing firms.

supplier would charge the same price. Even though the demand curve for the firm when all firms change their prices by the same percentage is D', the individual firm still faces demand curve d', since changing its price does not cause other firms in the market to follow suit.

EXPLORATION: Spatial Models of Monopolistic Competition

▼
3. Explain the role of distance and location as they relate to demand in spatial models of monopolistic competition.

One of the intrinsic problems of monopolistic competition is that there is no natural boundary for defining a group of highly substitutable products. This is because we often buy goods for different characteristics or for different uses to which they can be put. A screened-in porch might substitute for a back-yard electric bug zapper, which might substitute for using an insect-repellent spray, which might substitute for Avon Skin-So-Soft (regarded by many as a substitute for insect repellent), which might substitute for a lanolin-containing hand lotion to protect one's hands after gardening, which might substitute for wearing work gloves. However, work gloves don't seem to be much of a substitute for a screened-in porch.

Faced with the realities of why people demand their goods, firms need some way to explain how consumers change their demand or shift from one product to another in response to price changes. Although circumstances are too varied for any single explanation to apply in general, economists have come up with spatial models that tie demand to characteristics of goods in ways that determine degree of substitutability and response to price. To demonstrate the simplest one, let us return to the beach.

A Beach Economy. Assume that beachgoers are uniformly spread at the rate of 1,056 per mile (one every 5 feet) along the beach of length 2 miles. Demand by each person for ice cream depends on its price and the distance the person has to go to buy it. In this case, being distance i from the vendor has an *inconvenience cost* to the individual of $g = \$10.00$ per mile, so that the effective total cost of buying ice cream is $p + gi$, where p is the price of the ice cream and gi is the inconvenience cost.[1] Each beachgoer buys ice cream from the vendor with the lowest total cost. For simplicity, we will assume each beachgoer buys 3 units of ice cream per day, as long as total cost is below his or her reservation price, R.

Let's also assume that vendors buy their ice cream at a constant price of $f = \$1.00$ per unit and have quasifixed costs $FC = \$25.86$ per day (quasifixed costs are identical to fixed costs except that they are zero if the firm produces zero output). Total costs are therefore $C(q) = FC + fq$, with marginal cost $MC = f$.

Location Determines Purchases. Given price, each beachgoer has a preferred location for ice cream. However, location in this example really just represents a more general setup: we could imagine assigning each good a list of characteristics (price, size, color, quality, performance features, and so on) that would place it at some location on a multidimensional grid, with each axis of the grid measuring the amount of one of the characteristics (Figure 9.5, later in the chapter, shows such a grid). Consumers choose which good they buy by noting how "far away" the good is on the grid from their ideal configuration spot. If a good is too unlike what they are looking for—the price is too high, the color is too bright, or some combination of such factors is not right—they do not buy.

Implied Firm Demand Curve. These assumptions determine how demand shifts from one vendor to another on the basis of per-unit price the vendor charges. That is, the location model gives us a way to determine demand and substitutability among goods offered at different locations. Figure 9.3 schematically presents the information relevant to vendor 1, who is located at distance m_1 along the beach. The two closest vendors are located at distances

1. Think of the inconvenience cost as the amount beachgoers would be willing to pay to have someone go 1 mile to get an ice cream for them, rather than interrupt their sunbathing to do it themselves. This is roughly $.56 for someone to travel 100 yards.

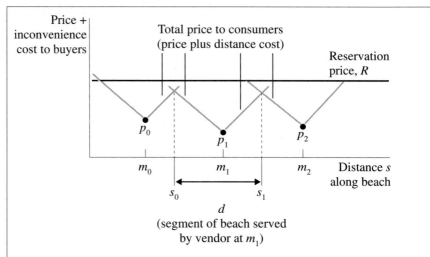

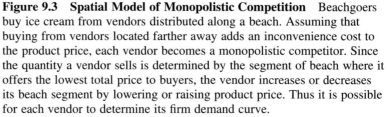

Figure 9.3 Spatial Model of Monopolistic Competition Beachgoers buy ice cream from vendors distributed along a beach. Assuming that buying from vendors located farther away adds an inconvenience cost to the product price, each vendor becomes a monopolistic competitor. Since the quantity a vendor sells is determined by the segment of beach where it offers the lowest total price to buyers, the vendor increases or decreases its beach segment by lowering or raising product price. Thus it is possible for each vendor to determine its firm demand curve.

m_0 and m_2. Vendors 0 and 2 charge prices p_0 and p_2, respectively. Buyers on the beach at distance s between m_0 and m_2 thus pay a total price (including inconvenience cost of g per mile) of $p_0 + g(s - m_0)$ if they buy from vendor 0 and $p_2 + g(m_2 - s)$ if they buy from vendor 2. The height of the total price lines starting at the price points p_0 and p_2 represents these total prices. If vendor 1 chooses price p_1, buyer total price can be computed in the same way, leading to the two total price lines emanating from price point p_1. Distance d in the figure shows the segment of the beach for which it is cheaper in total price to buy from vendor 1. Since lowering p_1 moves intersection point s_0 to the left and s_1 to the right, vendor 1's beach segment expands and the number of people served by the vendor rises with lower price.

The quantity of ice cream sold will be $q = d \times 1,056 \times 3$, where d depends on the price the vendor chooses. Since this is the firm's demand curve, the vendor can find marginal revenue and equate it to marginal cost f, determining its profit-maximizing price and quantity.

Social Costs. Having seen how to determine one vendor's demand curve (price, quantity, and profits follow from this), let's now see how many vendors there will be with free entry and exit and where they will locate along the beach. In this case, we start with a certain number of identical vendors, spread them evenly along the beach, and check to see if each vendor earns positive profits. If so, we keep adding more vendors to the beach until economic profits are zero for each one. We can then determine the price that each vendor charges and the distance between them (since we know the number of vendors on the beach). What do such computations tell us?

If we interpret the number of spatially distributed firms as representing differentiated products, we can check to see if monopolistic competition leads to too few or too many competing goods. Why does this matter? If you return to part (b) of Figure 9.2, you will see that the long-run equilibrium of a representative firm at point e' is necessarily at a point of declining average cost. Thus, $p >$ MC leads to monopoly social costs as discussed in Chapter 8. If there were fewer competing substitutes, the remaining firms would offer a higher quantity. They would then be able to achieve lower costs by moving down their AC curve.

In our beach economy, average costs, AC $=$ FC/$q + f$, decline uniformly so that a single vendor supplying the entire beach would have the lowest direct cost. However, having only one vendor would raise the consumers' inconvenience costs, which are just as important as the firms' production costs.[2] In addition to the monopoly social costs of each individual monopolistic competitor, therefore, we must consider the benefits from having more types of substitute goods around. Although more varieties decrease inconvenience costs, monopoly social costs rise with more varieties. Balancing the two welfare effects determines the right number of firms. In the case of ice cream, this number is the number of firms that minimizes the total costs (direct firm costs and consumer distance costs) of supplying ice cream.

In our beach economy, the market generates 70 vendors (roughly one every 50 yards) selling at a price $1.29. Since distance costs average $.07 per unit of ice cream, total costs per unit are $1.36. To minimize total costs, there should instead be 35 vendors present, leading to production costs of $1.14 per unit, average distance costs per unit of $.15, and lower total costs per unit of $1.29. In this case the number of firms provided by the market exceeds the social optimum. However, with different distance costs, the answer could just as easily go the other way. Thus, monopolistic competition could provide either too many, too few, or just the right number of firms. It depends on how strongly consumers feel about goods that are not at their preferred location and on how steeply the costs of individual firms decline. The greater the degree of substitutability among goods for consumers, and

▼
4. Summarize the two sources of loss from monopolistic competition. Do monopolistically competitive markets supply too many or too few competing substitute goods?

2. Central planners have sometimes been accused of being fixated by the idea that having many varieties of goods in a free market society is "wasteful," since production costs could be lower if only one variety were produced for everyone. The thought is, indeed, appealing, until one begins to contemplate the other kinds of costs associated with, say, everyone's wearing identical gray business suits, as was the case for Mao suits in the People's Republic of China for many years. Or imagine all sweaters being brown because the single color saved on production costs. The "distance" your preferred sweater color (blue, for instance) was from brown would represent your costs from not having a blue sweater. Such other costs are just as real as production costs registered in dollars.

the flatter the average cost curve at the point of firm production, the smaller the social costs of monopolistic competition. In practice, most economists believe that the inefficiencies of monopolistic competition are probably quite small. In the present example, total costs were higher by a little over 5 percent. As just noted, in some cases there may be no social costs at all.

The Effect of Different Distance Costs on Social Costs. The rate at which distance costs rise with distance describes how strongly the consumer is devoted to a particular variety of good. Quickly rising costs imply a strong attachment to a particular variety and hence little substitutability among goods. In the beach example, this would mean that a beachgoer strongly wants ice cream at a particular location—the one that's closest.

To see how different distance costs influence the monopolistically competitive equilibrium, assume that we are at the long-run monopolistically competitive equilibrium for the beach economy, with all vendors alike and distributed uniformly along the beach. Part (a) of Figure 9.4 shows the increasing total cost to vendor 1's buyers who are located between m_1, where vendor 1 is situated, and m_2. Part (b), in turn, shows vendor 1's production at point e_1 on firm demand curve d and average cost curve AC. In the original equilibrium, cost rises linearly on the straight line from point a to point b. The total distance costs of all buyers located between m_1 and half the distance to m_2, for example, would be the area under line ab and the price line.

Now, assume instead that consumers' distance costs rise according to the curved line from a to b'. Nonlinear distance costs change several things. First, given the number of firms in the market, distance costs are greater than they were before. This means that they now weigh more heavily in minimizing total costs. In other words, the social optimum favors more varieties (in this case, more competing vendors).

What about the effect of the nonlinear costs on the number of firms in long-run market equilibrium? When vendor 1 lowers product price from a to a', the beach area served increases, shifting by the horizontal distance from point b' to c'. This is smaller than the shift from b to c for the same price change when distance costs were linear. Thus the firm has a less elastic firm demand curve than before (lower price doesn't get as many new customers). In part (b) of the figure, the new firm demand curve d' becomes less elastic (steeper), implying that the vendor wants to contract production (serve a smaller beach segment). The only way all vendors can contract production, given their share of the market demand for ice cream, however, is if the number of firms decreases. The market demand curve D thus shifts to D'. In the new equilibrium, vendor 1 produces at e_2.

The social costs from producing where $p > $ MC at e_1 (shown by the shaded triangle between the firm demand curve d and MC) are lower than the costs at e_2, although the increased number of firms decreases some buyers' distance costs.

The linear-distance-cost equilibrium had too many firms relative to the social optimum. In the nonlinear-distance-cost equilibrium, there were more

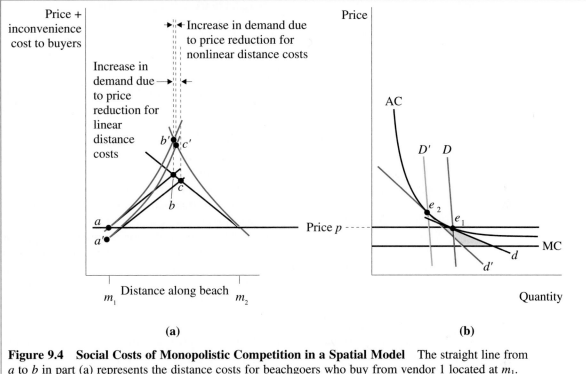

Figure 9.4   Social Costs of Monopolistic Competition in a Spatial Model   The straight line from
a to *b* in part (a) represents the distance costs for beachgoers who buy from vendor 1 located at m_1.
The curved line from *a* to *b'* represents different, nonlinear distance costs. When vendor 1 reduces
price to move from *a* to *a'*, the intersection at *b* moves to *c* for linear costs and to *c'* for nonlinear
costs. The distance along the beach served by vendor 1 therefore enlarges less for the nonlinear
distance costs, and the vendor perceives a less elastic firm demand. Point e_1 in part (b) represents
vendor 1 in long-run market equilibrium, given firm demand curve *d* when distance costs are linear.
With nonlinear distance costs, the firm demand curve through e_1 is less elastic than *d*, meaning that
the firm wants to raise price and contract production. This is possible only if there are more firms in
the new long-run equilibrium, each one producing smaller output at point e_2. At the old equilibrium,
the monopoly social costs equal to the shaded area are smaller than the equivalent loss at e_1/e_2.

firms but the number needed for the social optimum also rose. If the second
change was bigger, the different distance costs move the number of firms in
the right direction to achieve the social optimum. In fact, it is possible to
show that, depending on distance costs, the market equilibrium will be socially optimal.

Having spent some time examining the overall market implications of
monopolistic competition, we should now consider some of the implications
from the perspective of the firm manager. In the next section we review the
market forces at work at the firm level. ■

9.2 Market Forces in Imperfect Competition

The manager of the monopolistically competitive firm would like to do more than just set MR = MC to maximize profit given the firm's demand curve, but what?

Desire to Differentiate Product from Competitors' Products. In our beach example, if the vendor was located farther from the nearest competitor, and if there were more customers on its section of the beach, it would have a larger market and could charge a higher price without losing customers. The same principle applies to monopolistic competition in general. Distance in the spatial model represents the degree of differentiation from another product. In general, the monopolistic competitor wants to choose a "location" for its product (product characteristics) so that many consumers perceive that it meets their needs, and no competing product can substitute for it. The less consumers defect to competing products when the monopolistic competitor raises price, the closer the competitor comes to being a pure monopoly, with all the attendant rights and privileges. Inventing a better product or giving an existing product new, more desirable, and distinctive characteristics can enhance the firm's market position and profits.

Desire to Compete in as Many Niches as Possible. A corollary to the monopolistic competitor's desire to offer a differentiated product at a location of high demand is the desire to offer differentiated products at *multiple* "locations" where consumer demand is great. Sometimes a market is characterized by different areas of consumer demand, or "niches," so that the firm can raise its profit by offering a variety of products, each designed to supply a particular niche. Again, in each niche the firm would like consumers to be aware of the product's features and perceive the product to be better than, and nonsubstitutable by, competitors' products. This brings us to the next market force at work in monopolistically competitive markets, advertising.

Desire to Advertise. The firm can raise profits by shifting its firm demand curve to the right. One way to do this is to advertise. Perfectly competitive markets are characterized by perfect information, but imperfectly competitive markets may or may not be characterized by perfect information. Thus advertising can serve an information role, as well as seek to convince buyers of the desirability and distinctiveness of the firm's product. In this role, advertising is a tool to help the manager differentiate the firm's product and "locate" it in the minds of consumers where demand is greatest.

Before we discuss how the manager makes decisions about product variety and advertising, it is useful to review why these decisions are not relevant to perfectly competitive firms.

▼

5. Explain why some types of firm decisions are not relevant to perfectly competitive firms operating in markets with perfect information. Give an example.

Why Are Advertising and Variety Not Decision Issues in Perfectly Competitive Markets? A wheat farm producing red winter wheat does not need to advertise its product to the market. In fact, we would be surprised if it did. Since the wheat farm is one of many firms in a perfectly competitive market, it is already supplying as much wheat as it wants to at the going market price. It therefore has no desire to increase sales at current prices. Moreover, if its advertising somehow increased the demand for wheat enough to raise its price, the benefits of this increase would accrue not just to the farm that advertises, but to all wheat farms. If economic profits in wheat production rose above zero, for example, other farms could easily shift production to wheat, driving profits back to zero. Lastly, since red winter wheat is already graded for type and quality, there is no need to inform customers of product characteristics or to try to differentiate one farm's wheat from another's. In short, advertising would raise the farm's costs but provide few benefits.

The same reasoning applies to other choices that firms make, including choices about product differentiation, variety, and some types of research and development expenditures.[3] Firms make these decisions to develop a distinct product line that will give them a greater degree of monopoly power, to increase demand for the company's product relative to competing products, or to inform potential buyers about the product. But perfectly competitive firms like the wheat farm have few of these motivations. We would thus expect to see less money devoted to attempts at product differentiation for products such as table salt, refined sugar, or hydrochloric acid than, say, for products like colas or personal computers.

The relevant issue is whether the *expenditure generates benefits,* and whether the firm that pays the costs can *capture those benefits.* In the next two sections, we consider situations in which these conditions apply. We will examine choices of product variety and advertising by firms that have the ability to influence product price. In each case, the basic principles that apply are the same as those that govern the other types of decisions we have discussed for monopolistic firms.

9.3 Optimal Product Variety for Firms with Market Power

To begin our study of the firm's decisions about variables other than price and quantity, we can look at a breakfast cereal manufacturer that must decide how many types of cereals to offer. As noted, the approach that applies to variety also carries over to other decisions of the firm. We begin with the case of a firm that is a sole seller of its product, and then we see what happens when other firms enter the market.

Effect of Variety on Demand

You are the president of the American Foods Corporation, which has been in the flour business for two generations. In addition to flour and other products made from wheat, your company deals in corn, oats, and rice. A scientist in your product-quality division has come to your office excitedly

---

3. We will discuss research and development decisions in Chapter 16 as a part of the economics of time.

telling you of something that happened in his lab. The week before, while working with a mash made from corn, he accidentally spilled some of it onto a pan that was being heated for another purpose, and found that the flakes produced by baking the mash were delicious. He wants to call the pieces of cooked mash "corn flakes" and sell them as a breakfast cereal. You order some marketing surveys and wait for the report.

Nine months later, surveys and tests come back. They indicate that consumers would react favorably to the new flakes. Another surprising fact your marketers discover is that demand would be greater among some groups of potential buyers if the cereal were offered in different shapes (to retain crunchiness in milk better and to appeal to little children) and with different amounts of sugar coating and internal sweetness. What do you do now?

Since your function as company president is to operate the company as profitably as possible, selling a new breakfast cereal appears to be a good idea: even plain corn flakes alone would be profitable. If you want to do even better, though, you need to consider *how many varieties* to offer. The first question is how additional varieties will affect demand.

In this case your marketers have done a good job. They know that for a given price, the distribution of demand can be plotted as shown in the cells in Table 9.1 and graphed as on the three-dimensional Figure 9.5. They have determined what sales would be in millions of pounds for each cereal type if price were $1.00 per 1-pound box. They discovered, for example, that the market is made up of groups of buyers who prefer particular "locations" of cereal shape and sugar content, represented by the different cells in the table. If buyers of breakfast cereal could pick their own preferred varieties, they would array themselves into distinct locations as shown in the figure. Some would choose no-nonsense, unsweetened corn flakes, and others, such as mothers buying for young children, would want animal-shaped cereal.

When no cereal exactly matches the buyer's preference, the buyer chooses the cereal that comes closest. For the shapes and sugar contents tested, it appears that bear-shaped cereal is the most popular and does best with the highest sugar content plus a sugar coating, whereas plain flakes do best with a medium amount of sugar content. Star-shaped and doughnut-shaped cereals

Table 9.1   Sales in Millions of Pounds of Cereal

Shapes	*Sugar Content*				
	None	Low	Medium	High	High + Sugar-Coated
Bear-shaped	11	12	14	22	25
Stars	7	8	10	17	7
Doughnuts	5	6	8	4	5
Flakes	3	3	6	3	3

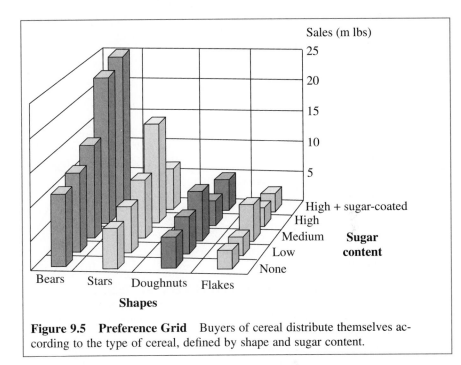

Figure 9.5 Preference Grid Buyers of cereal distribute themselves according to the type of cereal, defined by shape and sugar content.

seem to do best with high- and medium sugar content, respectively, but no sugar coating. Your marketers also tell you that they can predict what demand will look like for other shapes and levels of sugar content on the basis of their research to date.

To further organize this information and relate it more closely to profits, you ask your marketers to show you the demand curve if American Foods sold only the best-selling, sugar-coated, bear-shaped, high-sugar cereal. You then ask what demand would be if the firm sold two varieties, adding the next-best-selling variety, and so on, up to the limit of offering as many varieties as there are customer types. This procedure already contains one type of optimization by starting from the best-selling cereal and working down: it guarantees that demand will be as high as possible for each number of varieties offered. The remaining optimization involves choosing the best quantity to offer given the number of varieties and the *best* number of varieties.

Part (a) of Figure 9.6 shows the effect of variety on demand. As the product line expands, total sales increase but at successively slower rates. (Best-selling varieties were added first, and subsequent varieties are not as popular.) In addition, your marketing staff says that with each variety added, some of the

▼
6. Explain the steps optimizing firms engage in when they choose the number of varieties to sell.

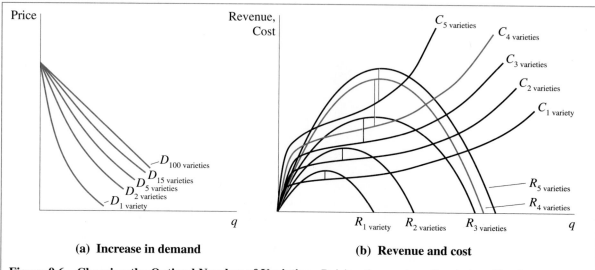

Figure 9.6 Choosing the Optimal Number of Varieties Raising the number of varieties offered for sale increases demand, according to part (a). This in turn implies higher total revenue, as shown in the revenue curves in part (b), although the increase in revenue eventually becomes smaller for the addition of new varieties. Providing greater variety also raises total cost, as shown by the rising total cost curves. For each number of varieties, part (b) shows maximum profit as the greatest vertical distance between the revenue curve and the cost curve. Choosing the best of the maximum profits determines the number of varieties to offer. In the diagram, offering four varieties is the profit-maximizing choice.

new sales come at the expense of previous lines, "cannibalizing" sales.[4] With more varieties, this effect is more pronounced. Demand eventually reaches an effective upper limit. For anything over 100 varieties, the demand is negligibly different from the $D_{100 \text{ varieties}}$ demand curve.

Effect of Variety on Cost and the Variety Choice Rule

Producing more varieties adds to cost because each variety uses different machines, different assembly lines, different packaging, and different input mixes. After a point, adding more varieties may add so much to your cost that it is not profitable to extend your product line further. From the demand curves in part (a) of Figure 9.6, you have your finance division prepare

4. Sales of complementary products can sometimes enhance sales of other varieties over a certain range of offerings. For example, if your company were selling gardening tools (each essentially a wooden handle with a shaped metal working end attached), offering two types of rakes, several shovel shapes, hoes, and a spade might cause buyers to buy *more* from your company in order to have a matching set. The decision about how many offerings to make can be broken down into the same steps as described in the breakfast cereal example: determine demand if just the single, best-selling item were offered, and then observe the effect of adding items. Eventually, however, new varieties would lead to little increase in demand.

American Foods' total revenue curve for each number of varieties offered. Your accounting division also provides cost information for producing each corresponding number of varieties. These curves are plotted together in part (b) of Figure 9.6.

You now have two remaining choices: You must decide how many varieties to offer and what quantity of output to sell. To decide, you compute the maximum profit and profit maximizing quantity for each number of varieties and choose the number of varieties that yields the highest profit. If you offer only bear-shaped cereal with sugar coating, the total revenue curve is $R_{1 \text{ variety}}$ and the total cost curve is $C_{1 \text{ variety}}$. The largest vertical distance between the two curves gives this combination's maximum profit at the profit maximizing quantity. If you offer two varieties, the total cost curve rises but the total revenue curve rises even more, allowing greater profits. As the number of varieties increases, the total cost curve eventually rises more quickly than the revenue curve so that additional variety will not improve profit. In Figure 9.6, a choice of four varieties yields the maximum profit. From R_4 and C_4, you have the corresponding marginal revenue and marginal cost curves, MR_4 and MC_4 (not shown). Since you are a monopoly, your profit-maximizing quantity occurs where $MR_4 = MC_4$.

Variety and Monopolistic Competition

How would our analysis be different if the market were not a monopoly but were monopolistically competitive? From the firm's point of view, the decisions would be very much the same. On the demand side, the firm would still have to determine how offering greater variety would affect the demand curve for the firm's products. On the cost side, whether the firm is a monopolist, a monopolistic competitor, or one of a small number of firms in the market makes little difference: regardless of market structure, technological considerations determine the firm's costs. Thus the effect of increasing variety on costs can be treated in these markets in the same way as in the monopoly case. Combining the effect of variety on demand and revenue with the effect of variety on cost generates the effect of variety on profit.

▼
7. What determines whether a monopoly would produce more or fewer varieties than monopolistically competitive firms, or more or less quantity for each variety, given the number of varieties?

From the point of view of the market, one question we can ask about monopolistic competition is whether it will lead to more or fewer varieties than monopoly and whether prices for each variety will be lower. For example, many individual firms, each producing a differentiated product, will produce greater quantity than they would if they operated as one giant firm. To see this, consider the following scenario: A number of independently operating firms come together as separate divisions under centralized management. Previously, when they were independent sellers, a price reduction for one firm increased sales of its product by increasing the purchases of existing consumers and by attracting new buyers, but also by taking customers away from other firms. When the companies become part of a centralized enterprise, the lost profit of other divisions (previously independent firms) will cause the monopoly to restrain the output of each division. The same number of firms operating independently would therefore each produce a larger quantity than they would under centralized management. This means that prices would be lower.

Will the just-created monopoly eliminate any varieties? If reducing the number of varieties primarily shifts demand to other varieties offered by the monopoly's remaining divisions (who can consequently raise their prices),[5] the costs of providing fewer varieties will decline more than revenues and the monopoly should reduce the number of varieties.[6] On the other hand, if reducing variety loses demand altogether but saves only a little on cost, it may be profitable for the monopolist to reverse direction and *increase* the number of varieties offered to raise profit. This outcome is even more likely if substantial economies of scope are present, meaning that the monopoly can supply more variety niches at lower cost than independent firms could.

APPLICATION: Product Differentiation and Demand Determination in Colas

Pepsi-Cola Company offers a number of different colas and soft drinks in its product line. So what did it do when it considered offering another?

In this case, the proposed extension of the Pepsi line was a colorless clear cola characterized by low sodium, no caffeine, no preservatives, 100-percent natural flavoring, and a lighter, less sweet taste. Pepsi-Cola hoped the new crystal cola would appeal to the growing number of consumers who want a light-tasting, all-natural beverage.

To ascertain demand for its new cola, Pepsi-Cola placed the cola in markets in Dallas, Providence, and several areas in Colorado, including Denver. The company chose a price close to that of regular colas, although the drink also competes with newer beverages like sparkling juices, flavored waters, and natural sodas that cost more.

Pepsi's plan was to attract consumers from different age groups and buying habits. Although market analysts believe that the product is unlikely to attain the sales of Coke or regular Pepsi, it could be a very profitable niche product and the first authentic change in colas in a great number of years.[7] ■

---

5. As a check, you might stop to verify where we took this into account in our description of the American Foods variety choice.

6. In the case of the beach economy, for example, we can show that a monopoly serving the beach would provide fewer vendors, each one charging a price so that the beachgoer furthest from the vendor would be paying total costs (price plus distance cost) equal to his or her reservation price R.

7. Data from Anson Fehey, "Seeing a Future in Crystal," *Advertising Age,* April 20, 1992, p. 4.

9.4 Advertising

▼

8. How does advertising make markets more competitive, and how might it make markets less competitive?

Economists identify two distinct functions of advertising: information and persuasion. If information were perfect, advertising would be unnecessary to relay information about a product; but since information is generally less than perfect, advertising helps to convey (1) the fact that the product exists and is available for sale, (2) its price, (3) its quality, attributes, and performance features, (4) the presence and content of seller warranties, (5) where the product may be bought, and (6) when the product may be bought. Informative advertising helps to make markets more competitive. In fact, studies have shown that advertising can *reduce prices* and *lower price variation across suppliers* for competing products or services.

Persuasive advertising, on the other hand, tries to convince the listeners, viewers, or readers that they *should* buy the product advertised (not just that they can). The advertiser may want to make the audience aware of a need for the product or even create a need for the product that did not exist before. For example, the message may be, ''If you buy this sports car, you will be attractive to the opposite sex,'' or ''Business leaders and other successful and admired people buy this type of wrist watch; since you deserve to be admired and successful, you should buy this wrist watch too.'' The advertiser also tries to create brand loyalty by convincing buyers that the brand-name product is better than non-brand-name products.

Sometimes the two types of advertising are difficult to tell apart. For example, when a company specializing in clothes washers advertises that its repairmen have nothing to do because its product rarely breaks down, is this trying to inform the buyer of a legitimate quality difference, or is it advertising to create brand loyalty?

To the extent that advertising attempts to change preferences or mislead consumers, economists have argued that persuasive advertising diminishes market competition. For example, false brand loyalty created through misleading advertising differentiates products in the consumer's mind and leads to monopoly power with its associated social costs. In such cases, the absence of advertising-induced loyalty might have resulted in a more competitive market structure. Persuasive advertising leads to two social costs: (1) the social loss from less competitive markets, and (2) the direct cost of the resources devoted to advertising.

The net economic merits of advertising have been under debate for over fifty years, and we are still learning about them. To the extent that advertising creates demand where there was none before or changes consumer preferences, its effects fall outside the models we have studied in this book, which take utility and preferences as given. There is little disagreement that misleading and false advertising is harmful, but attempts to separate the legitimate information function from the persuasion function are often hard to evaluate.

Without attempting to resolve this quesiton, we now turn to the question of advertising from the point of view of an imperfectly competitive firm with market power. The firm's objective is to balance the benefits and costs of advertising in such a way as to maximize firm profits.

Effect of Advertising on Demand

Imagine that several years have passed, and your American Foods Corporation has been profitably offering four varieties of breakfast cereal to the market. However, the market looks a little different: Other firms are now emulating American Foods by providing their own competing breakfast cereals. The marketing division says that the company needs to advertise to increase its market share and raise profits. The manager needs to decide how much of the firm's revenues to devote to advertising.

As president of American Foods, you know that the purpose of every advertising dollar is to increase sales of your breakfast cereal. You also know that the quantity sold depends on price. You can either lower price to increase sales or you can increase advertising to increase sales. Either method of increasing quantity is costly: reducing price loses revenue on the quantity sold, and advertising expenditures directly cost money.

▼
9. What is the elasticity of demand with respect to advertising, and how is it used in the advertising rule of thumb?

Letting q denote the quantity of cereal demanded and A the amount of money spent on advertising, we know that the quantity you can expect to sell is dependent on price p and advertising A, so that $q(p, A)$ represents your demand curve, taking advertising into account. Decreasing p or increasing A raises quantity demanded. With this in mind, we define the *elasticity of demand with respect to advertising,* ε_A, as the percentage increase in quantity per percentage increase in advertising,

$$\varepsilon_A = \frac{\dfrac{\Delta q}{q}}{\dfrac{\Delta A}{A}} = \frac{\Delta q}{\Delta A}\frac{A}{q}.$$

As president of American Foods, you want to know how selling an additional unit of output affects revenue. Since an additional unit is sold at price p and the cost of producing that additional unit is marginal cost (MC), selling Δq more units adds to net revenues in the amount of $\Delta q(p - \text{MC})$. That is, $\Delta q(p - \text{MC})$ is the gain you expect from increasing your sales, whether by advertising or by lowering price. To know how much to increase sales, you now need to balance this gain against the losses from lowering price or the costs of advertising.

Effect of Advertising on Costs

The cost of additional advertising is ΔA. Thus if $\Delta q(p - \text{MC}) > \Delta A$, you want to continue increasing advertising until the increase in revenue equals the increase in cost, $\Delta q(p - \text{MC}) = \Delta A$.[8] Multiplying both sides of the

---

8. If $\Delta q(p - \text{MC}) < \Delta A$ the firm wants to advertise less. If $\Delta q(p - \text{MC}) < 0$ for a firm currently doing no advertising, it means such a firm will not begin to advertise.

equality by $A/(pq\,\Delta A)$ and noting the definition of the elasticity of demand with respect to advertising gives us

$$\varepsilon_A \frac{(p-\text{MC})}{p} = \frac{A}{R},$$

where $R = pq$ is firm revenues.

If the firm had lowered its *price* to increase sales instead of advertising more, it would have cost the firm the amount $-q\,\Delta p$, because its sales q would be made at the lower price and Δp is the amount of price reduction. Following the same logic that we applied to advertising, the condition for the firm not to be able to raise profit by lowering or raising price is that $\Delta q(p - \text{MC}) = -q\,\Delta p$. Multiplying both sides by $-p/(q\,\Delta p)$ gives us $-(p/q)(\Delta q/\Delta p)(p - \text{MC}) = p$ or

$$-\varepsilon(p - \text{MC}) = p.$$

The equation in this form is already familiar to us from Chapter 8 as the MR = MC condition for the firm to maximize profits, but its different derivation here serves to highlight the similarity of the principle used in advertising.[9]

The Advertising Rule of Thumb

Combining the two conditions to eliminate $(p - \text{MC})$ gives us the *advertising rule of thumb,*

$$\frac{\varepsilon_A}{-\varepsilon} = \frac{A}{R}.$$

The rule says that the share of revenues devoted to advertising should equal the ratio of advertising elasticity of demand to the price elasticity of demand. For example, assume that the price elasticity of demand is -0.75 (that is, a 10 percent drop in price would cause a 7.5 percent increase in sales). Assume that an increase in the advertising budget of 10 percent causes a 1-percent increase in sales. Then ε_A is 0.1 and $\varepsilon_A/-\varepsilon = 0.1/0.75 = 0.133$. Hence, if advertising is less than 13.3 percent of the firm's revenues, the firm increases profit by raising its advertising expenditure.

Notice that as the price elasticity of demand gets further from zero, the share of revenues devoted to advertising declines. In a perfectly competitive market, the demand curve is perfectly elastic (the elasticity of demand is minus infinity). In that case, the formula says that the firm should spend no money on advertising, as we predicted would be true of perfectly competitive, pricetaking firms.

Advertising by Industry in the United States

Many firms engage in little or no advertising, but some firms spend more than one-fifth of their revenues on advertising. Judging from the formula we have developed, firms should devote more advertising expenditure to products

9. Rewriting, the equation takes the form $p(1 + 1/\varepsilon) = \text{MC}$, which is MR = MC.

Table 9.2	Advertising Expenditures as Percentage of Total Revenues for Major Users of Advertising in the United States	
Industry	**Advertising as Percentage of Revenues**	
Over-the-counter drugs	20.2	
Cosmetics	14.6	
Soft drinks	13.8	
Cutlery (including razor blades)	12.9	
Cereal breakfast foods	11.4	
Pet foods	11	
Distilled liquors	11	
Magazines and periodicals	10.3	
Cigarettes	8.8	
Soap and cleaning products	8	

Source: Federal Trade Commission, *Statistical Report: Annual Line of Business Report, 1977,* Washington, D.C., 1977. This is the latest year for which the industry breakdown of advertising figures is available.

whose price elasticity of demand is low compared to their elasticity of demand with respect to advertising. The amount of advertising therefore reveals something about the nature of the market. Over-the-counter drugs, for example, might be expected to have relatively low elasticity of demand, since they are used to treat sickness (purchase is determined by need more than by price). Table 9.2 shows that firms in that industry in fact spend over 20 percent of their revenues on advertising. Perfumes and cosmetics might be expected to have a high elasticity of demand with respect to advertising; they come in second in the list at nearly 15 percent of revenues. The other products shown in the table, such as cutlery, breakfast cereal, magazines and periodicals, and soap, have advertising-to-revenue ratios ranging from just under 14 percent down to 8 percent of revenues.[10]

APPLICATION: Tobacco Advertising and Demand Response

One of the more beleaguered industries in the United States and parts of the rest of the world, some would say with good cause, is the tobacco industry.[11] In spite of the fact that cigarettes are a health hazard—turning smokers into addicts and causing cancer that kills many users—cigarettes remain among

10. Since much of the advertising for soap and cleaning products has been targeted to viewers of daytime drama serials, these serials have come to be known as ''soap operas,'' or ''soaps'' for short.
11. See ''The Tobacco Trade: The Search for Eldorado,'' *The Economist,* May 16, 1992, pp. 21–24.

the world's most profitable consumer products. In Investigation I.B we examined how an excise tax on cigarettes would affect smoking in the United States. We now examine the tobacco industry to learn about the effects of advertising on demand.

Health advocates are having a gradual impact on smoking in the United States and Western Europe. American smoking has fallen by 2 to 3 percent annually for the past 10 years. Whereas average per-capita consumption of cigarettes was over 2,600 in 1982, the figure fell to around 2,100 in 1990. Consumption is lower in Western European countries like Great Britain, preunification West Germany, France, Italy, Spain, and Holland.

Faced with this situation, the tobacco industry has turned to advertising and other world markets to maintain and expand its sales. Tobacco companies spend $4 billion annually advertising in the $40-billion U.S. market ($\varepsilon_A/-\varepsilon = 0.1$)[12] and about the same in the $50-billion European market ($\varepsilon_A/-\varepsilon = 0.08$). The companies claim they advertise to introduce new brands and attract the 15 to 20 percent of smokers who change brands every year. The success of their advertising can be seen in the case of Joe Camel, the suave dromedary appearing on billboards and in magazines across the United States. Studies show that children as young as six can recognize Joe Camel as readily as Mickey Mouse. Camel Cigarettes' share of sales in the 18- to 24-year-old market targeted by the ads soared from 4.4 percent of the market to 7.9 percent in just three years of advertising. According to one analyst, before that the brand was in "free fall." "The turnaround has been miraculous."[13]

The attempt to enter new markets abroad has brought tobacco companies into conflict not only with health lobbies, but also with the governments of foreign countries, many of which maintain state-owned tobacco monopolies and do not want competition from outsiders. According to the General Agreement on Tariffs and Trade (an agreement governing trade practices to which most countries, including the United States, are signatories), a country has the right to control the importation and sale of goods for health reasons as long as competing domestic products are subject to the same rules as the foreign product. A ban on tobacco advertising is proposed in many countries, including Great Britain. How much would a total ban on advertising affect the quantity of smoking there? According to Britain's health department, smoking would drop between 2 and 5 percent a year. ■

9.5 Cartels

▼
10. Explain how a cartel works, the advantages to a firm of joining a cartel, and the incentives to cheat on the cartel.

As we have seen in this chapter and in the two preceding chapters, prices and markets differ on the basis of how firms compete with one another. Perfectly competitive markets (with standardized product) are at one extreme; monopolistically competitive markets (with differentiated product) are another basic type, and pure monopoly is a third. The assumptions of monopolistic competition tend to apply best to markets where the number of sellers

12. Notice that this figure is higher than the 8.8 percent reported for 1977 in Table 9.2.
13. "The Tobacco Trade," p. 21.

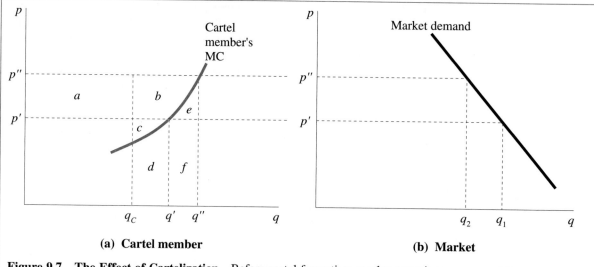

Figure 9.7   The Effect of Cartelization   Before cartel formation, market quantity was q_1, and the firm sold quantity q' at price p'. After cartel formation, cartel supply is restricted to quantity q_2, price rises to p'', and the cartel member produces assigned output q_C. The cartel member loses profit equal to area c, but gains profit equal to area a by being able to sell units q_C at the higher price. Since area a is greater than area c, the member gains. If the member cheats on the cartel by producing quantity q'' at price p'', it gains profit equal to areas $b + c$.

is relatively large, whereas monopoly deals with markets where there is a single seller. In the middle are markets in which relatively few firms, each taking account of the others' responses, must decide how they will compete. Competition among relatively few firms when they act noncooperatively is the subject of Chapter 10. But before leaving our discussion of monopoly and monopolistic competition, it is appropriate to discuss one way in which a relatively small or moderate number of firms might respond to the market—by agreeing not to compete at all. An industry where firms cooperate to set price and quantity according to a common plan is called a cartel.

> A **cartel** is a combination of independent producers of a common product that agree to limit competition in order to fix prices.

By agreeing to act jointly, cartel members limit their joint output and move to a point on the market demand curve with higher prices. Even though individual cartel members may sell fewer units as their assigned shares of the lower cartel quantity, they sell them at a higher price, which more than compensates them for the lower quantity.

Figure 9.7 illustrates the effect of cartelization. Without the cartel, market quantity is q_1, shown in part (b), and price is p'. The firm produces quantity q', shown in part (a). After cartelization, market supply is limited to q_2 and the firm, now a cartel member, is assigned the quantity q_C. This reduces the firm's profit by area c, since firm revenues fall by areas $c + d$ while costs of producing fall by area d. However, being able to sell output q_C at price p'' instead of p' adds area a to the firm's profit. Since area a is larger than area c, the firm gains by being in the cartel.

Cartels are notoriously unstable because the incentive is so great for a member to renege on its quantity commitment to the cartel. Tremendous profits are possible if the member is able to sell additional units at the higher cartel price. In Figure 9.7, the cartel member raises revenues by areas $b + c + d + e + f$ if it sells q'' units instead of the cartel allotment of q_C. The cost to the member of producing these additional units is the sum of the marginal costs (the area under the marginal cost curve), areas $d + e + f$. Areas $b + c$ are therefore the additional profit. If all cartel members attempt to overproduce their allotments, the cartel breaks down and prices return to their previous market level, p'.

Some of the conditions that appear to aid cartel stability include small numbers of firms (agreements are easier to reach and monitoring is easier), stable demand and costs (negotiations and changes to the cartel choices are less frequent), control of the market (little competition from noncartel firms), entry barriers (the cartel is not threatened by outside firms entering), and homogeneous product (members have greater incentive to increase profit by cartel activities than by going it alone with their own product varieties).

Cartels, Coffee, and College

There are many examples of cartel-like organizations that collude to fix prices, including the well-known Organization of Petroleum Exporting Countries (OPEC). We discuss two of them here.

Coffee. The now defunct International Coffee Agreement is a particularly interesting example of a cartel's effect on market prices. This agreement was an international treaty that set quotas to regulate member countries' coffee exports and imports. The agreement's stated objective was to reduce fluctuations in coffee prices, but most observers agreed that it also raised prices.

Although the United States is not a coffee producer (with the exception of a small amount produced in Hawaii), it agreed to lend its support to the coffee agreement. Partly this was to help certain South American and African coffee producers, and partly to win international friends. The last version of the agreement, renegotiated in 1983, ran until September 30, 1989. This was the fifth in a series of agreements in which the United States had participated since 1962. Because of the importance of the United States in world markets, American support was critical to continuation of the agreement. In the past, when an agreement was due to expire, the State Department had frequently argued for renegotiation on diplomatic grounds, whereas agencies such as the Council of Economic Advisers had wanted to abandon the agreement for economic reasons.

The different varieties of coffee are grouped into two main types. In recent years, demand has grown for mild Arabica coffees as opposed to the other basic type, Robusta. Since the coffee agreement specified production quotas for member countries, supplies of the two types of coffee through the years grew out of line with market demand. Importing countries also were allocated quotas for each type of coffee; these quotas had to be renegotiated each time the agreement was renegotiated.

Although the ostensible purpose of the coffee agreement was to stabilize coffee prices—by withholding coffee from the market in periods of high production and releasing it during periods of low production—observers concur that the agreement had the cartel-like net effect of raising coffee prices. Demand for coffee is relatively inelastic; econometric estimates put the price elasticity of demand for coffee, ε, in the -0.16 range. Withholding only 10 percent of available coffee from the market in a given year, a tactic that was not unusual, could imply an increase in price of $(\Delta q/q)/\varepsilon = 10/0.16 = 62.5$ percent. Termination of the agreement should therefore have been accompanied by the expectation of a drop in the price of coffee in the future, and this should have been reflected by a drop in the futures price of coffee.[14] How big was this effect when the agreement actually came to an end?

Figure 9.8 shows a time series for the coffee futures price in 1989. The price and export-quota clauses of the agreement were suspended in July of that year, largely because of difficulties with shipments of coffee to nonmember countries at discount prices and with the rigid export quotas that limited exports of mild coffee. In anticipation of the demise of the agreement, prices for green (unroasted) coffee started falling in June 1989, as the figure demonstrates. The cumulative result was a 50-percent drop in price, to below 70 cents per pound after the agreement effectively ended in July.

College. To a student looking for a college education, deciding which college to purchase one from is much like other market purchases, albeit more important than most. For many schools, the price that the student pays for education is determined by how much the college is willing to discount from its stated tuition in the form of financial aid. According to U.S. Attorney General Richard Thornburgh, "students are entitled to the full benefits of price competition when they choose a college . . . just as they would in shopping for any other service."[15]

In fact, Mr. Thornburgh found that 9 well-known Eastern colleges met annually along with 14 other schools to collude on a common student-aid policy, even to the point of deciding what price they would charge individual students admitted to more than one of the institutions. Evidence of cartel-like behavior included the fact that the colleges agreed not to award financial aid

---

14. A futures price is the price agreed to now for delivery of a product at a future time.
15. Paul M. Barrett, "U.S. Charges 8 Ivy League Schools and MIT with Fixing Financial Aid," *Wall Street Journal,* May 22, 1991, p. A16, and Peter Passell, "Fixing Prices for Virtue's Sake?" *New York Times,* May 13, 1992, p. D2.

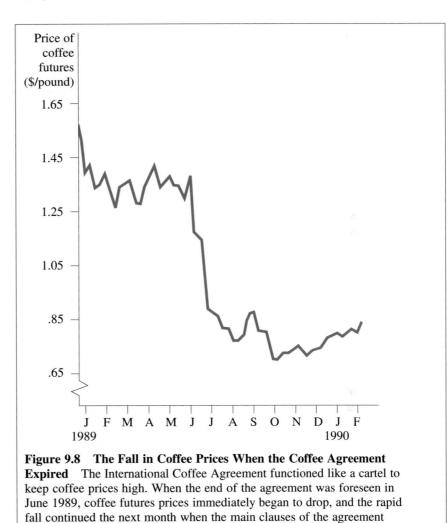

**Figure 9.8   The Fall in Coffee Prices When the Coffee Agreement
Expired**   The International Coffee Agreement functioned like a cartel to
keep coffee prices high. When the end of the agreement was foreseen in
June 1989, coffee futures prices immediately began to drop, and the rapid
fall continued the next month when the main clauses of the agreement
were suspended. Source: John Valentine, ''Prices Recover as Collapse of
Coffee Agreement Gives the Market a Chance to Allocate Supplies,''
Wall Street Journal, February 12, 1990, p. C12. Reprinted by permission
of the Wall Street Journal, © 1990 Dow Jones & Company, Inc. All
Rights Reserved Worldwide.

on the basis of merit, but only on the basis of ability to pay. Students who
were deemed able to pay more were charged more, and students deemed able
to pay less were charged less. During the period in which this system was
used, average tuition at the 9 schools rose nearly twice as fast as prices in
general. All but one of the colleges agreed to abandon their practices in
response to the Justice Department's probe.

In defense of its practices, the one dissenting school argued that since it was not-for-profit and charged lower prices to students less able to pay, it should be exempt from antitrust actions. Whether a private supplier should be able to operate as a mini-federal government in dispensing aid garnered from collusive practices may ultimately have to be settled by the courts. One economist quoted in the press likened the case to a hypothetical situation in which the Big Three automakers colluded to raise prices on luxury cars, promising to use the profits in some socially valuable manner, such as making a cheap fuel-efficient car. In such a situation, would we want these companies to be exempt from antitrust laws? Another economist argued that if banning merit-based financial aid *is* good public policy, it is a policy that should be set by government, not by colluding universities. The dissenting school lost its case in federal district court, although as of this writing the matter is being appealed.

Summary

Active Reading Guide numbers are given in parentheses at the end of each summary item.

1. Imperfect competition prevails when one or more of the assumptions of perfect competition are violated. Monopolistic competition describes markets in which sellers sell differentiated products that are imperfect substitutes for one another, and for which market entry is free. Information may or may not be perfect. Monopolistic competitors, facing downward-sloping firm demand curves, are not pricetakers. (1)

2. Monopolistic competitors maximize profits by setting MC equal to MR on the basis of their firm demand curves. Because of free entry, firm profits are zero in long-run monopolistically competitive markets. (2)

3. One of the issues in monopolistic competition is how firms determine their firm demand curves. Spatial models explain demand for differentiated products in terms of the location of the product in the grid of product characteristics, where each axis of the grid measures the amount of one of the characteristics. Consumers are assumed to have preferred locations in the grid for the differentiated product. They buy from the firm whose good is closest to their preferred location in the grid. (3)

4. The two sources of welfare loss from monopolistic competition are (1) the usual monopoly so-cial costs from each monopolistic competitor producing where $p >$ MC, and (2) the social costs of having too few varieties. Examination of spatial models tells us that monopolistically competitive markets could result in too many, too few, or the right number of varieties. (4)

5. Imperfectly competitive firms with the ability to influence market price have an incentive to differentiate their products from those of competitors, to supply a number of product varieties of their own, and to advertise. These decisions do not apply to markets with perfect competition, because a perfectly competitive firm selling a standardized product to informed buyers cannot differentiate its product and would receive little or no benefits from advertising. (5)

6. A firm offering more varieties of a product can increase its demand by appealing to the range of tastes of consumers more closely. The decision of how many varieties of a product to offer involves balancing the increase in demand (outward shift of the firm's demand curve) with the increase in cost from providing the additional varieties. The variety choice rule involves adding varieties, starting with the ones that are most important to demand, and for each number of varieties offered, finding the quantity at which profit is maximized. From the list of maximized profits obtained in the first step, the final

step is to select the number of varieties and corresponding quantity that give the highest of the maximized profits. The procedure is the same for a monopolist and for a firm in a market with few sellers, except that the latter must take into account the potential reactions of other firms in determining the effect of introducing greater variety. (6)

7. Given the same number of varieties, each monopolistically competitive firm would sell a larger quantity at lower price than would a monopolist. But monopolistic competition could result in more or fewer varieties than monopoly. If demand from discontinued varieties shifts to the remaining varieties offered by the monopolist, then the monopolist will offer fewer. If the demand is not shifted to other varieties offered by the monopolist, or if there are sufficiently strong economies of scope, the monopolist may offer more varieties. (7)

8. Advertising both informs and persuades. Greater information dissemination through advertising leads to more competitive markets, but advertising that falsely persuades consumers to believe products are more differentiated than they are diminishes competition. (8)

9. Firms advertise because advertising can increase demand for their products and lead to increases in price and quantity sold. Advertising also affects costs directly through the expenditures on advertising. The elasticity of demand with respect to advertising summarizes the effect of a percentage increase in advertising expenditure in terms of percentage increase in quantity sold at a fixed market price. According to the rule of thumb for advertising, the ratio of advertising expenditure to revenue should equal elasticity of demand with respect to advertising divided by the negative of the price elasticity of demand. (9)

10. A cartel is a group of sellers who agree to limit their joint quantity to fix prices. Cartel members raise their profits by producing a smaller, cartel-determined quantity and selling at the higher, cartel-fixed price. Since individual cartel members would make even greater profits by selling a larger quantity at the cartel-fixed price, there is an incentive for cartel members to cheat on the cartel. (10)

Review Questions

*1. Give an example of a market that you think might be monopolistically competitive, and justify your choice.

2. Construct a chart with three columns, labeled Perfect Competition, Monopolistic Competition, and Monopoly, and four rows labeled with the four conditions for perfect competition. For each column, indicate whether each of the conditions of perfect competition applies, and if not, what situation applies instead.

*3. Use the spatial model of monopolistic competition to explain what prevents a monopolistically competitive market from supplying each consumer his or her preferred variety. What prevents the market from supplying just one variety?

4. What conditions would you check for to determine whether a market was monopolistically competitive instead of perfectly competitive?

*5. What are the costs of having too many varieties of goods offered in a monopolistically competitive market? Of too few varieties?

6. What is a market niche? How does the distribution of demand matter in the formation of a market niche?

*7. Explain what sales cannibalism is. How exactly does it matter to the firm's choice of the number of varieties to offer?

8. What distinguishes the two functions of advertising as they relate to increasing or decreasing the amount of competition in the marketplace? Relate your answer to the four conditions for perfect competition.

*9. How does the advertising decision of the firm take into account the fact that the firm can increase sales revenue either by lowering price or by increasing advertising expenditures.

* Asterisks are used to denote questions that are answered at the back of the book.

10. Rank the following in terms of firm profits for a typical member of a cartel:
   a) Production at the cartel price and assigned firm quantity
   b) Production at MC = cartel price
   c) Production at precartel price and quantity
   d) Production at cartel quantity, but with other cartel members producing to the point where price = MC.

Relate your answer to the long-run stability of cartels.

Numerical and Graphing Exercises

*1. Draw a diagram and explain, using the theory of monopolistic competition, why the following graphical technique works to find marginal cost for any quantity on the declining part of the average cost curve: Given the average cost curve and quantity q_0 on its declining portion, draw the tangent to the average cost curve, calling its intercept on the price axis a and its intercept on the quantity axis b. Draw the chord from point a to the point on the horizontal axis that is half the distance to point b. Marginal cost of output q_0 is at the point where the vertical line through quantity q_0 intersects the chord. (Hint: How must average cost and the demand curve relate to one another in monopolistically competitive equilibrium?)

*2. A monopolistically competitive industry has 100 identical firms, each selling a differentiated product. Total market demand distributed over all firms is $q^D = 110 - p$. In equilibrium each firm produces 1 unit of output at price 10. For each firm, what is the elasticity of demand curve D?

3. Using the information from exercise 2, assume that the elasticity of firm demand d is -2. Draw d, D, and the firm's average cost curve assuming long-run equilibrium.

*4. Using the information from exercise 3, assume that a change in cost occurs so that every firm (and every potential entrant) sees its average cost curve shift rigidly downward. Draw a picture of the new long-run market equilibrium for a firm, using what you know of each firm's d curve, assuming there are more firms in the market. Will each firm's demand curve d be flatter or steeper in the new equilibrium?

*5. A firm finds that its demand curve has price intercept 100 and quantity intercept $100 - 50/n$,

where n is the number of varieties it offers. The curve's equation is $q^D/(100 - 50/n) + p/100 = 1$. How many varieties will the firm offer if its fixed cost is $50n$ and its marginal cost is zero? (Hint: Graph the firm's problem to guide your algebra.)

6. For the United States as a whole, advertising expenditure was just under 2.5 percent of Gross Domestic Product in 1988, although for some firms it ranged as high as 20 percent of revenues. Assuming that 20 percent of a firm's revenues are devoted to advertising and that price markup over marginal cost is between 10 and 50 percent, what would be the implied advertising elasticity of demand for a profit-maximizing firm?

7. Draw a diagram to represent the following facts. A firm has a marginal cost curve given by MC $= 5 + 2q$ and no fixed costs. In the precartel situation, it produces 5 units at price 18. In the cartel situation, price is 25 and the firm's assigned output is 3.
   a) What was the elasticity of demand for the firm in the precartel situation?
   b) What are the firm's precartel and postcartel profits?
   c) What would be the firm's profits if it produced as many units of output as it wanted at the cartel market price?

*8. Use section 9.1's beach economy example with linear distance costs to find the gross substitutability between ice cream products offered by neighboring vendors. In your answer you may assume that the locations of the vendor and its two nearest competitors are fixed, and you can use the resulting demand to compute the effect on vendor 1's quantity sold if vendor 2 changes its price.

CHAPTER 10

Oligopoly: Competitive Games That Firms Play

Many of the most interesting situations in the economics of firms arise when the outcome of the firm's choice depends not only on its own decision, but also on the decisions of a small number of competitors. Interactions of this sort can be described in terms of game theory. What the firm decides to do in a game situation depends greatly on what the firm thinks its competitor firms will do in response. In addition, the firm may employ strategies designed to change competitors' beliefs about how the firm itself will behave. This chapter explores the manager's choice of price and quantity in different "games" that firms play.

ACTIVE READING GUIDES

After reading this chapter, you should be able to answer the Active Reading Guides listed below. These guides also appear in the page margins, near the material to which they refer.

1. Define *oligopoly*, explaining why oligopolies don't become perfectly competitive or monopolistic.

2. Define a game in economic terms. Why can competition among firms be considered a game?

3. Relate oligopolistic competition to games of common interest, pure conflict of interest, and intermediate cases including the Prisoner's Dilemma.

4. Explain the differences among cooperative solutions to a game and dominant, rational, and maximin strategies.

5. Create a simple game that has a Nash equilibrium.

6. How do oligopolistic equilibria relate to firms'

choices of strategy and the solution to a game?

7. Construct an example of Cournot competition.

8. Relate Bertrand competition to Cournot competition and the Stackelberg leader-follower model.

9. What is the difference between a pre-emptive threat equilibrium and a Stackelberg leader-follower solution?

10. Give examples explaining the role of credibility and strategic choice in oligopolistic competition.

11. Theoretically, how might the domestic government use its first-player advantage to improve the position of the domestic firm relative to the foreign firm in international competition? How does credibility play a role?

12. Give four main reasons to be cautious about the use of activist, interventionist trade policy.

10.1 Oligopoly Versus Competition and Monopoly

▼

1. Define *oligopoly*, explaining why oligopolies don't become perfectly competitive or monopolistic.

As president of one of America's major airlines, you are responsible for setting strategic policy for your firm. Although the airline industry couldn't exactly be described previously as a sleepy backwater, deregulation in 1978 seems to have unleashed some pretty strong competitive jockeying for position. Since your firm is one of the more established airlines, you feel confident that you can handle whatever comes down the pike. However, some of your former rivals are no longer in operation, and you want to be careful. Should you compete aggressively, undercutting others' prices to expand market share, perhaps buying a few weaker regional rivals that might become available along the way? Should you turn instead to promotion and heavy advertising? Or should you perhaps try to seek some accommodation with other firms to produce a quieter but more stable market?

In fact, if you are the rough-and-tumble Robert Crandall, chairman of American Airlines, you have tried all of the above, including aggressive pricing, advertising and media appeals, and seeking price accommodation with rivals. The purpose of this chapter is to describe the forces that govern competition in markets such as these with a relatively small number of firms. These markets are called oligopolies.

> An **oligopoly** is a market situation in which each of a small number of interdependent, competing producers influences but does not control the market. A **duopoly** is an oligopoly consisting of only two producers.

In an oligopoly, each firm has the ability to determine its quantity and to affect price to some extent, but its choice cannot guarantee a given profit, because the outcome will also depend on what other firms in the market do. Unlike a firm in perfect competition or monopoly, the oligopolistic firm cannot treat its demand curve as given unless it knows for certain what its few competitors are doing. This mutual interdependence of firms distinguishes oligopolistic markets from monopolistic, perfectly competitive, and monopolistically competitive markets.

Entry Barriers and the Failure of Perfect Competition

Two main questions to ask of oligopolistic markets are: (1) Why don't they become perfectly competitive? and (2) Why don't they become monopolistic? A distinguishing feature of oligopoly is that, although there is enough entry to allow more than one firm, there is too little entry to lead to perfect competition. Oligopolistic entry barriers can take many forms. The market may not be large enough to sustain more than a few firms at efficient scale. The need for high start-up costs and capital requirements, which become sunk costs once paid, may impede entry, as can the presence of economies of scale, ownership or control of an essential input by one or a few firms, ease of product differentiation, and the intentional or unintentional effects of government regulations.

A good example of high start-up costs is the large-airframe market. Firms that make the largest commercial aircraft require as much as $4 billion or more to develop a new aircraft. The firm must recoup these expenses over the lifetime of the aircraft model, and average costs of production do not reach their lowest level until many hundreds of airplanes are made. In this market there is probably enough demand for two, perhaps three, efficient-sized firms, but not four. The market for large airframes is therefore likely to be characterized by few firms, and there is little chance that a new or fly-by-night manufacturer will suddenly come on the scene to compete with incumbent firms.

Actions by firms already in the market can also create entry barriers. If a new entrant faces higher costs because of its lower scale of operation or its setup costs, we would expect existing firms to do what they could to discourage the entrant (for example, by setting a low price) while using their experience, market position, and superior cost structure to continue to make positive profits. Even if the entrant and the incumbent face the same costs, the incumbent's best strategy may be to commit itself to a policy of strong entry deterrence.[1] If the entrant cannot dislodge the incumbent, and if it foresees losses for a long time, entry will be unprofitable.

With few firms in the market and barriers to entry, incumbent firms' profits may not be driven to zero in the long run as would be the case in perfectly

---

1. Such commitment can take any number of tangible or intangible forms, including sunk investments in excess capacity, or even generating a reputation for being ruthless in responding to new rivals. Entry can be made difficult on grounds other than just price. For example, if the incumbent firm has substantial control over the market for an essential input, it might prevent access to the input.

competitive or monopolistically competitive markets. Competition between firms will ensue, but it will be imperfect competition.

The Failure of Oligopolistic Collusion

Entry barriers keep oligopolies from turning perfectly competitive, but we still don't know why oligopolies don't become monopolies. In any market, sellers are able to get the most profit from the market using the monopolistic pricing strategies described in Chapters 8 and 9. The natural objective of oligopolistic firms therefore should be to collude with one another and form a cartel. If competing sellers can find ways to cooperate, they can maximize joint profit and then distribute it in such a way as to make each of the colluding firms better off.

One way to prove that collusion results in higher profits is to note that if the competing firms were all run under one roof, the single decision maker would retain the option of setting production and sales at the prices that prevailed in the absence of collusion. If the decision maker chose a different (and therefore better) choice, profit would rise.

If this were all there was to it, we would make a very short story for this chapter: firms in oligopolistic markets would prevent entry, collude, and enjoy monopolistic profits! However, there are many obstacles to successful collusion—some natural, some government-imposed. Since we observe more oligopolistic markets than we do cartelized or monopolistic ones, a reasonable conclusion is that forces leading to collusion are matched by equally strong or stronger forces against collusion. The incentive for cartels to break down was discussed in Chapter 9. Another way for cartels to break down is through the entry of new firms. However, if cartels do not break down on their own, there is still the issue of antitrust litigation. Since passage of the Sherman Antitrust Act in 1890, cartelization and collusion in restraint of trade have been of much less value to the firm because of the consequences if the firm is found in violation of the law.

APPLICATION: Demise of Collusion in Three Industries

For oligopolistic firms, collusion is not necessarily easy to initiate or to sustain. Nevertheless, a review of antitrust actions under section 1 of the Sherman Antitrust Act reveals that there is no lack of collusive activity.[2] In Chapter 9 we discussed the International Coffee Agreement and collusive behavior among colleges in terms of their effects on the price of coffee and tuition. We can now look at three examples that illustrate the making or

---

2. From 1974 to 1978, for example, the following list of well-known firms pled *nolo contendere* or guilty to price fixing for one or more of their products: Allied Chemical, Bethlehem Steel, Dean Foods, Du Pont, Gulf Oil, ITT, International Paper, Purolator, R. J. Reynolds, and Rockwell International.

breaking of cartels from the point of view of oligopoly interaction and industry structure. In one case, collusion died of its own causes; in another, government unintentionally provided the support for effective collusion, which died once government withdrew; and in the last case antitrust action intervened.

Tin. The first example of the demise of a cartel comes from international trade. In the preceding chapter, we saw that the coffee agreement failed because of the inability to renegotiate an agreement that allocated supplies to the members' satisfaction. In the case of tin, the attempt to fix prices failed because the cartel authority did not have sufficient financial backing to support the agreed-on price or sufficient ability to cause members to restrict supply.

The International Tin Council was originally formed to stabilize world prices in tin by establishing a buffer-stock operation that would buy and sell tin, taking it off the market when price fell, and putting it on the market when price rose. As is often the case, the objective of stabilizing prices was extended to trying to raise prices. The result was that, in the face of falling demand for tin in the late 1970s and early 1980s, the Tin Council accumulated 73,000 metric tons of tin and eventually exhausted its cash reserves. It managed to limp along for several years, until the need to resume stock accumulations in 1985 exhausted its money and borrowing ability. In this case, the existence of reserve stocks and the knowledge of the Tin Council's diminishing resources probably hastened the cartel's demise, because speculators predicting lower prices hastened to sell tin before the collapse in prices, thereby placing further pressure on price. In fact, with the Tin Council's collapse in 1985, tin prices fell nearly 40 percent.

Airlines. The next example comes from the American airline market, and it deals with government regulatory activity that inadvertently supported collusive-like pricing. The extent of the price-fixing effect became known only with deregulation of the industry.

Government regulation of the airline industry began in the 1920s with the granting of U.S. mail routes to airlines. Regulatory authority was passed to the Civil Aeronautics Board (CAB) upon its creation in 1938. At that time, the belief was that unregulated competition would keep fares too low to allow the industry to grow and prosper. The CAB therefore regulated fares; and before an airline began service on a new route, it had to get CAB permission. At the time of the CAB's formation there were 16 existing airlines. In spite of the enormous growth in airline traffic in the 1950s through '70s, not one new airline entrant was allowed to begin service on a major route until after October 1978, when Congress enacted the Airline Deregulation Act. By that time, mergers had reduced the number of original carriers to 11.

By the mid-1970s, the development of intrastate carriers—notably in Florida, Texas, and California, where state regulation was not as stringent—suggested that competition would have a major effect on reducing price.

(Intrastate routes with the same mileage as some interstate routes had substantially lower fares.) Academic studies, policy studies, and eventually government studies came out in favor of deregulation. In 1975 the CAB, which had previously been opposed to deregulation, also came out with a report in favor of it. After its report, the CAB began to allow airlines fare reductions that it had blocked previously. Legislative reform finally came in 1978 with the Airline Deregulation Act. In response to the act, new entry and meaningful competition were permitted. The CAB's authority over routes ended in December 1981; its authority over fares ended in January 1983; and the CAB itself was abolished at the end of 1984.

The extent to which the CAB had become a de facto enforcement mechanism for collusion can be seen by the evidence on fares in the wake of deregulation. One of the functions the CAB performed was setting standard fares between two points on the basis of airline costs, taking into account a standard load factor for flights, distance traveled, and other considerations. Fares charged by airlines did not have to conform to these rates exactly, but in fact they often did. In 1975 fares charged on the 90 top interstate routes averged 97 percent of the CAB formula. Five years later, after deregulation, fares on the same routes had dropped to 65 percent of the CAB formula for the 52 routes where entry had occurred, and to 92 percent of the CAB formula for the remaining routes where there was no entry.

Even stronger evidence was forthcoming in the years after 1980. One type of analysis divided routes into pairs so that routes in each pair differed in length by only a few miles and had equivalent passengers and fares in 1980. Four years later, the route pairs with entry had experienced fare reductions that averaged 27 percent. The paired routes without entry experienced fare *increases* that averaged 74 percent, for a total divergence in rates on the order of 100 percent![3]

Baby Formula. As of 1990, more than 90 percent of the greater than $1.6 billion baby formula market was served by three companies: Ross Laboratories (a division of Abbott), the maker of Similac, which controlled over 50 percent of the market; Mead Johnson Nutritional Group (part of Bristol-Myers Squibb Company), the maker of Enfamil; and Wyeth-Ayerst Laboratories (a division of American Home Products Corporation), the maker of Nursoy. Over one-third of the market quantity was bought by the federal government for its special supplemental food program for Women, Infants, and Children (WIC), run by the states with federal money.

In 1992 the Federal Trade Commission (FTC) reached a settlement with Mead Johnson and Wyeth-Ayerst,[4] having previously charged the companies

3. See Daniel P. Kaplan, ''The Changing Airline Industry,'' in *Regulatory Reform: What Actually Happened,* ed. Leonard W. Weiss and Michael W. Klass, Boston: Little, Brown, 1986, Table 3, p. 59.
4. Court charges were filed against Ross Laboratories, with which no agreement was reached. At the time of writing, the matter was not settled. See Robert Pear, ''Top Infant-Formula Makers Charged by U.S. Over Pricing,'' *New York Times*, June 12, 1992, p. A1.

with illegally limiting competition by agreeing to fix prices through rigged bidding. The case represented two years of investigation by the bureau of competition at the FTC. Evidence of collusion included the fact that prices had risen in a lock-step pattern for a decade. The companies were charged with signaling what they intended to bid on state contracts for formula and also with agreeing, through an industry group, to discourage consumer advertising for infant formula. For example, one of the companies sent open letters to state officials specifying what it intended to bid on new WIC contracts, even though the state had requested sealed bids and the company should have known that the information would become known to its competitors. According to the government, the companies' actions resulted in changed behavior and higher prices, costing millions of dollars to WIC buyers and providing formula to fewer babies than would otherwise have had it. Though none of the companies admitted wrongdoing, the government's policing action was intended to change the companies' behavior in the future. ■

Having explained *why* we might observe oligopolies that do not become perfectly competitive or collusive, we are left with the task of explaining what firms do as oligopolies. For this, we apply the theory and approach of games.

10.2 Why Discuss Games in Producer Theory?

▼
2. Define a game in economic terms. Why can competition among firms be considered a game?

Although perfect competition and monopoly represent powerful paradigms that are useful in many applications of microeconomics, few markets exactly fit the requirements for either extreme. Oligopolies contain elements of both competition and monopoly. A complete description of oligopolistic markets must therefore deal with the challenging and interesting cases where the *mutual interdependence* of distinctly recognizable sellers is a major feature. That is, your firm's profit no longer depends just on market prices and your decision about how much to produce; it also depends on what other firms do in response to your firm's choices. Moreover, you take their probable reactions into account when you make your choices. This is something you didn't do if you were a perfect competitor or a monopolist, because in those cases you considered your firm's demand curve as given. Once you begin to make your choices strategically with an eye to how they will affect your competitors, you are in a game situation.

Situations in which the payoff to you depends on what you choose, plus what your competitors choose, plus the rules of interaction, are called games.

*A **game** is a set of players, a description of payoffs for each player, and a set of rules for player interaction, such that the payoff to a player depends on the choices of the player and on the choices of the other players.*

According to this definition, a perfect competitor's profit-maximizing quantity choice would not involve a game, since knowing market price alone determines the outcome of the firm's choice. On the other hand, chess and checkers are games, as is competitive market interaction between a relatively small number of firms. The players are firms; the payoffs are profits; and the rules of the game are the determinants of prices and quantities for each firm given market demand and the choices of other firms. For example, if two firms sell a perfectly homogeneous good (for instance, two gas stations across the street from one another), the "rule" for sales would say that the firm quoting the higher price will have zero sales and the firm quoting the lower price will get all of the market. If the competing goods are imperfect substitutes, the rules can be a little different: in that case, prices of the two firms may differ somewhat without one firm's losing all of its sales, subject to the particular demand curve for the substitute goods in the case at hand. By using the framework of games for describing these interactions, and understanding something about game solutions, we can take advantage of one of the important changes in microeconomic thinking over the past 40 years.[5]

APPLICATION: Price Wars and Uniform Pricing

In 1992, Robert L. Crandall, the chairman of American Airlines to whom we have referred earlier, took to the newspapers to publicize steep price reductions for American.[6] With 20 percent of the domestic airline market,[7] American was leading an industry that had just lost $6 billion over the previous two years. Mr. Crandall explained that American's price reductions, which included half-price fares for nonbusiness travelers on most routes and a reduction in the advance purchase requirement from 14 to 7 days, were the natural result of "the most intense and savage competition found in any business I know of." Prominent in American's thinking was the issue of how its competitors would respond to its actions and how it should respond to theirs.

The previous fall, American had re-evaluated its pricing structure in light of traveler criticism that its restrictions were complicated and unfair.[8] It had decided to replace the complex structure with just four fares: first class, coach, and two more-flexible advance-purchase fares. "When we introduced our plan," writes Mr. Crandall, "we did not know what our competitors would do. We figured that some might choose to undercut our prices. And we knew that we would match them." In fact, in the weeks following American's new fares, America West, Continental, Northwest, TWA, and USAir all filed

5. The study of games dates back at least to John von Neumann and Oskar Morgenstern, *Theory of Games and Economic Behavior,* Princeton, N.J.: Princeton University Press, 1944.
6. Robert L. Crandall, "Behind Those Bizarre Air Fares" *New York Times,* June 14, 1992, Business Section, p. 13.
7. "America's Airlines: Offers Nobody Can Refuse," *The Economist,* June 6, 1992, p. 74.
8. We reviewed airline pricing schemes in Chapter 8 as a way to capture consumer surplus.

lower, special-purpose domestic fares, including Northwest's "Adults Fly Free" one-week 50-percent fare for pairings of adults with children. As planned, American did respond with the half-price fares we have mentioned.[9]

Mr. Crandall's news foray was not entirely based on a desire to advertise. He was also attempting to counter a suit filed by Continental, which, as part of its own strategic maneuvering, had charged that American's fare structure sought to drive competitors out of business. There was some irony in the charge, as we will see shortly, because not a decade earlier the same Mr. Crandall had been sued for too little competition rather than too much. Either way, it is clear that competition in the airline industry is well described as the strategic maneuvering of a small number of firms jockeying for a competitive edge—a game in which one firm's payoff depends on other firms' actions.

A similar story emerges in the consumer products industry. In 1992 Procter & Gamble announced it was jettisoning its old price list on nearly half of its products, for everything from Jif peanut butter to Cascade dishwashing soap, in favor of what it called "everyday low prices."[10] A dish soap like Dawn, for example, which might have sold between $.99 and $1.89, averaging $1.37 for a standard bottle, would now sell for a uniform $1.32. Procter & Gamble's new uniform pricing plan replaced an older system whereby grocery stores were offered periodic promotional allowances and concessionary prices to give them the flexibility to choose the best marketing tactics for particular areas. However, many distributors had taken advantage of the discounts to stockpile products, sometimes not reordering for half a year or more; they pocketed the savings with little benefit to Procter & Gamble.

The risks of Procter & Gamble's uniform-pricing gamble had to do with how supermarket chains would react and how rivals would respond. Since most analysts believed that P&G was so large that few supermarket chains could afford to drop its brands, the strategies of rivals had particular importance. Not surprisingly, Kraft General Foods (the nation's largest food company), Dial, Colgate, and Nabisco all were reported to be testing similar strategies of their own within a short time of P&G's decision. Again, the business maneuvers seem to fit our model of a game. ■

Games of Common Interest and Pure Conflict of Interest

▼

3. Relate oligopolistic competition to games of common interest, pure conflict of interest, and intermediate cases including the Prisoner's Dilemma.

Newspapers and the media are fond of portraying conflict and antagonism because they make good copy and arresting stories. This often carries over into their coverage of economic events. Foreign direct investment and country

9. Air fares are in an almost constant state of flux. Confronted with the special promotions and discounts offered by its rivals, American was forced to abandon its four-tier pricing in October 1992. Oligopolistic competition can, indeed, be tough. You may find it interesting to follow developments in the airline market as an ongoing application of microeconomic theory in an oligopolistic industry.

10. Eben Shapiro, "P&G Takes on the Supermarkets with Uniform Pricing," *New York Times,* April 26, 1992, Section 3, p. 5.

development in the colonial period, for example, might be erroneously described as purely exploitative. Bargaining between corporate management and a labor union might be described as a situation in which only one side can win. Howwever, such a one-sided view fails to appreciate the large number of economic and social interactions in which elements of *mutual benefit* appear.

It is just as easy to think of social interactions in which everyone wins as to think of cases in which one party wins at the expense of the other. Stopping at a red light and allowing traffic with a green light to proceed is a good example. Without such behavior, losses from accidents would be enormous. Likewise, when firms in an industry come together to form an industry association to share information about the industry, legislative concerns, information about foreign export opportunities, and so on, each firm benefits. In fact, industry associations are a common feature among U.S. industries.

Games of *common interest* are characterized by the fact that there is a unique assignment of choices for players that leads to a payoff that is best for all players. In this type of game, there is no question about what needs to be done to determine the best outcome for everyone. Assuming that all players understand the structure of the game—and there are no irrational or perverse decisions by firms that choose to accept lower payoff for themselves in order to lower the payoff to others—the choices of players will lead to the best outcome for all players as a group.

Games of *pure conflict of interest,* on the other hand, are characterized by the fact that there are no net gains to the players as a group, any increase in payoff to one player comes from a lower payoff to another player. *Zero-sum games,* so named because the payoffs to all players add to zero, are games of pure conflict of interest. Whereas in a game of common interest it may be possible for every player to win a positive payoff, in a game of pure conflict of interest there are losers as well as winners.

Oligopolistic competition, which involves elements of conflict as well as mutual benefits from collusion, lies between these two extremes. We can explain the presence of conflict and common interest in terms of a classic game: the story of the Prisoner's Dilemma.

Using the Prisoner's Dilemma to Model Oligopoly

In the scenario called the Prisoner's Dilemma, the police detain two robbery suspects and place them in separate rooms for questioning. Each prisoner is told that if he provides state's evidence to be used to convict his partner, he will be given a more lenient sentence. Each prisoner can choose whether or not to provide evidence. Figure 10.1 shows the payoff matrix.

If both prisoners refuse to provide evidence, each gets only a two-year term. However, if one prisoner provides evidence when his partner does not, his jail term is reduced to only one year while his partner gets four years. Similarly, if the partner provides evidence, the prisoner can reduce his jail

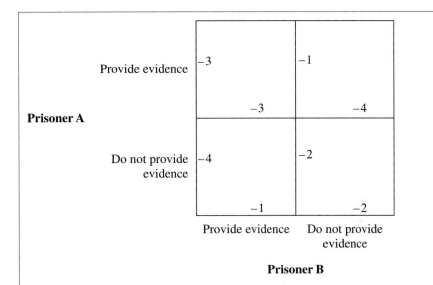

Figure 10.1 The Prisoner's Dilemma In the Prisoner's Dilemma game, the prisoners receive payoffs consisting of time in jail, represented by the negative numbers in the payoff matrix. Numbers close to zero are better: they represent fewer years in jail. Although the two prisoners together would be better off if neither provided evidence against the other, from each prisoner's point of view it is better to provide evidence than to refrain. Thus, in a one-time playing of the game, both prisoners tend to provide evidence.

term from four years to three by providing evidence himself. Since the game is symmetrical, both players have an incentive to provide state's evidence against the other, and the outcome will likely be that both receive three years in jail—even though cooperation (neither providing evidence) would have garnered each prisoner only a two-year term.

The benefits to oligopolistic firms from collusion, as well as the incentives for defection from collusion, have a structure that derives from the Prisoner's Dilemma.[11] In the Prisoner's Dilemma collusive behavior would be to refuse to provide state's evidence. For a firm it means agreeing to collusive (cartel) market pricing. For the firm, as for the prisoners, there is an advantage to collusion. However, successful deviation from the collusive solution—that is, deviation while the other player sticks to the agreement—leads to an even higher payoff for the deviating firm. At the same time, each firm's worst

11. Whereas the prisoners play their game only once, firms play their game in repeated trials. We will discuss later how repeated playing may change the outcome of the game, depending on what strategies the firms try to follow, whether it is possible to establish reputations over time for certain types of play, and so on.

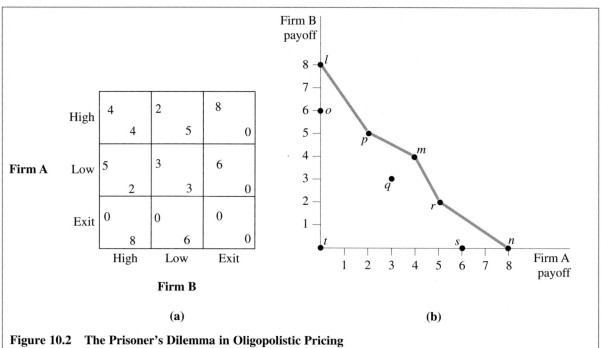

Figure 10.2   The Prisoner's Dilemma in Oligopolistic Pricing
Economic games generally include elements of both common interest and conflict. In the pricing game shown in part (a), in which each firm must decide whether to price high or low or leave the market, the outcomes include payoffs that are nonnegative for both firms, but it is impossible for both to achieve their most preferred outcomes simultaneously. If both firms remain in the market, they face a Prisoner's Dilemma pattern of payoffs. Part (b) plots the payoffs for each of the nine possible outcomes.

payoff results from sticking to the collusive solution while the other firm cheats. The ranking of payoffs for the firm is as follows:

1. Successful cheating on the collusive solution
2. Collusive solution
3. Noncollusive competitive solution
4. Successful cheating on the collusive solution by the other firm

In addition to the potental gain from collusion, therefore, there is a carrot-and-stick cause for collusion to break down: If you break the agreement while your partner does not, *you do better*; if your partner breaks the agreement and you do not, *you do worse*.

Figure 10.2 shows a game that might be played by two firms competing for sales of different brands of a product. Each firm has three choices shown in part (a): price its product high, price its product low, or exit the market. The profit that each firm earns depends on its choice and on the choice of the other firm. Assume, for example, that Firm B decides to price high. The profit to Firm A if it also prices high is 4. If Firm A prices low, however, it will capture market share at the expense of Firm B and receive profit of 5. If the firm leaves the market, it earns zero. If Firm B prices low, Firm A earns only 2 if it prices high, but earns 3 if it also prices low, and earns zero if it leaves the market. Finally, if Firm B exits the market, Firm A earns 8 if it prices high, 6 if it prices low, and zero if it exits the market. Firm B's options are identical to Firm A's.

In this game, each firm does better by playing than by not playing. If the other firm stays in the market, the best choice for each firm separately is to price low. If both firms price low, each firm earns payoff 3. However, if both firms could agree to price high with neither firm deviating, they could earn payoffs of 4. This game therefore has the following features:

1. Firms remaining in the market earn a positive payoff.
2. There is room for cooperation to improve the return to each firm.
3. Given the cooperative solution of both firms pricing high, there is incentive for each firm to deviate from this outcome to improve its payoff at the expense of the other.

These elements of common interest and conflict of interest describe important features of oligopoly.

Part (b) plots the payoff pairs for the game. For example, point *m* shows the outcome when both firms price high, and point *r* shows the outcome if Firm A decides to price low when Firm B prices high. The line forms a frontier, connecting those outcomes for which no other outcome provides gains for one firm without harming the other. Firm A would like to move the outcome from *m* to *r*, just as Firm B would like to move the outcome from *m* to *p*. If both firms try to do this by choosing to price low, however, they end up at point *q*, which lies below the frontier. Points on either axis are possible only if a firm exits the market.

Airlines and Oligopolistic Schizophrenia?

As noted earlier, Robert Crandall's American Airlines came under criticism in 1992 for its aggressively competitive pricing strategy. Yet less than 10 years earlier, the same American Airlines ran afoul of a prominently reported suit charging it with the opposite behavior: seeking to collude with its competitors in fixing price.[12] In late 1981 and early 1982, American Airlines and Braniff International, both based in Dallas, were engaged in a price war. Braniff had resorted to two-for-one sales, offering travelers one free trip for every full-fare ticket. In a conversation later made public in the national press, Mr. Crandall was reported as saying to Braniff's president, "I have a suggestion for you. Raise your . . . fares 20 percent. . . . You'll make more money and I will, too."[13]

12. Robert D. Hershey, Jr., "American Airlines Target of Suit: Head Is Accused of Overtures to Braniff on Raising Fares," *New York Times,* February 24, 1983, pp. A1, D4; and "Blunt Talk on the Phone," *New York Times,* February 24, 1983, p. D4.
13. "Blunt Talk on the Phone," *New York Times,* February 24, 1983, p. D4. Proposing to fix prices violates section 2 of the Sherman Antitrust Act, which deals with attempts to monopolize an industry. After a 1983 suit by the Justice Departrment, American promised not to engage in such activity in the future and apparently hasn't.

That American should find itself the target of complaints charging it with too little and too much competition might seem to indicate schizophrenia. Both responses, however, are natural consequences of oligopolistic competition.

10.3 Game Strategies and Solutions

Market outcomes for oligopoly depend on the way firms perceive their options and what they do on the basis of what they believe other firms will do. We have already described one strategy that firms in an oligopoly might follow if it is available: collusion or cooperation. We can now consider other strategies and a solution concept that allows us to determine the market outcome in oligopoly. The choice of strategies by firms determines the solution of the game, which in oligopolistic competition is the market equilibrium.

Cooperative Strategies

▼

4. Explain the differences among cooperative solutions to a game and dominant, rational, and maximin strategies.

Games in which players may choose cooperative strategies, as in the collusion between firms in oligopolistic markets, are often called *cooperative games.* Cooperative strategies are usually characterized by the ability of players to make payments to other players in addition to the payoffs listed in the game itself. We already know that if two players do not cooperate, the Prisoner's Dilemma game leads to the outcome in which each player plays the noncooperative strategy (provide state's evidence) and the payoff is low. Side payments would allow the players to distribute the joint benefits from playing cooperatively, so that each would be better off.

As we have discussed, cooperative solutions are not always possible in oligopoly, because of the difficulty of reaching and enforcing an agreement and because collusion runs afoul of antitrust law. We therefore turn our attention to noncooperative strategies and solutions for games.

Dominant Strategies

Without cooperation, a firm is no longer certain what the other firm will do. However, if there is one choice that is best for the firm regardless of what the other firm chooses, the game has a *dominant strategy* for that firm.

> In a game, a **dominant strategy** is a choice of action that leads to the best payoff for the player regardless of the other players' choices. If the player's best choice depends on the choices other players make, the player does not have a dominant strategy.

Dominant strategies, when they are available, provide the rational option for a player in a noncooperative game, because any other choice leads to a lower payoff. For a firm participating in an industry association, it may always be best for the firm to share information (perhaps even proprietary information) about, say, harmful consequences to the industry of a particular piece of legislation. If this is the best option regardless of what other firms in the industry do, sharing the information is a dominant strategy. Whether a firm is able to choose a dominant strategy depends primarily on the situation in which it finds itself.

APPLICATION: AT&T's Advertising Counterattack

Long-distance telephone service is provided by three main firms and a number of smaller rivals. AT&T, the industry long-distance giant, accounts for two-thirds of the market (66 percent of 1992 market revenues), followed by MCI at 15 percent; Sprint at 9 percent; Alascom, Allnet, ATC, Cable&Wireless, Metromedia/ITT, Williams and Wiltel/Telesphere with 1 percent each; and all others at 3 percent.[14] AT&T once controlled virtually all of the long-distance market; as a result of antitrust actions, however, other companies were able to enter the market, and AT&T's share declined. Industry observers believe that AT&T had to wait until its market share fell sufficiently so as not to raise the ire of Justice Department antitrust lawyers. Once that point had been reached, AT&T's dominant strategy involved heavy advertising along with price competition to slow down and reverse its loss of market share. This strategy was called for regardless of the actions of rivals, because as the established company AT&T could only lose by continuing a passive stance in the face of new competitive challenges.

In 1989 AT&T began a highly visible and massive advertising counterattack, making AT&T the seventh-biggest advertiser nationwide. The company spent $797 million on advertising in 1990, for instance, compared to Sprint's $155 million. Coupled with price reductions, including an average reduction of 40 percent on direct-dialed, state-to-state calls since 1984, the counterattack seems to have shown results. After 1989 Sprint gained only 1 percent in market share, and the share of the smaller carriers fell. ■

If dominant strategies were always available, game theory would be very simple: each firm would play the dominant strategy. Unfortunately, many games do not have a dominant strategy for each player. In these cases we must look for other rational strategies.

Rational and Maximin Strategies

Even though there may not be a dominant strategy for each player, there may nevertheless be a rational payoff-maximizing strategy for each player. For example, part (a) of Figure 10.3 shows a game in which the player we will call MCI/Sprint does not have a dominant strategy because MCI/Sprint is better off advertising heavily only if AT&T does not advertise. Otherwise, it

14. "The Loneliness of the Long-Distance Telephone Company," *The Economist,* June 6, 1992, pp. 73–74.

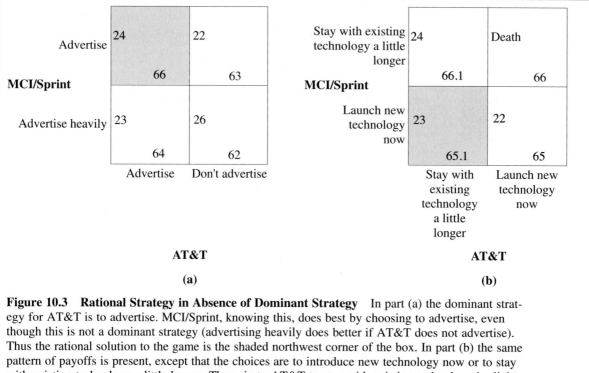

Figure 10.3   Rational Strategy in Absence of Dominant Strategy   In part (a) the dominant strategy for AT&T is to advertise. MCI/Sprint, knowing this, does best by choosing to advertise, even though this is not a dominant strategy (advertising heavily does better if AT&T does not advertise). Thus the rational solution to the game is the shaded northwest corner of the box. In part (b) the same pattern of payoffs is present, except that the choices are to introduce new technology now or to stay with existing technology a little longer. The gain to AT&T to stay with existing technology is slight, but the damage to MCI/Sprint is "death" (end of the company) if AT&T chooses new technology. To avoid death, MCI/Sprint may decide to maximize its minimum payoff. In that case, the solution to the game is the shaded southwest corner of the box.

should advertise at a lower level. In this case, we treat payoffs as revenues minus advertising costs, measured as a percentage of the market.[15] Is there a rational strategy for MCI/Sprint?

AT&T has a dominant strategy of advertising no matter what MCI/Sprint does. Thus MCI/Sprint might reason as follows: "AT&T is a rational firm, and so will choose to advertise because it is in its own interest to do so. Thus we definitely should choose 'Advertise' instead of 'Advertise heavily.'" The *rational* solution to the game would therefore be the shaded northwest box in part (a).

Notice that before we could determine the rational strategy, we needed to take into account how the firm believed the other firm would play. If the beliefs of MCI/Sprint about AT&T were different, the solution might have been different. To illustrate, part (b) of the figure reproduces the same game, leaving the structure of payoffs the same but modifying the relative sizes of

15. The way a firm chooses the profit-maximizing level of advertising was discussed in Chapter 9.

the gains and losses. The issue is whether to launch a new technology now or stay with existing technology a little longer. The dominant strategy for AT&T is to delay launch of the new technology, in which case it is better for MCI/Sprint to delay as well. However, the gains to AT&T from delay are slight, and if AT&T decides to launch the new technology while MCI/Sprint stays with the old, the results are devastating to MCI/Sprint—"death," meaning end of the firm.

To minimize its risk, MCI/Sprint might choose the action that *maximizes its minimum payoff.* This *maximin strategy* means in essence that the firm focuses its efforts on making the worst that can happen as acceptable as possible. It gives up the prospect of better payoffs at the high end to ensure that the worst payoffs are avoided. In the example, if MCI/Sprint chooses to stay with existing technology, the worst that can happen is "death." If it chooses to launch new technology, the worst that can happen is a payoff of 22. Since it wants to limit risk, MCI/Sprint will choose to launch the new technology unless it is absolutely certain that AT&T will choose to stay with existing technology. If MCI/Sprint plays the maximin strategy (which, under the circumstances, it might be expected to do!) and AT&T plays the dominant strategy, the solution to the game is in the shaded southwest panel.

Unfortunately, there is no simple rule for finding firms' rational strategies in every game; oligopolistic competition is too diverse for that. However, as we have just seen, it is sometimes possible to describe the competitors' actions in such a way that their best responses can be identified. In other cases, adding more information about the way firms compete allows us to find the equilibrium.

Nash Equilibrium

▼
5. Create a simple game that has a Nash equilibrium.

Firms should always follow rational strategies, but what is considered rational frequently depends on the firm's beliefs about how other firms may respond. Once chosen, strategies determine the solution of the game. In oligopolistic markets, the solution to the game is the market equilibrium. A solution or equilibrium implies that no firm believes it can improve its profit by doing something different than what it is doing, given its beliefs about other firms and what they are doing. The idea that equilibrium for a game requires each player's actions to be the best they can be, given what all other players are doing, comes from economist John Nash, who introduced this concept in 1951.[16]

> A **Nash equilibrium** *for a game is a choice of strategy by each player such that each player believes it cannot improve its payoff by any other choice, given the strategies of the other players.*

16. John F. Nash, "Non-cooperative Games," *Annals of Mathematics,* 54 (1951), pp. 286–295.

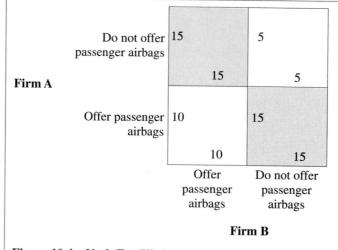

Figure 10.4 showing a payoff matrix for Firm A (rows) and Firm B (columns):

Firm A \ Firm B	Offer passenger airbags	Do not offer passenger airbags
Do not offer passenger airbags	15 / 15	5 / 5
Offer passenger airbags	10 / 10	15 / 15

Figure 10.4   Nash Equilibrium   In this game there is no dominant strategy for either firm. However, the two shaded boxes are Nash equilibria because, given the choice of the other firm, each firm's choice represents the highest payoff.

We can illustrate Nash equilibrium first in terms of a simple two-choice decision, and then in terms of the choice of quantity that a firm might make in an oligopolistic market.

In the game portrayed in Figure 10.4, two automobile firms are considering whether to offer standard passenger-side airbags. Offering airbags increases safety but raises cost. In this market the payoffs are symmetrical, but the two firms are better off appealing to different parts of the market. If one firm offers airbags for safety-conscious buyers, the other does better by offering cars without standard airbags for cost-conscious buyers. If both firms appeal to the same side of the market, they are better off offering airbags. To find a Nash equilibrium, we look for a strategy for each firm such that, given the strategy of the other, neither firm wants to change its own strategy. There are two such situations, in the shaded northwest and southeast boxes where one firm offers airbags and the other does not. Since each firm is doing the best for itself given the choice of the other, the shaded boxes are Nash equilibria.

APPLICATION: Wars in Snack Food and Pizza

The markets in snack food and pizza reveal information about Nash equilibria and rational strategies in oligopolistic markets under changing conditions. In the case of the snack food market, representing more than $12 billion per year in revenues in 1990,[17] the agent for change was Eagle Snacks, a division of Anheuser-Busch Company. A negligible player for years, Eagle displayed newfound aggressiveness, increasing its market share to 5 percent in 1990 and making no secret of ongoing plans for the following year to increase its shelf space in supermarkets by 30 percent and increase spending for feature displays by 15 percent.

What was described as a once-quiet market, accustomed to minor scrapes between the dominant Frito-Lay (the most profitable unit of PepsiCo, accounting for 41 percent of the market) and smaller regional rivals, found itself no longer quiet. Rational strategies that were appropriate in the earlier market equilibrium were no longer appropriate. New competitive strategies took the form of saturating stores with promotions for snack products, increased advertising (Eagle had increased its ad budget for tortilla chips by 50 percent), price reductions (eight national brands in an Atlanta supermarket discounted their prices from $1.39 to $.99), and competition for more supermarkets shelf space. In some cases, distributors were reported to be asking for, and getting, up to $1,000 per year for a single foot of shelf space. Although it had not lost market share, Frito-Lay responded vigorously, but the company suffered a 4-percent drop in profits in the first quarter of 1991, its first decline in five years. At Borden, Inc., the maker of Wise potato chips and other products, profit fell 12.4 percent, and market share was down by 1 percent of the market, as it was for Keebler, another major firm.

At the same time that more aggressive competition signaled the end of the previous Nash equilibrium in the snack food market, decreased competition appeared ready to characterize a new equilibrium in the pizza market. In this case the agent of change was an increase in the price of cheese, including a 27-percent jump in the price of mozzarella and a 20-percent jump for other varieties in little more than half a year.[18] For more than two years previous to the cheese price increase in 1991, pizza makers such as Domino's Pizza had steadily done battle with one another, discounting the price of pizza and offering more and more cheese on their products. In the case of a cheese pizza, cheese can make up over half the cost, and in the case of a pepperoni pizza, it can make up nearly 40 percent of cost.

The reactions to this cost increase illustrate the nature of oligopolistic competition from the perspective of national chains. Though earnings of firms such as National Pizza, Inc. (the franchisee of Pizza Hut) were already falling, no firm wanted to be the first to raise prices. ''The competition won't let you,'' said a representative of Godfather's Pizza Inc. The same sentiment applied to the other weapon of war, cheese: ''We're not about to jeopardize quality by reducing our cheese, so there's not a lot we can do.'' The translation is: Given what other firms are doing, our present strategy is Nash.

17. Laurie M. Grossman, ''Price Wars Bring Flavor to Once-Quiet Snack Market,'' *Wall Street Journal,* May 23, 1991, p. B1.
18. Richard Gibson and Scott Kilman, ''Cost of Cheese May Turn Pizza into Pricey Pie,'' *Wall Street Journal,* August 26, 1991, p. B1.

From the perspective of the market, however, the steep rise in cheese price, representing an increase of as much as 9 or 10 percent in the cost of ingredients per pizza, must eventually be reflected in prices. At that time the market will settle into a new Nash equilibrium—at least until such time as conditions change again. ■

Relating Game Solutions to Market Equilibria

Up to now, we have been able to describe the firm's oligopolistic strategy in terms of simple two-choice games. The same principles apply, however, to cases in which there are a large or even infinite number of choices, as when the firm must decide what quantity to produce. In this section we relate rational strategies and Nash equilibrium to competition in which the firm chooses from a range of alternatives.

Take a simple case where a number of firms, each with constant marginal cost of $10 and no fixed cost, compete for sales in a market whose demand curve is given by

$$q^D = 100 - p.$$

We want to look for a Nash equilibrium. The payoffs to each firm are the firm's profits. If q_i is the quantity of Firm i, market price is given by $100 - \Sigma_i q_i$, where $\Sigma_i q_i$ is the sum of quantities for firms in the market. The profit of Firm 1, say, is given by $\Pi = (100 - \Sigma_i q_i)q_1 - 10q_1$. Thus, given the quantity choices of other firms and the quantity of Firm 1, we can compute profit. To diagram the effect of firms' choices, we will assume that there are just two firms considering 16 options. The issue at stake is how much each firm should produce for sale, given that neither firm will be able to make a positive profit if price drops below $10. The $10 price is reached for a total quantity of 90 units. Instead of two alternatives, each firm has a list of 16 output quantities ranging from 0 units to 90 units from which it can choose. Nash equilibrium will consist of a quantity choice for each firm such that the firm does not want to change its quantity, given the choice of the other firm.

Figure 10.5 displays the game with the two firms' profits shown in the payoff matrix. The horizontal axis shows Firm 2's output choice, and the vertical axis shows Firm 1's output. Cells in the northeast part of the matrix show no profits, because the two firms' total output for these cells has driven the market price to zero. Since we know that neither firm will operate in the region of negative profits, these cells can be ignored as potential equilibria.

Rather than check cell by cell, we can find the Nash equilibria for this game by fixing the output of Firm 2 and finding the cell that gives the greatest profit for Firm 1. For example, fixing the output of Firm 2 at 24 units, we read Firm 1's profits for its different choices of output in the column of cells above Firm 2's output choice 24. The cell with the highest profit for Firm 1 is the border-shaded cell showing 30 units of output for Firm 1 and $1,080 profit. Doing this for each column (representing a different fixed level of output for Firm 2) leads to the downward-sloping line of border-shaded cells.

Firm 1's output choice (rows) vs. Firm 2's output choice (columns). Each cell shows Firm 1's profit (top) and Firm 2's profit (bottom).

Firm 1 \ Firm 2	0	6	12	18	24	30	37	44	49	54	62	66	74	78	85	90
90	0 / 0															
85	425 / 0	0 / 0														
78	936 / 0	468 / 36	0 / 0													
74	1184 / 0	740 / 60	296 / 48	0 / 0												
66	1584 / 0	1188 / 108	792 / 144	396 / 108	0 / 0											
62	1736 / 0	1364 / 132	992 / 192	620 / 180	248 / 96	0 / 0										
54	1944 / 0	1620 / 180	1296 / 288	972 / 324	648 / 288	324 / 180	0 / 0									
49	2009 / 0	1715 / 210	1421 / 348	1127 / 414	833 / 408	539 / 330	196 / 148	0 / 0								
44	2024 / 0	1760 / 240	1496 / 408	1232 / 504	968 / 528	704 / 480	396 / 333	88 / 88	0 / 0							
37	1961 / 0	1739 / 282	1517 / 492	1295 / 630	1073 / 696	851 / 690	592 / 592	333 / 396	148 / 196	0 / 0						
30	1800 / 0	1620 / 324	1440 / 576	1260 / 756	1080 / 864	900 / 900	690 / 851	480 / 704	330 / 539	180 / 324	0 / 0					
24	1584 / 0	1440 / 360	1296 / 648	1152 / 864	1008 / 1008	864 / 1080	696 / 1073	528 / 968	408 / 833	288 / 648	96 / 248	0 / 0				
18	1296 / 0	1188 / 396	1080 / 720	972 / 972	864 / 1152	756 / 1260	630 / 1295	504 / 1232	414 / 1127	324 / 972	180 / 620	108 / 396	0 / 0			
12	936 / 0	864 / 432	792 / 792	720 / 1080	648 / 1296	576 / 1440	492 / 1517	408 / 1496	348 / 1421	288 / 1296	192 / 992	144 / 792	48 / 296	0 / 0		
6	504 / 0	468 / 468	432 / 864	396 / 1188	360 / 1440	324 / 1620	282 / 1739	240 / 1760	210 / 1715	180 / 1620	132 / 1364	108 / 1188	60 / 740	36 / 468	0 / 0	
0	0 / 0	0 / 504	0 / 936	0 / 1296	0 / 1584	0 / 1800	0 / 1961	0 / 2024	0 / 2009	0 / 1944	0 / 1736	0 / 1584	0 / 1184	0 / 936	0 / 425	0 / 0

Figure 10.5 Nash Equilibrium for Oligopoly with Many Quantity Choices Available In this game each firm has 16 options for what quantity to produce. The payoff for each firm indicates the profit. The quantity corresponding to the border-shaded cell in each column is the profit-maximizing quantity for Firm 1, given the output of Firm 2. The center-shaded cell in each row gives the profit-maximizing quantity for Firm 2, given the output of Firm 1. The Nash equilibrium for this game is given by the one fully shaded cell, where each firm achieves highest profit given the quantity choice of the other firm.

Turning next to Firm 2, we can find the cells that give the highest profit for Firm 2 with the output of Firm 1 fixed. This means finding the cell of highest Firm 2 profit for each row in the box. These cells are marked by center shading. If Firm 1 produces 6 units of output, for example, the highest profit for Firm 2 is $1,760 at output quantity 44. The center-shaded cells form another downward-sloping string that cuts the border-shaded line of cells at the single darkly shaded cell, which corresponds to 30 units of output for each firm. This intersection is a Nash equilibrium: Given 30 units of output by Firm 2, Firm 1 cannot improve its profits by moving to any other cells in the column, and given 30 units of output by Firm 1, Firm 2 cannot improve its profits by moving to any other cell in the row.

Visually inspecting Figure 10.5, it seems reasonable to expect that if we increased the number of quantities from which each firm could choose, the shaded cells would get smaller and each string of shaded cells would begin to look like a line. This is in fact what happens. The intersection of the two strings of cells (now lines) would become a point, and this point would indicate the Nash equilibrium. In the next section we will apply our knowledge of game solutions to describe different Nash equilibria in oligopolistic markets. Instead of arrangements of cells and payoff matrices, however, we will work with lines of the type that Figure 10.5 should exhibit if we extended the range of choices.

10.4 Types of Oligopolistic Equilibria

▼
6. How do oligopolistic equilibria relate to firms' choices of strategy and the solution to a game?

In solving the game described in Figure 10.5, we have already applied the techniques needed to find the market equilibria in oligopolistic markets. In this section we reapply these techniques to describe different types of oligopolistic competition and their market equilibria, though the payoff matrices are replaced by their line equivalents. The different equilibria have in common the properties that (1) firms choose rational strategies to maximize profit given their beliefs about other firms' behavior, and (2) Nash equilibrium is the solution for the game.

Cournot Equilibria

Let's assume that you are the chief executive officer of a firm selling electric can openers. Again, so that we can draw the relevant diagrams, we assume that there are only two firms in the market, though the same principles apply if there are more. You and your competitor sell virtually identical products to a market with a demand curve (in units of thousands) given as

$$q^D = 100 - p.$$

If the price of the can opener is $40 per unit, for instance, 60,000 units will be demanded. How do you select the right price and quantity to maximize your profit?

To answer, you must be able to compute your firm's anticipated profit, which depends on what you think your competitor will do in response to a change in your price-quantity pair. In this case, assume that you and your competitor must choose ahead of time what quantity to produce before bringing it to market. Once brought to market, your quantity and the other firm's quantity are sold at the price that equilibrates demand and supply. Both you and your competitor know what quantity the other sold last year, but you have to decide what to do this year.

▼
7. Construct an example of Cournot competition.

Although we have not found out yet what the equilibrium in the can opener market is, let us assume that last year was an equilibrium and see what things look like from the firm's point of view. Assume that your competitor (Firm 2) sells 30,000 can openers. If you decide to increase the quantity of can openers that your firm sells, you believe that your competitor will still bring 30,000 units to market. Oligopolists that act as if other firms' quantities are fixed are often referred to as Cournot oligopolists or Cournot competitors, after French economist Augustin Cournot, who first described the implications of this type of behavior in 1838.

> In **Cournot competition,** firms assume that competitor's quantities are fixed and decide simultaneously what quantities to produce to maximize profit.

In the scenario we have described so far, you believe that the other firm will hold quantity fixed because you both must decide your quantity before bringing it to market. However, assuming that the other firm will hold sales fixed might also be justified by your belief that the other firm will do whatever is necessary to protect its sales, even if it has the ability to adjust quantity in response to your choice. Market share is important, and keeping sales from declining in response to a competitor's quantity increase might therefore be a reasonable response.

Assuming that the competitor sells 30,000 units allows you to determine what your profits will be for each output level you choose. You maximize profits by choosing the highest-profit quantity. Finding your profit-maximizing quantity for each quantity that Firm 2 might choose and plotting the quantity pairs, we graph the line through points *b, d,* and *e* in Figure 10.6.[19] Because the resulting curve portrays all of the responses or reactions of Firm 1 to the production level chosen by Firm 2, it is called Firm 1's *reaction*

19. If the other firm produces q_2 units, market price is $(100 - q_1 - q_2)$ if you choose q_1 units. Revenue for Firm 1 is therefore equal to $(100 - q_1 - q_2)q_1$. Maximum profit for Firm 1 occurs at the quantity where MC cuts MR for the demand curve $p = (100 - q_1 - q_2)$ from below (treating q_2 as constant throughout the computation of MR). For our example, MR is the straight line $MR = 100 - 2q_1 - q_2$. The marginal cost of can opener production is constant at \$10. This cuts the MR curve at $q_1 = 45 - q_2/2$. Thus, if the competitor produces 30,000 units, Firm 1 responds by selling 30,000 units. Since the market demand curve is $q^D = 100 - p$, we know that the price Firm 1 charges, which is also the market price, is given by $60 = 100 - p$, or $p = \$40$.

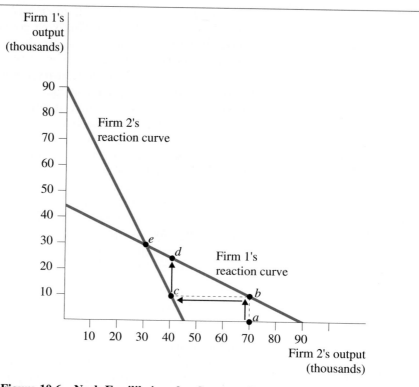

Figure 10.6   Nash Equilibrium for Cournot Competitors   Plotting all the quantities that Firm 1 would choose given the quantity of the other firm gives us Firm 1's reaction curve. The same method produces Firm 2's reaction curve. Because the curves represent each firm's highest profit for each choice by the other, Nash equilibrium occurs where the two reaction curves cross at point *e*. Only at point *e* is there no incentive for either firm to change its production. At point *a*, in contrast, Firm 1 would want to move to point *b*; then Firm 2 would want to move to point *c*; and so on.

curve.[20] Following the same procedure for Firm 2 gives us Firm 2's reaction curve. In the example shown here, Firm 2 was identical to Firm 1, so Firm 2's reaction curve is the same as Firm 1's except that it is oriented toward the other axis.

Exactly as we did when the firms had a limited number of choices, we find the Cournot equilibrium at the intersection of the two reaction curves,

20. In general, if demand is given by $q^D = a - bp$, where a and b are positive constants, and the quantity of Firm 1, q_1, plus the quantity of Firm 2, q_2, equals q^D, the revenue of Firm 1 is given by $pq_1 = [a/b - (q_1 + q_2)/b]q_1$. Marginal revenue for Firm 1 is therefore $MR_1 = a/b - (2q_1 + q_2)/b$. Firm 1's reaction curve consists of the values of q_1 that solve $MR_1 = MC$ given q_2. In the example of the text, $a = 100$, $b = 1$, and $MC = 10$. Thus the reaction curve is given by $q_1 = 45 - q_2/2$.

point *e*. At point *e*, each firm is maximizing its profit given the quantity chosen by the other. A quick check of other points shows that point *e* is the only possible Nash equilibrium. For example, at point *a* Firm 2 produces 70 thousand units. Firm 1 would raise its profit by producing 10,000 units at point *b*. Given production of 10,000 units by Firm 1, however, Firm 2 can raise its profit by producing 40,000 units at point *c*. Firm 1 would then want to produce 25,000 units to maximize its profit at point *d*, and so on. Only at the intersection of the reaction curves of both firms is the profit of each maximized given the output of the other.

The Cournot model of competition applies best in situations in which (a) firms make prior decisions about what quantity to bring to market on a more or less equal basis, meaning that no individual firm has an advantage in being able to choose quantity first (we discuss the effects of a first-mover advantage later in the chapter); and (b) once the quantity decision is made, the firm is committed. Products for which the size of the production run must be pre-determined—for instance, goods for a seasonal market, such as Christmas toys—may satisfy these characteristics. Once the product is available for sale, the market determines the market clearing price. If toy firms plan correctly, there will be little stock to clear out in January sales.

Bertrand Equilibria

▼
8. Relate Bertrand competition to Cournot competition and the Stackelberg leader-follower model.

In Cournot competition, each firm believes that the other firm will hold its quantity fixed. In other types of markets, price may be the more natural competitive variable, and firms will compete by choosing price in advance. Joseph Bertrand, a French economist of the late 1800s, suggested that price-competitive firms might behave differently than Cournot oligopolists, holding *price* (instead of quantity) constant in response to changes in the actions of their competitors.

> In **Bertrand competition,** *firms assume that competitors' prices are fixed and decide simultaneously what prices to charge to maximize profit.*

What sorts of markets fit the Bertrand model? If you are in a market where firms sell perfectly homogeneous goods, setting your price below your competitor's means that all of the market buys from you. However, very rarely do firms in oligopolistic markets supply *perfectly* homogeneous goods. Rather, the competing goods are more likely to be close substitutes. This means that prices can differ by an amount that depends on the degree of substitutability without driving all of the market demand to the lower-priced good. We can therefore discuss Bertrand competition in terms of competing substitutes.

As we did with Cournot competitors, we first characterize the rational strategy of each firm, given its beliefs about the other firm and the type of competition present, and then we find the Nash equilibrium. Let Firms 1 and 2 face the following demand curves:

Firm 1's demand: $\quad q_1 = 100 - 2p_1 + p_2,$

Firm 2's demand: $\quad q_2 = 100 - 2p_2 + p_1.$

As these equations show, (1) an increase in the price of the competing product increases demand; (2) an increase in price of the good itself reduces demand; and (3) dollar for dollar, a reduction in the price of the good has greater effect on demand than an equivalent increase in the price of the competing good. As before, we assume that each firm has a marginal cost of $10 per unit.

If Firm 1 believes that Firm 2's *price* will remain fixed, Firm 1's demand curve becomes a standard downward-sloping demand curve with the competing price determining its location. If the competitor keeps its price at $40, for example, Firm 1 maximizes profit by finding the point where MC cuts MR from below. This occurs at quantity 60 and price $40.[21] This is the response or reaction of Firm 1 to Firm 2's setting its price at $40.

Following the above procedure to find Firm 1's reaction to *every* price that Firm 2 chooses, we can generate Firm 1's reaction curve, plotted as curve *A* in Figure 10.7. The axes in Figure 10.7 represent the prices of each firm, because Bertrand competitors compete in price. If Firm 2 is expected to hold its price fixed at a low level, Firm 1's effective demand will be small. The best that Firm 1 can do, therefore, is to charge a low price. On the other hand, if Firm 2 chooses a high price, then Firm 1's demand curve will lie further to the right. In that event, Firm 1's best price response will be higher. The net effect is that Firm 1 has an upward-sloping reaction curve. Plotting Firm 2's reaction curve leads to the second curve in Figure 10.7, labeled *B*.

As before, the equilibrium must be a point that lies on both of the reaction curves. This requirement is met at the intersection of the reaction curves, point *e*, where neither firm has an incentive to change what it is doing given the other's choice.

Stackelberg Leader-Follower Equilibria

In Bertrand and Cournot competition, the two firms are more or less equivalent in that they make their choices at the same time. When one firm can make its choice (move) first, an inherent asymmetry enters that the first mover can exploit. This leads to yet another type of oligopoly equilibrium, which we will examine by returning to the can opener market.

In this case, you are the head of the company that first invented electric can openers and so had the exclusive patent on them for 17 years. Your

---

21. If demand for the output of Firm 1 is $q_1 = e - fp_1 + gp_2$, where e, f, and g are positive constants, $p_1 = (e/f) + (gp_2/f) - (q_1/f)$ and revenue is $[(e/f) + (gp_2/f) - (q_1/f)]q_1$. Assuming p_2 is fixed, marginal revenue for Firm 1 is $MR = (e/f) + (gp_2/f) - (2q_1/f)$. Firm 1 maximizes profit at $MR = MC = 10$, implying that $q_1 = (e + gp_2)/2 - 10f/2 = 60$, when $e = 100, f = 2$, and $g = 1$ as in the text. This, in turn, implies that Firm 1 chooses price $p_1 = \$40$ on its demand curve.

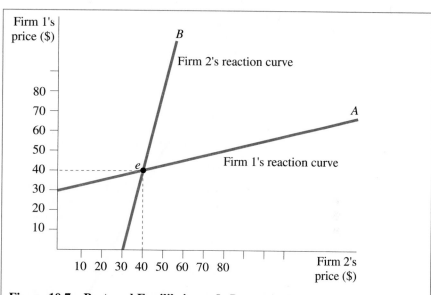

Figure 10.7 Bertrand Equilibrium In Bertrand price competition between substitute goods, each firm believes the others will hold their prices
fixed in response to changes in its price. This implies a demand curve for
each firm from which the best price can be found given the prices charged
by other firms. Plotting all such best prices gives each firm's reaction
curve, as shown in the two-firm case here. The reaction curves are upward-sloping because the higher one firm sets its price, the higher the
other firm's price can be.

patent has just expired, and a large manufacturer of other electric appliances
has entered the electric can opener market with the same manufacturing costs
that you have. Because your product was the first on the market, you have
the prior position in the market: you can pick an output quantity and hold to
it in the face of competition from your new rival.

To show how you would decide what quantity to produce, Figure 10.8
displays the reaction curve of your competitor, Firm 2. The figure assumes
the same market demand as in the Cournot example ($q^D = 100 - p$), and
the reaction curve is found using the same method as before. Given Firm 2's
reaction curve, you can now figure out what your profit will be for each
choice of output level, because you know that the other firm will react to
your choice with the quantity given by the reaction curve. Knowing each
firm's output means that you can calculate market price. From market price,
your output, and your cost function, you can calculate your firm's profits.

It follows that your firm has a profit level corresponding to each point on
Firm 2's reaction curve. For example, assume you decide to produce and sell

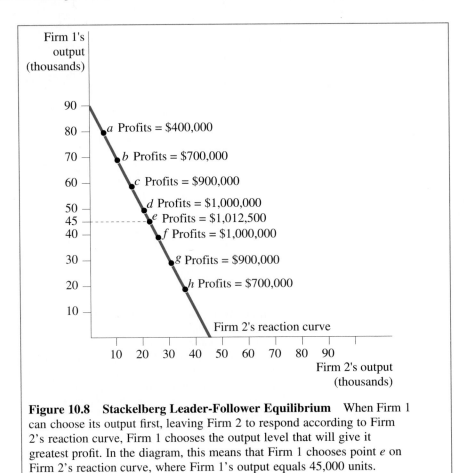

Figure 10.8   Stackelberg Leader-Follower Equilibrium   When Firm 1 can choose its output first, leaving Firm 2 to respond according to Firm 2's reaction curve, Firm 1 chooses the output level that will give it greatest profit. In the diagram, this means that Firm 1 chooses point *e* on Firm 2's reaction curve, where Firm 1's output equals 45,000 units.

80,000 can openers. Firm 2 will respond with 5,000 units, corresponding to point *a* on its reaction curve. With 85,000 can openers on the market, price will be given by $85 = 100 - p$, or $15 per unit. With a cost of $10 per unit, your firm's profits will therefore be

$$\Pi = \$15 \times 80,000 - \$10 \times 80,000 = \$400,000$$

This is the profit shown for point *a*. Proceeding in this way for other points generates the profits shown for points *b* through *h*.[22] The highest profit possible on the curve occurs at point *e*. Consequently, you decide to produce

22. In general, if Firm 2's reaction curve is given by $q_2 = d - cq_1$ and demand is given by $q^D = a - bp$, where a, b, c, and d are positive constants, then Firm 1's revenue is $pq_1 = (1/b)[(a - d) + (c - 1)q_1]q_1$, and the marginal revenue of Firm 1 (if Firm 2 acts as a follower) is $MR = (1/b)[(a - d) + 2(c - 1)q_1]$. Solving for $MR = MC$, where MC is Firm 1's marginal cost, determines the profit-maximizing Stackelberg leader output choice.

45,000 electric can openers, knowing that Firm 2 will respond by producing 22,500 and causing market price to drop to $32.50 from the level where it was when you were the only seller.

The type of oligopolistic competition just described is often called a *Stackelberg leader-follower solution* (named for yet another economist who first studied it). One firm (the first mover) acts as a *leader* in making its choice, and the other firms (the second movers) *follow* by choosing the corresponding points on their reaction curves.

> In **Stackelberg leader-follower competition,** *one firm (the leader) sets its output before other firms (the followers) set their output. Follower firms treat the output of other firms as constant in deciding what quantity to produce to maximize profit.*

A leader-follower model of quantity competition is appropriate when one firm is dominant in the market and makes its output choice in such a way that other firms are left to react as best they can. We can also apply the leader-follower approach to price competition. The dominant firm in the market sets its price, and follower firms choose their best responses.

Pre-emptive Threat Equilibria and Limit Pricing

▼
9. What is the difference between a pre-emptive threat equilibrium and a Stackelberg leader-follower solution?

Closely related to the Stackelberg leader-follower solution is the *pre-emptive* or *threat* solution. In this solution the leader benefits from *threatening* an action that induces the other firm to respond as the threatener wishes. Unlike the Stackelberg leader-follower solution, the threat itself need not be carried out—its presence is sufficient.

> In a **pre-emptive threat equilibrium** *the dominant or pre-empting firm induces other firms to make choices favorable to itself by threatening to take harmful actions if other choices are made.*

As an example, your can opener firm might threaten to raise production to 90,000 units if any new firm attempts to enter the market. The threatened increase in production would lower market price to $10, meaning that the entrant could not make positive profits. As long as other firms believe the pre-emptive threat, the existing firm can produce at whatever level it chooses, secure in the knowledge that it can prevent entry. In effect, its threat has converted the oligopolistic competition into a monopoly. Whether it can sustain its position depends on how firmly potential entrants believe the threat.

If the existing firm finds that economic profits at the monopoly level cause potential competitors to attempt entry, a variation on the threat equilibrium might be tried. Instead of fending off entrants by threat, the firm might decide to limit its price so as not to look too profitable or make the market appear too enticing. Limit-pricing equilibria of this type require the incumbent firm to balance higher profit against prospective costs from potential entry when it decides what price to charge.

The Kinked Demand Curve

Not all oligopolistic markets are as intensely competitive as others. Equilibrium in some industries might involve a degree of inertia and price stability that firms are reluctant to upset because of the potential losses that a heavy round of price wars might entail. As we saw in the case of the pizza market, when the price of cheese rose steeply, firms were loath to raise their prices because of the competitive disadvantage that would result. In an attempt to explain why some oligopolistic markets seem to exhibit more price stability than one might expect in the face of large changes in costs, economists have considered the possibility that competitors may match price decreases more closely than they match price increases. In this scenario, a firm matches declines in its competitors' prices in order to protect its market share. But if competitors' prices rise, the firm refuses to follow the increase, thereby positioning itself to gain a greater market share.

Consider an oligopolistic firm producing at point *e* in Figure 10.9. The asymmetric price response by rivals puts a kink in the demand curve at *e*, since the firm's quantity will fall faster if it raises price than the quantity will rise if it lowers price. The kink causes a gap in the firm's marginal revenue curve. (To the left of *e*, the MR curve shows marginal revenue for the demand curve left of *e*; and to the right of *e*, MR represents marginal revenue for the demand to the right.) Consequently, the firm's MC curve can rise or fall to any level within the gap and still lead the firm to choose price and quantity at *e*.

Although the kinked demand curve explains why the market equilibrium might be stable, it does not really explain how the equilibrium got to point *e* in the first place. For that, we need a complete description of the firms' competitive choices.[23]

10.5 Credibility and Strategic Choices

In pre-emptive equilibria, as we have seen, the dominant firm's threat may be designed to induce the competitor not to enter the market. The choice is aimed not at raising profit directly, but at changing the competitor's behavior in a way that allows higher profit. Success of the threat depends on its credibility to other firms. Such pre-emptive equilibria demonstrate two important elements in oligopolistic competition—credibility and strategic choices—that can lead to seemingly puzzling behavior until they are explained.

---

23. A complete treatment of the kinked demand curve, showing the full set of choices available to the firm, is beyond our scope here. Such a treatment can be found in D. Kreps, *A Course in Microeconomic Theory,* Princeton, N.J.: Princeton University Press, 1990, pp. 335–337.

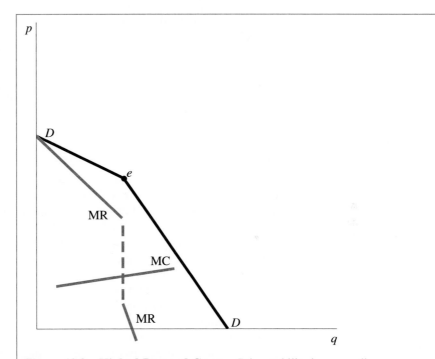

Figure 10.9 Kinked Demand Curve Price stability in some oligopolistic markets can be explained by firms' belief that competitors will match price reductions more closely than price increases. This results in a kink in the firm's demand curve and a gap in its marginal revenue curve. Consequently, the firm's MC curve can move up or down in the region of the gap in MR without inducing the firm to change its market price or quantity.

Establishing Credibility for Strategic Gain

▼
10. Give examples explaining the role of credibility and strategic choice in oligopolistic competition.

Can a firm ever *limit* its future options, and by so doing make itself better off? Such a possibility seems paradoxical unless limiting choice somehow improves the market setting for the firm in the future. In the case of *strategic choices,* however, that is precisely the situation. By committing itself to a particular course of action, the firm establishes credibility in the eyes of its rivals, inducing different behavior on their part, which works in the firm's favor.

> A ***strategic choice*** *in a game influences the choice of the other player or players in a direction that is favorable to oneself.*

We can illustrate this principle with a practice once known among some American Indians. The practice was known as staking oneself out. It worked like this: Occasionally, during the ongoing disputes between neighboring tribes, a crisis developed. At this point, a warrior might find an area where he was sure to be seen by his enemy and publicly tie himself with a leather thong to a stake pounded into the ground. This was both a challenge to his enemy and a statement: ''I care so strongly about this matter that I will either prevail here or die at this stake in the process of trying to achieve it.''

By limiting his range of movement, the warrior did two things. First, he prevented himself from choosing the option of retreat at a future time when he might otherwise have decided to give up the struggle. But, second, he let his enemy know that he was absolutely committed to his course of action. His enemy could either fight to the death or choose to avoid the conflict altogether. By being willing to limit his options, the staked-our warrior might end up winning the conflict without actually fighting. Without the staking out, the enemy might have underrated the strength of the warrior's commitment, and so might have engaged in combat, seeking an easy victory.[24]

Many other such examples, in which limiting one's options can improve circumstances by changing the behavior of other players in the game, are available from history. In A.D. 363 the Roman emperor Julian decided to burn the boats that had transported his army through the rivers and waterways to Assyria. Similarly, in 1066 William the Conqueror burned the boats that had brought his Norman fleet to England. In these cases, the main effect of losing the option of retreat was to create greater motivation for the troops to fight.

In addition to pre-emptive threat equilibria, we have seen an application of this principle in the Stackelberg leader-follower description of oligopoly. As long as the follower firm *believes* that the dominant firm's quantity choice is fixed, the best that the follower can do is stick to its reaction curve. On the other hand, if the follower *believes* that it can dislodge the leader from its chosen quantity, it may be in the interest of the follower to try to do so. The positions can be reversed if, for example, the former follower picks the leader's quantity and refuses to budge from it. The former leader, now accepting the former follower's quantity as given, can do no better than to respond as a follower. If both firms simultaneously try to act as leader, the leader-follower solution breaks down, and some other type of solution will prevail.

The conclusion is, the leader's position must be *credible* to the follower for the strategic benefit to be gained. One way the leader can establish credibility is by eliminating the possibility of other options. If the firm can establish credibility by restricting its options, this may be a worthwhile strategy.

Credibility and Tacit Collusion

Credibility may also be needed to establish tacit or explicit agreements between firms. One way to make a mode of action credible to other players is to develop a reputation for behaving in a particular way, by virtue of repeated

---

24. Interestingly, *The Art of War,* written by the Chinese military strategist Sun Tzu some 2,000 years ago and read by many business leaders today as a guide to strategic behavior, advocates that ''to win without fighting is best.''

choices in past games. Another way is to limit one's future options so that the course of action is the only one possible (the ''burning one's boats'' strategy). Still another way, however, is to *change the incentives* of the game so that the action that one desires to make credible is also the economically best choice. This strategy is best explained by an example involving tacit collusion.

In this game we consider the actions of two price-competitive firms. Since it is sufficient to make our point, we assume that each firm has the option of setting just one of two prices, either ''high'' or ''low.'' The game replicates the standard Prisoner's Dilemma pattern of payoffs: The best solution for each firm results if it prices low and the other firm prices high, because in that case it will get most of the market. The next-best solution occurs when both firms price high; the third-best solution is for both firms to price low. The worst outcome for each firm occurs when it prices high while the other firm prices low. A game with this pattern of outcomes is shown in part (a) of Figure 10.10.

If each firm could be sure that the other would price high, both would be better off doing so and receiving a profit of $2,000,000. The incentive to reduce price when the other firm prices high makes this outcome difficult to sustain, however. One way in which each firm could make credible its commitment to price high would be to create a cost that comes into play only if the firm prices low. How might such a cost be created? Let us suppose that your firm, Firm 1, issues a warranty to each buyer of its product, stipulating

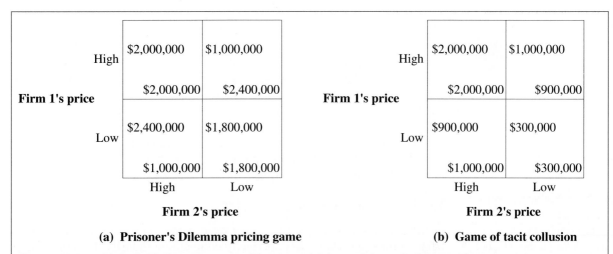

Figure 10.10 **Tacit Collusion** In part (a) Firms 1 and 2 face a Prisoner's Dilemma in their pricing strategy, making it difficult for them to enforce the mutually beneficial ''high-high'' outcome. One way to make credible their commitment to one another to price high is to announce an action that commits them to side losses of $1,500,000 if they price low. These losses, when combined with the payoffs, produce the game in part (b), which gives each firm a dominant strategy to price high.

that if the product is subsequently sold to another customer at any lower price within a certain period of time, the firm will rebate the difference in price to the original customer. The warranty would be enforceable in court and would be tremendously costly to the firm if it sold even one unit at a lower price.

What would be the effect of the warranty if both competing firms offered it? Assume that the number of previous customers who would be affected is such that pricing low will require $1,500,000 of rebates. This side payment, when combined with the payoffs in the game, changes the net profits of each firm to those shown in part (b). For example, assume Firm 2 prices high and Firm 1 prices low. Instead of receiving a profit of $2,400,000, Firm 1 will receive $2,400,000 − $1,500,000, or $900,000. This is less than the $2,000,000 Firm 1 would receive from pricing high, so Firm 1 no longer has an incentive to deviate from the high-high solution. A check shows that Firm 1 is also better off pricing high when Firm 2 prices low; thus the warranty makes pricing high a dominant strategy for Firm 1. Since a similar argument applies to Firm 2, the two firms can make their commitment to high prices credible. Pricing high becomes the best choice for each, regardless of what the other firm does.

It is interesting that in this case the warranty, sometimes called a most-favored-customer warranty because it guarantees that a customer will get the product at the same price as the most favored customer would, appears to serve the purpose of providing a service to the customer. In reality, it allows the firm to charge high prices to everyone and to collude implicitly. It seems that when a monetary reward is at stake, individuals will eventually find clever ways to get it.

EXPLORATION: Intervention in Trade for the National Advantage

One controversial issue that has gained international prominence is the use of government intervention to aid selected domestic industries in their competition with foreign counterparts. The role of such intervention can be understood in terms of oligopoly theory. Intervention is generally of two types. The first helps the domestic firm or industry improve its competitive position by changing the type of oligopolistic competition that prevails in the market; the second helps the domestic firm or industry in its entry into a targeted market. We will examine examples of each type of intervention.

The Country as Stackelberg Leader

▼
11. Theoretically, how might the domestic government use its first-player advantage to improve the position of the domestic firm relative to the foreign firm in international competition? How does credibility play a role?

In many cases a country's firms may have market power on world markets because they operate in an imperfectly competitive industry. Certainly large commercial aircraft manufacturers (discussed in Investigations III) are one example. In these cases, there may be a role for the domestic government to play in improving the position of the domestic firm. When the government intervenes in such situations, it becomes a player in the economic game; its

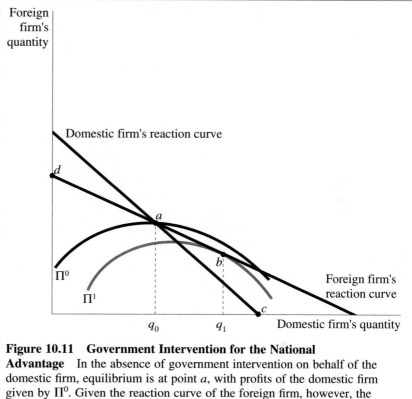

Figure 10.11   Government Intervention for the National Advantage   In the absence of government intervention on behalf of the domestic firm, equilibrium is at point a, with profits of the domestic firm given by Π^0. Given the reaction curve of the foreign firm, however, the domestic firm's profits would be highest at point b. There is an incentive, therefore, for the government to intervene with subsidies to induce the domestic firm to produce the greater quantity corresponding to point b, the Stackelberg leader quantity.

choices are the levels at which to set trade taxes or subsidies. Moreover, the government often has a first-player advantage in the sense that its choice of tax or subsidy is taken as given by the domestic and foreign firms when they choose their own plays. By choosing a tax or subsidy that will support the domestic firm in some way, it can make the domestic firm a stronger player in the oligopolistic competition.

The effect of government industrial policy can be illustrated with the help of Figure 10.11, in which we consider two firms, one domestic and the other foreign, that compete for sales to a third country in a Cournot oligopoly. In the absence of government intervention, the outputs of the domestic and foreign firms on the world market are given by the intersection of their reaction curves at point a. Since the two firms compete in Cournot fashion, each takes the quantity of the other as given when it makes its decision about how much to produce. For each point in the diagram we can calculate the profit of the domestic firm. The curve labeled Π^0, for example, gives the combinations of output for both firms for which the profit of the domestic firm is the same as it is at point a. Such a curve is called an *isoprofit curve* (*iso* is Greek for "same" or "equal"). Since point a is on the domestic firm's reaction curve, we know that any change in domestic firm output given foreign output (that is, movement from a to the right or left) lowers the domestic firm's profit. Further, we know that the domestic firm's output reaches its highest level if the foreign firm produces zero output and the domestic firm produces the monopoly quantity at point c. It follows that there is a family of isoprofit curves, downward-sloping like Π^0 but showing increased profit as we move to the southeast along the firm's reaction curve. Π^1 is one such curve in the family.

Inspecting isoprofit curves Π^0 and Π^1 shows that the domestic firm could raise its profit above the level at point a if it were credibly to commit to produce at point b, thereby lowering output of the foreign firm and increasing its own output. Since quantity q_1 corresponding to point b gives the highest profit to the domestic firm of all points on the foreign firm's reaction curve, it is the Stackelberg leader quantity. Consequently, if the domestic government used production subsidies (or export subsidies) to cause the domestic firm to raise quantity to q_1, it would raise the profits of the domestic firm. Such a move would be in the national advantage because, even though taxes would have to be levied to pay for the subsidies, the tax loss to citizens would be canceled by the fact that shareholders of the domestic firm (most of whom presumably are domestic citizens) receive the subsidies, leaving the increase in profit as a net gain to the domestic country.

The subsidy leaves the foreign firm no choice but to accept the new output of the domestic firm as credible and respond with a lower output in accordance with its best interests, given the domestic firm's higher output. Since producing at point b was in the domestic firm's interest, why did it not move to the Stackelberg leader position without government help? Presumably it could not, because the higher output would have required making its commitment to stay at that higher level credible to the foreign firm. If the foreign firm found the domestic firm's higher output not credible, it could cause a drop in domestic firm profit by holding its output constant, or even increasing it. Sustaining lower profits may have been too great a hurdle for the domestic firm without intervention to make its higher output credible.

Unequivocal examples of such government strategy are difficult to produce, because it is hard to separate strategic intervention from more traditional protectionist actions that favor domestic industry. In traditional protectionism, the benefits to the industry may be present, but at the expense of overall harm to the intervening country in the form of taxes and higher prices paid by consumers. Many countries have tried to nurture their domestic steel industries through subsidies and import restrictions, for example. The benefit from intervention in our example came from inducing the foreign firm to reduce output to the Stackelberg follower level, an outcome that is unlikely under competitive conditions in the international steel industry. In this event, government subsidies would indeed help local steel, but at a cost to the country that exceeds the benefits.

Government Support for Market Entry

So far, our analysis has highlighted the role that government can play in an oligopolistic setting to enhance the market position of its domestic firm. The government can also play a role in the entry process.

As we learned previously, oligopolistic markets are characterized by few competitors, positive economic profits, and some entry barrier or other reason why additional firms do not enter. The idea behind government intervention to aid entry is that if some firms are making positive economic profits, then one or more of them might as well be domestic. For example, let us say that the world supercomputer market is big enough for three efficient-sized firms, and that these are all foreign. Firms supplying supercomputers make economic profits, but should a fourth firm try to enter, the competition would drive profits to negative levels.

Your country would like to produce supercomputers. But if a domestic firm in your country tried to enter the market, its entry would not be credible because, as a newcomer, it would face startup costs exceeding the costs of firms already in the market. Firms already in the market would recognize their advantage and make countermoves that would make the entry attempt unprofitable.

In the face of this situation, the domestic government decides to subsidize the entry of its firm into the supercomputer market. It makes known its intention to support the domestic firm as much as necessary until the firm is profitable. With the domestic government as a player, the foreign firms have no choice but to take the entry threat as credible and choose their best responses. Inevitably, in the circumstances described, the weakest of the three foreign firms will leave or be driven from the market. The end result of the government intervention is that there are three firms producing supercomputers in the world market, as before, except that now one of them is a domestic firm.

Activist Trade Policy: An Evaluation

▼
12. Give four main reasons to be cautious about the use of activist, interventionist trade policy.

Even when a nation increases its welfare by intervening in trade, it usually does so at the expense of the welfare of one or more other nations. In the case of the domestic government using a subsidy to increase the domestic firm's output, the profits of the foreign firm decline. In the case of government support for the domestic firm's entry into an oligopolistic market, success must come at the expense of the market position of one or more foreign firms.

Even if we ignore the effects on foreign welfare, it is often difficult to use microeconomic theory as a precise guide to activist trade policy. The nature of the prescription is often specific to the circumstances. Applying the cure for one disease may end up killing the patient if the problem is improperly diagnosed.

For example, assume that the domestic firm and foreign firm operating in the duopolistic market of our Stackelberg leader example are not quantity competitors, but are Bertrand price competitors instead. In Bertrand competition the two firms would like to collude to charge a high price, but are prevented from doing so by their competitive environment. If the domestic government taxes the exports of its domestic firm, this would limit the quantity of the country's good on world markets, raising the price and making it possible (and credible) for the foreign firm to raise its price, too. Both the domestic and foreign firm can now more effectively collude in extracting higher prices from the third-country buyers. While this possibility is interesting in itself, the most sobering aspect is that the prescription is an export *tax,* whereas in the case of Cournot competition we found that the appropriate policy was an export *subsidy.* What improved the domestic welfare in one case would harm it in another. Since it is not always such an easy thing to distinguish the circumstances of Cournot competition from those of Bertrand, it is entirely possible that activist trade intervention could have unintended consequences that harm the domestic country instead of helping it.

Rationales for government intervention may also be misused and misapplied by domestic firms seeking public support. In the supercomputer example, the government's help enabled the domestic firm to enter the world supercomputer market by dislodging a foreign firm already in the industry. The reward for the up-front support (paid for through taxpayer dollars) was the future profits of the domestic firm. What if the profits never materialize, either because they were overstated originally, because other countries drive them to zero in the future, or because new developments in the field of supercomputers reduce them to zero? Then we are left with the domestic firm having received from the public coffers with nothing to show in return. Moreover, firms that are in perfectly competitive markets (where entry does not need public support and economic profits are zero) will rightly claim that they too would benefit if they received government help. Finally, if up-front support will allow enough future positive profits to repay the initial costs, why aren't private investors and the private capital markets snapping up such stupendous opportunities? Could it be that the glowing claims of future benefits made by government lobbyists are not convincing to business people who must part with their own money to support a firm's entry into the market?

Another problem is that foreign activism and retaliation are possible. If one government can intervene on behalf of its households and firms, so can another. If the foreign government enters the business of subsidizing its private firm, the whole structure of the market on which the analysis was based breaks down. We then enter the realm of a game with *four* players (two governments and two private firms), with much more complicated strategies and outcomes. It is conceivable that in the ensuing trade war, both countries could lose.

In the final analysis, the strongest argument against a selfishly nationalistic trade policy is that governments intervening on behalf of their domestic interests place the common interest in a free trading environment in jeopardy.

In short, when everyone tries to win at others' expense, all may lose. For these and other reasons, the general consensus among those who have studied this problem is that, although there may be cases in which such intervention is theoretically helpful, it is difficult and probably unwise to make use of this fact in practice. A hands-off policy, in the long run, may be the best. ■

Summary

Active Reading Guide numbers are given in parentheses at the end of each summary item.

1. Oligopoly is the competition of a few firms in a market. In an oligopoly a firm influences but does not control the market. Common features of oligopoly include barriers to entry, which explain why more firms are not present; the existence of positive economic profits because of the absence of perfect competition; and the incentive for oligopolistic firms to collude to produce the monopoly outcome for maximum joint profits. The difficulties of sustaining collusive agreements, as well as the illegality of agreements in restraint of trade, act as deterrents to successful collusion. (1)

2. A game consists of a set of players, a set of rules, and a list of payoffs for each player depending on the choices of the players. Games can be (a) games of common interest, in which all players benefit from the same outcome; (b) games of pure conflict of interest, in which what one player wins the other players lose; or (c) games with mixtures of both elements. Game theory describes the choices of each player, taking into account the actions of other players. Oligopolistic competition can be described in terms of a game with mixtures of conflict and common interest, often including elements of the Prisoner's Dilemma, because firms have an incentive both to attempt collusion and to desert it. (2, 3)

3. A cooperative solution to a game requires that players be able to agree among themselves about taking cooperative actions, an ability which may not always be present. Strategies in noncooperative games include dominant strategies (strategies that give the best payoff regardless of the strategies of other firms), maximin strategies (strategies that maximize the minimum possible payoff, given the other players' choices), and other rational strategies that often depend on the beliefs of the players about other players' intentions and the features of the game. (4)

4. A solution to a game in which each player makes the best choice, given the strategies chosen by other players, is called a Nash equilibrium. It is a fundamental equilibrium or solution concept for noncooperative games that has been applied to different types of oligopolistic markets. (5)

5. If we specify the beliefs of each firm about how its competitors choose their strategies, and if we assume that firms choose the best strategy given the strategies of other firms in equilibrium, the Nash solution to the game becomes the market equilibrium in oligopolistic competition. Different beliefs lead to different solutions, but the basic structure is the same whether firms choose from a small number of choices (strategies), a large number, or even an infinite set of choices. (6)

6. In noncooperative oligopolistic games, Cournot competition is characterized by the choice of quantities; firms make their choices simultaneously, each believing that others will hold their quantities fixed. (7)

7. Bertrand competition is characterized by the choice of prices; firms make their choices simultaneously, each believing that others will hold their prices fixed. When one firm can make its choice before the other firm and commit itself to a given quantity, a Stackelberg leader-follower solution to the oligopoly problem is the result. The firm that moves second has no option but to react to the choice of the lead firm by following its reaction curve. The lead firm, taking into account the follower's reaction, chooses its quantity to maximize its profit. (8)

8. Other types of equilibria include the pre-emptive threat equilibrium, in which the dominant firm, moving first, threatens to take an action that will harm the rival if the rival chooses a disliked strategy. For example, an existing firm might threaten to lower price greatly if another firm enters the market. (9)

9. In games, a strategic choice is one that is taken with the intention of influencing the behavior of other firms in a favorable manner. Strategic choices can involve developing a reputation for ruthlessly competitive behavior and making credible threats and statements about the firm's future behavior. By taking action that eliminates the possibility of some choices, a firm sometimes can make credible a remaining move. Tacit collusion by firms to charge high prices and increase their profits, for example, might be one result of firms' committing themselves to extra costs if they lower prices. Such an action can lead to strategic benefits by changing the behavior of other players. (10)

10. Government intervention in oligopolistic trade markets can aid domestic firms either to improve their positions relative to foreign firms or to enter a new market. The government often has a first-player advantage in such situations. (11)

11. Successful government intervention in oligopolistic markets requires that the government be able to assess the nature of oligopolistic competition (the right intervention in one situation may be exactly the wrong intervention in another) and to assess the magnitude of future gains that its costly intervention would achieve. Often neither assessment is possible or likely to be accurate. Other reasons for being cautious about the use of interventionist trade policy are that it often achieves success at the expense of foreign countries, it does not take into account the effect of foreign retaliation, and it could damage the trading system that benefits all countries. (12)

Review Questions

*1. Why is oligopoly typically explained by non-cooperative games involving elements of common interest and conflict of interest?

2. Explain the following statement: "Entry barriers and barriers to collusion are necessary to prevent oligopoly from becoming perfect competition at one extreme and monopoly at the other."

*3. Why is the cooperative or collusive solution "best" from the point of view of the oligopolist firm?

4. Why is the Prisoner's Dilemma game relevant to oligopoly theory?

*5. What is a dominant strategy? Does a dominant strategy always exist?

6. What is a maximin strategy? Does a maximin strategy always exist?

*7. What is a Nash equilibrium? Does it require a particular set of beliefs by the firm about how other firms behave?

8. Why is a Cournot equilibrium more suited to describing firms that must make their choices simultaneously, whereas the Stackelberg leader-follower equilibrium is more suited to describing situations in which one firm moves first?

*9. How does a Cournot competitor differ from a Bertrand competitor? How are they similar?

10. What is a strategic choice by a firm? How could a firm limit its options and improve its situation?

*11. How are credibility and reputation important to successful strategic choices by the firm?

* Asterisks are used to denote questions that are answered at the back of the book.

Numerical and Graphing Exercises

*1. For the following game, determine whether each player has a dominant strategy and find the Nash equilibria, if any.

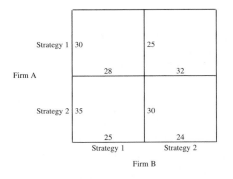

Firm A

	Strategy 1	Strategy 2
Strategy 1	30 — 28	25 — 32
Strategy 2	35 — 25	30 — 24

Firm B

*2. Assume that demand is given by $q^D = 100 - p$ and that two firms each have fixed costs of 0 and marginal costs of 0. If each firm has the choice of producing only 30 or 50 units, find the profit for each firm under each of the four possible outcomes. Plot your information in a payoff matrix as in exercise 1. Find the Cournot equilibrium if there is one.

3. Redo exercise 2 with the firms' choices limited to 30 or 40. How does the equilibrium change?

*4. Use the information from exercise 2 but assume each firm can supply any quantity. If these are the only two firms supplying product, find the equilibrium price and quantity if:
   a) The firms collude to form a cartel
   b) The firms act as Cournot competitors
   c) The firms act as pricetaking perfect competitors

(Hint: You may want to use computation information from the chapter footnotes.)

*5. Using the information from exercise 2 and from footnotes 19, 20, and 22, compare the oligopoly price and quantity if Firms 1 and 2 act as Cournot competitors and if Firm 1 acts as a Stackelberg leader. Assume each firm can choose any output it wants.

6. Use the information from problem 2 but assume each firm can supply any quantity. Solve for the pre-emptive threat equilibrium.

*7. Find the formula for the reaction curves shown in Figure 10.7. The demand curves are:

Firm 1's demand: $q_1 = 100 - 2p_1 + p_2$;
Firm 2's demand: $q_2 = 100 - 2p_2 + p_1$.

Solve for the Bertrand equilibrium. (Hint: You may want to use computation information from the chapter footnotes.)

8. Use the description of a cartel in Chapter 9 to model the decision of a cartel firm to either abide by the rules of the cartel or to cheat. Consider this a two-player game in which the second player is the rest of the cartel firms. Is there a Nash equilibrium? (You may give each player two options.)

*9. Trade policy analysts frequently use the Prisoner's Dilemma to describe the situation of countries that must decide whether to engage in free trade or to adopt interventionist policies. Explain this in terms of a two-country game in which each country has two choices. In what units are the payoffs measured?

CHAPTER 11

The Firm as Demander

This chapter looks behind the firm's output decision to consider the firm's profit-maximizing factor demand. We find a rule describing how much of each factor the firm should use, and from that rule we derive the firm's factor demand curve. Combining the factor demands of all firms, we find the factor demand for the industry as a whole and then for the entire market. After examining the nature of equilibrium in factor markets, we consider factor markets with monopsony power and monopoly power and their implications for bargaining. The last section looks at the effect of asymmetric information, relating the efficiency wage model to unemployment.

ACTIVE READING GUIDES

After reading this chapter you should be able to answer the Active Reading Guides listed below. These guides also appear in the page margins, near the material to which they refer.

1. What primary characteristic do buyers in a competitive factor market exhibit?

2. Explain the firm's hiring condition in the one-factor case.

3. Relate MRP and the firm's factor demand curve in the one-factor case. Distinguish between firms with and without market power in the product market.

4. Derive the output expansion path. Explain how it changes for different factor prices.

5. Describe the effect of a factor price change on firm use of the factor in terms of the substitution and output effects.

6. What is the difference between complements in production and substitutes in production? Using these concepts, derive the firm's factor demand curve.

7. What effects influence the derivation of industry and market demand curves (and their price elasticities) from firm demands? Draw diagrams showing how each effect works.

8. Interpret the market equilibrium wage and the $w = pMP_L$ condition.

9. What is marginal factor cost (MFC)?

10. Contrast the effects of a minimum wage in competitive and monopsonistic labor markets.

11. What determines the boundaries of the wage-employment point when a monopolistic labor union bargains with a monopsonistic employer?

12. Why do the asymmetric information conditions of the efficiency wage model require unemployment in market equilibrium?

11.1 The Firm as Demander of Factor Inputs

According to the vice president for sales, demand for the specialty electronic control devices produced by your firm, Control Electronics Incorporated (CEI), will be growing for the foreseeable future. Your assignment is to plan for expansion by deciding how many more engineers, scientists, and assembly-line laborers to hire for the company's new plant to be located in the other half of the country. Most prices for different job descriptions and grades of labor are determined by the market in that part of the country, but there are some skills that your company is the major buyer for. CEI's founder has always followed a policy of paying a fair wage, and your instructions are to see to it that hiring in the current expansion is no exception. Just how do you decide how many employees of various types to hire, you wonder, and in what sense can the wage you offer be described as fair?

The purpose of this chapter is to address questions of the type facing CEI. The preceding five chapters have discussed the firm manager's output decisions under perfect and imperfect competition. But, as we saw in Part Two, just as households act as *consumers* of goods and *suppliers* of factor inputs such as labor, firms act as *suppliers* of goods and *demanders* of factor inputs. In this chapter, therefore, we complete the description of the firm by discussing it as the demander of factor inputs such as skilled and unskilled labor, capital, land, and raw materials. The firm manager has to determine their value to the firm and the combination and quantity of factor inputs to use.

Competitive Factor Markets

A factor market is a market for the buying and selling of goods or services used as inputs in the process of production. In making the distinction between inputs and outputs, we recognize that the dividing line is sometimes blurred. For example, an automobile usually would be considered an output because it is a final product for auto companies and a consumption good for households, but it would be an input from the point of view of a traveling sales representative who used it for business. Alternatively, sheet metal might be a steel firm's output, but it is an input for a heating and air conditioning firm that uses it for duct work. Whether a good or service is an input or an output, therefore, is not so much a function of the product itself as of how it happens to be used. The firm's demand for a factor is called a *derived demand* because it is derived from the firm's primary object, namely, to produce output and maximize profit.

▼
1. What primary characteristic do buyers in a competitive factor market exhibit?

In Chapter 7 we described the conditions for perfect competition among sellers in terms of standardized product, pricetaking, contestability and free entry, and perfect information. These conditions would continue to hold in a perfectly competitive factor market. However, in this chapter we are concerned with buyers of a factor, so we can initially describe the firm's demand for factors without reference to the conditions of supply. As with product markets, we assume that firms in perfectly competitive factor markets are *pricetakers* with respect to the price of inputs they buy. No firm is able to influence the market price. A factor such as labor, for example, is used as an input in most—if not all—industries and is sold by many different people. Even adjusting for skill grades within labor, it is often the case that a single firm would be unable to influence the market price of its labor input. When the firm treats input prices as fixed, the firm's goal of maximizing profit reduces to deciding how much of each factor input to hire.

If there is only one factor of production, that is the end of the story. Listing how much the firm hires for every alternative factor price gives the firm's factor demand curve. For firms that use multiple factors, matters are a little more involved, because the firm must decide what *technique* (combination of inputs) it will choose to produce each level of output. Choice of technique is inextricably linked to the choice of how much to produce and how much of each factor to use to do it. Nevertheless, you should find the firm's behavior fairly easy to understand from the point of view of hiring's effect on profits.

The Firm's Factor Demand: The One-Factor Case

The first step in finding the firm's factor demand is determining what the factor is worth to the firm in terms of output that the firm can get from using the factor. Firm managers can compare this value to what the factor costs. Balancing benefits and costs determines the firm's hiring condition in the one-factor case.[1] After we have derived the firm's hiring condition, we will see how it determines the firm's factor demand curve.

▼

2. Explain the firm's hiring condition in the one-factor case.

The Hiring Condition. Consider a firm hiring only one factor of production. The relevant production function for the firm is $q = F(L)$, where output, q, is determined by how much input, L, is used. We will refer to this single factor as labor, but our discussion applies equally to nonlabor factors such as raw materials or capital. Firm profit is

$$\Pi = pq - \text{FC} - wL$$
$$= pF(L) - \text{FC} - wL,$$

where FC is the fixed cost for other factor inputs (if any), and w is the labor wage rate. The decision about how much labor to hire determines the firm's profits by increasing both revenue and cost. If the firm hires another worker, the additional revenue it gets is called the *marginal revenue product of labor,* MRP_L.

> The ***marginal revenue product of factor*** L, ***MRP***$_L$**,** *is the additional revenue earned by the firm from selling the output generated by an additional unit of* L.

Since additional output is given by the marginal product, MP_L, and the revenue from selling additional output is MR, marginal revenue product is given by $\text{MRP}_L = \text{MR} \times \text{MP}_L$. In the event that the firm sells its output in a perfectly competitive market, marginal revenue is the same as price, and the marginal revenue product equals the *value of marginal product,* $p\text{MP}_L$.

> The ***value of marginal product*** *for factor* L *is price times marginal product:* $VMP_L = pMP_L$.

Since marginal revenue product describes the marginal benefit to the firm from hiring an additional unit of labor, and the wage, w, gives the marginal cost, profit maximization requires that the firm hire to the point where the marginal revenue product MRP_L equals the wage,

$$\text{MRP}_L = w.$$

This condition is called the firm's *hiring condition.* To illustrate, Figure 11.1 shows the firm's marginal product of labor curve, MP_L, in part (a) and its MRP_L curve in part (b). The curve in part (b) is derived from the curve in part (a) by multiplying MP_L by MR for each labor input. In the case drawn,

1. Though most firms have more than one input, a firm might find itself in a position to hire only a single factor if it is in the short run and all factors are fixed except one. A single-input firm might also find itself deciding how much of the single factor to use in the long run. Thus the analysis in this chapter can be applied to either short-run or long-run situations, depending on how many variable factors are being hired. Firms selling pure labor services, such as management consultants, psychologists, migrant farm laborers, and home cleaning services, might be considered to use only labor input. In most cases, however, it is hard to imagine that some other input does not enter in some significant way.

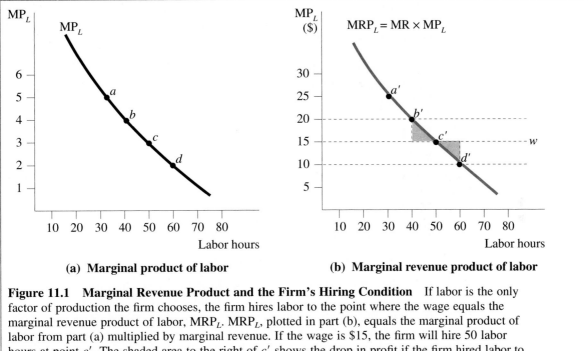

Figure 11.1   Marginal Revenue Product and the Firm's Hiring Condition   If labor is the only factor of production the firm chooses, the firm hires labor to the point where the wage equals the marginal revenue product of labor, MRP_L. MRP_L, plotted in part (b), equals the marginal product of labor from part (a) multiplied by marginal revenue. If the wage is $15, the firm will hire 50 labor hours at point c'. The shaded area to the right of c' shows the drop in profit if the firm hired labor to point d', and the shaded area to the left shows the firm's drop in profit if it hired to point b'. In the case shown, the firm sells output in a perfectly competitive market at price $5, so MR = p = $5.

▼

3. Relate MRP and the firm's factor demand curve in the one-factor case. Distinguish between firms with and without market power in the product market.

we have assumed that the firm sells output in a perfectly competitive market at price $5, so MR = p = $5. Thus, if 30 labor hours are used, MP_L is 5 at point a in part (a), and the corresponding MRP_L at a' in part (b) is $25. The same computation applies for other points. Were the firm a monopolist in its output market, we would multiply by MR from the product demand curve for the output quantity associated with the labor input level.

Part (b) of the figure also shows how a $15 hourly wage affects hiring. The height of MRP_L gives the value of the extra output produced for each unit of labor hired, and the wage rate gives its cost. The difference between MRP_L and the wage rate shows the addition to profit from hiring another unit of labor. At point b' MRP_L is greater than w, so the additional profit earned by moving from b' to c' is the shaded area between the MRP_L and the wage curve to the left of c'. At point d' MRP_L is *less* than w, so by moving to c' the firm increases profit by the shaded area to the right of c'. Point c', where MRP_L = $15, shows the firm's only profit-maximizing choice.

The Firm's Demand Curve.   In the one-factor case, it is easy to see that the marginal revenue product of labor curve is the firm's demand curve for labor. If the firm has market power in the product market MRP_L = $MR \cdot MP_L$, and if the firm is perfectly competitive, $MRP_L = p \cdot MP_L$. If the wage were $25 per hour, the firm would hire labor to point a', corresponding to 30 labor hours. At lower wages the firm hires more workers because the value of the extra output will cover the cost of the additional labor time. The demand curve is downward-sloping because of the downward slope of the MP_L curve and declining MR for larger output. The steeper the marginal product curve and marginal revenue curves, the steeper the factor demand curve will be.

The Firm's Factor Demand: The Multiple-Factor Case

With two or more variable factors, we must extend the single-factor hiring condition to multiple factors and evaluate how the hiring of one factor affects the use of other factors. To be able to draw the relevant curves, we assume that the firm uses just two factors, although the principles we find will apply to any number of factors. Assuming that the firm simultaneously hires capital, K, and labor, L, the equation

$$\Pi = pF(K, L) - wL - rK$$

gives the firm's profits, where $F(K, L)$ is the production function, w is the wage rate, and r is the rental rate on capital services.[2] Since the firm's goal is still profit maximization, the hiring logic used in the one-factor case applies to each factor considered separately. Thus the firm maximizes profits if the marginal revenue product for each factor equals that factor's hiring price,

$$MRP_L = w \quad \text{and} \quad MRP_K = r.$$

Although these hiring conditions are the same as the hiring condition we derived in the single-factor case, the firm's factor demand curve is no longer the MRP curve for each factor. Interaction between the use of one factor and the use of the other will affect the demand curve. To find the curve, we first describe the effect that a change in price of one factor has on the firm's hiring of all factors; then we relate the hiring conditions to the derived factor demand.

Output and Substitution Effects on Choice of Technique

If there is only one factor being chosen by the firm, the combination of inputs used to produce a given output level is not an issue. With more than one factor, however, the firm has different combinations of capital and labor from which to choose in producing a given output. For example, if labor costs rise, the firm may try to minimize them by using more capital in its production process. Using a different combination of inputs to produce a given output is referred to as using a different technique. We now examine how the firm's demand for factors relates to its production technique and output level.

---

2. Recall from Chapter 6 that r is the rental rate (leasing rate) on units of capital if the firm explicitly pays for its input, or the opportunity cost of capital if the machines are owned by the firm.

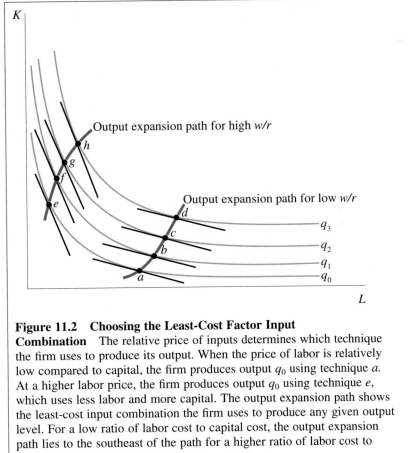

Figure 11.2   Choosing the Least-Cost Factor Input Combination   The relative price of inputs determines which technique the firm uses to produce its output. When the price of labor is relatively low compared to capital, the firm produces output q_0 using technique a. At a higher labor price, the firm produces output q_0 using technique e, which uses less labor and more capital. The output expansion path shows the least-cost input combination the firm uses to produce any given output level. For a low ratio of labor cost to capital cost, the output expansion path lies to the southeast of the path for a higher ratio of labor cost to capital cost.

▼

4. Derive the output expansion path. Explain how it changes for different factor prices.

The Output Expansion Path. Figure 11.2 shows the firm's isoquants for capital and labor, curves q_0 through q_3. The horizontal axis measures the amount of labor used in production, and the vertical axis measures the amount of capital. How are factor prices related to the choice of technique?

From Chapter 6 we know that the point of tangency between the isocost line and the isoquant shows the firm's least-cost input combination. For example, the least-cost input combination for output q_0 occurs at point a when the price of labor, w, is low relative to the rental rate, r (the price of capital input). If the firm were to produce output level q_1 at the same w/r ratio, least-cost production implies that the firm would move to point b. Continuing in this way by finding the least-cost input combinations for output levels q_2 and q_3 and connecting the points, we construct the *output expansion path* (defined in Chapter 6), shown as the line through points a, b, c, and d.

What happens if input prices change? The output expansion path through points *e, f, g,* and *h* represent the firm's input choices when *w/r* is higher. Notice that at the higher wage rate the output expansion path lies closer to the *K* axis, because the firm saves in production costs by using less labor and more capital. The output expansion path behaves in a way completely analogous to the income consumption path discussed in Chapter 4. For instance, the firm produces q_0 more cheaply at point *e* when the *w/r* is high. Because the technique represented by point *e* uses less labor, the firm substitutes capital to make up for it. Similarly, points *f* through *h* show the least-cost combinations of capital and labor for higher output levels at the higher *w/r* ratio.

Factor Substitution and Output Effects. The output expansion path allows us to describe two adjustments the firm makes when the price of a factor such as labor rises. First, it moves to a new output expansion path by substituting other factors for a costlier one; second, it can change its output level by deciding how far out on the expansion path to go. These two choices, the *substitution effect* and the *output effect,* determine the firm's use of labor.

> *(i) The **factor substitution effect** is the change in use of a factor resulting from a change in its factor price, holding output constant by adjusting the level of other factors.*

> *(ii) The **output effect** is the change in use of a factor at fixed factor prices that result from the firm's change in output quantity.*

Figure 11.3 illustrates the substitution effect and the output effect. In part (a) the firm initially produces at point *a.* The line tangent to isoquant q_1 is the isocost line, indicating that *a* is the firm's least-cost input combination. Assume now that the wage rate rises. The isocost line rotates clockwise to *dd.* Given the new isocost line, the least-cost input combination for producing q_1 moves to point *b,* where the tangent line has the same slope as *dd;*[3] since it is further from the origin, though, we see that a higher wage rate increases the cost of producing output q_1.

The higher wage rate changes the firm's marginal cost of production at output q_1. Since the firm chooses output where MR = MC, this causes a change in quantity produced. In the case in part (a), the wage increase causes the firm to shift production to point *c.* At point *c,* the firm's use of labor has dropped and its use of capital increased from the original levels at point *a.* Total output for the firm has fallen from q_1 to q_0.

To break the total change in employment of labor into the substitution effect and the output effect, we first hold output constant at q_1. The shift in labor use from point *a* to point *b* represents the substitution effect. It shows how labor use declines solely from the higher price of labor when there is no

▼
5. Describe the effect of a factor price change on firm use of the factor in terms of the substitution and output effects.

3. The cost of producing q_1 goes up, but not as much as it would have gone up had the firm not adjusted its technique to point *b.* Had the firm continued to produce output q_1 at *a,* the isocost line would have had the same slope as *dd,* but it would have passed through point *a.* The line through *a* would have been further from the origin than the line through *b,* indicating a higher cost.

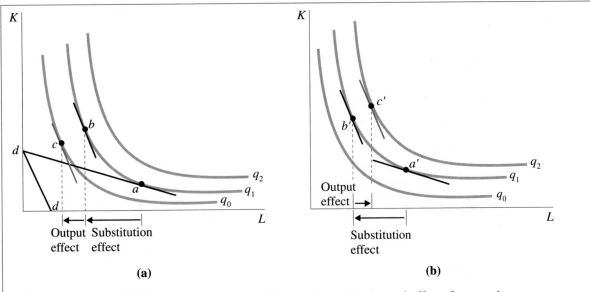

Figure 11.3   Factor Substitution and Output Effects   In part (a) the total effect of a wage increase shifts production from point *a* to point *c*. The firm chooses a more capital-intensive process and *reduces* output; marginal cost must therefore have risen. In part (b) the total effect of the wage increase shifts production from *a'* to *c'*. The firm chooses a more capital-intensive process and *increases* output; marginal cost must therefore have fallen. Arrows show the breakdown of the total effect into a substitution effect and an output effect. The substitution effect always moves in the "normal" direction of using less of the more expensive factor. The output effect can either decrease or increase output.

change in output. The shift from point *b* to point *c* is the output effect, showing the separate effect of the change in output on labor use.

The firm's factor substitution effect and the output effect should remind you of the household's income and substitution effects illustrated in Figure 4.6 of Chapter 4. In either case, the substitution effect causes the firm or household to move in the "normal" direction of buying relatively less of the good or factor that has become more expensive while holding utility or production constant. The output or income effect measures the impact of changing the production level or utility level, keeping prices fixed at their new levels. The same diagrams are used for each.

Part (b) of Figure 11.3 shows the unusual case in which the overall effect of the increase in the wage rate causes the firm to *increase* production of the good from q_1 to q_2. The substitution effect in this case is the drop in labor employment corresponding to the shift from point *a'* to point *b'*, and the output effect is the change in labor employment corresponding to the shift in production from point *b'* to point *c'*. Although an increase in the price of a factor could cause the firm to expand output, we generally expect that an increase in the price of a factor raises marginal cost and therefore causes the firm to lower production at the fixed product price.[4]

Figure 11.4 shows the effect of a wage increase on total cost and marginal cost. In part (a) the increased wage causes total cost to rise. This causes marginal cost, total cost's slope, to increase, too. With increased marginal cost in part (b), the firm produces less output at the fixed output price p_0. In part (a) the firm moves from point a to point b, and in part (b) it moves from c to d. In the usual case just discussed (also corresponding to part (a) of Figure 11.3), the substitution effect and the output effect work in the same direction, causing the competitive firm to hire more of a factor whose price has gone down and less of one whose price has gone up. However, even if the output effect goes in the other direction, it is never large enough to outweigh the substitution effect.[5] Thus factor demand curves always slope down.

The Factor's Effect on Other Factors' Marginal Products

Now that we know how factor prices cause the firm to alter its production technique and output level, we could select the price of a factor, plot the firm's resulting factor use for a range of prices, and sweep out points on the firm's factor demand curve. If we look at how changing the use of one factor affects the marginal product of the other, we can also show that the firm's factor demand curve is more elastic than the factor's MRP curve. We therefore want to examine the interaction between factors and their marginal products.

Rising worker productivity from the time of the Industrial Revolution seems to be associated with accumulation of capital. Thus it is natural to think that the marginal product of a given amount of labor should rise when more capital is present. In this case, labor and capital would be *complements* in production. However, there is also the possibility of factors that are *substitutes* in production, meaning that the marginal product of one falls with more of the other.

▼
6. What is the difference between complements in production and substitutes in production? Using these concepts, derive the firm's factor demand curve.

4. Expansion of output when a factor price rises requires that the marginal cost curve fall at the initial output quantity. Could this unusual event occur? Consider a firm whose output expansion path is described by $L = 200 - q$ and $K = (q - 100)^2$ in the region $105 \leq q \leq 110$, where $w = r = 1$. Isoquants with obtuse corners along the described path might give rise to such an expansion path, for example. The firm's total cost is $C(q) = w(200 - q) + r(q - 100)^2$, and its marginal cost is $MC(q) = 2r(q - 100) - w$. Thus, when w rises, MC falls. Intuitively, what is happening is this: In this production process the firm uses less labor and more capital as output rises. Thus, when the wage rises, the firm's cost of production at lower levels of output rises more than its cost at higher levels of output. The *increase* in cost as the firm moves to increased output, MC, is therefore not as great after the wage increase.

5. We know that the firm chooses its production to maximize profits for each set of prices. If, after the wage rate was higher, the firm raised profits relative to its original choice of inputs by hiring more labor, then it could have done so before the wage rose. But this would contradict the fact that the firm was maximizing profits initially. Exercise 6 at the end of this chapter gives hints to work through this question.

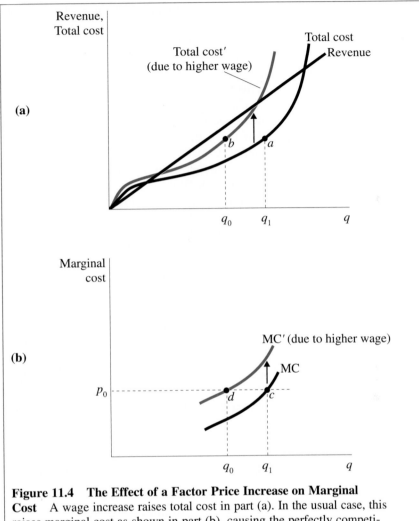

Figure 11.4   The Effect of a Factor Price Increase on Marginal Cost   A wage increase raises total cost in part (a). In the usual case, this raises marginal cost as shown in part (b), causing the perfectly competitive firm to produce a smaller output q_0 (the shift in quantity from a to b or from c to d) at the given output price.

*Two factors are **complements in production** if the marginal product of one factor rises when employment of the other increases. They are **substitutes in production** if the marginal product of one factor falls when employment of the other increases.*

In this definition, factors other than the one being increased are held constant when measuring marginal product.

As noted, capital and labor might be complements in production because having more machines makes each worker more productive. An engineer gets more done with a computer than without; the productivity of a business analyst is greater with a spreadsheet program than without; a worker on a partially automated assembly line has a higher marginal product than one on a manual assembly line.[6]

Conversely, two types of machines may be substitutes in production if increased use of one type of machine replaces the function of the other, so that using more of the second machine type has less effect on increasing output. Consider a short-order cook who uses a conventional oven to heat food. Another conventional oven would increase the cook's speed of food preparation. With a microwave oven, however, the cook finds that another conventional oven has little impact on increasing the speed of food preparation. Because the microwave is so much faster, it almost replaces the conventional ovens. In this case, more microwave ovens imply a lower marginal product for conventional ovens.

Figure 11.5 shows the difference between the two cases in terms of the firm's isoquants. In part (a) the marginal product of labor is related to the vertical distance between the isoquants for uniform increments in output. A smaller vertical distance implies a larger MP_L because it takes less additional labor to increase output by one unit. Increasing capital by moving from point a to point c reduces the vertical distance between isoquants (distance cd is smaller than distance ab), showing that capital and labor are complements— increased capital raises the marginal product of labor. In part (b), on the other hand, increasing the input of microwave ovens increases the distance between isoquants distance ($c'd'$ compared to distance $a'b'$). Since the $MP_{\text{conventional ovens}}$ is smaller with greater microwave use, the two factors are substitutes.

The Firm's Factor Demand Curve in the Multiple-Factor Case

How do factor substitution and complementarity cause the factor demand curve to differ from the MRP curve in the multiple-factor case? To see, refer to Figure 11.6. Part (a) shows the marginal revenue product curve for labor, and part (b) shows the marginal revenue product curve for capital. In part (a) the wage rate initially is w_0 and the quantity of labor hired is L_0. In part (b) the rental rate on capital is r_0 and the capital hired is K_0.

How would a lower wage rate affect the firm's labor demand? Because of the lower wage, the firm can raise profit by increasing its hiring to L_1,

---

6. If there are only two factors of production and production exhibits constant returns to scale, the two factors must be complements in production. This can be shown using the relationship for constant returns to scale functions proved by the mathematician Leonhard Euler, $F(K, L) = MP_K K + MP_L L$. For small changes we have $0 = (\Delta MP_K/\Delta L)K + (\Delta MP_L/\Delta L)L$. Since MP_L falls with increasing L by the law of diminishing marginal returns ($\Delta MP_L/\Delta L$ is negative), it must be that MP_K rises with increasing L to satisfy the above equation. A symmetrical argument shows that MP_L rises with increase in K.

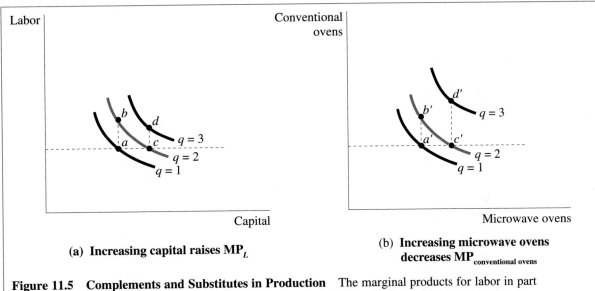

(a) **Increasing capital raises MP$_L$**

(b) **Increasing microwave ovens decreases MP$_{conventional\ ovens}$**

Figure 11.5 **Complements and Substitutes in Production** The marginal products for labor in part (a) and conventional ovens in part (b) correspond to the vertical distances between isoquants: the smaller the distance, the greater the marginal product. In part (a), increasing capital by moving from point a to point c raises MP$_L$ by decreasing the distance between isoquants (distance cd compared to ab). Thus, capital and labor are complements. In part (b), increasing microwave ovens lowers MP$_{conventional\ ovens}$ because $c'd'$ is greater than $a'b'$. In this case, microwave ovens and conventional ovens are substitutes.

corresponding to point b. This is not the end of the story, however, because if capital and labor are *complements* in production the MRP$_K$ curve in part (b) shifts to the *right* to MRP$_K'$. Consequently, the use of capital rises to K'. The MRP$_L$ curve in turn shifts to the right. The firm now hires labor to the right of L_1. The shift in labor to an amount above L_1 shifts the MRP$_K$ curve a small amount further to the right; this again increases the amount of capital used, so the adjustments shift back and forth until the two curves reach their final positions. Assume that MRP$_L'$ is that final curve for labor. Since we know that points a and c in part (a) are both on the firm's demand curve for labor, the firm's derived labor demand curve is therefore the line connecting points a and c. This curve is more elastic than the marginal revenue product curve.

If capital and labor are *substitutes* in production, the MRP$_K$ curve shifts to the *left* when labor employment increases to L_1. This decreases the quantity of capital used to K''. The drop in capital used increases the marginal product of labor (remember that capital and labor are substitutes in production in this case) and causes the MRP$_L$ curve to shift to the right. This further increases labor hired, which in turn shifts the MRP$_K$ curve to the left, and so on until each curve reaches its final position. Assuming again that MRP$_L'$ is the final curve for labor, it follows that point a and point c are on the firm's derived

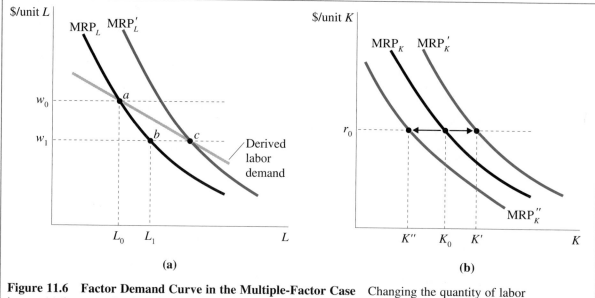

(a)

(b)

Figure 11.6   Factor Demand Curve in the Multiple-Factor Case   Changing the quantity of labor
in part (a) from *a* to *b* when the wage rate drops affects the demand for capital in part (b), which in
turn shifts the MRP$_L$ curve to the right in part (a). The end result is that the firm's derived labor
demand curve passing through points *a* and *c* is more elastic than the MRP$_L$ curve through point *a* in
part (a). This holds true regardless of whether factors are substitutes or complements in production.

labor demand curve. Thus, regardless of whether factors are complements or
substitutes in production, the derived demand curve for a factor is more elastic
than the marginal revenue product curve for that factor.

Relating the Hiring Conditions to MR = MC and the Least-Cost Tangency Condition

In Chapters 6 and 7 we described the firm's decisions in terms of the least-
cost tangency condition and the requirement that marginal revenue equal
marginal cost (p = MC in perfect competition). In this chapter we have
described the firm's decisions in terms of the hiring conditions for factors.
Since we derive both sets of conditions from the assumption that firms maximize profit, they are different aspects of the same thing. That is, requiring
that the firm satisfy the hiring conditions is the same as requiring that the
firm (1) produce its output at least cost, and (2) choose quantity where price
equals marginal cost.

The two hiring conditions we have derived can be expressed as

$$\text{MR} \times \text{MP}_L = w \quad \text{and} \quad \text{MR} \times \text{MP}_K = r.$$

Dividing the left-hand equation by MR $\times$ MP$_K$ and r and rewriting the right-
hand equation gives us the two equivalent equations,

$$\frac{MP_L}{MP_K} = \frac{w}{r} \quad \text{and} \quad MR = \frac{r}{MP_K}.$$

However, MP_L/MP_K is the slope of the isoquant, and w/r is the slope of the isocost line. Therefore, the left-hand requirement is the familiar least-cost tangency condition (see Chapter 6). The right-hand equation represents the $MR = MC$ rule, since it can be shown that marginal cost equals the cost of a factor divided by its marginal product.[7]

11.2 Market Demand for Factors

Market demand for a factor depends on the industries that use it. An industry is a group of firms producing like product and frequently using similar sets of inputs. Factors include well-known and widely used inputs like electricity or labor, which virtually every firm uses; less widely used inputs such as pyrogenic silica, used to control material flowability by industries producing silicon rubber, paints and coatings, pharmaceuticals, and personal care products such as toothpaste; and specialized inputs such as chicle, which the chewing-gum industry uses. When the price of an input changes, this changes costs for all firms that use that input, causing their output and demand for other inputs to change. The induced changes in the output price and the other inputs' prices change the user firms' factor demand curve. Thus it is not possible to get to the market demand curve for a factor just by horizontally summing all the demand curves of user firms. Changes in these demand curves must be accounted for to reach market demand. The process of getting to market demand for a factor can be broken into two steps: (1) Deriving the industry factor demand curve for industries that use the factor, and (2) adding the demand of all industries to get to market demand. We will consider each step in turn, also relating the material to market factor demand elasticity.

Before beginning, however, we should first take note of the most obvious determinant of market factor demand elasticity: the factor demand elasticities of individual firms. Because we build market factor demand from demands of individual firms, the more easily a firm can substitute another input for the

---

7. Marginal cost is defined as the change in total cost per unit of change in output. Thus, since total cost changes according to the change in variable costs, and output changes according to the change in productive inputs ($\Delta q = MP_L \Delta L + MP_K \Delta K$), $MC = \Delta VC(q)/\Delta q = (w \Delta L + r\Delta K) / (MP_L \Delta L + MP_K \Delta K)$. Continuing, using the fact that $MP_K/r = MP_L/w = 1/p$ from the hiring condition for factors,

$$MC = (w \Delta L + r \Delta K) / (MP_L \Delta L + MP_K \Delta K)$$
$$= (w \Delta L + r \Delta K) / [(MP_L/w)w \Delta L + (MP_K/r)r \Delta K]$$
$$= [(w \Delta L + r \Delta K) / (w \Delta L + r \Delta K)](r/MP_K)$$
$$= r/MP_K.$$

factor, the more elastic the demand for the factor will be.[8] If the individual firm can easily substitute a second factor for one whose price has risen, quantity demanded of the first factor will be extremely price-sensitive and therefore elastic. If the firm cannot substitute another factor, its demand will not be as price-sensitive.

Deriving Industry Factor Demand

▼
7. What effects influence the derivation of industry and market demand curves (and their price elasticities) from firm demands? Draw diagrams showing how each effect works.

As was the case in Chapter 7 when we derived market supply from individual firm supply, the industry factor demand curve differs from the sum of individual firm demand curves. To get from individual firms' demand to industry factor demand, four effects need to be taken into account: the product price effect, the effect of other factor price changes, the effect of externalities, and the entry and exit effect. Because the way these effects work is mostly familiar to us from our study of supply, we can briefly discuss each effect and then wrap up the discussion in terms of the market factor demand curve.

The Product Price Effect. Assume we are finding the industry demand for labor in a competitive industry. At a lower wage rate, each individual firm increases the quantity of labor hired and increases its output at a fixed product price. When *one* firm increases its output, market price is not appreciably affected. However, when the entire *industry* increases its output, market supply increases and market price decreases. In Figure 11.7, the curve going through points *a* and *b* shows the sum of individual firms' labor demand. Demand for labor at wage *w* corresponds to point *a*. If the wage rate drops to *w'*, the sum of individual firms' demand moves to point *b*, and the industry expands its output because of the lower costs. Increased industry output means reduced product price. Thus $MRP_L = pMP_L$ is lower for each firm. This shifts the MRP_L in and shifts the sum of individual firms' demands to the curve left of *ab* passing through point *c*. The resulting industry labor demand is the curve connecting points *a* and *c*. The product price effect implies that the industry labor demand curve is steeper (less elastic) than the sum of individual firms' demand.

The product price effect also relates the price elasticity of factor demand to the price elasticity of demand for the output. A product with high price elasticity of demand has a relatively small change in product price associated with a large change in quantity. A change in market quantity therefore induces a small change in product price, and hence a small product price effect.

The Effect of Other Factors' Prices. Industry factor demand is also less elastic than the sum of individual firm demand curves because the increased industry output resulting from a wage decline increases demand for other

---

8. We saw in Chapter 6 that the degree of factor substitutability is measured by the curvature of the isoquant. An L-shaped isoquant implies zero substitutability at its corner point, whereas a straight-line isoquant implies perfect substitutability. Firms with straight-line isoquants will have much more price-elastic factor demands than firms with L-shaped or curved isoquants.

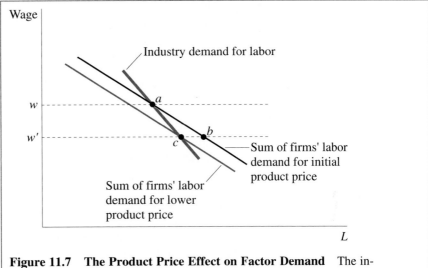

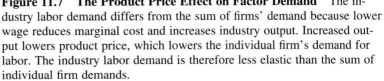

Figure 11.7   The Product Price Effect on Factor Demand   The industry labor demand differs from the sum of firms' demand because lower
wage reduces marginal cost and increases industry output. Increased output lowers product price, which lowers the individual firm's demand for
labor. The industry labor demand is therefore less elastic than the sum of
individual firm demands.

factors of production and raises their price. Think of the effect of a drop in
the wage of Wall Street financial analysts. As individual firms on Wall Street
seek to hire more analysts, they also demand more Wall Street office space,
driving its price up. Faced with higher costs of space, firms hire fewer analysts
than they would have at the original price for space, making labor demand
less elastic.

The factor price effect says that the price elasticity of factor demand
depends on the price elasticity of supply of other factors. A high price
elasticity of factor supply for other factors means that the price of other
factors changes very little as firms demand more of them. Since there is less
change in the price of other factors, there is a smaller factor price effect and
a more elastic demand for the original factor.

The Impact of Externalities. Sometimes industry size can directly affect
the production processes and productivity of individual firms. Such direct
effects are called *externalities,* a topic we cover in more depth in Chapter 14.
To illustrate with a simple example, think of a group of mining firms operating
in a valley and using the valley's water under high pressure for removing
earth. Once water is used in this way, it is filled with silt and unusable for
other firms, lowering their marginal product of labor. What effect would this
externality have on the industry labor demand curve? Consider the effect of
a lower price for labor. Individual firms would increase their hiring and

output. This would increase the silting of available water, however, and reduce firms' marginal product of labor (MP_L curves would shift to the left). Consequently, industry demand for mining labor (equal to the demand of all mining firms in the valley) would be less elastic than the sum of individual mining firms' labor demand. An externality that raised the marginal product of labor would have worked in the opposite direction, making the industry factor demand more elastic.

The Impact of Firms' Entry and Exit. The fourth way in which industry demand differs from the sum of firms' demand is through the entry and exit of firms. When we sum individual firms' demand curves, we include only the demands of existing firms in our calculations. As the wage rate falls, however, firm profits rise and new firms enter the market. Demand for labor by new firms tends to increase demand above the sum of the (original) firms' demand, making the industry demand curve more elastic (flatter). Because this effect works in the direction opposite to the product price effect and factor price effect, how do we know whether industry demand is more or less elastic than the sum of the demand of currently producing firms? The answer depends on which of the two effects is stronger. At one extreme is a case in which product demand is inelastic and firms are in the short run, so entry and exit are slight.[9] In this case, the product price effect dominates, and industry factor demand is less elastic than the sum of firms' demand. At the other extreme is a case in which the product demand is almost perfectly elastic (a nearly horizontal demand curve) and entry and exit are large. In this case, the product price effect disappears; since the entry effect dominates, the industry demand curve is more elastic than the sum of individual firms' demand.

The entry and exit effect says that the price elasticity of factor demand is greater in the long run than in the short run. The more time available to adjust to a factor's price change, the more time there is for new firms to enter or exit the market. The number of firms demanding the original factor expands when its price decreases and contracts when its price increases, flattening the factor demand curve and increasing its elasticity.

Deriving Market Factor Demand

Once the factor demand of every industry is determined, market demand is obtained by horizontally summing the demands of all industries. To the extent that (1) changes in one industry's output do not affect the product price or prices of other factors used in another industry, (2) there are no cross-industry externalities (in which the size of one industry directly affects the production of another), and (3) the entry or exit of new industries is not a factor, this gives the correct market demand curve.

---

9. Inelastic product demand implies little change in market quantity for large changes in market price. Thus the market could not absorb much output of new firms.

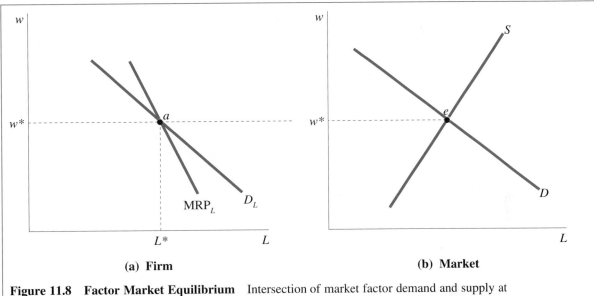

Figure 11.8 Factor Market Equilibrium Intersection of market factor demand and supply at point e determines the price of the factor, w^*. The individual firm perceives that it can buy any quantity of factor it chooses at w^*. The firm buys L^* units at point a on its factor demand curve, which also passes at that point through the firm's final MRP_L curve, which is consistent with its use of other factors.

 ## 11.3 Factor Market Equilibrium

We are nearly at the end of our story for factor markets. Thus far we have described the derived demands for factors by pricetaking firms and the market demand curve. Chapter 5 described the supply of factors such as labor owned by households. Many factors used by some firms are produced as outputs by other firms. The supply of these factors by perfectly competitive firms was described in Chapter 7, and the supply of these factors by imperfectly competitive firms, given the market demand curve, was described in Chapters 8, 9, and 10. Combining the demand curve derived in this chapter with the appropriate supply conditions from those earlier chapters allows us to describe factor market equilibrium.

The Pricetaking Firm and the Market

The relationship between factor market equilibrium and the individual firm can be shown in terms of equilibrium in a competitive market. Figure 11.8 shows factor curves for the individual firm in part (a) and the market demand and supply curves for the factor in part (b). The intersection of demand and supply at point e determines w^*, the market price of the factor. The individual firm perceives that it can buy as much factor as it wants at the going market price. It therefore chooses the point where price w^* cuts its demand curve at a. This point will also be where w^* cuts the firm's marginal revenue product curve, consistent with the firm's level of use of other factors. If the firm uses only one factor, then its factor demand curve and marginal revenue product curve coincide, as we saw previously.

The existence of a supply curve for this factor market indicates that the market is supplied perfectly competitively by firms and/or households, and the existence of a demand curve indicates that demanders are pricetakers. If the factor were supplied monopolistically or oligopolistically, there would be no supply curve. Instead, equilibrium would be determined by the output choice or choices of the monopolist or oligopolist suppliers as described in Chapters 8 and 10. From the point of view of the individual pricetaking firm, however, the description in part (a) would still apply.[10] It follows that the factor's price is determined both by its marginal revenue product to the user firm and by the relevant market demand and supply conditions.

APPLICATION: Education, Earnings, and the Eighties

The 1980s witnessed tremendous changes in the American economy, including the longest peacetime expansion in history and the creation of over 18 million new jobs out of a total labor force of 127 million. In recent years, however, attention has been given to explaining the noticeable trend toward increasing income inequality. For example, in 1967 43.8 percent of household income was produced by the top 20 percent of households, whereas in 1989 the equivalent figure had risen to 46.8 percent. In contrast, the lowest 20 percent of households produced 4.0 percent of household income in 1967 and only 3.8 percent in 1989. For the top 5 percent of households, the figures for 1967 and 1989 were 17.5 and 18.9, respectively.[11]

Inspection of the data for the period 1964 to 1989 shows that the years from 1964 to 1969 were marked by a decline in income inequality, followed by a longer period (1969–1989) during which inequality increased.[12] For most groups the changes have not been great, especially in terms of changes

---

10. We will consider the case where the firm can influence the price of its factor input later in the chapter.
11. U.S. Department of Commerce, *Money Income of Households, Families, and Persons in the United States: 1988 and 1989,* Current Population Reports, Consumer Income Series P-60, No. 172, Washington, D.C., U.S. Government Printing Office, July 1991, p. 358. The second, third, and fourth household quintiles produced the following percentages of household income in 1967: 10.8, 17.3, and 24.2. The equivalent figures in 1989 were 9.5, 15.8, and 24.0. Thus all but the top quintile produced less of total household income in 1989 than they did in 1967.
12. U.S. Department of Commerce, *Trends in Relative Income: 1964–1989,* Current Population Reports, Consumer Income Series P-60, No. 177, Washington, D.C., December 1991, p. 4.

in absolute real incomes over the period, but they raise certain questions, especially in light of the fact that real incomes at the lowest end of the spectrum show absolute declines. What could explain the changes?

One obvious explanation is the compositional change in the population being measured. For example, 21.6 percent of the population was elderly in 1990, compared to only 19.3 percent in 1970; 29.2 percent of households were living in nonfamily situations in 1990, compared to only 18.7 percent in 1970; and the percentage of female householders with no husband present was 16.5 percent in 1990, compared to only 10.8 percent in 1970. Since each of these groups is well known to have significantly lower incomes relative to the population at large, their increase in the population causes greater income disparity.[13]

Compositional changes, however, are not the major explanation for changing relative wages. Instead, evidence points to changes in the market demand curves for different types of workers. In particular, technological change over the period increased the productivity of educated workers compared to the less educated.[14] Changes in technology that increase the MRP of educated workers shift the market demand for educated workers to the right, raising their real wages. Were it not for the fact that the American labor force became more educated by the 1980s than in the 1960s and 1970s, the relative disparity in earnings would be even greater. In short, the nation is producing more educated workers than in the past, as measured by years of schooling (the supply curve is shifting to the right), but market demand for workers with greater education is growing even faster (the demand curve is shifting further to the right).

The effect of education on income and standard of living differs according to the type of living unit we measure. Since more than 70 percent of households are families (two or more individuals living together related by blood, marriage, or adoption), we will examine the relationship between education and family income first and then look at data for individuals corrected for the size of household in which they reside. Table 11.1 shows family income for different education levels of the family head. Families with 5 or more years of college for the head have seen their real incomes rise from $58,431 in 1969 to $66,277 in 1989 (measured in 1990 dollars). Relative to all families, this represents an improvement from 171 percent of median family income

13. U.S. Department of Commerce, *Money Income of Households,* p. 6. The ratio of elderly to nonelderly median income was 0.48 in 1989; of nonfamily householder income to median family income, 0.49. Data also show that half of female householder families with no husband present were in the lowest income quintile.

14. See Peter Passell, "The Wage Gap: Sins of Omission," *New York Times,* May 27, 1992, p. D2. The link between education and earnings shows up strongly in labor force data. In 1989, for example, 54.1 percent of those with five or more years of college were in the top quintile for family income, compared to 41.2 percent of those with four years of college, and only 13.4 percent of those with four years of high school. In contrast, nearly half (45.7 percent) of those with eight years or less of school and one-third (34.6 percent) of those with one to three years of high school were in the lowest quintile for family income (U.S. Department of Commerce, U.S. Government Printing Office, *Money Income of Households,* p. 56).

Table 11.1   Absolute and Relative Family Income by Education, 1969–1989

Year	Elementary (8 or fewer years)	High School (12 years)	College (4 years)	College (4 or more years)	College (5 or more years)	Median Income— All Families
1989	$18,321	$34,253	$55,208	$60,308	$66,277	$37,133
	49%	92%	149%	162%	178%	
1984	$18,783	$33,359	$52,441	$54,285	$61,350	$34,815
	54%	96%	151%	156%	176%	
1979	$20,642	$37,086	$48,929	$53,856	$55,085	$34,308
	60%	108%	143%	157%	161%	
1974	$21,581	$37,138	$50,633	$54,490	$57,020	$34,626
	62%	107%	146%	157%	165%	
1969	$22,735	$36,989	$49,575	$52,169	$58,431	$34,230
	66%	108%	145%	152%	171%	

Note: Absolute incomes expressed in 1990 dollars. Relative incomes expressed as percentages of median income for all families.

Source: *Author's calculations from data in two U.S. Department of Commerce reports:* Trends in Relative Income: 1964–1989, *Current Population Reports, Consumer Income Series P-60, No. 177, Washington, D.C., December 1991, p. 25; and* Money Income of Households, Families, and Persons in the United States: 1988 and 1989, *Current Population Reports, Consumer Income Series P-60, No. 172, Washington, D.C., July 1991, p. 53.*

to 178 percent. Families of college-educated heads show similar increases from $49,575 to $55,208 in absolute terms, and an increase relative to all families from 145 percent to 149 percent of median family income. In absolute terms, those with only high school degrees have declined in income ($36,989 in 1969 versus $34,253 in 1989) and have lost ground relative to the median (108 percent in 1969 versus 92 percent in 1989). The least educated, those with 8 or fewer years of education, show the greatest drops in absolute and relative incomes over the same period of time ($22,735 to $18,321 and 66 percent to 49 percent).

The 1989 data underscore the importance of education to family income. Finishing high school nearly doubles family income (from roughly $18,000 to $34,000), and completing a college degree adds another $21,000. Although it is difficult to predict the extent to which the technological changes raising the productivity of more highly educated workers will continue, it does not seem hard to predict that a policy geared toward education will help to raise family incomes in the least productive portion of the population.

Table 11.2 reports median relative income for persons 25 to 64, again based on education. This table corrects for the fact that households of different sizes need different incomes for members to have a given standard of living. For example, a two-person household needs less than twice the income of a one-person household to have an equivalent living standard. In the table,

	Table 11.2	**Median Relative Incomes of Persons 25 to 64 by Education, 1969–1989 (as Percentages of Median for All Persons)**	
Year	*Did Not Finish High School*	*High School (12 years)*	*College (4 or more years)*
1989	65%	108%	175%
1984	72%	111%	171%
1979	80%	117%	161%
1974	85%	117%	167%
1969	91%	120%	170%

Source: U.S. Department of Commerce, Trends in Relative Income: 1964–1989, *Current Population Reports, Consumer Income Series P-60, No. 177, Washington, D.C., U.S.G.P.O., December 1991, Table D, p. 10.*

everyone in a given household is attributed the same equivalence-adjusted income. The percentages indicate each group's median equivalence-adjusted income relative to the median equivalence-adjusted income of all persons. As the table shows, both those with 12 years of high school and those with 4 or more years of college fare better in relative terms than in the family data reported in Table 11.1. But the declining trend from 1969 to 1989 is still evident for those with 12 years of high school or less. The trend for those with 4 or more years of college to increase their equivalence-adjusted income is less pronounced over the same period than in the family data, but still evident. ■

The Fair Wage?

▼

8. Interpret the market equilibrium wage and the $w = pMP_L$ condition.

At the start of the chapter, we established a scenario in which you were a manager of Control Electronics Incorporated who needed to know what quantities of labor to hire. We have answered that question in terms of the firm's hiring condition and its demand for factor curve. We also referred to the founder of CEI, who wanted to follow the policy of paying a fair wage to CEI employees. Is there any sense in which the equilibrium wage w^* in Figure 11.8 is a ''fair'' wage, and should we be concerned if the wage is different from this level?

From the point of view of economics, we perhaps cannot give a definitive answer acceptable to everyone in the moral sense, but we can shed considerable light on the wage from an efficiency standpoint. In the case of a factor—labor in this case—demanded by perfectly competitive firms in the output market, equilibrium implies that $w = pMP_L$. In other words, the last unit of labor hired produces MP_L units of output having value pMP_L. This is precisely what the unit is paid. Since the labor was willingly supplied at wage w, payment at that level is revealed to be sufficient to cover the laborer's disutility of supplying it (or to cover the costs of the factor's production if it is a nonlabor factor).

If the firm tries to pay more than $p\mathrm{MP}_L$, this extra must come at the expense of payments to other factors or of the owners of the firm. Figure 11.9 shows the relationship between payments to labor and those to capital. At market wage w^* the firm hires L^* units of labor corresponding to point a. Total payments to labor are given by the shaded area. By the definition of marginal product, the firm's total output equals the area under the MP_L curve and thus firm revenues are the area under the $p\mathrm{MP}_L$ curve. Why doesn't labor get paid the full value of the output out to L^*? The answer is that other factors also contributed to production, and their payments must come from the area of triangle abc. Assuming that capital and labor are the two factors, $wL = p\mathrm{MP}_L L$ will be paid to the firm's labor and $rK = p\mathrm{MP}_K K$ will be paid for the firm's use of capital services. If the firm has money left over after these payments, it accrues to the owners of the firm as economic profit. If the firm is unable to make these payments, even choosing the least-cost combination of K and L, it suffers economic losses and closes down in the long run.[15]

Figure 11.9 also shows what happens if the firm has market power in the output market. Since $\mathrm{MR} < p$, $\mathrm{MRP}_L < p\mathrm{MP}_L$ and the firm will hire L' units of labor instead of L^*, moving to point d. The firm still pays wage w^*, which is less than VMP_L at w'. We have already covered the social cost of monopoly in Chapter 8. We can now see from Figure 11.9 that the monopolist earns monopoly profits by employing less labor and paying it *below* the value of its marginal product. The same argument applies to other factors. In this sense, the monopolist's profits come partly at the expense of factors whose value of marginal product is higher than their rewards.

Applying the Market Model

On first consideration, the demand and supply model for factor markets often seems too simple to explain many of the phenomena we observe daily. For example, why does a janitor who sweeps floors in the neighborhood grade school earn less than the unskilled construction worker who sweeps at the construction site? Why does one Olympic sports star whose time is only one-tenth of a second faster than another's earn millions in product endorsements while the close second earns virtually nothing? Or, in the university setting,

---

15. If the firm exhibits constant returns to scale, least-cost production and perfect competition in the output market imply that the firm's payments to its factors—both labor and capital—according to the value of their marginal product just equal the firm's revenues and the firm makes zero economic profit. That is, $p\mathrm{MP}_L L + p\mathrm{MP}_K K = pq$. If the firm exhibits decreasing returns to scale, $p\mathrm{MP}_L L + p\mathrm{MP}_K K < pq$ and the firm makes positive economic profit. Perfect competition is incompatible with firms' exhibiting increasing returns to scale, since with downward-sloping AC, setting $p = \mathrm{MC}$ implies economic losses with $p\mathrm{MP}_L L + p\mathrm{MP}_K K > pq$.

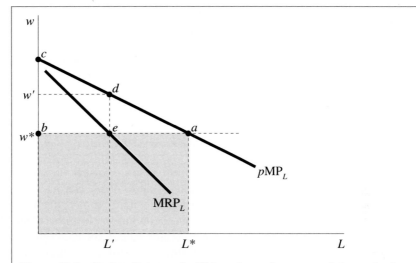

Figure 11.9   Factor Price and $p\,\mathrm{PM_L}$ At market wage w^* the perfectly competitive firm hires L^* units of labor at point a, so that $w = p\,\mathrm{MP}_L$. Total payments to labor are shown by the shaded area. If the firm is a monopolist in the output market but a pricetaker in the input market, it reduces its labor to L' units at point d but still pays wage w^*. Thus it pays a wage lower than labor's value of marginal product: $w < p\,\mathrm{MP}_L$.

why does the economics or electrical engineering professor earn more than the English or classics professor, when all appear to perform similar duties?

Compensating Wage Differentials. Economists, too, have puzzled over these questions, and in so doing have discovered that the market approach to factor payments works far better than it might appear. In the case of labor markets especially, there is a great variety of job descriptions and skills, so one cannot really consider labor to be a single market. In the case of the janitor and construction worker, sweeping the ground floor of the grade school is not the same thing as sweeping the same area 100 stories up in a windy building that is not yet closed in! In this case, economists talk of *compensating wage differentials,* which reflect jobs' different hazards or degrees of unpleasantness. Other things being equal, jobs with greater risk or more unpleasant working conditions pay higher than similar jobs with better working conditions. Once these different conditions are taken into account, many variations in wages can be explained.

Wages and Economic Marginal Productivity. In the case of the sports star, our discussion in Chapter 5 of the rent frequently earned by those who are best in their field touched on the fact that such workers often command large incomes far out of proportion to the extent of their superior skill. We can now explain the reason for this in terms of the demand for their labor and their marginal productivity. Take the Olympic gold-medal winner. If you were a firm, would you want the gold-medal winner to endorse your product, or would you select the silver- (or bronze-) medal winner? If you were honest, you said the gold. Why? Because you know the endorsement of the winner will carry much more weight with consumers. How *much* more is often unrelated to the extent of the physical superiority of the athlete—being the best, by however slim a margin, is enough. This explains the difference in earnings.

Next, let's apply the model to the earnings of electrical engineering and classics professors. Even assuming the two types of professors perform identical jobs at the university, we still would expect the electrical engineer to command a higher salary. Why? Because the electrical engineer has higher productivity in nonuniversity employment, so a higher salary is needed to warrant removing the engineer from the other sector and to justify that shift to the engineer. Trying to pay the electrical engineer the classics professor's salary would ultimately result in an empty electrical engineering department. Thus, what appeared to be identical productivity in fact is not. Said another way, the electrical engineer and the classics professor are in different job markets, though they are both professors.

Comparable Worth. Heightened awareness since the 1960s of racial discrimination, coupled with the observation that many jobs that appear to have the same requirements nevertheless pay different wages, has prompted some observers to conclude that the cause of the difference must be illegitimate discrimination. Others note that often what appears as inequitable is not when the labor market is understood properly. While it is generally agreed that cases of inequity do exist, remedying them without causing greater problems will not be a simple process. One proposed remedy consists of passing laws requiring employers to offer equal pay for jobs of comparable worth, where *comparable worth* is defined in terms of job characteristics rather than demand and supply. For the most part, economists have not been sympathetic to this notion because of difficulties that can arise from applying it. In essence, the comparable worth doctrine asserts that it is possible to predict the fair market wage (the wage applying in a market without improper discrimination) on the basis of characteristics of the job, such as how much formal education is needed, how much training is needed, how much prior experience is required, how unpleasant the working conditions are, and so on. By assigning points to the different components of the job description, employers would come up with scores that would determine the right wage for the job, replacing the function of the labor market. Jobs with the same scores would automatically be paid the same.

In general, comparable worth cases have not fared well in federal courts. To date, only a few scattered state and local governments have made pay adjustments on the basis of comparable worth, although many others are investigating whether their pay scales reflect the jobs' relative contributions. Just as we would not expect two artists to be paid the same for their paintings because they both filled the same size canvas with paint, had the same art training and so on, our examples of the sweepers, the Olympic stars, and the university professors show some of the pitfalls of trying to measure productivity and economic worth solely in terms of external measures such as credentials, apparent job descriptions, and so on. These external measures can be helpful, but in many cases they are misleading and are no substitute for economic determinants. In each of our examples, a more thorough consideration of marginal productivity and the proper functioning of demand and supply explained the pay differences.

APPLICATION: Who's Chicken About Chickens?

Certainly the American public is not chicken about chickens, if the decades-long increase in poultry demand is any indication. Between 1977 and 1987, for example, poultry production rose 67 percent, from about 12 billion pounds to 20 billion pounds.[16] Americans now eat more chicken and turkey than red meat. At the same time, the poultry industry has undergone major changes, including shifting to new breeds of chickens that can be raised in factory farms, converting to large-scale plants and assembly-line operations for processing, mechanizing tasks, and simplifying the remaining steps that are still done by hand. Whereas a skilled worker in the 1960s could slaughter about 66 birds a minute, today a machine can handle five times as many, or five per second.

Because of these changes, output per worker in the poultry processing industry rose 43 percent between 1975 and 1985. Reflecting changes in the industry, poultry worker wages are higher than what the workers could earn in convenience stores or fast-food restaurants, and many poultry workers find their jobs steadier and easier than field work.

From the description thus far, it would appear that the industry represents a success story. It has succeeded in raising productivity, efficiency, and wages in the labor markets of Arkansas, Georgia, Alabama, and North Carolina, where three-fourths of the processing is done. Indeed, higher marginal product implies higher market wages. There are two other aspects to the story, however. In the process of converting to faster production methods, firms such as Perdue, Cargill, and others have created jobs that require workers to perform simple repetitive tasks, such as drawing out viscera, cutting wings, or popping thigh bones, 25, 40, even 90 times per minute, hour after hour, day after day, in rooms that vary from below 32 to 95 degrees, depending on the type of processing done. Workers are assigned to the assembly line except for lunch and two 10- to 15-minute breaks, and they are pressured not to leave the line otherwise, even for bodily functions. Given the unpleasant

16. Information in this section is taken from Barbara Goldoftas, ''To Make a Tender Chicken: Poultry Workers Pay the Price,'' *Real World Micro,* 3d ed. September 1989, pp. 44–46.

aspects of the working conditions, compensating wage differentials would be another explanation for the relatively high level of wages. But the third aspect of the story is more troubling.

Working conditions in the plants have resulted in a large number of repetitive motion injuries. For example, Mary Smith worked at Cargill only seven months before her hands began to swell, hurting day and night. Fourteen of her coworkers had surgery for carpal tunnel syndrome, and the plant estimates that one third of the workers have trouble with their hands.[17] Other plants report that it is common procedure for 60 percent of their workers to go to the nurse each morning for painkillers and to have their hands wrapped. Complaints allege that processors ignore injuries, underreport them (fewer reported injuries keep firm worker compensation costs down), intimidate those who speak up about injuries, and fire workers who develop repetitive motion injuries. Wages would not appear to be fair compensation for what workers actually give up. Workers, in turn, appear not to be aware of the extent of the risks they are taking.

In recent years the government has levied huge fines against poultry firms for underreporting of repetitive motion injuries, and advocacy groups are becoming increasingly involved in the workers' behalf. These groups argue that firms can do a better job of educating their workers to the risks of the job, increase their responsiveness to worker needs, rotate workers, give them longer breaks, redesign tools and working conditions, take more care to keep tools sharp to reduce strain in their use, and even retrain workers disabled by poultry work.

Although the results of mechanization, industry restructuring, and marginal-productivity-based labor demand theory contribute to the industry's wage determination, the obvious signs of dysfunction, and perhaps even calculated malfeasance by some companies, suggest a more important feature in this case: the lack of full information by poultry workers, many of whom become aware that they are making a choice between their health and their job after the "choice" has already been made. ■

Minimum Wage Legislation

The Fair Labor Standards Act of 1938 established a minimum wage for certain workers, primarily those employed by firms engaged in interstate commerce. Periodically since that time, the level of the minimum wage has been raised and the coverage extended, so that today most full-time workers are included.

If Congress is able to raise the income of workers just by passing minimum wage legislation, a natural question to ask is: Why stop at a minimum wage of $4 or $5 per hour? Why not raise the minimum wage to $100 or even

---

17. Overuse of the tendons passing through the carpal tunnel in the wrist causes swelling and pressure on the nerve that serves the hand.

$1,000 per hour so that all workers can benefit? In fact, the minimum wage operates in competitive labor markets in the same way that a price floor does (see Chapter 2). For this reason, economists have criticized minimum wage legislation for the social costs it imposes and for its unemployment-creating effects, especially among teen-agers and young workers in unskilled occupations that are most affected by the minimum wage. Because of the downward-sloping demand curve for factor inputs, raising the wage for unskilled workers causes firms to move up their demand curves, hiring fewer workers and shifting to other types of inputs. Those who have jobs benefit, but at the expense of those who lose their jobs, are made to work part-time instead of full-time, or never get a job at all. The individuals who lose out are often concentrated in the ranks of the young, less skilled, and less educated—the very groups often most in need of employment.

For comparable worth supporters, the objective is often to equalize men's and women's wages by raising women's wages (men's could just as easily be lowered, but for obvious reasons that is typically not the objective). Since legislating an increase in one job's wages above market levels is equivalent to imposing a price floor, the effect would be to reduce employment in the affected occupation. For example, assume that clerk-typist and warehouse worker jobs are assigned the same comparable worth score, although clerk-typists had formerly earned less than warehouse workers. The effect of the wage floor would be to reduce employment of clerk-typists, forcing some of those who would have had clerk-typist jobs to be out of work or to take other work at lower pay or with less pleasant working conditions. A better policy would be to ensure that clerk-typists who want to work as warehouse workers and are qualified to do so can get such jobs in a freely and fairly functioning labor market.

In spite of being told about the effect of price floors, some members of government continue to support minimum wage and comparable worth legislation. If we can assume that their reasons are sincere and not political, (i.e., we assume voters understand that there is no free lunch when it comes to wages), are there any valid circumstances for supporting minimum wage legislation for which decreased employment might *not* be the result? One obvious answer is that employment would not decline if the elasticity of the labor supply curve were zero. However, since most studies indicate that the relevant labor supply has an elasticity much closer to 1 than to zero,[18] this would appear not to offer much hope. Another such circumstance would occur if the demand for labor were not competitive. To evaluate this possibility, we need to consider the demand for labor by firms with the ability to influence price. We take this up next.

---

18. See Jacob Mincer, "Unemployment Effects of Minimum Wages," *Journal of Political Economy,* August 1976, and Finis Welch, *Minimum Wages: Issues and Evidence,* Washington, D.C.: American Enterprise Institute, 1978. Labor supply was discussed in Chapter 5.

11.4 Firm Demand in Monopsonistic Factor Markets

The theory of *monopsony*—markets with a single buyer—is nearly identical to the theory of monopoly we looked at in Chapter 8. In this section we will see how a single buyer of a factor input decides which point on the factor supply curve to choose. We will then briefly consider the effect of a minimum wage on such a firm, before we turn in the following section to the interesting case of what happens when a labor union (a monopolist seller) sells to a monopsonistic firm.

Setting Input Price: MRP and Marginal Factor Cost

▼

9. What is marginal factor cost (MFC)?

The monopsonist knows that employing an additional unit of labor adds to revenues according to the marginal revenue product, MRP_L. If the firm is a pricetaker in the output market, $MRP = pMP_L$. If it is a monopolist in the output market, $MRP = MR \times MP_L$. To know whether employing an additional unit of labor increases profits, the monopsonist must also know how much employing the additional unit adds to *cost*. The change in total payments to the factor is called the *marginal factor cost*.

> Let factor L *be paid wage* w. *Then the change in total factor payments* wL *due to the employment of an additional unit of* L *is the* ***marginal factor cost****, MFC* = $\Delta wL/\Delta L$.

To see how to compute marginal factor cost, let labor be the representative factor and let the supply of labor be $L = 10 + 0.5w$, where L is the quantity of labor supplied and w is the wage rate. As the wage rate rises, the labor supplied increases. Writing the supply curve to show how the wage rate depends on the number of workers hired, we get $w = 2L - 20$. Now consider the effect on the wage bill, wL, of raising the number of workers hired from 20 to 21. First, the wage rate must rise from \$20 to \$22. The employer therefore must pay \$22 for the additional worker, plus raise the wage by \$2 for the other 20 workers, which will cost \$40. The total marginal factor cost is therefore \$62.[19]

Marginal factor cost can be written in terms of the elasticity of factor supply. We know that adding a unit of labor raises total payments because of the wage paid to the extra labor unit, w. Hiring an additional labor unit also moves the employer up the supply curve of labor and raises the wage that needs to be paid to all previous units of labor hired, $L \Delta w/\Delta L$. Combining both effects gives us

---

19. This can also be computed directly. At wage \$20, 20 workers are hired, for a total wage bill of \$400. To employ 21 workers, the wage rate must be \$22, which means a total wage bill of \$462. The marginal factor cost is the difference in the wage bill that results from hiring the additional worker, or \$62.

$$\frac{\Delta wL}{\Delta L} = w + L\frac{\Delta w}{\Delta L}$$

$$= w\left[1 + \left(\frac{L}{w}\right)\left(\frac{\Delta w}{\Delta L}\right)\right]$$

$$= w\left(1 + \frac{1}{\varepsilon_L}\right),$$

where ε_L is the price elasticity of labor supply. Since ε_L is a positive number, the marginal factor cost is higher than the wage. The formula for marginal factor cost is the same as the formula for marginal revenue, except that the elasticity of factor supply replaces the elasticity of demand. In the event that the firm faces a horizontal factor supply curve (this is what the pricetaking firm perceives, for example), $\varepsilon_L = \infty$ and MFC $= w$; otherwise MFC $> w$.

In the same way that the marginal revenue curve lies below the demand curve, the MFC curve lies above the supply curve. To draw the marginal factor cost curve for a linear supply curve, find the supply intercept on the vertical axis (point *a* in Figure 11.10). Next, draw a horizontal line from the

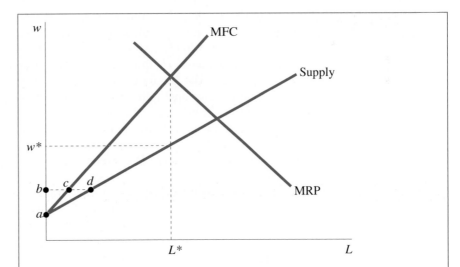

Figure 11.10 Monopsony and Marginal Factor Cost The marginal factor cost is higher than the supply curve because hiring an additional unit of labor requires raising the wage as the employer chooses quantities further out on the supply curve of labor. This means paying higher wages to all units of labor. For a linear supply curve, the marginal factor cost has the same intercept on the vertical axis as the supply curve (point *a*) and passes through a point half the horizontal distance from the vertical axis to the supply curve (distance *bc* equals distance *cd*). The monopsonistic firm hires to the point where the marginal revenue product equals the marginal factor cost. This leads to employment of *L** units of labor at wage *w**.

vertical axis to the supply curve, such as line *bd* in Figure 11.10. Bisect the line at point *c* and draw a new line through points *a* and *c*. This is MFC.

The difference between the increase in revenues to the firm, MRP, and the increase in factor costs, MFC, is the change in profit to the firm. Only when MRP = MFC can the firm not raise profit by changing the quantity of the factor employed. The monopsonist therefore chooses to employ the factor up to the point where MRP = MFC.

In Figure 11.10 MRP cuts MFC at employment level L^*. The monopsonistic firm therefore hires L^* units of labor and pays w^*, the wage that corresponds to L^* units of labor on the supply curve. Since $p\,MP_L \geq MRP_L > w$, we also note that by employing less labor at a lower price, the monopsonist pays a wage that is below the value of labor's marginal product.

Monopsony and the Minimum Wage

▼
10. Contrast the effects of a minimum wage in competitive and monopsonistic labor markets.

We saw earlier that a minimum wage created an excess supply of labor (unemployment) when the labor market was in competitive equilibrium. In the case of a labor market characterized by monopsony, a minimum wage may have a different effect.

Figure 11.11 shows the effect of a minimum wage in a monopsonistic labor market. With no minimum wage, the monopsonist chooses the wage-employment point *a* on the supply curve of labor with wage w^*. Now consider the effect of a minimum wage w' that is above w^*. The firm must pay the minimum wage w' for employment of labor up to quantity L', corresponding to point *b* on the supply curve. Since the wage is fixed, the marginal factor cost of an additional unit of labor is just the wage rate w'. To employ labor above L' units, however, the monopsonist must pay a higher wage determined by the supply curve above point *b*. The line labeled MFC in the figure is the marginal factor cost corresponding to the supply curve of labor for levels of employment above L'. The effective marginal factor cost curve is therefore *fbde*.

Comparing the MRP curve to the effective MFC curve shows that MRP cuts the effective MFC curve in the gap between points *b* and *d*. Consequently, the firm chooses the wage-employment pair at point *b* in response to minimum wage w'. As w' is raised, the point chosen by the monopsonist travels up the supply curve from point *a* until it reaches point *c*. For higher minimum wages, the wage-quantity pair moves up the MRP curve from point *c* toward point *g*, since the firm will not hire to the right of MRP. The overall conclusion is that wages and employment follow the heavy curve from *a* to *c* to *g* as the minimum wage is increased. In segment *ac*, both wages and employment rise without unemployment (unlike the effect of a minimum wage in a competitive market). After point *c*, however, the minimum wage causes a drop in employment and excess supply of labor.

What can we conclude from this? If one believes that labor markets are characterized by monopsony, a minimum wage (up to a point) might be able to increase employment at the same time that it raises wages (this corresponds

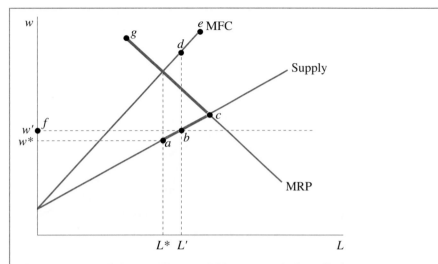

Figure 11.11   Minimum Wage and Monopsony Labor Choice   The heavy curve passing through points *a, b, c,* and *g* traces the path that the wage-employment pair follows as the minimum wage is raised from *w** for a monopsonist with the marginal revenue product curve labeled MRP.

to segment *ac* in Figure 11.11). However, with the possible exception of the classic company town, where all workers are hired by one firm and cannot leave for work elsewhere, the monopsony model would not appear to be the best model of the labor market. In any case, even though finding a pure monopsony may be difficult, the model offers useful insights into the relationship between wages and employment and into the interactions of laborers and firms.

11.5 Monopsonistic Firm Versus Monopolistic Union: Bargaining Implications

What happens when an irresistible force meets an immovable object? Or what happens when a monopsonistic buyer faces a monopolistic seller? The answer is that bargaining results within certain parameters that can be described in economic terms. One such case occurs when a labor union bargains with a monopsonistic firm about wages and employment.

Figure 11.12 shows the MRP curve, the supply curve of labor, and the MFC curve for a representative firm and labor union. The supply curve shows a horizontal segment at wage *w'* because union members can take jobs elsewhere in the economy for wage *w'*, and so will not accept union employment at less than this amount. The horizontal segment is also the MFC curve

▼
11. What determines the boundaries of the wage-employment point when a monopolistic labor union bargains with a monopsonistic employer?

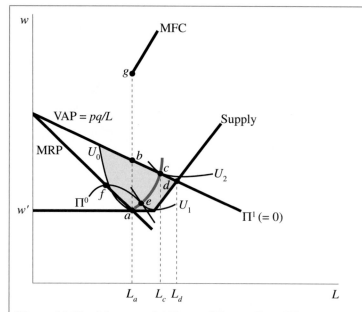

Figure 11.12 Monopsonist Versus Monopolist   When the monopsonistic firm meets the monopolistic seller of labor (the labor union), the two must bargain to reach a solution acceptable to each. Given the supply curve, the firm prefers point *a*. The union wants higher wages and employment for its members, trading off the two according to its particular objectives indicated by indifference curves U_0, U_1, and U_2, but not such high wages as to put the firm out of business and not more employment than union members desire on the basis of their supply curve. The ''battleground'' therefore becomes the shaded region, where these constraints are met and the union is no worse off than if it lets the firm choose its preferred point. The union prefers point *c* as its best point in the shaded region. The set of points describing the preferred point for the union, given the level of profit for the firm, is the line connecting points *a* and *c*. Whether point *a*, point *c*, or some point between the two is chosen depends on the relative strength of the two parties in their bargaining.

for that portion of the supply curve. Higher wages induce greater labor supply, in the usual fashion, as given by the upward-sloping portion of the supply curve. Since the firm's MRP curve cuts the supply curve in its horizontal section, the firm's preferred wage-employment pair is point *a*.

In contrast to point *a*, what is the labor union's preferred point? Possible union objectives include maximizing the wage of employed union members, increasing economic rent to union workers (payments above what is needed to keep workers on the job), or establishing some trade-off between *w* and *L* (maximizing total wages of union members, wL, is one example of the last objective). In fact, unions do not seem to maximize their members' wages without consideration to employment, since this implies shrinking the number of workers employed and diminishing the power and even the viability of the union.

There is a limit to what the union will demand, whatever its objectives. If it seeks too high a wage, the firm will not be able to pay its other factors of production and could earn negative economic profits, exiting the market and taking the union with it. The labor union therefore would never seek a wage rate higher than the *value of the average product of labor,*[20] which is the curve labeled VAP in Figure 11.12. At the same time, the union would not seek employment levels for a given wage to the right of the supply curve, since they would exceed what its members want to supply. In the region to the left of the supply curve and below VAP, the other objectives of the union imply that increased union employment given the wage, or increased wage given the employment level, is beneficial. Thus the union trades off wages and employment, as the indifference curves labeled U_0 and U_1 show. These indifference curves become horizontal when they touch the supply curve, since increasing employment beyond the supply curve level at the given wage no longer is beneficial.

Since the union reaches indifference curve U_0 passing through point *a* by simply letting the firm choose its preferred point, the shaded region bounded by VAP, the supply curve, and U_0 contains the potential set of points that the labor union might want to select. (For simplicity's sake we will assume that VAP forms the upper bound of the union's objectives, even though we recognize that the true upper bound would typically lie below VAP, since the union would not seek to claim all firm revenues.) The highest indifference curve that the union can reach in this region is U_2. Point *c*, therefore, would be the union's preferred point.

Since the union (a monopolist) must bargain with the firm (a monopsonist), we can characterize the quality of the outcome for each in terms of union utility and firm profits. Firm profits are at their highest level at point *a* (that is why the firm chose it in the first place!), and they are zero at point *c* (all of the firm's revenues are being paid out to union labor). In between these two extremes, one can draw isoprofit curves showing the combinations of the wage rate and employment level that give the same firm profit.[21] One such curve is drawn as the curve Π^0. Higher profit for the firm lies below Π^0 and lower profit above. For example, if the firm has to hire more labor at a fixed wage than it would choose on the basis of its MRP curve, its profits will fall (a move to the right of *f* puts the firm in the region above Π^0). To hold profit constant, therefore, the wage rate must fall as employment increases. Points *e* and *f* have the same profit, for example.

---

20. Recall from Chapter 6 that the average product of labor is q/L where q is firm output. The value of the average product of labor is pq/L. Setting $pq/L = w$ implies that all firm revenues are paid to labor, $pq = wL$.

21. We discussed isoprofit curves in Chapter 10 in terms of duopolists' output levels.

Given profit Π^0, the highest indifference curve that the labor union can reach is U_1 at the tangency point e. Conversely, given indifference level U_1 for the union, point e is the point with highest profit that the firm can reach. Points like e therefore form the set of bargaining solutions that we would expect from the firm and union if we eliminate outcomes where the firm could increase profit without lowering union utility and vice versa. Collecting all such tangency points for all profit levels gives us the line connecting points a, e, and c. However, we cannot tell from this line what particular agreement the firm and the union will reach.

With better union bargainers, the solution will lie closer to point c, whereas better firm bargainers move the agreement closer to point a. In the event that an agreement is not reached, the union can threaten that it will strike, lowering firm profits. Strikes are also costly to union membership in lost wages, however, so the prospect of the firm's closing, shutting out workers, or hiring replacement workers is also a threat to the union. The bargaining is a game in which elements of both common interest and conflict of interest appear: both sides benefit from reaching a cooperative solution, but each side prefers the outcome to be as close to its preferred position as possible.

APPLICATION: Unionism and Worker Participation in the United States

At the peak of union membership in the early 1950s, nearly 40 percent of workers in the United States were unionized. That fraction fell gradually but steadily until the 1970s, when it began to drop dramatically. Today, only about one in six workers in the United States belongs to a union, even though the number in nearby Canada remains 35 to 40 percent.[22]

Causes of the decline in unionism are still being debated. Some critics point to organizing complacency on the part of union officials, and others cite lowered union effectiveness. The effects of unionism's decline are just as difficult to assess. Although fewer than 2 percent of contract negotiations result in strikes, old-style unionism evinces images of antagonism and conflict between workers and management. Today, new research shows that productivity can be raised by greater *cooperation* between workers and management and *participation* by workers in decision making. This suggests a role for organizations that enhance worker-management cooperative interaction.

Productivity-increasing worker participation includes activities of the type successfully demonstrated by the Japanese and now being learned by American firms in the auto industry and elsewhere. Giving workers a say in the production process, including them in the training of new workers, having workers participate in the work-pace decision and quality control effort, and

---

22. Patricia Horn, ''Labor After Reagan,'' *Dollars & Sense: Real World Micro,* September 1988, pp. 67, 70.

even letting them help keep the firm's financial records are among the types of participation that seem to pay off in increased productivity.[23] Worker participation seems to work best when it involves workers in essential shop-floor decisions, where they are often better informed than supervisors who have less intimate contact with the floor. Purely consultative arrangements, such as quality circles or token ownership plans, seem to be less effective than direct arrangements such as work teams that give workers a say in making their own assignments and determining their own work routines.[24]

The many dozens of studies already published seem to indicate that worker participation usually produces at least small short-run improvements in productivity, sometimes can lead to significant long-lasting productivity improvements, and virtually never leads to losses in productivity.[25] In that event, cooperative worker participation would appear to be a no-lose proposition. ■

EXPLORATION: Asymmetric Information and Factor Market Equilibrium

Our description of the labor market (and other factor markets) thus far is based on two assumptions:

1. Once we know how households decide how much labor to supply, we sum to get to the market supply curve (see Chapter 5).
2. Once we know how much labor to use, we can sum to get to the industry and market labor demand curves (with appropriate modifications, the subject of this chapter).

Combining demand curves with supply curves then gives us market equilibrium.

This description assumes that labor is a well-defined entity, equally known by both buyer and seller. In many cases, perhaps most cases, this is a good assumption. After all, there is no reason why firms would not be able to observe what they get any less than households know what they sell.

However, this assumption sometimes fails. An example might be a buyer purchasing a lawyer's services. The buyer cannot easily observe everything the lawyer does, and thus may not know for sure how much real effort the lawyer is expending on the case. Because of this lack of information, the perfect information equilibrium breaks down, so the analysis must be modified. Labor contract theory provides one such modification: the efficiency wage model. This model shows how asymmetric information affects labor demand, labor supply, and equilibrium.

23. David I. Levine and Laura D'Andrea Tyson, "No Voice for Workers: U.S. Economy Penalizes Worker Participation," *Dollars & Sense: Real World Micro,* September 1988, pp. 70, 71.
24. Ibid., p. 71.
25. Ibid.

Labor Contract Theory: The Efficiency Wage Model

The efficiency wage model assumes that *workers* decide how much effort to put in on the job and that employers cannot easily monitor their employees to ensure a given level of effort. For simplicity, we assume that there are just two options available to the worker: ''shirking'' or ''not shirking.''[26] The firm eventually discovers workers who shirk and fires them. Similarly, in our example of legal services, lawyers who are discovered to shirk will find it harder to attract and retain clients.

In order for the market to meet firms' expectations that hired workers will not shirk, there must be some mechanism to encourage workers not to shirk and to encourage firms to pay more for the nonshirking workers they get. A wage at which no shirking occurs is called an *efficiency wage,* and a model generating this wage is called an *efficiency wage model.* An incentive not to shirk exists if fired workers bear an unemployment cost for being fired. Assume therefore that fired workers, instead of finding immediate employment elsewhere, must pass through a period of unemployment. In general, the larger the pool of unemployed workers, the longer the expected period of time before any newly fired worker gets new employment. Since the wage workers receive while employed is higher than the unemployment wage, they have an incentive not to be caught shirking. Longer periods of unemployment and higher wages on the job mean that the advantage of retaining one's job by not shirking is greater.

Labor Market Equilibrium and the Efficiency Wage

▼

12. Why do the asymmetric information conditions of the efficiency wage model require unemployment in market equilibrium?

We can now explain why equilibrium cannot occur at the intersection of the demand and supply curves under the asymmetric information conditions of the efficiency wage model. Figure 11.13 shows the labor demand curve as curve D_L and the labor supply curve as S_L. At point e', where labor demand equals labor supply, all workers who want to work at wage w' are employed. A worker who is discovered shirking and is fired, however, can immediately present himself or herself for new employment at another firm at wage w' and suffer no harm from the transition. Because there is full employment in the labor market, employees can get replacement jobs without any transition cost. Given this situation, workers have no incentive not to shirk. With all workers shirking, however, the equilibrium breaks down because firms are willing to pay only for workers who do not shirk. Hence, e' cannot be the equilibrium.

---

26. The shirking terminology may not be the best in all circumstances because it implies a conscious choice not to perform at an acceptable level. In some cases, neither the worker nor the employer may know whether an employee's work will be acceptable, and so the matter is one of inherent ability or quality. In either event, the issue is one of acceptable job performance or unacceptable job performance. However, because the shirking terminology is commonly used, and because it is concise, we will follow that lead.

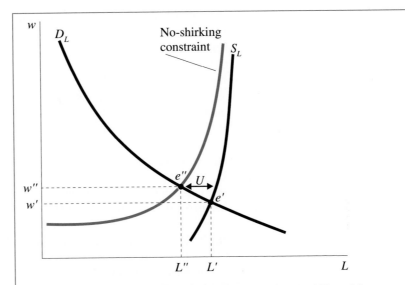

Figure 11.13 Efficiency Wage Equilibrium The inability of firms to know how well their workers will perform when hired prevents market equilibrium from occurring where the labor demand curve (D_L) and the labor supply curve (S_L) intersect. Unemployment is the result in the efficiency wage model. The labor demand curve assumes that hired workers perform at an acceptable level (they don't shirk). To ensure that workers do not shirk, their pay must equal the level determined by the no-shirking constraint. For a given quantity of labor, the no-shirking wage is high enough that the threat of unemployment if the worker is fired for shirking induces workers not to shirk. Equilibrium occurs where the labor demand curve and the no-shirking constraint intersect at point e''. Unemployment (distance U) equals the difference between the number who want to work at wage w'' and the number hired.

Considering the need for a cost of being fired, we can construct a curve showing the wage needed to ensure that hired workers do not shirk. Figure 11.13 shows this no-shirking constraint as the heavy upward-sloping line. What determines the shape of the no-shirking constraint? At high wages, having a job is so advantageous relative to not having a job that workers will not shirk even if there is little unemployment. For a given quantity of employed workers, then, there need be only a small number of workers seeking employment above the number with jobs. The extra workers create a small pool of unemployed that acts as the inducement not to be fired. At lower wages, however, there is less advantage in having a job compared to not having a job, so the associated pool of unemployed—and the associated spell of unemployment for a fired worker—must be greater. Thus the no-shirking constraint must lie further to the left of the supply curve for lower wages.

In fact, we presume that even at the no-shirking wage, some workers will shirk and be fired. Recognizing this, assume that the no-shirking constraint generates a sufficiently reduced level of shirking so firms are generally satisfied with the workers they hire.

What happens if equilibrium occurs where the no-shirking constraint and the labor demand curve intersect? At wage w'' in Figure 11.13, firms assume that the workers they hire shirk at a suitably low level and demand L'' units of labor at point e'' on their demand curve. Wage w'' meets the firms' expectations because e'' is also on the no-shirking constraint. At point e'' workers earn their marginal revenue product, but this is higher than wages would have been at the full-employment, full-information equilibrium e'. At wage w'', $L'' + U$ workers seek work at the going wage (U is the number of unemployed), but firms demand only L'' of them.

Firms cannot lower their wages in the face of the unemployment, because if they did, the level of shirking would rise and firms would again find that the labor they hired shirked too much. The only sustainable equilibrium imposes a penalty for shirking. Since the no-shirking constraint always lies to the left of the labor supply curve, equilibrium will always entail some degree of unemployment.

To summarize, asymmetric information can play a major role in factor markets. As the efficiency wage model shows, asymmetric information may be a contributing cause of unemployment.[27] Moreover, it may help explain why market wages do not drop even though unemployed workers want to work at the going wage.

The efficiency wage model represents just one of the ways that asymmetric information may play a role in factor markets, but remember that in this model no single firm or worker is responsible for the unemployment-ridden equilibrium. They are simply players in a larger drama. Under different market conditions, the equilibrium might be different. For example, if firms could easily monitor the final product, there would be no need for unemployment or the threat of firing to provide the incentive for workers not to shirk. In many labor markets, factors need not be paid if their work is not satisfactory. (Consider piecework employment or home repairs. In each case, pay is given after inspection of the product.) This provides the necessary

27. In the model, we have implicitly assumed that workers either have jobs or are unemployed. More generally, all that is needed to prevent shirking in a particular type of job is the possibility that the wage a worker will get if fired is lower than the working wage. For example, the same principles apply to skilled mutual fund managers whose alternative if fired is to accept boring jobs writing financial reports in the research division. Fund managers want to do their best as fund managers so as not to lose their jobs; there are more individuals competent to manage funds who want positions than there are positions available; and those who lose their jobs suffer a reduction in their well-being. You might check to see how the model would work applied to television network news anchors, Hollywood actors and actresses, or other jobs where more competent individuals are available than positions.

incentive against shirking. It follows that asymmetric information is not a problem in these cases, and equilibrium occurs at the competitive point where the demand curve crosses the supply curve.[28] ∎

Having completed in this chapter our study of supply and demand for inputs and outputs under various market conditions, we are ready to turn our attention to the economy-wide question of optimality. That is, we know how market economies function, but do they function well? Are there ways for determining whether an economy could do better than it is doing? Is there one best way to organize production and supply in an economy so that its citizens are as well off as possible? These are questions that we take up in Part Four.

28. Another way for the market to ensure no shirking might be for firms to require workers to post bonds (pay a sum of money to the firm upon hiring), which the firm could then confiscate if the worker were found shirking. This, of course, introduces different monitoring problems. For example, how do we know the firm will not always claim the worker is shirking in order to claim the money?

Summary

Active Reading Guide numbers are given in parentheses at the end of each summary item.

1. Although the primary role of firms in the economy is to provide goods and services, firms also buy factor inputs. Firm factor demand is an indirect or *derived* demand, because the firm buys factors not for their own sake, but in order to produce goods and services for sale. In perfectly competitive factor markets, the firm takes the prices of inputs as given and decides what quantity maximizes firm profits. The decision about how much of a factor to employ is therefore directly tied to the decision about how much output to produce to maximize profits. (1)

2. The firm's decision about how much of a factor to use is simplest for the single-input case. The firm's hiring condition says that the firm hires factor L to the point where the marginal revenue product, MRP, of the factor is equal to the factor's price, where $MRP = MR \times MP_L$. (2)

3. In the one-factor case, the firm's factor demand curve is the marginal revenue product curve of that factor. (3).

4. In the multiple-factor case, the firm decides which technique (or combination of factors) to use in production. Given factor prices, it minimizes production costs by finding the least-cost input combination to produce each output level. The collection of least-cost input bundles over all production levels is the output expansion path for that set of factor prices. (4)

5. When a factor price increases or decreases, the firm correspondingly reduces or increases its use of the factor to continue to minimize costs at the new factor price. The overall impact of a factor price change on factor employment is separated into two parts, called the *factor substitution effect* (the change in use of the factor while holding output constant) and the *output effect* (the remainder of the total change, determined by the firm's decision to produce more or less output). (5)

6. If the firm hires multiple factors, the hiring condition for each factor is that the marginal revenue product of the factor equal its price. The firm's factor demand curve in the multiple-factor case, however, is more elastic than the marginal revenue

product curve, whether factors are complements or substitutes in production. Factors are complements in production if using more of one raises the marginal product of the other. Factors are substitutes in production if using more of one reduces the marginal product of the other. The firm's hiring conditions for factors contain the same information as the requirements that the firm produce at least cost and that it produce where price equals marginal cost. (6)

7. To go from the firm's factor demand curve to industry demand curves and the market factor demand curve, we take into account the product price effect, potential effects of other factor prices, externalities, and the entry and exit effect. A change in the factor price changes the factor-using industry's output, which in turn affects its demand for other factors. This can change the product price, the price of other factors, and the level of positive or negative externalities, and it can cause firms to enter or exit the industry. Each of these effects influences the location of individual firms' factor demand curves and can also alter the number of firms in the market. The industry factor demand curve and the market factor demand curve (the sum of industry demand curves) therefore differ from the simple horizontal summation of individual firms' demand curves. From the effects that determine the market factor demand, we know that market factor demand becomes more elastic with greater substitutability of other factors for the factor in question, with greater price elasticity of demand for the output produced by the factor, and with greater price elasticity of supply of other factors. Market factor demand will also be more elastic in the long run than in the short run. (7)

8. The intersection of the market factor demand curve and the factor supply curve determines market equilibrium. In equilibrium, the factor's price equals the value of the factor's marginal product for firms that are pricetakers in the output market. The factor is therefore paid the value of its marginal contribution to output. Many elements operating through market demand and supply curves contribute to explaining the equilibrium level of wages. For example, seemingly similar jobs sometimes pay different wages because the worker with more un-

pleasant working conditions receives higher pay. This higher pay is called a *compensating wage differential* (were pay equal, not enough workers would opt for the more unpleasant job, affecting supply). At the same time, trying to set market wages based on pre-chosen job characteristics, as the notion of comparable worth attempts to do, is difficult because what matters to the market is often different than what one might think should matter. (8)

9. The theory of monopsony is closely related to the theory of monopoly. A single buyer chooses the point on the factor supply curve leading to maximum profits. This implies hiring the factor to the point where the marginal factor cost equals the marginal revenue product of the factor. Marginal factor cost is the increase in the firm's total factor payments from hiring an additional unit of the factor. (9)

10. In a monopsonistic labor market, a price floor (minimum wage) can raise employment and the wage simultaneously, provided the floor is not too high. But if the floor exceeds a certain level, the market behaves like a competitive market, leading to employment declines and unemployment. (10)

11. When a labor union (monopolist) faces a monopsonistic labor buyer, the outcome depends on the solution to a bargaining problem. Within a restricted set of possibilities that both bargainers want to preserve, the relative strength of the two bargainers determines the wage-employment point chosen. The boundaries are the firm's VAP curve, the factor supply curve, and the union's indifference curve for wage and employment passing through the wage-employment pair corresponding to the point where the firm's MRP curve cuts the MFC curve. (11)

12. If the factor market exhibits asymmetric information, unemployment in equilibrium may sometimes result. This is the case in the efficiency wage model of the labor market. Firms cannot be sure that workers will not shirk on the job. To ensure nonshirking workers, the market equilibrium must include unemployment so that the threat of being fired if caught shirking induces workers not to shirk. (12)

Review Questions

*1. What is the firm's output expansion path in the short run? In the long run? Is the output expansion path likely to show greater response to a change in factor prices in the short run or the long run? Explain.

2. In consumer theory the income consumption path bent back on itself when one of the goods was inferior. Define and discuss an analogue in terms of an inferior factor.

*3. A firm hires both capital and labor. The product price is 1, the marginal product of capital is 5, and the marginal product of labor is 2. The price of capital is 10, and the price of labor is 8. Does this firm satisfy its hiring condition? What should happen to this firm's hiring of capital and labor in order for the firm to produce at least cost?

4. In a competitive factor market, a factor is paid the value of its marginal product by a pricetaking firm in output markets. In what sense is this a "fair" wage to pay?

*5. Assume that the ratio w/r rises. Will the firm use a technique with a higher or lower capital-to-labor (K/L) ratio?

6. If factor B is a complement to factor A, what happens to the demand for A when the firm uses more B? If A and B are substitutes, what happens to the demand for A when the firm uses more B?

*7. Is the industry demand for a factor input likely to be more elastic or less elastic as a result of a less elastic demand for the industry's output?

8. Two lines of work have the same prospects for diminishing supply of labor. Other things being equal, would you rather work in the line of of work for which the product demand is highly inelastic or the one for which product demand is elastic? Explain.

*9. Two lines of work have the same prospect for diminishing supply of labor. Other things being equal, would you rather work in the line of work for which there is (a) a close substitute input for your labor with highly elastic supply, (b) a close substitute with moderately elastic supply, or (c) no close substitutes. Explain.

10. State and explain the employment condition for a monopsonistic buyer of labor.

*11. For which market structure, monopsonistic or competitive, would a minimum wage be more sensible? Do you think most markets are of this type?

Numerical and Graphing Exercises

*1. A firm faces a product price of $5 per unit of output, and each additional worker produces a marginal product of $100 - 4L$, where L is the number of labor hours hired and labor is the only input. The wage rate is $15 per hour. The firm is currently hiring 23 labor hours. Should the firm increase or decrease its labor use? Why?

2. In exercise 1, what would be the quantity of labor demanded if the wage rate were zero? If the wage rate were $100? Can you use this information to draw the firm's labor demand curve?

*3. A firm's marginal product for factor A is $MP_A = (50/A) + B$, and its marginal product for factor B is $MP_B = (100/B) + A$. The product price is $2/unit, and the costs for factors are $p_A = \$30$, $p_B = \$50$.

a) Are the factors substitutes or complements in production?

b) How much of each factor should the firm use?

4. Use the information from exercise 3 to draw the firm's value of marginal product curve for factor A when the firm hires 5 units of factor B by plotting pMP_A at each price of A: $40, $35, $30, and $25. Next, plot the firm's demand for factor A at each of the same prices. Is the firm demand more or less elastic than the value of the marginal product curve? (Hint: If the firm adheres to the hiring conditions, what is the price of factor B?)

*5. ABC Corporation produces its single product at a market price of $5 per unit according to the following table. Its only input is labor. From this information draw ABC's demand for labor curve.

* Asterisks are used to denote questions that are answered at the back of the book.

Hours of Labor (thousands)	Output (hundreds)	Hours of Labor (thousands)	Output (hundreds)
0	0	11	142.5
1	19	12	151.5
2	36	13	160
3	51	14	168
4	65	15	175.25
5	78	16	181.5
6	90	17	186.5
7	101.5	18	190.25
8	112.5	19	192.5
9	123	20	192.5
10	133		

*6. A Giffen good is a good with an upward-sloping demand curve, as we discussed in Chapter 4. Use the hints below to show why there cannot be "Giffen" factors for a competitive firm (that is, a factor for which demand increases when its price goes up).

Let there be two inputs, capital and labor. Let the firm's initial choice of production be q_0, K_0, L_0 when prices are p, r, w_0. Now let prices change to p, r, w_1, where w_1 is greater than w_0, and assume that the firm's new production choices are q_1, K_1, L_1.

a) Write profits in the final situation, and write what profits would have been after prices changed if the firm had continued to produce using its original choices.

b) Write the formula for the increase in profits to the firm from changing its production.

c) Using the facts that $w_1 > w_0$ and that the firm increased its profits by changing its production after prices changed, show that if $L_1 > L_0$, the firm could have increased its profits *before* prices changed by producing output q_1 using inputs K_1 and L_1. [Write the change in profits before the price change so that it equals the answer to part (b) plus another term. Then consider the signs of the terms.]

This leads to a contradiction: Since the firm was said to be maximizing profits initially, producing q_1 with inputs K_1 and L_1 cannot raise profits. Thus, when the factor price rises, the employment of the factor cannot also rise.

7. Use a graph to explain why a minimum wage set above the market clearing wage causes unemployment and leads to an increase in labor productivity of those remaining at work in a full-information, competitive labor market. Is this different from the effects of a minimum wage in the efficiency wage model of the labor market?

*8. Assume that $w = r = \$1$ initially. Draw an isoquant for each of the following production functions: $q = \min(K, L)$ and $q = K + L$. Assuming initial output of 10 units and $K = L$, what is the substitution effect of an increase in the wage to \$2 for each function?

*9. A firm finds that its marginal products are $MP_L = 1/MP_K = k$, where k is the capital-to-labor ratio (K/L). Write the formula for the firm's output expansion path as a function of w and r. (Hint: What does the least-cost tangency condition tell you?)

10. Assume that a firm uses a single input L. The firm's demand for labor is given by $D_L = 100 - w$, and the supply of labor is $S_L = -10 + 4w$. Graph the relevant curves and find the equilibrium wage and quantity of L if:

a) The firm is a monopsonist

b) The firm is the only firm in the market, but nevertheless acts as a pricetaker with respect to inputs.

*11. Model the bargaining between a union and a monopsonist as a game with three choices for firm and union and payouts indicated by firm profit and union utility. One of the choices for the union is to strike, and one of the choices for the firm is to lockout. Is there a Nash solution? How is the game different if the firm has the added ability to fire workers and hire nonunion replacements?

INVESTIGATIONS III

A. Manipulating an Oligpolistic Market for National Advantage: The Airbus Industry

Since Lockheed left the commercial market in 1981, the oligopolistic market in large-jet transport aircraft has been dominated by the remaining U.S. firms, Boeing and McDonnell-Douglas. The need for highly technical aerospace expertise in design and production, the existence of increasing returns to scale, and tremendously high up-front costs of developing a new large-scale aircraft are natural entry barriers to the aerospace market. To ensure a European presence in the industry, Great Britain, West Germany, France, and Spain joined in 1967 to form Airbus Industrie, subsidizing its market entry and position. In this investigation we examine the circumstances surrounding their decision and its consequences.

The Industry

Commercial large-jet passenger transport aircraft, defined as aircraft over 5,600 pounds in weight and sometimes referred to as wide-bodied aircraft, are the most important segment of the civil aircraft industry, accounting for 92 percent of the value of U.S. civil aircraft shipments in 1990.[1] At the beginning of the 1970s, the U.S. companies Boeing, McDonnell-Douglas, and Lockheed almost totally dominated the large-jet aircraft market (controlling over 90 percent of market share)[2] and appeared likely to continue to do so. Boeing's 727 and 737 and McDonnell-Douglas's DC-9 entered service in the 1960s. Boeing's 747 was introduced in 1970, with Lockheed's TriStar L-1011 and McDonnell-Douglas's DC10 introduced shortly thereafter.[3]

European nations wanted their own aerospace industry, although they knew that surmounting formidable natural entry barriers in the form of aerospace design and production expertise, increasing returns to scale, and R&D development costs would be difficult for private firms in light of the uncertainty of reaching a viable market share at the end of the process. Anglo-French government collaboration on the Concorde began in 1962, resulting

1. U.S. Department of Commerce, ''Aerospace,'' *U.S. Industrial Outlook 1991,* Washington, D.C., 1991, p. 22-5. The total value of shipments of complete civil aircraft in 1990 was $25.3 billion, of which $23.2 billion was accounted for by large transport aircraft.
2. U.S. Department of Commerce, *A Competitive Assessment of the U.S. Civil Aircraft Industry,* Boulder, Colo.: Westview Press, 1986, p. 10.
3. Ibid., p. 21.

in flight testing in 1969 and delivery of the first plane in 1976. Although the Concorde ultimately proved uneconomic and only 16 were produced,[4] the collaboration provided a pattern for negotiations in 1965 between England and France to produce a European answer to the L-1011 and DC-10 then on the U.S. drawing boards. This ultimately led to the creation of Airbus Industrie as a four-nation consortium of English, French, German, and Spanish companies with government involvement.[5]

After large infusions of money from member governments and a series of delays, the A-300, with a typical seating capacity of 250 to 260, finally entered service in 1975. Whether Airbus would ever be commerically profitable was in doubt, however. Boeing had sold 270 747s by 1977; McDonnell-Douglas had sold 244 DC-10s; and Lockheed had sold 151 TriStars; yet Airbus had sold only 34 planes.[6] Eventually, orders from member-country airlines and a breakthrough purchase by a major U.S. airline in 1978 (Eastern Airlines) encouraged Airbus. From this point on, it devoted itself to developing a series of airliners, of which models A-310, A-320, A-330, and A-340 are already in service or production.

The 1970s were hard years for aircraft manufacturers in general. Prompted by higher oil prices, an emphasis on more fuel-efficient engine and aircraft design, and a slowdown in world growth rates, demand for aircraft was insufficient to support four companies. Experiencing losses of $2.5 billion and anticipating sales of only 24 planes per year from 1985 to 1990, Lockheed phased out its TriStar and announced its decision to cease production of the L-1011 (the last planes were delivered in 1985). Since 1981, only two American companies and one foreign company have accepted orders for large commercial jets.

Rationale for the European Action

Bringing a large commercial jet aircraft to market is estimated to cost more than $4 billion.[7] To break even, approximately 400 aircraft must subsequently be sold, and 600 to 700 planes are needed to return a respectable profit on the venture. Table III.1 shows that this number of planes could take a decade or more to achieve, whereas the development costs are up-front and can be spread out over six or more years. The entire process can therefore take 15 or even 20 years.

Given the view of many industry analysts that the market in large aircraft is big enough to support only two or possibly three firms, European govern-

4. Daniel Todd and Jamie Simpson, *The World Aircraft Industry,* London: Auburn House, 1986, p. 199.
5. British Aerospace is 50 percent government owned; Deutsche Airbus is 50 percent government owned; Aerospatiate of France is 100 percent government owned; and Construcciones Aeronauticas, CASA, of Spain is 100 percent government owned.
6. Todd and Simpson, op. cit., p. 51.
7. ''Aerospace and Air Transport,'' Standard and Poor's *Industry Surveys,* June 20, 1991, p. A16.

Table III.1   Unit Deliveries of Large Commercial Aircraft

	1982	1983	1984	1985	1986	1987	1988	1989	1990
Boeing 707	8	8	8	3	4	9	—	5	4
727	26	11	8	—	—	—	—	—	—
737	95	82	67	115	141	161	165	146	174
747	25	23	16	24	35	23	24	45	70
757	2	25	18	36	35	40	48	51	77
767	20	55	29	25	27	37	53	37	60
Boeing total	176	204	146	203	242	270	290	284	385
McDonnell-Douglas									
MD-80	44	50	44	71	86	95	121	118	139
DC-10	5	4	2	0	5	3	10	1	—
MD-11	—	—	—	—	—	—	—	—	3
McDonnell-Douglas total	49	54	46	71	91	98	131	119	142
Lockheed L-1011	14	6	4	2	—	—	—	—	—
Airbus A-300	46	21	19	16	10	11	17	24	19
A-310	—	17	29	26	20	21	28	23	18
A-320	—	—	—	—	—	—	16	58	58
Airbus total	46	38	48	42	30	32	61	105	95
Grand total	285	302	244	318	363	400	482	508	622

Source: Data from "Aerospace and Air Transport," Standard and Poor's Industry Surveys, *June 20, 1991, p. A17. Reprinted by permission of Standard & Poor's.*

ments knew that major support would be needed to establish Airbus as a world aircraft supplier. Further, such support would have to be sustained over a long period of time and might entail forcing another manufacturer out of the market. Estimates place Airbus government support from its inception at $26 billion.[8] For comparison, the entire capitalization of Airbus was estimated at $7.5 billion in 1980, compared to $5.9 billion for Boeing and $3.9 billion for McDonnell-Douglas. Both the support and the costs of development are large relative to company size.

Since the large aircraft market is an oligopoly, there are two ways in which government support enhances Airbus's market position with respect to its rivals. First, by providing funds for initial development and production, European governments have ensured an Airbus presence in a market where there very likely would not be such a presence otherwise. In addition to making Airbus's entry possible, the European governments' ongoing support, buy-national policies, and subsidies to foreign sales[9] have established the credi-

8. "Aid to Airbus Called Unfair in U.S. Study," *New York Times,* September 8, 1990.
9. Concerning Airbus sales, one report stated that "Airlines have received purchase financing at favorable prices and, at times, highly advantageous operating leases. One attention-getting example of these practices was Airbus' loan of $500 million to Northwest Airlines in October 1990, firming up an order for 75 A-320s." "Aerospace and Air Transport," p. A17.

bility of Airbus's market presence and scale of operations. This discourages American companies from either entering or enlarging their presence in the market.[10] Whether a third American firm would now be in the market if Airbus didn't exist can never be known with certainty, but it is clear that the size and support of Airbus strongly affect competitors' planning. The fear that McDonnell-Douglas might leave the commercial wide-body market or fail to develop its MD-11 seems not to have materialized, at least for the time being, largely because of the surge in aircraft demand in the 1980s. With enough market for everyone, there is no reason for firms to exit.

The U.S. Response

The U.S. government has objected strongly to Airbus subsidies and has conducted talks with the European governments since 1987. At issue was the U.S. view that subsidies were incompatible with standard market practices and the GATT (General Agreement on Tariffs and Trade) Subsidies Code, to which the European governments were signatories. The European Community (EC) negotiators in turn said that American companies received indirect subsidies through defense contracts, a view that American negotiators denied because commercial and military divisions of the American companies are kept carefully separate. In fact, sometimes commercial aircraft could be said to subsidize the military, as when the Boeing 707, developed for commercial use, was modified for military use in a subsequent version. Either way, the issue was commercial aircraft, said the American negotiators, not America's costs for defending the free world.

Since many people believed that Airbus would die without continued government support, Europeans were loath to promise elimination of subsidies. The intensity of negotiations varied inversely with the strength of the worldwide aircraft market, which improved greatly in the latter part of the 1980s. Nevertheless, the talks remained strained, and they broke down in 1991 when the United States rejected an EC proposal to eliminate production subsidies and cap development subsidies at 45 percent of development costs (the U.S. negotiators wanted a 25 percent cap).[11] The United States requested a GATT panel to rule on certain subsidies by the German government; the ruling was returned in favor of the U.S. position in January 1991. Later, negotiations resumed, resulting in a tentative agreement in 1992 to cap development subsidies at one-third of developmental costs, eliminate production

---

10. Planes are designed for market slots defined by passenger capacity and distance. European trade journals indicate that one strategy of Airbus is to anticipate what planes its American competitors will produce and then produce a comparable plane "on top" of the American one a year or two earlier (see U.S. Department of Commerce, *A Competitive Assessment,* p. 68). Such a strategy ultimately could cause the competitor to abandon its planned market slot or plane if it perceived that building the plane could not be profitable.
11. "The United States and the EC Reach Tentative Agreement on Subsidies to Aircraft Manufacturers," *International Economic Review,* May 1992, p. 13. Development costs are estimated to be between 75 and 90 percent of costs.

subsidies, cap indirect subsidies at 5 percent of aircraft sales, and require repayment of subsidies received on a royalty basis at interest rates ranging between 8.5 and 9.5 percent.

Assessment

The last chapter on Airbus subsidies has not been written. In oligopolistic markets, government support to aid firms in the entry process and to increase market share relative to rivals can sometimes be in the national interest if the domestic firm eventually pays back in increased profits the costs to the government. Since data for American companies tell us that aerospace profits are not substantially different from those in all manufacturing (if anything they are lower), the objective of having a national producer of aircraft seems not primarily to be financial.[12] Will Airbus eventually become profitable as an independent manufacturer without government support? If so, will it ever become sufficiently profitable to pay back the enormous initial investment for Airbus's entry into the market? We may not know for many years.

Suggestions for Further Investigation. (a) If you were Boeing or Mc-Donnell-Douglas, how would Airbus's market presence affect your planning? (b) Who are the main groups to gain and lose from the Airbus situation? Think in terms of competing companies, users of aircraft, air travelers, and taxpayers in the United States, Europe, and the rest of the world. (c) Assume that aircraft sales are down worldwide. If you were in a position to advise the U.S. government regarding a response to Airbus, what would you recommend?

B. You Don't Know What You've Got Till It's Gone: Lessons from the Coke-Pepsi Wars

> Strategic competition in oligopolistic markets challenges its participants strenuously because conditions are constantly changing. What won the game for you one day may no longer keep you on the board on another. The subsequently reversed Coca-Cola formula change introduced in 1985 demonstrates the effect of changing market conditions on oligopolistic competition and on Nash equilibrium. It also shows the effect of lack of perfect information by participants about payoffs. It is important to define the game properly so that you ultimately choose from the correct set of options.

---

12. For U.S. firms, aerospace after-tax profits as a percentage of sales were lower in 1989 (3 percent) than for all manufacturing, as they had been every year since 1971. Measured as a percentage of stockholder equity, 1989 after-tax profit was 10.5 percent, compared to 13.5 percent for all manufacturing. Since 1971, this comparison shows aerospace lower more than half the time, even though the high risks in aerospace would suggest that there should be a higher return to compensate. See "Aerospace," p. 22-3.

Establishing a Market Share Supremacy in Colas

In 1886, pharmacist John S. Pemberton introduced a product that he called Coca-Cola. A modification of his nerve stimulant and tonic, it was distributed to soda fountains in beer bottles and thought of primarily as a headache cure. It wasn't long before users discovered that the syrup tasted better mixed with carbonated water. Before he died in 1888, Pemberton sold his rights to Coca-Cola to Asa Candler, who in 1892 organized the Coca-Cola Company that still exists today.

Under Candler, the product was sold as a beverage. Although the company faced periods of difficulty, profits grew, reaching $25 million by the start of the Depression years. In 1930 there were 64 bottlers associated with Coca-Cola in 28 countries.[13]

Coca-Cola's policy during World War II was to see that everyone in uniform could get a Coke for 5 cents, regardless of the cost to the company. Coke received its reward after the war, dominating the soft drink market throughout the 1950s, 1960s, and early 1970s. Coca-Cola outsold Pepsi-Cola, its main rival today, by margins better than two to one.

The Pepsi Challenge: Changing Market Conditions, Changing Payoffs

In the second half of the 1970s, market conditions began to change. For one thing, Pepsi-Cola was running its successful ''Pepsi Generation'' ads to appeal to baby boomers, who were becoming the largest consumer group for soft drinks. Pepsi also mounted its ''Pepsi Challenge,'' in which it advertised blind taste tests showing that consumers preferred the taste of Pepsi to Coke. Whereas Coke and Pepsi's respective market shares were 24.2 and 17.4 percent in 1975, they were 21.1 and 18.9 in 1985.[14] Worse yet from Coca-Cola's perspective, the market share for all of Coca-Cola's products was falling relative to Pepsi's. Clearly, Pepsi's advertising and its sweeter formula were making inroads.

Finding the Nash Equilibrium Response

From Coca-Cola's point of view, what had worked in the past was not working now. Since the company's own taste tests revealed that consumers *said* they liked a sweeter-tasting cola, the options looked like those in part (a) of Figure III.1. Pepsi-Cola has positioned itself in the market by offering a highly carbonated, sweeter, more syrupy cola. Coca-Cola's traditional formula, dating back to 1886, was tarter and less syrupy. At least until the 1980s, the upper-left-hand cell, where Coca-Cola chose to market its traditional

---

13. Robert F. Hartley, *Management Mistakes and Successes,* 3d ed., New York: John Wiley and Sons, 1991, p. 68.
14. Thomas Oliver, *The Real Coke, the Real Story,* New York: Random House, 1986, p. 21, and *Beverage Industry Annual Manual 1989/90,* Cleveland, Ohio: Magazines for Industry, 1990, p. 24.

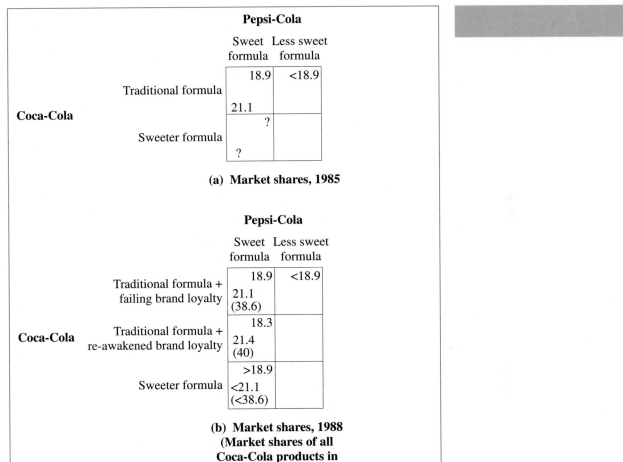

(a) Market shares, 1985

**(b) Market shares, 1988
(Market shares of all
Coca-Cola products in
parentheses)**

Figure III.1 Nash Equilibrium with Market Share Payoffs and Partially Unknown Cells In 1985, Coca-Cola's 21.1 percent market share exceeded Pepsi-Cola's by only 2.2 points, having been much higher in the past. Given Coca-Cola's choice to market its traditional formula, Pepsi-Cola optimized by choosing to market sweet formula. To Coke, on the other hand, the upper-left-hand cell in part (a) did not appear to be a Nash equilibrium any longer, because tests seemed to indicate that changing to a Pepsi-like sweeter formula would raise market share. In fact, as events revealed, Coke had a better option, which was to reawaken brand loyalty and retain its traditional formula. By 1988 market equilibrium had settled in the left-hand middle cell of part (b), with Coke's market share at 21.4 percent and market share for all Coca-Cola products at 40 percent.

formula and Pepsi marketed its sweeter formula, seemed to be a Nash equilibrium: given the other firm's choice, each firm did better by marketing its own type of product. Since the rewards to each firm are profits not just in one year, but spread over future years, payoffs in this game can be represented by market shares, which indicate the size of the firm's revenues relative to others in the market. Given Coke's traditional formula, against which Pepsi was gaining ground, Pepsi was reasonably sure that shifting its formula to one less sweet (moving to the upper-right-hand cell) would lower its market share below the percentage it currently enjoyed. Coca-Cola, on the other hand, began to suspect that, given Pepsi's choice, its traditional formula was no longer the best option. However, Coca-Cola was not certain of the payoff from shifting to a sweeter formula (shown in the bottom-left-hand cell).

The Decision to Shift Strategy and the Results

After conducting extensive taste tests and carefully considering the ramifications of a change, Coca-Cola announced that it was introducing "New Coke" in April 1985. At first the results looked good. News of the change quickly spread, and over 150 million people tried the new Coke, more than ever before for another new product.[15] However, news coverage was negative, and the realization that Coke was discarding a product that had been known and loved by Americans for nearly 100 years began to change public reaction. The company started to receive calls and letters with sentiments like the following:

> *It is absolutely* TERRIBLE! *You should be ashamed to put the Coke label on it. . . . This stuff is worse than Pepsi.*

> *It was nice knowing you. . . . Yesterday I had my first taste of new Coke, and to tell the truth, if I would have wanted Pepsi, I would have ordered a Pepsi, not a Coke.*[16]

As negative reaction grew, company executives even began to worry about a boycott. In July 1985 they announced the reintroduction of traditional Coca-Cola as Coke Classic. For several years thereafter, both products were sold, along with Cherry Coke, Diet Coke, and other combinations of Coke with or without caffeine, and with or without sugar.

Unintentionally, Coca-Cola had stumbled onto the right strategy to respond to the Pepsi challenge. Sales of Coke Classic rose, and company profits increased. Best of all, market share for all Coke products increased. By 1988 the company could boast that 5 of the top 10 best-selling soft drinks were Coca-Cola products, and that its product market share had risen to 40 percent.

Coca-Cola learned that, rather than shift to a sweeter formula, it could do better by using publicity to reawaken its consumers' brand loyalty to a venerable product. In this case, publicity came serendipitously as a result of

15. Hartley, op cit., p. 73.
16. Ibid.

the company's earlier error, but it came nevertheless. The real game involved more choices than Coke had originally accounted for. Although a change from the initial equilibrium was needed, the change was to the middle cell of part (b) in Figure III.1. As shown in the figure, Coca-Cola's new options were to use publicity to reawaken brand loyalty or to shift to a sweeter formula. As events proved, market share was higher for the first of these options.

Coca-Cola learned other valuable lessons from this episode of competition. It learned, for example, that what people say in a taste test is not always a good indication of long-run commitment to a product. The company also came to understand that the best strategy may involve maintaining a market niche while introducing new varieties to compete for other niches. Consumers, perhaps, learned a valuable lesson too, as evidenced by their much-increased purchases of Coke after it was almost removed from the market forever: sometimes you don't know what you've got till it's gone.

Suggestions for Further Investigation. (a) Put yourself in the shoes of the Coca-Cola president in 1982. What would you have done? (b) If you were the Pepsi president in 1985, was there anything you could have done to turn this situation to your advantage?

C. Competition in Pharmaceutical Preparations

America is a world leader in the pharmaceutical industry, which includes a number of different types of products and market conditions. Pharmaceutical competition ranges from monopolistic competition to oligopoly to monopoly. Information plays a large role in determining the nature of competition, even in cases where products are chemically similar. This investigation looks at the determinants of competition in this evolving industry.

The Industry

The United States leads the world in discovering and developing new medicines. The country produces 42 percent of the major pharmaceuticals marketed worldwide and constitutes the world's largest single market.[17] Of the world's 20 largest drug producers, half are located in the United States, the rest being primarily in Western Europe.[18] U.S. exports of pharmaceuticals totaled $5.1 billion in 1990, exceeding imports by $1 billion, with Western Europe accounting for nearly half of the exports, followed by roughly one-sixth for Japan and one-eighth each for Canada and Mexico.

17. U.S. Department of Commerce, "Drugs," *U.S. Industrial Outlook 1992,* Washington, D.C., 1992, USGPO p. 44-1.
18. "Health Care," *Standard and Poor's Industry Surveys,* August 2, 1990, p. H19.

Certain features of the pharmaceutical market—especially of pharmaceutical preparations (medicinal drugs), which account for 75 percent of the pharmaceutical industry[19]—make this industry an ideal candidate for examining the nature of competition discussed in Chapters 8 through 10. First, pharmaceutical products are highly patented, and innovation is the driving force behind success in the prescription or "ethical" drug sector. Second, price is often not a highly significant component of the competition.[20] On the other hand, the industry contains a growing generic drug sector that competes on the basis of identical chemical compounds. In each case, the circumstances of the product and its development determine the nature of the competition that prevails.

Perfect Competition and Monopolistic Competition

The U.S. pharmaceutical industry consists of over 1,200 pharmaceutical manufacturers producing four basic types of drugs: (1) Prescription drugs, available to the public only through prescription by the medical profession; (2) nonprescription, over-the-counter drugs that may be purchased directly by the general public; (3) generic drugs, prescription products no longer covered by patents; and (4) imitative drugs whose active ingredient is nearly the same as that of a prescription drug, but whose formulation is differentiated by the manufacturer.

Firms producing generic drugs sell a standardized chemical product. Further, there are a large number of competing manufacturers, including some 600 generic pharmaceutical manufacturers. This increasing segment of the industry represents a shift toward uniform prices and perfect competition.

However, perfect competition also requires perfect information and the perception of perfect substitutability of competing products by consumers. According to a study of the effects of generic drug competition on the price and market share of previously patented drugs, 29 percent of drugs in 1989 were single source (provided by one firm), 58 percent were multisource but written by brand name in prescriptions, and 13 percent were multisource and written generically.[21] Prices of generic substitutes range from 60 percent of the brand-name drug, when only one generic alternative is available, to 20 percent when as many as 20 generic alternatives are available. Over this range the market share of the brand-name drug declines from 97 percent to 66 percent.[22] Competition therefore has the predicted effects of reducing price

---

19. Shipments of pharmaceutical preparations in 1989 were $32.7 million, compared to $43.8 for the industry as a whole (U.S. Department of Commerce, "Drugs," p. 44-1). The rest of the industry consists of the markets for medicinals and botanicals, diagnostics, and biologicals.
20. U.S. Department of Commerce, *A Competitive Assessment of the U.S. Pharmaceutical Industry,* Boulder, Colo.: Westview Press, 1986, pp. 1–3.
21. Richard Caves, Michael D. Whinston, and Mark A. Hurwitz, "Patent Expiration, Entry, and Competition in the U.S. Pharmaceutical Industry," *Brookings Papers on Economic Activity: Microeconomics 1991,* p. 6.
22. Ibid., p. 36.

and lowering the market share of higher-priced drugs, but the situation by no means has led to perfect competition.

Part of the difficulty lies in the fact that drugs are usually prescribed by one group (physicians), paid for by another (private medical insurance or government welfare), but consumed by a third (the patient). It is difficult for physicians, who often have become familiar with a particular brand-name drug through its promotions while under patent, to become knowledgeable about the many generic alternatives and their prices, nor is there much incentive to do so. A study of prescriptions shows that only 20 percent of prescriptions for multisource drugs are generic; an equal percentage prohibit generic substitution. Of the 60 percent that could be filled with either brand-name or generic drugs, about 40 percent are filled with generic drugs. There is some indication that the market is still changing, and that generics will come to play a larger role, but for the moment the degree of price difference between generics and brand alternatives remains large given the relatively small market share of generics.

Because brand names and the different ''packaging'' of active ingredients (combining them with other agents) can provide product differentiation even for products long out of patent, monopolistic competition is often a good description of competition in the drug market.[23] Ordinary aspirin and acetaminophen serve as examples. The formula for aspirin, acetylsalicylic acid, has been the same since its discovery in 1897. This means that all aspirin brands have the same active ingredient. Companies such as American Home Products (Anacin), Bristol-Myers (Bufferin and Excedrin), Sterling (Bayer), and others have turned to advertising and combining aspirin with other compounds such as caffeine and antacids, changing the shape of the tablets, and placing different coatings on them to differentiate their products, and claim a larger slice of the analgesics, or pain relievers, market. This market, $2.7 billion in 1990, is about one-fourth of the entire over-the-counter drug market and larger than the market for shampoos, deodorants, toothpastes, or any other single category of health or beauty product.[24] With so much at stake, it is not surprising that each aspirin product claims to be the safest, fastest, strongest. As any quick check at a drug store can verify, the presence of nonbrand generic aspirin has not eliminated the higher-priced brands.

As a drug, aspirin competes not just with differentiated versions of itself but also with over-the-counter analgesics such as acetaminophen, marketed most widely under the brand name Tylenol by Johnson and Johnson. Acetaminophen was discovered in 1878, even before aspirin; but in spite of

23. As noted, even for chemically equivalent drugs, many druggists do not automatically substitute a generic product for a brand name, even when permitted by the prescribing doctor and even when the price is lower. Patients, in turn, are often unaware of the alternative or are reluctant to insist on it. The Commerce Department reports that ''patients with the most education, highest incomes, and who are professionals or business owners appear to purchase generics more often than others'' (U.S. Department of Commerce, *A Competitive Assessment of the U.S. Pharmaceutical Industry,* p. 13).
24. Charles C. Mann and Mark L. Plummer, *The Aspirin Wars: Money, Medicine, and 100 Years of Rampant Competition,* New York: Alfred A. Knopf, 1991, p. 7.

marketing attempts over the years, it did not become a major commercial product until advertised successfully as "the strongest pain reliever you can buy without a prescription" in 1977 by Johnson and Johnson. Although this claim was technically true, since Tylenol was equally as effective as aspirin (which could make the identical claim), it *seemed* to imply superiority, and the market share of Tylenol rose quickly at aspirin's expense.

As emphasized in Chapter 9, product demand and hence product differentiation frequently occur on the basis of the list of characteristics or capabilities of the product. Aspirin manufacturers were quick to exploit in their advertising the 1988 finding that aspirin can significantly reduce the chance of second heart attacks, something that Tylenol could not claim. Although aspirin has been known for nearly 100 years, and has been out of patent for over 70, efforts continue to differentiate it from competing products and from the identical compound sold by competing manufacturers.

Oligopoly and Monopoly

The pharmaceutical manufacturing industry as a whole exhibits below average concentrations of market share, with no one firm accounting for more than 8 percent of sales and the largest four companies accounting for 23 percent.[25] The life blood of the prescription drug industry, however, is new patentable drugs to replace old.[26] In the market for selected therapeutic treatments, concentration is significantly higher. A study of 30 leading therapeutic categories of drugs, for example, found that the market leader might have as much as 80 percent of the market, two companies as much as 94 percent, and four companies virtually all of the market in some categories.[27] Every company's dream is to discover a new, technologically advanced drug whose action is not duplicated by existing medicines, giving the company a monopoly. More likely, the drug will provide the company better market position relative to its rivals, but leave it facing oligopolistic competition from a few other patented products that overlap in usefulness.

Such competition usually takes the form of promotional competition[28] and further innovation rather than price competition. As one analyst explains, "Medicines are a necessity and as such an increase in price will drive relatively few people from the market nor will a fall attract very many in. The

25. "Health Care," p. H18.

26. A list of major drug patents with company and year of expiration would include Aldomet (Merck, 1984), Inderal (American Home Products, 1984), Motrin (Upjohn, 1985), Valium (Hoffmann-LaRoche, 1985), Keflex (Eli Lilly, 1987), Naprosyn (Syntex, 1989), and Procardia (Pfizer, 1992), at least some of which are probably familiar names to the reader. An equally long list of new introductions each year could also be given ("Health Care," *Standard and Poor's Industry Surveys,* March 27, 1986, p. H21).

27. Stuart St. P. Slatter, *Competition and Marketing in the Pharmaceutical Industry,* London: Croom Helm, 1077, p. 49.

28. Promotion is primarily direct advertising, brand-name promotion, and solicitations with doctors.

level of consumption is determined by the requirements imposed by disease incidence, not by price.''[29] Research and development spending by the pharmaceutical companies that engage in R&D totals 15 percent of sales, a larger figure than for any other industry.[30]

When a company patents a new chemical compound, competitors try to find a patentable chemical variant. The outcome could be no success, discovery of a variant with a small improvement over the original patent, discovery of a variant with a substantial improvement over the original patent, or even discovery of a drug that has effects determined to be helpful against another disease than the one treated by the original patent. In the case of an improvement over the original patent, the new drug will steadily increase market share and even eventually displace the original drug. This will force the losing company to respond with a new innovation of its own.

National Industrial Policies

As indicated in Chapter 10, actions by government can have the effect of favoring domestic industry at the expense of foreign. In the case of pharmaceuticals, U.S. companies face obstacles to overseas sales, including price controls, regulations on marketing and R&D, and pirating of patents and copyrights. Some foreign nations, for example, offer only process patents, protecting the way in which a product is made, rather than the product itself. Since a company is usually required to disclose the process when it files for patent, competing firms of the domestic country have access to records describing the process and can attempt to patent their own, slightly altered versions to get to the same end product. Other types of regulations can also favor a country's domestic industry. As examples, until 1975 Japan prohibited wholly owned foreign pharmaceutical subsidiaries in Japan,[31] and French law requires that all drugs sold in France must be manufactured in that country.[32] Other regulations involving testing and certification of drugs (such as not accepting foreign tests or studies, as is the case in Japan) can add to trade barriers and act to favor domestic industry at the expense of foreign. Since pharmaceuticals are so intimately tied to health, it is hard to separate national oligopolistic industrial policy from simple protectionism of domestic industry,

29. W. Duncan Reekei, *The Economics of the Pharmaceutical Industry,* New York: Macmillan Press, 1975, p. 35. One might also add that demand is determined by the doctors who prescribe and not the patients who use the drugs.
30. According to a study by the Center for the Study of Drug Development at Tufts University (reported in ''Drugs,'' p. 44-1), it takes 12 years and $231 million to create one new drug.
31. U.S. Department of Commerce, *A Competitive Assessment of the U.S. Pharmaceutical Industry,* p. 80.
32. Suresh B. Pradhan, *International Pharmaceutical Marketing,* Westport, Connecticut: Quorum Books, 1983, p. 195.

and both from actions taken for health and safety reasons. In any case, to the extent that government intervention restricts trade, it tends to lessen competition.

Suggestions for Further Investigation. If you managed a pharmaceutical company, how would you evaluate your choices of price, advertising budget, and research and development as they relate to (a) a drug that has many years of patent life left, and (b) a drug that is near the end of its patent life?

PART FOUR

WELFARE ECONOMICS

What firms do, how prices are formed, what effect taxes have—such issues are ultimately secondary compared to being able to determine whether an economy is doing as well as it can in providing utility for its member households. Welfare economics is the study of the utility-providing ability of the economy. There are three parts to this study: (1) deciding what we mean by an economy that does as well as it can, (2) determining whether a particular economy, especially a market economy, meets those standards, and (3) locating the impediments, if any, to maximum economy functioning and describing how they might be corrected. We tackle these issues in the next three chapters.

CHAPTER 12

Optimality and Efficiency in Any Economy

Thus far we have discussed *how* the economy works: we have seen how consumers choose what goods to buy and what factor services to sell; we have seen how firms decide what goods to sell and what factor services to buy; we have seen how demand and supply interact to determine price and quantity in output markets and in factor markets. In this chapter we ask *how well* the economy works. To answer this question, we examine what we mean by an economy operating well, and we describe the requirements of meeting that standard. In Chapter 13 we apply the standard to the market economy described in this book.

12.1 Types of Economies and Resource Allocation

For those of us accustomed to living in a market economy, with prices determined by market conditions and incomes determined by our jobs, it is sometimes difficult to separate the elements of an economy related to markets from elements present in *any* economy. For example, a common way to distribute goods is to let households buy them at the going price. Prices, however, imply the existence of markets. To talk at the most general level, we should focus not on prices but on the fact that *any* economy, market or not, needs a rule to distribute goods. The distinction between market economies and other types of economies is therefore an important one, especially if you ultimately want to consider how to have society do its "best." Perhaps market economies are not the best way to produce human happiness. If so, then we must be able to recognize elements that are unique to a market system and separate them from elements that are not.

Although we now know a great many positive facts about a market economy—including how consumers choose the goods they buy and decide what factor services to sell, how firms operate to maximize profits, and how demand and supply interact to determine equilibrium prices and quantities in both output markets and factor markets—this information is not very valuable if we have no way to determine whether these economic interactions perform well or perform poorly in producing happiness for the members of society. Studying the *optimality* properties of an economy provides us with ways to evaluate an economy's performance; it also alerts us to things that may go wrong, so that we can fix them.

In this chapter we have two main tasks. The first is philosophical in nature: to discuss and define what we mean by a "healthy" or efficient economy, that is, an economy that generates as much welfare for its members as possible. Once we know what a healthy economy is, we can examine the conditions guaranteeing economic health. These conditions must apply to any economy. We will reserve for Chapter 13 the more specific task of evaluating whether a market economy is healthy.

Since one objective of this part of the course is to think more perceptively about how economies respond to common economic contraints, it is useful to start with a brief discussion of the considerations that arise in any type of economy and how they have been met. We will then be able to appreciate the simplicity and power of the rules for economic health.

A Quick Survey of Economic Organizations

▼
1. What are the three main issues that any economy, regardless of organization, must address?

History reveals that there have been many ways to organize an economy. Whatever its organization, however, any economy has to decide three main issues: (1) What will be produced? (2) How will resources be allocated to different types of production? (3) How will the goods produced be distributed to households? In simple terms, these questions involve *what* to produce, *how* to produce it, and *for whom* to produce it. In the most basic form of society, with individual household units acting as hunter-gatherers, each household decides how to allocate its resources to hunting and gathering. Each family consumes what it produces and cannot consume what it does not produce. Only if households engage in some form of rudimentary trade with other households do prices enter the economy, in the form of rates of exchange of one good for another.

More complicated economies also must decide how to allocate their resources and distribute their goods. In general, a *market economy* is one in which households determine the distribution of goods and services by buying what they need at market prices. Each household earns income at market prices by providing labor services or other factor services (including services from physical capital or other assets that the household may own). The government in a pure market economy restricts itself to basic tasks: protecting personal freedoms, such as the right to practice religion and express one's thoughts through free speech, press, and assembly; guaranteeing law and order; ensuring competition; and providing public goods such as national defense and highways (we will look at public goods in Chapter 14). In such an economy, firms determine how much of each type of good to produce and what resources to use on the basis of what will earn the greatest profit. Households see the benefits of working and saving in the form of market payments such as wages, salaries, interest, and dividends.

A very different form of economic organization is a *centrally planned economy.* As its name implies, a centralized plan for the economy determines the assignment of resources and distribution of output. In addition to providing public goods, the state in such an economy writes the plan directing where households will work, which resources will be used in which production activities, and how the output will be distributed. Households in such a society are not necessarily rewarded for their work commensurately with their respective contributions.

A common misconception is that market economies do not do as much planning as centrally planned economies. This mistakes the absence of *central* planning for the absence of planning. A simple story makes this point. American farmers have often been host to foreign visitors wanting to learn from U.S. farming experience. When a delegation of farmers on such a visit from the former Soviet Union asked their hosts who decided how much of each type of crop American farms were to produce each year, they couldn't believe the answer they got: Nobody tells us, we plant whatever we want. To the visitors, who were accustomed to central planning, letting each farmer decide what to plant seemed nonsensical. Would it not surely lead to chaos, if not disaster? In fact, a great deal of planning was being done: each farmer carefully calculated which crops to plant and what inputs to use to yield the greatest return. Quite possibly, there was *more* planning going on, but it was decentralized.

It would be difficult to find examples of a pure market economy or a pure centrally planned economy. In most market economies the government is involved in some form of planning, and most centrally planned economies have some markets in operation. To a purist, the economies of most parts of the world would be classified as *mixed market economies,* differing from one another by their varying degrees of central planning as well as the extent of their operating markets.

Other types of social organization have existed throughout history. A feudal society, for example, was organized along very different lines than a hunter-gatherer economy, a market economy, a centrally planned economy, or a mixed market economy. In a feudal system, social structure was based on land rights plus the associated loyalties and obligations. Barons and feudal landlords owned the land and were entitled to specific services and payments from the serfs, who worked the land and kept most of their crops. Although the manorial landlords often exercised various rights over the peasants, including judicial and tax rights, they also were expected to provide protection for the serfs and thus were subject to risks of sudden death in battle or political intrigues. Many of our modern notions about the balance of rights between government and the governed, such as the principle of consent of the governed, derive from feudal origins.

Economies also have varied greatly according to each household's degree of control over what it does and the authority it retains over the fruits of its labor. In a slave society, slaves and their output were the property of their owners, who decided what work would be done and how output would be distributed. Many societies have had slaves, often taken from the population of defeated peoples. Ancient Rome used slaves; eighteenth- and nineteenth-century Europe, Africa, and America used slaves; and so did pre-Columbian American cultures, such as that of the Aztecs. The book of Genesis describes how Egypt of 1800 B.C. was converted into a society in which property, authority, and even ownership of the Egyptian people became vested in the pharaoh. Though the pharaoh was the ultimate authority, such a society could function because it was in the pharaoh's interest to provide for his subjects' needs so that they would be able to meet his objectives.

Although we could discover even more variations of societal organization, it is unnecessary to do so to establish that most types of economies work to some extent, in the sense that they usually keep their members from starving and seem able to provide for their own continuation by raising the next generation. The real question is whether they *work well* and whether one (or more) of them *works best*. In the next section we develop a way to approach these questions.

12.2 Pareto Optimality

There are different views about what a properly functioning society should accomplish. Some cultures have taught that society's highest purpose is to exalt the leader or the national honor, that the state's success overrides the welfare of individual members of society. Most Western-based culture, however, is founded on a social compact for collective rule, rooted in the notion that the state's success is defined in terms of the success of its constituent members. Measuring welfare in terms of the welfare of households that make up society is the starting point for our definition of economic health or efficiency. Though this principle may seem noncontroversial, not all cultures and peoples have started from this premise.

We still need to define what we mean by welfare. Welfare, or well-being, is determined by many things, such as giving love and receiving it, engaging in honorable behavior, being aware of spiritual values, having access to justice, freedom and so on. Since this is an economic discussion, however, we will limit household welfare to the utility received from consumption of goods and services. Our approach is *individualistic,* meaning that we evaluate the welfare of each household according to what the household itself says its welfare is.

> ***Household welfare*** *is measured by utility,* $U^i = U^i(X^i)$, *where* X^i *represents the goods consumed by Household* i.

Having effectively represented the household by its utility function, we can now define the components that constitute an economy. *Households, production technologies,* and *endowments* make up an economy. How these components are organized and how they interact with one another determine whether the economy is a market economy, a centrally planned economy, or some other type of economy.

> *An **economy** consists of its households; its production technologies and technical knowledge; and its endowments of goods, factors, and natural resources inherited from the past or from nature.*

▼
2. What are the elements that make up an economy?

In an economy, various allocation or assignment decisions need to be made, such as where goods will be produced and what goods households will consume. In most contexts there will be no confusion about which type of assignment we are discussing. We say that produced goods and services are distributed to households according to an *allocation*.

> An **allocation** *is an assignment of consumption bundles to* **all** *households in the economy.*

Later, we will also talk about the assignment of production to different locations in the economy, using the term *production allocation*. Depending on how the economy is organized, an allocation can come about in different ways. Given an allocation and each household's utility function, we can tell how each household ranks different allocations.

Comparing Allocations

We can rank two allocations, *A* and *B*, according to a rule developed by Italian economist Vilfredo Pareto, who worked on the problem of ranking social outcomes at the end of the nineteenth century. The Pareto approach is individualistic in the sense that it takes into account how members of society themselves think about the alternatives.

▼
3. What is meant by Pareto optimality?

> *(i) Allocation* A *is* **Pareto superior** *to allocation* B *if at least one household has higher utility in allocation* A *than in* B *and no household has lower utility. If* A *is Pareto superior to* B, *then* B *is also said to be* **Pareto inferior** *to* A, *or to be* **Pareto dominated** *by* A.

> *(ii) Two allocations are* **Pareto noncomparable** *if neither is Pareto superior to the other.*

Thus a Pareto ranking does not look at the assignment of physical goods and services directly, but at how the assignment affects the recipients' utilities.

Figure 12.1 displays a set of points that indicate the utilities of two people in alternative allocations. Both people are better off at point *a* than at *b* because point *a* lies strictly to the northeast of *b*. Point *a* is therefore Pareto superior to point *b*. In comparing points *c* and *b,* we see that person 2 has higher utility at point *c*, whereas person 1 has equal utility at both points. Since one person is better off at *c* and no one is worse off, point *c* is Pareto superior to point *b*. *In general a point is Pareto superior to another if it lies to the northeast of the other point.*

Comparing points *b* and *d*, we find that neither point lies to the northeast of the other. Since neither point is Pareto superior to the other, points *b* and *d* are Pareto noncomparable.

Achieving a Pareto Optimal Allocation

Pareto ranking is fairly noncontroversial in its essentials. It suggests that an economy is not doing as well as it can if it is possible to make at least one person better off without hurting another. If it is impossible to achieve a Pareto superior allocation, then the economy is *Pareto efficient.*

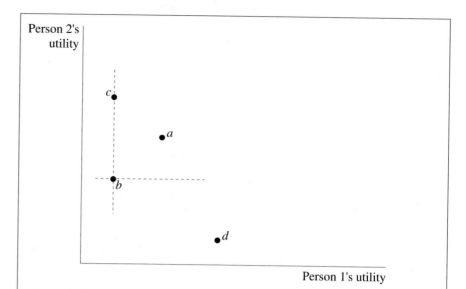

Figure 12.1   Pareto Rankings   Pareto rankings depend on the utilities of the economy members. Point *a* is Pareto superior to point *b* because both individuals have higher utility at *a* than at *b*. In general, points to the northeast of a point are Pareto superior to that point. Point *c* is also Pareto superior to point *b* since person 2's utility is higher at *c* than at *b* and person 1's is the same. Allocations *b* and *d* are Pareto noncomparable because neither ranking is Pareto superior to the other.

> An allocation is **Pareto optimal** or **Pareto efficient** *if it is feasible and if there is no other feasible allocation Pareto superior to it. That is, an allocation is Pareto optimal if it is impossible to raise any household's utility without lowering the utility of another.*

Any change in an allocation must do one of three things: make everyone better off or no worse off; leave everyone indifferent; or harm one or more people. Since the definition of Pareto optimality rules out the first possibility, we can say that an allocation is Pareto optimal if any change harms at least one household or leaves all households indifferent.

Notice that Pareto optimality is not a measure of what seems *right* or what seems *fair*. (We have not even defined these words for our economy.) Rather, it is a statement that helping someone without hurting someone else is desirable, regardless of who is being helped. Those with little and those with much are treated impartially by the Pareto ranking.

For example, let us say that you are the totalitarian despot of a small island in the Pacific inhabited by 99 other people and yourself. As supreme ruler of the island, everything is devoted to your pleasure, and the utility of the other inhabitants is met only at the subsistence level necessary to keep them alive (in order to serve your needs). If the only way to improve the lot of the 99 is to take something away from you, then the original outcome is Pareto

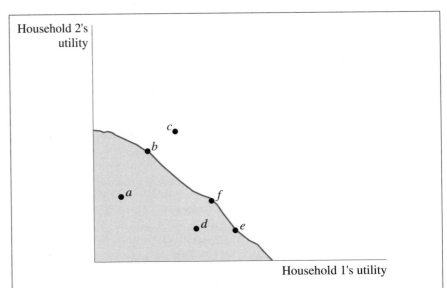

Figure 12.2 Pareto Optimal Allocations   In this two-household economy we allocate all possible output to the two households, producing the
shaded area that indicates all feasible allocations. Only shaded points that
have no Pareto superior points are Pareto optimal. Points *a* and *d* have
Pareto superior feasible points, since at point *b* both households have
higher utility than at *a*, and at point *f* both households have higher utility
than at *d*. All other shaded points to the northeast of *a* and *d* are also
Pareto superior. Points *b*, *f*, and *e* are Pareto optimal because no feasible
point is Pareto superior to them (they are as far to the northeast as possible). Even though point *c* has no point to its northeast, it is not Pareto
optimal because it lies outside the feasible set.

optimal. Now assume that a way is found to adjust the use of the resources
of the island to make you a little better off without hurting the 99. By the
Pareto ranking criterion, the change should be made since it will lead to a
Pareto superior outcome.

Figure 12.2 illustrates Pareto optimality in a two-person economy. Allocating all the physically possible outputs of the economy between the two
people leads to their set of feasible utilities. The shaded area shows this set.
Points *a* and *d* are not Pareto optimal because there are shaded (feasible)
Pareto superior points to the northeast of them. For example, point *b* is Pareto
superior to point *a*, and point *f* is Pareto superior to point *d*.

Points *b*, *f*, and *e* lie as far to the northeast as is possible for this economy.
The set of all such points is sometimes called the utility possibility frontier.
Since it is not possible to raise one person's utility without lowering the
other's, these points are Pareto optimal. Point *c* has no point Pareto superior
to it, but because it is infeasible for the economy it is not Pareto optimal.

As Figure 12.2 shows, Pareto optimality does not necessarily lead to a *unique* allocation that is *the best* for an economy. In Figure 12.2 any point on the northeast frontier is Pareto optimal. Moreover, all Pareto optimal points are Pareto noncomparable (since a Pareto optimal point has no feasible Pareto superior points, it follows that another Pareto optimal point is not Pareto superior). Thus, in considering two economies that are identical except that one has chosen one Pareto optimal allocation and the other another, it is not possible to say which economy is doing better by this ranking. We can narrow down our search for the best outcome for an economy to the set of Pareto optimal allocations, but we do not yet have a way to select among those allocations.

Finally, it is important to reiterate that Pareto optimality is not defined in terms of a fair division of goods and services based on physical quantities of the various goods. True, Pareto optimality depends on which goods and services are given to each household, but its relevance to the social ordering comes from the value that the household itself places on the goods, not from some external planner's rule about what the household should like or what the household needs. In that sense, the Pareto rule takes the gentlemanly course: it lets people evaluate their utility for themselves, and it counts the attainment of higher utility as socially good as long as no one is hurt in the process.

The Edgeworth Box

To illustrate Pareto optimality and become more acquainted with its underlying logic, we can make use of an Edgeworth box. The Edgeworth box is named for the English economist Francis Edgeworth, who worked with it around the end of the nineteenth century. The Edgeworth box provides a convenient way to draw the possible allocations of two goods between two individuals so that the welfare effects on each can be seen. The dimensions of the box are the total quantities of two goods held by the two individuals. If we plot in the box the point showing how much of each good the first individual has, we automatically allocate the remaining goods to the other individual. Moving the chosen point changes the implied allocation. Since indifference curves can be drawn in the box for the two individuals, we can see the effect of changing the allocation on each person's utility.

Imagine that there are two consumers, whom we shall call Country Mouse and City Mouse, who have two types of food available to them, 200 ounces of grain and 100 ounces of cheese.

To plot possible divisions of the grain and cheese between the two mice, we construct the box in Figure 12.3. The horizontal axis measures the total amount of grain available, 200 ounces, and the vertical axis measures the total amount of cheese, 100 ounces. Country Mouse and City Mouse, together with their stocks of grain and cheese, can be considered an economy: there are two consumers, there is no production technology, and the endowments are the stocks of grain and cheese. Though it is a simple economy, we can use it to illustrate Pareto optimal allocations.

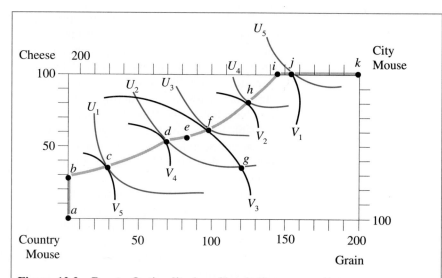

Figure 12.3 Pareto Optimality in a Simple Economy Country Mouse's indifference curves are labeled U_1 through U_5, City Mouse's V_1 through V_5. To see whether an interior point is Pareto optimal, we look for other points that are better for both mice. At point g, for example, we look for points to the northeast of curve U_2 *and* to the southwest of V_3. Since the intersection of the two sets contains such points (for example, e), g cannot be Pareto optimal. Only if the original point in the interior of the box represents a *tangency* between the two mice's indifference curves is it impossible to raise the welfare of one mouse without hurting the other. Some points on the edge of the box, such as j, are Pareto optimal because moves outside of the box are infeasible and any move into the interior or along the edge would harm one or both parties. The line from point a to point k therefore shows the complete set of Pareto optimal points.

Since this simple economy has no production, the only decision is how to allocate the grain and cheese between the two mice. To know what is best for the economy, we need to know what the mice prefer. We label Country Mouse's indifference curves U_1 through U_5, measuring quantities consumed from the lower left origin of the box. That is, quantities of grain for Country Mouse are measured by distance to the right of point a, and cheese is measured by vertical distance from point a. Utility rises for indifference curves further to the northeast. Since the total stocks of grain and cheese are fixed at 200 and 100 ounces, any assignment of goods will be limited by these quantities, as indicated by the dimensions of the box. Indifference curves extend to points outside the box that represent points of positive consumption of both goods for a mouse, as is the case for curve U_5; but these points are not feasible because they represent quantities that are not available.

Indifference curves for City Mouse are labeled V_1 through V_5. For this mouse, quantities consumed are measured from the origin at the upper right corner of the box (point k). Quantity of grain for City Mouse is measured by the horizontal distance to the left of point k, and cheese for City Mouse is measured by the distance below point k. City Mouse's utility rises for indifference curves further to the southwest.

Choosing a point in the Edgeworth box automatically determines the allocation of grain and cheese between the two mice, because it shows what quantities of each good the two mice consume. To find the Pareto optimal points, let's consider an arbitrary point in the interior of the box, such as point g. To see if g is Pareto optimal, we ask whether we can increase the utility of one mouse without hurting the other. Points that have higher utility for Country Mouse lie to the northeast of indifference curve U_2, whereas points having higher utility for City Mouse like to the southwest of indifference curve V_3. Any point in the region bounded by these two curves (such as point e) has higher utility for both mice. Since e Pareto dominates g, g is not Pareto optimal. Proceeding in this fashion, we find that the only points in the interior that cannot be dominated are points such as c, d, f, and h, where City Mouse's and Country Mouse's indifference curves are tangent to one another. Any move from one of these points harms at least one mouse, so they cannot be Pareto dominated. Trying to move from point c to the northeast of U_1, for example, harms City Mouse. Moving southwest of V_5, on the other hand, harms Country Mouse, and moving between both curves to the southeast or to the northwest harms both mice. Connecting all points of tangency gives us the curve starting at point b and going to point i.

Since the slope of an indifference curve is the negative of the marginal rate of substitution between goods, tangency is the same thing as the two mice having the same marginal rate of substitution between goods. In economic terms, if both mice place the same marginal value on one good in terms of the other, it is not possible to reassign goods to improve one mouse's welfare without harming the other.

Look again at the curve connecting the points of tangency. For any point off this curve (such as g), there is some point on the curve (such as e) for which each mouse would be better off. This means that unless they are on the curve, they have an incentive to trade with each other. Because this curve represents the set of points that the mice would move to through their trade, it is called the *contract curve*.

▼
4. What is the contract curve? How does it relate to Pareto optimality in a two-person economy without production?

Given two households with a fixed quantity of goods between them, the **contract curve** *is the set of Pareto optimal allocations of goods to the two households.*

To evaluate points on the edge of the box, we must first consider whether any move into the interior can improve one mouse's utility without harming the other, and then check moves along the edge. Point j, for example, is on indifference curve U_5 for Country Mouse and V_1 for City Mouse. Although we cannot extend indifference curve V_1 above the box (that would represent negative consumption of cheese for City Mouse), it is clear that the slopes of the two indifference curves are unequal at point j. Moving from j to outside the box is impossible; moving into the interior of the box harms Country Mouse if the move is to the southwest of U_5 and City Mouse if it is to the northeast of V_1. Since this covers all possible moves into the interior, no point in the interior can be Pareto superior to j. Since any move to the right along the edge of the box hurts City Mouse, and any move to the left hurts Country Mouse, no move along the edge can Pareto dominate j either. Thus j is Pareto optimal even though it is on the boundary and not a tangency. Adding the Pareto optimal points on the edge to the interior Pareto optimal points extends the contract curve along the edge.

The Difference Between Efficiency and Equity

▼
5. Relate efficiency and equity to Pareto optimality.

Assuming that consumers value all goods, an easy way to find at least one Pareto optimal allocation in an economy without production is to give all of the goods to one consumer. Such an allocation must be Pareto optimal, because any other allocation requires taking goods from the consumer with everything; no consumer can be made better off without hurting the consumer with everything. Although Pareto optimality is desirable, few people would recommend giving one consumer a claim to everything. This fact underscores the difference between Pareto optimality, which deals with economic *efficiency,* and fairness, which has to do with *equity.*

Efficiency is a performance measure. It is concerned with getting the desired output or results from the least expenditure of effort or input. Alternatively, it is getting the most output from a given amount of inputs. In loose terms, we would say that an efficient economy is one that gets the most utility from its available inputs and technology.

Equity is concerned with whether the utility of each household seems right according to some notion of justice. There are many elements that might go into determining a just distribution of goods. For example, fairness might include some notion of distribution according to the size of contribution to social output: households would be expected to receive in proportion to what they earn through their own effort. Another principle might be that no household in the social compact should be allowed to fall below a minimal level of well-being if it is behaving responsibly to the limit of its abilities. The fact that these two principles conflict with each other (Should the second principle be followed, for example, if a family is not responsibly living up to its abilities or if following the principle requires taking excessively from other families?) demonstrates the extent to which choices must be made, either consciously or unconsciously, by any economy.

Economists have no value-free way to resolve the problem posed by the existence of many possible Pareto optimal allocations. It appears to be desirable for society to reach some Pareto optimum; but government intervention in the economy to choose a particular one is unavoidably controversial.[1]

---

1. Economists sometimes use an individualistic social welfare function as a way to summarize beliefs about which allocation in an economy is preferred. An individualistic social welfare function is a rule that assigns welfare numbers to an allocation based on the utilities of households in the economy, $W = W(U^1, U^2, \ldots, U^m)$, such that raising any household's

12.3 Necessary Conditions for Pareto Optimality

▼
6. What are the necessary conditions for Pareto optimality?

Now that we know what we mean by a "healthy" or efficient economy (one that attains Pareto optimality), we can turn to the second task posed at the start of the chapter, which is to describe conditions guaranteeing economic efficiency. When you go for a physical exam, the doctor usually does a number of things, including taking your temperature, listening to your heartbeat, and looking at your retina. These tests evaluate necessary but not sufficient conditions for your health: having a temperature of 98.6° F does not guarantee that you are healthy, but having a temperature of 103° F guarantees that you are not. In the same way, there are conditions that are necessary for an economy to be Pareto optimal. If an economy achieves a Pareto optimal allocation, all of the conditions will be satisfied. If the economy achieves an allocation that is *not* Pareto optimal, one or more of the conditions must be violated.

In order to assess the efficiency of an economy, all aspects of it—consumption and production—must be analyzed. Consumption is what matters to utility, but it is production that determines how much is available for consumption. Thus both elements must be examined. The first three conditions for Pareto optimality all relate to efficiency in production, so we group them together.

Productive Efficiency

In simple terms, productive efficiency means that an economy is using its resources in such a way that it is not possible to increase the output of one good without lowering the output of another. If the economy could produce more of a good without lowering the output of any other, it could use the extra output to raise someone's utility; hence it would not have been Pareto optimal to begin with. Achieving productive efficiency requires satisfying three conditions, each of which addresses a different aspect of the production process.

▼
7. Explain why full employment is needed for Pareto optimality. Relate the notion of full employment to exhaustion of renewable and nonrenewable natural resources.

Full Employment. The first necessary condition for productive efficiency is that all resources of production must be fully employed. If an economy found that it had unused stocks of raw materials, for example, it could put them to work, produce more output, and use the extra output to raise someone's utility without hurting anyone.

utility, while holding constant utilities of the others, raises social welfare. Ranking allocations by their social welfare numbers and choosing an allocation with the highest one is equivalent to choosing from among the set of Pareto optimal allocations. This requires making normative utility comparisons across households, however, and unlike the scales held by justice, which is supposed to be blind, the social welfare function has eyes wide open in deciding whose utility matters most: what you get depends on *who* you are, rather than on impersonal characteristics describing *what you have done.*

For example, let's assume that the economy uses capital, K, as a factor of production. If the economy produces goods x, y, and z, the condition for full employment would be

$$K_x + K_y + K_z = K,$$

where K_x, K_y, and K_z are the quantities of capital devoted to production of goods x, y, and z, respectively, and K is the total available quantity of capital. By saying that all capital is accounted for in the production of some good, we say that the economy has zero unemployed capital.

We can use Figure 12.4 to illustrate the effect of full employment on the economy's production. The figure shows two *production possibility frontiers*. At curve AA, the economy has some unemployed factors of production, so output is limited to points on or below AA. If the economy fully employs all factors of production, however, the frontier expands to curve BB. Exactly which bundle the economy produces depends on how the factors are assigned to production tasks, but the area enclosed by the frontier indicates the overall set of feasible bundles, given the level of factor usage. Clearly, a frontier further from the origin is better than one closer to the origin.

Full Employment and Labor Supply Although we want inputs like physical capital and land to be fully employed, what about other types of factors? In the case of labor, greater work effort is generally utility-reducing, as we saw in Chapter 5. Thus, ever-greater employment of labor is beneficial only if the utility gain from the increased output compensates for the utility loss of the labor expended. What does full employment mean in this case?

In a market economy, labor time is rewarded by the direct results of the labor or by the payment of wages. In either case, the benefits more than compensate for the utility loss from the labor expended. A worker is unemployed if he or she wants to work for the going wage (or in return for the direct benefits produced by the work) but is prevented from doing so. Since workers want to increase their labor supply only if it means higher utility, the presence of unemployed labor signifies that there is an unexploited opportunity to raise utility.

The Role of Time and Resource Depletion In addition to factors whose supply directly reduces utility, we must also consider what full employment means for depletable factors. If the U.S. economy has unused stocks of oil underground, does that mean we should immediately pump them all out and use them up to meet the full employment condition? A similar question can be asked about renewable natural resources such as forestry products and fisheries. Were we to attempt full employment by cutting down all trees today, we would have no lumber for tomorrow. Can this be what full employment means?

To answer this question requires the introduction of time into the analysis, something that we shall do in Chapter 16. The idea behind the interpretation of full employment is that when the effective period of economic activity is over (or, to be blunt, when the earth ceases to exist), there should not be any unused factors of production left.

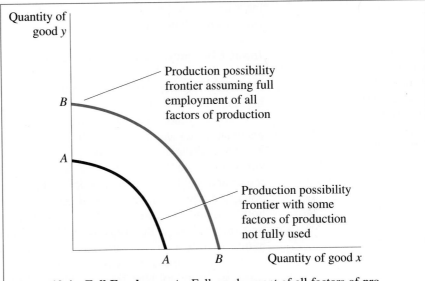

Quantity of good y

B

A

Production possibility frontier assuming full employment of all factors of production

Production possibility frontier with some factors of production not fully used

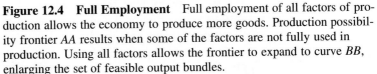

A   B   Quantity of good x

Figure 12.4   Full Employment   Full employment of all factors of production allows the economy to produce more goods. Production possibility frontier *AA* results when some of the factors are not fully used in production. Using all factors allows the frontier to expand to curve *BB*, enlarging the set of feasible output bundles.

Worrying about whether all inputs will have been fully employed before the economy ends may seem to suggest undue devotion to the importance of Pareto optimality, but this view is only partly right. We expect that life will continue for many years, but there are still valid questions concerning how fast the world's nonrenewable resources such as oil should be depleted and how intensely its renewable resources such as forests should be farmed. Although such analyses are beyond the scope of this book, we can consider them a special case of the general Pareto optimality condition for "full employment."

In general, there are certain rules that explain how fast a resource should be used under different conditions, and neither complete depletion today nor complete conservation today is typically correct. If we use up all oil in our lifetimes, there will be none available for our children. On the other hand, oil may become an unimportant resource a generation from now, and we would needlessly deny ourselves its benefits today by failing to use it. Moreover, stressing conservation could impede the development of new, more efficient technologies.

In the 1840s whale oil was the major source of oil for lighting. We would not be particularly grateful to our great-great-grandparents if they had reacted to the diminishing supplies of whale oil relative to its demand by restricting its use and trying to stockpile it for the future. Rather, we *are* grateful to them for having found alternative sources of energy in response to the limited supplies of whale oil.

Input Efficiency. Fully employing all factors of production will not be of much value if the factors are not being used as efficiently as possible. Input efficiency requires using the factors of production so that they yield the highest possible output.

▼

8. What happens if the wrong assignment of factor inputs is made to productive tasks? Relate this to the mathematical condition for input efficiency.

Consider road repair and jewelry making. Road repair uses labor and pneumatic jackhammers to break up concrete and asphalt road surfaces; jewelry making requires labor and tiny jewelry hammers for tapping out silver and gold fittings. Assume that we assign jewelry hammers to road repair and jackhammers to jewelry making. How much road repair will get done, and how much jewelry will get made? Before answering, consider that both types of labor are hard at work, that all workers are doing the absolute best they can with the tools available, and that there is no waste of either hammers or workers. Yet not much is being accomplished.

The reason is that the wrong kind of input was assigned to do each job. There is a subtlety here that should not be overlooked. Were you asked to testify to a congressional committee about the losses involved in assigning jackhammers to jewelry making and jewelry hammers to road repair, what would you say? If you were asked, ''Were there any wasted or unemployed inputs?'' you would have to say no. If you were asked, ''Were there any workers who were not working to the best of their ability?'' you would have to say no. If you were asked whether any output was being destroyed or mistreated, you would have to say no. So what is the problem? The problem is that things could be improved by rearranging the assignment of inputs to the different production tasks. If the same amount of inputs can produce more outputs, then this is a ''gift of goods'' that can be distributed to make someone in the economy better off.

*An economy satisfies the condition of **input efficiency** if, given the available supply of productive inputs, it is impossible to reassign inputs to the production of different goods so as to increase the output of one good without lowering the output of another.*

Figure 12.5 uses an Edgeworth box to demonstrate how the example of jackhammers and jewelry hammers generalizes to other cases. The horizontal and vertical dimensions of the box represent the available supplies of jewelry hammers and jackhammers, respectively. Since we assume that jewelry hammers are not useful in road repair, the road repair isoquants labeled z_1 through z_3 are horizontal lines with the direction of output increase pointing downward (more jackhammers assigned to road repair). Similarly, the isoquants for jewelry output are vertical lines with output increasing to the right (more jewelry hammers assigned to jewelry).

If the economy had initially assigned both factors to both tasks, as at point b, we know that removing jewelry hammers from road repair and removing jackhammers from jewelry making in order to assign each factor to the

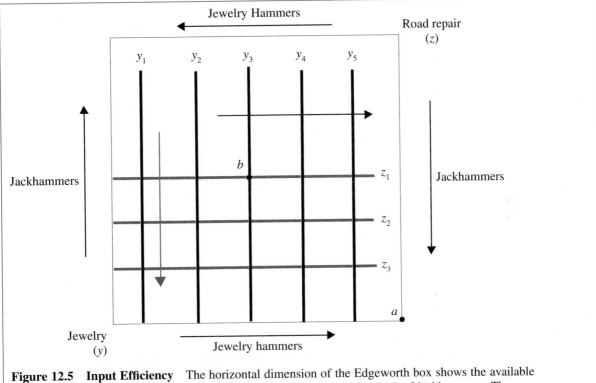

Figure 12.5 Input Efficiency The horizontal dimension of the Edgeworth box shows the available stock of jewelry hammers; the vertical dimension shows the available stock of jackhammers. The vertical lines, measured from the origin at the lower-left-hand corner, show isoquants for jewelry output. The horizontal lines, measured from the origin at the upper-right-hand corner, show isoquants for road repair. The arrows inside the box indicate directions of output increase. In this example, assigning all jewelry hammers to jewelry production and all jackhammers to road repair (this is the lower-right-hand corner of the box, labeled point a) yields the highest quantity of both outputs. At any other point in the box or on its edge, we can increase the output of one good without lowering output of the other by shifting more jewelry hammers to jewelry making or more jackhammers to road repair. Point a is therefore the only input efficient assignment of factors to the two tasks.

''right'' task would increase the output of both types of goods. This would be a move to the southeast of point b in the figure. Since this shift increases the output of one good without lowering output of the other, it follows that point b could not have been input efficient. Continuing to eliminate all input inefficient points leaves us with point a.

The same principles apply in less extreme cases, where the factors have positive marginal productivity in both uses. Figure 12.6 shows an Edgeworth box for two factors, capital and labor, both of which are inputs into the production of chemicals and automobiles. As before, the dimensions of the box represent all the capital and labor available to the two industries. We

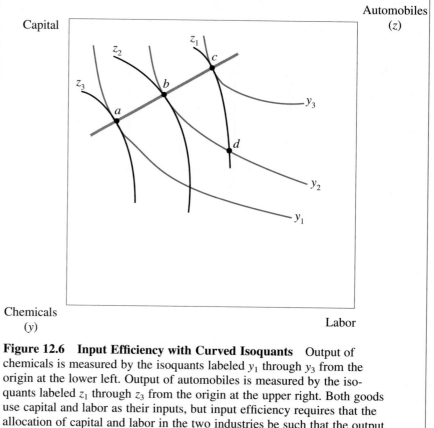

Figure 12.6 Input Efficiency with Curved Isoquants Output of chemicals is measured by the isoquants labeled y_1 through y_3 from the origin at the lower left. Output of automobiles is measured by the isoquants labeled z_1 through z_3 from the origin at the upper right. Both goods use capital and labor as their inputs, but input efficiency requires that the allocation of capital and labor in the two industries be such that the output of neither good can be increased without lowering the output of the other. Points *a, b,* and *c,* where the isoquants are tangent, satisfy this requirement. (Any move from point *b,* for example, lowers the output of one or both goods.) Since the slope of the isoquant determines the marginal rate of technical substitution between labor and capital, tangency requires that marginal rates of technical substitution be equalized across industries for any two factors. In the figure, chemicals are the capital-intensive industry; that is, the industry uses more capital per unit of labor than the automobile industry.

measure the chemical industry's isoquants from the lower left and the automobile industry's isoquants from the upper right. The degree of curvature of the isoquants is related to the degree of substitutability between capital and labor in each industry, as discussed in Chapter 6. To check whether an assignment of capital and labor to the two industries is input efficient, we must find out whether we could reassign existing supplies of capital and labor to increase the output of chemicals or autos without lowering the output of the other good. Point *d* is *not* productively efficient, because moving to a point between curves z_1 and y_2 can increase the output of both goods. Any move from tangency points *a, b,* or *c,* on the other hand, lowers the output of one or both goods. These points are therefore input efficient.

Tangency of two isoquants means that the slopes of the isoquants, given by the marginal rate of technical substitution between labor *L* and capital *K,* $\text{MRTS}_{L,K}$, is equal across industries, or

$$\text{MRTS}_{L,K}^C = \frac{\text{MP}_L^C}{\text{MP}_K^C} = \frac{\text{MP}_L^A}{\text{MP}_K^A} = \text{MRTS}_{L,K}^A,$$

where superscript *C* refers to the chemical industry, superscript *A* refers to automobiles, and MP is the marginal product of the relevant factor. At point *d* in Figure 12.6, for example, $\text{MRTS}_{L,K}^C = \text{MP}_L^C/\text{MP}_K^C < \text{MP}_L^A/\text{MP}_K^A = \text{MRTS}_{L,K}^A$. Labor is thus relatively more productive in the automobile industry at point *d.* We can increase the output of both goods by moving to the northwest of *d,* shifting labor away from chemicals and capital away from automobiles. If the inequality went the other way, then the reverse shift would be needed to raise output.

The only input efficient assignments occur when the two industries reach equality of their marginal rates of technical substitution (or when they reach an edge of the box where any move lowers output of one or more goods or leaves both the same). The collection of all input efficient points in Figure 12.6 forms a curve much like the contract curve of Figure 12.3. The line through points *a, b,* and *c,* for example, would be part of this curve.

If the condition for input efficiency holds for the inputs for *any* choice of goods, the economy is input efficient.

Sector Production-Allocation Efficiency. So far, to ensure productive efficiency we have considered full employment of factors and reassigning inputs to get more output. We now consider another requirement of productive efficiency, which involves changing the *output assignments among sectors* to get more output. That is, having each *sector* of the economy produce the right quantities of goods can increase available output, even if factors are fully employed and every sector is input efficient when considered separately. This type of productive efficiency is particularly important because it applies both to domestic production and to international trade.

Domestic Sector Production-Allocation Efficiency Imagine an economy that produces potatoes and corn in two separate regions or sectors that we will call Idaho and Iowa. Both sectors use capital and labor to produce both goods. We further assume that each sector is input efficient. Sector production-allocation efficiency deals with production assignments in different sectors, so we consider the available capital and labor in each sector to be fixed.

> *A **sector** is any firm or group of firms producing two or more goods, plus the fixed quantity of inputs used by those firms.*

▼
9. What is a sector, and what is sector production-allocation efficiency? What does sector production-allocation efficiency mean with respect to international trade?

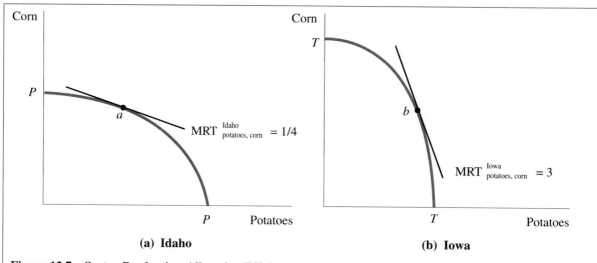

Figure 12.7 Sector Production-Allocation Efficiency Input efficient Idaho produces at point *a* on its production possibility frontier *PP*. Idaho cannot increase the output of corn or potatoes without lowering the output of the other good. Input efficient Iowa is in the same situation, producing at point *b*. However, the sectoral allocation of production of the two goods is inefficient, as shown by the fact that the marginal rate of transformation between potatoes and corn is different in the two sectors. Giving up 1 unit of corn production in Idaho allows production of 4 additional units of potatoes, whereas giving up 1 unit of potatoes in Iowa allows production of 3 additional units of corn. More of each good could therefore be produced by having Idaho produce more potatoes and Iowa produce more corn. As long as the two sectors have unequal marginal rates of transformation, we can increase output by reassigning the sectoral productions. When the sectors have equal marginal rates of transformation, we achieve sector production-allocation efficiency, because output gains in one sector would be canceled by losses in the other, indicating that no further net gains are possible.

A sector is not necessarily associated with a geographical region. A sector might be any distinctive part of an economy. One might speak of the Idaho farm sector, the chemical sector, or even the foreign trade sector (meaning firms engaged in international trade).

Since Idaho is input efficient, we cannot increase production of Idaho corn without decreasing production of Idaho potatoes, and vice versa. The same holds true in Iowa. The convex production possibility frontier *PP* in part (a) of Figure 12.7 shows all possible combinations of potatoes and corn that Idaho can produce from the available stocks of capital and labor. Part (b) shows Iowa's equivalent frontier *TT*. Although both regions can produce both goods, the two sectors' frontiers look different because Idaho is a relatively better potato-growing region and Iowa is a relatively better corn-growing region.

Since any point on *PP* or *TT* is the result of an input efficient allocation of factors, we check to see whether production at point *a* in Idaho and at point *b* in Iowa leads to a productively efficient outcome for the economy. If the sectoral assignment of production is productively efficient, it must be the case that no sectoral reassignment can increase the output of one good without lowering the output of another. However, we see from Figure 12.7 that the transformation rate between potatoes and corn in Idaho (the number of units of corn that must be given up if one more unit of potato is produced) is $\frac{1}{4}$, and the same marginal rate in Iowa is 3. In general, the rate at which another good must be reduced in order to increase the output of a good is called the marginal rate of transformation between the two goods.

> The **marginal rate of transformation** of good x *for good* y *is the rate at which good* y *must be reduced as output of good* x *is increased.* $MRT_{x,y} = -\Delta y/\Delta x.$

For efficient production on the production possibility frontier, the marginal rate of transformation is just the absolute value of the slope of the frontier. $MRT_{x,y}$ can be thought of as the opportunity cost of good x in terms of units of y needed to be foregone for another x. Sectors with low $MRT_{x,y}$ are said to have a comparative advantage in production of x, while sectors with high $MRT_{x,y}$ have a comparative advantage in y.

The difference between the marginal rates of transformation for the two regions suggests that Iowa finds it less costly in potatoes given up to produce an additional unit of corn and that Idaho finds it less costly in corn given up to produce an additional unit of potatoes. Can we take advantage of this difference?

The answer is yes. For example, consider having Idaho produce 1 fewer unit of corn. This allows Idaho to produce 4 more units of potatoes. The ledger for the economy now reads

Corn	Potatoes
−1	+4

Now have Iowa produce 1 fewer unit of potatoes. This allows Iowa to produce 3 more units of corn. The ledger for the economy now reads

Corn	Potatoes
−1	+4
+3	−1
+2	+3

The economy has more of both goods without using more resources to produce them! The explanation for this seemingly miraculous creation of goods from nothing is that assigning each sector to produce more of what it does best allows greater total output from increased productivity in each sector.

> An economy satisfies the conditions for **sector production-allocation efficiency** *if, given the use of factor inputs within any two sectors, it is impossible through reassignment of sectoral output levels to increase the economy's output of one good without lowering the output of another.*

Although it may seem restrictive to define sector production-allocation efficiency in terms of just two sectors, we can always choose one sector in the economy and let the other sector be everything else. Sectors might consist of two geographically distinct regions between which factors cannot travel, or they might consist of geographically intertwined groupings of firms between which factors can move. The relevant point is that each sector has a set of feasible production bundles that defines its ability to increase output of one good at the expense of other goods. In our discussion of corn and potato production in the Idaho and Iowa sectors, we saw that different marginal rates of transformation between goods implied an opportunity to increase the output of one good without lowering the output of another. Thus sector production-allocation efficiency requires that marginal rates of transformation be the same across any two sectors,

$$\text{MRT}^1_{x,y} = \text{MRT}^2_{x,y}.$$

We can use a simple graphical technique to find the proper assignment of output between sectors. In Figure 12.8, draw the production possibility frontier (PPF) for sector 1 in the usual fashion with the origin on the lower left. Then draw the production possibility frontier for sector 2 inverted, so that its origin is in the upper right. Part (a) shows the two frontiers' orientations. To find an efficient assignment of production for each sector, move sector 2's inverted production possibility frontier until its edge is tangent to the edge of the first production possibility frontier, as in part (b). The tangency ensures that the two sectors have the same marginal rate of transformation, and the tangency point shows the efficient quantities of output to be produced by each sector when measured relative to each sector's origin. For example, at point *a* the inverted production block for sector 2 has its origin at point *b*, and both sectors have the same marginal rate of transformation, given by the absolute value of the slope of the line labeled MRT. For production at point *a*, the combined output of the two sectors can be read as the distance from sector 1's origin (point *O*) to point *b*. Shifting sector 2's production block to other locations, we can generate other output assignments that show sector production-allocation efficiency—for example, at tangency point *c*.

Part (c) of Figure 12.8 shows what happens if the assignment is at a point where the two sectors have different marginal rates of transformation. At point *e*, sector 2's production block has a different slope than sector 1's. Point *f* indicates their combined output. You can see that point *f* is inefficient because it generates less of each good than point *b*, reproduced from part (b).

Transforming by International Trade As no man is an island, so no nation is an island unto itself. From the perspective of a national economy, trading with other nations is another way to convert some types of goods into other types of goods. An open economy is one that can trade with other nations. When the United States produces more video cassette recorders by diverting components from other uses, it in essence transforms the output that would have been produced with these components into VCRs. In the same way, when the United States exports goods to the rest of the world and imports

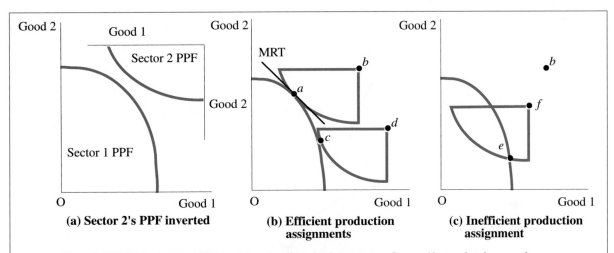

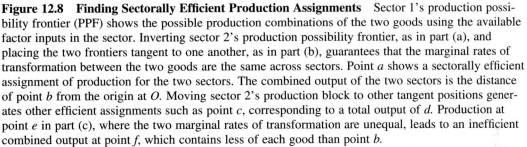

Figure 12.8   Finding Sectorally Efficient Production Assignments   Sector 1's production possibility frontier (PPF) shows the possible production combinations of the two goods using the available factor inputs in the sector. Inverting sector 2's production possibility frontier, as in part (a), and placing the two frontiers tangent to one another, as in part (b), guarantees that the marginal rates of transformation between the two goods are the same across sectors. Point a shows a sectorally efficient assignment of production for the two sectors. The combined output of the two sectors is the distance of point b from the origin at O. Moving sector 2's production block to other tangent positions generates other efficient assignments such as point c, corresponding to a total output of d. Production at point e in part (c), where the two marginal rates of transformation are unequal, leads to an inefficient combined output at point f, which contains less of each good than point b.

VCRs, it transforms the exported goods into VCRs through international trade. The marginal rate of transformation of one good into another in international trade is the rate at which the rest of the world is willing to trade one type of good for another.[2]

If we think of trading with the foreign sector as one way to produce a given good, and producing it domestically as another, sector production-allocation efficiency implies that the domestic marginal rate of transformation should equal the marginal rate of transformation through foreign trade. Such a rule does indeed lead to the greatest quantity of goods for the domestic economy, as shown in Figure 12.9.

Figure 12.9 shows a standard production possibility frontier for the economy as the curve PP. Without foreign trade, the economy could produce any bundle of goods contained inside or on the frontier PP. The foreign economy, however, is willing to trade 2 units of good y for 1 unit of good x. Thus, if the domestic economy produces at point b, say, it could trade units of x to

---

2. We will assume that the country is unable to influence that rate of exchange, so the marginal rate of transformation in trade is a fixed number for the country.

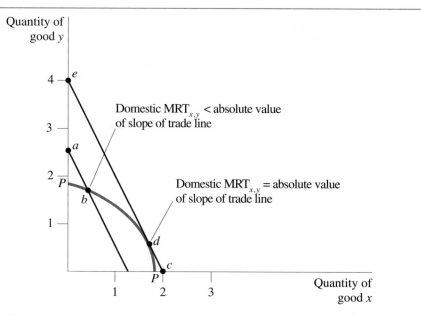

Figure 12.9   Sector Production-Allocation Efficiency and Foreign Trade   The production possibility frontier *PP* shows the economy's capability to produce domestically. Since the rest of the world is willing to trade 2 units of good *y* for 1 unit of good *x*, the marginal rate of transformation in foreign trade is 2, given by the absolute value of the slope of the trade lines *ec* and *ab*. In an open economy, sector production-allocation efficiency requires that the domestic marginal rate of transformation be equal to the foreign marginal rate of transformation. When the domestic economy produces at point *b*, trading with the rest of the world allows the economy to reach bundles on line segment *ab*. However, if the country sets the domestic marginal rate of transformation equal to the foreign marginal rate of transformation by producing at point *d*, the economy can reach bundles on line segment *ec*, a better outcome.

the foreign economy in exchange for *y* and achieve bundles on the line segment *ab*. The domestic marginal rate of transformation equals the absolute value of the slope of the tangent line to *PP* at point *b* (not shown). The figure shows that at point *b* the two sectors have different marginal rates of transformation,

$$\text{Domestic MRT}_{x,y} < \text{Foreign MRT}_{x,y} = 2.$$

If we set the two rates equal by producing domestically at point *d*,

$$\text{Domestic MRT}_{x,y} = \text{Foreign MRT}_{x,y} = 2,$$

and the economy can get to bundles on the line *ec,* which is further out than the line through points *a* and *b.* Therefore, sector production-allocation efficiency implies that the domestic marginal rate of transformation should equal the marginal rate of transformation in foreign trade.

As we have just seen, full employment, input efficiency, and sector production-allocation efficiency are necessary conditions for Pareto optimality. We group them together under the title of productive efficiency since they relate to efficiency in production. However, there are two other conditions that also must be satisfied for Pareto optimality, one relating to consumption and the other relating consumption to production. We turn to the consumption condition next.

Distributive Efficiency

▼

10. What is the mathematical condition for distributive efficiency?

Imagine an economy that produces goods and distributes them to households, which then consume them. Without more information, we do not know if the economy produces the ''right'' type of goods or if the economy is productively efficient, but we can assert the following: if the economy achieves a Pareto optimal allocation, it must be true that, given the bundle of goods produced, it is not possible to make one household better off through redistribution of the available goods without harming another.

As a simple example, assume that we list everything consumed in a given year's time by U.S. households, and that among these products are avocados and grapefruit. Furthermore, assume that we can divide the population into four groups: those who like both fruits; those who like avocados but not grapefruit; those who like grapefruit but not avocados; and those who like neither. The U.S. economy obviously already has a way to decide which consumers get grapefruit, which get avocados, which get both, and which get neither, but let us assume for the moment that a new mechanism is at work that assigns avocados and grapefruits to everyone equally, and that consumers can consume no more than what they are assigned of the two fruits. (Such a mechanism would be a silly way to distribute avocados and grapefruit, since it takes no account of preferences, but we can imagine why it might be chosen since it *sounds* like a reasonable way to allocate.)

The economy could not achieve a Pareto optimal allocation according to this mechanism: we could easily raise every group's utility by transferring grapefruit from those who like only avocados to those who like only grapefruit and by sending avocados in the reverse direction. This will be true independently of the distribution of other goods. Satisfying the conditions of distributive efficiency for the entire economy simply requires repeating the process for *any* choice of goods.

> *An economy satisfies the conditions of **distributive efficiency** if, given the available goods and services, it is impossible to redistribute them among households so as to increase the utility of one household without lowering the utility of another.*

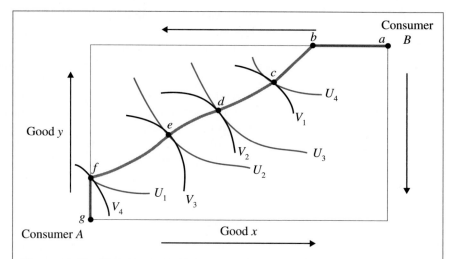

Figure 12.10 Distributive Efficiency Distributive efficiency requires that for any two goods, x and y, and any two consumers, A and B, it is impossible to redistribute the goods to improve one consumer's utility without harming the other. In this example the dimensions of the box are the quantities of goods x and y distributed to consumers A and B. Except on an edge of the box, distributive efficiency occurs only at points of tangency between the two consumers' indifference curves. At point d, for example, the slope of indifference curve U_3 is the same as the slope of V_2, so any move to raise A's utility will harm B, and vice versa. Tangency is characterized by equality of the two consumers' marginal rates of substitution of good x for good y. The set of points representing distributive efficiency is the contract curve from point a through point g.

The Edgeworth box gives us another way to characterize distributive efficiency. Figure 12.10 shows an Edgeworth box for two consumers, A and B, and two goods, x and y. The total quantity of good x for the two consumers is indicated by the horizontal dimension of the box, and the quantity of good y by the vertical dimension. The indifference curves of A are labeled U_1 through U_4, and the indifference curves of B are labeled V_1 through V_4. As in the case of City Mouse and Country Mouse, unless the allocation is on the contract curve we can raise the utility of one household without lowering the utility of the other. As indicated before, in the interior of the box the contract curve connects points of tangency, meaning that the slopes of the indifference curves, given by the marginal rate of substitution of good x for good y, are the same across households. Thus

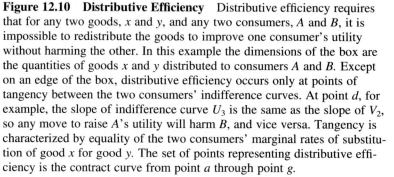

$$\text{MRS}^A_{x,y} = \frac{\text{MU}^A_x}{\text{MU}^A_y} = \frac{\text{MU}^B_x}{\text{MU}^B_y} = \text{MRS}^B_{x,y}.$$

Distributive efficiency requires that this condition apply to *any two goods* and *any two consumers.*[3]

When distributive efficiency fails to hold, the two consumers involved have an incentive to trade goods with one another, thereby improving each other's utility. Only after all such trades have taken place is there no further room to improve utility. Thus another interpretation of distributive efficiency is that it requires *exhausting all potential benefits from interpersonal trade.*

Distributive efficiency tells us the "right" allocation of existing goods, and productive efficiency tell us that no more of any good could be produced without lowering the output of another, but we still can't guarantee Pareto optimality. We now turn to the last necessary condition for Pareto optimality, relating production to consumption.

Consumer Sovereignty

▼

11. Explain the role of consumer sovereignty in Pareto optimality.

Given full employment, input efficiency, sector production-allocation efficiency, and distributive efficiency, it seems an idle question to ask what other aspect of an economy might need correction to achieve Pareto optimality. Everyone is working; all factors are assigned to the right tasks; no change in output assignments among sectors can increase overall output; and the goods being produced are efficiently distributed. What could still be wrong with the economy?

The answer is that the economy might produce the wrong *selection* of goods. Regardless of how efficient it may be at production and distribution, an economy is not doing a good job if it does not produce what households want. Consumer sovereignty, the last necessary condition for Pareto optimality, stipulates that the consumer rules.

*An economy achieves **consumer sovereignty** if it is impossible to change the selection of goods produced in such a way as to increase any household's utility without harming another household.*

Figure 12.11 shows production possibility frontier *PP* for the economy. Consider point a' on the frontier. As indicated earlier, the marginal rate of transformation for the economy equals the absolute value of the slope of the production possibility frontier. Since the frontier is relatively flat at point a', $MRT_{x,y}$ at point a' is low. The economy can thus produce relatively large amounts of additional good x at little cost in y given up. Now look at the right-hand portion, which shows indifference curve U_0 passing through point a for an arbitrary household, where point a is the household's consumption bundle when the economy produces at a'. The absolute value of the slope of

---

3. On the edge of the box, as at point f, distributive efficiency can be satisfied without equality between marginal rates of substitution. For example, $MU_x^A/MU_y^A < MU_x^B/MU_y^B$ at point f, which would imply distributing less of good x to A. This is impossible, though, because A's holdings of good x have already been reduced to zero.

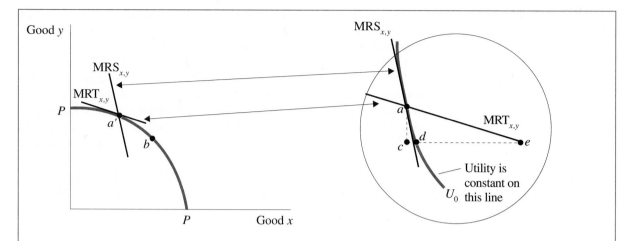

Figure 12.11   Consumer Sovereignty   Consumer sovereignty requires for any two goods x and y that the marginal rate of transformation of good x for good y be the same as an arbitrary household's marginal rate of substitution of good x for good y. Let U_0 be the indifference curve of an arbitrary household, passing through the household's consumption bundle at point a. Point a represents the household's consumption when the economy produces at point a'. The marginal rate of transformation for the economy is determined by the slope of the production possibility frontier at a', whereas the household's marginal rate of substitution is determined by the slope of its indifference curve at a. Since $\text{MRS}_{x,y} > \text{MRT}_{x,y}$, the diagram on the right shows that lowering the production of good y would increase utility. For example, if production of y were lowered from point a to point c, the household would need cd units of good x to hold utility constant. However, the economy can produce ce units of good x, leaving de units with which to raise the household's utility. Similar comparisons could be made for other households. Only if $\text{MRS}_{x,y} = \text{MRT}_{x,y}$ for any household and any choice of two goods is it impossible to raise any household's utility without harming any other by adjusting the mixture of goods produced.

the indifference curve at a gives the household's marginal rate of substitution. Since this line is steeper than the frontier, for this household

$$\text{MRS}_{x,y} = \frac{\text{MU}_x}{\text{MU}_y} > \text{MRT}_{x,y}.$$

This means that if good y were reduced by a small amount, the economy could produce more good x than the household would need to keep its utility from dropping. The leftover good x could then be used to raise utility higher than at point a.

The right-hand side of Figure 12.11 shows that if the economy reduced production of good y by amount ac, the household would need amount cd to stay on the initial indifference curve U_0. The marginal rate of transformation curve, on the other hand, shows that the economy could produce ce units of good x with the resources freed up by producing less y. The excess, equal to *de*, could then be divided among households to raise one or more's utility. If the inequality went the other way, $\text{MRT}_{x,y} > \text{MRS}_{x,y}$, utility could be raised by producing more *y* and less *x*. Thus, only if

$$\text{MRT}_{x,y} = \text{MRS}_{x,y}$$

is the economy producing the mix of goods that consumers want, meaning that it is impossible to adjust production to improve any household's utility without harming another household.

12.4 Combining the Necessary Conditions for Pareto Optimality

Now that we have described the necessary conditions for Pareto optimality, we can show how they work together.

The *full employment* condition states that for any factor *F*, the sum of factor usage over all uses—for instance, production of goods *x, y,* and *z*—equals the available stock of the economy,

$$F_x + F_y + F_z = F.$$

Full employment guarantees that the economy has a production possibility frontier extended out as far as possible, since it puts all factors of production to work. In part (a) of Figure 12.12, this means that the economy's frontier is $P''P''$ rather than $P'P'$.

Input efficiency and *sector production-allocation efficiency* guarantee that, given the factors of production used, the economy assigns them to the right tasks and assigns the sectors to produce the right quantities of each good. In part (a) of Figure 12.12, this means that domestic production takes place on the production possibility frontier at point *a* rather than in the interior, and that the economy uses the international trade sector optimally to generate feasible bundles for the economy on line *cab*.

Distributive efficiency guarantees that the economy distributes available goods in such a way that no redistribution can raise one household's utility without lowering another's. In part (b) of Figure 12.12, the available goods are shown by the dimensions of the Edgeworth box with corners at the origin and point *d*. Within the box, distributive efficiency occurs at a point such as *e*, where the two households' indifference curves have equal marginal rates of substitution.

Finally, *consumer sovereignty* guarantees that the economy chooses a proper selection and mix of goods from the set of feasible bundles. In part (b) of Figure 12.12, this is point *d*, where the marginal rate of transformation (which equals the marginal rate of transformation in foreign trade, because of sector production-allocation efficiency) equals the marginal rate of substitution of households.

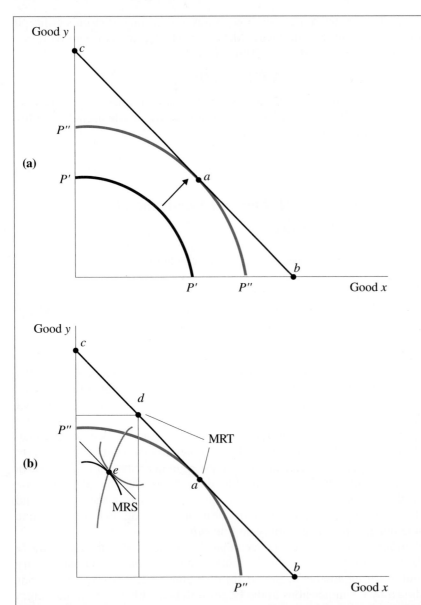

Figure 12.12   Combining the Necessary Conditions for Pareto Optimality   The two parts of the figure bring together the various conditions for Pareto optimality. In part (a), full employment guarantees that the economy's production possibility frontier is as far out as possible (at $P''P''$ instead of $P'P'$). Input efficiency and sector production-allocation efficiency guarantee that domestic production takes place on the frontier (point a). Sector production-allocation efficiency also guarantees that the domestic marginal rate of transformation equals the marginal rate of transformation in foreign trade, so that the economy chooses its goods bundle from the line segment cab. In part (b), consumer sovereignty guarantees that the choice of production is the right mixture of goods by setting the marginal rate of substitution equal to the marginal rate of transformation (MRS = MRT at point d). Distributive efficiency guarantees that the goods are distributed in the right way by equalizing all consumers' marginal rates of substitution (point e).

Combining the mathematical summaries of the necessary conditions for sector production-allocation efficiency, consumer sovereignty, and distributive efficiency gives us

$$\text{MRT}^{\text{foreign trade}} = \text{MRT}^{\text{domestic production}} = \text{MRS}^{\text{I}} = \text{MRS}^{\text{II}} = \text{MRS}^{\text{III}} = \cdots,$$

where the Roman numerals refer to different households. We express input efficiency as

$$\text{MRTS}^x_{L,K} = \text{MRTS}^y_{L,K} = \text{MRTS}^z_{L,K} = \cdots,$$

where *x, y,* and *z* represent goods and *K* and *L* represent factors of production. We represent full employment by the condition that the economy uses all available factors to produce output,

$$F_x + \cdots + F_z = F,$$

where *F* is a factor of production and *x* through *z* are goods.

In summary, we have described what we mean by economic "health" in terms of Pareto optimality and have found necessary conditions for its attainment. We are now in a position to apply what we have learned to a market economy. Whereas this chapter did not even refer to prices once we finished the quick survey of types of economies, in Chapter 13 we will refer to prices often as the key mechanism for determining whether a market economy attains Pareto optimality.

Summary

Active Reading Guide numbers are given in parentheses at the end of each summary item.

1. Regardless of its organization, an economy has to decide three main issues: (1) what to produce, (2) how to allocate resources to different types of production (how to produce), and (3) how to distribute goods and services to society members (for whom to produce). A market economy is only one of many ways in which the questions of "what," "how," and "for whom" can be answered. (1)

2. An economy is made up of households, production technologies, and endowments of goods, factors, and natural resources. (2)

3. To determine how well an economy performs, we need to specify what its goals are. Pareto optimality defines economic success in terms of the welfare of the economy's constituent members. An economy achieves Pareto optimality if it is not possible to raise one household's utility without lowering that of another. An equivalent definition of

Pareto optimality is to say that an allocation is Pareto optimal if any move from it harms someone or leaves everyone indifferent. In a two-person economy without production, Pareto optimal allocations are represented by the contract curve, showing the points for which beneficial trade is impossible for the two people. (3, 4)

4. Pareto optimality deals with efficiency rather than equity or fairness. A Pareto optimal outcome does not indicate that the distribution to households is necessarily equitable according to some criterion of justice. In addition, there may be more than one, or even an infinite number, of Pareto optimal outcomes for an economy. (5)

5. The necessary conditions for Pareto optimality are productive efficiency, encompassing full employment, input efficiency, and sector production-allocation efficiency; distributive efficiency; and consumer sovereignty. Productive efficiency relates to efficiency in production; distributive efficiency

relates to consumption; and the final condition, consumer sovereignty, links production to consumption. (6)

6. Full employment implies that the economy's production possibility frontier is extended out as far as possible because there are no unused factors of production. Full employment for labor means that no one who wants to work at the going wage is prevented from working. In the case of renewable and nonrenewable natural resources, full employment implies that the resources are used at the appropriate rate through time. In many cases, the appropriate rate to use resources is unknown or difficult to determine. (7)

7. Input efficiency requires that it be impossible, by reallocating the existing supply of factors, to raise the output of any good without lowering that of another. The mathematical condition is that producers' marginal rates of technical substitution between inputs be equal across firms. (8)

8. Sector production-allocation efficiency requires that it be impossible to raise the economy's output of any good without lowering that of another by reassigning production levels for the goods across sectors. The mathematical condition is that the marginal rate of transformation between two goods be the same across any two sectors. When one of the sectors is a foreign country with which the economy trades, sector production-allocation efficiency requires that the domestic marginal rate of transformation be equal to the foreign marginal rate of transformation, which is the rate at which one good can be traded for another. (9)

9. Distributive efficiency requires that it be impossible, by redistributing the existing supply of goods, to raise the utility of any household without lowering that of another. The mathematical condition is that households' marginal rates of substitution between any two goods be equal across households. (10)

10. Consumer sovereignty requires that it be impossible, by increasing the output of one good at the expense of another, to raise anyone's utility without lowering someone else's. The mathematical condition is that the marginal rate of transformation between any two goods should be equal to the consumers' marginal rate of substitution. (11)

Review Questions

*1. Discuss the following statement: "All economies are alike in that they have to solve the same fundamental problems, but they can be quite different in how they solve them."

2. In an ideal world, define what it would mean to you for an economy to be working as well as it could. Relate your definition to Pareto optimality.

*3. How does an individualistic approach to measuring an economy's success differ from other approaches?

4. Prove or disprove that the following definitions are equivalent to one another. Prove or disprove that each is equivalent to the definition in the text.
   a) An allocation is Pareto optimal if it is feasible and if there is no other feasible allocation in which everyone is better off.
   b) An allocation is Pareto optimal if it is feasible and if any move from it harms someone.

*5. Does limiting the economy to Pareto optimal allocations completely determine what the economy should do? Why or why not?

6. "Even though two individuals might have different marginal rates of substitution between two goods, distributive efficiency might still be satisfied." Explain.

*7. Explain the following statement: "Most of the conditions for Pareto optimality seem to involve tangencies of one sort or another."

8. "Consumer sovereignty is the necessary condition for Pareto optimality that is most difficult for central planners to get right." Discuss.

*9. Assume that there are three people in an economy. Prove that if an allocation is Pareto optimal, there must be at least one person who does not strictly prefer any other person's allocation over his or her own. Is this true for an economy with any number of people?†

* Asterisks are used to denote questions that are answered at the back of the book.
† (Hint: Think about what you might mean by a cycle of size n and what that implies.)

Numerical and Graphing Exercises

*1. Draw an Edgeworth box and locate the Pareto optimal points for a two-person economy with no production. The utility of person 1 is given by $U_1 = X + Y$, and the utility for person 2 is given by $U_2 = \min(X, Y)$, where X and Y are consumption levels of the two goods, and $\min(X, Y) = X$ when $X \leq Y$, and Y when $Y \leq X$. Available quantity of X is 2 units, and available quantity of Y is 1 unit.

*2. Answer exercise 1 when the utility of *both* individuals is given by $U = \min(X, Y)$.

3. For each definition in review question 4, and for the corresponding definition in the text, find the set of Pareto optimal points for the following two-person economy. (The *utility possibility frontier* gives the upper bound for the economy of combinations of utility that it can provide for the two people.)

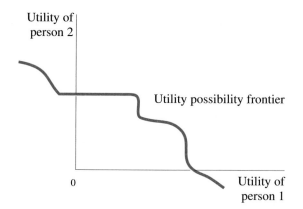

*4. An economy consists of two sectors. The first has a production possibility frontier given by $X + Y \leq 100$; the second has a frontier given by $X^2 + Y^2 \leq 25$, where X and Y are each nonnegative. Draw the overall production possibility frontier for both sectors combined, using the condition for sector production-allocation efficiency.

5. Danielle and Rachel have convex-to-the-origin indifference curves and have positive marginal utility for both goods X and Y. Assuming each woman has the same endowment of X and the same endowment of Y, draw their contract curve in an Edgeworth box and show the trades that Danielle and Rachel would willingly make.

*6. Assume that utility is directly proportional to income. Draw a two-person utility possibility frontier that is consistent with the following statement: "For everybody to get the same income, total income must be less than half what it would be if complete inequality were allowed."

CHAPTER 13

▼

Welfare in Competitive Market Economies

In *An Inquiry into the Nature and Causes of the Wealth of Nations,* Adam Smith posited that the separate actions of households and firms, each working to improve its own station, join together as if led by an invisible hand to achieve the social good of everyone. This "invisible hand" doctrine remains one of the most enduring issues of economics. In a market economy, prices provide incentives for households' and firms' actions and perform important coordination and information roles. This chapter shows that a perfectly competitive market economy with private ownership can in fact provide maximum welfare to its members by achieving Pareto optimality. We discuss two fundamental theorems of welfare economics that link Pareto optimal outcomes to competitive equilibria. We also look at government's role in ensuring competition and market function.

13.1 Market Economies: General Equilibrium and the Function of Prices

The Declaration of Independence states that "all men are created equal, that they are endowed by their Creator with certain unalienable Rights, that among these are Life, Liberty and the pursuit of Happiness." High on the list of freedoms needed for "Liberty and the pursuit of Happiness" is personal economic freedom, including enforceable property rights, the opportunity to make a living for oneself without interference or fear of expropriation by other citizens or government, and the ability to enjoy the fruits of one's labor and enterprise. A related consideration is whether the economy's organization enhances its members' abilities to provide for themselves through their economic interactions.

A *market economy,* the subject of this chapter, can be considered society's natural working out of both concerns: that households be able to keep the fruits of their labor and that they be able to garner the benefits of joint activity. Households initially produce for themselves. They then begin to trade with other households for products, rent out their land, hire neighbors for labor services, and so on. The development of firms soon follows. In each step of the progression, households exchange goods and services for other goods and services of value, eventually leading to prices and a market. The prevalence of markets across time, place, and culture (whether highly sophisticated stock exchanges for trading financial assets or simple bazaars for food) suggests that the market is a natural response to economic forces that are common to all mankind.

The Rules of the Game

▼

1. What are the "rules of the game" for production and consumption in a market economy?

In Chapter 12 we learned that an economy consists of households, productive technology, and endowments of goods, factors, and natural resources inherited from the past or from nature. How these elements are organized to generate output and how that output is distributed vary with the economy. Since the purpose of this chapter is to talk about how well a *market* economy provides for its members' needs, it is important to know the "rules of the game"—that is, the rules of production and distribution in a market economy.

First, by a market economy we simply mean any economy with functioning markets present.[1]

> A ***market economy*** *is an economy characterized by significant voluntary market exchange and well-defined property rights.*

This definition is broad enough to cover economies with perfectly competitive markets (discussed in Chapters 7 and 11), for example, as well as other market forms.

The rules of the game specify that households are free to maximize their utility by spending their income on consumption of goods and services. The ability of a household to consume is determined by the household's flow of income, which is determined by what the household provides to the market. As we saw in Chapter 5, every household can sell its labor hours to produce a flow of income, and households may own other factors that generate income. The rules of the game also say that firms use inputs to produce goods with the objective of maximizing profits. Firms choose what to produce and what inputs to use in production. Household purchases determine firm revenues, and firm payments determine households' income.

Since households make their decisions in their own best interest without consulting firms, and firms likewise make their decisions without consulting households, what ensures that the decisions of households and firms are coordinated with one another in any consistent way? We turn to this next.

General Equilibrium and Coordination

▼

2. Describe four roles that prices play in a market economy.

In fact, the market acts in a decentralized way to coordinate the production and distribution decisions households and firms make: the action of prices sets demand equal to supply for each market in equilibrium. For the rules of the game just described to determine the *what* (production) and *for whom* (distribution) for the entire economy, a *general equilibrium* of markets must be found. This means finding prices for each good and service so that, when these prices apply, every market is simultaneously in equilibrium. Naturally, this is a much larger task than the partial equilibrium analysis used extensively in previous chapters, where we found equilibrium for only one market, holding constant the conditions in others.

1. A market was defined in Chapter 2, which also included a discussion of the role of common price in a market.

In a market economy, prices both *coordinate* (between markets) and *equilibrate* (move the markets to equilibrium). Reaching equilibrium in one market depends on conditions in many others. We know from our study of cross-price effects on consumer demand in Part Two, and from the analysis in Part Three of the effects of input prices on firm output and demand for other inputs, that conditions in one market influence demand and supply in another. For example, consider the following brief excerpt from a report on feeder cattle prices at the end of 1991. (Feeder cattle are cattle to be fattened for market, as opposed to fed cattle, which are cattle at market weight at the end of the fattening process.) How many markets do you find mentioned in these two sentences?

> Feeder cattle prices continued to slide in early December, reflecting disappointing fed cattle prices. Relatively low priced feed and lower interest rates did little to encourage cattle feeders.[2]

If you said four markets, you were right. Feeder cattle prices (market 1) depend on the prices of fed cattle (market 2), the price of feed (market 3), and interest rates (the market for borrowing, market 4). Since the price of fed cattle was low, the report is saying that there was little incentive to fatten cattle. Thus demand for feeder cattle was down. The report also allows for the fact that low feed prices and interest rates[3] typically increase demand for feeder cattle, but in this case they were not low enough to counteract the lower price for fed cattle. To find equilibrium in the feeder cattle market therefore requires that we know equilibrium prices of at least three other markets. This in turn requires knowing the prices of yet other markets related to them. Finding equilibrium in all markets simultaneously is what economists call *general equilibrium analysis.*

Understanding the function of prices is essential for appreciating the power of markets. Consider what happens in the following situation: If the demand for fed cattle suddenly rises, demand for feeder cattle also will rise. For the supply of feeder cattle to go up, more resources must be made available to feed them. This requirement is met by the action of prices! Increased demand for fed cattle raises the price of fed cattle. This raises the profitability of fattening cattle for market, and the number of cattle in feeder lots goes up. As the demand for feed rises, this puts upward pressure on feed prices, which induces suppliers to increase the quantity of feed supplied. At each step, prices move in the right direction to induce the needed change in quantity, at the same time causing each market to adjust to a new equilibrium.

Prices, Information, and Incentives

At the market level, then, prices coordinate and equilibrate. At the level of the firm or household, prices perform two other functions: they provide information and incentives. That is, a high price tells the household, "This

2. "The Farm Picture." The Bankvertising Company, Champaign, IL: January 1992, p. 1.
3. Interest rates matter if the feeder must borrow money to purchase cattle or feed.

is a costly product. Economize. Use it only when its benefits are high.'' It is in the household's best interest to act accordingly, because the household has to pay for what it consumes. The price *provides information* to the household by telling it the costliness of the product relative to other products. At the same time, it *creates an incentive* to the household to use the product wisely.

A high price serves a similar function for firms. A high price tells the firm, ''This product is highly desirable and valued by consumers. Try to provide as much of it as possible.'' Firms respond because they can increase profits by doing so. The high price gives the firm information about the relative worth of providing this product compared to others. It also provides an incentive to respond because profits rise with the price of output.

It is worth pausing momentarily to digest what we have said about prices. Prices (1) coordinate, (2) equilibrate, (3) provide information, and (4) create incentives. In each function, the market tends to move prices in the right direction to respond to the ultimate needs of households and firms. Although these observations seem promising, can we be sure, given all the complexity present in the entire economy, that we will reach a good outcome overall? This is a deep question, but we can say a considerable amount about it using what we learned about Pareto optimality in Chapter 12.

13.2 The Fundamental Theorems of Welfare Economics

▼

3. What is Adam Smith's invisible hand doctrine?

The publication in 1776 of *An Inquiry into the Nature and Causes of the Wealth of Nations* by Scottish economist Adam Smith marked the birth of economics as distinct from philosophy or political science. Much of Smith's book was devoted to showing that a nation's wealth came from elevating and unloosing the industry and energies of its people rather than from acquiring gold through foreign trade, as the then-popular mercantilist notion asserted.[4] By seeking to better themselves, firms and households would be led by the market to actions that also promoted the public good. In a justly celebrated passage in *Wealth of Nations,* Smith wrote:

> As every individual, therefore, endeavors as much as he can both to employ his capital in the support of domestic industry, and so to direct that industry that its produce may be of greatest value; every individual necessarily labours to render the annual revenue of the society as great as he can. He generally, indeed, neither intends to promote the public interest, nor knows how much he is promoting it. By preferring the support of domestic to that of foreign industry, he intends

4. *Mercantilism* is the term used to describe an economic system prominent after the fall of feudalism in Europe. It was designed to acquire bullion through the development of manufactures and establishment of foreign trading companies and a favorable balance of trade. It tended to rely heavily on regulations by the government to secure these ends.

> only his own security; and by directing that industry in such a manner as its produce may be of the greatest value, he intends only his own gain, and he is in this, as in many other cases, led by an invisible hand to promote an end which was no part of it.[5]

In modern language, Smith's invisible hand passage avows that a market economy *would* be led to achieve a Pareto optimum. We now examine conditions under which this assertion is true.

Equilibrium in the Perfectly Competitive Market Economy

The first step is to be more precise about the type of market economy to which we are referring. We talked about the conditions for a perfectly competitive market in Chapters 7 and 11; we now need to explain what perfect competition means for equilibrium in an entire economy where households choose their own consumption and firms choose their own production. To describe the equilibrium, we need to consider the consumption, production, and ownership arrangements for the economy as a whole.

▼

4. How are production and consumption plans chosen in a market system? In what way must they be consistent?

In Chapter 12 we defined an *allocation* as the *consumption* bundles for all households in the economy. We can now expand that definition to include each household's supply of factor services that directly enter into the determination of utility such as labor. For example, if household h consumes C_1 units of good 1 and C_2 units of good 2, and supplies 160 units of accounting services, its consumption bundle X_h includes $+C_1$ and $+C_2$ units for consumption of goods 1 and 2, respectively, and -160 for the supply of accounting services, $X_h = (+C_1, +C_2, -160)$. (The sign convention reminds us what the household consumes and what it supplies.) All households' consumption $X = (X_1, X_2, \ldots)$ is therefore the allocation for the economy.

Firms similarly must decide what their inputs and outputs will be. If firm j produces, say, 20 tons of glass using 10 units of labor, 5 units of machine time, 20 tons of sand, and 15 units of natural gas, its production plan, Y_j, includes $+20$ for the output of glass and -10, -5, -20, and -15, respectively, for the use of inputs. (Again, the sign convention reminds us which goods are inputs and which are outputs.) We will refer to all such firm plans $Y = (Y_1, Y_2, \ldots)$ as the *production plan* for the economy.

Finally, we said that a market economy has well-defined property rights. Each household owns endowments (its own labor time and possibly other endowments as well); many households also own claims to income from firms (for example, through owning shares of stock in firms or bonds that firms issue). The property rights associated with this ownership entitle the household to receive income from the sale of its endowments or endowment services and to receive a portion of the revenues of firms according to the claims held.

5. Adam Smith, *An Inquiry into the Nature and Causes of the Wealth of Nations,* Chicago: William Benton Publishers, Encyclopaedia Britannica Incorporated, 1952, p. 194.

Equilibrium requires that firm production plans and household allocations be consistent. That is, the total amount of goods households consume annually cannot exceed the amount that firms make available. Similarly, the total hours of labor that firms use cannot exceed what households supply. Households cannot spend more on consumption than their income allows,[6] and so on. When households and firms take prices as given and do not act strategically,[7] when firms choose their production plans to maximize profits and households choose their consumption to maximize utility, and when production and consumption plans are consistent (quantity demanded equals quantity supplied in every market), we have what we call a *competitive equilibrium.*

▼

5. List the requirements for a competitive equilibrium.

*A **competitive equilibrium** for an economy consists of prices P for all outputs and inputs, a production plan Y, an allocation X, and ownership by households of endowments and claims to firm profits, where the following conditions are met:*

(i) Firms and households take prices as given and do not act strategically.

(ii) Each firm's production plan is feasible, given its technology, and maximizes the firm's profits, given prices P.

(iii) Each household's consumption is feasible for the household and maximizes the household's utility, given its income.

(iv) In each market there is market clearing, meaning that consumption of goods and services by households and firm use of inputs equals the supply available.

With respect to our earlier discussion of the role of prices, this definition not only tells us what we mean by a competitive equilibrium, but suggests where in the economy planning takes place: *the firm plans when it maximizes its profit, and the household plans when it maximizes its utility.* Because firms and households base their decisions on prices, and because prices must cause markets to clear in general equilibrium, the two sectors' plans coordinate. The incentive for firms and households to act comes from their desire to maximize profits and utility. We are now in a position to introduce two theorems that can help us see how well the perfectly competitive market economy succeeds.

---

6. In a one-period economy, spending cannot exceed income in that period. In a multiperiod economy, households may be able to borrow or lend so that their consumption can differ from their period-by-period income. We discuss multiple-period consumption choices in Chapter 16.

7. In Chapter 10 we saw that a strategic choice is one taken with the intention of causing other firms to change their behavior in a manner favorable to the one making the choice. In principle, households could also act strategically. For example, if I particularly enjoy a restaurant in town because of its quiet atmosphere, I might reduce my use of it (also telling others that I do not go there much) in the hope that others would choose to go elsewhere and leave me with an even quieter and lower-priced restaurant when I do use it. Such behavior, because its motive was to alter others' behavior in a manner favorable to myself, would be considered strategic.

The Two Theorems

The *First Fundamental Theorem of Welfare Economics* basically says that Adam Smith was right under appropriate conditions. If the economy reaches a position that is a competitive equilibrium, then the allocation corresponding to the position is a Pareto optimum: there is no way to reorganize the economy to increase any household's utility without harming another's.[8] The theorem is remarkable because it indicates that a perfectly competitive market economy automatically does the enormous coordination and planning needed to get to a Pareto optimum. The theorem reveals the close relationship between competitive equilibria and Pareto optimality: every time you find a competitive equilibrium, you find a Pareto optimum. The identification also works in the reverse direction: the *Second Fundamental Theorem of Welfare Economics* says that every time you find a Pareto optimum, no matter how the economy achieved it, you also could have reached the same Pareto optimum by setting up the economy as a market system, assigning appropriate property rights and letting the economy move to competitive equilibrium. In this sense, the collection of all allocations that are Pareto optimal is the *same set* as the set of all competitive equilibria.

▼

6. State the First and Second Fundamental Theorems of Welfare Economics. Relate them to one another.

The First Fundamental Theorem of Welfare Economics: *If a set of prices* P, *a production plan* Y, *and an allocation* X *represent a competitive equilibrium, then allocation* X *is Pareto optimal.*

The Second Fundamental Theorem of Welfare Economics: *If* Y *is the feasible production plan corresponding to a Pareto optimal allocation* X, *then there is an assignment of property rights and a set of prices* P *such that* P, X, *and* Y *form a competitive equilibrium.*[9]

Proof of the two theorems is beyond the level of this book, but we can use them as reference points in our discussion of how well a market system performs. To link the welfare theorems to our discussion in Chapter 12, the next section shows how market prices cause the conditions for Pareto optimality to be satisfied in general equilibrium. We center our discussion on the same necessary conditions developed in Chapter 12, but we're answering a different question this time: now we want to show how *market prices* cause the conditions to be satisfied.[10]

8. We also require that there be no externalities. For example, we rule out situations where one firm's production directly affects the ability of another firm to produce. We will discuss the effect of externalities in more detail in section 13.5 and in Chapter 14.

9. The theorem requires that households and firms in the economy satisfy certain standard assumptions about their indifference curves and preferences or their isoquants and production functions, as discussed in Chapters 3 and 6.

10. Remember, the economies we discussed in Chapter 12 may not have had prices or markets.

13.3 Pareto Optimality in a Perfectly Competitive Market Economy

▼
7. How does a competitive equilibrium meet each of the conditions for Pareto optimality?

To relate the necessary conditions for Pareto optimality to market prices, we can characterize each condition except full employment in terms of marginal rates of substitution or marginal rates of transformation. We will see that the market causes households and firms to adjust their decisions in such a way that their marginal rates of transformation and substitution are led as if by an invisible hand to satisfy the requisite conditions. Full employment, which we take up first, operates somewhat differently, but it too can be shown to respond to market forces in a perfectly competitive setting.

Full Employment

Most market economies have some unemployment even in periods of expansion, if only because some workers are always going to be between jobs and the transition takes some time to accomplish. This type of unemployment is often called *frictional unemployment* because it relates to unemployment that occurs when workers move between jobs and sectors. The efficiency wage model discussed in Chapter 11 also helps explain why unemployment might occur.

If both sides of the labor market had perfect information about job opportunities and workers' qualifications, and if prices were perfectly flexible, there would never be any need for unemployment. Although the world is not that perfect, we can refer to the demand and supply diagram in Figure 13.1 to see how a competitive equilibrium eliminates unemployment. Since unemployment in the labor market is the same thing as excess supply, market clearing automatically implies zero excess supply and therefore zero unemployment. The same argument applies for other factors, too.

Although market clearing does not require us to describe what happens if the market is not in equilibrium, we can describe a process by which unemployment is eliminated. Assume for some reason that there is an excess supply of labor at wage w'. Because surplus labor competes for work with employed labor and there are no informational constraints, competition causes the market price to fall. It continues to fall as long as there is excess supply. When the price reaches w^*, unemployment is zero, the price stops falling, and the market clears. Under these price dynamics, therefore, only full employment prices are compatible with market equilibrium. The same story applies for nonlabor factors.

Input Efficiency

Productive efficiency implies that the marginal rate of technical substitution between two inputs must be the same across firms. Letting the marginal rate of technical substitution of labor for capital be given by $MRTS_{L,K}$, the condition is

$$MRTS_{L,K}^x = MRTS_{L,K}^y = MRTS_{L,K}^z = \cdots,$$

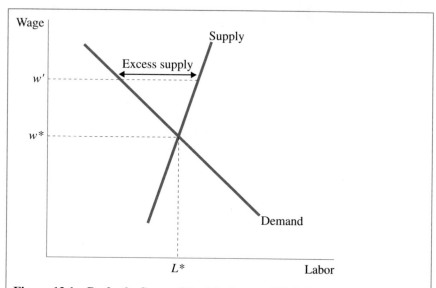

Figure 13.1 Perfectly Competitive Markets and Full Employment
In markets with flexible prices and no informational asymmetries or constraints, excess supply is associated with falling prices and excess demand with rising prices. Equilibrium therefore occurs where demand equals supply and unemployent is zero, as at price w^* in the figure.

where the superscripts refer to the different industries producing goods x, y, z, and so on.

When a firm buys its inputs in the factor markets, it chooses least-cost production techniques to maximize profits. Figure 13.2 shows the input decision of a representative firm producing q_0 units of output. As discussed in Chapter 6, the tangency between the isoquant and isocost line for cost minimization requires equality between the firm's marginal rate of technical substitution and the ratio of input prices,

$$\text{MRTS}_{L,K}^x = \frac{w}{r}.$$

However, *all* firms in the economy face common input prices, so that

$$\text{MRTS}_{L,K}^x = \frac{w}{r} = \text{MRTS}_{L,K}^y = \text{MRTS}_{L,K}^z = \cdots,$$

satisfying the condition for productive efficiency.

When there are competitive input markets, each firm has the same marginal rates of technical substitution, not because its isoquants are the same, but because it purchases inputs to produce at a final position where its marginal rate of technical substitution equals the factor price ratio w/r. In terms of

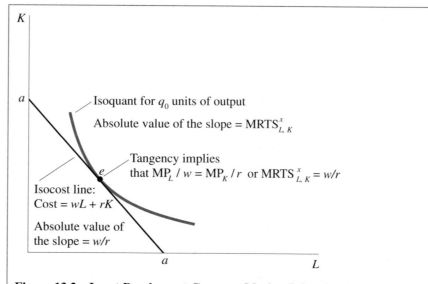

Figure 13.2   Input Purchase at Common Market Prices Leads to Productive Efficiency   To maximize profits, firms choose the least-cost production techniques. In the figure, the firm produces q_0 units of output at least cost using capital and labor at tangency point e. Since the slope of the isoquant is the same as the slope of the isocost line, we have $\text{MRTS}^x_{L,K} = w/r$ (the factor price ratio, wage rate divided by rental rate). Since other firms buy at the same prices, equality of marginal rates of technical substitution of labor for capital is assured across firms.

Figure 13.2, the firm's isoquant is tangent to the cost line aa at point e, and thus has the same absolute slope (w/r) as the cost line aa. Another firm with different technology could have chosen a different input point, but its marginal rate of technical substitution would still have equaled the common factor price ratio, because it would have selected inputs where its isoquant was tangent to a cost line having the same slope.

Sector Production-Allocation Efficiency

As we learned in Chapter 12, sector production-allocation efficiency requires that the marginal rate of transformation between two goods x and y, $\text{MRT}_{x,y}$, be the same in different sectors of the economy. How does a market achieve this?

Remember that perfectly competitive profit-maximizing firms set $p\text{MP}_L = w$ and $p\text{MP}_K = r$. We also know that price equals marginal cost. Since

$$\text{MRT}_{x,y} = -\frac{\Delta y}{\Delta x} = -\frac{\text{MP}^y_L \, \Delta L_y + \text{MP}^y_K \, \Delta K_y}{\text{MP}^x_L \, \Delta L_x + \text{MP}^x_K \, \Delta K_x}$$

for a sector, we have[11]

$$\text{MRT}_{x,y} = \frac{MC_x}{MC_y} = \frac{p_x}{p_y}.$$

The sector's marginal rate of transformation thus equals the ratio of the goods' prices. The last step to notice is that if sector 1 satisfies

$$\text{MRT}^1_{x,y} = \frac{p_x}{p_y},$$

and other sectors satisfy the same condition, then

$$MRT^1_{x,y} = \frac{p_x}{p_y} = MRT^2_{x,y} = \text{MRT}^3_{x,y} = \cdots,$$

which is none other than the condition for sector production-allocation efficiency.

We can also explain graphically how the market leads to satisfaction of the condition $\text{MRT}^1_{x,y} = p_x/p_y$. Figure 13.3 shows the production possibility frontiers for two sectors labeled 1 and 2. Each sector produces the two goods x and y. Sector 1 has a production block with frontier $T_A T_A$, and sector 2 has a production block with frontier $T_B T_B$. We draw the origin for sector 2 at point a on the production possibility frontier of sector 1 to allow us to add graphically the output of both sectors.

Profit maximization by firms in sector 1 implies that they maximize the value of sectoral production in terms of prices p_x and p_y. The income corresponding to the budget line passing through the production point gives the value of production. At point a, the marginal rate of transformation $\text{MRT}^1_{x,y}$ is equal to p_x/p_y, and the budget line is as far out from the origin as possible, indicating that output value has been maximized at that point. Because sector 2 also maximizes profits at the same prices, its production takes place on $T_B T_B$ at tangency point b, where the marginal rate of transformation also equals p_x/p_y. Thus profit maximization implies that both sectors have the same marginal rate of transformation, satisfying the sector production-allocation efficiency condition.

Sector production-allocation efficiency implies that the two sectors, by individually maximizing the value of their output, jointly maximize the value of their combined output. In the figure, we placed the origin of the production block for sector 2 at point a. The combined output of both sectors therefore passes through point b on the curve labeled $T_{A+B} T_{A+B}$. Frontier $T_{A+B} T_{A+B}$

---

11. Since factor supply is fixed for the sector to when checking for sector production-allocation efficiency, $\Delta K_x + \Delta K_y = 0$ and similarly for other factors. Simple substitution and canceling produce the expression in the text:

$$-\frac{MP^y_L \Delta L_y + MP^y_K \Delta K_y}{MP^x_L \Delta L_x + MP^x_K \Delta K_x} = \frac{-(w \Delta L_y/p_y + r\Delta K_y/p_y)}{w \Delta L_x/p_x + r\Delta K_x/p_x} = \frac{p_x(w \Delta L_x + r\Delta K_x)}{p_y(w \Delta L_x + r\Delta K_x)} = \frac{p_x}{p_y}.$$

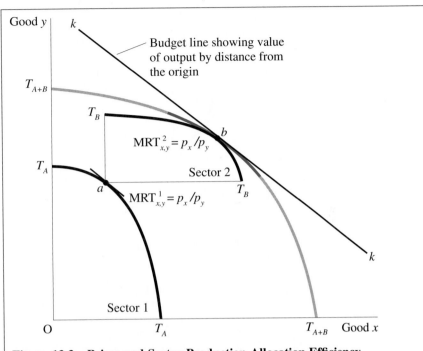

Figure 13.3   Prices and Sector Production-Allocation Efficiency

Sector 1 has production possibility frontier $T_A T_A$, and sector 2 has production possibility frontier $T_B T_B$ (whose origin has been placed at point a). Profit maximization by firms in sector 1 leads to production at point a, where the marginal rate of transformation of good x for good y equals the price ratio p_x/p_y. Profit maximization in sector 2 leads to production at point b, where the marginal rate of transformation also equals p_x/p_y. This satisfies the condition for sector production-allocation efficiency. Moreover, the marginal rate of transformation for the combined sectors also equals the price ratio, as shown by the production possibility frontier for the combined sectors $T_{A+B} T_{A+B}$ passing through point b.

is also tangent to the price line at point b and therefore has a marginal rate of transformation equal to p_x/p_y.

Distributive Efficiency

The condition for distributive efficiency implies that households have equal marginal rates of substitution for any two goods x and y,

$$\text{MRS}^{\text{I}}_{x,y} = \text{MRS}^{\text{II}}_{x,y} = \text{MRS}^{\text{III}}_{x,y} = \cdots.$$

In the absence of market exchange, each household would have a different marginal rate of substitution. In a market economy, though, the household maximizes its utility with respect to its budget constraint, which leads to a

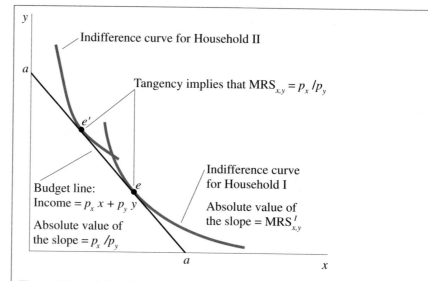

Figure 13.4   Prices Equalize Households' Marginal Rates of Substitution   Because households maximize utility subject to their budget constraints, they choose consumption at point of tangency e or e'. Even though the different households have different preferences and different indifference curves, their budget lines have a common slope determined by market prices. Buying at market prices, therefore, forces the marginal rates of substitution of different households to equal the common slope of their budget lines, satisfying the condition for distributive efficiency.

tangency between the budget line and the household's indifference curve, as we saw in Chapter 3. Tangency implies that $\mathrm{MRS}^{\mathrm{I}}_{x,y} = p_x/p_y$. However, other households in the economy face the same set of prices. Their market purchases also lead to a tangency so that

$$\mathrm{MRS}^{\mathrm{I}}_{x,y} = \frac{p_x}{p_y} = MRS^{\mathrm{II}}_{x,y} = \cdots,$$

and the condition for distributive efficiency is satisfied.

In a market economy, consumers have the same marginal rates of substitution, not because their preferences are the same but because they have traded to a final position where their marginal rate of substitution equals the price ratio. For example, Figure 13.4 shows two households with the same income but different preferences. Household I chooses point e on the budget line, whereas Household II, with different preferences, chooses point e'. In equilibrium both households' marginal rates of substitution equal the common slope of the budget line. Were household incomes different, each household would have a separate budget line. However, each budget line would have the same slope, so the households' marginal rates of substitution would still be equal.

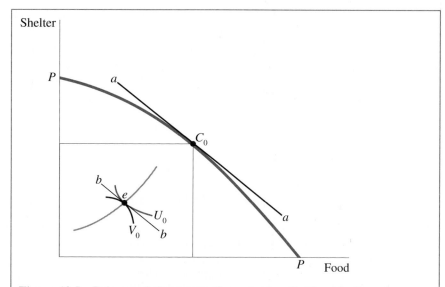

Figure 13.5 Prices and Consumer Sovereignty Total production of food and shelter in a two-person economy is given by bundle C_0 on the production possibility frontier. Profit maximization by competitive firms implies that $\text{MRT}_{\text{Food,Shelter}}$ equals $p_{\text{Food}}/p_{\text{Shelter}}$. Point e distributes food and shelter between the two households by allocating goods in the Edgeworth box with its lower left corner at the origin and upper right corner at point C_0. Consumer sovereignty is satisfied because aa and bb have the same slope, $-p_{\text{Food}}/p_{\text{Shelter}}$, and therefore the slope of the indifference curves at e (MRS) and the production possibility frontier at C_0 (MRT) are the same.

Consumer Sovereignty

As we just saw in the discussion of sector production-allocation efficiency, market equilibrium with perfectly competitive firms implies that firms' profit maximization decisions cause the marginal rate of transformation to equal the price ratio, $\text{MRT}_{x,y} = p_x/p_y$. Likewise, our discussion of distributive efficiency showed that households' marginal rates of substitution equal the price ratio, $\text{MRS}_{x,y} = p_x/p_y$. Since firms and households face the same prices,

$$\text{MRT}_{x,y} = \frac{p_x}{p_y} = MRS_{x,y}.$$

This is the condition for consumer sovereignty. Since the marginal rate of substitution is equalized across households, the equality holds for all households.

Figure 13.5 shows the economy's production possibility frontier PP for the two goods food and shelter. The price ratio, $p_{\text{Food}}/p_{\text{Shelter}}$, equals the absolute value of the slope of line aa tangent to the frontier at production point C_0 as well as the absolute value of the slope of the budget line bb

passing through point *e*. The division of goods between consumers is given by point *e* in the Edgeworth box, whose horizontal dimension equals total consumption of food and whose vertical dimension equals total consumption of shelter. Maximization of utility subject to the consumers' budget constraints implies that $\text{MRS}_{\text{Food,Shelter}}$ equals $p_{\text{Food}}/p_{\text{Shelter}}$. Thus consumer sovereignty is satisfied,

$$\text{MRT}_{\text{Food,Shelter}} = \frac{p_{\text{Food}}}{p_{\text{Shelter}}} = \text{MRS}_{\text{Food,Shelter}},$$

as shown by the fact that lines *bb* and *aa* have the same slope.

Summary of Market Achievement of Pareto Optimality

Table 13.1 summarizes how market prices achieve the necessary conditions for Pareto optimality. The first column lists the condition, the second characterizes it, and the third details how the market satisfies the condition. Three basic assumptions underlie the market's attainment of Pareto optimality: (1) households maximize utility subject to their budget constraints, setting household marginal rates of substitution equal to the price ratio; (2) firms cost minimize by purchasing inputs at market prices, setting marginal rates of technical substitution equal to the input price ratio; and (3) firms profit maximize, setting the marginal rate of transformations equal to the price ratio. In addition, our figures have assumed that profit maximization by firms leads to maximum output value at market prices. This places the budget lines as far as possible from the origin, given the production possibility curve.

APPLICATION: Incentive and Coordination Failure in Central Planning

As noted at the outset, the purpose of this chapter is to develop an understanding of how markets and prices can work to lead the economy to function efficiently. To appreciate how something works, sometimes it helps to examine circumstances in which it didn't work. In this respect, the experience of central planning in communist countries during the past two generations offers abundant material. We will look at an example involving failure of incentives and coordination—two of the four basic functions that are performed by prices in a market economy.

In November 1991, only months before having to leave power as leader of what was then the Soviet Union, Mikhail Gorbachev commented in the world press that by the early 1980s "the command system of management had shown that it had totally exhausted its potential, and the people did not gain the appropriate benefits from the enormous resources that were expended." He went on to say that "the total grip of state property destroyed the natural motivation, the natural incentives, to work. . . . It also generated

Table 13.1	Market Satisfaction of the Necessary Conditions for Pareto Optimality	
Condition	*Characteristics*	*How the Market Satisfies the Condition*
Full employment	Demand for inputs equals supply.	Market clearing in factor markets sets demand equal to supply.
Input efficiency	Marginal rates of technical substitution are equal across firms.	Cost minimization by firms buying inputs at common market prices sets $MRTS_{L,K} = w/r$ for all firms.
Sector production-allocation efficiency	Marginal rates of transformation are equal across sectors.	Profit maximization by firms causes sectoral marginal rates of transformation to equal the market price ratio, $MRT_{x,y}^{Sector} = p_x/p_y$, for all sectors.
Distributive efficiency	Marginal rates of substitution are equal across consumers.	Utility maximization subject to the household budget constraint at market prices sets $MRS_{x,y} = p_x/p_y$ for all consumers.
Consumer sovereignty	Marginal rate of transformation equals consumers' marginal rates of substitution.	Profit maximization by firms causes the marginal rate of transformation to equal the market price ratio, and utility maximization by consumers causes the marginal rate of substitution to equal the market price ratio, so that $MRT_{x,y} = p_x/p_y = MRS_{x,y}$.

the mentality of equalization, lack of initiative, and it gave birth to a certain kind of worker who is not interested in much of anything."[12] Gorbachev's sad assessment publicly confirmed what Western observers of the communist system of central planning had known for decades. The following story, an example of what Gorbachev meant, is only one of many that could be described.[13]

Lonnie Berger, an American student of agricultural economics, traveled to Cluj, Napoca, Rumania in 1980–82 to study at the Babes Boli Rumanian University. There he noticed that the milk sold in state-run stores was rationed and that long lines would form as early as 4:00 A.M. in advance of the opening of the store at 8:00 A.M. The system was apparently designed to be fair to everyone, with milk rationed to mothers and others with special needs; but there were obviously too many coupons issued for everyone to get milk, even if all were willing and able to pay the price and had ration tickets.

The milk came from a dairy some 30 miles out of town. There Lonnie observed that although each barn had 200 cows, only 60 were lactating. A herd of that size normally would have 180 or so of its cows lactating at any one time. The dairy seemed unmotivated to change this situation, however,

12. Interview with Mikhail Gorbachev, *U.S. News and World Report,* December 2, 1991, reported in Champaign-Urbana News-Gazette, 24 Nov. 1991, p. A1.
13. Related by L. Berger, December 1991; used by permission.

even with the great demand for more milk only 30 miles away. Rumanian state regulations, apparently designed for proper dairy management, required that cows be let out of the barns at least 2 hours per week. Since it was easier to leave cows in the barn and there was no gain to the dairy to do otherwise, the dairy followed regulations at the minimal level. Little time out of the barn and little access to bulls meant few cows became pregnant, and thus few were giving milk at any one time.

How does Mikhail Gorbachev's statement apply to the Rumanian dairy? Although the Rumanian system claimed that it wanted to provide milk to those who needed it most, and although it set rules to ensure that dairies followed certain standards in their operation, state operation (which kept the dairy running regardless of any measure of profitability) eliminated the incentives for dairy suppliers to provide more milk, even though they were capable of it. The natural coordination between demanders of milk in the city and suppliers of milk in the country was broken, causing a failure of consumer sovereignty: milk that had high value to consumers (MRS) was not being provided, even though its cost of provision (MRT) was low. On the distribution side, the Rumanian system also failed to distribute what milk it had in the manner it claimed, leading to a failure of distributive efficiency. Instead, those who were able to stand in line the longest got milk and others didn't. ■

13.4 Competition and Price Failures in Market Economies

The First and Second Fundamental Theorems of Welfare Economics seem to provide a fairly optimistic assessment of the market system in contrast to other systems. However, we must note that these theorems describe a world in which (1) markets exist, (2) perfect competition prevails, and (3) information is perfect. They therefore represent an idealized benchmark to which actual market economies can be compared. Failure of any of the conditions of the theorems leads to failure of the economy to achieve Pareto optimality. Although the many ways in which an economy can fail to achieve Pareto optimality are too numerous to present, we can select a few examples to show how deviation from a perfectly competitive economy leads to loss of efficiency and violation of one or more necessary conditions for Pareto optimality.

Monopoly and Imperfectly Competitive Markets

One of the most important requirements of the fundamental theorems is that there be perfect competition. Competition "polices" the marketplace, in essence keeping firms in line and seeing that they maximize profits in the interest of the consumer rather than at the consumer's expense. Imperfectly competitive markets, such as oligopolies or monopolies, violate the requirements of perfect competition by allowing firms to charge prices that are above

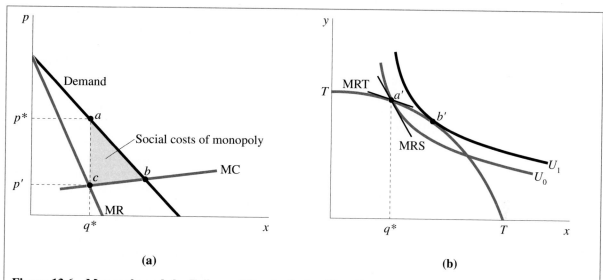

(a)   **(b)**

Figure 13.6   Monopoly and the Failure of Pareto Optimality   Part (a) shows the social costs of monopoly provision of good x as the shaded triangle. Part (b) shows the same social costs of monopoly as the drop in utility from indifference curve U_1 to U_0. Because the monopolist sets price above marginal cost, the value to society of additional units of good x are greater than the cost of providing them, so $MRS_{x,y} > MRT_{x,y}$. This violates consumer sovereignty. Points a and b in part (a) correspond to points a' and b' in part (b). At a' $MRS_{x,y} > MRT_{x,y}$, consumer sovereignty is violated, and utility is lower than it could be if production took place on the production possibility frontier TT at point b'.

▼
8. Which necessary condition for Pareto optimality does monopoly violate, and why?

marginal cost. We will examine how this violates the conditions for Pareto optimality in the case of monopoly, although essentially the same argument applies to other imperfectly competitive markets.

From Chapter 8 we know that monopoly leads to social costs equal in dollar magnitude to the area of the shaded triangle in part (a) of Figure 13.6. The monopolist limits output in order to raise price to p^*, thereby causing price to exceed marginal cost at point a. Were the monopolist to act like a perfect competitor, it would produce where price equaled marginal cost at point b.

The social costs of monopoly imply that the economy is not achieving a Pareto optimum, violating one or more necessary conditions for Pareto optimality. But how do we identify which one?

If a condition does not come to mind immediately, one way to tell which condition (or conditions) is violated is to go down the list of conditions one at a time to see which ones are satisfied. Distributive efficiency, for example, is not violated by the existence of monopoly, because consumers buy and sell at common market price and can freely trade existing goods, whether or not they were produced in the wrong quantities by monopolists.

A similar argument applies to productive efficiency: producers can freely buy and sell factor inputs at common market prices whether one firm is a monopolist or not. Monopoly in the output market does not affect the ability of firms to choose factor inputs at common marginal rates of technical substitution in the input market.

Sector production-allocation efficiency is also not violated, because the monopoly good is produced in only one sector. Sector production-allocation efficiency requires comparing the marginal rates of transformation between two different sectors; if only one sector exists, the condition is irrelevant.

Full employment is not violated by the existence of monopoly because monopoly has to do with too little output rather than with hiring conditions for factors. Market demand for factors by a monopolist may be smaller than it would be if the monopolist produced more output, but this does not prevent the factor markets from clearing, given the different demand curves.

That leaves consumer sovereignty. Since the economy's marginal rate of transformation between two goods equals the ratio of marginal costs for firms,

$$\text{MRT}_{x,y} = \frac{\text{MC}_x}{\text{MC}_y},$$

the price ratio p_x/p_y is greater than $\text{MRT}_{x,y}$ if industry x is a monopoly. This follows from the fact that $p_y = \text{MC}_y$, but $p_x > \text{MC}_x$ in the monopolistic x industry. Since households buy and sell at prices p_x/p_y, we have

$$\text{MRS}_{x,y} = \frac{p_x}{p_y} > MRT_{x,y},$$

violating consumer sovereignty.

Look again at Figure 13.6, which shows the graphical implication of the monopolist's violation of consumer sovereignty. Part (a) should look familiar from our earlier study of the monopoly problem (see Figure 8.7): the demand curve and marginal revenue curve are the downward-sloping straight lines with identical vertical intercept. Point a on the demand curve shows the monopolist's price-quantity choice. At quantity q^*, corresponding to point a, marginal cost equals marginal revenue. In contrast, a perfect competitor would produce at point b. Because the monopolist limits production to q^*, the monopoly results in social costs equal to the area of the shaded triangle.

Part (b) of the figure shows the economy's production possibility frontier, TT. The horizontal axis shows the quantity of good x, and the vertical axis shows production of other goods, y. Production at points a and b in part (a) corresponds to production on the production possibility frontier at points a' and b', respectively. When the monopolist produces at a' rather than at b' by limiting production to q^*, household utility drops from U_1 to U_0.[14] Part (b) also shows that the marginal rate of substitution at point a', given by the

---

14. For simplicity, assume that this economy has just one consumer. The same principles apply with many households.

slope of indifference curve U_0, is different from the marginal rate of transformation, given by the slope of the production possibility frontier.

Efficiency Cost of Taxes in a Competitive Market

The efficiency loss from taxes in a competitive market can be evaluated in a manner similar to the analysis for monopoly. We know that a tax causes the price paid by buyers to exceed the price received by sellers, so that $p_{buyer} >$ $p_{seller} = $ MC in competitive markets. As we saw above, $p > $ MC leads to violation of the consumer sovereignty condition. The efficiency cost of such a tax is the loss in consumer and producer surplus that exceeds the amount of money collected by the tax. This loss, called the *tax deadweight loss,* reflects the net loss in utility from failure of the economy to reach Pareto optimality.

For example, assume that the firm in part (a) of Figure 13.6 is perfectly competitive, so that the marginal cost curve is the supply curve for good x. Imposing a tax on x equal to the difference between p^* and p' causes the buyer price-quantity point to move to a and the seller price-quantity point to move to c. The shaded area is the amount by which lost consumer and producer surplus exceeds the amount of tax revenues collected. Since the economy produces too little of the taxed good at a, utility drops from U_1 to U_0 in part (b). Thus, taxing a competitive market leads to losses similar in principle to those from monopoly.

Import Duties

▼

9. Which necessary condition for Pareto optimality does an import duty violate for a country that faces fixed world prices?

We can also consider the effect of import duties. An import duty is a tax paid by importers for the right to import a good.[15] Because of the duty, the importing country pays a higher price than the world price for that good. Because prices inside the country differ from prices outside the country, the domestic marginal rate of transformation differs from the marginal rate of transformation in foreign trade, the rate at which one good can be converted to another through foreign trade. Since we assume that the country faces fixed world prices, the marginal rate of transformation in foreign trade and the world price ratio are the same. Unequal marginal rates of transformation in the domestic sector and the foreign trade sector therefore imply failure of sector production-allocation efficiency.

How does this failure affect utility? The absolute value of the slope of budget line $b'b'$ in Figure 13.7 shows the world price ratio. At these prices, profit maximization by firms maximizes the value of output at point e'. The country consumes at point f' on its budget line. If a duty is imposed on imports of good y, however, the domestic price is higher than the world price of good y. The absolute value of the slope of line cc shows the postduty domestic price ratio. Profit maximization at domestic prices therefore implies

---

15. Since an import duty generally raises the prices buyers pay, part or all of the tax is usually passed on to the importers' customers.

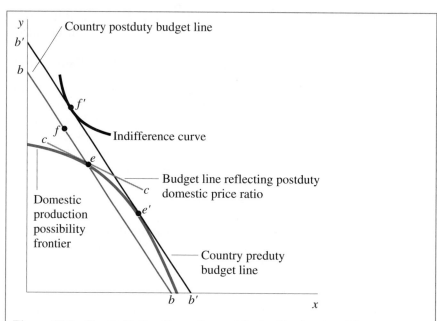

Figure 13.7 **Trade Duties Cause Loss of Sector Production-Allocation Efficiency in an Open Economy** When there is no import duty on good y, domestic prices and world prices are the same. Production takes place at point e', where the value of output is as large as possible, and consumption takes place at point f' on the country's budget line $b'b'$. With an import duty on good y, however, the domestic price rises above the world price. Domestic production shifts to point e, where the flatter slope of the new budget line cc implies a relatively higher price for good y. Since the domestic marginal rate of transformation at point e differs from the marginal rate of transformation in foreign trade (still given by the slope of budget line $b'b'$), sector production-allocation efficiency is violated. Given production at e, the country consumes at point f on its new budget line bb, which gives lower utility than f'.

production at point e and country consumption at point f on the postduty budget line bb. If there were no duty imposed, utility would be higher than at f.

Differential Factor Costs

▼

10. Under what circumstances might input efficiency be violated, and why?

Congress has mandated that businesses larger than a certain size must provide their employees with health and retirement benefits that are not mandated for smaller businesses. For our purposes it is not important what these mandated costs are, but only that they differ across business types. How do these differential costs affect input efficiency?

Assuming that a small business and a large business hire labor from a common pool, the immediate effect of the government mandates is that larger businesses will have to pay a higher cost for the same labor. Larger businesses will therefore have a greater incentive to economize on the use of labor than will smaller businesses. Let w^y be the effective wage that large businesses must pay for labor of a given type, and let w^x be the wage that smaller businesses pay, where $w^y > w^x$.

Both large and small business also employ capital at cost r. Cost minimization therefore implies that

$$\text{MRTS}_{L,K}^y = \frac{w^y}{r} > \frac{w^x}{r} = MRTS_{L,K}^x.$$

Since larger and smaller businesses have different marginal rates of transformation, the different prices for labor violate input efficiency.

Missing Markets

Finally, for a market to operate at all there must be a well-defined good or service and a group of buyers and sellers able to trade in that good or service. Markets can fail to exist for a number of reasons, including information asymmetries, high costs of trading (transaction costs), or absence of appropriate legal rules about ownership. For example, there is generally not a market in breathable air. We all take what we need from the atmosphere without making a monthly payment. This sometimes leads to problems, as when a smoker and nonsmoker want to use the same airspace. Missing markets can lead to violation of any of the conditions for Pareto optimality because markets equalize marginal rates of substitution across consumers, equalize marginal rates of technical substitution across producers, and equate marginal rates of transformation with marginal rates of substitution.

To give one small example, consider the market in used household items such as clothing, furniture, kitchenware, children's toys—the types of things often found in garage sales. Because of the small benefits relative to costs for an individual trying to organize a citywide market in these items, the price at which a given item sells may differ from garage to garage. This means that marginal rates of substitution are not equalized across buyers, and therefore distributive efficiency is not satisfied. In principle, therefore, we know that there is a way to redistribute these items to make at least one person better off without harming another. The possibility of gains in such situations has not gone entirely unnoticed, however. It is interesting that many individuals make a hobby of visiting garage sales to buy items whose prices they think are low in order to resell those items in their own sales later. The activity of such spontaneous "middlemen" has an equalizing effect on prices, tending to make the markets more efficient. Greater efficiency can also be achieved when a neighborhood association arranges to have a garage sale for the entire neighborhood at a certain time each year. We will discuss the effects of missing markets in more detail in Chapter 14 when we look at the economics of externalities.

13.5 The Role of Government in a Market System

The message of the past few sections is that, if there is perfect competition, market equilibrium will achieve a Pareto optimum. The right market conditions must be present; but if they are, it follows that actions by government cannot possibly help matters. In such cases, government cannot find a Pareto superior outcome, but it could *worsen* the situation by producing a Pareto inferior outcome.

Then what role is left for government other than insuring perfect competition? This section recapitulates some of what we have said in order to suggest several answers to this question and broaden our understanding of the relationship between the marketplace and other social structures. The discussion in this chapter also leads in to the treatment of externalities and public goods in Chapter 14.

Law and Order and Contract Enforcement

▼

11. What legitimate functions can government serve in a market economy? Explain why they are compatible with the First and Second Fundamental Theorems of Welfare Economics.

Most of us take for granted that when we buy a carton of skim milk, the contents of the carton are milk. There were periods in our nation's history, however, when buying milk in some places meant buying a disease-laden product that might even have been adulterated with chalk! The fact that you would never take part in an evil scheme to make money selling adulterated milk does not mean that someone else somewhere in the economy would not.

Thus far in our study of microeconomics, we have pretty much ignored issues of legality, law and order, and contract enforcement because we take these to be foundational for the operation of a successful market system. Some markets, such as the diamond-cutting business,[16] for example, are able to operate with thousands and even millions of dollars changing hands on the basis of a handshake. On the rare occasions when a diamond merchant tries to cheat or steal, the closely knit association of diamond dealers worldwide is able to exclude the offending merchant from further business in diamonds. The unwritten code of honest and decent conduct is thereby enforced in New York, Antwerp, Hong Kong, and other diamond centers around the world.

Such internal enforcement mechanisms, however, are not feasible in general. The Depression-era American gangster Al Capone is reported to have said, "You can make more friends with a gun and a smile than you can with just a smile." (Though the remark may be true, it makes us wonder what kind of friends Mr. Capone had!) In commerce the message is the same: it might seem easier to take what you want, force others to trade at your terms, or cheat them by subterfuge and falsehood than to earn your profits honestly. This, however, is the law of the jungle and leads to the rule of pirates and brigands. If one person's property is not safe, then no person's property is

16. Diamond cutting is distinguished from the raw diamond market, which is dominated by the DeBeers near-monopoly.

safe, and commerce grinds to a halt. It follows that a government is needed to maintain ground rules so that commerce can flourish.

The need for government to serve everyone's needs by establishing rules of law and conduct does not contradict the First and Second Fundamental Theorems of Welfare Economics because neither theorem addresses the need for ethical and moral behavior to undergird the functioning of markets. Being outside the scope of the theorems, and in some sense prior to them, the law-and-order function of government *complements* the First and Second Fundamental Theorems by giving to government the task of establishing an environment in which morality can be taught in the private sector and buying, selling, and competition can take place.

Market Failure and Government Actions to Bolster the Economy

Property rights relate to the ability of markets to exist. As we have already noted, missing markets can lead to a breakdown of the necessary conditions for Pareto optimality. By establishing appropriate legal structures to protect property rights, government can help establish markets.

A second role of government not inconsistent with the First and Second Fundamental Theorems has to do with the failure of the market (when it does exist) to be perfectly competitive. As we saw in Chapter 7, no market is likely to meet all of the conditions of perfect competition. By acting to foster greater competition, the government can support the operation of the First Fundamental Theorem of Welfare Economics.

Monopoly, Cartels, and Competition Enforcement. Competition is the regulating element of the marketplace. Competition guides the actions of firms to keep them operating for the social good instead of against it. Because a perfectly competitive firm is unable to control market price, for example, profit maximization causes the firm to set marginal cost equal to price. The consumer, therefore, pays for the product exactly what it costs to produce an additional unit and no more.[17]

Oligopolistic or monopolistic firms, on the other hand, face imperfect or no competition. As we saw in Chapters 8, 9, and 10, their market choices enhance profits partly at the expense of the consumer, because they set price above marginal cost. In that case, the First and Second Fundamental Theorems of Welfare Economics do not really apply because the theorems require perfect competition.[18]

Where imperfect competition prevails, the government can help ensure Pareto optimality by encouraging competition. The Sherman and Clayton

17. Recall from Chapter 7 that economic profits include a normal rate of return to productive activity, so that costs in this case also include the normal return to the firm.
18. We must recognize that there are cases in which monopoly serves a useful social purpose, as when it is granted as the reward for development of new products. Monopoly profits, allowed for a short time under the protection of patent law, encourage innovation. Research and development are discussed in more detail in Chapter 16.

Antitrust Acts, for example, give the government authority to prohibit practices that act in restraint of competition. The breakup of the Standard Oil Company and the similar action against AT&T are examples of the exercise of this authority. Regulating monopoly and cartel behavior in favor of competition is therefore a justified exercise of government authority that does not contradict the First and Second Fundamental Theorems. When the government can correct some but not all of the imperfections in the market, however, care must be taken that the actions of government do not worsen welfare in the attempt to improve it.

Information. In some cases, incomplete or imperfect information can lead to market failure. In this text we have discussed information asymmetries involving price and quality, for example. If a law or regulation can address the problem, the government can rectify information asymmetries to restore competition. One example might be a truth-in-labeling law; another might be the establishment of rules about making financial information public. In other cases, in which government may not be able to restore perfect competition fully, it can still try to move the operation of the market in the right direction by regulation, the setting of standards, or taxation.

Externalities and Public Goods. A third area in which the government can move the economy in the right direction involves the provision of public goods and the treatment of externalities. An externality is anything, whether harmful or beneficial, that affects profits or utility and that does not operate through markets. Public goods can be considered a special case of externalities. For example, when the government provides for a public good such as national defense, there is an externality: the utility of every household rises because household security is enhanced, but the degree of enhancement is independent of the household's market decisions. We will also see in Chapter 14 that externalities and public goods can lead to a failure of the economy to achieve Pareto optimality.

Since the First and Second Fundamental Theorems of Welfare Economics describe an economy of *private* goods, there is a role for the government to provide *public* goods supported by coercive taxes. The private markets would not be able to deliver such goods.

The Theory of the Second Best

In principle, as we have just demonstrated, we can identify ways for government to improve the operation of the economy in accord with the First and Second Fundamental Theorems of Welfare Economics. Because of the complexity of the economy, however, policymakers often must implement their policies on a piecemeal basis, and they are incapable of estimating the full effects on the general economic equilibrium. In response to this situation, many economists urge a view of intervention that highlights the potential for harmful government actions as well as helpful ones. For example, if certain imperfections cannot be eliminated, should government nevertheless try to enforce as many of the remaining necessary conditions for Pareto optimality as possible? Unfortunately, the answer is no.

The *theory of the second best* examines conditions for an economy to do as well as it can, given the presence of certain imperfections that cannot be removed. According to this theory, if one or more imperfections must be present, the economy should satisfy a different set of conditions than those required for unencumbered Pareto optimality. Even marginal cost pricing might not be the right objective any longer.[19] In other words, well-meaning but unenlightened intervention by the government could made matters worse. The theory of the second best is not entirely encouraging on this point. In general, there is no simple way to say what different set of conditions the economy should seek to fulfill when some of the conditions for Pareto optimality cannot be fulfilled.

Equity

Last of all, we note that there may be a role for government to try to decide which Pareto optimum the economy should achieve. This role is controversial compared to the roles already described because it is openly redistributive in nature. As we saw in Chapter 12, Pareto optimality does not make judgments about the equity of social outcomes. Decisions about distribution in a market system are made by the impersonal operations of the market. A market system rewards those who produce more with greater income. What is considered productive work is determined by the price that the work can command in the market. If the economy rewards a rock guitarist with 100 times the income of a concert violinist, we must presume that an additional rock concert is contributing more to society from an *economic* point of view than an additional violin concerto.

Nevertheless, many people think that equity justifies taking wealth or income from those who have acquired wealth or who earn high incomes and giving it to those who earn less. To the extent that this is true, and if taxes can be collected without causing inefficiency, redistribution would not technically contradict the First and Second Fundamental Theorems of Welfare Economics because those theorems do not deal with equity. However, taxes generally *do* lead to efficiency loss by imposing social costs that exceed the revenues collected by government. These losses, estimated to be on the order of $.17 to $.56 of extra social cost per marginal tax dollar collected, must be taken into account in evaluating the overall merits of any redistributive scheme.[20] ■

---

19. See William J. Baumol and David F. Bradford, ''Optimal Departures from Marginal Cost Pricing,'' *American Economic Review,* 60 (1970), pp. 265–283, for a classic treatment from the perspective of the theory of the second best.

20. See Charles L. Ballard, John B. Shoven, and John Whalley, ''General Equilibrium Computations of the Marginal Welfare Costs of Taxes in the United States,'' *American Economic Review,* 75 (1985), pp. 128–138; and E. K. Browning, ''On the Marginal Welfare Cost of Taxation,'' *American Economic Review,* 77 (1987), pp. 11–23. Ballard, Shoven, and Whalley estimate the cost to be in the range of 17 to 56 cents per dollar of extra revenue for the United States, whereas Browning's preferred estimate is between 31.8 and 46.9 cents per dollar.

Summary

Active Reading Guide numbers are given in parentheses at the end of each summary item.

1. A market economy decides what to produce by allowing firms to choose their production levels to maximize profits; it decides how to distribute goods and services by allowing households the choice of what to buy to maximize their utility. The household's income, in turn, is determined by its earnings from its supply of goods and services to the market, including work that the household does. (1)

2. In a market economy, prices perform four basic roles: coordinating producers' and consumers' plans; moving the market toward equilibrium; providing information about the cost and value to society of an additional unit of a good; and providing incentives for firms and households in their decision making. (2)

3. The question of optimality for a market economy is whether firms and households, acting independently to choose their production and consumption in their own self-interest, will be led by the marketplace to choose actions that lead to a Pareto optimum. Adam Smith's doctrine of the invisible hand was the earliest statement that this would be the case. (3)

4. A production plan is a listing of inputs and outputs for each firm. An allocation is a listing of all goods and services consumed and factor services supplied by households. Property rights determine who will get the income from supply of factor services and who will receive a flow of income from firms based on such claims as stocks and bonds. A competitive equilibrium occurs when (a) firms and households act as nonstrategic pricetakers; (b) firms choose their production plans to maximize profits, given prices; (c) households choose their consumption to maximize utility, subject to their budget constraints; and (d) production and consumption are consistent in that demand equals supply in all markets. (4, 5)

5. The First Fundamental Theorem of Welfare Economics states that a competitive equilibrium achieves a Pareto optimum. In the reverse direction, the Second Fundamental Theorem of Welfare Economics states that any Pareto optimum can be achieved as a competitive equilibrium with appropriate assignment of ownership rights. (6)

6. Market prices are the key to a competitive equilibrium's achieving each of the necessary conditions for Pareto optimality:
   a) Full employment is satisfied by the requirement of market clearing in each market.
   b) Cost minimization by firms implies that each firm's marginal rate of technical substitution between factor inputs is equal to the factor price ratio, which implies that firms' marginal rates of technical substitution are equal to one another. This satisfies the requirements for input efficiency.
   c) Profit maximization by firms implies that the marginal rate of transformation in a sector equals the output price ratio. This implies that the marginal rates of transformation are equal across sectors, since they face the same output prices. This satisfies the requirements for sector production-allocation efficiency.
   d) Utility maximization by households implies that each household's marginal rate of substitution is equal to the price ratio, which implies that household marginal rates of substitution are equal to one another. This satisfies the requirements for distributive efficiency.
   e) Since the household's marginal rate of substitution and the economy's marginal rate of transformation are each equal to the ratio of output prices, they are equal to one another in a competitive equilibrium. This satisfies the requirements of consumer sovereignty. (7)

7. Each failure of the economy to achieve Pareto optimality can be associated with one or more failures of the five necessary conditions for Pareto optimality. Monopoly violates consumer sovereignty, for example, and differential factor costs violate input efficiency. An import duty violates sector production-allocation efficiency by improperly limiting use of the international trade sector. (8, 9, 10)

8. Since a perfectly competitive economy in general equilibrium achieves a Pareto optimum, any intervention in the marketplace moves the economy to a Pareto inferior position or, at best, to another Pareto optimum. Although this seems to imply that there is no room for government in a market economy, we recognize that there are also no guarantees that the economy will meet the conditions for the First and Second Fundamental Theorems of Welfare Economics. Thus government can play a role in a market economy. One role for the government is to provide the necessary law and order, property rights, and contract enforcement for a market system to function. Another role for government is to foster competition where monopolistic or imperfectly competitive markets would otherwise prevail, either by direct enforcement of antitrust measures or by regulations designed to reduce such problems as information asymmetries. A final role for government is to provide public goods, which competitive markets would not do, and to respond to externalities and other such market failures. None of these functions of government are incompatible with the First and Second Fundamental Theorems. (11)

Review Questions

*1. How does a market economy solve the two main problems of any economy, determining *what* to produce and *for whom* to produce it? How does a hunter-gatherer society of isolated families solve these two problems?

2. What is the basic idea behind Adam Smith's invisible hand doctrine? Relate this to the assertion that if firms take prices as given and maximize profits, they will maximize the value of the economy's output.

*3. How does a competitive equilibrium coordinate household and firm choices?

4. Comment on the following statement: "The First and Second Fundamental Theorems of Welfare Economics say not only that competitive equilibria and Pareto optimal outcomes are related, but that they are the same thing."

*5. What is the effect on distributive efficiency if citizens under the age of 65 are made to pay higher prices for public transportation than are senior citizens?

6. What role does profit maximization play in assuring consumer sovereignty in a competitive equilibrium?

*7. What role does cost minimization play in assuring productive efficiency in a competitive equilibrium?

8. Mikhail Gorbachev said that the people did not gain the appropriate benefits from the enormous resources that were expended in the Soviet economy. Failure of which of the necessary conditions for Pareto optimality do you think would lead to this state of affairs?

Numerical and Graphing Exercises

*1. In an Edgeworth box, draw an allocation of goods that does not satisfy distributive efficiency and find an allocation that is Pareto superior to it.

*2. A market equilibrium for an economy without production consists of a position in which each household does not want to trade its consumption bundle for any other, given its budget constraint. Using an Edgeworth box for a two-person economy without production, draw a market equilibrium. What determines the income of each household in equilibrium?

3. Using the relationship between the contract curve (see Ch. 12) and Pareto optimal allocations in a two-person economy without production, demonstrate the First and Second Fundamental Theorems of Welfare Economics in an Edgeworth box.

* Asterisks are used to denote questions that are answered at the back of the book.

*4. Assume that FRT stands for the ratio of prices in foreign trade, MRS is the ratio of prices seen by consumers, and MRT is the ratio of prices seen by domestic producers. In general, Pareto optimality requires that FRT = MRS = MRT; when one or more equality is violated, the economy suffers a welfare loss. Using budget lines whose slopes correspond to FRT, MRS, and MRT, draw production possibility frontiers, budget lines, and indifference curves showing the following suboptimal situations: (a) FRT = MRT ≠ MRS; (b) MRT ≠ FRT = MRS; (c) FRT ≠ MRS = MRT. In each case, show how utility would rise if equality of all three were achieved.

CHAPTER 14

Externalities and Public Goods

In this chapter we discuss the economics of externalities and a new type of good called public goods. Public goods and externalities both involve situations in which the use or production of a good by one economic agent directly affects the utility or production of another. We look at how externalities affect the efficient assignment of resources and what to do to correct the problems externalities may create. We then examine public goods in terms of what quantity of them should be provided and how society should pay for them.

ACTIVE READING GUIDES

After reading this chapter, you should be able to answer the Active Reading Guides listed below. These guides also appear in the page margins, near the material to which they refer.

1. What is an externality? Give several examples.

2. How does the absence of property rights, whether because of legal or physical limitations, lead to a missing market and an externality? Give examples.

3. State and explain Coase's First and Second Theorems. Give examples.

4. Apart from direct bargaining, what are three primary ways to correct an externality?

5. What are some informational problems of regulation?

6. How do rivalry and excludability distinguish private from public goods?

7. Use a two-household economy to derive the condition for optimal provision of a public good.

8. How is the economy's demand curve for a public good derived?

9. Explain the need for tax-financed provision of public goods and why it might lead to a Pareto suboptimal level of provision.

10. Why is demand revelation so important for provision of public goods? What basic problem must it overcome?

11. Is voting a solution to the problem of deciding what quantity of public goods to provide? What are the relevant considerations?

14.1 Externalities

What do garbage disposal, Tappan Zee Bridge traffic congestion, nitrous oxide, and water management have in common? Nothing, you say? In economic terms, each is a current example of an externality. The purpose of this chapter is to explain what externalities are and how to deal with them.

The Problem

The major thrust of our study of microeconomics thus far has been the workings and advantages of unfettered markets. One routinely encounters situations, however, in which markets don't seem to produce happy results. For example, the Environmental Protection Agency estimates that America's landfills will be full by 2010.[1] Most Americans are aware of the solid-waste disposal problem and say they are willing to contribute to alleviate it; a poll reveals that 74 percent of respondents would favor even mandatory recycling.[2] Yet products continue to be packaged, bought and sold, and discarded pretty much as always. In Los Angeles, air quality experts estimate the annual health cost of smog at $3.65 billion, but many consumers and firms continue to operate as if it were zero.[3] In the Midwest, an Ohio utility plant emits

1. "Throwing Things Away," *The Economist,* October 5, 1991, pp. 13, 14. Similar reports predict that Japan's landfill space will be exhausted by 2005, and other countries like Holland basically have no space now.

2. John Holusha, "Mixed Benefits from Recycling," *The New York Times,* July 26, 1991, p. D2.

3. Patricia Horn, "Natural Enemies: Private Profits, Public Interests at War over the Environment," *Dollars and Sense,* October 1989, p. 81.

sulfur and nitrous oxides that result in harmful acid rain in the Northeast; yet it, too, continues to operate as if there were no costs to its emissions. With respect to the Atlantic and Pacific fishing banks, major fishing nations recognize that declining fish populations might spell lower sustainable harvests for all, yet find it in their private interests to continue fishing at maximum levels. Why?

In each of these cases, an externality is present; that is, an action taken by one household or firm has a direct effect on another that is not registered in the prices or costs paid by the action-taking firm. Solid-waste producers—manufacturers, you, and I—place burdens on our municipalities' trash disposal, but in most cases bear no extra costs when we create extra trash. Los Angeles air polluters and the Ohio utility do not pay more for their activity when air conditions are worse, though they harm others' air quality. Fishing boats overfish the ocean, reducing the catch for others, yet do not pay a higher price for the damage their activity does to the catches of others. In each case, the critical feature is the presence of an effect not registered in market prices.

▼

1. What is an externality? Give several examples.

*An **externality** is an effect on a firm or household arising from the action of another firm or household and operating directly rather than through market prices.*

Positive externalities create beneficial effects, and *negative externalities* create harmful effects. If a logging company's freshly cut areas provide better browse and habitat for woodland animals that you enjoy, you experience a positive externality. On the other hand, if my company's decision to dispose of toxic wastes in the river affects your ability to swim or fish there, you have suffered a negative externality because of my waste disposal. However, if my company's decision to contract for waste disposal in the regional landfill raises landfill costs and therefore the price you pay for your own waste disposal, you have not suffered an externality because the effect on you has operated through prices.

An anomymous pundit once restated Henry David Thoreau by saying that if a man does not keep pace with his neighbors, it isn't that he marches to the sound of a different drummer, but that he probably doesn't hear any drummer at all! In the same way, a thoughtful review of the externalities mentioned so far reveals that they represent not so much the *failure* of markets as the *absence* of markets and the consequential failure of costs and benefits to be registered to those creating them. In the next section we discuss how the deviation of benefits and costs seen by agents from true benefits and costs leads to inefficiency. After that, we take up the question of why the necessary markets failed to exist.

Externalities and Inefficiency

Part (a) of Figure 14.1 depicts the situation for a firm engaging in a negative-externality-producing activity. This could be the Ohio utility plant emitting air pollution, for example. The horizontal axis shows the quantity of electric-

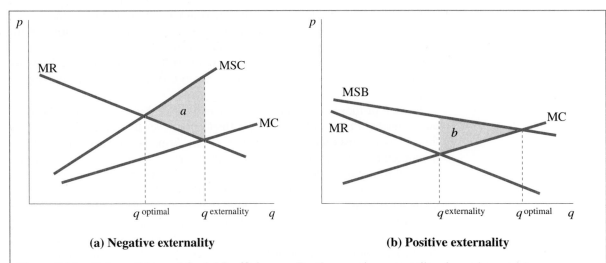

(a) Negative externality   **(b) Positive externality**

Figure 14.1   Externalities and Social Inefficiency   For the negative externality shown in part (a), the firm's marginal cost, MC, is lower than the marginal social cost, MSC, because the firm does not take into account the value of damage imposed on others by the externality. The firm sets MR = MC at $q^{\text{externality}}$ instead of producing at the social optimum q^{optimal}, where MR = MSC. Area *a* is the resulting social inefficiency. For the positive externality in part (b), the marginal benefit seen by the firm is its own marginal revenue, MR. MR is lower than the marginal social benefit, MSB, because the firm does not take into account the value of benefits its activity creates for others by the external- ity. Instead of choosing the social optimum where MSB = MC, the firm produces too little output where MR = MC. The resulting social loss equals area *b*.

ity generated, and the vertical axis measures the marginal revenue and mar- ginal costs. Taking its benefits and costs into account, the firm sets its quantity where MR = MC. However, producing output also imposes an externality cost on others that is not reflected in the firm's MC. For example, effluent from electricity-generating plants is known to increase the amount of nitro- gen- and sulphur-based acids in rain, acids that corrode buildings and cars. More corrosion means higher costs. Adding the marginal costs experienced by others to the firm's MC gives us the higher curve labeled marginal social cost, MSC. *Marginal social cost* reflects the costs imposed on everyone in society because of an increase in the firm's activity. Taking *all* costs into account, the firm should not produce beyond the quantity where MR = MSC, since costs from units produced above this quantity exceed benefits. When the firm produces at $q^{\text{externality}}$ rather than at q^{optimal}, the total social loss from the externality is the shaded area *a*, which equals the excess of costs over benefits for the units above the optimal level.

Social losses also occur from positive externalities (helpful side effects of the firm's activity that have value to others), but there the problem is that too little of the externality-producing activity is undertaken. A pharmaceutical manufacturer that knows its costly basic research on how to develop drugs for tropical diseases would confer great direct benefits on other firms that could benefit from its knowledge has little incentive to engage in such basic research unless it provides sufficient benefits to the firm itself. In part (b) the benefit to the firm is again MR, but this time the marginal social benefit MSB, exceeds MR by the value of the positive externalities associated with the units produced. *Marginal social benefit* reflects the sum of marginal benefits accruing to everyone in society as a result of the firm's activity. The social optimum occurs at the quantity where MSB = MC, but the firm sets its quantity where MR = MC since it does not get the value of the positive externalities. The social loss is equal to area *b*, reflecting the excess of marginal social benefit over marginal cost that could have been attained with higher output.

14.2 Property Rights and Externalities

The key feature of each inefficiency described in Figure 14.1 is that the value of the externality did not enter into the firm's computation so that it could make the socially correct decision about how much to produce. In the history of economics, as the study of externalities progressed, those thinking about the problem began to realize that it was the *absence of a market* that caused the externality, especially the absence of a market price connected with the level of the externality. For example, if a polluting firm had to pay a price for each unit of its pollution, then the cost of the pollution would be taken into account in the firm's computation of how much to produce.

Linking Property Rights to Missing Markets

▼
2. How does the absence of property rights, whether because of legal or physical limitations, lead to a missing market and an externality? Give examples.

Once the problem was diagnosed as a missing market, attention focused on why markets failed to exist. The answer seemed to be inextricably linked to property rights. This insight was found to unify a host of seemingly disparate problems. To see why this is so, we will review a few of the classic examples of externalities along with some modern counterparts. We will then be ready to tackle the fascinating question of how to convert this knowledge into policy prescriptions to correct the problem of externalities.

English Enclosures, Common Property, and Congestion. Between 1700 and 1845, some 6 million acres of English fields were enclosed for ownership and use by individual farmers, an action that removed them from use in the thousand-year-old system of open fields. The enclosure movement later spread to the Continent, and it is generally regarded as one of the milestones in the move to modern and more productive farming.

Prior to enclosure, fields used in common were overgrazed and under-productive. Social losses took the form of inefficient agriculture. No one owned the common land (property rights in the land were absent), so those using it for traditional livestock grazing had no reason to take account of the effect their use had on the productivity of the land for others. This system encouraged overgrazing and other such negative externalities. In contrast, the more productive Norfolk system of agriculture required farmers to rotate their acreage through a four-year cycle of wheat, turnips, barley, and clover or ryegrass. The fodder-crop emphasis allowed more productive feeding of cattle and sheep in yards and eliminated the usual fallow year for land. On open land, however, farmers growing clover, ryegrass, or other legume or root crops would find themselves providing additional feed for their neighbors' animals (a positive externality) without compensation.

The inefficiencies were eliminated by enclosure. Benefits of improvements now accrued to the one undertaking the investment. Owners were vested with property rights, including the right to keep others off the land or to charge for its use. The result was that the effect of land use on productivity was taken into account by the owner, whether the land was managed for self-use or for maximum rental value.[4]

Modern counterparts include the already-mentioned problem of common fishing in the world's oceans. Some nations, including the United States, have taken the step of establishing sovereign "economic exclusive-use zones" within 200 miles of their coastlines. Under this system, other nations wishing to fish must pay for the right, and the sovereign control insures that the resources within the exclusive-use zones will be managed with an eye to overall productivity. The right to exclusive use is a property right.

Traffic congestion on the Hudson River's Tappan Zee Bridge connecting Westchester and Rockland counties, New York, is another example of the same phenomenon. Traffic has increased from 10.5 million vehicles in 1960, five years after the bridge was built, to 40 million vehicles per year today. The bridge has become so crowded that commuters complain it can take as long as 68 minutes to cross.[5] How does this relate to property rights? The answer is that if all commuters whose travel time on the bridge would be slowed by the addition of another car had the right (a form of property right) to charge the added car for the increased time costs, there would be no externality. If the additional congestion cost to cars using the bridge were $10, say, from the addition of another car, then the new car would enter only if its benefit from crossing exceeded $10. Of course, enforcing such a property right would be difficult, if not impossible, so we will talk later about using tolls to deal with this type of congestion problem. The important insight here is that congestion is an externality that can be explained in terms of property rights.

Trains, Sparks, and Pollution. The importance of knowing *which* rights property owners can enforce by law was emphasized in Nobel Prize–winning

4. To be sure, not everyone was pleased with the conversion of common land to private use. Many viewed it as stealing, and the conversions were often accompanied by force.
5. Lisa Foderaro, "Tappan Zee Traffic Enrages Commuters, Worries Planners," *New York Times,* November 15, 1991, p. B5.

economist Ronald Coase's seminal analysis of externalities.[6] Among his examples was the problem caused by the sparks emitted by coal- and wood-powered steam engines.

At issue was the problem that fires sometimes caused by the sparks damaged nearby property. In the absence of rules governing compensation for fire damage—another form of property right—a negative externality was present, since railroad companies would have little incentive to prevent sparks and an unnecessarily large number of fires could be expected. On the other hand, requiring trains to pay full compensation would leave property owners with little or no incentive to protect themselves, and too few defensive measures would be taken. Is it better for trains to take defensive measures or for farmers to take defensive measures? Which is done depends on whether farmers can sue for damages (what their property rights are). We will return to this issue later, but for now we should note once again the central role played by property rights.

A modern counterpart is the question of liability rules for pollution. In the case of waste disposal, for example, the Environmental Protection Agency has been criticized because it pursues companies that once dumped hazardous waste (often quite legally) to make them pay for cleaning up the old sites. In effect, this interpretation of property rights says: "Current owner can make old dumper pay regardless of previous dumping legality." If extended litigation means that only the litigating lawyers clean up (these are social costs, too), then those who determine property rights must consider court costs as well as the effect on future dumping.

Apples and Bees. Another classic example relating property rights to externalities deals with a positive externality. Bees produce honey, and they also help pollinate fruit crops such as apples. Consider the effect when beekeeper Betty locates her hives next to the fence separating her land from Alice's apple orchard. As the bees travel over the fence in search of nectar, they alight on apple blossoms and pollinate them. The more bees that Betty has, the more blossoms are pollinated for Alice. In this case, there is a positive externality because Alice receives a direct benefit from the decision of Betty to raise more bees. Since Betty does not benefit from the increased apple production of her neighbor, Betty is likely to choose too few beehives to maximize the value of the total apple and honey output.

Several solutions exist for this externality, one of which is to have Alice raise both apples and bees. In fact, orchards that sell honey on the side are not uncommon. Another solution, however, is to have Alice pay Betty to put her beehives in the orchard during the spring pollinating season. This invests Betty with a property right for the pollinating services of her bees. Now Betty receives payment for the benefit that her bees provide in pollinating Alice's apple blossoms, and she can take this into account when she decides how many hives to have. Orchards commonly use services of this type.

6. Ronald Coase, "The Problem of Social Cost," *Journal of Law and Economics,* October 1960, pp. 1–44.

Each of these examples shows that an externality is *not* something that is intrinsic to the activity in question. We cannot say, for example, ''Dumping waste into a river is always a negative externality.'' Sometimes dumping waste into a river is a negative externality, and sometimes it is not. What makes the difference is the presence of appropriate property rights and market payments for grazing rights, fishing congestion, traffic congestion, property damage, hazardous waste disposal, pollination services, and the like. Dealing with negative externalities such as air pollution does not mean simply finding ways to stop them; rather, it requires using our knowledge of property rights to affect the causes of pollution so that socially efficient quantities are chosen.

Designing Property Rights for Social Efficiency: Coase's Two Theorems

When there are externalities, the process of setting up markets and arranging for the legal rights of damaged parties is crucial to achieving an efficient use of resources. Among the available options is always the choice of doing nothing and letting the involved parties act on their own to correct the problem. Another option is setting up laws so that aggrieved parties can ask the courts to enforce specified property rights. Either option can be the right choice, depending on the circumstances. For example, as a property owner, do I have the right to prevent you from building a wall on your adjoining land because it creates a negative externality for me by blocking my view? Could you and I solve the problem without going to court?

To answer these and other questions, this section considers two propositions that describe the principles of intervention called for in different circumstances. We will refer to them as Coase's theorems because they are concepts that first appeared, though not as formal theorems, in the article by Ronald Coase cited earlier.

▼

3. State and explain Coase's First and Second Theorems. Give examples.

Coase's First Theorem: An economy where information is perfect, where no costs are incurred for bargaining about arrangements or for enforcing them, and where property rights are clearly set will achieve an optimal assignment of resources, regardless of how property rights are assigned and without need of government intervention.

In this theorem, the assignment of property rights refers to whether the party damaged by the externality is legally entitled to restitution from the damaging party. The basic insight of the theorem is that, if affected parties can negotiate, the prospect of a net gain is sufficient that they will make the proper choice *without government intervention.* Take again the issue of air pollution. Assume that everyone who is harmed can get together with everyone who pollutes (bargaining is costless) and discuss the cheapest way to reduce or eliminate pollution (information is perfect). If the cheapest way to reduce pollution is less costly than the potential gain, then the action will be taken. The only remaining issue is how the net gains from eliminating the externality will be distributed among the parties, and this can be settled by bargaining.

In many cases the no-bargaining-cost assumption makes perfect sense. You want to build your wall next door to me. I believe that the damage it will do to me is worth $10,000, so I am willing to offer you up to $10,000 not to build. Regardless of whether my best offer is sufficient to induce you not to build, the fact that it was made guarantees that your choice about building will be socially optimal. How can I be sure? Let's say the wall is worth $12,000 to you. Then you build, and society is better off by a net $2,000. If the wall is worth only $9,000 to you, then you don't build, and society is again better off because the optimal choice has been made.

What would be different if the property rights, in the form of legal liability rules, said that you had to compensate me for damages? In this case you would have to pay me $10,000 before I gave you permission to build. If the wall were worth $12,000 to you, you would pay me $10,000 and build. Society would be better off by a net $2,000, and the optimal choice would have been made. If the wall were worth only $9,000 to you, you would not offer me enough, the wall would not be built, and once again the optimal choice would have been made. Comparing who has what in these four cases, we see that with costless bargaining the only effect of the liability rule is to change the distribution of the gains and losses. The socially optimal choice is made regardless.

Although Coase was criticized initially because he seemed to contradict popular wisdom that externalities require government intervention, his emphasis on bargaining costs and property rights as the key to externalities ultimately proved correct. If bargaining is costless, property rights don't matter, and externalities are eliminated by self-interested agents. Coase, however, did not claim that bargaining costs *were* zero. His second theorem shows that when bargaining is costly, property rights matter a great deal.

> ***Coase's Second Theorem:*** *If bargaining is costly and information is imperfect, then liability rules help achieve optimality, and the party that has the least costly way of dealing with the harmful effects of an externality should be made responsible for paying the costs associated with the externality.*

To explain Coase's Second Theorem, let's apply it to a case reported in the news concerning an area two blocks from the city hall in Jersey City, New Jersey. A sign was placed there reading, ''This area contains dangerous and contaminated materials that are harmful to human life.''[7] A chromium refinery that once operated at the site had contaminated the area with 46 times the carcinogens considered by the state to be safe. If we want to choose a solution that prevents future repetitions of this episode elsewhere, we first have to admit that it is not possible for a contemporary firm to bargain with people who may be harmed in the future. If the firm is not liable for future damage, the likely outcome is that the firm will leave carcinogens. On the other hand, if the rule is that the firm and its directors are liable for future damage traced to their actions, then the firm will not leave carcinogens when

7. Horn, op. cit., p. 80.

prevention costs to the firm are cheaper than the anticipated liability costs. Thus the particular liability rule matters.

So should the chromium plant have to pay for future damages or not? The second part of Coase's theorem says that the choice depends on whether the chromium plant has the cheapest way to prevent damage. Let's say that future users have only to wait one week for the toxic wastes to disappear naturally, but that forcing the chromium plant to produce in such a way that no carcinogens are left on the site would cost millions of dollars. Since waiting one week is far cheaper, the firm should *not* be made liable. On the other hand, if future cleanup of the plant site costs millions of dollars, and the firm could adjust production at little cost to leave no toxic wastes, then the firm should be made liable.

Coase's Second Theorem provides a natural link between economics and law, offering an efficiency rationale for deciding externality liability rules. Returning to the classic example of the train and sparks, where the fire damage is valued in terms of the amount of crops burned, there are at least three different ways to deal with the problem of sparks: (1) limit the amount of train traffic; (2) have trains install some type of spark-inhibiting device; or (3) have farmers plant their crops several yards farther away from the tracks. Did the courts make the damaging party liable, or did they recognize the principle of Coase's Second Theorem? Halsbury's *Laws of England*, cited in the original article by Coase, indicates in this case that efficiency and common sense concerning the relative costs of remedy prevailed:

> If an engine is constructed with the precaution which science suggests against fire and is used without negligence, they [railroad companies] are not responsible at common law for any damage which may be done by sparks. . . . In the construction of an engine the undertaker is bound to use all the discoveries which science has put within its reach in order to avoid doing harm, provided they are such as it is reasonable to require the company to adopt, having proper regard to the likelihood of the damage and to the cost and convenience of the remedy; but it is not negligence on the part of an undertaker if it refuses to use an apparatus the efficiency of which is open to bona fide doubt.[8]

We have come a long way in our understanding of externalities. We now know that the presence of an externality implies (1) the failure of full social costs and benefits to be included in the decision-making computations of the externality-producing party, (2) the absence of a market, (3) high bargaining costs, and (4) absent or inappropriate assignment of property rights (liability rules). In the next section we use this understanding to develop a list of remedies for externalities.

8. Coase, op. cit., p. 30.

14.3 Ways to Correct Externalities

▼

4. Apart from direct bargaining, what are three primary ways to correct an externality?

How can the social costs implied by externality be eliminated? In general, there are only three avenues: (1) market structural changes or changes in the market roles of affected parties, (2) corrective taxes, or (3) direct regulation. The second two of these have received the most attention, but as the insights of Coase and others show, the first should not be overlooked. We consider each briefly in turn.

Market Structural Changes

As Coase's First Theorem reminds us, permanent government intervention may be unnecessary to deal with an externality. Where there is a missing market, the natural response to the externality is to establish a market in the externality, if possible. In the honey bee–apple blossom externality, the establishment of a market in pollination services eliminated the externality. In the case of the commons, establishing land ownership with associated property rights eliminated the externality because land services would be bought and sold. In the case of ocean fishing, the establishment of a 200-mile economic exclusive-use zone implies a marketable right that can be bought and sold by other nations wanting access to the zone.

Figure 14.2 illustrates the ocean fishing example. The total catch is equal to the area between the VMP curve and the horizontal axis, and the opportunity cost of sending an additional boat to the fishing area is C. When the fishing grounds are common property, boats enter until the catch per boat, given by the VAP curve, equals C. If the fishing grounds become a privately owned resource, however, it is worthwhile to send additional boats only as long as the marginal catch, VMP, exceeds C. Under private ownership, therefore, the number of boats is q^* instead of the inefficiently large $q^{\text{externality}}$. The social gain from eliminating the externality is area $a + b$, while the reduction in total catch is area $d - b$. If the fishing rights are sold, their market value will equal MP, since that is the opportunity cost to the owner of giving them up. Firms will bid for fishing rights to the point where VMP $= C$, again insuring the optimal use of the fishing grounds.

If we look at Figure 14.2 in terms of the English commons example, we can see that ownership rights and a market in land (or water) services ensure efficiency in another way. Since owners who happen to work their own land will select the field treatment and the degree of grazing that are in their best interest, productivity will increase, meaning the VAP and VMP curves will shift upward from the ones shown. Correcting the externality results in the benefits explained in Figure 14.2, plus the benefits of higher productivity. The establishment of the market "internalizes" the externality, either by valuing the externality with a market price used by the externality-causing party or by having the externality-causing party be the recipient of the externality.

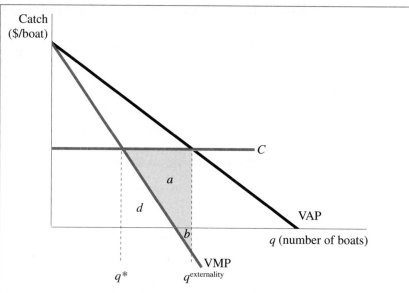

Figure 14.2 Congestion Externality When the fishing grounds are common property, boats enter the fishing area until catch per boat, VAP, equals the opportunity cost of devoting an additional boat to the fishing ground, C, at $q^{externality}$. Under private ownership, the number of boats fishing is q^*, where VMP $= C$. Since the total value of fish taken is the area between the marginal product curve, VMP, and the horizontal axis (area below the axis is treated as negative), and costs are the area between C and the horizontal axis, the social gain from private ownership equals area $a + b$. The catch is smaller by area $d - b$, and costs are lower by area $d + a$.

APPLICATION: Land Privatization and Water Markets

Two contemporary examples will help demonstrate the role of market structural changes in correcting externalities. The first involves land use, and the second deals with water rights.

Mongolia. About 77 percent of Mongolian land is used for herding, and the social tradition favors communal grazing. Since grazing is communal, all of the problems discussed earlier of common property are present. In addition, communal grazing may not be the best use of the land. In 1992 the Mongolian parliament grappled with new land laws and a legal framework for natural resource use, as well as guidelines for privatization and dispute settlement.[9] State farms had previously cultivated the arable land, and Mongolian experts feared that no one would know how to cultivate it if it were taken out of state

9. "Mongolian Land Reform: The Legal Framework," *Institutional Reform and the Informal Sector Update* (University of Maryland), May 1992, pp. 1, 6.

control. According to policymakers, under the previous system most farmers became more like workers who knew isolated tasks but did not have the knowledge or skill to run an entire farm operation. Moreover, in Mongolian society animal husbandry is more prestigious than farming, and there is little tradition of crop production. Only 1 percent of the land is arable.

The original idea was to continue to vest in the state control of the arable land, so that the state would make decisions about the crops to be grown and the techniques to be used. If land was not actively cultivated, the state would have the power to terminate ownership rights. After Western advice was sought, however, alternative solutions included agricultural extension services to educate farmers and greater reliance on the use of natural economic incentives to encourage crop production. According to Mongolians working on the problem, much of the re-education must also involve legislators, who are not well acquainted with the legal foundations for a market-based economy.

California. Another case in which establishing different property rights can deal with the social costs of externalities comes from water use rights in agriculture in the American West. California agriculture currently consumes 90 percent of the water used in the state.[10] Farmers might pay $20 to $30 (sometimes the price is even less) for an acre-foot of water, whereas coastal communities might have to pay ten times that amount. An acre-foot is the amount of water that would cover an acre (roughly the area of a football field) with water one foot deep. In this case, an externality is present because farmers do not pay the true cost of their water (private costs are below social costs) and therefore overuse it. In 1988, for example, 215,000 acres were devoted to rice, a product whose price is subsidized by the government at many times the world price, and which is far better suited to moist areas of Southeast Asia than to dry California. Cheap prices for water also discourage careful irrigation practices that could save large amounts of water. The limited water supply for nonagricultural uses creates hardships on communities. The federal government has spent nearly $4 billion in today's dollars to collect water from Northern California and send it to the central valleys. Since water contracts (some of them obtained before the turn of the century and renewed since) govern who is entitled to water at what price, allowing a market in the sale of water rights—a type of trade that is currently restricted—would quickly alleviate the problem. ■

Taxes

When establishing a self-perpetuating market is impractical, another solution is to tax the externality. Setting the tax equal to the marginal social cost of the externality causes the firm or household to take into account the social costs of the externality and choose its production and abatement activity at the socially optimal level. Figure 14.3 shows how the process works. On the

---

10. Peter Passell, ''Soaking Lawns, Not Taxpayers,'' *New York Times,* February 5, 1992, p. D2.

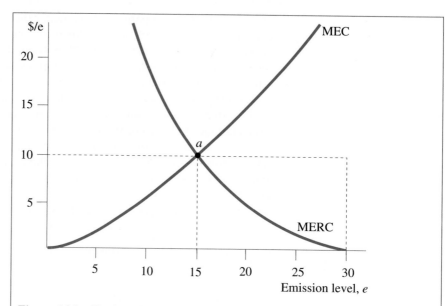

Figure 14.3   Taxing Harmful Emissions   At the firm's profit-maximizing output, it produces 30 units of harmful emissions. The socially optimal level of emissions occurs at 15 units at point *a*, where the social marginal externality cost, MEC, equals the firm's marginal externality reduction cost, MERC. Limiting emissions below 15 units costs more to the firm than the cost savings to society. Taxing emissions at $10 per unit makes it cheaper for the firm to limit emissions to 15 units than to pay the tax, so this tax causes the firm to choose the optimal emission level.

horizontal axis we measure the amount of the externality—in this case the level of a polluting emission—and on the vertical axis we measure the firm's marginal cost of reducing the externality and the marginal social cost of the externality. When the firm produces without concern for its emission level, output is 30 units of emissions. Limiting emissions to smaller amounts costs the firm increasingly more in the form of direct emission abatement costs and/or lost profit from reduced sales of the good. Marginal firm costs incurred in the abatement of emissions are measured by the *marginal externality reduction cost* curve, MERC. For example, at 30 units of emissions, the marginal externality reduction cost is zero, since the firm is doing nothing to reduce emissions. But if the firm is emitting 15 units of emissions and wants to reduce the emissions by a small amount from this level, this will cost the firm something—in this case, $10 per additional unit of emission reduced.

   Marginal externality cost, MEC, measures the damage done by additional units of emission. If there are zero emissions, MEC is zero since no damage is being done. As emissions increase, however, damage from additional emissions increases and MEC rises. Balancing reduced damage from emissions against the cost of reducing emissions determines the desired quantity of emissions: the point where MEC and MERC cross. At point *a*, further emission reduction will cost more than the additional benefits in reduced damage. The firm can be induced to choose point *a* if it is taxed at a rate of $10 per unit of emission.[11] If the firm continued to produce 30 units of emissions, for example, it would pay more in the emission tax than if it took efforts to reduce emissions. As long as MERC is lower than the tax, the firm is better off reducing its emissions further. When MERC equals the tax, it is more costly to the firm to reduce emissions below 15 units than to pay the tax, so at this level the firm chooses to pay.

Until the Coasian analysis of externalities, the *Pigovian tax* just described[12] was considered to be the appropriate solution to externalities. In the case of traffic congestion, for example, a toll set equal to the marginal social cost of an additional car crossing at that time of day would be the right solution because it would cause drivers to internalize the social costs of their crossing. In general, it was more or less taken for granted that a tax levied on the polluter at the right level would induce the proper response. However, as we know from our discussion of Coase, there are cases in which the party causing the externality does not have the least costly way of limiting it. In these cases, taxing the perpetrator causes the *wrong* outcome, and the costs of the externality should be allowed to fall on the party that has the least costly way to alleviate it.[13]

Direct Regulation

The last way that an externality can be dealt with is through direct regulation. For example, if automobile emissions cause air pollution, it is possible to set an emission standard by legislative fiat that achieves the objective of pollution

---

11. With the emission tax F, firm profits are $\Pi = pq - C(q, a) - Fe(q, a)$, where q is quantity of output, a is the level of emission abatement activity by the firm, and $e(q, a)$ is the level of emissions as a function of quantity of output and abatement activity. Since the firm can limit emissions by reducing quantity and/or increasing abatement efforts, it chooses the mix of the two that is least costly in terms of forgone profit. The firm chooses output so that $p = MC + F \Delta e/\Delta q$ and $\Delta C/\Delta a \geq F \Delta e/\Delta a$. The first condition says that price equals marginal cost, where marginal cost now includes the marginal cost of paying the emission tax. The second condition says that the marginal cost of reducing emissions by direct abatement efforts must be greater than or equal to the marginal benefit to the firm in terms of savings on emission charges. If $\Delta C/\Delta a < F \Delta e/\Delta a$, the firm saves more in emission tax than it costs to reduce emissions by abatement activity a; hence its current choice of a cannot be profit-maximizing. If $\Delta C/\Delta a > F \Delta e/\Delta a$, the firm pays more trying to reduce emissions than by paying the tax. In that case, direct abatement activity a is set equal to zero.

12. Named for A. C. Pigou, an early-twentieth-century economist, who advocated corrective taxes for externalities.

13. As a matter of *efficiency,* it is better that farmers be left to deal with the damage of burned crops on their own, so they have an incentive to take the countermeasure of planting a few yards farther from the railroad track. Though such a policy might still be deemed *inequitable* or *unfair,* since farmers were not the cause of their losses, a useful comparison is to ask how things would be different if the identical damages were caused, say, by lightning and the relative costs of countermeasures by railroad companies and farmers were the same. Would we want railroads or farmers to take action?

reduction. This method of dealing with an externality is actually identical to internalizing the externality, except that the agent that internalizes the externality is the entire community, operating through the government or legislature. Presumably the legislature has the interests of the entire society at heart (though this cannot always be assumed) and will direct that the right activities at the right levels be pursued. Nonmarket forms of regulation, however, have other problems relating to informational needs, and we will consider these next.

Informational Problems of Regulation

▼
5. What are some informational problems of regulation?

In a perfect world, applying emission taxes or setting emission standards might be the end of the story. In reality, legislatures and governments often do not have the necessary information to adequately carry out so ambitious a regulatory task. To get the information they need about relative pollution control costs, for example, governments often must turn to the very parties they seek to regulate: the externality-causing firms. This can create two problems. First, government may set its regulatory tax or standards at the wrong level; and second, it may impose regulatory standards uniformly when not all firms should be treated alike.

To illustrate the first problem, consider the two regulatory situations shown in Figure 14.4. In part (a) the social optimum of 10 units of emissions would be reached by an emission tax of $10 per unit. But since the government is not sure where the marginal externality cost curve MEC and the marginal externality reduction cost curve MERC intersect, it erroneously sets the emission tax 10 percent too high at $11. Because the curves are shaped as they are, this leads to an enormous social cost equal to area $a + a'$. Social costs are high because the tax causes firms to spend large sums of money reducing emissions to levels that have relatively small harmful consequences. Had the government set a *quantity* standard that was 10 percent too low, the social costs would only have been area a'. However, under the conditions in part (b) the situation is reversed: making a 10-percent quantity mistake is enormously costly to society, resulting in losses $b + b'$, rather than only b' for a 10-percent price mistake. How is the government to know which situation applies, so that the "cure" is not worse than the original problem? If information is poor, there is no good answer to this question.

To illustrate the second problem of insufficient information and uniform standards, consider the case of Plastics Anonymous and Chemical Compost Technologies, two firms that each create serious negative externalities with their effluents. To reduce the total effluents by 40 units, the legislature decides to enact an ordinance that no firm can emit more than 10 units of effluent per year. Although such a rule appears fair since it requires the same standard of each firm, it fails to take into account the different abilities of the two firms to reduce their emissions. If the goal of the standard is to achieve a target level of emissions at least cost, then a better way is to impose a tax or to allow trading rights in emissions.

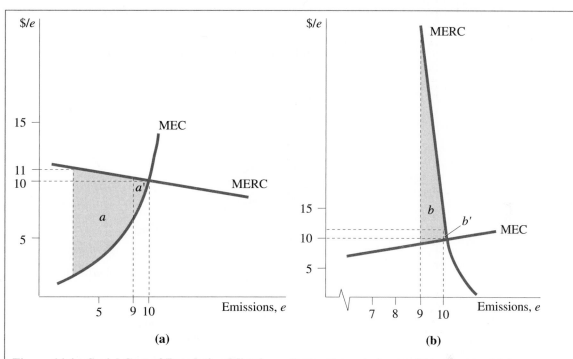

Figure 14.4   Social Cost of Regulation Mistakes   Setting the emission tax 10 percent too high leads to social losses of $a + a'$ in part (a), but only b' in part (b). Setting an emission *quantity* limit 10 percent too low leads to social losses equal to area $b + b'$ in part (b), but only a' in part (a). Conditions in part (a) are therefore unforgiving of emission tax mistakes, and conditions in part (b) are unforgiving of quantity regulation mistakes. In many cases the government may not know the shape of the MEC curve or the MERC curve, so it runs the risk of error whether it sets an emission tax or a quantity limit.

Figure 14.5 shows that each firm was originally emitting 30 units of effluent. The marginal externality reduction costs of Plastics Anonymous, however, are significantly lower than those of Chemical Compost. Imposing the uniform emission standard of 10 units per firm produces a total cost equal to the area under the two curves between 10 units and 30 units.

If a tax of $7 per unit of effluent is imposed instead, each firm decides whether it is cheaper to pay the tax or to reduce emissions. Plastics Anonymous finds it advantageous to reduce emissions *below* the original standard, to 5 units, rather than pay the tax. Chemical Compost, on the other hand, finds it saves most by emitting 15 units of effluent and paying the fee. The same total effluent is emitted, but the savings to Chemical Compost (the area under its curve between 10 and 15 units) are greater than the increase in cost to Plastics Anonymous. Society gains the net savings.

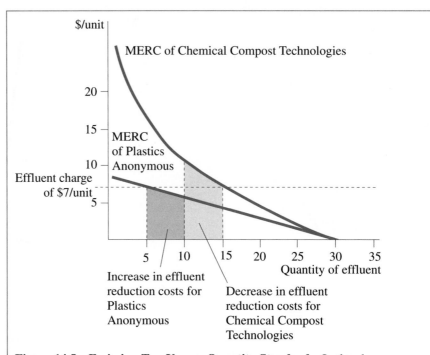

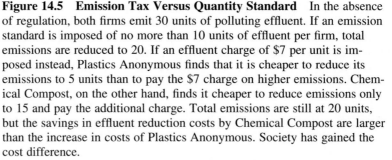

Figure 14.5 Emission Tax Versus Quantity Standard In the absence
of regulation, both firms emit 30 units of polluting effluent. If an emission
standard is imposed of no more than 10 units of effluent per firm, total
emissions are reduced to 20. If an effluent charge of $7 per unit is im-
posed instead, Plastics Anonymous finds that it is cheaper to reduce its
emissions to 5 units than to pay the $7 charge on higher emissions. Chem-
ical Compost, on the other hand, finds it cheaper to reduce emissions only
to 15 and pay the additional charge. Total emissions are still at 20 units,
but the savings in effluent reduction costs by Chemical Compost are larger
than the increase in costs of Plastics Anonymous. Society has gained the
cost difference.

Notice that the government did not have to know which firm had the better
technology for reducing emissions. The tax automatically caused the firms to
choose the right amount of emission reduction. The same thing could have
been accomplished if the government had assigned effluent standards as
before, but allowed firms to trade in effluent rights. To show how trading in
effluent permits works, Figure 14.6 redraws the marginal externality reduction
costs, MERC, of both firms in such a way that the effluent of Plastics Anonymous is measured from the right origin and the effluent of Chemical Compost Technologies from the left. When the government arbitrarily assigns the
firms effluent permits of 10 units each, Chemical Compost is paying $10 to
reduce its last unit of effluent (point *a*), and Plastic Anonymous is paying $5

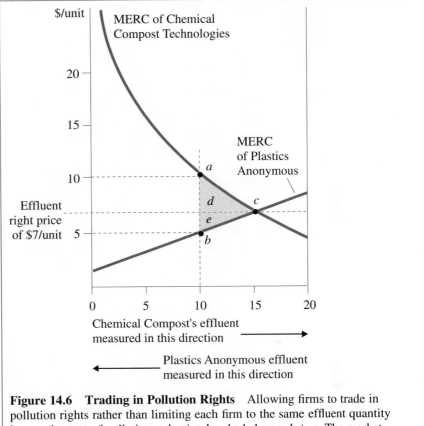

Figure 14.6 Trading in Pollution Rights Allowing firms to trade in pollution rights rather than limiting each firm to the same effluent quantity lowers the cost of pollution reduction by shaded area *d* + *e*. The market price of one unit of effluent right settles at $7, where the two firms have equal MERCs.

(point *b*). Therefore Chemical Compost can save money by buying an effluent permit from Plastics Anonymous at a price between $5 and $10; with that permit to emit an extra unit, Chemical Compost saves the $10 cost of reducing its last unit of effluent. At the same time, Plastics Anonymous is paid more than its cost of reducing its effluent by an additional unit. Such trading, carried to the most profitable conclusion for both firms, would result in a market price of $7. The firms would end up at point *c*, where there is no further advantage to trading. Since it pays less in buying permits than it would have spent to reduce its effluent, Chemical Compost saves area *d*. Plastics Anonymous gains area *e*, the amount by which its sale of effluent permits exceeded its cost of reducing effluent further. Total social gain is therefore area *d* + *e*. Comparing this to the outcome in Figure 14.5, where the effluent charge was set at $7, shows that the same final position is reached.

APPLICATION: The Clean Air Act and Trading in Pollution Rights

Economists have been espousing the virtues of trading in pollution permits for decades, and it appears that their message is beginning to get through. In June 1989, President Bush asked Congress to strengthen the 1970 Clean Air Act by allowing generators of acid-rain gases a certain level of emissions. If a firm achieved a lower level than its permit specified, it could sell the unused portion of its allowance to other firms. The excess of one firm's emission would be offset by the lower emissions of another. Congress responded in 1990, and the new provision of the Clean Air Act is now law.

Similar proposals are being considered for solid-waste disposal and for other types of pollution in states such as California.[14] Although the prospect that firms would be able to pay their way to a right to pollute is offensive to some, it makes good economic sense. In the case of solid-waste disposal, landfill fees have been rising in many highly populated areas, but some parts of the country have abundant landfill space. It makes little sense to force these latter areas to follow the same stringent set of national standards for recycling and waste disposal that make economic sense in other parts of the country. Areas for which continued dumping is the least costly way to dispose of waste should continue dumping—and selling their excess capacity to other areas. The money saved, both by the regions that buy dumping privileges and by the areas that sell, can be put to other good uses.

In a 1992 California proposal, Southern California air quality regulators have suggested the creation of an air quality district to replace the current company-by-company restrictions. The plan would initially apply to the 2,000 companies in the area that account for 85 percent of the smog-forming hydrocarbons and to the 700 companies, such as oil refineries and utilities, that account for 95 percent of the nitrogen oxide emissions. Smaller companies would be added to the plan later, with a small number exempted. Most companies see the plan as giving them greater flexibility in dealing with the requirement to reduce pollution, though some critics are concerned about the way the credits would be given out. The possession of pollution permits would become a valuable asset to companies that had surplus pollution rights to sell. Would the assignment of pollution rights become an object of lobbying? What long-term rights to permits would companies have? Would a company be allowed to leave the district but continue to sell its pollution rights to other companies, for example? If *all* companies were made to buy their permits from the air quality authority to circumvent such problems, the program would become equivalent to an effluent tax. Either way, however, the costs of achieving a given level of pollution reduction would be minimized. ▪

14. See Richard W. Stevenson, "California Proposal Would Let Industry Sell Pollution Rights," *New York Times,* January 30, 1992, p. A1; Sylvia Nasar, "Can Capitalism Save the Ozone?" *New York Times,* February 7, 1992, p. D2; and Holusha, op. cit.

Although most of our discussion of externalities has dealt with the problem of negative externalities, an equally important class of issues arises with respect to positive externalities. Next we consider cases in which the provision of a good generates benefits to more than one individual.

14.4 Public Goods

In this part of the chapter, we turn our attention to a class of goods that we have not yet considered in depth: public goods. We begin by discussing the externality characteristics that distinguish public goods from private goods. We then use the microeconomics that we learned in Chapter 12 to find the rule for Pareto optimal provision of public goods, and finally we discuss the features that make public goods difficult for private markets to provide.

Rivalry and Excludability

▼
6. How do rivalry and excludability distinguish private from public goods?

When you eat a plate of toast and eggs for breakfast, it necessarily means that your friend cannot eat the same plate of toast and eggs. The same is true when you burn gasoline in your car or use toothpaste. These goods have the property of *rivalry* in consumption, because the act of consuming them necessarily prevents anyone else from consuming the same unit. The dictionary defines a rival as one of two or more striving to obtain something that only one can have. Thus a *rival good* is a good that only one household can consume.

There are also nonrival goods. For example, a radio broadcast is nonrival because it can be received by any number of listeners without any reduction in the ability of other listeners to tune in. A weather forecast is nonrival because, once it is readied, it can be disseminated to benefit additional consumers without lessening its usefulness to anyone or requiring additional forecasting expense.

For nonrival goods there is also the issue of *excludability: can* other consumers be prevented from consuming the good? For example, when the nation provides for its security through national defense measures, it automatically secures and protects the lives and property of each household in the country. One area realistically cannot be prevented from benefiting if all other areas are protected. Goods that are nonrival and nonexcludable are called *pure public goods.*

> A ***pure public good*** *is a good that is nonrival and nonexcludable. Consumption by one household does not prevent other households from consuming the same unit at no additional cost of provision, and excluding others from consumption is prohibitively costly.*

We use the term *pure* public good in recognition of the fact that some goods have varying degrees of rivalry. For example, a concert performed in a 1,000-seat auditorium allows up to 1,000 people to listen to the same concert with little or no additional provision cost or deterioration of the quality of the listening experience (at least if the concert hall is well designed!). On the other hand, trying to place more people into the room than the capacity it was designed for would eventually cause congestion problems that would diminish the ability of others to enjoy the concert.

Nonrivalry and congestion are related issues with respect to public goods. A pure *private* good of the type that we have discussed in earlier chapters is characterized by rivalry in use and an *infinite* degree of congestion once a single household consumes the good. A pure *public* good, at the other extreme, is nonrival and has *zero* degree of congestion for any number of consumers of the same good. Goods that are intermediate between pure private goods and pure public goods exhibit increasing congestion with more users and increasing costs of providing the same unit to multiple individuals. Intermediate goods are often called *club goods* because there is an optimal number of people or "club size" for consuming a given quantity of the good.

Providing a club good requires knowing how much of the good to provide and how many people should share in its consumption. A hunting club and country club are examples of "goods" that present a congestion problem if the membership becomes too great. Although the principles for club goods and pure public goods are similar, describing in detail the provision rules for club goods is beyond our scope of treatment here, so we will devote ourselves to pure public goods. The number of individuals sharing a pure public good is always the number of people in the economy.

If everyone consumes the same units of public good, how do we know when the right amount has been provided? We tackle this question next.

Optimal Provision of a Pure Public Good

The Pareto optimal level of a public good occurs when the sum of all households' marginal rates of substitution of public good for private good equals the marginal rate of transformation,

$$\text{MRS}^1 + \text{MRS}^2 + \cdots = \text{MRT},$$

where the sum is taken over all households. What does this mean? Since the marginal rate of substitution of public good for private good is the household's marginal benefit from consuming an additional unit of public good measured in units of private good, and MRT is the marginal cost of producing another unit of public good in terms of private good, the condition says that the sum of everyone's marginal benefits from the public good should equal the marginal cost of supplying it.

▼

7. Use a two-household economy to derive the condition for optimal provision of a public good.

To see how the condition comes about, consider a two-person economy in which g is the quantity of pure public good and x^1 and x^2 are the quantities of private good x consumed by Households 1 and 2, respectively.[15] The total quantity of private good in the economy is given by $x^1 + x^2 = x$, and the total quantity of public good is given by g. Part (a) of Figure 14.7 shows the

15. Think of x as a composite good representing consumption of all private goods.

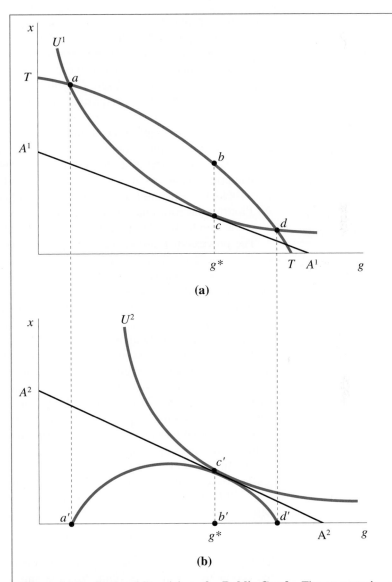

Figure 14.7 Optimal Provision of a Public Good   The economy's
production possibility frontier for public good g and private good x is TT.
If Household 1 is to be kept at utility level U^1 in part (a), it must be given
a combination of x and g lying on its indifference curve, such as point c.
This leaves quantity bc of the private good for Household 2, plotted in
part (b) as $b'c'$. Doing this for all possible distributions in part (a) gives us
curve $a'c'd'$. Picking the best point for Household 2 leads to point c'.
Pareto optimal provision of the public good therefore corresponds to production at point b, with Households 1 and 2 consuming at c and c', respectively.

economy's production possibility frontier, TT, and an arbitrarily selected indifference curve of Household 1. Our strategy for finding a Pareto optimum is to hold utility constant for the first household at the level indicated by the indifference curve and then find the maximum utility for the second household. The result will be a Pareto optimum, because any increase in utility for the second household will require a reduction in utility for the first, and vice versa.

Assigning consumption at point c to Household 1 keeps its utility at U^1 and is feasible for the economy because it is inside production frontier TT. Choosing c means the other household can consume g^* units of public good (consumption is nonrival) and bc units of private good x (the remainder after household 1's consumption of x is subtracted from the economy total at point b). Plotting the combination of g^* and bc units of x in part (b) gives us point c' as the bundle that Household 2 can consume if Household 1 is at c.

The process of plotting points in part (b) can be repeated for every point on Household 1's indifference curve between a and d. This leads to curve a' $c'd'$ in part (b), whose height at each choice of x equals the vertical distance between TT and U^1 in part (a). That is, vertical distance $b'c'$ in part (b) equals vertical distance bc in part (a), and so on. Since Household 1 is indifferent, we select the point on $a'c'd'$ that gives Household 2 the highest utility. This is point c', which is tangent to Household 2's indifference curve U^2. If the economy produces at point b, Household 1 consumes at point c, and the remainder of good x is given to Household 2, we have reached a Pareto optimum because it is impossible to make Household 2 better off without harming Household 1. Likewise, making Household 1 better off would lower curve $a'c'd'$, making Household 2 worse off. To find other Pareto optimal points, we would simply start with a different indifference curve for Household 1 and repeat this procedure.

The most important feature of Figure 14.7 is the tangency of Household 2's indifference curve with $a'c'd'$. Because the slope of $a'c'd'$ is the rate at which TT and U^1 approach each other as g increases, the slope of U^1, $MRS^1_{g,x}$, equals the difference $MRT_{g,x} - MRS^2_{g,x}$, or

$$MRS^1_{g,x} + MRS^2_{g,x} = MRT_{g,x}.$$

This is the condition we are looking for. Visually, it means that the slope of the production frontier at point b is the sum of the two indifference curve slopes at c and c'. Verbally, it means that the public good should be provided to the point where the sum of all marginal benefits by consumers of the good equals the marginal cost of providing it. Notice that if the two consumers had the budget lines A^1A^1 and A^2A^2, they would choose points c and c' as market choices. We will make use of this observation shortly when we discuss the possibility of market purchases of public goods.

Also notice that if our economy had more than two households, every household's MRS would be included in the sum. If the economy had one consumer, the condition would become $MRS^1_{g,x} = MRT_{g,x}$, which we recognize from Chapter 12 as the consumer sovereignty condition for provision of good *g*. The difference when *g* is a public good, then, is that beneficiaries of the good include *all* households in the economy rather than just one. Equating the sum of the marginal rates of substitution to the marginal rate of transformation is therefore a generalization of the consumer sovereignty condition for public goods.

Market Purchases of Public Goods

The consumer sovereignty condition for public goods describes how much of a public good should be provided, but does not tell us much, except indirectly, about the arrangements to pay for it. Since everyone benefits from the public good and cannot be excluded from consuming it, we must look for a sensible way to share the cost of providing it. Our starting rule is the principle that in an ideal world, households should pay for the public good in proportion to how much benefit they receive from it. For example, if a city park that benefits one region of the city is going to be constructed, it makes sense, other things being equal, that households nearer the park should pay, and should be willing to pay, more for it.

Our approach in this section is hypothetical, in the sense that we act as if we know every household's preferences in order to find out what an ideal outcome would look like. After we have arrived at a method of paying for the public good, we will decide whether the payment system could be implemented.

For the purposes of the exercise, let's assume the public good is national defense, with annual spending around $300 billion. The number of tanks, ships, planes, and personnel associated with various levels of national defense can be represented by units of *g*. Now assume that you are the only person deciding how much national defense and private good *x* to buy, just as if you were buying *x* and *g* off the shelf at a local store. For each price of *g* there is a quantity that you would buy, so we can construct your private demand curve for the public good in the usual way.[16] For any given quantity of public good, however, all families consume the same units, so the total price paid by the economy would be the *sum* of the individual household prices. Constructing the *economy* demand curve for a public good, therefore, means summing individual demand curves *vertically* (in the price dimension). This is shown in Figure 14.8 for two consumers. Curves D^1 and D^2 are the individual demand curves, and $\Sigma_i D^i$ is their vertical sum. At *g**, for example, the height of point *e* is the sum of the prices on the individual demand curves for quantity *g**. We also find the supply curve for the public good in the usual way from the marginal cost curve of the supplying firm or firms.[17]

▼
8. How is the economy's demand curve for a public good derived?

16. Remember, your choice and no on else's determines how much national defense you get in this exercise. How many units of *g* would you buy if you paid $100 per year? $1,000 per year?
17. From the perspective of production, a public good is just like a private good. The externality that distinguishes a public good from a private good applies just to the consumption side.

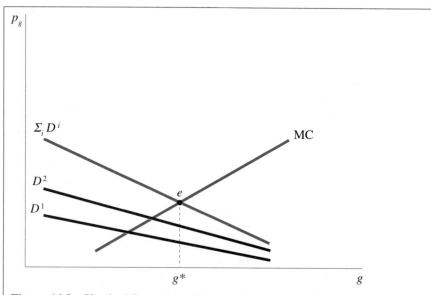

**Figure 14.8   Vertical Summing of Demand Curves for Public
Goods**   Households 1 and 2 have demand for the public good given by
demand curves D^1 and D^2, respectively. Adding the demand curves *vertically* leads to the summed demand curve labeled $\Sigma_i D^i$. The supply curve
for the public good is given by the marginal cost curve labeled MC.
Choosing the level of public good g^* given by the intersection of the
summed demand curve and supply curve at e satisfies the consumer sovereignty condition that the sum of marginal rates of substitution of public
good for private good equal the marginal rate of transformation of public
good into private good.

Taking the intersection of supply and demand gives us a quantity for the
public good.

Does the intersection at e satisfy the consumer sovereignty condition? The
answer is yes, since (1) every household buys a common quantity of public
good at the price of its demand curve for that quantity, and (2) the market
demand curve is the *vertical* summation of the individual demand curves, so
aggregate price satisfies $p_g^1 + p_g^2 + \cdots = MC_g$, where MC_g is the marginal
cost of providing the public good. However, we know from the consumer's
choice problem that each household sets $MRS_{g,x}^i = p_g^i/p_x$ and $p_x = MC_x$ for
good x. Dividing the left-hand side of the public good equation by p_x and the
right-hand side by MC_x gives us

$$\frac{p_g^1}{p_x} + \frac{p_g^2}{p_x} + \cdots = MRS_{g,x}^1 + MRS_{g,x}^2 + \cdots = \frac{MC_g}{MC_x} = MRT_{g,x},$$

where the last equality comes from noting that the ratio of marginal costs equals the marginal rate of transformation.[18]

In terms of Figure 14.7, what we have done is to select a price of the public good for each household so that the household budget lines are the tangent lines A^1A^1 and A^2A^2 at points c and c', respectively. Since we have not mentioned anything yet about assigning households different income levels, we now note that if we wanted to reach a different Pareto optimum—for example, one where the utility of Household 1 was lower and that of Household 2 higher—then we would need to start in Figure 14.7 with a lower indifference curve for Household 1, find the new consumption and income assignments, and use the different incomes to construct the demand curve for the public good.

Let's review what we have found. Constructing each household's demand curve for the public good and summing vertically gives us the market demand curve for the public good. Setting demand equal to supply leads to a Pareto optimal level of the public good. The price on each household's demand curve for that quantity is what the household pays. So far this is encouraging. The problem is that we need the household's demand curve both to know how much good to produce and how much to charge. It doesn't take much to see that the household has an incentive to say the public good is tremendously valuable (high MRS) if it thinks that will get the good provided. On the other hand, it has an incentive to say the good is worthless (low MRS) if it thinks its answer will determine how much it has to pay for the good. If there is no way to keep the household from *free riding*—benefiting from a public good provided by or for others without paying—the information problem is quite serious. We briefly review this aspect of public goods next.

The Free Rider Problem

The problem of free riders is really a problem of excludability and information. Consider the financing of public television, for example. Most of us enjoy at least to some degree the alternative programming that public television offers. Most of us are also aware, during the periodic public appeals for viewer support, that we can choose to free ride on the support of other viewers or voluntarily send in a contribution. If we could be excluded in a simple and costless way from watching public television if we didn't pay, financing could be handled like an admission fee. On the other hand, if we were taxed for public TV exactly what it was worth to us, it could be fairly financed in that way. The problem arises because the good is nonexcludable and because we lack information about individuals' valuation of it.

---

18. The additional cost of supplying amount Δg of public good is equal to $MC_g\Delta g = w\,\Delta L_g + r\,\Delta K_g$, where ΔL_g and ΔK_g are the additional factor inputs and w and r are their prices. Likewise for the private good, $MC_x\Delta x = w\,\Delta L_x + r\,\Delta K_x$. Since the inputs from additional public good must come from production of private goods, $\Delta L_g = -\Delta L_x$ and $\Delta K_g = -\Delta K_x$. Taking the ratio of $MC_g\Delta g$ and $MC_x\Delta x$ and substituting implies that $MC_g/MC_x = -\Delta x/\Delta g$, which is the definition of $MRT_{g,x}$.

Whereas nonrivalry is the key *defining* feature of public goods, nonexcludability is the key feature relating to *provision.* A private firm that incurs the cost of producing a public good must sell its product to make a profit. If households cannot be prevented from consuming the product (whether they have paid for it or not), the firm may not be able to collect from enough consumers to make a profit, and it will have to cease operation. Asking for voluntary contributions runs into the free rider problem. Nonvoluntary taxation runs into the information problem: those who do not pay for the public good will say they want and need it very much, while those who pay for the good will have no incentive to say anything that increases their payment. For these reasons, private markets, which operate on voluntary interactions, are not the usual vehicle for providing public goods.

14.5 Practical Provision of Public Goods

Although tax-supported government provision of public goods is not generally efficient, it does do better than no provision. Few of us would choose to give up public highways, for example, in favor of attempting to pay for them by subscription. In this section we first discuss the economics of taxes and public goods and then turn to issues of demand revelation and voting.

Taxes and Provision of Public Goods

▼
9. Explain the need for tax-financed provision of public goods and why it might lead to a Pareto suboptimal level of provision.

In light of the free rider problem, public goods are generally provided under the auspices of government and paid for through involuntary taxes. There are several consequences of this that deserve mention. First, since tax payments are not closely related to the degree of benefit that a household receives from public goods, heavily taxed households will generally pay more for the public good than they should, and lightly taxed households will pay less than they should. The tax structure will then have an impact on the political desires of the households, with lightly taxed households favoring greater spending and heavily taxed households favoring less. Unlike the equilibrium constructed from the intersection of the demand and supply curves for public goods, a situation will exist in which households generally want different quantities of tax-supported public goods, and the equilibrium will not be Pareto optimal.

To show how taxes affect the provision of public goods, consider again the two-household economy. Part (a) of Figure 14.9 shows the indifference curve of Household 1 passing through point c as before, but now we assume that Household 1 has a higher income and pays taxes for the provision of the public good. (For reference, the economy's production possibility frontier TT is also shown, and the total economy income is indicated by the vertical intercept of the line tangent to point b.) If no public good is produced, household 1's income is given by the vertical intercept of budget line B^1B^1. Taxes are relatively high, since the income left for the household to spend on private good x falls rapidly along B^1B^1 as g increases. Part (b) shows the budget line B^2B^2 for Household 2, which has a lower income and lower taxes.

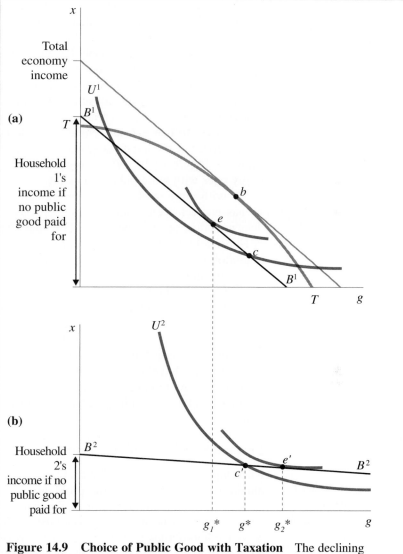

Figure 14.9 Choice of Public Good with Taxation The declining budget lines B^1B^1 and B^2B^2 reflect different taxation levels of the two households to pay for the public good. Household 1, which must pay a large tax when the public good is provided, prefers g_1^* units of public good. Household 2, which pays little tax for the public good, prefers g_2^* units of public good.

Given the income and tax rates of the two households, Household 1 prefers that the public good be provided at quantity g_1^* and Household 2 prefers g_2^*, as shown by the tangencies between their budget lines and indifference curves at e and e'. Both households agree that levels of public good below g_1^* are too low and levels above g_2^* are too high. In between those levels, however, Household 2 wants more public good and Household 1 less. What this means in terms of the consumer sovereignty condition is that the sum of household MRS values is greater than MRT at g_1^*; the sum of MRS values falls below MRT at g_2^*; and equality would occur only at g^*.[19]

The effect of the fixed tax structure on the utility of the two households is shown in Figure 14.10. When no public good is provided, each household's utility rises with more public good. At $g = g_1^*$, Household 1's utility begins to fall with more public good even though the Pareto optimal level of $g = g^*$ has not yet been reached. This happens because the fixed tax structure does not allow taxes to be reduced on heavily taxed Household 1. The utility of Household 2 continues to rise until $g = g_2^*$, after which the utility of both households falls. Even though one point, $g = g^*$, is Pareto optimal, the economy may not choose that point. If taxes could be set optimally, the economy could choose points on the utility frontier to the northeast.[20] A fixed tax structure, however, forces a choice somewhere on the curve between g_1^* and g_2^*. If the economy chooses closer to g_1^* it will please Household 1, and if it chooses closer to g_2^* it will please Household 2.

Given that households' choices are partly determined by how much or how little they have to pay for the public good, there might be a problem in eliciting true preferences for the public good. We can now review some of the more important results that have been found concerning demand revelation.

Demand Revelation Mechanisms

▼
10. Why is demand revelation so important for provision of public goods? What basic problem must it overcome?

Knowing the true demand for a public good is key to finding the optimal quantity to provide. Given the problem just described, that how much one says he likes the public good is dependent on how much what he says determines what he will pay, economists have thought long and hard about ways for households to send ''messages'' revealing their true preferences to decision makers. After all, consumers cast dollar votes that are quite effective in expressing their wishes in competitive markets. Are there not similar mechanisms that might be devised for public goods? Unfortunately, most of the answers that have been found are ''impossibility theorems,'' meaning that a preference revelation mechanism having a minimal set of desirable properties can be shown *not* to exist.

---

19. We know that g^* is Pareto optimal from our discussion of Figure 14.7.
20. Recall from Chapter 12 that the utility frontier is the boundary for possible combinations of household utility in the economy. Points on the utility frontier are Pareto optimal, and points inside the frontier are Pareto suboptimal.

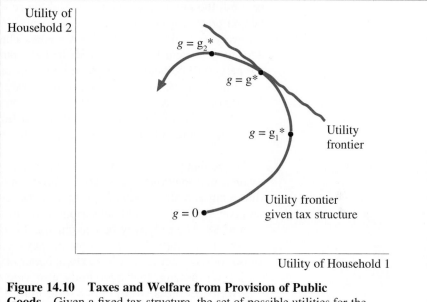

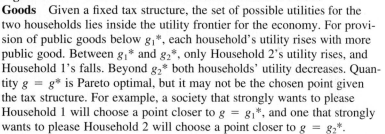

Figure 14.10   Taxes and Welfare from Provision of Public Goods   Given a fixed tax structure, the set of possible utilities for the two households lies inside the utility frontier for the economy. For provision of public goods below g_1^*, each household's utility rises with more public good. Between g_1^* and g_2^*, only Household 2's utility rises, and Household 1's falls. Beyond g_2^* both households' utility decreases. Quantity $g = g^*$ is Pareto optimal, but it may not be the chosen point given the tax structure. For example, a society that strongly wants to please Household 1 will choose a point closer to $g = g_1^*$, and one that strongly wants to please Household 2 will choose a point closer to $g = g_2^*$.

The general nature of these problems can be shown in terms of one of the simpler possible mechanisms. Imagine that a club of 100 members has a meeting to decide whether to arrange a party with a private showing of *Animator II,* a popular but expensive movie. The total cost will be $2,000. In this simple case, all that is needed is for the members to tell what dollar value they place on the party and movie. It is agreed that if the party is held, all members must attend, so the possibility that some people place a negative value on the movie must be taken into account in deciding whether to hold the party.

One member comes up with the following scheme. Since the cost per person is $20, each person starts out paying a subscription fee of $20. Each member then writes down on a piece of paper how much *more* he or she would be willing to pay to have the event. We refer to this as the tax. Negative numbers are permitted. Only if the sum of the votes is greater than zero is the event held. Should the event not be held, the subscription is returned to everyone, but the tax is still paid. To insure that what each person writes is truthful, the member who has devised the scheme explains that the tax each person pays will be adjusted to equal only the additional ''burden'' placed on everybody else by that person's vote. That is, if everybody else's vote adds to $-\$5$, and Jim's vote is $6, he has ''put the project over the top'' and the party will be held. The burden he places on everybody else is $5, so that is the tax he pays. Alternatively, if everybody else's vote sums to $+\$8$, and Jim's vote is $-\$13$, he has stopped the project and caused a burden on everybody else of $8 in lost enjoyment, so Jim pays $8 in tax. If Jim's vote isn't large enough to put the project over the top or to pull it down, he pays zero tax.[21]

To see that this causes Jim to tell the truth, consider each possibility. First, assume that everybody else votes $+\$48$ and Jim's true vote would be $8 (the event is really worth $28 to him). If he tells the truth, he pays no tax, so he gives up only his $20 subscription for an event worth $28 to him, a net gain of $8. The only way he can change this outcome is to vote negative by $-\$48.01$ or more. In that event, he pays a tax of $48 but gets back his subscription, a net loss of $28. He is better off telling the truth.

Second, assume that everybody else votes $+\$9$ and Jim's true vote is $-\$10$ (the event is worth only $10 to him). If he votes the truth, he causes the event not to be held and pays only the tax, a net loss of $9. The only way he could alter this outcome is to vote $-\$8.99$ or higher—that is, a number closer to zero or positive. In that case, the event is held, he pays no tax, but he does pay a subscription fee of $20 for an event that is worth $10 to him, a net loss of $10. Again, he is better off telling the truth.

Performing the same comparisons when everybody else's vote sums to a negative number shows that Jim should always tell the truth. In fact, this mechanism is the only mechanism that (1) induces him to tell the truth regardless of how others vote, (2) causes the party to be held only if the sum of everyone's taxes is nonnegative and if everyone's value from the party exceeds its cost, and (3) guarantees that no one will be worse off than the value he or she places on the party minus the $20 subscription.[22]

Although the mechanism induces everyone to tell the truth, it has several serious failings. First, condition (3) still allows for the fact that some individuals could suffer a significant loss, equal to the subscription fee plus the disutility of the event. There is no guarantee that payment for the public good will be equitable. Second, the scheme may collect too much money (the budget is unbalanced). If a surplus is collected, the outcome will not be Pareto optimal because any use of the money cannot be based on the revelations of the members (they will then have an incentive to misrepresent). On the other hand, if it is used arbitrarily, it will be wasteful. Any attempt to change the scheme to balance the budget will violate one of the three conditions in the

21. For example, if everyone else's vote sums to $-\$5$ and Jim's vote is $4, Jim's vote does not change the outcome and he pays no tax. Likewise, if everybody else's vote sums to $+\$14$ and Jim's vote is $-\$7$, his vote does not change the outcome and he pays no tax.
22. See David M. Kreps, *A Course in Microeconomic Theory,* Princeton, N.J.: Princeton University Press, 1990, pp. 704–713, for a discussion of this mechanism.

preceding paragraph. In short, the only possible mechanism satisfying the three conditions forces us to give up Pareto optimality and an equitable distribution of payments, the very reasons we wanted to find a true revelation of preferences in the first place.

Voting and Provision of Public Goods

▼
11. Is voting a solution to the problem of deciding what quantity of public goods to provide? What are the relevant considerations?

What about straight voting to decide about the quantity of public goods? Will the political process lead to predictable outcomes, and will those outcomes have any particular desirable properties?

Cycle Problems. One problem is that voting does not lead to a consistent ranking of projects, even in simple cases. For example, assume that voters must choose one of thee alternatives for funding: education, roads, or space exploration. Voter 1 ranks the alternatives as (education, roads, space); voter 2 ranks them as (roads, space, education); and voter 3 ranks them as (space, education, roads). Now what happens if a vote is taken between education and roads? Voters 1 and 3 favor education, so it wins. Similarly, if a vote is taken between space and education, voters 2 and 3 favor space, so space wins. Finally, voters 1 and 2 favor roads over space, so roads will beat space in a direct vote. Since there is a cycle, no alternative is unquestionably best. Further, the outcome can be manipulated by controlling the ordering of comparison votes and deciding which run-off should be last.

The Median Voter Result. The problem of cyclicity can be ruled out if there is a common listing of alternatives so that each voter has a preferred position and chooses among the alternatives on the basis of how close they are to the preferred position. In the education, roads, space example, there was no such ordering. Assume now that the issue is what quantity of a public good to provide, for quantities ranging between 0 and 100. A voter whose preferred level of public good is 50 will select between alternatives of, say, 65 and 91 by choosing 65, since that is closer to 50. In this case, it can be shown that the level preferred by the median voter will always win over any alternative. The proof is simple. Assume that 50 is the choice of the median voter (half want a higher number, half want a lower number). Then 50 will win in a vote against any alternative, because the alternative must lie to one side of 50. If the alternative is above 50, for instance, all the people who prefer a lower level will vote for 50, as will all those who have higher preferences that lie closer to 50 than to the alternative. Since 50 gets more than half the votes, it wins. The same result applies regardless of the alternatives or where the median position happens to be in the listing. Although the median voter result gives a definite answer about how much good to provide, conditions for the result to apply do not always hold, and the choice of median voter need not be Pareto optimal, as we will see next.

The Effect of Progressive Taxes on Voting. Although certain voting schemes and preference revelation mechanisms can solve some of the problems inherent in providing public goods, no arrangement deals with all of them. As noted, the median voter result does not apply in all cases, for example. When it does, there is still the problem that voters base their preferences on their perceptions of how much they benefit from the public good compared to how much they pay for it. In this case, the progressivity of the tax system unavoidably becomes relevant to political decisions. In the United States, for example, the highest-earning 5 percent of the population pays 44.2 percent of federal income taxes, while the lowest-earning 40 percent of the population pays 1.7 percent![23] Simple arithmetic tells us that the latter group is eight times larger than the former. Therefore, votes for a government-provided public good will usually be disproportionately reflective of those who pay little for it, though they receive benefits.

Economic science tells us that we would like to have a system for preference revelation that meets three conditions: what is said is divorced from tax payments (so that the truth is told); taxes are charged in proportion to the preference-related benefits received from the public good (the same ones truthfully revealed in the mechanism); and a Pareto optimal quantity of the good is provided without waste. So far, it doesn't seem possible to satisfy all three conditions.

Given the realities of missing markets and public goods, we should not be surprised to see externalities figure prominently in the nightly news and in state houses and capitol buildings around the country. This is microeconomics in action. There *are* correct answers and approaches for dealing with externalities and public goods, just as there are incorrect ones. Understanding the microeconomics allows us to see who has what to gain and what to lose by each course of action, what the trade-offs are, and what principles lead to efficiency.

Summary

Active Reading Guide numbers are given in parentheses at the end of each summary item.

1. Externalities arise when the economic choices of one economic agent have a direct affect on another that does not operate through a market. Externalities can be positive or negative. They can occur between producer and producer, consumer and consumer, or producer and consumer. (1)

2. The presence of an externality indicates a missing market. The missing market could result from ill-defined property rights or from some physical limitation. (2)

3. Coase's theorems show that if bargaining among agents is costless, externalities will be self-correcting, because there will be a joint gain to the agents in changing their behavior. Arrangements

23. *Economic Report of the President, 1992,* Washington, D.C.: U.S. Gov't Printing Office, 1992, pp. 140–141.

can be made to spread the gain in such a way that everyone is better off after the externality is eliminated. In this case, the legal system and property rights rules about who should pay for the damage of externalities do not matter to the resolution. When bargaining is costly, however, the property rights and liability rules affect the resolution of the externality. In general, the legal system should create an incentive for action by the party that has the least costly way of eliminating the externality. (3)

4. Apart from direct bargaining, there are three main ways to eliminate externalities. These are (a) changing the market structure by adjusting property rights so as to establish a market in the externality or internalize the externality through single ownership; (b) instituting a corrective tax; and (c) applying direct regulation. (4)

5. Regulation imposes information demands on the government that the government is not always able to meet. Because government taxes or quantity standards might be set too high, they could cause more social inefficiency than the original externality. In addition, a quantity standard does not generally distinguish which firms are able to help eliminate an externality at least cost, so it can lead to more costly solutions than a tax or a system of marketable emission rights. The size of a tax (or price of a marketable right) shows firms the social cost of an externality and allows them to select in a decentralized way the least costly response. (5)

6. Public goods differ from private goods because they are nonrival and nonexcludable. Nonrival goods are ones that can be consumed by more than one household simultaneously. Pure public goods can be consumed by any number of households, whereas pure private goods can be consumed by just one. Goods in between are sometimes called club goods; they can be consumed effectively by more than one household (as a musical concert can be seen by more than one person), but congestion eventually prevents them from being consumed by more than a limited number of people. Nonexcludability refers to the inability to prevent people from consuming a good they do not pay for. (6)

7. The necessary condition for Pareto optimal provision of a public good is that the sum of marginal rates of substitution of public good for private good across all households be equal to the marginal rate of transformation of public good for private good. This is the consumer sovereignty condition for public goods. (7)

8. Since multiple households benefit from a public good, household demand curves for public goods are added vertically to produce market demand. Providing the public good at the quantity where demand equals supply leads to a Pareto optimum. (8)

9. Nonexcludability leads to the free rider problem, which is that households may avoid paying for a public good but "free ride" on others' provision of it. Because of the free rider and nonexcludability problems, relatively few public goods are provided by private markets. Public provision of public goods, with payment through taxes, is the norm. Given the tax structure, the quantity of public good supplied may not be Pareto optimal, because demand for the public good will vary with the household's tax burden and different households will want different quantities of the good. (9)

10. Economists have searched for demand revelation mechanisms that would induce true reports of household preferences for public goods. The basic problem to be overcome is that those who benefit most should also pay the most for the public good, but what they pay will influence their report about their preferences. Mechanisms exist for which reporting true preferences is the best choice of the household, but they lead to Pareto inefficiency in provision of the public good, and they do not set tax burdens in accordance with relative benefits. (10)

11. Simple voting schemes for choosing public goods can lead to cycle problems, except in special cases such as the median voter case in which alternatives can be clearly ordered. In any event, the progressivity of the tax structure implies that voting for public goods and for the size of government spending will be influenced by how much the household pays for the additional provision of goods and by how many households are in the respective tax groups. (11)

Review Questions

*1. Compare the following two situations:
   a) XYZ Company spills industrial waste into the Salmon Run River, limiting your fishing business to the upstream portion of the river.
   b) XYZ Company buys rights to place its industrial waste in the Salmon Run River, raising the price you have to pay for your use of the upstream part of the river.
In each case, the value of the loss to you is the same. Is an externality present in each case, and if so, what is the social cost?

2. Your neighbor's tree annoys you by leaning over into your yard. You want the tree cut down, and your neighbor does not care whether the tree stays or goes, but neither of you wants to pay for cutting it. As a result nothing happens. Is this Pareto optimal, and does Coase's First Theorem apply?

*3. If Coase's First Theorem is applied to the problem of monopoly, would costless bargaining lead to the elimination of all monopoly? In principle, would Coase's First Theorem imply that *any* equilibrium must be a Pareto optimum?

4. In what way is a tax imposed as a response to an externality a disguised way to ''internalize'' the externality?

*5. How does the use of a tax require less information by the government to achieve least-cost elimination of an externality than the use of direct regulation?

6. Compare the equity and efficiency aspects of a rule that assigns payment of the costs of an externality to the party that has the least costly way to avoid the damage.

*7. Pure private goods are rival and excludable, whereas pure public goods are nonrival and nonexcludable. Are there goods that are nonrival and excludable? Rival and nonexcludable? If so, give examples. If not, explain why not.

8. If not for the excludability and free rider problems, would private provision of public goods be possible? Would private provision lead to a social optimum? Discuss.

*9. Explain in terms of total marginal benefits why individual demand is summed horizontally for pure private goods and vertically for pure public goods.

10. Do you think the distribution of different tax burdens across the population is a significant problem in voting on the level of government-provided public goods? Why or why not?

*11. Explain the following statement: ''In tax-financed public provision of public goods, it is sometimes best not to choose a Pareto optimum, even when one may be feasible.''

Numerical and Graphing Exercises

*1. Describe the externality involved in the problem of pedestrians walking across the grass in a busy college quad, and draw the relevant curves showing the extent of the externality.

2. Community members have two ways to get to the downtown area where most residents work. The land route, costing $1 per trip, is slightly longer but never suffers traffic jams or delays. The second route is by way of a bridge that can become congested. The total cost of using the bridge is $.20n + $.01n^2$, where n is the number of trips taken across the bridge.

   a) If there are 100 trips per day, what percentage of trips will take the bridge and what percentage the land route, assuming that drivers take the route that is cheaper?
   b) What percentage of trips should take the bridge, and what percentage the land route, if the total number of trips is to be accomplished at least cost? (Hint: A graph may be helpful. The MC of the bridge is $.20 + $.02n$.)
   c) What toll on the bridge would induce the right number of trips to take the bridge?

* Asterisks are used to denote questions that are answered at the back of the book.

*3. Shelly and Diane each have to pay $350 per month if they live separately, but they could share an apartment for $500. Unfortunately, an externality is present in that early-riser Shelly disturbs the morning sleep of night-owl Diane. The value to Diane of her lost sleep is $40 per month, and Shelly would be willing conform her sleep habits to Diane's for $100. Analyze the following:
   a) What is the Pareto optimal outcome in this situation?
   b) What will the bargaining outcome be?
   c) What happens if liability is placed on Shelly for the externality of her early rising? If liability is placed on Diane?

4. Two firms produce 50 units each of harmful emissions. The marginal externality reduction cost (MERC) of the first firm is $50 - e$, where e is the level of emissions, and that of the second firm is $25 - e/2$. Permits for 30 units of emissions are issued to each firm.
   a) If the permits are not tradable, what will be each firm's emissions and MERC?
   b) If permits *are* tradable, how will the emissions and MERC change for each firm? Also, what will be the market price of a permit for one unit of emissions and the overall cost savings? (Hint: You may find it helpful to draw a diagram.)

*5. The MERC for a firm emitting harmful emissions is $100 - e$, where e is the level of emissions. The marginal harm to society from additional emissions is given by the marginal externality cost $-20 + e$.
   a) What is the level of emissions without any government intervention, and what is the optimal level of emissions?
   b) If the government sets an emission tax to induce the optimal level of emissions, how high should it be set per unit of emission?
   c) Assume the government sets an emission standard 10 percent below the optimum level

of emissions. What is the social cost of this relative to the optimum?
   d) Assume that the government sets an emission charge that is 10 percent too high, compared to the level that would elicit the optimal emission level. What is the social cost of this relative to the optimum?

*6. The marginal cost of providing a public good g is $200 per unit. Household 1's demand for the good is $100 - p_1/2$; Household 2's demand is $200 - 2p_2$; and Household 3's demand is $100 - 2p_3$.
   a) What is the Pareto optimal quantity of the public good?
   b) How much should each household pay for it? (Hint: How does total price paid for the good relate to the prices individual households pay when demand curves are added vertically?)

*7. Using the information in the preceding problem, assume that the three households are deciding whether to provide the optimal quantity of the public good. What will the outcome be if they use the demand revelation mechanism described on pages 573–574? Describe each person's payments and revealed value for that quantity of good.

8. Assume that public and private goods can be provided according to the production possibility frontier given by $x^1 + x^2 + g = 20$, where x^1 and x^2 are the quantities of the private good going to Households 1 and 2, respectively. Each household has the utility function $U = xg$.
   a) If the first household's utility is held at 50, and g units of public good are provided, how many units of private good are available for the other household?
   b) What is the utility of the second household in terms of units of g chosen?
   c) Find the choice of g that maximizes the second household's utility, given that the first household is held at utility 50.

INVESTIGATIONS IV

A. Economic Aspects of a Greenhouse Gases Tax

Growing worldwide awareness of environmental changes brought on by gaseous emissions has led to proposals to tax the more problematic airborne pollutants. This investigation looks at economic aspects of these proposals.

The Scope of the Problem

Greenhouse gases get their name from the potential they possess to create a greenhouse-like effect in the earth's atmosphere by trapping solar energy and causing global warming. The main greenhouse gases are carbon dioxide (CO_2), chlorofluorocarbons (CFCs), methane (CH_4), and nitrous oxide (N_2O). Because most greenhouse gases involve carbon—or are closely related to the emission of carbon in the burning of coal, oil, or gas—controlling carbon emissions is the main object of economic policy and scientific study.

Table IV.1 displays data showing the change in greenhouse gas concentrations in the past 250 years. As shown there, carbon dioxide, methane, and nitrous oxide are present today in significantly larger concentrations than in the preindustrial era. Chlorofluorocarbons, moreover, were unknown in the earlier period. The growth rates are also shown. In 1950, global carbon dioxide emissions were an estimated 1.5 billion tons per year. Today, emissions are more than 6 billion tons per year.[1]

Estimates of future emissions depend on the growth of world economies and the corresponding growth in demand for fuel. One study estimates growth in total final energy demand and fossil-fuel demand at 1.4 and 0.9 percent a year, respectively.[2] Likely growth in global CO_2 emissions is between 0.5 and 1.5 percent per year for the foreseeable future. By the year 2075, estimates place carbon emissions somewhere between 50 percent higher and more than double present levels. Some projections say that carbon emissions could reach as high as 25 billion tons per year by 2100 if no steps are taken to reduce emissions.

Higher emissions will lead to an increase in global temperatures between 0.2° C and 0.5° C per decade over the next century, according to current

1. Peter Hoeller, Andrew Dean, and Jon Nicolaisen, "Macroeconomic Implications of Reducing Greenhouse Gas Emissions: A Survey of Empirical Studies," *OECD Economic Studies,* No. 16 (Spring 1991), p. 55.
2. W. D. Nordhause and G. W. Yohe, "Future Carbon Dioxide Emissions from Fossil Fuels," in National Academy of Science, *Changing Climate,* Washington, 1983; cited in Hoeller, Dean, and Nicolaisen, op. cit., p. 54.

Table IV.1   Summary of Major Greenhouse Gas Concentrations

Era	Carbon Dioxide (ppmv)	Methane (ppmv)	CFC-11 (pptv)	CFC-12 (pptv)	Nitrous Oxide (ppbv)
Preindustrial era (1750–1800)	280	0.8	0	0	288
Present day (1990)	353	1.72	280	484	310
Current growth rate per year	1.8	0.015	9.5	17	0.8
	(0.50%)	(0.90%)	(4.00%)	(4.00%)	(0.25%)
Average atmospheric lifetime (years)	50–200	10	65	130	150

Notes: ppmv = parts per million by volume; ppbv = parts per billion by volume; pptv = parts per trillion by volume.

Source: Peter Hoeller, Andrew Dean, and Jon Nicolaisen, "Macroeconomic Implications of Reducing Greenhouse Gas Emissions: A Survey of Empirical Studies," OECD Economic Studies, *No. 16 (Spring 1991), Table A1, p. 74. © by OECD Economic Studies.*

estimates.[3] Cumulative effects of increased emission of greenhouse gases imply total warming between 1.5° C and 4.5° C by the end of the next century, with the width of the range reflecting uncertainties about future emission levels and about interaction effects involving the atmosphere and the world's oceans. Slowing warming to 0.1° C per decade (half the low-end estimate of current increase) would require halving greenhouse gases from current levels.

For comparison, global temperatures are reported to have increased 0.3° to 0.7° C over the last century, although the increase cannot be ascribed with certainty to the greenhouse effect. According to scientists, the 1991 eruption of Mount Pinatubo in the Philippines, a natural event, appears to have spread enough dust and ash into the higher atmosphere to lower the earth's temperature as much as 1° C by blocking some of the sun's rays. Thus the exact size of the greenhouse effect is still in question, though even conservative estimates say it is potentially large enough to warm the global climate twice as many degrees in the next 100 years as in the past century.

The Policy Response

As we learned in Chapter 14, economic theory would say that emissions of greenhouse gases should be reduced to the point where the marginal externality reduction cost equals the marginal social benefits from lower emissions. Unfortunately, little is known about the effects of global warming, and the lower estimates of warming may in fact be within the range of variation observed from natural phenomena. Consequently, the marginal benefits from avoiding global warming are difficult to estimate.

3. Peter Hoeller and Markku Wallin, "Energy Prices, Taxes and Carbon Dioxide Emissions," *OECD Economic Studies,* No. 17 (Autumn 1991), p. 92.

In spite of the lack of firm evidence on the costs of warming, advanced countries have agreed to phase out most CFCs by the end of this decade,[4] and the 1988 climate-change conference in Toronto proposed that countries reduce their CO_2 emissions by 20 percent from 1988 levels—this target to be achieved by 2005—and by 50 percent from 1988 levels in the longer run.[5] Without further data, economists are unable to estimate the benefits of reducing greenhouse gases, but they can estimate the effects of higher prices caused by higher taxes on emission levels. In other words, we can examine the costs of reaching the target levels of emission reduction by means of different types of taxes.

Fuel Prices and Carbon Emission Levels

Most proposals for reducing greenhouse gases involve taxing carbon emissions. We therefore need to know how higher prices relate to the use of carbon-containing fuels. Evidence that energy use would be susceptible to tax-induced higher prices includes the fact that the ratio of aggregate energy input to aggregate output *fell* in advanced countries by more than 20 percent between 1970 and the late 1980s. We also observe different levels of energy use per unit of output across countries where prices are different, suggesting that energy use can be reduced if there is a cost incentive. The United States, for example, has energy prices much lower than those of most other advanced countries, and it has higher carbon emissions per unit of GDP. Switzerland and Norway, on the other hand, have prices for fuel (measured per ton of carbon emission) approaching three times that of the United States and emission levels per unit of GDP about one-third that of the United States. Letting e be kilograms of carbon emissions per unit of GDP and p the price of fossil fuel per ton of emission, countries seem to fall somewhere on the algebraic relationship $\ln e = -2.51 - 1.04 \ln p$.[6] Applying our knowledge of demand and elasticity from Chapter 2 and Investigations I, we know that this equation implies nearly a unit elastic relationship between price and energy use, since a 1-percent increase in the price of fossil fuels leads to a 1.04-percent reduction in use in the long run.

Economic Costs of Emission Reduction

In Chapter 14 we talked about taxing emissions to raise their price so that firms and households would reduce emissions or cut their use of emission-causing fuels. How large does the tax on the carbon content of fuels have to be to achieve target emission reductions, and how costly are taxes of that magnitude? Applying a uniform $100 tax per ton of carbon emissions on

4. The countries include the United States, Canada, the United Kingdom, Australia, New Zealand, Norway, Finland, Denmark, Germany, France, Japan, Italy, Austria, Belgium, Greece, Ireland, Luxembourg, the Netherlands, Portugal, Spain, and Sweden (ibid., p. 93).
5. A 20-percent reduction relative to 1988 levels implies approximately a 40-percent reduction from the level that is predicted for 2005 in the absence of any action.
6. Hoeller and Wallin, op. cit., p. 95.

countries in the Organization for Economic Cooperation and Development (OECD, comprised essentially of the advanced countries of the world) would result in a reduction of emissions by about 25 percent. The United States would go from its 1988 effective tax on carbon content of $207 to a tax of $307, resulting in emission reductions of 34 percent. For countries like Norway and Switzerland, where prices are already high, the same absolute increase would lead to reductions of only about 15 percent. Cutting global emissions by 50 percent would require a tax of about $300 per ton.

Increasing the price of a fuel by $100 per ton of carbon content would raise the price of oil by about $12 per barrel from its market price of $15 to $20 per barrel in the late 1980s and early 1990s. The same tax on carbon content would increase the price of coal from $44 per metric ton to about $104. For comparison, the price of oil reached $50 per barrel in 1981 (in 1990 dollars), which would be the equivalent of adding $245 tax per ton of carbon to a price at $20.

Studies indicate that to stabilize emissions at 1990 levels, emission taxes would have to grow over time, ranging between $30 and $150 per ton of carbon up to the year 2020. Taxes to achieve a 20-percent reduction, the Toronto recommendation, would need to be higher, over $200 per ton of carbon in North America and Europe and over $900 in some areas.

The effect of such higher fuel costs would show up in lower GDP and lower growth rates. Most studies assume long-run growth of around 2 percent over the next century, with decreases from the baseline of between zero and 0.3 percentage points for achieving carbon emission reductions on the order of 20 percent. For example, a Congressional Budget Office study estimated that the effect in the United States would be to lower growth between 0.1 and 0.2 percentage points annually to the year 2000, and to lower GDP at the end-year relative to the baseline by 0.6 to 2 percent.[7] (For comparison, the recessions of 1974, 1975, 1982, and 1991 involved drops in real GDP of 0.6, 0.8, 2.2, and 0.7 percent, respectively.) Thus the costs, measured either in terms of the effect on the price of oil or in terms of the potential effect on output, appear to be quite high, but within the range of costs experienced in the past by the United States.

Welfare and Distributional Aspects

As Chapter 14 explained, an important issue in dealing with externalities and the provision of public goods involves the distribution of costs and benefits: who pays the costs and who reaps the benefits? If carbon emission taxes are instituted worldwide, we must ask *where* the taxes should be levied (in what countries), *who* should get the revenues, and whether all regions should reduce emissions to the same absolute level per capita. Collecting production taxes from fossil fuel exporters would have much the same effects as having

7. Congressional Budget Office, *Carbon Charges as a Response to Global Warming: The Effect of Taxing Fossil Fuels,* Washington, D.C., August 1990; cited in Hoeller, Dean, and Nicolaisen, op. cit. p. 59.

oil exporters institute cartel-like prices on oil, since the taxes would result in higher market prices. Higher prices result in lost consumer surplus. Assuming a global reduction in emissions averaging 50 percent for the 40-year period ending in 2030, welfare would decline in all regions of the globe except for oil-exporting countries. Estimates suggest drops in welfare of 4.3 percent for North America, 4.4 percent for the world as a whole, and 7.1 percent for the less developed countries (LDCs).[8] On the other hand, if a consumption tax were levied, importing countries would retain the tax collections, and the cost to North America would be a 1.2-percent drop in welfare, compared to 2.1 percent for the world as a whole and 4.5 percent for LDCs.

The differences in welfare effects also depend on how the taxes affect the relative prices of goods traded internationally and on the efficiency of the taxes themselves in achieving a 50-percent reduction in emissions. If a global production tax on carbon content of fuels were instituted, with the revenues redistributed worldwide according to population rather than according to who paid the taxes, the loss to North America would be 9.8 percent, compared to a loss of 4.2 percent for the world as a whole and a *gain* of 1.8 percent for LDCs. The most costly scenario, as we would expect from our study of corrective taxes for externalities in Chapter 14, would result from requiring all regions to reduce emissions to the same absolute standard, a per-capita emission ceiling. In that case, North America would suffer a whopping welfare loss of 18.6 percent and the world a loss of 8.5 percent, whereas LDCs would decline in welfare by 1.2 percent. Table IV.2 provides the breakdown by region and by proposal.

Suggestions for Further Investigation. (a) Do you think we should go ahead with plans to tax carbon emissions, or should we wait for further information? Why? (b) Assuming self-interest as the motivation, what plan do you think LDCs would favor for reducing global emissions? How do you think they would justify their position to the rest of the world?

B. Economies in Transition from Plan to Market

The techniques and methods of economic management used for more than sixty years in the USSR and for more than forty in other socialist countries have proved their ineffectiveness and nonrationality.

Wojciech Pruss, East European expert[9]

---

8. See John Whalley and R. Wigle, ''The International Incidence of Carbon Taxes,'' paper prepared for ''Economic Policy Responses to Global Warming,'' a conference held at Torino, Italy, September 1990; cited in Hoeller, Dean, and Nicolaisen, op. cit., p. 66.
9. Wojciech Pruss, ''Market Is the Only Escape,'' *Eastern European Economics,* 28 (Spring 1990), p. 30.

Table IV.2 Regional Welfare Effects of Reducing Global Carbon Emissions by 50 Percent (Percentage Change in Welfare)

Country	National Production Taxes	National Consumption Taxes	Global Production Tax Distributed by Population	Per-Capita Emission Ceiling
North America	−4.3	−1.2	−9.8	−18.6
Oil Exporters	4.5	−16.7	−13	−15.1
LDCs	−7.1	−4.5	1.8	−1.2
European Community (EC)	−4	1.4	−3.8	−6.4
Japan	−3.7	3	−0.9	−2.5
World	−4.4	−2.1	−4.2	−8.5

Source: John Whalley and R. Wigle, "The International Incidence of Carbon Taxes," paper prepared for "Economic Policy Responses to Global Warming," a conference held at Torino, Italy, September 1990; cited in Hoeller, Dean, and Nicolaisen, "Macroeconomic Implications" (referenced in Table IV.1), p. 66.

Under the conditions of a planned economy with a preponderance of state property, there was no such thing as consumer sovereignty anyway.

> *Fred S. Oldenburg, East European expert[10]*

The work ethic changed completely in East Germany. . . . After forty-five years of communist regime . . . [today we begin] the transformation of a society based on feelings of jealousy into an achievement-oriented society.

> *André Leysen, member, Chairman's Committee of the Treuhandanstalt (German Transition Agency), Berlin[11]*

The coming down of the Berlin Wall on November 9, 1989, signified more than the end of a repressive communist regime. Along with the toppling of five other communist regimes in Eastern Europe by the end of 1989, it marked the beginning of a great economic experiment to see how effectively and quickly the catalogue of failures of central planning

10. Fred S. Oldenburg, "The October Revolution in the GDR—System, History, and Causes," *Eastern European Economics*, 29 (Fall 1990), p. 59.
11. André Leysen, "Privatization: East Germany," *Eastern European Economics*, 30 (Fall 1991), p. 29.

could be reversed. There was no turning to the textbooks; everything had to be done for the first time. Chapter 13 claimed that a perfectly competitive market system achieves Pareto optimality. Exactly how great a difference does a market system make? This investigation looks both at the effects of central planning in Eastern Europe and at the first steps to undo past damage. The end of the process will not be reached until the beginning of the next century, but initial results will be seen in many countries before then.

The Economic Consequences of Socialist Central Planning

The inherent problems of socialist central planning have been observed first-hand for over two generations in communist countries, especially in Eastern Europe, as well as during periods of social experiment in other countries.[12] The failures are ideological as well as economic.

Causes of Planning Inefficiency. The economic inefficiencies in central planning have been attributed by scholars to a number of causes.[13] In Chapter 13 we learned that the price system performs an information- and incentive-creating function that guides profit-maximizing firms and utility-maximizing households to achieve a Pareto optimum. However, nationalized production leads to usurpation of the decision-making function of the proprietor by the state, so that producers are unable to determine the aims of production. The constraints imposed on economic planning by social ideology are another factor inhibiting performance. The state becomes an instrument of the ruling elite, while a larger, ever more unwieldy and lifeless bureaucratic administrative structure replaces the market. The tendency of central planning to use monopolistic enterprises also leads to noncompetitive production units and ineffective competition. In Hungary, for example, one enterprise provided all of the sugar refining for the entire country. Even after this was broken into separate companies for each county, regional monopolies still prevailed because of the high costs of transporting sugar beets to refineries in other countries.[14]

The reliance on large firms compared to small and medium-sized ones is a separate but related problem deriving from (1) the fact that planning is simpler for a smaller number of relatively homogeneous units, (2) the empire-building tendencies of planning managers, and (3) ideological preferences.[15]

12. See, for example, John Jewkes, *The New Ordeal by Planning,* New York: St. Martin's Press, 1968. Motivated by British experiences in the late 1940s and early 1960s, Jewkes seeks to explain the intrinsic forces leading to the problems of central planning.
13. See Jurgen Junger, Werner Maiwald, and Siegfried Stotzer, ''Economic Reform in the GDR,'' *Eastern European Economics,* 30 (Fall 1991), p. 32.
14. Marvin Jackson, ''Promoting Efficient Privatization: The Benefits of Small Enterprises Versus Large Ones,'' *Eastern European Economics,* 30 (Fall 1991), p. 9. We discussed the social costs of monopoly in Chapter 8.
15. Ibid., p. 4.

Table IV.3	Relative Sizes of Industrial Plants, Central Planning Versus Market Systems		
	Capitalist Countries		*Socialist Countries*
	Small	Large	
Total industry			
Percentage of workers employed in large firms	19	36	50
Average firm employment	80	138	197
Heavy industry			
Percentage of workers employed in large firms	30	48	62
Average firm employment	89	176	293
Light industry			
Percentage of workers employed in large firms	7	17	35
Average firm employment	55	90	146

Note: Large firms are defined as those with over 1,000 employees.

Source: Eva Ehrlich, "The Size Structure of Manufacturing Establishments and Enterprises: An International Comparison," Journal of Comparative Economics, 9.3 (September 1985), pp. 278–283; Used by permission of Academic Press, Inc.

Table IV.3 compares the relative employment sizes of manufacturing units in socialist countries and comparably sized Western countries. In socialist countries, the percentage of workers employed in large firms is twice that of large Western countries for light industry, 30 percent higher for heavy industry, and 40 percent higher for manufacturing as a whole. The figures are even more disparate if the comparison is made between socialist countries and small capitalist countries.

Unlike the market system we studied in Chapter 13, in which prices are an important signal for efficient resource use, planned economies often have distorted prices. Prices in East Germany at the end of 1989, described by one expert as having "developed into a perfect schizophrenia," serve as an example.[16] Planners considered it a proof of their success if they could keep the price of bread stable. On the other hand, they felt the need to discourage their citizens from buying certain foreign products (using scarce foreign currency). Thus bread rolls costing 10 pfennigs to make were being stubbornly sold for 5 pfennigs, while the price of a Mark Sanyo videocassette recorder was set at an enormous 7,350 marks!

Central planning also was not very kind to its environment. "An especially sad manifestation of the resolute exploitation of all production factors was

16. Irwin Collier, "GDR Economic Policy During the Honecker Era," *Eastern European Economics,* 29 (Fall 1990), p. 20.

not only the neglect of workers' safety, but also the incredible environmental devastation,'' writes one observer. ''Pollution of the rivers, the destruction of the forests, and an utterly unparalleled overexploitation of human health'' was the result.[17]

The Human Element. Ultimately, inefficiency takes its toll in terms of its human impact. Labor productivity in West Germany, for example, was 40 percent higher than in East Germany at reunification, and the East German infrastructure, including water, sewage, electricity, gas, heating, roads, and highways, and transportation in general, was especially backward.[18] Estimates of the standard of living[19] in the planned economies of Eastern Europe show dramatic differences when compared to their Western European counterparts. Table IV.4 reports the standard of living of the European socialist countries in 1980, compared to countries in the rest of the world. As the table shows, the socialist countries had a standard of living roughly half that of the initial members of the European Economic Community (EC), and less than one-third that of the United States.

Table IV.5 presents more information about the effects of central planning by comparing centrally planned economies with market economies that were roughly equivalent in 1937. The centrally planned economies failed to keep pace with their market counterparts as measured in the years 1960, 1970, and 1980. For the planned economies, the end of the 1980s saw the plants out-dated, the buildings not suitable for modern production, the warehouses too large, and the personnel unacquainted with modern production processes.[20] As just one example of the differences in lifestyle implied by these figures, we can compare the housing stocks of the two Germanies. In 1970 to 1971, only 39 percent of East German dwellings had a bath or shower, compared to over 68 percent for West Germany. Only 39 percent in East Germany had a private toilet, compared to 79 percent for West Germany. By 1978, 86 percent of West Germany's dwellings had bath or shower and 92 percent had a toilet; in contrast, only 72 percent had a toilet in East Germany and 79 percent a bath or shower at the time of unification.[21]

The Privatization Process

How does one go about shifting a planned economy to a market system? In broadest terms, one has to legalize diverse forms of ownership to replace state ownership. As the discussion of Ronald Coase's ideas reminded us in

---

17. Oldenburg, op. cit., p. 60.
18. Ibid., p. 59.
19. Many socialist planned economies did not record GDP, and exchange rates with Western currencies were often unreliable indicators of relative purchasing power. Hungary, Poland, and the former Soviet Union began recording GDP in national currency only in 1970, 1986, and 1988, respectively, for example. See Eva Ehrlich, ''The Competition Among Countries, 1937–1986,'' *Eastern European Economics,* 29 (Winter 1990–1991), p. 80.
20. Leysen, op. cit., p. 32.
21. Collier, op. cit., p. 11.

Table IV.4   Living Standards of Major Country Groupings, 1980

Countries	GDP (U.S. $/capita)	Scale (U.S.A. = 100)
North European developed economies	8,650	74.7
Initial members of the EC ("the Six")	6,970	60.2
Present members of the EC ("the Twelve")	6,291	54.3
European market economies	5,837	50.4
South European market economies (without Turkey)	3,623	31.3
European small socialist countries	**3,476**	**30**
Less developed European market economies	2,504	21.6

Source: Eva Ehrlich, "The Competition Among Countries, 1937–1986." From the Journal of Comparative Economics, 9.3, September 1985 issue. Used by permission of Academic Press, Inc.

Table IV.5   Comparison of Development Levels of Socialist and Market Economies

Country Pairings	Relative Dollars per Capita GDP			
	1937	1960	1970	1980
West Germany/East Germany	1	1.42	1.41	1.55
Austria/Czechoslovakia	1.12	1.1	1.29	1.43
Italy/Czechoslovakia	0.8	0.7	0.94	1.02
Italy/Hungary	1.12	1.16	1.43	1.36
Spain/Hungary	0.79	0.78	1.04	1.12
Spain/Poland	0.95	0.8	1.14	1.3
Greece/Yugoslavia	1.15	1.03	1.2	1.24
Greece/Rumania	1.13	1	1.29	1.28
Spain/Soviet Union	0.9	0.75	0.99	1.04
Average	0.99	0.97	1.19	1.26

Source: Ehrlich, "The Competition Among Countries" (cited in Table IV.4). From the Journal of Comparative Economics, 9.3, September 1985 issue. Used by permission of Academic Press, Inc.

Chapter 14, social infrastructure and properly functioning markets require property rights. The first phase of transition to a market economy therefore requires defining the laws concerning enterprise, property rights, foreign investment, and so on.[22] At the same time, new private enterprises need to be encouraged and state firms returned to the private sector. This may include encouraging foreign firms to bring in capital and embarking on joint ventures

22. Ibid., p. 10.

with foreign enterprises.[23] Methods for transferring state firms into private hands include the two-stage process of first converting state firms into joint-stock companies, then selling the shares to private investors. Other methods include breaking up the larger state enterprises and selling the smaller units, and reprivatizing, meaning returning land, buildings, and companies to their previous private owners.[24] In this process, the shortage of trained managers, accountants, bankers, entrepreneurs, and lawyers has been a major hindrance. Foreign joint ventures partly compensate for this lack. In the case of East Germany, a manager of a state enterprise directing 40,000 people was asked what depreciation method he used. The response was, "What is depreciation?"[25]

In the second phase of economy conversion, as many prices as possible must be brought into line with market levels. Prices in nearby market economies offer a guide, as do world prices for many items. Initially, certain subsidies and taxes are needed to keep the dislocations from becoming too great in a short space of time.

After enterprises begin operating on the basis of price incentives, the third phase involves gradually diminishing the subsidies and letting labor and other inputs be allocated on the basis of price. Capital markets also become fully functional in this stage.[26]

East Germany. East Germany offers a glimpse of the privatization process when it is attempted in as short a time as possible. Germany had to react speedily to prevent major movements of the East German work force into West Germany, the collapse of the East German productive system, massive unemployment, and social stress. The common background and language and the application of the legal structure of West Germany to East Germany provided benefits in the transition that other countries did not have.[27] Nevertheless, the problems associated with shifting East Germany to a market system have proven to be significant.

The feelings of the people of the two Germanies were characterized by the statements quoted in one contemporary report. In the East, people said such things as "We lost the war along with you but we suffered forty-five years longer. We have to be compensated." In the West, a typical reply was: "It's time the East Germans learned to work. Nothing was given to us for free after 1945. We had to work hard for everthing."[28] Much of the trans-

23. Jan Svejnar, "A Framework for the Economic Transformation of Czechoslovakia," *Eastern European Economics,* 29 (Winter 1990–1991), p. 12.
24. Jackson, op. cit., p. 3.
25. Leysen, op. cit., p. 32.
26. Svejnar, op. cit., p. 26.
27. The speed of progress varied in different countries. As of the fall of 1991, Hungary had privatized only 8 to 10 percent of the companies (330), compared to 70 percent of its enterprises (2,200) that it planned to privatize. In Czechoslovakia, the privatization of large-scale enterprises was barely under way. In Poland, only 100 to 150 enterprises of more than 3,500 had been privatized by April 1991, though the figure rose to 250 by May and 650 more privatizations were planned for the remainder of the year (Jackson, op. cit., pp. 11, 12).
28. Leysen, op. cit., p. 29.

formation to a market economy was a transformation of the mind as well as of the physical and legal structures.

To supervise the incorporation of East Germany into West Germany, a trust institution (Treuhandanstalt) was created; its supervisory board was made up of ministers from the new state regions, civil servants, secretaries of state from the finance and economics ministries in Bonn (West Germany's capital), a representative of the central bank, an East German head of *kombinate* (an East German enterprise unit), West German and foreign entrepreneurs, and high-level representatives of the union of the two previous governments—23 members in all. The Treuhand, as it was commonly called, was given oversight of some 8,000 enterprises with 6.9 million employees, 10 million acres of land (1.3 times the size of Belgium), 30,000 commercial outlets, 700 bookshops, 900 movie theaters, and holiday centers with more than 40,000 beds.[29]

Conversion of these enterprises to private hands was hindered by the fact that there were only 100 telephone lines to the West at the beginning of the process. Moreover, if all uneconomical enterprises had been closed, some 3 to 4 million people would have became unemployed immediately. The shipbuilding plant in Rostock, for example, representing 60 percent of the work force of the region of Mecklenburg, was uneconomical and capable of losing some 2 billion marks per year if no changes were made. Even if restructured, it was considered to be a money loser. Therefore, the decision to close it or keep it running a little longer had to take into account the effect of turning 60 percent of the area's work force out of a job.[30] In the initial phase after reunification, from July to September 1990, the Treuhand gave financial help to ailing industries, 27 billion marks, without asking many questions, just to keep things afloat. In the few months following, this aid was dropped to 3 billion marks, and eventually support was restricted to the most pressing and necessary privatization proposals in enterprises that could survive on their own after a year or two.

The strongest need was to establish many small and medium-sized firms. The missing ingredient was usually experienced personnel. For example, under the old system firms could not trust their supply and distribution system. As a result, firms tried to achieve a sort of autarky, producing for themselves as much as possible. The firms often made their own tools, even their own nails. Yet a firm with a large technical staff and purchasing department might have only *one* sales staff person, because under the old system the only buyer was the government.[31] Another constraint was found to be the treatment of property confiscated by the old regime. Under the unification treaty, the restoring of confiscated property was to take priority over compensation. The result was that the courts became clogged with over 1 million cases for

29. Ibid., p. 30. Treuhand property is estimated at 500 billion marks in value, but since East German debts from the past are much higher, "all that is left of the ex-GDR is debris and a mountain of debts" (p. 40).
30. Ibid., p. 33.
31. Ibid., p. 32.

restitution, 50,000 in Berlin alone.[32] This slowed the transfer of firms to the private sector and impeded investment, because title to land and property could not be obtained.

The Germans gave top priority to property privatization. Everything that could be sold was sold immediately, when buyers were available. To speed matters, privatization was decentralized by transferring decisions to some 15 regional suboffices of the Treuhand, accounting for 5,000 firms, leaving 2,000 to 3,000 companies to be handled in the Berlin office. Some 30 percent of the Treuhand's holdings were disposed of by the fall of 1991; 40 percent of the enterprises were to be discontinued as soon as circumstances permitted (probably within several years); and the remainder were to be restructured and then sold. The total extent of the transformation is suggested by fact that East Germans before unification had 55 percent of their work force in industry, compared to about 25 percent in the West. Shifting to Western standards would mean that about 2 million of 7 million East German members of the work force will have to change sectors.

It is too soon to report on the effects of privatization on East Germans' income and standard of living. However, those currently engaged in the process feel the transition can be fully accomplished by the end of the decade if five elements are present: (1) a commitment to shift to private enterprise; (2) the legal framework to permit the transition; (3) complete elimination of the communist power structure; (4) government funds for infrastructure building; and (5) private investment to build up industry.[33]

Suggestions for Further Investigation. (a) If you were a West German considering investing in East Germany, what would be your most important concerns? What if you were an American investing in Poland or Russia? (b) In disposing of state firms after converting them to joint-stock companies, do you think the proceeds of the sale should be kept by the government, or do you think shares should be distributed to citizens who would then be able to sell them and keep the proceeds? (c) In a country making the transition from a socialist to a market economy, should foreign firms be able to bid for shares of domestic firms? Would this be good or bad for the price of the shares?

32. Ibid., p. 35.
33. Ibid., p. 38.

PART FIVE

RISK AND TIME

Up to now, our models have not taken into account the roles that risk and time play in household and firm decision making. The following two chapters extend our basic model by applying the tools we have already learned to deal with both issues. We will see that with proper reinterpretation of variables our existing theory can handle both topics quite well.

CHAPTER 15

Decision Making Under Risk

In this chapter we extend the household's decision making to conditions of risk. After discussing what we mean by risk and different degrees of aversion to it, we characterize the household's decision making under risk as a maximization problem, subject to a budget constraint involving the risky assets available to the household. The next section explains how market prices for risky assets are determined and the strategies that households use to manage risk in their purchases. The last section discusses another important risky asset, insurance.

ACTIVE READING GUIDES

After reading this chapter, you should be able to answer the Active Reading Guides listed below. These guides also appear in the page margins, near the material to which they refer.

1. What makes a given decision risky?

2. Give an example of computing expected value and standard deviation.

3. Define, and give the formula for, expected utility.

4. Draw representative utility of income curves for (a) a risk averse investor, (b) a risk neutral investor, and (c) a risk loving investor.

5. What is a risk premium?

6. Explain the economic arguments against gambling.

7. How do demand and supply determine a security's price and its risk premium?

8. How can a diversification strategy reduce risk?

9. Give an example showing how an insurance company uses risk pooling.

10. Explain moral hazard and adverse selection in insurance markets in terms of asymmetric information.

15.1 What Is Risk?

Every homeowner faces risk, the chance that a natural disaster—a flood, a hurricane, a tornado, an earthquake, a fire—will damage or destroy the home. Households also face risk when they must decide where to place their retirement savings: should the money go into stocks or bonds, this pension fund or that pension fund? College students face risk when they choose their major: will their choice lead to a well-paying job upon graduation and a career in which they can be productive and happy? Households respond to the inevitable vicissitudes of life by developing ways to manage and reduce risk. Describing household attitudes toward risk, their decision making in the presence of risk, and the market devices that have arisen to manage risk is the purpose of this chapter.

Risk and Probability

Our first task is to make clear what we mean by risk. When you make a decision that leads to a sure outcome, you have made a *deterministic* decision. When you make a decision that leads to an unsure outcome, you are dealing with *risk*. In the case of risk, your choice does not determine the outcome with certainty; it determines only that one of a set of random possible outcomes will occur. There is a risk that the outcome may not be the one you prefer.

For example, when you flip a coin you know two things: either the coin lands with heads showing, or (equally likely) it lands with tails showing. You thus know the *set of possible outcomes* (heads or tails) and the *probability* of each type of outcome occurring (a 50–50 chance). Betting on the flip of a coin therefore entails risk.

> ***Risk** is the possibility of different outcomes occurring, some of which are less desirable than others and may entail loss, when the probability of different outcomes is known.*

▼
1. What makes a given decision risky?

To describe decision making under risk, it is necessary to know the list of possible outcomes and the probability that each will occur. For example, assume you buy a corporate discount bond for $791 today in return for being able to turn in the bond for its $1,000 face value two years from now. If you know that you will not sell the bond before its redemption, the possible outcomes are that you will get your $1,000 (most likely) or that the corporation will go bankrupt and you will get nothing (less likely). What you are really buying, then, is an asset that pays you $1,000 in a certain circumstance (that the firm does not go bankrupt) and zero otherwise. How you decide to buy such a commodity is just another example of the household optimization problem we discussed in Chapters 3 and 4. Once we learn how to think of decisions under risk as buying particular assets, we can apply the same optimization techniques. The process also applies to other risky choices that can entail almost anything—whether you get rained on if you do not take your umbrella to the game, or whether a particular question will be on the next test.

How much you take a particular outcome into account in your decision making depends partly on how likely you think that outcome is. Every time you cross the street, for example, there is a small chance that you will not see a car coming your way and be run over. Because the probability of that happening is low (if you are fairly careful in looking both ways), you cross the street frequently. The likelihood of an outcome occurring is its probability. For example, a die has six faces, so the probability of rolling a 3 is $\frac{1}{6}$ or 16.7 percent. The probability of rolling two 3s in a row is $0.16667 \times 0.16667 = 0.02777$, or about 2.8 percent, and the probability of rolling a particular sequence of four numbers drops to less than eight one-hundredths of one percent! We can determine the probabilities governing the roll of a die by performing repeated trials.

> ***Probability*** *is the percentage of outcomes in which a particular outcome would occur in repeated trials of the identical decision.*

Philosophers disagree about the meaning of probability when it deals with a unique situation that leads to a set of uncertain outcomes. Without the ability to repeat the experiment, the usual meaning for probability would seem not to apply. Thus, some economists distinguish between *risk,* in which a random set of outcomes can occur for which one knows the probabilities, and *uncertainty,* in which a random set of outcomes can occur for which one does not know the probabilities. Though we will follow this distinction in the chapter, many economists believe the distinction is unimportant because we can always *imagine* repeated trials and from them select *subjective probabilities.* (The word *subjective* means related to a person's belief, as opposed to objective probabilities, which have their existence independent of individual beliefs.) Probabilities, regardless of their subjective or objective origin, are the cornerstone of our description of choice under risk.

APPLICATION: The Shopper's Pennies

Taking the decreased purchasing power of the dollar into account, a penny in 1945 would be the equivalent of more than 6 cents today. The inconvenience in the 1990s of dealing with coins of such small value has not gone unnoticed by consumers, many of whom leave their pennies in dishes at checkout counters for other consumers to use. But until such time as the venerable penny goes the way of the no-longer minted mil (one-tenth of a penny coin), there is a probability-based alternative that might work just as well in providing convenience.

Thanks to inventor Michael Rossides, we have the suggestion that purchase amounts at the cash register can simply be rounded up or down to an even dollar.[1] To insure that neither the consumer nor the store loses by this or is able to manipulate the rounding, the shopper provides a random number between 1 and 100 and the store provides a random number between 1 and 100. The two numbers are added and, if the sum exceeds 100, 100 is subtracted from it. The resulting number is compared to the amount of change in the purchase. If it is greater, the bill is rounded down to the nearest dollar. Otherwise, it is rounded up to the nearest dollar.

For example, assume your bill is for $10.58. If the sum of the store's number and your number is greater than 58, you pay $10. If the sum is 58 or less, you pay $11. Shoppers don't need to carry coins, and stores don't need to make change in coins. Tests in Evanston, Illinois, where half of the shoppers chose to use the system, confirm that over many purchases shoppers pay the same amount as they would if they were paying to the penny every time.

Since neither party controls the number picked by the other, the numbers don't really need to be picked randomly to provide the same outcome. All that is needed is that neither party know the other's number ahead of time. In this case, taking on a little short-term risk can provide long-term convenience at no long-term expense. ▪

Measuring Risk

Investment advisers often talk as if risk can be measured on a straight scale: "This investment is riskier than that investment," for example. In reality, anything that has random outcomes where some outcomes are preferred to others is risky. The nature of risk is so varied that no single scale can suffice. There are, however, some descriptive measures that capture valuable information about risk. To discuss two of the most important of these measures, we can focus on two carefully chosen risky investments and one riskless alternative.

Table 15.1 shows two risky investments, A and B, and a riskless investment, C. Each investment requires a $1,000 payment today in return for a

---

1. See "Heads I Win, Tails You Lose," *The Economist,* June 13, 1992, p. 74.

Table 15.1 Payouts for Three Investments of $1,000 Each

Outcome and Probability	Investment A	Investment B	Riskless Investment C
Good times (1/3)	$1,350	$1,550	$1,070
Average times (1/3)	$1,065	$1,000	$1,070
Bad times (1/3)	$800	$750	$1,070
Expected value	$1,071.67	$1,100.00	$1,070.00

payout in one year. The dollar amounts in the table indicate each investment's payouts. For each investment there are three possible outcomes listed, corresponding to whether the next year represents "good times," "average times," or "bad times." We assume for simplicity that each outcome is equally likely, so that the probability of each is 1/3.

Investment C is riskless because no matter what occurs over the next year, the investor receives $1,070. Comparing $70 to $1,000, we see that the investor receives a sure return of 7 percent. Investments A and B, on the other hand, are risky because the return is dependent on which outcome occurs. Investment B pays the most ($1,550) if "good times" occur, but it also pays the least ($750) if "bad times" occur.

Expected Value. How would you decide which of these three investments to pursue? One thing you might ask is, "If I were to make the same investment repeatedly, which one would leave me with the most money?" If so, you would be looking at the *expected value* or *average payout* of the investments.

▼

2. Give an example of computing expected value and standard deviation.

Expected value is the average value of a set of random numbers, where the weights used to average represent the probability that each number will occur.

Thus, to compute the expected value for the investments in Table 15.1, we take the probability that each outcome will occur times the payout and sum over all outcomes. For example, the expected value of A is

(probability good times × payout good times) + (probability average times × payout average times) + (probability bad times × payout bad times)

$$= (1/3)\$1,350 + (1/3)\$1,065 + (1/3)\$800$$
$$= \$450 + \$355.00 + \$266.67$$
$$= \$1,071.67.$$

Performing the same calculation for investment B, we find an expected value of $1,100. Repeated investments in investment A would therefore earn $1,071.67 on average, whereas repeated investments in B would earn $1,100. Riskless investment C earns $1,070.

On the basis of expected value, investment A would be better than C, but only by $1.67. On the other hand, investment A might lose $200 if bad times occur. Is $1.67 extra in expected value worth taking that chance? Similarly,

Table 15.2 Computing Standard Deviations for Investments

	Investment A	Investment B	Investment C
Deviation from Expected Value			
Good times (1/3)	$278.33	$450.00	$0.00
Average times (1/3)	($6.67)	($100.00)	$0.00
Bad times (1/3)	($271.67)	($350,00)	$0.00
Squared Deviation from Expected Value			
Good times (1/3)	$77,469.44	$202,500.00	$0.00
Average times (1/3)	$ 44.44	$10,000.00	$0.00
Bad times (1/3)	$73,802.78	$122,500.00	$0.00
Probability-Weighted Sum = Variance	$50,438.89	$111,666.67	$0.00
Standard Deviation	$224.59	$334.17	$0.00

investment B has an expected value $28.33 higher than that of investment A, but two-thirds of the time it pays less by $50 or more. Is $28.33 in expected value enough to compensate? To answer, we must evaluate the risk attached to each asset.

Standard Deviation. One measure for evaluating the amount of risk is its standard deviation, the typical or representative amount by which a group of numbers is above or below its expected value. If payouts for an investment range from wildly above to wildly below the expected value, you might not view that investment as favorably as one that had the same expected value with less fluctuation of payouts. Table 15.2 computes the deviation of payments for each investment. Because it is risk free, investment C has no payout deviation. Figure 15.1 plots the deviations for investments A and B, showing positive deviations to the right and negative ones to the left.

Figure 15.1 shows that the deviations of investment B are larger than those for investment A for every outcome. Investment B would therefore be considered the riskier investment. Is there a way to summarize the greater variability of B's payout compared to A's in a concise measure? One way of generating this measure is to use the probability-weighted average of the squared deviations or the square root of this number. The first measure is called the *variance,* usually indicated by the Greek symbol σ^2. The square root of the variance is called the *standard deviation,* usually indicated by the Greek symbol σ.

*The **variance** of a set of random numbers is computed by squaring their deviations from the expected value, multiplying each by the probability and summing. The **standard deviation** of a set of random numbers is the square root of their variance.*

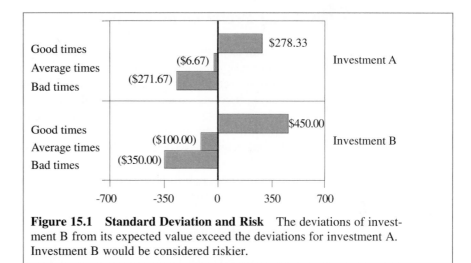

Figure 15.1 Standard Deviation and Risk   The deviations of investment B from its expected value exceed the deviations for investment A. Investment B would be considered riskier.

For example, to compute the standard deviation of investment B we take the three deviations given in Table 15.2 (450, − 100, − 350) and square them to get $202,500, $10,000, and $122,500. These numbers are weighted by the probability for each number and then summed, to get (1/3)$202,500 + (1/3)$10,000 + (1/3)$122,500 = $111,666.67. The square root of this number is $334.17. Thus the standard deviation of the payout in investment B is $334.17.

You may have noticed that the standard deviation gives positive weight to both negative and positive deviations, but it is *not* the average of the deviations. The variance and standard deviation give more weight to deviations that are large than to deviations that are small by squaring them before taking the average. (In essence, the squaring is "undone" by taking the square root of the average when we compute the standard deviation, but this still attaches more importance to large deviations.) In the case of investment B, the absolute deviations are $450, $100, and $350, which have an average value of $300. The standard deviation for investment B, however, was $334.17 because the large deviation of $450 weighed more heavily in the computation than the smaller deviations.

How an investor responds to an investment's inherent risk depends on the investor's preferences for risk, which we consider next. Most people prefer to avoid large variations in their payouts. Although standard deviation and variance are not synonymous with risk, they are reasonably good summary measures of the degree of variability, emphasizing the large deviations that most people want to avoid.

15.2 Preferences for Risk

As with any other decision, households' preferences enter into their decisions among risky alternatives. Some households are more willing to take risks and some households less. For each household, however, the process of decision making involves attaching to each alternative a number called expected utility, which represents the alternative's value to the household. Then the household chooses the alternative that has the highest expected utility among those that are feasible. Expected utility incorporates the household's attitudes toward the payoffs and the risk embodied in them. We therefore model decision making under risk in terms of finding the highest expected utility subject to the budget constraint.

Expected Utility

The numbers that households use to choose between risky alternatives are called *expected utility*. Since the household's expected utility depends on its utility, and utility depends on goods and services, we start there to describe the construction of expected utility.

In the presence of different outcomes (called *states of nature*), a good is specified not only by its description but by the state of nature in which it is consumed. To take a simple example, let's look at an umbrella. I can use an umbrella in two states of nature tomorrow: rain or shine. If you offer me an umbrella to use tomorrow, I would pay more for (umbrella, rain) than I would for (umbrella, shine). This behavior is not unusual. It is corroborated by the fact that in some cities it is common for street vendors to sell the same umbrella for $5 on a sunny day and $8 during a sudden downpour. They could not sell at the higher price unless consumers were willing to pay it. Other things being equal, then, your utility and mine will be different in one state of nature compared to another.

In general, if we use s to stand for states of nature, my utility in state s can be written as $U_s = U(X_s)$ where X_s is the list of all goods and services consumed in state of nature s. Because I do not know today which state of nature will occur, I look at my average utility or expected utility.

> *Expected utility is the expected value of the household's utility across states of nature,* U_s.

▼

3. Define, and give the formula for, expected utility.

Expected utility depends on the consumption of goods and services in each state of nature plus the probability that each state of nature will occur. Expected utility replaces utility as the thing the household maximizes when it chooses among risky alternatives. There are several ways in which working with expected utility differs from using utility, however.

First, as we learned in Chapter 4, the quantity of goods and services consumed depends on income and prices. Including each state of nature in the decision, U^s can be written as a function $V(I_s, p)$, where I_s is income in state s and p is the list of prices. As long as prices are the same in each state of nature, we can ignore them and write $U_s = V(I_s)$. Thus, preferences for risk represent attitudes about the household's *income* available in different states of nature. With this in mind, we can look at how preferences for risk relate to income across states of nature.

Second, we will see that renumbering the expected utility scale in a way that retains ordinal rank does not necessarily lead to the same choices by the household. Thus, although utility is ordinal (any renumbering preserving ordinal rank gives the same choices), expected utility is cardinal, meaning that the exact curvature and scale chosen matter to the choices of the household.

▼
4. Draw representative utility of income curves for (a) a risk averse investor, (b) a risk neutral investor, and (c) a risk loving investor.

Risk Averse Behavior. Figure 15.2 graphs four shapes for the utility function $V(I)$. Each one represents a different preference for risk. The slope of the curve shows the individual's marginal utility of income, the rate at which utility rises with additional income. We will see that the type of curvature (concave, convex, or straight depending on whether marginal utility of income falls, rises, or is constant) determines whether the individual is risk averse, risk loving, or risk neutral. To study attitudes toward risk, let's look at Julie, a student deciding which career to pursue. If Julie goes into medicine, we assume that over the course of her career she will earn $120,000 annually. On the other hand, if she goes into business, we assume that she has a 50 percent chance of becoming a corporate head, at which point her annual income would be $180,000. If she fails to become a corporate head, we assume that her income would instead be $60,000 annually. At this point we also assume that income is the only important consideration in deciding which route she takes. The expected income from choosing business is therefore $(0.5)\$180,000 + (0.5)\$60,000 = \$120,000$ per year. This is equal to the sure income she would receive from choosing medicine. How should Julie value these two options?

If Julie is risk averse, her preferences might be represented by the concave curve in part (a) of Figure 15.2. A risk averse individual will always choose a sure thing over an alternative having the same expected value. If Julie chooses business and succeeds in becoming a corporate head, her utility will be 148,000 utils (a util is our unit of utility). If she does not become a corporate head, it will be 72,000 utils. Her expected utility from choosing business is the probability-weighted average of utilities, $(0.5)148,000 + (0.5)72,000 = 110,000$ utils. Comparing this to the 120,000 utils from medicine, we see that the risk in the corporate choice reduced Julie's expected utility by 10,000 utils. Risk averse Julie therefore chooses the sure thing (medicine) over the risky alternative (business).

An easy way to find expected utility on a graph is to draw the line *ab* between the two risky alternatives at points *a* and *b* and find the midpoint. The vertical height of the midpoint gives the expected utility. If probability is unequal, one uses a different point on the line *ab*. The location of the point is determined by the fraction of the probability that applies to the upper endpoint. For example, if the probability of the upper income is $\frac{1}{2}$, the midpoint

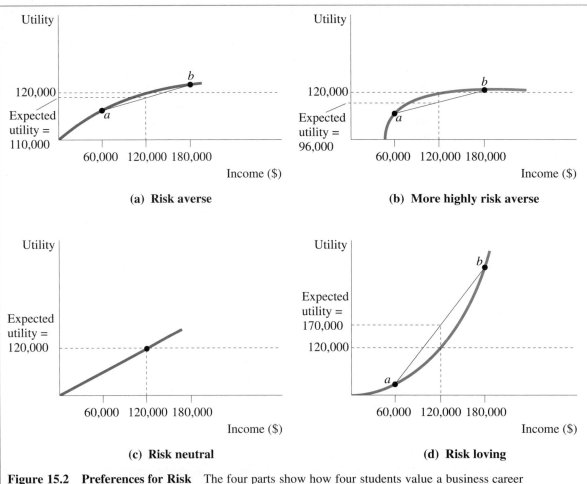

Figure 15.2   Preferences for Risk   The four parts show how four students value a business career with expected income of $120,000 but equal chances that income will be $60,000 or $180,000. Each student values a sure income of $120,000 at 120,000 utils. Risk averse Julie in part (a) values the risky option at expected utility of 110,000 utils, whereas the more highly risk averse student in (b) values it at 96,000 utils. In part (c), the risk neutral student values it at 120,000 utils, the same value as for the sure income. Finally, in (d), the risk loving student values the risky alternative at 170,000 utils, indicating a positive utility from risk itself.

of the chord is chosen. If the probability of the upper income is $\frac{2}{3}$, then the point on the chart is two-thirds of the distance from the lower income point to the upper income point, and so on. If the upper endpoint is certain (probability 1), all weight is on the upper endpoint and the point chosen moves to the upper endpoint.

The curve is concave for a risk averse individual, indicating that the marginal utility of income is declining. That is, the first units of income increase utility at a faster rate than subsequent units of income. Notice that the utility scale in part (a) of Figure 15.2 is set such that the utility of $120,000 income is $V(\$120,000) = 120,000$ utils. $V(\$60,000) = 72,000$ utils, and $V(\$180,000) = 148,000$ utils. A concave curve also implies, as it did for Julie, that expected utility is lower for a random outcome than for a certain one having the same expected value.

The other three parts of Figure 15.2 show utility curves for students with different attitudes toward risk. Each one is scaled so that $V(\$120,000) = 120,000$ utils. Part (b) shows a curve for a student who is more risk averse than Julie. In this part the utility curve is again concave, but the curvature is greater. In the case of the more highly risk averse student, utility rises more steeply with income until income reaches the $80,000 to $90,000 range, after which the curve flattens out considerably. The greater curvature lowers expected utility for risky alternatives that produce some income below the $80,000 to $90,000 range and some above. This is because income below $80,000 lowers utility more than the same amount of income above $90,000 raises it. The connecting line for this student shows that he values the risky business career at 96,000 utils, a number lower than Julie's valuation of business.

Risk Neutral Behavior. Part (c) shows a linear utility curve that is a ray from the origin. Such a student is risk neutral. A risk neutral individual will always be indifferent between a sure thing and a risky alternative having the same expected value, because expected utility for the two will be the same. For a risk neutral student, the expected value of the business career is 120,000 utils, which equals the expected utility of the (sure) medical career. A risk neutral student sometimes would take the business career, whereas the risk averse student would never take it.

Since changing the curvature did not change the ordinal ranking of alternatives but it did change the choices made by the student, we see that expected utility is cardinal rather than ordinal. As noted previously, in this respect expected utility differs from utility.

Risk Loving Behavior. Finally, part (d) shows a convex curve. This student is risk loving, meaning that the student will choose a risky alternative over a sure thing having the same expected value. That is, the expected utility of the risky alternative will be higher than the expected utility of the sure thing. For this student, we find that the expected value of the risky business career is 170,000 utils. Since this exceeds the 120,000 utils from the sure thing (medicine), the student chooses business. Why does this student have higher expected utility from a risky alternative than from a safe one paying the same expected value? It is because the individual receives utility from risk taking itself.

Combinations of Degrees of Risk Aversion. For the most part we assume that households are risk averse. Psychologists explain that risk avoidance is one sign of maturity, and indeed, we observe that people typically buy insurance to lessen their risk. Yet the same person who buys insurance might think nothing of buying a raffle ticket. The evidence is that some people seem to be willing to take small risks at the same time that they avoid large ones. (This implies a utility function that curves upward for small changes in income above the current level but is concave downward for large changes in income.) People who own house and auto insurance have in fact been known to spend money to buy state lottery tickets. In one interesting case, a lottery held for charity used a drawing to reduce the list of potential winners to four individuals, each of whom had a one-in-four chance of winning the $10,000 prize. Though each had taken part in the lottery, thereby indicating a willingness (albeit for the benefit of charity) to take on a small amount of risk, when the risk became significant, the four agreed to split the prize equally rather than complete the drawing. The individuals showed risk aversion for a large risk.

Risk Aversion, Fair Gambles, and the Risk Premium

▼

5. What is a risk premium?

If most individuals (and firms) are risk averse, then why would they ever invest in risky projects? We call an asset or a project with a certain payout a riskless asset. Why wouldn't they restrict themselves to riskless assets? Often it's because they have an incentive to take the risk. "No pain, no gain," might be restated as "No risk, no reward." The incentive to take risk, called the *risk premium*, relates a project's expected payout to the expected payout that would be needed by a risk neutral household to accept the project. In other words, it measures the "extra" payout or premium that the project gives to compensate for its risk.

To calculate the risk premium we need to talk about gambles and fair gambles.

> A **gamble** is a certain payment made in return for receiving a risky payout later. A **fair gamble** is a gamble in which the expected payout equals the amount paid for playing.

A simple example of a fair gamble would be betting $1 on the flip of a coin if you receive $2 for heads and nothing for tails. Your expected payout is $(0.5)\$2 + (0.5)\$0 = \$1$, exactly what you paid to play the game. Over a large number of plays, your net expected gain would be zero.

The fact that a gamble is fair does not mean that you would want to play without receiving some premium for the risk. To demonstrate the need for a risk premium, let's look at the St. Petersburg paradox, a game in which a player flips a coin until the first tail appears. If the first flip shows tails, the player wins $1 and the game ends. If the first tail appears on the second flip, the player wins $2 and the game ends; if the first tail appears on the third flip, the player wins $4, and so on. In general, if n heads in a row are flipped before the first tail appears to end the game, the player wins $\$2^n$.

The paradox is that individuals will not pay an unlimited amount of money to play this game, even though the expected value of the game is infinity dollars. The probability of winning $1 is 0.5, the probability of winning $2 is 0.25, and so on. Adding all payouts times their probabilities to compute expected value therefore produces an infinite sequence of .5s, which add to infinity. Why don't people pay more to play the game? Daniel Bernoulli, a Swiss mathematician of the eighteenth century, resolved the paradox by suggesting that risk averse gamblers valued the game at less than its expected value. They therefore needed a risk premium to play.

> The **risk premium** is the amount by which the expected payout from a gamble exceeds the expected payout for a riskless asset or a fair gamble that costs the same.

To calculate the risk premium for a representative household, our version of the game will allow up to four coin flips. If n heads appear before the first tail or end of the game, the payout is $\$10^n$. This is a serious game: the player could win $10,000. How much would you pay to play this game, or equivalently, how large a risk premium would you need to play this game?

Table 15.3 lists the five possible outcomes in column 1, using H to indicate heads and T for tails. The probability that the first flip will be a T (ending the game) is 0.5. The probability that the first flip will be a head, followed by a tail (ending the game on the second flip), is 0.25, and so on. Column 3 shows the payout for each outcome. Column 5 multiplies each dollar payout by its probability and sums the numbers at the bottom of the column to compute the expected payout, $703.

A risk neutral household would be willing to pay exactly $703 to play this game, since that is the game's expected payout. Paying $703 makes the game a fair gamble. A risk averse household, however, would be willing to pay less. To demonstrate, we assume that our risk averse household initially has $40,000 income and that its utility is $V(I) = -40,000 + 400I^{1/2}$. Since

Table 15.3 Calculation of Expected Utility for a Coin Game

(1)	(2)	(3)	(4)	(5) Calculating Expected Payout (col. 2 × col. 3)	(6) Calculating Expected Utility (col. 2 × col. 4)
Event	Probability	Payout	Utility		
T	0.5	$1	39,328.11	$0.50	19,664.05
HT	0.25	$10	39,337.18	$2.50	9,834.29
HHT	0.125	$100	39,427.88	$12.50	4,928.49
HHHT	0.0625	$1,000	40,329.25	$62.50	2.520.58
HHHH	0.0625	$10,000	48.841.37	$625.00	3,052.59
Totals				$703.00	40,000.00

Note: The household's initial utility is 40,000 utils. The utilities for individual payouts in column 4 are based on a cost to play of $670.07. Column 6 shows that these utilities produce an overall expected utility of 40,000, matching the household's initial utility. Thus, at a cost of $670.07, the household may choose to play the game. Comparing this cost to the game's expected payout of $703 (column 5), we see that the risk premium is $703.00 − $670.07 = $32.93.

utility depends on the square root of income (a concave function), this function has the right curvature to be risk averse. Initial marginal utility of income for this household is 1, and it declines with income.[2]

How much less than $703 would this risk averse household have to pay to be willing to play the game? By checking its expected utility for different payouts, we find that paying $670.07 for the gamble leaves the household with expected utility equal to its pregame 40,000. Column 4 in Table 15.3 calculates the risk averse household's utility after paying $670.07 to play the game and receiving the payout in column 3. Multiplying each utility by the probability and summing as in column 6 gives the expected utility of 40,000. Paying $670.07 for this gamble means that the game's expected payout is more than a fair gamble; the "extra" earned by this gamble is $703 − $670.07 = $32.93. $32.93 would therefore be the risk premium for this gamble at that price.[3]

APPLICATION: Legalized Gambling

The more things change, the more they stay the same. The recent trend across the United States to increased legalized gambling in the form of state-sanctioned lotteries, casinos, on-track and off-track betting facilities, riverboats, and video gambling machines is a throwback to an earlier era before gambling was outlawed in the United States.[4] Gambling was known to ancient cultures thousands of years before the time of Christ. In terms of its antiquity, it might be described as the world's second oldest profession. Yet in the first economics book written in 1776, Adam Smith inveighed against the evils of gambling. Economists continue to do so today. Why?

Organized gambling is an activity that adds to the gambler's risk at the same time that it reduces the expected return. This is because gambling providers must skim from the "handle" (the amount bet) to cover their costs and make a profit. Smaller pots mean that the bets gamblers make are unfair gambles.

▼
6. Explain the economic arguments against gambling.

2. $MU_I = \Delta V/\Delta I = (0.5)400I^{-1/2} = 1$ if $I = 40,000$.

3. In this example, initial payments and payouts were made in the same time period. If an investment's payouts are made in a later time period, then the time value of money based on the interest rate must be taken into account in computing the risk premium. (See Chapter 16 for a discussion of the interest rate and Investigations V for a dicussion of present value.) For example, if a riskless investment costing $100 today pays back $105 next period, a fair gamble would also need to pay back $105 in the next period. Thus a risky investment costing $100 today and paying an expected return of $107 next period has a risk premium of $2 (2 percent of the original investment), which is the amount by which its return exceeds that of a riskless investment costing the same.

4. In 1833 Pennsylvania, New York, and Massachusetts led the move to eliminate state-authorized lotteries. First the northeastern states, then the southern and western states followed suit. In 1860 only Delaware, Missouri, and Kentucky retained lotteries. By 1894 no state permitted the operation of lotteries. With a few exceptions, such as casinos in Nevada and horse tracks in Kentucky, there was no legalized gambling in the United States between 1894 and 1964. See Charles T. Clotfelter and Philip J. Cook, *Selling Hope: State Lotteries in America,* Cambridge, Mass.: Harvard University Press, 1989, pp. 37–38.

To the extent that recreational gamblers know the odds are against them and that they are likely to lose their money but want to gamble anyway for entertainment, there is probably little to condemn. On the other hand, the allure of gambling for many people is that they view it as a way to earn money. Since gambling simply transfers money from one individual's pocket to another, nonrecreational gamblers gamble to acquire money without producing anything tangible. The economic costs of this type of gambling are the wasted time and resources that could have been used in productive activity.

Economists distinguish between *investing* (placing money in risky productive ventures, as in stock market purchases) and nonrecreational gambling. Investors place their money in projects that ultimately produce goods and services as the source of the payouts they get. Investors also try to choose projects with expected payouts larger than what they paid in. Finally, investors are risk averse in the sense that they try to avoid risk when possible and minimize the risk that they do take on. None of these attributes characterize gamblers.

Currently 33 states and the District of Columbia operate some form of state-sanctioned gambling, collecting more than $20 billion a year from lotteries alone.[5] Opponents of gambling point to the high costs associated with collecting taxes through the medium of gambling. One cost is the observed increase in crime rates associated with gambling. Another problem is the 1.5 to 4 percent of the population who are known to be subject to compulsive gambling disorders. Computing the public costs from addicted gamblers shows that state outlays for this problem can run on the order of $30,000 per addicted gambler.

Another strong objection is that lower-income and less-educated households engage in lotteries and other forms of gambling disproportionately to their income. One study found that low-income households (those earning less than $10,000 per year) spent between 5 and 6 percent of their income on lottery tickets, for example.[6] Why would households that clearly need their money place this much cash in a lottery, where the chances of winning anything are frequently less than the chances of being struck by lightning? According to Adam Smith, lotteries exploit the hope of winning and the fact that the true probabilities are often incorrectly assessed.

> That the chance of gain is naturally overvalued, we may learn from the universal success of lotteries. The world neither ever saw, nor ever will see, a perfectly fair lottery; or one in which the whole gain compensated the whole loss; because the undertaker could making nothing by it. . . . The soberest people scarce look upon it as a folly to pay a small sum for the chance of gaining ten or twenty thousand pounds; though they know that even that small sum is perhaps twenty or thirty percent more than the chance is worth. . . . There is not,

5. Marj Charlier, "The Payoff: Casino Gambling Saves Three Colorado Towns But the Price Is High," *Wall Street Journal,* September 23, 1992, p. 1.
6. Clotfelter and Cook, op. cit., p. 99.

however, a more certain proposition in mathematics than that the more tickets you adventure upon, the more likely you are to be a loser. Adventure upon all the tickets in the lottery, and you lose for certain; and the greater the number of your tickets the nearer you approach to this certainty.[7]

Interestingly, the degree to which gamblers today are willing to accept an unfair gamble is the same as it was in Adam Smith's day. Smith reports that gamblers of his day were willing to pay 20 to 30 percent more than a gamble was worth. The equivalent figure can be checked today by considering the figures for a state-sanctioned off-track betting establishment. In pari-mutuel betting[8] in the state of Illinois, for example, gambling promoters remove 22 percent of the handle. A $5 bet by two gamblers on each side of a fifty-fifty proposition, therefore, would produce a net pot of $7.80. The expected value of such a gamble is $0.5 \times \$7.80 = \$3.90$. The gambler pays $5 for the privilege of this unfair bet. Since $\$5/\$3.90 = 1.282$, the modern gambler pays 28.2 percent ''more than the chance is worth''—well within the 20–30 percent overpayment reported by Adam Smith more than two centuries ago.

In the case of state lotteries, the amount paid back by the state in winnings varies. For instance, New York returns 56 cents on the dollar, New Jersey 58.7 cents, and Connecticut 57 cents.[9] Some states return even less. A lottery ticket is therefore a pretty hefty hidden tax, where the tax rate exceeds the highest marginal tax on federal income. The more tickets you buy, the more tax you pay. ■

15.3 Risk Trading

Although one can avoid gambling if one chooses, there are other situations where risk effectively cannot be avoided. In these cases, markets can allow the household to manage its risk. In a market, households with different risk aversions trade claims or securities that entitle the owner to receive random payments. Such a claim might be a share of stock, but it also could be a bond, for example, or a life insurance policy, which pays only if the death of the insured occurs. In this section, we examine how the market brings together the different attitudes toward risk of individual households and generates the market price and from it the risk premium for traded assets. We then examine

---

7. Adam Smith, *An Inquiry into the Nature and Causes of the Wealth of Nations* (Chicago: William Benton, 1952), p. 194.
8. Pari-mutuel betting refers to betting whereby the winners divide the total amount bet, after deducting management expenses, in proportion to the sums they have wagered individually, according to the *American Heritage Dictionary*. Horse races are a common vehicle for such gambling.
9. N. R. Kleinfeld, ''Many Dreams, Fewer Dollars in Lotteries,'' *New York Times,* November 5, 1991, p. B-1.

how the household uses the market for risk to manage the total amount of risk that the household faces.

We use the word *security* to describe any risky asset.

> A **security** is any asset providing its owner with a claim to risky payments that vary by the state of nature.

The price of a security is determined by demand and supply, just as for a good or commodity. By establishing the relationship between the security's price and its expected payout, market price also determines the security's risk premium.

Market Determination of Security Prices and Risk Premia

▼

7. How do demand and supply determine a security's price and its risk premium?

To demonstrate how the market determines security prices and risk premia, let us construct a two-states-of-nature example. Laurel and Hardy, our two traders, have two securities that they can trade between them. Laurel is risk averse and Hardy is risk neutral (and thus would be willing to hold any amount of risk so long as the expected value of his holdings is the same). In the example we will do two things: First, we will show that trade in securities, which allows each trader to change the profile of his risky holdings, can be explained with the same tools that we have used to explain trade in goods. We can then show that this trade leads to demand and supply curves and equilibrium prices for securities, and hence determines risk premia.

Figure 15.3 plots the information that we will need in an Edgeworth box. Remember from Chapter 12 that an Edgeworth box shows the possible allocations of two commodities between two consumers and allows us to depict the allocations and trades that would benefit a given consumer. The horizontal axis measures Laurel's income in state of nature 1 as the distance from the lower left corner; it also measures Hardy's income in state of nature 1 as the distance to the left from the upper right corner. The vertical distance from the lower left of the diagram measures Laurel's income in state of nature 2, and the vertical distance from the top right measures Hardy's income in state of nature 2. Point a gives the initial endowment of each investor. Laurel has $40,000 income if state 1 occurs and $10,000 if state 2 occurs. Hardy has $15,000 and $10,000, respectively. We assume that the probability of state of nature 1 is 0.6 and the probability of state of nature 2 is 0.4.

Point a involves uncertain income for both investors. Hardy has income with standard deviation $2,449.49, and Laurel has income with standard deviation $14,696.94. If each investor had certain income, income for the two states would be equal. The points of equal income for Laurel lie on the 45-degree line from the lower left corner, and the points of equal income for Hardy are on the 45-degree line passing through the upper right corner.

Since Hardy is risk neutral, his utility as a function of income is a ray from the origin like that shown in part (c) of Figure 15.2, represented by the equation $V(I) = I$. Thus Hardy's expected utility is $0.6I_1 + 0.4I_2$. Plotting the combinations of (I_1, I_2) that provide constant expected utility generates

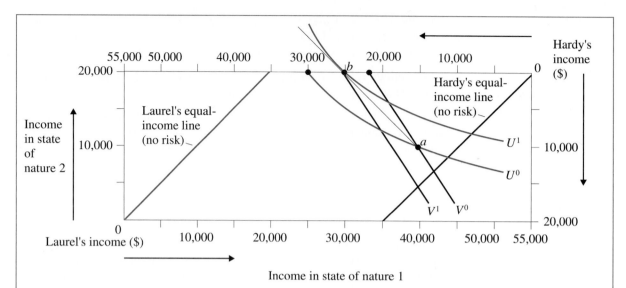

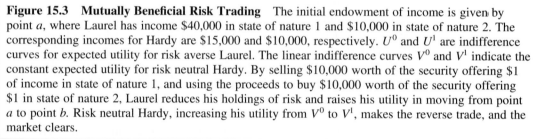

Figure 15.3 Mutually Beneficial Risk Trading The initial endowment of income is given by point a, where Laurel has income $40,000 in state of nature 1 and $10,000 in state of nature 2. The corresponding incomes for Hardy are $15,000 and $10,000, respectively. U^0 and U^1 are indifference curves for expected utility for risk averse Laurel. The linear indifference curves V^0 and V^1 indicate the constant expected utility for risk neutral Hardy. By selling $10,000 worth of the security offering $1 of income in state of nature 1, and using the proceeds to buy $10,000 worth of the security offering $1 in state of nature 2, Laurel reduces his holdings of risk and raises his utility in moving from point a to point b. Risk neutral Hardy, increasing his utility from V^0 to V^1, makes the reverse trade, and the market clears.

the linear indifference curve labeled V^0 passing through point a. Other indifference curves are lines parallel to V^0, with higher expected utility for lines further from the upper right corner such as V^1. Risk averse Laurel's utility is given by $U(I) = \ln I$. This is a concave function of the type shown in Figure 15.2 (a) or (b) for risk averse individuals. Thus Laurel's expected utility is $0.6 \ln I_1 + 0.4 \ln I_2$. Plotting the combinations of Laurel's incomes for the two states of nature that give the same expected utility as point a generates the indifference curve labeled U^0. Risk averse preferences in general give rise to concave indifference curves because they are derived from concave functions, whereas risk neutral indifference curves give rise to straight lines because they derive from linear functions.

We assume that Laurel and Hardy can trade two securities. The first pays $1 if state of nature 1 occurs and nothing if state of nature 2 occurs. This can be summarized by the payout list (1, 0). The second security with payouts

(0, 1) is identical except that it pays only if state of nature 2 occurs.[10] Let p_1 and p_2 stand for the prices of one unit of the two securities. That is, if Laurel buys security 1, he pays the purchase price p_1, and his income goes up by $1 (the payout of the security) if state of nature 1 occurs. If he sells security 1, he receives purchase price p_1 and his income falls by $1 from what it would have been if state of nature 1 occurs. Laurel's budget constraint is the number of units of each type of security he can buy and still be able to pay for them.[11]

Let's see how trade in securities allows both investors to raise their expected utility. From the figure we see that by moving from point a to point b, Laurel and Hardy can both raise their expected utility. This involves Laurel selling 10,000 units of security 1 (lowering his income from $40,000 to $30,000 in state of nature 1) and using the proceeds to buy 10,000 units of security 2 (raising his income from $10,000 to $20,000 in state of nature 2). This assumes the securities have equal prices, which in fact will be the case in equilibrium, as we will show shortly. Hardy makes the reverse trades. Further, point b satisfies distributive efficiency and is on the contract curve for trading income in one state of nature for income in the other.[12] In particular, the budget line passing through points a and b indicates the rate of exchange for income in the two states. Laurel's indifference curve U^1 is tangent to the budget line at point b, showing that the trade leads to highest utility for him given the budget line; similarly, Hardy's indifference curve V^1 is the highest attainable for him (measuring from his northeast origin) given the budget line. Were Laurel and Hardy trading state-dependent income directly, they would both be willing to make the trade from a to b. Will trade in the securities also cause them to reach point b?

To verify that point b is the market equilibrium for Laurel and Hardy when they trade securities, we construct the demand and supply curves for security 1. Figure 15.4 shows the number of units of security 1 on the horizontal axis and the price ratio p_1/p_2 on the vertical axis. At a very high price for security 1, neither investor wishes to buy security 1, so the demand curve corresponds to the vertical axis. As the price falls, however, Hardy becomes willing to buy units of security 1 when the price ratio reaches 1.5. This is because 1.5 is Hardy's marginal rate of substitution of income in state

10. For simplicity we assume that the assets pay in dollars commensurate with first-period income. The expected value of payouts can then be compared directly to the asset's price when we determine the risk premium without adjustment for the value of income in different time periods, the subject of Chapter 16.

11. We assume that Laurel has certain current income of $22,000. He receives endowments of $40,000 if state of nature 1 occurs and $10,000 in state of nature 2. Because he can sell 40,000 units of security 1 at price p_1 and 10,000 units of security 2 at price p_2, he has $22,000 + p_1 40,000 + p_2 10,000$ that he can spend on the two securities or use as income before the state of nature is revealed. His budget constraint is therefore $\$22,000 + p_1 40,000 + p_2 10,000 = p_1 s_1 + p_2 s_2 + I$. The utility from his choice of (s_1, s_2, I) is $\ln I + 0.6 \ln s_1 + 0.4 \ln s_2$, where $\ln I$ is utility from current income and the rest is expected utility from income in the two states of nature.

12. We discussed distributive efficiency and the contract curve in Chapter 12.

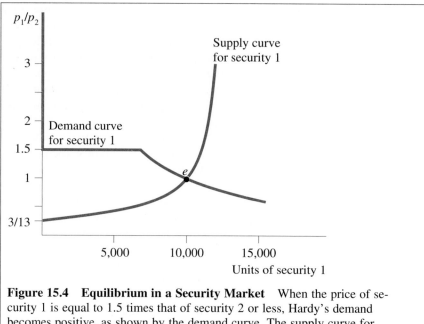

Figure 15.4 Equilibrium in a Security Market When the price of security 1 is equal to 1.5 times that of security 2 or less, Hardy's demand becomes positive, as shown by the demand curve. The supply curve for security 1 by Laurel is the upward-sloping curve that intersects the demand curve at point e. By selling 10,000 units of security 1 and buying 10,000 units of security 2, risk averse Laurel is able to reduce his holdings of risk and to increase his expected utility.

1 for income in state 2, given by the slope of his indifference curve through point a in Figure 15.3. At this price, proceeds from selling a unit of security 2 allow him to buy just enough security 1 that increased income in state 1 compensates for reduction in state 2 income. At price p_1/p_2 below 1.5, supplying security 2 allows him to buy more security 1 than needed to compensate him, so he supplies 10,000 units of security 2—the maximum that his income in state 2 will allow. The 10,000 units of security 2 allow Hardy to buy $10,000 p_2/p_1$ units of security 1, generating the downward-sloping portion of the demand curve in Figure 15.4.

Computing what Laurel does for prices p_1 and p_2 shows that he supplies security 1 for price ratios higher than $\frac{3}{13}$, as shown by the supply curve in Figure 15.4.[13] Setting demand equal to supply at point e reveals that equilib-

13. This is more difficult to derive graphically, but we use the same optimizing principles we discussed for consumer choice of goods subject to a budget constraint. In this case, given $U = \ln I + 0.6 \ln s_1 + 0.4 \ln s_2$, Laurel maximizes his utility subject to the budget constraint $I_0 \equiv \$22,000 + p_1 40,000 + p_2 10,000 = p_1 s_1 + p_2 s_2 + I$ by taking half of I_0 as current income I and spending the other half on s_1 and s_2, where $0.3 I_0 = p_1 s_1$ and $0.2 I_0 = p_2 s_2$. Laurel's net supply of security 1 is then $40,000 - s_1$, which leads to the supply curve shown in Figure 15.4.

rium occurs when Laurel sells Hardy 10,000 units of security 1 at $p_2/p_1 =$ 1. One can also show that both markets for securities clear when $p_1 = p_2 = \frac{11}{25}$, with Hardy selling Laurel 10,000 units of security 2. The trade in securities therefore moves Laurel and Hardy from point a to point b in Figure 15.3, as suggested earlier.

In this example, demand and supply of securities determine their price, just as in conventional commodity markets. Once we know a security's price, we can substract it from the security's expected payout to find the risk premium. In this case, for example, the risk premium is $(0.6 \times 1) - \frac{11}{25} =$ 0.16 for security 1 (that is, a buyer pays \$.44 for the security that pays an expected return of \$.60). The same principles would apply in finding the equilibrium prices and risk premia in other situations. For example, if Laurel's endowments were reversed so that he held 10,000 units of state 1 income and 40,000 of state 2 income, Laurel's demand and supply for securities would change. As we might expect, the lower initial supplies of state 1 income and higher supplies of state 2 income would result in a higher equilibrium security 1 price, $p_1 = 0.6$, and a lower security 2 price, $p_2 = 0.4$. The risk premium on security 1 would also change, dropping to zero.[14]

Having seen how the market determines security prices and risk premia, let's turn our attention again to individual households and see how they use risk markets to manage the risk they face.

Diversification

In Laurel and Hardy's case, Laurel's objective was to use securities to rearrange his income between states of nature in a more desirable way. He was not interested so much in the risk of an individual asset as he was in the risk of his overall income. Risky assets can have payouts that are uncorrelated (one's payout is high or low independently of whether the other is high or low), positively correlated (one's payout is high when the other's payout is high), or negatively correlated (one's payout is high when the other's payout is low). By carefully selecting assets, one can change the payout pattern of one's total holding across states of nature, thereby reducing risk.

One way to reduce risk is *diversification.* Households following a diversification strategy spread their purchases over many different kinds of assets, so that if one asset does poorly, some other asset or group of assets will be doing well. In this way, the risk of the entire portfolio can be significantly less than the risk of its individual assets.

In order for the diversification strategy to reduce risk, the payouts of the assets must properly relate to one another. A simple example serves to demonstrate the role of diversification. Assume that asset 1 pays \$10 if the economy booms and \$5 if it does not. Asset 2 pays \$5 if the economy booms and \$10 if does not. Since each asset has a random payout, depending on

▼

8. How can a diversification strategy reduce risk?

14. Laurel buys 12,000 units of security 1 and sells 18,000 units of security 2. His after-trade income is therefore \$22,000 in each state of nature. As in the first example, trade with neutral Hardy allows Laurel to reduce his risk—in this case to zero.

whether the economy booms or not, each asset is risky. The payout of both assets combined, however, is $15 regardless of how the economy does. A household that diversifies by holding both assets, therefore, has zero risk, even though each asset separately is risky.

In the above example, diversification would not work if the two assets had returns that were positively correlated. If both assets paid $10 if the economy boomed, and $5 otherwise, the portfolio consisting of both of them would be just as risky as the individual assets. The general rule is that as long as a number of assets are held whose payouts are not highly correlated, it is possible to eliminate some risk.

Many people diversify by buying mutual funds. There are two basic types of mutual funds. An *open-end mutual fund* uses the money of investing households to buy a collection of stocks. Each participating household owns a part of the entire collection in proportion to how much money the household paid in. If new households supply money to the fund, the new cash is used to buy more stocks. A *closed-end mutual fund* operates in a similar fashion except that once the fund is started new households wanting to buy fund shares must buy them from another household that wants to sell. The fund manages only the assets derived from the original start-up.

Mutual funds are a way to provide the household with the lowest risk, given an expected payout. For example, if there is a set of assets with expected payouts E_i and standard deviations σ_i, it is possible to construct from these assets two mutual funds so that investors who choose only efficient portfolios (ones with as low a standard deviation as possible given the expected payouts) will be indifferent choosing between the two mutual funds and the original list of stocks. What this means is that the two mutual funds themselves must be efficient to be able to replicate the efficient returns of any combination of stocks the investors might choose on their own.[15]

Mutual funds also serve another purpose by offering an asset that can target a particular type of investment and provide payouts for that investment type with as little risk as possible. If I want to invest in Mexico, for example, but want as little risk as possible given the expected payouts for the types of investments Mexico offers, I might buy a mutual fund of stocks chosen from Mexico. This mutual fund would give lower risk than selecting one or two Mexican stocks by themselves.

 ## APPLICATION: Stock Mutual Funds

Should one use managed or indexed mutual funds? A *managed fund* is one whose managers attempt to selectively pick stocks to provide superior performance, given the constraints of the fund's objectives. An *indexed fund* is one that does not actively pick stocks, but simply buys a representative

---

15. See Robert C. Merton, ''An Analytic Derivation of the Efficient Portfolio Frontier,'' *Journal of Financial and Quantitative Analysis,* September 1972, pp. 1851–1872.

collection of stocks. An example of an indexed fund is the Standard and Poor's 500, which does not use managers to actively change the content of the portfolio through time. The evidence on whether managed funds perform better is sometimes hard to interpret. For example, if one took 64 coins and tossed each six times, by chance one would expect to have one give six straight heads. Would this mean that the tosser was better at throwing heads? The same problem arises in evaluating mutual fund performance.

The top ten performing mutual funds provided returns between 768 percent (Fidelity Select Health) and 543 percent (SteinRoe Investors Special) for the 10-year period between June 1982 and June 1992.[16] This converts to an annual return between 22.6 and 18.4 percent. However, there is no guarantee that the same funds will again be the best performers in the next ten years. It is extremely rare for a mutual fund to remain in the top group of performers for many successive years. Standard and Poor's 500 earned an annual return of 18.48 percent over the same period.

In cases where a particular managed fund, such as Fidelity's Magellan Fund, seems to consistently outperform the market, analysts have found that the higher return can be explained because the fund took a larger position in riskier stocks. Riskier stocks provide a higher risk premium and hence have higher expected returns. Between 1977 and 1983, for example, a study by Morningstar, a specialist research firm, found that Magellan's average returns varied by far more from month to month than returns on the Standard and Poor's 500.[17] Fidelity's stable of mutual funds also seems to consistently provide a large number of the top performing funds. However, of the $30 billion that Fidelity manages, 47 percent is invested in equity funds (stocks), compared to other fund companies that have 20 to 25 percent in equity funds.

Since actively managing funds is costly (analysts' and managers' time must be paid for, the costs of investigating companies must be borne, and trading costs must be covered), the more actively a fund is managed, the more money must be taken from returns of the stocks held and the less will be left for the investor. For this reason, many economists recommend that the wise investor simply buy indexed funds and save the management costs.[18] These economists assert that the indexed fund is just as likely to perform well as the comparable managed fund, so one should be ahead in the long run. ■

15.4 Insurance

A second major way in which households reduce risk is by buying insurance. Insurance reduces the household's overall risk because a payout is given when the insured-against loss occurs (that is, the policy's payout is negatively

16. See ''Finance: Fidelity Changes Tack,'' *The Economist,* August 8, 1992, pp. 67–68.
17. Ibid., p. 67.
18. ''The Stock Picking Fallacy,'' *The Economist,* August 8, 1992, pp. 15–16.

correlated with the insured loss). From the point of view of the household, the insurance buyer replaces an uncertain event (the loss being insured against) with a certain event, the payment of the premium. Even though the payout of the insurance contract is risky, when combined with the household's other circumstances it reduces overall risk.

Insurance Risk Pooling

▼

9. Give an example showing how an insurance company uses risk pooling.

How is the insurance company able to accept a certain payment in return for taking on a risky commitment? Doesn't this mean the insurance company is doing the opposite of what it should by *adding* to its risk? The answer is that by insuring large enough numbers of households for risks that are both independent of one another and uncorrelated, the insurance company reduces its risk to very little compared to the amount of insurance offered. This procedure is called *risk pooling*. Risk pooling takes advantage of the law of large numbers, which says that if an event happens with probability p in a large number of independent events, the fraction of the events in which it actually happens will approach arbitrarily close to p as the number of events gets large.

To see how this works, consider the situation of 1,000 homeowners, any one of whom runs a one-in-a-thousand chance of fire destroying his or her home in a given year. If a fire occurs, the homeowner suffers a loss of $100,000, the value of the home. If no fire occurs, the loss is zero. Since such a situation is inherently risky, each risk averse homeowner would prefer a *certain loss* equal to $100 each year (the expected value of the loss for a given year) to having the same unexpected loss from fire with the risk.

Fortunately, by pooling their experiences, the homeowners can collectively offer insurance contracts that meet their risk-reducing needs. If the states of nature are "fire" and "no fire," the insurance contract says that it will pay the owners $100,000 if fire occurs, and nothing otherwise. Denote this by the payout list ($100,000, $0). In return, the insurance buyer pays $100 whether or not the fire occurs (this is the annual insurance premium). Denote this by the payout list ($-$100, $-$100). Writing the cost and the payouts of the insurance contract in this way reminds us that purchase of an insurance contract is a purchase of a risky asset, just as buying a stock is. The net effect of the insurance purchase is that the homeowner's risky original holding ($-$100,000, 0) is converted to a certain payment: ($-$100,000, 0) + ($-$100, $-$100) + ($100,000, 0) = ($-$100, $-$100).

Out of the annual premiums collected from the 1,000 insurees (1,000 × $100 = $100,000), homeowners collectively are able to make payouts to homeowners whose homes burn. The arrangement works because the loss from fire for any given home is uncertain, but for the group as a whole it is not.

In reality, even the loss for a large group will still contain some risk. However, the law of large numbers says that the overall losses can be predicted with much greater accuracy for a large group than for an individual.

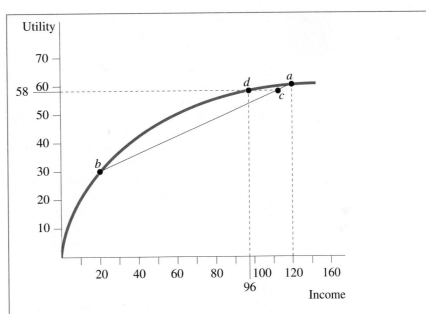

Figure 15.5   The Household's Willingness to Buy Insurance   A
household has $120 income and utility 60 if no accident occurs (point *a*),
but faces a 1 in 20 chance of a $100 loss (utility 30, point *b*). Its expected
income is (0.95)$120 + (0.05)$20 = $115, and its expected utility is 58,
the same as it would have if its income were $96 and there were no possi-
bility of loss. The household is therefore willing to pay up to $120 − $96
= $24 for full insurance against a contingency whose expected loss is $5.

Because an insurance company must cover the costs of administration and
selling, the premium charged by the insurance company is typically larger
than the expected value of the policy payout. However, buyers of insurance
are more than willing to pay a little extra, because they get the benefit of the
reduced risk.

Figure 15.5 shows how much the household is willing to pay for insurance.
In this case the household has income $120 and utility 60 if no accident
occurs. This is point *a*. It has a 1 in 20 chance, however, of a large $100 loss,
leaving it with income $20 and utility 30. This is point *b*. The household's
expected income–expected utility pair is ($115, 58), given by point *c*. If the
household had certain income of $96, its utility would be 58 at point *d*. The
household is therefore willing to pay up to $120 − $96 = $24 for complete
insurance (which would leave it with certain income of $96). Notice that
actuarially fair insurance (insurance whose cost exactly equals the expected
payout) would be just $5. There is room therefore for a large group to insure
using the law of large numbers, charge prices for insurance close to the
actuarially fair rate, and leave each insuree better off. The welfare gains come
from eliminating risk.

APPLICATION: Risk Pooling and the Aftermath of Hurricane Andrew

Hurricane Andrew, passing through southern Florida in August 1992 and then moving west to Louisiana, was the most costly natural disaster in American history. Prudential Insurance Company of America placed its losses alone at more than $1 billion. "We have the capital to absorb major one-time hits like this," Eugene O'Hara, Prudential's chief financial officer, said as he reported that the company had $10 billion available to pay for the loss.[19] Even though the industry has $160 billion overall to deal with losses of this type, the effect will be to raise property and casualty rates nationwide.

What makes losses of the Hurricane Andrew type so hard to prepare for is that they cause claims to be highly correlated among policyholders. All households in the path of Andrew insured by Prudential filed claims at the same time. High correlation of insuree claims works against the basic principle of risk pooling on which insurance is based. For this reason, most insurance companies stipulate that they will not pay property and casualty claims resulting from war or insurrection. For a similar reason, earthquake insurance, when offered, is relatively expensive compared to insurance for damage from other causes. ■

▼
10. Explain moral hazard and adverse selection in insurance markets in terms of asymmetric information.

EXPLORATION: Insurance and Asymmetric Information: Moral Hazard

Home and automobile insurance companies often stipulate that the policyholder can obtain lower rates if a fire detector is present in the home or if the car is equipped with an air bag, an automatic restraint system, or antilock brakes. Each condition can be verified by simple observation and is likely to reduce the probability and magnitude of a claim. On the other hand, automobile insurance rates are higher if the driver lives in a congested or high-accident part of the country, has a history of citations and moving violations, or has had numerous previous accidents.

The above facts remind us that precautions undertaken by the insuree often have a significant bearing on the probability that a loss will occur. Whether a manufacturing firm periodically spends the time and money to hold a safety training course for its employees, for example, can make a great deal of difference to the number of accidents that occur. What happens if there is asymmetric information between the insurer and insuree about the amount of preventive activity undertaken by the insuree? In this case, a situation can arise called *moral hazard*. Moral hazard arises when the behavior of the insuree changes upon obtaining insurance in such a way that the probability of a claim goes up.

19. See Greg Steinmetz, "Prudential Lifts Loss Estimate from Hurricane," *Wall Street Journal,* September 24, 1992, p. A3.

For example, if the manufacturing firm just mentioned gets full accident coverage, it may decide not to hold safety seminars any longer. In the same way, a homeowner may decide not to install a lightning rod or fire detector if the house is fully insured for replacement for either hazard, and a driver may not be as careful in his driving habits if he has full replacement coverage on his automobile. If the effects of moral hazard are great enough, insurance companies may find that they have to raise their premiums or be forced not to offer insurance at all.

The costs of moral hazard to society as a whole arise because the inability of the insurance company to know who is careful to avoid claims and who is not means that it must charge all policyholders alike. With no rate incentive, those who have the least-cost way to prevent accidents may not take the needed action. More costly accidents occur, but those whom they happen to and who could have prevented them at low cost do not care since they are covered by insurance.

Insurance companies try to deal with moral hazard by devising better ways to monitor their policyholders' claim-reducing behavior and by segmenting their policyholders as well as they can into higher-risk and lower-risk categories. The better the segmentation, the better the company's ability to charge each group the right premium based on the true probabilities of claims. Segmenting into higher- and lower-premium groups creates the proper incentive for insurees to undertake the right amount of preventive activities, because they can gain the benefit of lower premiums by placing themselves in the lower-risk group.

The attempt to segment markets into groups of policyholders, each of whom has the same probabilities of claims as any other in the group, leads us to the second problem caused by asymmetric information faced by insurance companies: adverse selection. ■

EXPLORATION: Insurance and Asymmetric Information: Adverse Selection

The life insurance policy I hold has an inflation clause that allows me to increase my insurance each year by an amount that matches the inflation-induced loss in purchasing power of the death payment to my family. However, the policy stipulates that I can exercise the inflation option only if it was exercised the previous year. Why is this requirement present?

The answer has to do with *adverse selection*, the problem that an insurance policy may disproportionately attract buyers whose claims will be larger than the average for the group for which the policy was designed. As a simple example, let us say that I know only 1 in 10,000 college students is likely to die in the year after reaching age twenty. I therefore offer a policy that pays $1 million if death occurs between the twentieth and twenty-first birthdays, charging $101 for the policy. If 10,000 average students take the policy, I collect $1,010,000 in premiums. Since only one student dies, in a typical year

I pay $1 million in claims and keep the extra $10,000 to cover my expenses. However, in a large population there are students who know they have a higher than 1 in 10,000 chance of dying between their twentieth and twenty-first birthdays (maybe they have a serious disease, or maybe they have just taken up hang-gliding or technical climbing). Instead of getting an average group of students buying the policy, I get many more of the latter type. If I am unable to screen them out because of asymmetric information (they know their true probabilities but I know only the probabilities for the population at large), I will get a self-selected or adversely selected group that is heavily weighted toward those with high claims. If the problem is large enough, I go broke and am able to offer insurance to no one.

Insurance companies try to eliminate adverse selection by designing insurance policies that minimize it and by screening insurance buyers. For example, in the case of my policy with the inflation option, limiting use of the option to those who used it in the previous year designs the policy so that someone who has just learned his probability of imminent death has increased can't suddenly enter the market for more insurance. The design of the policy limits adverse selection from occurring. Similarly, medical insurance policies ask about prior medical conditions so that they can screen those with likelihood of large claims into groups with similar probabilities, charging these groups higher rates. This also helps reduce adverse selection.

Private companies frequently offer medical insurance policies to their employees without worrying greatly about adverse selection because membership in the group is determined for purposes (suitability for work in the company) that are largely unrelated to risk of a claim. In some cases, however, insurance coverage might be sufficient to induce some workers who know they have high risks to seek work in the company because it has a good medical plan. If this behavior became prevalent, adverse selection would again become a concern, and the company would want to screen out those with prospective costs far above the norm. ■

Summary

Active Reading Guide numbers are given in parentheses at the end of each summary item.

1. Risk is used to describe a situation when a household or firm encounters the possibility of random outcomes for which the probabilities are known and some outcomes are preferred to others. The description of risk requires a listing of possible outcomes and their probability of occurrence. (1)

2. Apart from the description of all possible outcomes and their probabilities, two key descriptions of a random number are its expected value and its standard deviation. The expected value measures the average value of the random number that would occur over repeated trials, and the standard deviation records the typical dispersion above or below the expected value. Expected value is computed as

the probability-weighted average of the random numbers, and the standard deviation is the square root of the probability-weighted sum of squared differences between the random numbers and the expected value. Standard deviation is often used as an indicator of the quantity of risk, though it is not synonymous with risk. (2)

3. Households select among risky alternatives by choosing the alternative that maximizes their expected utility. Expected utility is the probability-weighted average of utility over all possible outcomes. (3)

4. Since consumption depends on goods and services that, in turn, depend on income and prices, much of a household's risk depends on its utility of income, assuming prices are constant across different outcomes. Risk averse households are characterized by concave (downward-curving) utility functions of income; risk neutral households are characterized by utility functions of income that are straight lines; and households that are risk loving are characterized by utility functions of income that curve upward. (4)

5. Risk averse investors have expected utilities for risky outcomes that are less than the expected utility they would receive for a sure outcome with the same expected payout. The risk premium is the amount by which the expected payout for the risky alternative exceeds the payout for a riskless alternative costing the household the same. (5)

6. Nonrecreational gambling is distinguished from risky investing in that (a) investing puts money into projects that produce tangible goods and services; (b) investors place money in projects where their expected payout is greater than the amount they invest; and (c) investors try to avoid or minimize risk when possible. Legalized gambling entails social costs in the form of gambling addictions and associated crime, and the hidden taxes involved in legalized gambling particularly affect low-income and less-educated households, which spend a higher proportion of their income on gambling. (6)

7. A security is any asset providing the owner with a claim to risky payments. Equilibrium of de-

mand and supply for securities determines their market price. The risk premium for a security is the difference between its expected payout and the payout on a riskless asset costing the same. (7)

8. Purchasing securities with different payouts across states of nature allows investors to change the nature of the risk in their portfolios. Diversification, meaning spreading one's money over the purchase of many types of assets, can reduce the holdings of risk in comparison to buying just one type of asset. When one asset does poorly, another is doing well; so overall variability is reduced. (8)

9. Pooling independent risks is another way to reduce overall risk. For example, insurance companies take on the risks of their policyholders when they sell insurance. They reduce their overall risk through the law of large numbers, which says that if an event occurring with probability p is repeated a large number of times, the proportion of the trials in which the event actually occurs will approach arbitrarily close to p. The insurance company can therefore compute with near certainty what its claims will be over a large number of policyholders. (9)

10. Asymmetric information presents two types of problems to insurers. If policyholders are able to influence the probability of a claim's occurring and the insurance company is unable to observe their actions, moral hazard may occur. This means that, once insured, the policyholder will take fewer precautionary measures, thereby raising the probability of a claim. A second problem is called adverse selection, meaning that an insurance policy disproportionately attracts buyers whose claims will be larger than the average for the group for which the policy was designed. To combat each problem, the insurance company can screen applicants for insurance and try to design policies that reward risk-reducing behavior. The insurance function works best when insurance buyers are homogeneous in their likelihood of claims. When those wanting insurance cannot be separated into groups on the basis of their different risks and expected costs, it becomes impossible in some cases to offer insurance at all. (10)

Review Questions

*1. Given two risky assets, is it possible that investor A could think the first is riskier and investor B think the second is riskier? Does this conflict with the use of standard deviation as a measure for risk?

2. Why is expected value useful to know in repeated investments?

*3. In what way does standard deviation give more weight to large deviations than to small deviations?

4. If demand for a security falls, all else being constant, will its risk premium change?

*5. How does diversification reduce risk?

6. What is the different principle governing risk pooling as compared to diversification?

*7. When Adam Smith speaks of there being no such thing as a "fair" lottery, what does he mean? What is the "worth" of the tickets bought in a lottery?

8. Some people claim investing in the stock market is no different from gambling. In what ways are they alike, and in what ways different?

*9. Why does insurance require that those insured be grouped into homogeneous groups on the basis of probability of a claim? What happens if *non*-homogeneous groups are insured together?

10. Use moral hazard to explain why insurance companies will not insure an object for more than it is worth.

Numerical and Graphing Exercises

*1. Compute the expected value of the toss of a die. Prove or disprove that the expected value of the toss of two dice is twice that for one.

2. Gamble 1 pays $100 with probability $\frac{1}{4}$ and $1,000 with probability $\frac{3}{4}$. Gamble 2 pays $200 with probability $\frac{1}{2}$ and $300 with probability $\frac{1}{2}$. For two investors whose utility reaches the same level at income = $1,000, draw a graph to prove or disprove that both will always prefer the same gamble.

*3. If $a + bV(I)$ is a transformation of $V(I)$ where a and b are constant, determine graphically or mathematically whether it gives the same ranking of risky alternatives as $V(I)$.

4. An individual is risk neutral for small gambles and highly risk averse for large gambles. Draw $V(I)$ for such an individual.

*5. A household's utility curve is $V(I) = \sqrt{I}$. How much would the household be willing to pay to insure against a 50-percent chance of losing $200 if the household's income is originally $600?

6. Two dice are rolled and the payoff is equal to $\$(s^2 - 25)$, where s is the number of spots showing. If a household's utility function is $V(I) = I^2$, where I is its income and initial income is $100, at what price will the household accept such a gamble?

*7. A household is given the choice between receiving $100 outright or taking a $\frac{3}{4}$ chance to win $220. It chooses the latter. The same household is given a choice between a $\frac{1}{3}$ chance to win $100 and a $\frac{1}{4}$ chance to win $220. It chooses the former. Prove that this is inconsistent with expected utility maximization.

8. A traveler has $1,000, which has a 1 in 2 chance of being seized by robbers if she places it all in one place in her purse. If she divides her money into two $500 stashes and hides them in separate places, each one has a 1 in 2 chance of being discovered and stolen. How much does she expect to have stolen under either alternative? What is the standard deviation of her loss under each alternative?

*9. In the preceding exercise, if the traveler's utility function is $V(I) = \sqrt{I}$ where initial income is $30,000, which alternative is she better off choosing? How does your answer relate to the rule, "Don't put all of your eggs in one basket"?

10. An investment costing $110 pays returns of (150, 120, 90, 80, 70) with probabilities (0.6, 0.1, 0.1, 0.1, 0.1). What is its risk premium?

* Asterisks are used to denote questions that are answered at the back of the book.

Intertemporal Decision Making

Language and literature are filled with references to the importance of time to consumers and producers alike. Benjamin Franklin coined the phrase "Time is money" in his *Advice to a Young Tradesman* in 1748. In this chapter we extend our study of microeconomics to include intertemporal decision making, the decisions that consumers and producers make that depend on future time periods. We focus our discussion on the two prime intertemporal decisions: the household's decision to save and the firm's decision to invest, including spending on research and development. In addition, we examine the special prices that apply to time, real and nominal interest rates, to see how they are formed by the market.

16.1 The Household's Intertemporal Budget Constraint

Investors in money market funds discovered to their amazement in September 1992 that the average fund was offering interest rates below 3 percent for the first time in years. This was a far cry from the heady days of the early 1980s, when such funds often offered interest rates of 13 and 14 percent. The new rates were symptomatic of a shift in the balance between borrowers and lenders. Retired households, wealthier on average than the population at large and accustomed to higher earnings on their assets, found that their investment-derived income was lower. In contrast, young households borrowing for a first home suddenly found that their interest costs had dropped. How does one analyze changes of this type? The answer requires taking explicit account of time in the household budget process.

In the first sections of this chapter, we examine how households decide to save or to borrow, what difference it makes to their utility, and what determines the market interest rate. We then look at the investment decision of firms as it relates to research and development.

The Intertemporal Model

▼
1. Relate intertemporal choice to standard household choice and derive the intertemporal budget constraint.

The models we examined in previous chapters assumed that the household spends all of its income in the current period. That is, if the household chooses goods x and y, its budget constraint is

$$p_x x + p_y y = \text{income},$$

where p_x and p_y are "spot" prices (the price for buying the good on the spot, or at that moment) for goods x and y, both assumed to be consumed in the present. We now relax that constraint and allow the household to spend more or less than its income and to allocate its consumption among different periods. If a household spends less than its current income, it can save the difference for later consumption. If it spends more, it needs to borrow or consume its savings.

Although it might seem that adding the possibility of saving would complicate our utility-maximizing model, we can still analyze intertemporal decisions using conventional budget lines and indifference curves. To do so, we define our two goods a little differently. As in Chapter 5, when we looked at consumers choosing between labor and leisure, we can portray intertemporal choices in terms of two composite goods. This time, the composite goods are made up of all present goods (C_1) and all goods in the future period (C_2). As long as the prices of goods making up the composite are fixed relative to one another, this poses no problem for drawing conventional indifference curves. We let p_1 and p_2 be the spot prices for the composite good in each period.

The key tool that we use to describe the household's decision to save or consume at a particular point in time is the intertemporal budget constraint.

*The household's **intertemporal budget constraint** describes the constraints on the household's purchases over multiple time periods.*

The word *intertemporal* comes from the two root words *inter,* for "between," and *tempus,* for "time." It therefore relates choices between time periods. To derive the intertemporal budget constraint, we start with the household's first-period budget constraint

$$p_1C_1 + S = I_1,$$

where S indicates income the household devotes to savings (negative S indicates borrowing) and I_1 indicates the household's period 1 income. In the second period, the household can spend its second-period income I_2 plus the principal and interest from what it saved in the first period. Thus the second-period budget constraint is

$$p_2C_2 = I_2 + (1 + r)S,$$

where r is the rate of interest earned on the household's savings. *Principal* refers to the amount saved by the household and *interest* to the percentage of the amount saved that the household receives as payment for its savings.

*An **interest rate** is the charge for borrowing money or a commodity (alternatively, the payment for loaning money or a commodity), expressed as a percentage of the quantity borrowed.*

Later in the chapter we describe what determines the interest rate. For now, we take the interest rate as given and assume that the household can borrow or lend at the same interest rate.

We discussed in Chapter 5 the fact that households earn income from various sources, such as from supplying labor or supplying other resources or assets that they might own. For our discussion here, we will have the household's income each period determined entirely by its endowment of the two composite goods. Then $I_1 = p_1E_1$ and $I_2 = p_2E_2$, where E_1 and E_2 are the household's endowments of the composite good in the first and second period, respectively.

Deriving the Intertemporal Budget Constraint

Dividing the second-period budget constraint by $(1 + r)$ gives us $p_2C_2/(1 + r) = I_2/(1 + r) + S$. Adding this to the first-period budget constraint, we get $p_1C_1 + S + p_2C_2/(1 + r) = I_1 + I_2/(1 + r) + S$. Subtracting S from both sides then gives us

$$p_1C_1 + \frac{p_2C_2}{(1 + r)} = I_1 + \frac{I_2}{(1 + r)},$$

which is the household's intertemporal budget constraint because it relates the household's spending in the two time periods. In the intertemporal budget constraint, it is no longer the household's current income that determines what can be spent, but the sum of incomes over the two time periods, modified by the interest rate so that a dollar of second-period income is equivalent to $1/(1 + r)$ dollars of first-period income.

Plotting the intertemporal budget constraint gives us Figure 16.1. The horizontal axis shows the household's consumption in the first period, and the vertical axis shows second-period consumption. If the household spends $I_1 + I_2/(1 + r)$ in the first period, it can consume $[I_1 + I_2/(1 + r)]/p_1$ units of C_1, for example.[1] If it saves all of its first-period income (consuming nothing in the first period), the household can spend $(1 + r)I_1 + I_2$ in the second period, which allows it to buy $[(1 + r)I_1 + I_2]/p_2$ units of C_2. The budget line connecting these two intercept points shows the combinations of consumption in the two periods that satisfy the intertemporal budget constraint. The absolute value of the slope of the budget constraint is $(1 + r)p_1/p_2$. Thus a higher interest rate would make the budget line steeper, whereas a lower interest rate would flatten it. Later in the chapter we will discuss in more detail how a change in the interest rate and market equilibrium are related.

The Household's Intertemporal Choice

Figure 16.1 also shows a household indifference curve for bundles of C_1 and C_2 providing equal utility. Given its intertemporal budget constraint, the household makes its consumption choice in the same way that a utility-maximizing household usually does. The household reaches the highest in-

---

1. This involves borrowing $I_2/(1 + r)$ in the first period and paying I_2 in the second period to pay off the loan. This leaves nothing for second-period consumption.

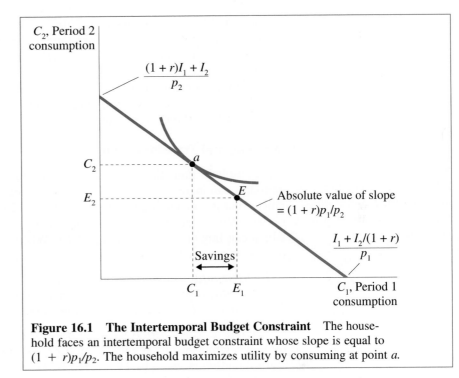

Figure 16.1   The Intertemporal Budget Constraint   The household faces an intertemporal budget constraint whose slope is equal to
$(1 + r)p_1/p_2$. The household maximizes utility by consuming at point a.

difference curve possible at point a, given the intertemporal budget constraint.
The choice of consumption at point a leads to a tangency. Thus the household's marginal rate of substitution of period 1 good for period 2 good (the
absolute value of the slope of the indifference curve) equals the absolute
value of the slope of the budget line, or

$$\text{MRS}_{C1,C2} = \frac{(1 + r)p_1}{p_2}$$

at point a. This corresponds in the intertemporal model to the tangency
condition relating consumption of two goods in the single-period model that
we derived in Chapter 3. In the present setting, however, $\text{MRS}_{C1,C2}$ represents
the household's *marginal rate of time preference*. The higher $\text{MRS}_{C1,C2}$ is,
the greater the household's impatience to have period 1 good relative to
period 2 good; the lower $\text{MRS}_{C1,C2}$, the greater is the household's patience,
meaning its willingness to give up period 1 good for period 2 good.

> The **marginal rate of time preference**, $MRS_{C1,C2}$, *measures the num-
> ber of units of period 2 good that the household requires to compen-
> sate for forgoing a unit of period 1 good.*

The intertemporal budget constraint also gives us a convenient way to
evaluate saving by the household. In the figure, C_1 is smaller than E_1. Since

the household consumes less in the first period than it has available, it is saving the difference. In dollar terms the amount of savings is $S = p_1(E_1 - C_1)$. Had C_1 been to the right of E_1, it would have indicated that the household was borrowing in the first period.

By saving, the household effectively converts period 1 consumption into period 2 consumption. By borrowing, it does the reverse. Next we examine this intertemporal transformation in more detail.

Intertemporal Transformation

▼

2. Explain what intertemporal transformation is, distinguishing between the nominal and real interest rates.

The household finds that by giving up one unit of consumption in the first period, it can increase its consumption in the second period by $(1 + r)p_1/p_2$ units. That is, consuming one fewer unit in period 1 generates p_1 dollars of saving. With interest, this savings becomes $(1 + r)p_1$ dollars in period 2, which can buy $(1 + r)p_1/p_2$ units of C_2. When the household borrows, this process is reversed.

> **Intertemporal transformation** is the act of changing the quantity of a commodity available in one time period (or periods) by altering the quantity available in some other time period(s).

The rate at which period 1 *dollars* transform into period 2 dollars is given by $1 + r$, while the rate at which period 1 *consumption* transforms into period 2 consumption is given by $(1 + r)p_1/p_2$. To distinguish between the two, r is called the *nominal (or money) interest rate,* and $\rho = (1 + r)p_1/p_2 - 1$ is called the *real interest rate.* We subtract 1 from the formula because we want the interest rate to measure only the consumption increment over the period. Real interest rates are the relevant variable for making utility comparisons because consumption goods are what enter into utility. For example, if I decide not to buy a $17,000 automobile this year and place my money in the bank at 3 percent interest ($r = 0.03$), I will be able to buy the same automobile next year and have money left over if the price of the automobile rises less than 3 percent ($p_2 < 1.03p_1$). In other words, the condition for being able to have more in the second period is $p_2 < (1 + r)p_1$, which is equivalent to $\rho > 0$: One automobile forgone today implies $1 + \rho$ automobiles tomorrow.

The Nominal Interest Rate in Intertemporal Transformation. As indicated above, higher nominal interest rates lead to steeper intertemporal budget lines for given prices. A good example relating the nominal interest rate to the slope of the budget line is the case where the (nominal) interest rate at which the household borrows, r_B, is greater than the (nominal) interest rate on savings, r_S. Many consumers are in exactly this position when they use a credit card charging 14 percent interest to buy something even though they have cash or savings in the bank earning only 3 percent. They would be better off not using the credit card and taking their money out of the bank.

If we distinguish between borrowing and saving, the household's budget constraints become $S + p_1C_1 = I_1 + B$ in the first period and $p_2C_2 = I_2 + (1 + r_S)S - (1 + r_B)B$ in the second period. It is easy to show that if the household is borrowing, say, $10 at the same time it is saving $5, it is better off reducing its saving to zero and borrowing only $5. Similarly, if the household is saving $10 and borrowing $5, it is better off reducing its borrowing to zero and saving only $5. Thus the household that is borrowing at the same time it is saving will increase its income in the second period by $(r_B - r_S)$ times the minimum of S and B if it reduces both saving and borrowing by whichever of the two is smaller. In short, the rational household will either borrow or lend but not both. When the household borrows, its transformation of goods between periods is indicated by $(1 + r_B)p_1/p_2$, which gives a steeper slope than the transformation rate $(1 + r_S)p_1/p_2$ that applies if the household saves.

The resulting intertemporal budget constraint is shown in Figure 16.2. If the household borrows, it moves to the right of endowment point E by giving up $(1 + r_B)p_1/p_2$ units of C_2 for each unit of C_1. If it moves to the left by saving, it gains $(1 + r_S)p_1/p_2$ units of C_2 for each unit of C_1 forgone. The corner in the intertemporal budget constraint occurs because $r_B > r_S$.

The Importance of Prices. In the example just completed, we didn't need to worry about prices much because p_2/p_1 was the same whether the household borrowed or saved. This does not mean that price changes are unimportant, however, as our discussion of the real interest rate earlier indicated.

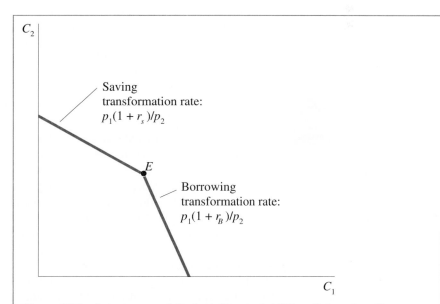

Figure 16.2   Intertemporal Budget Constraint When Interest on Borrowing Is Higher Than Interest on Saving ($r_B > r_S$)   Starting at endowment E, the household's budget line is steeper to the right than to the left because it must pay a higher interest rate on borrowing than it receives on saving.

To see the importance of prices, consider the story of Rip Van Winkle VI (descendant of the original Rip). In the 1990s, Rip goes hunting in the Catskills and falls asleep for 200 years. He wakes up in the 2190s and finds his shotgun rusted beyond help and his clothes in shreds. He remembers, though, that he had a bank account with $100 in it when he went to sleep, and that the account was drawing nominal interest of 5.25 percent per year. Hurriedly he finds the nearest pay phone and calls his bank to ask what his account balance is. The teller informs him that his balance is $2,782,408.56. He is two times a millionaire! (Maybe this sleeping jag was not so bad after all.) Just then, the operator breaks in and tells him, "That will be $1,209,800 for the first three minutes, please." Because inflation has been 8 percent per year ($p_2/p_1 = 1.08$), what would pay for 400 local calls when he went to sleep would pay for precisely 2.3 local phone calls 200 years later!

What happened to Rip was that his real interest rate was negative. Let p_1 and p_2 be the prices for the good in periods 1 and 2 (for Rip this is the price of a phone call). Use π to stand for the percentage price increase between periods, $p_2/p_1 - 1 = \pi$. From the intertemporal budget constraint, the rate of converting period 1 good into period 2 good is $(1 + r)/(1 + \pi)$. In Rip's case, r was 5.25 percent and π was 8 percent. Thus Rip Van Winkle's savings were earning him a real return of $(1.0525)/(1.08) - 1 = -.0255$ or -2.55 percent. Rip's purchasing power was dropping with every year he slept. For his purchasing power to rise, the nominal interest rate r would have to exceed the rate of price increase π. In terms of the intertemporal budget line, a high p_2/p_1 means a flatter transformation frontier.

We will examine the savings implications of a steeper or flatter transformation frontier after we see how the basic intertemporal model can shed light on other matters in addition to household saving.

APPLICATION: Gasoline Prices and Intertemporal Choices

In Chapter 2 we explained that expectations of demand and supply changes in the future can have an immediate effect on prices today. As an example, we cited the increase in gasoline prices due to the Iraqi invasion of Kuwait in August 1990. By using our intertemporal model, we can now give a fuller explanation of why prices would rise immediately, even though supplies of oil were not immediately reduced.

Figure 16.3 displays the quantities of oil available to the domestic market in each of two time periods at point a. The slope of line l_1 equals the intertemporal transformation rate $p_1(1 + r)/p_2$, where p_1 and p_2 are the prices of oil in each period and r is the interest rate. Viewing this from the point of view of a representative household, this rate also equals the marginal rate of transformation between oil in one period and oil in the other, given by the slope of the representative indifference curve at point a.

When production of oil in Kuwait was cut off, current supplies of oil were unaffected, but the supply of oil in the future period was expected to be

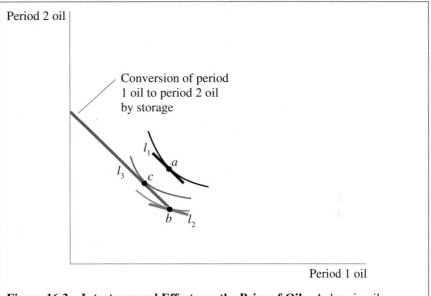

Period 2 oil

Conversion of period
1 oil to period 2 oil
by storage

l_1

l_3

a

c

b l_2

Period 1 oil

Figure 16.3   Intertemporal Effects on the Price of Oil   A drop in oil
availability in period 2 (the shift from point a to point b) implies a higher
price of period 2 oil relative to period 1 oil (l_2 is flatter than l_1). This
raises the demand for oil for storage, moving point b to point c and returning the oil price ratio to its original level, with the period 1 and period
2 oil prices both being higher.

lower. This moved point a to point b. Were no action taken, oil supplies in
the second period would be drastically reduced from their original levels and
the price of oil in the second period would rise. The increase in p_2 relative
to p_1 shows up in the flatter slope of line l_2 at point b (this is consistent with
the marginal rate of substitution at point b).

This is not the end of the story, however. Oil suppliers and oil distributors
have the option of converting one barrel of period 1 oil into a barrel of period
2 oil by storage. This gives the intertemporal transformation frontier indicated
by the line with slope minus 1 through points b and c. Revenues from selling
period 2 oil are determined by p_2, and the cost of oil for storage is given by
p_1. If price p_1 stays the same while p_2 rises, the profitability of storing oil
rises. In a competitive market, overall demand for oil rises as the storage
demand for oil rises. Recall, too, that some of this storage demand comes
from households themselves, who also anticipate higher future prices. Increased first-period demand raises the price of first-period oil until such point
as additional storage is unprofitable. Since we assume that the changes in the
oil market do not change the interest rate r, and originally prices were such
that additional storage was unprofitable, this occurs at point c, where the
slope of l_3 equals the slope of l_1.

What is the net effect? The availability of storage to transform period 1 oil into period 2 oil implies that $(1 + r)p_1/p_2$ is unchanged, so that prices in both periods rise proportionately. Thus expectations of higher future prices lead to price increases today. The price system, firm profit maximization, and storage act to alleviate the shortage of oil in the second period. Further, such conservation is exactly what one wants. In effect, the price rises today so that it will not have to rise so much tomorrow. One can also see that point c is on a higher indifference curve than point b, so that the price increase today raises utility by providing more even use of oil in the two periods.

Using the intertemporal model helps us explain why the observed oil price increase of 1990 (30 percent above the prewar price at the peak) was more the result of normal market functions than of conspiratorial opportunism by oil companies.[2] ∎

Having described the intertemporal model, we see that a number of elements interact to determine intertemporal choices, given the transformation opportunities between periods as measured by the real interest rate. However, we have not said where the real interest rate comes from. To see how the economy determines the real interest rate, we first consider a one-person economy and then the general case of a market economy with multiple households.

16.2 Time Preference, Time Productivity, and the Interest Rate

▼
3. What three main elements determine the household's saving or borrowing?

There are three main components to consider with respect to the household's intertemporal consumption: its time preference for goods (the period in which it wants to consume), its time endowment of goods (when the goods are available, apart from adjustments made by the household), and its time productivity of goods (how it can transform goods in one time period into goods in another time period). We can look at how these elements interact in the simplest possible society to determine the real interest rate.

2. For further reading see David A. Butz, ''Intertemporal Resource Allocation: Distributive Issues Surrounding Gasoline Price Hikes,'' *Economic Inquiry,* 29 (July 1991), pp. 591–600, and Matthew L. Wald, ''Gas Is at Historic Low, Reckoning for Inflation,'' *New York Times,* July 26, 1991, p. D1. Butz writes, ''Afraid of bad publicity, oil companies tried with only limited success to keep prices low. Unsatisfied with these efforts and unswayed by efficiency arguments in favor of price-induced conservation, many people expressed outrage and often called for more aggressive efforts to reign in oil company profits. By showing that hoarding by itself in all likelihood helped consumers and hurt oil company profits, this paper may blunt some of these calls for a return to the failed policies of the past.''

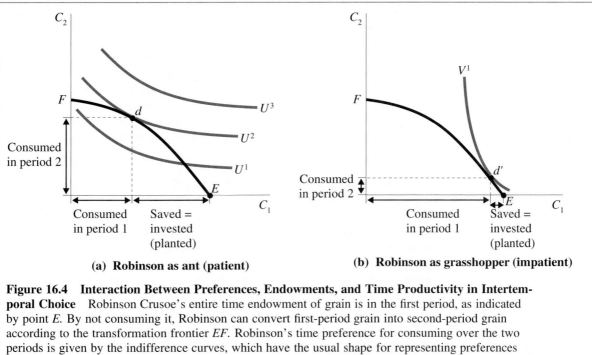

(a) Robinson as ant (patient)

(b) Robinson as grasshopper (impatient)

Figure 16.4   Interaction Between Preferences, Endowments, and Time Productivity in Intertemporal Choice   Robinson Crusoe's entire time endowment of grain is in the first period, as indicated by point *E*. By not consuming it, Robinson can convert first-period grain into second-period grain according to the transformation frontier *EF*. Robinson's time preference for consuming over the two periods is given by the indifference curves, which have the usual shape for representing preferences between two goods. The highest indifference curve attainable determines the quantity of grain consumed in each period. In part (a), a patient Robinson's relatively high marginal rate of substitution of grain in period 2 for grain in period 1 leads to a tangency at point *d*. In part (b), impatient Robinson's relatively high marginal rate of substitution of grain in period 1 for grain in period 2 leads to a tangency at point *d'*. Like the grasshopper in Aesop's fable, impatient Robinson has little period 2 food because he ate most of it in period 1, instead of saving it to plant for the following year.

Operation of a One-Person Economy

Robinson Crusoe, whom we visited in Chapter 3, lives alone on a South Seas island. We assume that he consumes only grain from a bag of grain that he rescued from his shipwreck. He can also plant the grain to produce more the following year. For simplicity, we assume that Robinson allocates his consumption between only two periods: this year, C_1, and next year, C_2.

Figure 16.4 shows Robinson's consumption problem in terms of his time preferences, his endowment in each period, and his ability to convert goods from one period to the next. In part (a), the indifference curves labeled U^1 through U^3 each show the trade-off between consumption in the two periods that Robinson is willing to make. Point *E* gives Robinson's *time endowment of goods*. That is, if Robinson did nothing to change his consumption pattern, he could consume a quantity of C_1 equal to the horizontal distance of point E from the origin. He could not consume any C_2, because his endowment does not provide him with grain in the second period.

Faced with this state of affairs, Robinson can respond in different ways. On one hand, he can behave like the grasshopper in Aesop's fable, who enjoyed the easy life in summer when food was readily available. In economic terms, the grasshopper consumed his endowment quantity of C_1. This option displays a high marginal rate of time preference for consumption today. However, when winter came (period 2), there was no food (zero endowment of C_2), so the grasshopper starved.

On the other hand, Robinson could behave like the ant in Aesop's fable, who worked in summer to store some of his food for winter. By not consuming today, the ant kept food available for the second period. In Aesop's fable, the technology for converting food today into food tomorrow was simple storage (one unit of food stored = one unit of food available next period). In Robinson's case, the technology for converting grain today C_1 into grain next year C_2 is the planting and harvesting process. We assume unplanted grain would rot, so he doesn't have the ability to convert period 1 grain into period 2 grain, except by planting.

If Robinson uses some grain for planting, he moves to the left of point E and upward along curve EF. The rate at which EF rises as one moves left measures the *time productivity* of his technology for converting C_1 into C_2. A steeper EF indicates a more productive technology. This *intertemporal transformation frontier* acts like the production possibility frontier we studied in Chapter 12. It also plays the same role for Robinson as the intertemporal budget constraint did for the household in our previous discussion.

Robinson has relatively flat indifference curves in part (a) of the figure: a high marginal rate of substitution of C_2 for C_1 indicates great willingness to give up consumption in period 1 for consumption in period 2. Given his technology, the highest indifference curve he can reach is U^2, which is tangent to frontier EF at point d. In this case, by saving Robinson consumes even more in period 2 than he does in period 1.

Part (b) displays the same circumstances except that Robinson's preference for consumption in period 1 is higher: $MRS_{C1,C2} = 1/MRS_{C2,C1}$ is higher at any given point than it is in part (a). The technology and endowment are the same, but now Robinson chooses point d' on indifference curve V^1, eating most of his grain in period 1 and having little available in period 2.

What conclusions can we draw from this simple model? First, the location of endowment E, Robinson's preferences for period 1 and period 2 consumption, and the technology available for converting goods in one period into goods in another jointly determine how Robinson allocates his consumption. By using the figure, we can see the effect of changing any one (or more) of the three components.

Second, the goods in the two periods differ only in the time of their delivery. Since grain is the same good, the rate at which period 1 grain would be given up for period 2 grain is a rate based on time alone. This rate determines the real interest rate. That is, an individual who borrows a quantity

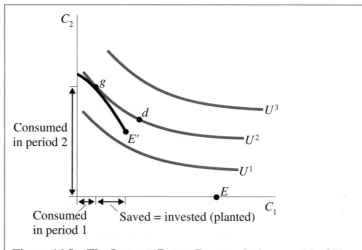

Figure 16.5   The Interest Rate By reproducing part (a) of Figure 16.4 and moving the endowment from E to E' (increasing C_2 and decreasing C_1), we can see the effect of altering the time endowment on Robinson's consumption and the interest rate. Robinson's consumption correspondingly shifts to point g. Since the indifference curve is steeper at point g than at d, the interest rate has risen (more units of second-period good C_2 are needed to compensate for a loss in first-period good C_1).

of grain in period 1 repays in a quantity of period 2 grain that has equivalent value.[3] The excess of period 2 grain needed to compensate for the period 1 grain is the real interest rate.

Relating the Interest Rate to Time Preferences and Time Productivity

Robinson Crusoe would not borrow from himself, but we can still talk about his marginal rate of time preference. If Robinson forgoes one unit of period 1 grain, he needs MRS_{C_1,C_2} units of period 2 grain to compensate. The excess of MRS_{C_1,C_2} over 1 is the real interest rate: that is, $MRS_{C_1,C_2} = 1 + \rho$, where ρ is the real interest rate. Since $MRS_{C_1,C_2} - 1 = \rho$, the interest rate is determined by the slope of the indifference curve at point d in part (a) of Figure 16.4.

Looking at part (a) again, we see that anything that flattens the slope of the indifference curve (raises the value of period 2 grain relative to period 1 grain) lowers the interest rate, and anything that does the reverse raises the interest rate. As an example, what happens if we change the time endowment so that Robinson has more period 2 grain and less period 1 grain? This should raise the interest rate because it lowers the relative value of the period 2 good. Figure 16.5 reproduces part (a) of Figure 16.4, except that we shift the lower

3. When a household receives today and pays today, it makes a spot purchase; when it receives today and pays next period, it borrows.

right origin of the transformation frontier from point E to point E'. This moves Robinson's consumption from d to g. The slope of the indifference curve indicates that point g's MRS_{C_2,C_1} is lower than point d's. Thus the relative value of period 2 good is lower at g (it takes more period 2 good to compensate for period 1 good) than at point d, and the real interest rate is higher.

Figures 16.4 and 16.5 have another property: at the final point Robinson chooses, the marginal rate of substitution (i.e. marginal rate of time preference) and the slope of the transformation frontier (i.e. time productivity of production) *each* determine the interest rate. This is because the indifference curve is tangent to the transformation frontier. Making the transformation frontier steeper in Figure 16.5, for example, would raise the interest rate because the new tangency with the indifference curve, wherever it occurs, must be on the steeper curve.

Having seen in this simple economy how endowment, time preferences (degree of impatience), and time productivity determine the interest rate, we now consider the formation of interest rates in a market setting.

16.3 Market Determination of the Interest Rate

In a market economy with multiple households, the supply and demand for savings in the financial market determine the real interest rate. A *financial market* is a market where households with savings (money to lend) loan their savings to other households or firms for a period of time, after which their money is repaid with interest. Firms in a financial market invest the money they borrow by using it in productive ventures. In an economy without financial markets, each household provides its own investment funds through personal saving. Such was Robinson Crusoe's lot. With a financial market, however, savers can link up with borrowers.

Since *money* is borrowed and lent in financial markets, the interest rate that is quoted is the nominal interest rate. However, in making their decisions, firms and households take prices into account to compute the real interest rate. The market therefore determines the nominal interest rate, which, given prices, also determines the real interest rate. How does the market see to it that savers are willing to provide the money for investments that the borrowers want to undertake?

The answer is that the intertemporal budget constraint, operating through the interest rate, enables borrowers and savers to make their decisions independently yet still moves the market to equilibrium. Borrowers know only that they must borrow at the going interest rate. For example, a firm seeking funds does not need to know the preferences of its lenders, since the market interest rate accurately reflects those preferences for period 2 good relative to period 1 good. The firm chooses the proper investment by maximizing the profits from its investments given the market interest rate.

▼
4. Explain how the interest rate represents both the household's marginal rate of time preference and the time productivity of production.

Households, on the other hand, make their savings decisions solely on the basis of the interest rate without knowing about the investment project that will generate that rate of return. The interest rate tells them the productivity of invested resources in terms of future compensation. Equilibrium in the financial markets ensures that the interest rate satisfies both roles: it accurately reflects the productivity of investment projects, *and* it accurately reflects the utility value of first-period good in terms of second-period good. It accomplishes these roles by causing the slope of the indifference curve to equal the slope of the transformation frontier in equilibrium.

This description of equilibrium assumes that projects are riskless, but if projects are risky, then different interest rates reflecting different risk premia for each class of risk are needed (we discussed risk premia in Chapter 15). Assuming that investors and households both know the risk involved, however, and that a market exists for projects of each type of risk, the financial market can still reach equilibrium in matching savers to borrowers.[4] We now can explain how the supply and demand curves of savings are formed.

Household Savings and the Interest Rate

▼
5. Graphically explain the effect of an interest rate change on the household's savings, including the income and substitution effects.

Figure 16.6 shows the intertemporal budget line *tt* for three households with endowment *E*. Each household's initial consumption is at point *a*, where the indifference curve is tangent to *tt*. Since *a* is to the left of *E* in part (a), the household is saving in the first period. In part (b), point *a* corresponds to *E*, so the household neither borrows nor lends. Finally, in part (c), *a* is to the right of *E*, so the household is borrowing in the first period. Now consider for each household the effect on savings of a higher nominal interest rate.

When interest rate *r* increases, the budget line becomes steeper for given prices as the curve labeled *t′t′* shows. Since the household can always consume its entire endowment each period, the budget line rotates clockwise around the endowment point *E*.

When the interest rate increases, the household in part (a) moves from point *a* to *a′*. Since *a′* is to the left of *a*, this household increases its savings in response to the increase in interest rates. The economics of this shift can be explained in terms of the standard substitution and income effects. Because the interest rate rose, the cost of first-period consumption relative to second-period consumption rose. By the substitution effect, therefore, the household buys less first-period consumption (saves more). This is the shift from point *a* to point *b*, found by rotating the budget line along the original indifference curve, as we learned in Chapter 4. However, the increase in cost of first-period goods (which the household sells by lending) also means that the

---

4. If enough markets do not exist to provide pricing for all the different types of risk available, then it is possible that different households might place values on certain types of risky projects that differ from the values other households place on them. A firm owned by several such households would not know how to evaluate an investment project by referring to market prices. Instead, such a firm would have to know the specific preferences of its shareholders.

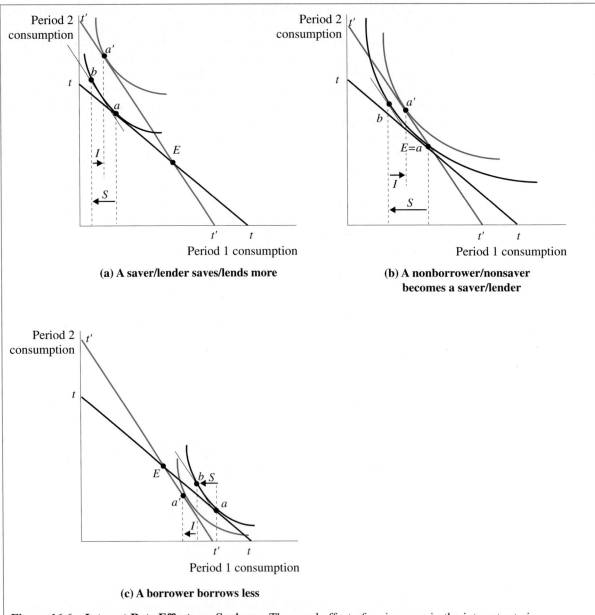

(a) A saver/lender saves/lends more

(b) A nonborrower/nonsaver becomes a saver/lender

(c) A borrower borrows less

Figure 16.6 Interest Rate Effects on Savings The usual effect of an increase in the interest rate is to increase saving. In part (a), those who are savers increase their saving as long as the substitution effect is larger than the income effect. The income and substitution effects are labeled I and S, respectively. In part (b), those who are nonsavers and nonborrowers become savers, and in part (c) those who are borrowers borrow less with a higher interest rate.

household's real income has risen. A rise in income tends to increase consumption of the first-period good, assuming it is a normal good. This is the shift from point b to point a'.

The consumer in part (b) is neither a borrower nor a lender in the initial situation. An increase in the interest rate in this case causes the household to move to point a', which lies to the left of point E. Since this implies a drop in period 1 consumption, the household has become a saver in the first period. As before, the substitution effect works in the usual direction of increasing saving, and the income effect works to reduce saving when consumption in period 1 is a normal good.

Finally, when the budget line in part (c) rotates clockwise through E, the borrowing household moves its consumption to point a'. Point a' implies less consumption in the first period, thus less borrowing by the household. Since a decrease in borrowing can be considered an increase in saving, the net supply of savings rises as a result of the increase in interest rate.

Although there is always a theoretical possibility that an increase in the interest rate could lead to a *reduction* in the supply of savings through operation of the income effect, we expect that an increase in the interest rate leads to an increase in savings over the relevant range of interest rates.[5]

Change in the interest rate affects the utility of households, just as any price change would be expected to affect household utility. Figure 16.7 portrays the effect of an interest rate decline on the utility of a retired household and a young working household. Part (a) shows the endowment of the retired household as E_R. The position of E_R indicates that period 1 consumption would be higher than period 2 consumption if the household consumed at its endowment point. This is because retired households are wealthier as a group than the rest of the population, but they do not work. Their ability to consume in period 1 is therefore high, but with only income from unearned sources (such as social security) in period 2 they would be able to consume less in period 2. The young working household in part (b) has higher income in period 2, when its wages and salary will be higher, but lower in period 1 because it is assumed to be at the start of its working career. The initial budget lines are labeled tt, passing through the endowment points E_R and E_W.

When interest rates drop, the budget lines shift to $t't'$. The utility of the wealthier retired household drops, because the income it derives from its saving is lower. Point b is on a lower indifference curve than point a. Young working households, on the other hand, see a rise in their utility because the cost to them of borrowing (home mortgages make up roughly two-thirds of household borrowing) has gone down. Point d is on a higher indifference curve than point c.

---

5. For the most part, interest rates are too low to cause people to pull back on their saving when the rate rises. Should the interest rate get so high that by saving 1 penny the interest would make available to the investor a very large amount of money next period, say $1 billion, it is possible that nearly all people would save less than they currently do, but the rates are not likely to get anywhere near such a level.

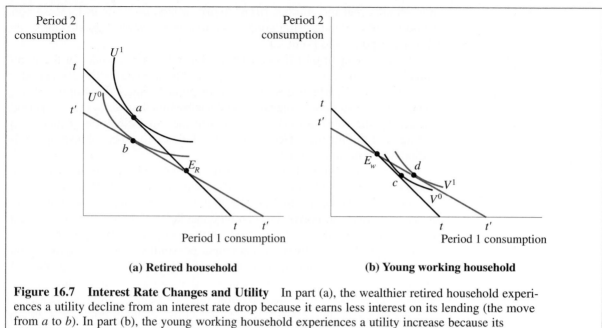

Figure 16.7   Interest Rate Changes and Utility   In part (a), the wealthier retired household experiences a utility decline from an interest rate drop because it earns less interest on its lending (the move from a to b). In part (b), the young working household experiences a utility increase because its interest cost on borrowing goes down (the move from c to d).

The Market Supply Curve of Savings

▼

6. Give the steps for constructing the market supply and market demand curves for savings.

By finding the savings of the household and plotting household savings for each interest rate, we can determine the household savings curve. Horizontally summing the supply curves for all saving households generates the market savings supply curve. Figure 16.8 shows such a curve as the curve S, which is upward-sloping over most of its range until it reaches point a. At point a it becomes backward-bending because of the income effect discussed earlier.

The Market Demand Curve for Savings

When Robinson Crusoe lived alone on his desert island, he did all of the borrowing (investing) and all of the saving. In a market, however, people who invest in a project frequently are not the same people who provide the money. Savers can lend money to borrowers, who pay back savers out of their future income (including the earnings of the investment projects).

We have discussed one type of borrower already: those households that want to borrow to spend more than their current income allows. Young households that have low incomes today but expect their income to rise over time might be in this category, for example. Borrowing households were depicted in part (c) of Figure 16.6. As indicated there, the higher the interest that borrowing households have to pay, the less they want to borrow. This

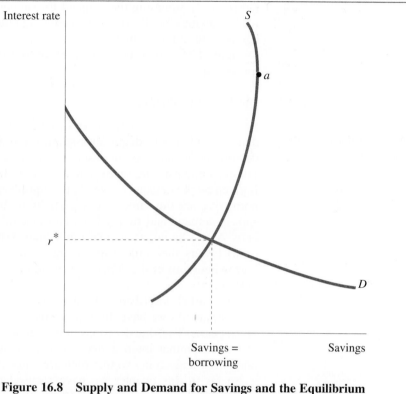

Figure 16.8   Supply and Demand for Savings and the Equilibrium Interest Rate   The market savings supply curve is the horizontal summation of all saving households' supply curves. The savings supply curve slopes upward in the normal range. It could become backward bending, as at point *a*, if the income effect becomes larger than the substitution effect and consumption in the first period is a normal good. Plotting the demand for loanable funds as curve *D* with the savings supply curve *S* determines the equilibrium interest rate r^* at the point of intersection.

implies a downward-sloping demand curve for borrowed funds in the usual demand curve diagram with the interest rate (price) on the vertical axis and quantity on the horizontal axis.

Another group of borrowers consists of firms that want to use the money for investment projects. The higher the interest rate, the more the firm has to pay out of the project's earnings in the second period to repay the borrowing. A higher interest rate means fewer projects will be able to earn enough in the second period to make it worth the firm's while to borrow the funds. If the interest rate is high enough, no project could be profitable enough to allow the borrower to pay the interest on the borrowing, whereas a lower interest rate means more projects will qualify. Thus the demand curve for borrowed funds by firms for investment purposes is also downward-sloping.

Horizontally summing the demand for savings (in other words, the demand for borrowing) by all firms and borrowing households determines the market demand curve for savings.

Figure 16.8 shows the demand curve for savings, *D*, with the supply curve for savings.

Market Equilibrium

▼

7. How does the interest rate bring about equality of saving and borrowing?

As was true for the markets we discussed in Chapter 2, the intersection of demand and supply determines equilibrium. In Figure 16.8 the intersection determines the nominal interest rate, *r*, and the quantity of savings/borrowing. For each interest rate, savings are given by the supply curve, and borrowing is given by the demand curve. At the equilibrium interest rate r^*, savings and borrowing are the same. We already know how to analyze the effects of a shift in demand and supply from Part One of the book, so little need be said here. As we know, an increase in savings (shift of the savings curve to the right) lowers the equilibrium interest rate, and an increase in demand for borrowing (shift of the demand curve to the right) raises the interest rate, and vice versa.

The market described in Figure 16.8 determines the nominal (or money) interest rate. As we have discussed, this also determines the real interest rate, given prices. Thus the decisions of households and firms interact to determine real and nominal interest rates, and the equilibrium interest rate balances borrowing and saving so that both are equal as required by equilibrium.

So far in this chapter we have focused primarily on the intertemporal model and the decisions of households as they related to saving, borrowing, and the determination of the interest rate. Firms have entered the picture primarily as demanders of household savings for use in investment projects. In the last part of the chapter, therefore, we spend some time discussing the nature of the firm's investment decision as it relates to one of the more important types of investments—the decision to undertake research and development. For this decision, market structure as discussed in Chapters 7 through 10 plays an important role.

EXPLORATION: Research and Development

Televisions, telephones, videocassette recorders, compact disk players, personal computers, automobiles, and airplanes are all products that play a large role in American society, yet none existed 150 years ago. Each product had to undergo a process of creation, development, and refinement to bring it to its current state. The importance of innovation cannot be overstated. Edward Denison estimates that between 1929 and 1982, well over half of the observed increase in value of output produced per worker in the United States was due to technological change, with the remainder explained by factors such as better education and increase in the capital stock per worker.[6]

Although no one can adequately describe how ideas arise, economics plays a large role in the innovation process. More than two-thirds of the research and development undertaken in the United States, totaling 2 to 3 percent of GDP, is conducted by industry. The next few pages are devoted to discussing some of the economic considerations that are relevant to firms.

Benefiting from Innovation

▼
8. Why is the ability to appropriate future benefits important to the level of R&D? How can the ability to appropriate be influenced to encourage investment?

No firm spends money on research and development (R&D) without some hope of receiving a future benefit from its expenditures. From the point of view of the firm, therefore, R&D expenditures are an investment: firms hope to recoup today's costs through future economic profits. Without that hope, there is no investment.

Consider the case of a television manufacturer that is considering whether to pursue high-definition television (HDTV). If it spends money on researching and developing a new generation of television products today, the future profitability to the company depends on (1) the prospects for success of the basic research itself, (2) the ability of the firm to appropriate the benefits of its invention, and (3) how large and far into the future the benefits will be. The second of these considerations depends on the marketplace, patent laws, and the type of competition the firm faces, whereas the third depends on the intertemporal nature of the project. It follows that the amount of research and development conducted depends on the interaction between market structure (the nature of competition) and the intertemporal aspects.

For example, assume that the company spends a lot of money on creating an improved type of television system and then test markets it to learn how it will sell. If the company knows that domestic and foreign competitors will be able to copy whatever it does and quickly enter whatever market niche it discovers with respect to HDTV, its potential economic profits will be zero. Similar considerations apply with respect to other potential hazards. The system the firm devises might ultimately be ''orphaned'' by regulations or government standards that favor a competitor's choice of technology, or perhaps the standard in other countries will be purposely chosen to thwart the company's selection of technology. How soon might these events happen? If the answer is too soon, the company's best strategy in that case is not to innovate, but to copy whatever innovation other firms may create. Since other firms face the same market environment, innovation as a whole is delayed or prevented.

At the opposite extreme, we can imagine situations in which the innovating firm is able to keep its process secret, close substitutes are infeasible, and uncertainty about standards is not an issue. In this case the firm will have a

6. Edward F. Denison, *Trends in American Economic Growth, 1929–1982,* Washington, D.C.: Brookings Institution, 1985, p. 113.

monopoly of its product, and the costs of R&D, if they are not too great, can be covered by the stream of monopoly profits running infinitely into the future.

The first of the two situations—the one in which the future benefits of R&D are short-lived and low—is not good from society's point of view because there is no incentive for innovation. Too little is invented, and society loses the benefits of new and better products. In the second situation, timing and market structure combine to encourage innovation to the maximum extent, but society does not do as well as it could because it has to sustain the social costs of monopoly forever.

Neither extreme is an accurate description of reality. Some innovation would take place whether or not monopoly rights to the invention were possible, and no invention is likely to remain secret from rivals forever. As we saw in Chapters 8, 9, and 10, monopolistic and oligopolistic markets are too dynamic to stay the same for very long. Time, in the form of windows of opportunity to innovate today and reap the benefits of innovation in a future period or periods, is therefore a key element in the firm's R&D decisions.

Judging that we benefit from greater innovation, Americans have chosen from our nation's founding to encourage invention by the granting of patents. American patents give the holder exclusive right to make, use, or sell a discovery for a period of 17 years. Today, infringers of patents are as likely to be foreign as domestic, so American law provides for the patent holder to use the court system to protect against either source of infringement.[7]

How R&D Affects Demand and Costs

▼
9. What are the two main ways in which R&D can benefit the firm in the future?

There are two types of innovation that can be distinguished on the basis of their economic effects: innovation that creates a new product and innovation that reduces the costs of producing an existing product. Figure 16.9 shows the benefits of a new product. When the product did not exist, there was no market in the good; a market price, strictly speaking, did not exist. However, there was latent demand for the product given by the demand curve D. At zero quantity, the most consumers would have been willing to pay for the product was the reservation price p_R. Because p_R was a high price, the inventor anticipates revenues in future periods equal to area $a + b$ by producing $q*$ at price $p*$. Area a shows the variable costs of production. Area b is therefore available for covering fixed costs and repaying the product's first-period sunk costs of research and development. Consumers are better off by area c, consumer surplus, due to the product being available at price $p*$.

In this case, we assume that the inventor has taken out a patent on the new product. By granting exclusive rights for 17 years, the patent system gives

7. Foreign firms that infringe American patents may always be prohibited from selling their products in the American market, though the nature of other sanctions depends partly on the legal system of the other nation and the governing treaties to which the United States and the other nation are party.

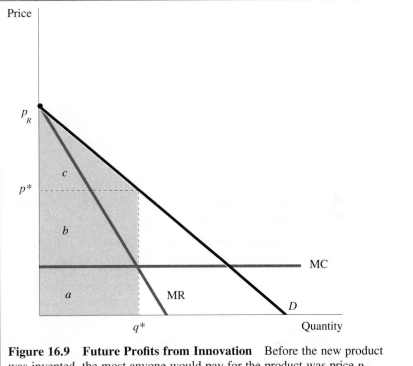

Figure 16.9 Future Profits from Innovation   Before the new product
was invented, the most anyone would pay for the product was price p_R.
After the product becomes available, price drops to p^* and quantity q^* is
made available. The patent-protected supplier is able to earn revenues in
the future period equal to area $a + b$ to cover the variable costs of production a, fixed costs, and the sunk costs of research and development.
Consumers are better off by the increase in consumer surplus, area c.

the inventor opportunity to earn enough future economic profits to recoup
the costs of invention. Figure 16.10 displays the profit stream from the inventor's perspective.[8] In part (a) the firm is assumed to have a stream of
profits for the full 17 years, after which competition drives the economic
profits to zero. In part (b) the firm is assumed to introduce the new product
at time zero. It takes 3 years before any competitors can offer their own
products, after which profits to the original firm drop as competitors meet
some of the demand. After 10 years the market has enough firms competing
that economic profits of the original firm are driven to zero.

It is important to note that although a patent system may reserve more
benefits of the invention for the inventor who bore the costs of development,
it is still not a perfect tool. Why? Any spillover benefits to consumers in the

8. We will discuss future profit streams and how to compare them in more detail in Investigation V.B.

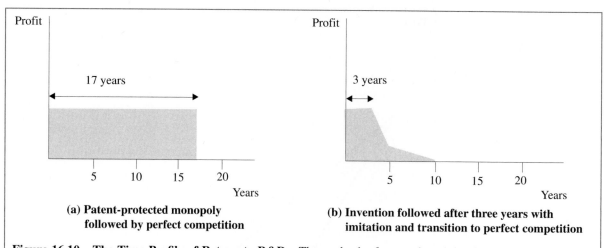

(a) Patent-protected monopoly followed by perfect competition

(b) Invention followed after three years with imitation and transition to perfect competition

Figure 16.10   The Time Profile of Return to R&D   The payback of research and development costs must come from the future economic profits earned after the product is put on the market. The shaded areas represent the profits earned by the inventor of a new product after its introduction on the market. In part (a), a patent protects the inventor from competition for 17 years, allowing monopoly profits for that period of time. In the absence of patent protection, as in part (b), the inventor is not assured a period of monopoly profits, though competitors may need a certain amount of time for preparation before they can engage in competition.

▼
10. Give an example in which a cost-reducing invention leads to a lower market price and one in which it does not.

form of consumer surplus (area c in Figure 10.9), and to other firms in the form of increased profits attributable to the innovation (firms may benefit from having the product available, for example, meaning their gains are part of area c in Figure 10.9, too), are benefits that the inventor creates but does not receive. In deciding to balance the future benefits of additional research against the additional current costs of development, the inventor will see only part of the benefits and may therefore underallocate resources to invention.

The second type of technological change that we spoke of was cost-reducing innovation. We can analyze the effects of this type of innovation on the consumer and the firm in much the same way as we did for a new product. Any benefit to the consumer comes through a change in product price.

Figure 16.11 illustrates a perfectly competitive market in which a cost-reducing innovation has taken place. Originally, price is p_1 and quantity is q_1. After innovation the firm's costs drop to MC_2. Because the innovating firm is able to produce at lower cost than its rivals, the firm might be able to drive its competitors from the market and convert the market to a monopoly. However, in this case MC_2 cuts MR from below at quantity q_2 (this is profit-maximizing for the monopolist, as we saw in Chapter 8), for which the monopoly price would be p_2. Since this is above the competitive price, other firms would be able to undercut p_2. The effective demand curve for the innovating firm, therefore, is the horizontal line segment from point a to point

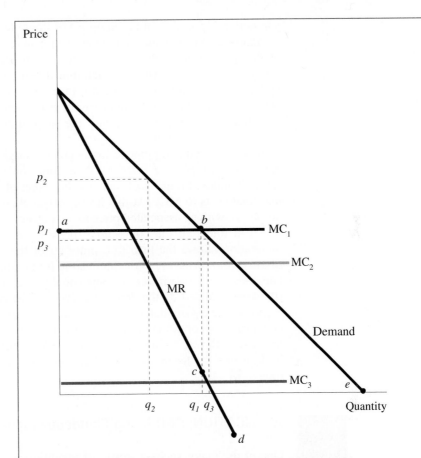

Figure 16.11   Future Benefits from Cost-Reducing Innovation
Starting from the competitive market price p_1, the innovating firm reduces
its future marginal cost to MC_2 through a cost-reducing invention. Although the firm would like to price at the monopoly price p_2, it cannot
because other firms will undersell it at price p_1. The effective demand
curve for the firm is therefore the horizontal segment from point a to point
b and from there down the market demand curve to point e. The marginal
revenue curve for the effective demand curve is segment ab with a jump
to segment cd. MR equals MC for the innovating firm at quantity q_1. In
this case, the innovating firm gains the amount $p_1 - MC_2$ on each future
unit it sells, and the consumer does not benefit at all. If the cost-reducing
invention is great enough to lower costs to MC_3, however, the monopoly
price p_3 is under the competitive price, and consumers benefit from the
innovation through price reduction.

b, and from there down the demand curve to point e. The marginal revenue
curve for this demand curve consists of the two segments ab and cd with a

gap between points *b* and *c*. Setting MR equal to MC_2 therefore implies that the innovating firm leaves market price and quantity unchanged.[9] The benefits of the innovation in this case accrue only to the firm, which receives the economic rent $p_1 - MC_2$ on each unit it sells. It is in the firm's interest to undertake the innovation if these future rents are sufficient to pay the first-period costs of innovation and earn the firm a satisfactory return on its R&D investment. Since consumers buy the same quantity at the same price, no benefits accrue to them.

If the cost-reducing innovation is great enough that the monopoly price is *below* the competitive price p_1, then both consumers and the firm receive future benefits. Figure 16.11 shows the effect of an innovation that reduces marginal costs to MC_3. At this level, marginal cost cuts marginal revenue at output q_3, with an associated price to the consumer of p_3. Since the innovating firm can undercut the competitive price p_1 at the monopoly price p_3, the innovation allows the firm to capture all of the market. The future benefits of the invention accrue to the innovating firm in the form of monopoly profits, and consumers gain future benefits equal to the increase in consumer surplus (the area bounded by the demand curve and the two prices p_1 and p_3).

As we have seen, determining the future benefits from innovation involves considerations of demand, market structure, patents, and the type of innovation itself. Before turning to the other side of the coin, financing R&D, we look at one of the innovations that continues to greatly improve our lives today. ■

APPLICATION: R&D in the Photocopy Industry

One of the major success stories of invention, research, and development in recent years relates to the American photocopy industry. It involves individual initiative, corporate support, and large-scale development and refinement before a finished product could finally be brought to market.

The story begins with Chester Carlson, a California Institute of Technology graduate, whose work in the patent division of a company in the 1930s convinced him of the need for cheaper and faster ways to make copies of drawings and documents.[10] In the mid-1930s he began to devote his spare time to looking for ways to make a copy machine. By 1938 he had a machine that was able to copy the first photocopied message: ''10-22-38 Astoria,'' which marked the date and place (Astoria, New York), that the feat was accomplished.

Working from his original design, which combined elements of electrostatics with photoconductivity, he was eventually able to patent his ideas in

---

9. Since other firms are unable to produce at marginal cost lower than p_1, the innovating firm lowers its price marginally below p_1 to capture sales in the market.
10. See John Jewkes, David Sawyers, and Richard Stillerman, *The Sources of Invention,* 2d ed., New York: Norton, 1969, pp. 321–323.

four patents issued between 1940 and 1944. Carlson then began to approach companies to get funding to work on a photocopier for commercial application. He met with rejection after rejection from some of the largest companies of the day, including IBM, Eastman Kodak, and others. Battelle Memorial Institute took up the project for a short while and made a number of innovations to the original patents, but the nonprofit research institute ultimately did not have the resources to carry the project further.

Carlson again sought funding from a larger company, meeting with another spate of rejections before Haloid Company agreed in 1946 to undertake the project. Haloid was a small company with sales in today's dollars of well under $750,000 per year. Led by Haloid's Joseph Wilson, the company brought the concept of photocopying to fruition after yet more years of work, development, and refinement. An industrial-use copier was first marketed in 1950. After a change of the company name from Haloid to Xerox, the year 1957 saw the firm produce a prototype office copier. Finally, in 1959 the immensely successful 914 copier was introduced by Xerox: the modern photocopy era had begun.

Commenting in 1990 on Haloid's development of the photocopier at the bicentennial celebration of the patent office, one observer summarized the process.

> After Haloid acquired the rights to xerography, the company set forth on its mission to develop the invention, and to explore and fulfill its promise. The crucial fact is that it took 14 years between the time Haloid obtained the first license on the Carlson patents and the successful introduction of the first truly commercial product, the Xerox 914. They were years of anguish, uncertainty, disappointment, frustration and only occasional satisfaction during which we were never entirely sure that xerography would ever be a success. It took truly tenacious commitment to bring it all to pass.
>
> How did it happen? I think there were several qualities that gave Haloid and later Xerox its special character.
>
> First, there was faith in the idea. . . .
>
> A second essential characteristic of the company was its enthusiasm . . . about what was being done and what might yet be done. . . .
>
> Third, there was a sense of idealism. . . . We sensed not only a copying revolution but also the nascent information revolution. . . .
>
> None of this could have happened without our antitrust laws and the patent system which provided the incentive for investment.[11]

All told, it is reported that the development of Carlson's xerography required the investment of $20 million in 1950s dollars and generated well over

---

11. From a speech by Washington lawyer S. M. Linowitz, given at the Bicentennial Celebration of the United States Patent and Copyright Laws in Washington, D.C., May 1990. Reported in the *Wall Street Journal,* May 31, 1990.

100 subsequent patents. Today, photocopy machines can copy in color, enlarge and reduce, convert from one-sided to two-sided and the reverse, collate and staple, and the revolution to better and faster machines continues. ■

Financing R&D

The last question we raise has to do with financing the up-front costs of invention. Funding R&D requires that someone be willing to part with first-period dollars (that is, give up consumption of some first-period goods) in return for future-period dollars (consumption in the future). The ability to draw funds for a particular purpose depends on the prospect of the funds' yielding a high enough real return. Intertemporal financing considerations are independent of the form of market structure: as long as properly functioning capital markets are available, firms that cannot finance their research and development internally can turn to borrowing in the financial market or to selling ownership rights to whatever is discovered.

It is possible that firms that can internally finance their research and development have a slight advantage over firms that must resort to outside financing. At the critical time when someone (or some group) with money must part with some of it to pay for the project, that individual or group must be convinced that the money ultimately will be repaid. This requires transmission of information to convince the necessary parties of the worth of the project. A self-funded organization is spared the costs of informing and convincing an outside group of the viability of the proposed project. Regardless of whether the research and development effort is internally or externally funded, however, predicting the speed of invention is not easy to do. In many areas of science and business, it is simply not possible to predict how long it will take to make a technological breakthrough given a certain amount of expenditure, time, and study.

Much research and development has unexpected side benefits. Space technology developed in the 1960s through 1980s has made available new products ranging from lightweight emergency ''space blankets'' and new heat-resistant materials to satellite capabilities that have revolutionized the communications industry. To the extent that positive externalities are present (see Chapter 14), market funding of R&D is likely to be too low. There is therefore a potential role for government financing in addition to the market.

Government Support of National R&D

▼
11. List some pros and cons of extensive government funding of R&D.

Setting national policy for funding R&D is difficult because the externality benefits from research are hard to quantify. Also, critics convincingly argue that government funding gets abused in pork-barrel politics so much that it may not deliver benefits to match its costs. In Chapter 14 we noted that an extra dollar collected in taxes is estimated by researchers to cause roughly $1.45 to $1.56 in costs to the private economy. Earning enough from a government-sponsored project to repay those costs therefore requires a high rate of return. Finally, though private investing is based on the principle that those who pay the costs reap the rewards, government-sponsored investing faces the problem of ensuring that the benefits and externalities generated accrue to those who paid the taxes.

In 1991 R&D funding by the federal government was $68 billion (this represents average annual taxes of about $575 for every working individual). Of this, 12 percent went to aeronautics and space research, 11 percent to energy research, 14 percent to health and human services, 53 percent to the military, and 10 percent to other research projects.[12] Of the total, 4 percent is devoted to general science under the auspices of agencies like the National Science Foundation. Nine congressional committees oversee different parts of the funding process, so it is probably inaccurate to describe funding as the result of a unified agenda. For example, among its many programs, the National Institute of Standards and Technology in the Department of Commerce administers an advanced technology program (ATP) to encourage development of promising but risky technologies. Winners of ATP support from the $68 million budget in recent years range from those working on switches for optical computers to those dealing with new plastics for cars. The fact that the program supports on individual merit so diverse a range of technologies (27 in one year) raises numerous questions: Is the government any better able to pick desirable investments, or should it be more willing to fund them, than the private sector? Is a broadly directed policy better than a focused one? Would fostering a proresearch, probusiness attitude be better than trying to channel taxpayer dollars into private ventures?

Since so much of government funding of R&D is administered for national defense, the Defense Department provides the country with the closest thing to a national technology policy. Its Defense Advanced Research Projects Agency (DARPA), relying on a few hundred people and spending some $1.5 billion per year, gets high marks from some observers for spending on dual-use technologies—projects that may prove useful to defense as well as be profitable for civilian purposes. Another area that receives good reviews is the country's array of national laboratories, some 700 across the country. Staffed with first-rate scientists, many of them having military missions, the national laboratories have entered into cooperative research and development agreements (CRADAs) with the private sector. These partnerships attack specific projects in commerce, the environment, transportation, energy, agriculture, and health and human services. Since CRADAs have well-defined goals (for example, achieving a certain supercomputing capability), it is felt that their output can be evaluated and measured. Because private industry is involved in the CRADAs, CRADAs also have an incentive to fund only profitable ventures.

Is the current amount of funding too big or too small? Benefits from R&D are indisputable, but whether the benefits are worth the cost is the difficult question. Regardless of how that question is answered, since the time of

12. See ''American Technology Policy: Settling the Frontier,'' *The Economist*, July 25, 1992, pp. 21–23.

Lewis and Clark it appears that the opening of new frontiers has fallen partly within the purview of government. As with aviation and space technology, other advances developed with the encouragement and help of government are being appropriated by the private sector. According to Vannevar Bush, a science and technology adviser who marshaled much of the nation's scientific contribution to the successful Manhattan Project in World War II,

> . . . government should foster the opening of new frontiers. It opened the seas to clipper ships and furnished land for pioneers. Although these frontiers have more or less disappeared, the frontier of science remains. It is in keeping with American tradition—one which made the United States great—that new frontiers shall be made accessible for development by all American citizens.[13]

If Dr. Bush is right, costs paid in taxes today represent an investment for which we will get a greater return tomorrow.

Summary

Active Reading Guide numbers are given in parentheses at the end of each summary item.

1. The choice to save or borrow (consume less or consume more than one's current income) depends on the household's time endowment of income (when it receives its income), its ability to convert goods in one period into goods in another period (given by its intertemporal budget constraint), and its time preferences. The intertemporal budget constraint determines the combinations of good in period 1 and good in period 2 that can be paid for by the household's income in periods 1 and 2, with borrowing and lending allowed. If the good in period 2 is placed on the vertical axis, the steepness of the intertemporal budget constraint increases with the interest rate earned on savings. (1)

2. Intertemporal transformation relates to the ability to convert goods or dollars in one period into goods or dollars in another. The rate of intertemporal transformation is governed by nominal and real interest rates. An interest rate is the charge for borrowing money or a commodity, expressed as a percentage of the quantity borrowed. The interest rate on money is called the money interest rate or

nominal interest rate. By saving, one dollar is transformed into $1 + r$ dollars in the following period, where r is the nominal interest rate. The real interest rate, the rate at which one unit of consumption today is converted into one unit of consumption tomorrow, is given by $(1 + r)p_1/p_2 - 1$, where p_1 is the price of the consumption good today and p_2 is the price of the consumption good tomorrow. Giving up one unit of consumption today and saving the money that would have been spent allows the household to buy $(1 + r)p_1/p_2$ units of consumption in the following period. (2)

3. The interaction between time endowment, time productivity, and time preference can be shown by plotting indifference curves for goods consumed in periods 1 and 2 along with the intertemporal transformation frontier (the curve showing the ability to trade off good in period 1 for good in period 2), in much the same way that indifference curves and frontiers are plotted for goods in the same time period. The household chooses the point on the frontier that gives highest utility. (3)

4. Since the marginal rate of substitution between good in period 2 and the same good in period

---

13. Vannevar Bush, ''Science, the Endless Frontier'' (1945), quoted in ''American Technology Policy,'' p. 21.

1 (MRS_{C_1,C_2}, called the marginal rate of time preference) gives the number of units of good in period 2 needed to compensate for a unit of good in period 1, $MRS_{C_1,C_2} - 1$ is the real interest rate. Since the indifference curve is tangent to the intertemporal transformation frontier at the household's choice, the interest rate is also determined by the slope of the intertemporal frontier, which depends on the time productivity of production. (4)

5. The intertemporal budget constraint passes through the household's time endowment point, which indicates the household's units of good in period 1 and good in period 2. Higher interest rates rotate the budget constraint clockwise around the endowment point. In the usual case, the response of borrowers to a higher interest rate is to borrow less; the response of nonborrowers/nonlenders is to lend; and the response of lenders is to lend more. The substitution effect of a higher interest rate always means that the household consumes less first-period good (saves more). The income effect, however, depends on whether consumption in each period is normal. If the good in period 1 is normal, the income effect leads to higher period 1 consumption (lower saving) for a household that is initially saving. In general, however, we expect the substitution effect to dominate, so that the supply of savings rises with the interest rate. (5)

6. Plotting the household's savings for each choice of interest rate produces the household savings supply curve for households that save (or the borrowing demand curve for households that borrow). Horizontally summing the supply curves of all saving households produces the market supply curve of savings. Similarly, plotting each firm's demand for savings (demand for loanable funds) for each interest rate produces the firm's demand curve. Horizontally summing the demand curves of all firms and borrowing households produces the market demand curve for savings. (6)

7. Plotting investment demand and the supply of savings on the same diagram leads to a conventional demand and supply diagram. Equality between investment and savings occurs at the interest rate where the two curves cross. The interest rate therefore adjusts so that borrowing demand equals savings supply in equilibrium. In a market, firms can make the right project decisions without knowing the preferences of households, so long as they know the interest rate. Similarly, households can make the right savings decisions without knowing about firm's investment projects, so long as they know the interest rate. This separation of decision making is possible because the interest rate provides the necessary information about time preferences to firms and about time productivity to households. (7)

8. A firm's decision to invest in research and development depends on the extent to which it can collect benefits from developing a new product or process and how soon it can do so. A firm that expects its innovation to be quickly copied in the future, for example, typically would not receive significant competitive advantage from developing new products or processes. Patents granted by the government and efforts by the firm itself to prevent competitors from copying its technology represent attempts to direct a greater portion of the benefits of invention to those who expended the work of invention. (8)

9. The future benefits of research and development depend on whether R&D creates a new product or provides a lower-cost method for producing an existing product. (9)

10. The benefits of a new product accrue both to the firm and to the consumer, unless the firm can perfectly price-discriminate (see Chapter 8) to capture all of the consumer surplus from sale of the new product. Cost-reducing innovations, on the other hand, provide benefits to the consumer only if the cost reduction lowers the market price. If the market is monopolistic, cost-reducing innovations may raise market price. In perfectly competitive markets, cost-reducing innovations may either leave the market price unchanged or lower it. If market price does not change, all of the benefits of the cost reduction accrue to producers using the new process. (10)

11. Since the benefits of new knowledge often spill over into many parts of the economy outside the developing firm, there are positive externalities from research and development. Since private investors do not see all of the benefits directly, and

are therefore likely to underinvest in research and development, there is an argument for public funding of research and development. However, it is difficult to know how much public funding the external benefits are worth. Moreover, government may not be very good at deciding which projects to fund, and the funding process can be abused by private firms eager for taxpayers' dollars. (11)

Review Questions

*1. If two isolated countries were identical in every respect, except that the second one had more patient households (those willing to wait for future consumption because their utility functions valued it more highly), which one would have higher interest rates?

2. In the California gold rush of 1849, interest rates in California were extremely high during the period before the market was well connected to the East. If we assume that gold miners had the same time preferences that households in the East did, what would explain the much higher interest rates?

*3. Historians have sometimes observed that high real interest rates are the sign of a decaying society. In fact, in the declining years of Rome, interest rates rose substantially. Assuming that the higher interest rates are not compensation for more risk, why might the historians be right?

4. Assume that there is no technology for converting goods in one period into goods in another except simple storage that causes the destruction of 10 percent of whatever is saved. Would households do any saving under these circumstances? (A simple example or counterexample is sufficient.)

*5. Referring to the preceding question, what does the intertemporal budget constraint look like in this case?

6. In forming the market savings supply and demand curves, we can group borrowing households with firms as demanders. What would be different in the equilibrium demand and supply diagram if we instead treated household borrowing as negative savings and grouped all households together? Would the equilibrium interest rate or the quantity of savings be different? Explain.

*7. In what sense is the real interest rate a "commodity bundle interest rate," and what is the technology in this case for converting one commodity bundle into another?

8. In some countries the inflation rate can be as high as 20 percent *per month,* making computation of real interest rates very important. Assuming that the interest rate that money can earn in savings is 200 percent per year, and the rate of inflation is 185 percent, what is the real interest rate?

*9. Explain how appropriability of the future benefits of R&D, spread of new knowledge to competitors, and market structure might be related.

Numerical and Graphing Exercises

*1. Johnson earns $85,000 in period 1 and $100,000 in period 2. If there is no borrowing and no lending, what is Johnson's intertemporal budget constraint?

*2. Smith earns $100,000 income in period 1 and $85,000 income in period 2. Write the formula for Smith's first-period, second-period, and intertemporal budget constraints and graph the intertemporal budget constraint if:
a) Borrowing and lending are both done at $r = 0.10$ (10 percent interest).
b) The interest on borrowing is 12 percent, and the interest on savings is 5 percent.

---

* Asterisks are used to denote questions that are answered at the back of the book.

*3. For the household in exercise 2, how much will Smith consume in each period and save or borrow in period 1 under each alternative if Smith's marginal rate of time preference is $MRS_{C_1,C_2} = C_2/C_1$?

4. Rip Van Winkle finds that prices rise each month by 2 percent and that the monthly nominal rate of interest is 4 percent. What is Rip's annual real interest rate?

*5. Johnson and Smith from exercises 1 and 2 live in a world without storage for physical commodities. Johnson has a constant marginal rate of time preference whereby 1 unit of period 2 consumption is worth 1 unit of period 1 consumption. Smith has preferences $U = \min[C_1, C_2]$. If the price ratio is $p_2/p_1 = 1$, and the two can trade with one another, draw a diagram showing the trades they will make. In your answer indicate the nominal interest rate that will arise.

6. Robinson Crusoe's bag of period 1 grain allows him intertemporal transformation of period 1 grain into period 2 grain through planting and harvesting. Friday has time preferences identical to Robinson's but has a bag of grain that is 50 percent more productive (planting one seed produces 50 percent more period 2 grain). If Robinson and Friday each live alone on separate islands, which of the two will have the higher interest rate? Draw a diagram to explain.

*7. Assume everything is as described in the preceding exercise except that Robinson's and Friday's bags of grain are identical and Friday has a marginal rate of time preference (MRS_{C_1,C_2}) that is 50 percent higher than Robinson's. The rate at which additional planted grain produces additional period 2 grain falls as more is planted. Which of the two will have the higher interest rate? Draw a diagram to explain.

8. Assume all households are savers. Starting from the intertemporal diagram for the household, describe the effect on the household, on the market supply and demand curves for savings, and on the interest rate of an increase in all households' marginal rate of time preference (MRS_{C_1,C_2}) at any consumption point.

INVESTIGATIONS V

A. Security Valuation in the Capital Asset Pricing Model

One of the chief applications of the theory of decision making under risk is to the stock market. This investigation presents a brief review of how to evaluate the risk in stock market equities.

Asset Returns

Rates of return express the payouts of a security as a percentage of the security's initial value. Since they are unit free, returns are convenient to work with in evaluating securities. If V_i is the payout of the asset in question in state of nature i and V its initial value, then V_i is related to V and the asset's return in state i, r_i, according to the formula

$$V_i = (1 + r_i)V,$$

where $r_i = (V_i - V)/V = V_i/V - 1$. We see next how security risk and return are compared.

The Efficient Frontier for Risk and Return

Consider a group of securities, each of which has a particular expected return and standard deviation of return. An investor who purchases one or more securities can create portfolios with different expected returns E depending on the stocks chosen. A portfolio refers to a grouping of stocks or a mutual fund. An *efficient portfolio* is one that provides its expected return E with the smallest standard deviation σ.

Figure V.1 shows the efficient frontier for a group of risky assets as the heavy curved line. The market portfolio at point a (the portfolio consisting of all stocks) is always on the efficient frontier. The riskless asset with return r_f (at point b) is also an efficient portfolio. Since buying a combination of two efficient portfolios always results in an efficient portfolio, an investor spending part of his or her money on the risk free asset and the rest on the market portfolio produces a new efficient portfolio. Portfolios consisting entirely of the riskless asset will be at point b on the axis, and portfolios consisting entirely of the market portfolio will be at point a. Portfolios with half of each asset type will be at a point on the line connecting a and b midway between the two. By increasing the share of the portfolio devoted to

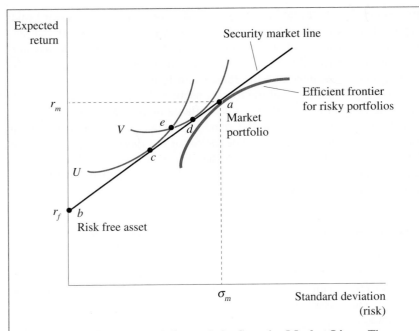

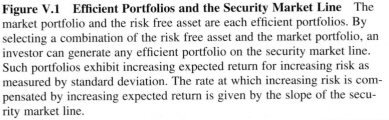

Figure V.1 Efficient Portfolios and the Security Market Line The market portfolio and the risk free asset are each efficient portfolios. By selecting a combination of the risk free asset and the market portfolio, an investor can generate any efficient portfolio on the security market line. Such portfolios exhibit increasing expected return for increasing risk as measured by standard deviation. The rate at which increasing risk is compensated by increasing expected return is given by the slope of the security market line.

the market portfolio, the investor selects a point closer to a, and by increasing the share devoted to the risk free asset, the investor moves closer to b.[1]

The Security Market Line

The line through a and b in Figure V.1 is called the *security market line*. It gives the trade-off between risk and return available to investors in the market. Figure V.1 also shows two different investors' indifference curves. The slope of investor I's indifference curve, labeled U, shows a higher marginal rate of substitution of expected return for risk at point e than that of investor II, whose indifference curve is labeled V. Higher indifference curves for each investor lie to the northwest (higher return and/or lower risk). Investor I is more risk averse than investor II; that is, investor I requires greater expected

1. Points to the northeast of a on the frontier are reached by *borrowing* at the risk free rate and using the proceeds to purchase the market portfolio.

return to compensate for taking on higher risk. Consequently, investor I finds the optimal mix of risk and return at point *c*, which shows lower risk and return than investor II's choice at point *d*. In equilibrium the two investors have equalized marginal rates of substitution of risk for return because both move to points of tangency on the same security market line.

By referring to the slope of the market security line, we can determine the rate at which higher expected return is available in the market to compensate for greater risk. The increase in the standard deviation from point *b* to point *a*, for example, is σ_m, the standard deviation of the market portfolio at point *a*. The corresponding increase in expected return is $r_m - r_f$, where r_m is the expected return on the market portfolio. It follows that the trade-off between risk and return is given by

$$\text{Compensation rate of risk by expected return} = \text{price of risk} = \frac{(r_m - r_f)}{\sigma_m}.$$

When this return for risk trade-off is more favorable than the investor requires, the investor takes on more risk by moving out the security market line, away from the riskless asset, until a point of tangency is reached, as shown at points *c* and *d*.

The Use of β as a Measure of Stock Riskiness

The previous discussion focused on the investor's choice of portfolio based on the available security market line. A common situation, however, is that the investor has optimally chosen a portfolio on the basis of the stocks available, and then a new stock becomes available for review. How should the investor decide whether the new stock is worth adding to the portfolio?

The first thing the investor needs is a measure of the amount of risk the stock will add to the portfolio. The stock's own standard deviation of return is not a good measure because it does not tell the investor how a purchase of the stock would affect the standard deviation of the entire portfolio.

One general measure of the additional risk contained in a stock is the amount by which the standard deviation of the market portfolio would rise if the stock were added to the market portfolio. To compute this, a number β (beta) is assigned to each stock. This number measures the way in which the stock's return varies with the market return. If the stock tends on average to go up 2 percent when the market goes up 1 percent, and drop by a similar proportion when the market goes down, we say that the stock has a β of 2. In this sense it is "twice as risky" as the market. Stocks with βs of 0.5 are half as risky as the market, and so on.

Multiplying the stock's β by the standard deviation of the market portfolio, σ_m, tells us the *total amount of additional risk contained in the stock*, meaning the rate at which it increases the standard deviation of the market portfolio

Table V.1   Security βs for Selected Well-Known Stocks, 1992

Stock	β
Compaq Computer	1.4
U.S. Health Care	1.3
Digital Equipment Corporation	1.2
General Electric	1.2
Xerox	1.2
General Motors	1.0
Bristol Myers	0.9
Mobil Corporation	0.8
IBM	0.7
Consolidated Edison	0.4

Data from ''Market Scope,'' New York: Standard & Poor's, September 24, 1992. Reprinted by permission of Standard & Poor's.

when a small amount of the stock is added to the market portfolio.[2] Table V.1 presents a list of some well-known stocks and their βs.

With β information we can answer the question of whether or not a particular stock is a good buy. Let r_s be the expected return on the stock, and $r_s - r_f$ be the excess expected return relative to the risk free return. If we buy the stock, our β measure tells us that we add $\beta\sigma_m$ units of risk to the market portfolio. According to the security market line, this should be compensated by $(r_m - r_f)/\sigma_m$ units of additional expected return. Thus if

$$r_s - r_f > \frac{(\beta\sigma_m)(r_m - r_f)}{\sigma_m}$$
$$= \beta(r_m - r_f),$$

the stock offers a better return for its added risk than the market security line. It is a good buy. If the inequality goes the other way, the stock does not offer sufficient reward to make the additional risk worthwhile. The investor can get better risk-return combinations in existing stocks. Finally, if the relation is an equality, the stock offers the going rate of reward for risk.

2. β is defined as cov $(s, m)/\sigma^2_m$, where cov (s, m) is the covariance of the market return m and the return on the stock s. For those mathematically inclined, let k be the number of shares of stock with return s. Then the variance of return for the portfolio consisting of the market and the stock in amount ks is $\sigma^2 = k^2\sigma^2_s + 2k$ cov $(s, m) + \sigma^2_m$. Using this to compute how σ rises with an increase in k, starting at $k = 0$, gives $\Delta\sigma/\Delta k =$ cov $(s, m)/\sigma_m = $ [cov $(s, m)/\sigma^2_m]\sigma_m = \beta\sigma_m$. Thus $\beta\sigma_m$ measures the rate of increase in the standard deviation of the market portfolio from adding the stock.

An important implication of this analysis is that for traded stocks to be in equilibrium (meaning that investors are willing to hold them in their portfolios), it must be true that for any stock s with risk content β_s

$$r_s - r_f = \beta_s(r_m - r_f).$$

This result is one of the main conclusions of what has come to be called the *capital asset pricing model.*

Today, if you go to a stockbroker and ask for background information on a stock, you will often routinely be given the stock's β to help you in your analysis of its risk-return mix. For example, say you are considering buying some shares of GeoCo. Your broker tells you that GeoCo's β equals 1.2, it has a dividend yield of 3.5 percent, the risk free interest rate is 7.5 percent, and the return on the market is 15 percent. In terms of our model you write

$$r_s - r_f = \beta_s(r_m - r_f)$$
$$r_s - 7.5 = 1.2(15 - 7.5),$$

where r_s equals the dividend yield of 3.5 percent plus the expected appreciation in the price of GeoCo's stock over the coming year.

Putting these numbers together you quickly compute that the excess return on the market is $15 - 7.5 = 7.5$ percent. Your stock is 1.2 times riskier, so its excess return over the risk free rate should be $1.2 \times 7.5 = 9$ percent. To get an excess return this high, you need an expected return on the stock of $9 + 7.5 = 16.5$ percent, of which the dividend yield accounts for 3.5 percent. Unless you expect the stock to appreciate in value by 13 percent, GeoCo does not offer enough return to warrant the risk.

Capital Gains and Losses

What happens to a stock if its return is too low to compensate buyers for the added risk it contains? The answer is that with too few buyers, the stock is in excess supply and its price drops, just as for any other commodity. Lower price affects the return of the asset in each state of nature i according to the formula derived earlier, $V_i/V - 1 = r_i$. Given the payout of the stock V_i in state i, a decrease in today's value V due to the drop in price means that the return r_i rises. The lower price (and higher return) makes the asset more desirable. Eventually the price drops enough (and the return rises enough) that the stock's return puts it back on the security market line, where demand for the asset equals supply. The increase or decrease in the value of the investor's holding (this is represented in the price of the stock) is called a *capital gain or loss.*

We end with a happy example of how you can use the security market line, hard work, and valuation of a capital asset to make a million dollars. After finishing your education, you strike out on your own to start a small business. After some years of hard work, you reach the point at which your business, year in and year out, produces a profit of $75,000 per year, after paying you a market wage for your time.

One day you decide to sell stock and go public, intending to use the money to franchise the idea of your business to other locations. You remember some microeconomics training you had, so you decide to see what your business might be worth on the open market. Writing the capital asset pricing equation in return form, you have

$$r_s - r_f = \beta_s(r_m - r_f).$$

In your case, the business does well through thick and thin. Since its earnings are not related to the return on the market portfolio, its β is zero. Thus the return on your business should equal the risk free rate of interest, which is 7.5 percent, so $r_s = r_f = 0.075$.

If V is the value of the firm, someone who becomes owner would have at the end of a year an asset worth V plus $75,000. Writing $V_i/V - 1 = 0.075$, where $V_i = V + \$75,000$, and solving gives $V = \$75,000/0.075 = \$1,000,000$! You are a millionaire. If your franchise idea is worth anything to investors, then your company, with franchise prospects, is worth even more.

Suggestions for Further Investigation. (a) Even if all investors do not know the capital asset pricing model or the security market line model, would market forces nevertheless cause efficient stocks to be described by the model? (b) Select a stock, find its β, and check its price movements for the past year. Considering dividends and price changes, did it perform well enough to warrant its risk?

B. Present Value

Firms and households often have to compare values across points in time. If a stream of payments is available in a business investment, how does the firm know whether it is worth undertaking? In other cases, the firm or household must choose only one stream of payments from a mutually exclusive list of choices. Which one should be picked? Finally, if a number of alternatives are available that interact with one another, how should this be handled? This investigation considers these questions and uses the concept of present value to answer them.

Chapter 16, which focused on the theory of intertemporal decisions, restricted the perspective to two time periods so that we could draw diagrams, but the principles apply to many time periods. In this investigation, we assume the existence of a real interest rate, r, and two or more time periods.

Using Present Value to Evaluate an Investment

Assume that you have the opportunity to rent a storefront property for $3,000 per month. If you spend $160,000 in the first year to buy rental stock, you can begin a video rental business. Each year thereafter you will need to spend $10,000 on new videos. To hire staff, you will have to pay $25,000 annually in salary and fringe benefits. Since you are renting the property, you pay no property taxes, but the shopping center where the store is located charges tenants a fee for grounds maintenance of $50 per month. You check the experience of similar video operations and find that sales in your store are likely to reach their maximum level of $103,000 per year in the third year and remain at that level thereafter. In the first and second years the sales are smaller, $25,750 and $81,650, respectively. You plan to operate the store for nine years, including the first year of operation, and at the end of the nine years your surviving stock will be worth $30,000. Assuming that your figures are accurate, and that risk is negligible, is this a good investment?

To evaluate, you arrange your information in a format like Table V.2, which allows you to see what will happen to you if you invest. Each column shows the expenses and revenues for one year. Although the first year makes a loss, the years after that make profits. Performing a simple sum of profits over all nine years, you find that the investment earns $34,000. Is this worth pursuing further?

You remember that your money could be invested in other projects at a 7 percent rate of return. Earning $1.07 one year from now is the same to you as earning $1 now (because the $1 now could be invested to become $1.07 in one year). Thus a year 2 dollar is not the same as a year 1 dollar, and so on for dollars earned in later years. A dollar earned *two* years from now is worth $1/(1.07)^2 = 0.873$ dollars today, because investing $.873 for two years at 7 percent produces $1 two years from now. You decide that you need to calculate the *present value* of your stream of profits for the nine years:

$$\text{Present value} = E_0 + E_1\left[\frac{1}{(1 + r)}\right] + E_2\left[\frac{1}{(1 + r)^2}\right] +$$
$$E_3\left[\frac{1}{(1 + r)^3}\right] + \cdots + E_8\left[\frac{1}{(1 + r)^8}\right],$$

where $r = 0.07$ is the interest rate, $1/(1 + r) = 1/1.07 = 0.9346$, and E_i is the profit of the store in year i. (If there were more periods, you would continue to add terms of the same form.) You know that this calculation tells you how many dollars today are the equivalent of the earnings in the future years. For example, having $31,400 in year 8 is the same as having $18,275.09 today because that amount of money would become $31,400 in eight years at 7 percent interest.

Performing the calculations shown in the table tell you that the present value of the total business earnings over nine years is −$28,304.50! In other words, the present value of the future positive profits is not great enough to

Table V.2 Using Present Value to Evaluate an Investment in Video Rental Property

	Year 0	Year 1	Year 2	Year 3	Year 4	Year 5	Year 6	Year 7	Year 8
Stock	($160,000.00)	($10,000.00)	($10,000.00)	($10,000.00)	($10,000.00)	($10,000.00)	($10,000.00)	($10,000.00)	($10,000.00)
Rent	($36,000.00)	($36,000.00)	($36,000.00)	($36,000.00)	($36,000.00)	($36,000.00)	($36,000.00)	($36,000.00)	($36,000.00)
Salary + fringe	($25,000.00)	($25,000.00)	($25,000.00)	($25,000.00)	($25,000.00)	($25,000.00)	($25,000.00)	($25,000.00)	($25,000.00)
Cleaning service	($600.00)	($600.00)	($600.00)	($600.00)	($600.00)	($600.00)	($600.00)	($600.00)	($600.00)
Sales	$25,750.00	$81,650.00	$103,000.00	$103,000.00	$103,000.00	$103,000.00	$103,000.00	$103,000.00	$103,000.00
Profit	($195,850.00)	$10,050.00	$31,400.00	$31,400.00	$31,400.00	$31,400.00	$31,400.00	$31,400.00	$31,400.00
Present value of year's profit	($195,850.00)	$9,392.52	$27,425.98	$25,631.75	$23,954.91	$22,387.77	$20,923.15	$19,554.34	$18,275.09
Interest rate			7.00%						
Simple sum of annual profits			$34,000.00						
Present value of annual profit stream			($28,304.50)						
Stock value at end of year 8			$30,000.00						
Present value of year 8 stock			$17,460.27						
Net value of the investment			**($10,844.23)**						

exceed the loss in the first year. The investment is not looking as good as it did before.

As a final check, you compute the present value of the $30,000 remaining stock at the end of the last year.[3] Unfortunately, it has present value of only $17,460.27. The net value of the investment, therefore, is −$10,844.23. Investing in the project is like throwing away $10,844.23 today. You wisely decide not to invest your money in this project, but to invest it in another project that earns 7 percent or better.

The Fundamental Theorem of Present Value

In evaluating the video business, we saw that present value was the proper measure to evaluate a stream of payments arriving at different times because future dollars are not worth as much as dollars today, as long as dollars today can be invested to earn positive interest. Present value can also be used to compare two different streams of income because the stream with the higher present value could always be converted, using borrowing and lending at the going interest rate, into the stream with the smaller present value, with some income left over. If stream of income 1 allows you to have everything that stream 2 does, plus more, then stream 1 must be better. Let's state this proposition formally and then look at an example.

> ***Fundamental Theorem of Present Value:*** *Let stream of income 2 have a higher present value than stream of income 1 when evaluated at interest rate* r. *Then, if an investor can borrow or lend at interest rate* r, *the investor can use the proceeds of income stream 2 to cover the costs of borrowing and lending needed to reproduce stream of income 1, and still have money left over in stream 2.*

To demonstrate the theorem, let us take two income streams that are four periods long. Table V.3 displays them and the relevant information. We assume that payments are made at the beginning of each period. Income stream 1 pays $50 at the start of year 2, $250 at the start of year 3, and $10 at the start of year 4. Income stream 2 pays $75, −$100, and $375, respectively, in the same periods. The interest rate for borrowing or lending is 7 percent.

For each income stream, the present value of the future payment is displayed under the payment. For example, the present value of receiving $250 at the start of year 3 (two years into the future) is $250/(1.07)^2 = $218.36. Summing the present values of all the payments making up the stream gives the present value of the entire stream reported in the right-hand column. As shown in the table, the present value of income stream 2 is $288.86, and the present value of income stream 1 is $273.25.

---

3. Present value of $30,000 eight years from now at 7 percent interest is $30,000/(1 + 0.07)^8.

Table V.3   Converting a Larger-Present-Value Income Stream into a Smaller One

	Year 1	Year 2	Year 3	Year 4	Present Value of Stream
Income stream 1	$0.00	$50.00	$250.00	$10.00	
Present value of future payment	$0.00	$46.73	$218.36	$8.16	$273.25
Income stream 2	$0.00	$75.00	($100.00)	$375.00	
Present value of future payment	$0.00	$70.09	($87.34)	$306.11	$288.86
Changes to income stream 2					
Borrow	$15.61	$0.00	$350.00	$0.00	
Lend	$0.00	($25.00)	$0.00	$0.00	
Repay borrowing	$0.00	$0.00	$0.00	($393.62)	
Receive payment for lending	$0.00	$0.00	$0.00	$28.62	
Income stream 2 after borrowing and lending	*$15.61*	*$50.00*	*$250.00*	*$10.00*	

Note: The calculations assume that the interest rate $r = 0.07$.

To apply the theorem, we borrow money in any future period when income stream 2 is less than income stream 1, and lend when the reverse is true. In the first period, however, we borrow an amount equal to the difference in the present values of the two streams and set this aside. The remaining income of stream 2 is sufficient to reproduce the income payments in stream 1.

Following this rule, we borrow $15.61 at the start of year 1 and $350 at the start of year 3. Repaying the loan at the start of year 4 means that we will have to pay $15.61 $\times$ $(1.07)^3$ + $350 $\times$ 1.07 = $393.62, because the $15.61 is borrowed for three years and the $350 is borrowed for one year. The amount $-$393.62 is listed in the row "Repay borrowing."

At the same time, we lend $25 at the start of year 2 and collect repayment of $25 $\times$ $(1.07)^2$ = $28.62 at the start of year 4. The amount $28.62 is listed in the row "Receive payment for lending."

The bottom row of the table shows the cumulative effect of the borrowing and lending. The income stream after borrowing and lending now exactly replicates income stream 1, except that income stream 2 is larger in the first year by the difference between its present value and the present value of the other stream. Any two income streams can be related to one another with this process. In general, the stream with the larger present value can replicate the income of the stream with the smaller present value, plus have more income in the first period by the difference in the two present values. The conclusion, therefore, is that present value provides a way to rank the desirability of income streams, with larger-present-value streams preferred over smaller ones.

Using Present Value to Select from Multiple Projects

The rule of thumb for using present value in project evaluation depends on the type of interaction among projects. That is, does undertaking one project influence the payment streams that can be obtained from other projects? The simplest cases arise when there is no interaction or there is mutual exclusion (undertaking one project prevents others from being undertaken), since then only one project needs to be evaluated at a time. More generally, the present value of a combination of projects needs to be evaluated to reach the right conclusion.

No Interaction When projects do not interact with one another, all projects with positive present value should be undertaken.

Mutual Exclusion When projects interact with each other in such a way that only one project can be chosen from a list of projects, the investor should choose that project that has the highest present value. For example, if a piece of land can be developed as a shopping center or as a residential neighborhood, but not both, choosing the alternative with the higher present value is preferred.

Other Situations Finally, if interaction is such that undertaking one project increases or decreases the present value of another project, the situation becomes more complicated. For example, one might have a parcel of land that can be developed as a shopping center or an airport or left vacant, and a second parcel that can only be developed as residential housing. Interaction might take the form that building the airport affects the housing value of the other parcel. In this case, undertake that project or *combination* of projects that gives the largest present value among all feasible combinations of projects.

Suggestion for Further Investigation. If present value is based on a dominance rule (through borrowing and lending, the income stream with higher present value can be made to duplicate the income stream of a lower-present-value project and have income left over), how might present-value comparisons be modified if borrowing and lending take place at different rates? (Hint: Try evaluating two streams that are only two periods long.)

Answers to Selected Problems

▼

Chapter 1
Review Questions

1. The price of rock salt will not be inaccurate to the homeowner because any additional costs caused by salt damage to the driveway will be known to the homeowner and thus can be taken into account in the homeowner's decision. The difference between the homeowner's case and the public case is that in the public case the costs from salt damage were incurred by people different from those making the decisions about the use of salt; thus more salt was used than if the additional damage had been taken into account.

3. Price reflects the interaction between demand and supply, not an object's intrinsic worth based on some other measure. Diamonds have high prices and water has a low price because people are willing to pay a lot for diamonds and little for water under current market conditions. Were market conditions to change considerably—for instance, if diamonds became common and water very scarce—price theory would be consistent with the prices of diamonds and water changing places.

5. Knowing that consumers optimize allows us to say only that the consumer will never buy a bundle of goods that provides less satisfaction than another bundle that the consumer gave up in its stead. For example, an optimizing consumer would not pay more for a good if it is possible to buy the good for a lesser price.

7. a) The objective is to spend as little as possible obtaining a given quantity of gasoline; the constraint is that you must choose from a limited selection of suppliers and their prices.

b) The objective is ingesting as little fat as possible in conjunction with a given quantity of meat; the constraint is that you have a limited selection of types of meat from which to choose.

c) Your objective is to earn as much money as possible; your constraint is that you must

work in a field that you are trained for (financial planning or accounting).

9. Comparative statics simply means comparing an equilibrium situation based on one set of circumstances to an equilibrium based on another. Comparative statics is closely tied to the use of models because models allow one to change a variable and see how the rest of the variables respond. Two equilibrium situations can therefore be compared.

11. The statement is false. Although in principle one could always do general equilibrium analysis rather than partial equilibrium analysis, in practice there are times when much additional effort and information would be needed and the relative benefit would be small or zero. In such cases, partial equilibrium analysis is preferred.

13. If by "harming" a family we simply mean taking tax dollars from them, then it is a matter of empirical fact whether families with children would have a greater fraction of their income taken by a sales tax on clothing than would other families. Item a) is therefore a positive statement. Each of the other statements involves personal opinions derived from different objectives or constraints of the opinion holder.

Chapter 1
Numerical and Graphing Exercises

1. Using the information given we can arrange the following multiplication:

$$\frac{5 \text{ bolteros}}{1 \text{ cuggle}} \times \frac{1 \text{ cuggle}}{5 \text{ askorgs}} \times \frac{3 \text{ askorgs}}{2 \text{ goutarks}} =$$

$$\frac{15 \text{ bolteros}}{10 \text{ goutarks}} = 1.5 \frac{\text{bolteros}}{\text{goutark}}.$$

Thus 15 goutarks requires 15 goutarks $\times$ 1.5 bolteros/goutark = 22.5 bolteros.

3. The data are from the linear relationship $y =$

1.5x − 2. The graph is a line passing through x-intercept 1.5 and y-intercept −2.

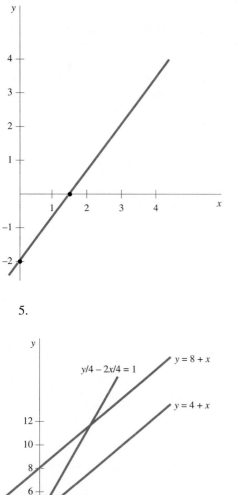

5.

7. Let A = allowance, B = number of blowpops, and p_B = price of blowpops. Then from a) we have $p_B B = 0.2A$. From b) we have $p_B = \$.10$. These two equations form the model.

9. If x = distance east and y = distance north, distance from home is $\sqrt{x^2 + y^2}$. Plotting the constraint $\sqrt{x^2 + y^2} \leq 500$ gives the following figure. Staying within the circle is Jon's constraint.

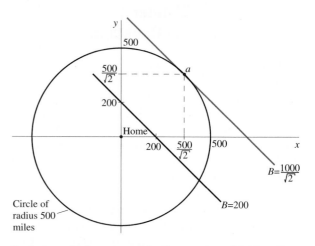

Jon's benefit from travel is $B = x + y$. Making B as large as possible is his objective. The largest B he can obtain, staying within 500 miles of home, is at point a, where $x = y = 500/\sqrt{2}$.

Chapter 2
Review Questions

2. U.S. computer makers supply laptop computers that use display screens as one of their costliest components. Every major U.S. manufacturer relies on Japanese sources for display screens. A U.S. duty on display screens would raise the cost of this input to American manufacturers above the cost that their Japanese competitor manufacturers pay for the input, shifting the U.S. supply curve to the left.

4. Demand does not go up when price falls. (An *increase in demand* indicates a shift in location of the demand curve.) Rather, the *quantity demanded* goes up when price falls; this is a movement of the price-quantity pair on the demand curve.

6. Demand depends on expectations about future oil prices as well as on the current price. Belief that the future price will be higher, for example, may cause

some buyers to buy more oil today to store for future use or resale. If D is the demand for oil today and S the supply today, an expectation-induced shift of D to the right raises today's price of oil even though no change in supply has occurred.

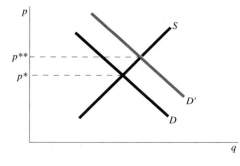

The higher price does not imply that oil companies and retailers are taking advantage of the situation to price-gouge.

9. Demand for California navel oranges is inelastic. Lowering quantity therefore raises price by more than enough to cause an increase in value of the remaining crop, as shown in the figure.

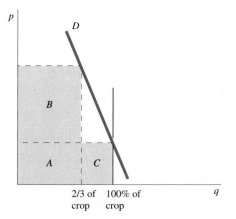

The value of two-thirds of the crop, with the other third destroyed, is shown by area $A + B$. This is greater than the value of a full crop, area $A + C$.

11. If every buyer could determine at a glance the quality of a used car, there would be no asymmetry of information. The markets for different-quality used cars would be separate. If buyers could not distinguish

car quality at a glance, they would be willing to pay for such information. We do not always observe such information offered for sale because the costs of supplying it in inconvenience, time, and money are frequently greater than the perceived value of the information to the prospective buyers.

Chapter 2
Numerical and Graphing Exercises

2. If $p = 500$, then $q^S = 2,000$ and $q^D = 1,000$. Excess supply is therefore 1,000 units.

4. Since refining costs are the same and there is a world market in oil causing domestic and foreign oil to sell for the same price, gasoline refined from domestic oil and gasoline refined from foreign oil cost the same to produce. A tax only on sales of gasoline refined from foreign oil would cause its price to rise above the price of comparable gasoline refined from domestic oil. No gasoline from foreign oil would be bought at the higher price.

5. Demand at each station depends on the price it charges and the price charged across the street. At station A, for example, $q^D = F(p_A, p_B)$, where p_A is the price charged by station A and p_B is the price charged by station B. Quantity demanded at station A drops to zero if $p_A > p_B$. If $p_A = p_B$, total demand for gasoline at the intersection is shared by the two stations; and if $p_A < p_B$, all demand at the intersection goes to station A. The diagrams at the top of p. 672 show the relationship between total demand for gasoline at the intersection and the demand for gasoline at station A.

Total demand for gasoline at the intersection when both stations charge the same price is q^*. Demand for gasoline at station A is zero if it charges a price higher than station B, and equals the entire demand at the intersection if A charges a lower price than B. If station A's price is the same as charged by station B, station A's share of the demand is q^D. The demand for gasoline at station B could be graphed analogously.

7. $-0.2 = \epsilon = (\Delta q/q)/(\Delta p/p)$. Thus, if $\Delta p/p = 0.02, 0.02(-0.2) = -0.004 = \Delta q/q$. Food purchases will fall .4 percent.

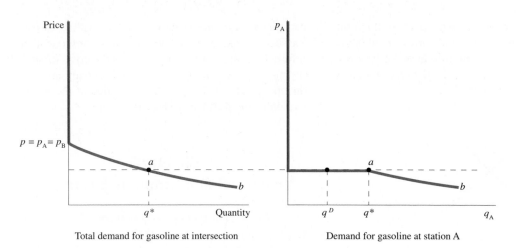

Total demand for gasoline at intersection

Demand for gasoline at station A

11. a) If $p = 3$, $q^D = 350 - 50(3) = 200$, and $q^S = -500 + 200(3) = 100$. Thus domestic demand exceeds domestic supply by 100 units. 100 units are therefore imported.

b) If a quota of 50 units is imposed, we must find a domestic price such that $q^D - q^S = 50$. Thus

$$350 - 50p - (-500 + 200p) = 50$$
$$800 - 250p = 0$$
$$p = 800/250 = 16/5 = 3.2.$$

Domestic price rises above the world level to 3.2. Domestic quantity consumed drops from 200 units to $350 - 3.2(50) = 350 - 160 = 190$ units.

12. Train trips to Key West and use of resort services are complementary goods for vacationers. By subsidizing train tickets to Key West, the developers hoped to shift the demand for resort services to the right from D to D'. By increasing the price they could

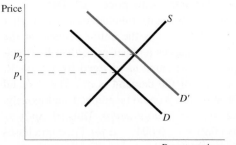

charge for resort services, they hoped to more than make up the cost of their subsidies.

Chapter 3
Review Questions

1. Consumers are irrational if they do not choose in their own best interest or if they are inconsistent. Consider points a and b on the two budget lines.

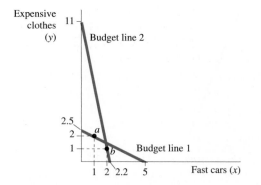

When fast cars were cheaper (budget line 1), the consumer chose bundle a consisting mostly of expensive clothes, even though bundle b was affordable (b is inside budget line 1). However, when fast cars become more expensive (budget line 2), the consumer chooses bundle b, even though the previously preferred bundle a is affordable. Choices of a and b, given the budget lines, are therefore irrational. The graph is based on the following assumptions.

	Budget line 1	Budget line 2
Income	100,000	110,000
$p_{fast\ cars}$	20,000	50,000
$p_{expensive\ clothes}$	40,000	10,000
x	1	2
y	2	1

3. I like strawberry shakes better than vanilla; I like vanilla shakes better than chocolate; and I like chocolate shakes better than strawberry shakes. I am pulling into the drive-in where all these kinds of shakes sell for $1.50. Which will I buy? My choice cannot be predicted because, for any of the three flavors, I like another flavor better.

4. Strict prioritizing implies devoting all effort to attaining the first priority, devoting any remaining effort to the next priority only after no further gains are possible on the first, and so on down the chain of priorities. In reality, very few decisions are made on the "all or nothing" basis of prioritizing. Rather, we choose mixtures or combinations of things (as when we seek the highest indifference curve) in order to do as well for ourselves as possible. In this type of decision making, there are trade-offs between objectives rather than rigid hierarchies.

7. The marginal rate of substitution between two bads might exhibit an increasing marginal rate of substitution. Consider a consumer who is eating Brussels sprouts and prunes, both of which are economic bads. Say that we plot prune consumption on the horizontal axis. Initially, the consumer is willing to eat one additional prune to avoid a Brussels sprout, and the consumer stays on the same indifference curve ($MRS_{prune,\ sprout}$ = 1). However, as the consumer moves along the indifference curve toward more prunes, the trade-off changes to the point where the consumer will accept only 1/2 prune to avoid a Brussels sprout ($MRS_{prune,\ sprout}$ = 2). MRS therefore increases as we move to the southeast on the graph.

9. Essentially the two conditions apply as before: when the highest utility bundle in the choice set is not on a corner, Robinson selects a point of tangency between his convex choice set and his indifference curve at point a.

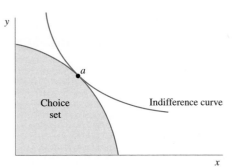

If the frontier is concave, two cases must be distinguished. Frequently the same conditions apply as in case 1, where the indifference curve is tangent to the concave shaded set at point a. However, we must be alert to the possibility of case 2, where being on the frontier and tangent at point b does not maximize utility. Instead, point c does better, raising utility to U_1.

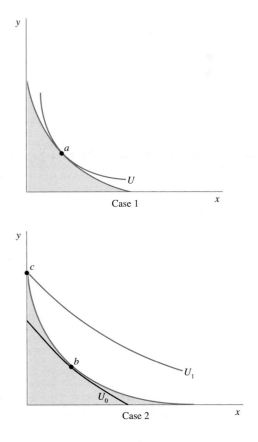

Chapter 3
Numerical and Graphing Exercises

2.

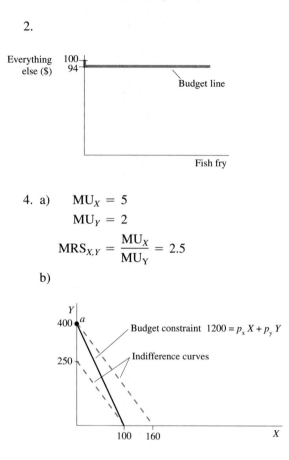

Everything else ($)

Budget line

Fish fry

4. a) $MU_X = 5$
$MU_Y = 2$

$MRS_{X,Y} = \dfrac{MU_X}{MU_Y} = 2.5$

b)

Budget constraint $1200 = p_x X + p_y Y$

Indifference curves

The highest utility bundle is point a, where $X = 0$, $Y = 400$.

6. Since each type of legion costs the same (assume its price is 1) and the Conqueror has enough for only 12 legions total, his budget constraint is $A + F = 12$, where A is the number of legions of archers and F is the number of legions of foot. Utility maximization implies choosing A and F so that $MU_A/MU_F = MRS_{A,F} = p_A/p_F = 1$. The only combination of A and F satisfying both requirements is $A = 8$, $F = 4$, where $MU_A = MU_F = 22$.

8. Graphing lexicographic preferences in the case of two goods leads to the following figure. The only bundle giving the same utility as a given bundle is the bundle itself. Hence there can be no indifference curves.

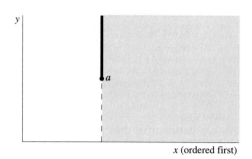

x (ordered first)

Points directly above or to the right are strictly preferred to a. Points directly below or to the left are strictly less preferred than a.

Chapter 4
Review Questions

1. Utility rises for points further out on a price consumption path. For price consumption paths to cross, there must exist an indifference curve for which points a and b in the figure reverse their relative positions. Given that indifference curves are concave and that the steeper budget line will always have the higher price of x, this is impossible. Price consumption paths could touch, however, as when an indifference curve had a sharp corner at an intersection, c.

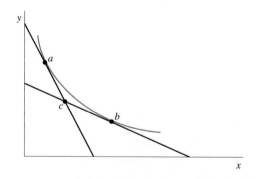

3. Probably not, for two reasons. First, brand-name clothing is often of higher quality than nonbrand clothing. Second, purchasers of brand-name clothing are

often buying a bundled good consisting of the clothing plus the prestige from having others know that they are wearing the higher-priced, brand-name item.

5. If there are only two goods, they must be substitutes because holding utility constant means that more of one must be consumed when less of the other is consumed.

7. If domestic and foreign crude oil are perfect substitutes, the higher-priced oil would not be bought. The elasticity of demand of domestic crude oil with respect to the price of foreign would be infinite.

9. Points corresponding to lower price are associated with higher utility on the individual demand curve. By construction, all points on the income-compensated demand curve are associated with the same utility level.

11. Horizontal summation of two curves means that for each vertical distance the horizontal distance to the point on the summed curve is the sum of horizontal distances on the individual curves. Vertical summation simply reverses the axes in the above description. Market demand curves are horizontal summations of individual demand curves.

Chapter 4
Numerical and Graphing Exercises

2. Let family income be I. Initial demand is

$$x_0 = \frac{0.3I}{p_x}$$

where x is housing and p_x its price. If p_x drops 10 percent to $0.9p_x$, demand becomes

$$x_1 = \frac{0.3}{0.9}\left(\frac{I}{p_x}\right).$$

The formula to approximate the area bounded by the demand curve and the two prices is

$$x_0 \, \Delta p_x + \frac{1}{2} \, \Delta p_x \, \Delta x =$$

$$\frac{0.3I}{p_x}(p_x - 0.9p_x) + \frac{1}{2}(p_x - 0.9p_x)(x_1 - x_0) =$$

$$(0.3)(0.1)I + \frac{1}{2}(0.1p_x)\left[(0.3/0.9 - 0.3)\frac{I}{p_x}\right] =$$

$$0.03I + \left(\frac{0.03}{18}\right)I =$$

$$0.03\left(\frac{19}{18}\right)I.$$

4. From the definition of price elasticity of demand we have

$$\frac{\Delta q^f}{\Delta p^f} = -3\left(\frac{q^f}{p^f}\right),$$

where q^f is the quantity of foreign apparel and p^f its price. We also know from the one-to-one shift that

$$\frac{\Delta q^f}{\Delta p^f} = -\frac{\Delta q^d}{\Delta p^f},$$

where q^d is the quantity of domestic apparel. From the market shares we have

$$\frac{q^f}{q^f + q^d} = 0.3 \quad \text{or} \quad \frac{q^f}{q^d} = \frac{3}{7}.$$

Combining the above information, we have

$$\left(\frac{\Delta q^d}{\Delta p^f}\right)\left(\frac{p^f}{q^d}\right) = \left(-\frac{\Delta q^f}{\Delta p^f}\right)\left(\frac{p^f}{q^d}\right)$$

$$= 3\left(\frac{q^f}{p^f}\right)\left(\frac{p^f}{q^d}\right)$$

$$= 3\left(\frac{q^f}{q^d}\right) = 3\left(\frac{3}{7}\right) = \frac{9}{7}.$$

5. Being on the budget line implies that

$$p_1 x_1 + p_2 x_2 = I,$$

and being tangent to the indifference curve implies that

$$\frac{MU_{x_1}}{MU_{x_2}} = \frac{0.5/x_1}{0.5/x_2} = \frac{p_1}{p_2}.$$

Since tangency implies that $p_1 x_1 = p_2 x_2$, we have

$$x_1 = \frac{0.5I}{p_1} \quad \text{and} \quad x_2 = \frac{0.5I}{p_2}.$$

The price consumption path tells us how x_1 and x_2 relate to one another as p_1 changes. Since p_1 does not enter the formula for x_2, we have

$$x_2 = \frac{0.5I}{p_2} = \frac{0.5(100)}{4} = 12.5.$$

In other words, the price consumption path is a vertical line at $x_2 = 12.5$. The Engel curve tells us how consumption of a good changes with income. Since $x_1 = 0.5I/p_1 = 0.5(100)/1$, we have $x_1 = (1/2)I$ as the Engel curve.

6.

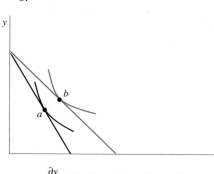

$\dfrac{\partial y}{\partial p_x} < 0$, y is a substitute for x and a gross complement to x.

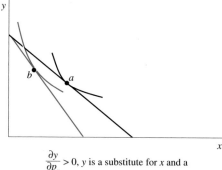

$\dfrac{\partial y}{\partial p_x} > 0$, y is a substitute for x and a gross substitute for x.

9. Positive income elasticity means that the demand curve shifts to the right at the given commodity price. This shift could also be accompanied by a flattening of the curve, causing greater price elasticity.

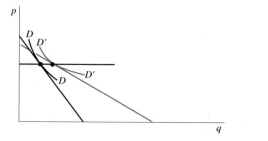

11. The Laspeyres price index can be written as the budget-share–weighted percentage change in prices. Thus

$$L_P = 0.2(1.04) + 0.4(1.01) + 0.4(1.10)$$
$$= 1.052.$$

On average, then, prices rose 5.2 percent. If the household's income rose 8 percent over the same period, the household is better off. We know this because Income index > Laspeyres price index implies that the household has more than enough income to buy the initial bundle.

Chapter 5
Review Questions

1. If the wage rate rises, leisure is more expensive so the substitution effect implies less leisure purchased. When the wage rate rises, the household also has higher endowment-time income. If leisure is inferior, the household buys less leisure. Since both effects imply less leisure (more labor), the supply curve must be upward-sloping at the point in question.

3. a) A head tax of $100 per year acts like a reduction in endowment income. If leisure is a normal good, leisure drops (implying that labor increases). If leisure is inferior, the reverse happens.

b) A wage tax has both an income and a substitution effect. The substitution effect leads to more leisure (less work), while the income effect leads to less leisure (more work), if leisure is a normal good. The outcome depends on which effect predominates. If leisure is inferior, both effects imply less work.

5. a) and b) Since a 64-year-old is likely to have greater wealth and thus higher non-labor income (in anticipation of retirement), the income effect is likely to imply more leisure (less work) compared to the 28-year-old. The preferences of a 64-year-old might

also be expected to favor leisure relative to the 28-year-old.

c) and d) An unskilled female head of household with a preschool child is likely to have low nonlabor income and a low wage coupled with a need for income to support herself and her child. Low nonlabor income and need for goods suggest that additional income would tend to be spent more on goods than on leisure. On the other hand, a low wage suggests a low price of leisure, which would work toward the spending of additional income more on leisure than on goods.

The college-educated female head of household is likely to have a higher wage. A higher wage raises the cost of leisure, working to shift the income effect toward greater purchase of goods rather than leisure.

e) The same consideration as in c) and d) apply to the male. If his wife works and earns a high income, this probably would shift the income effect in favor of greater purchase of leisure compared to the income effect if there were low or no income from his wife's earnings.

6. The budget constraint is $I = I_0 + wL$. The condition that the worker's indifference curve be tangent to the budget constraint is

$$-\mathrm{MRS}_{L,I} = w \quad \text{or} \quad \frac{-I}{(L - 17)} = w.$$

Since $I_0 = 0$, this implies that

$$\frac{wL}{17 - L} = w \quad \text{or} \quad L = 8.5.$$

7. Workers whose labor supply is zero at low wages, but whose labor supply becomes positive at higher wages, will have their labor supply added to market supply for wages where their supply is positive.

Chapter 5
Numerical and Graphing Exercises

1. $p_C C = I_0 + wL$

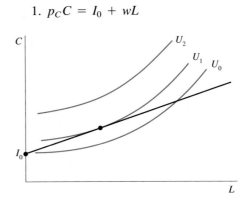

Labor is an economic ''bad.'' Welfare increases to the northwest when the diagram is oriented in this way.

3.

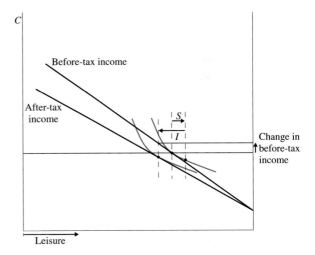

Since work hours rise, the worker's before-tax income rises.

4. See graph at the top of p. 678.

Worker consumer surplus as a percentage of initial labor income is

$$\frac{\Delta w(L_0) + 1/2\, \Delta L\, \Delta w}{w_0 L_0} = \frac{\Delta w}{w_0} + \frac{1}{2}\left(\frac{\Delta L}{L_0}\right)\left(\frac{\Delta w}{w_0}\right)$$

$$= 0.05(1 + 0.025\epsilon_S),$$

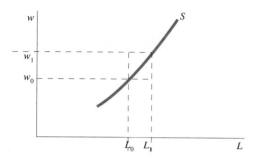

where we use the facts that $\Delta w/w_0 = 0.05$ and $\Delta L/L_0 = \epsilon_S(\Delta w/w_0) = \epsilon_S(0.05)$. For the three values of ϵ_S specified, this number becomes (a) 0.05, (b) 0.050625, and (c) 0.0525 (that is, 5 percent, 5.06 percent, and 5.25 percent, respectively).

7. See graph below.

Before the program, worker utility is U_1. After the program, worker utility is U_2 for those who can partake, and U_0 for those who cannot.

Chapter 6
Review Questions

1. A specialized activity requires a larger market to support it as a stand-alone enterprise because specialization of service limits the product that is sold. A large city could support a medical practice devoted to a highly specialized subdiscipline, for example, where a small town could not. Benefits from coordination encourage firms to bundle related activities, whereas greater profitability for stand-alone activities encourages unbundling.

2. A firm might pursue sales maximization, larger market share, or increased stock market value. Under certain circumstances, each objective might imply profit maximization for the firm in the long run or in the future.

4. The cost function represents the least cost of producing a given level of output at given input prices.

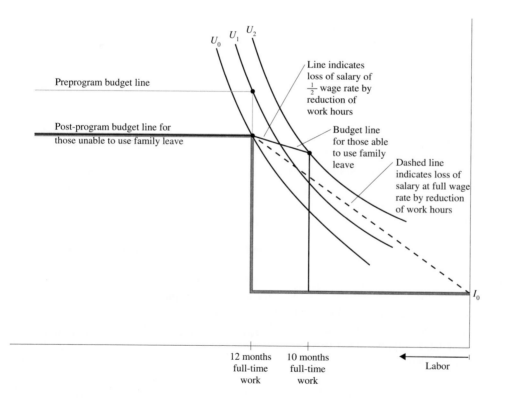

It therefore represents the result of a cost minimization problem—a form of optimization.

7. Yes. Constant returns to scale imply that output per unit of input is constant at any point on a ray from the origin. For example,

$$\frac{F(K, L)}{L} = F\left(\frac{K}{L}, 1\right).$$

Since K/L is constant on a ray from the origin, output per unit is constant on that ray.

9. If only labor is variable in the short run, Cost $= wL +$ Fixed cost. Since $\Delta q/\Delta L = MP_L$, we have

$$\Delta \text{Cost} = \left(\frac{w}{MP_L}\right)\Delta q \quad \text{or} \quad MC = \frac{w}{MP_L}.$$

If MP_L declines for larger q, then MC must rise with larger q.

11. Yes.

$$
\begin{aligned}
VC(q) &= C(q) - C(0) \\
&= C(q) - C(q - 1) \\
&\quad + C(q - 1) - C(q - 2) \\
&\quad + C(q - 2) - C(q - 3) \\
&\quad + \cdots \\
&\quad + C(1) - C(0) \\
&= MC(q) \\
&\quad + MC(q - 1) \\
&\quad + MC(q - 2) \\
&\quad + \cdots \\
&\quad + MC(1)
\end{aligned}
$$

13. For fixed input prices, the firm increases output by moving out on the output expansion path. Increasing returns to scale imply that isoquants for a given increment in quantity are closer together as one moves out from the origin, so cost per unit of output falls. As one moves to higher levels of output, isoquants are further apart if production experiences decreasing returns to scale. This requires more inputs, and thus more cost, per unit of output as output increases. U-shaped cost curves are therefore consistent with increasing, then constant, then decreasing returns to scale as output is increased.

Chapter 6
Numerical and Graphing Exercises

1. a)

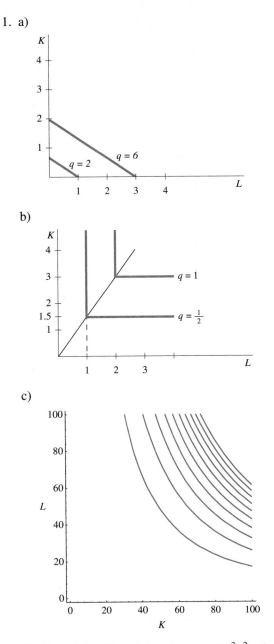

b)

c)

d) Since $3 \log K + 2 \log L = \log (K^3 L^2)$, the isoquants are the same as in c) except that the levels of output are logarithms of the levels in c).

3. a) If $T_0 + K_0 + L_0 = q_0$, then $2T_0 + 2K_0 + 2L_0 = 2(T_0 + K_0 + L_0) = 2q_0$. Production exhibits constant returns to scale.

   b) If $(T_0 + K_0)^{1/2} + L_0 = q_0$, then $(2T_0 + 2K_0)^{1/2} + 2L_0 = \sqrt{2}(T_0 + K_0)^{1/2} + 2L < 2[(T_0 + K_0)^{1/2} + L_0] = 2q_0$. Production exhibits decreasing returns to scale.

   c If $(T_0K_0)^{1/2} + L_0 = q_0$, then $(2T_02K_0)^{1/2} + 2L_0 = 2[(T_0K_0)^{1/2} + L_0] = 2q_0$. Production exhibits constant returns to scale.

   d) If $(T_0^{-3} + K_0^{-3} + L_0^{-3})^{-1/3} = q_0$, then $[(2T_0)^{-3} + (2K_0)^{-3} + (2L_0)^{-3}]^{-1/3} = (2^{-3})^{-1/3}(T_0^{-3} + K_0^{-3} + L_0^{-3})^{-1/3} = 2q_0$. Production exhibits constant returns to scale.

5. Let K_0 be the fixed quantity of capital. Since $q = \min(K_0, L/2)$, no extra output is produced for hiring labor above $2K_0$ units. Thus the firm will use labor quantity only from zero to $2K_0$, where

$$q = \begin{cases} L/2 & 0 \le L \le 2K_0 \\ K_0 & 2K_0 < L \end{cases}.$$

K_0 is the most the firm can produce. Thus

Cost $= wL + rK_0 = L + K_0$

$$= \begin{cases} 2q + K_0 & 0 \le q \le K_0 \\ \infty & K_0 < q \end{cases}$$

This relationship is shown in the graph.

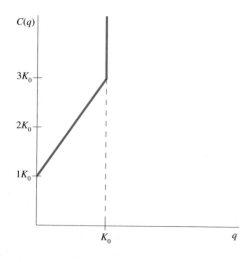

7. In the long run capital is adjustable. The firm sets $K = L/2 = q$. Thus the long run cost function is

$$C(q) = wL + rK$$
$$= L + K$$
$$= 2q + q$$
$$= 3q.$$

Chapter 7
Review Questions

1. If firms in the market knew that positive economic profits would induce entry, driving their profits to zero and possibly dislodging them from the market in the ensuing competition, firms might keep their prices at such a level that economic profits were zero or close to zero.

3. Firm profits equal $q(p - \text{AVC}_{SR}) - \text{FC}$, where AVC_{SR} is average variable cost in the short run and FC is fixed costs. If $q = 0$, profits are $-\text{FC}$. Thus, as long as $p - \text{AVC}_{SR} > 0$, the firm is better off producing in the short run than making larger losses by shutting down.

5. Yes. The market curve is determined by entry and exit of firms as well as by the shape of firm supply curves. If all firms produce at minimum average cost and entry is free, the market supply curve could be horizontal at a price equal to the common minimum average cost.

7. $\Pi = pq - \text{VC}(q) - \text{FC}$. Thus $\Pi + \text{FC} = pq - \text{VC}(q) = q[p - \text{AVC}(q)]$. Profit plus fixed cost is thus shown to equal revenue minus variable cost. Since the firm is better off by producing and selling its output at market price only if $q[p - \text{AVC}(q)] > 0$ (its profits would be lower if it chose $q = 0$ under this condition), condition (b) is also equivalent to $\Pi + \text{FC}$. If this firm leaves production in the industry, it earns $-\text{FC}$. This is the minimum needed to keep the firm producing in the industry. The excess above this amount is $\Pi - (-\text{FC}) = \Pi + \text{FC}$, which, as shown before, equals the other three definitions.

9. If industry size does not affect the price of inputs

to the industry, either the industry must use inputs whose supply curve is perfectly horizontal, or the industry must be too small in input markets to have appreciable impact on the prices of inputs.

Chapter 7
Numerical and Graphing Exercises

1. MC and AVC are fixed. However, AC moves up the MC with higher fixed costs.

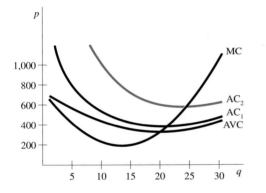

3. Finding MC and AC for each level of output gives us the following:

q	MC	AC	q	MC	AC
0			7	12	10.4
1	6	16	8	13	10.75
2	7	11.5	9	14	11.1
3	8	10.3	10	15	11.5
4	9	10	11	16	11.9
5	10	10	12	16	12.25
6	11	10.16			

Finding the quantity for which $p = MC(q)$, we get

p	q	Π
7	2	-9
9	4	-4
12	7	11
15	10	35

Each profit is higher than -10 (what Howard would make if he shut down). Minimum AC occurs at $10

per unit, so prices greater than $10 per unit are where Howard makes positive profit.

5. In the short run the 150 firms continue to operate as long as $p \geq$ minimum AVC = $12/unit. The condition $p = MC(q)$ implies that one firm's supply curve is

$$p = 10 + 3q^S \quad \text{or} \quad q^S = \frac{1}{3}p - \frac{10}{3}.$$

150 such firms would supply $q^{\text{market supply}} = 150(1/3p - 10/3) = 50p - 500$ for prices above or equal to 12, and zero for prices below 12.

7. In the short run, $C_{SR}(q) = 1/4q^2 + 4$ implies that $MC_{SR}(q) = 1/2q$. Short-run average cost is $(4/q) + (1/4)q$, which has its lowest value of $2/unit when $q = 4$. The equation $p = MC_{SR}(q)$ implies that the firm's short-run supply curve is $p = (1/2)q$ or $q^S = 2p$ for $p \geq $2, and 0 otherwise. 100 such firms have the short-run supply curve

$$q^{\text{market supply}} = 100(2p) = 200p \quad \text{for } p \geq 2$$

and

$$q = 0 \quad \text{for } p < 2.$$

In the long run, $C_{LR}(q) = 2q$ implies that $MC_{LR}(q) = 2$. Individual firms therefore supply any quantity for $p = 2$ and zero for $p < 2$. The market long-run supply curve is a horizontal line at $p = 2$.

9. If a common product is sold in two markets for fixed prices p_1 and p_2, and output for each market is produced in separate plants, firm profit is $\Pi = [p_1q_1 - C_1(q_1)] + [p_2q_2 - C_2(q_2)]$. The firm therefore sets $p_1 = MC_1$ and $p_2 = MC_2$ separately. We are effectively back to the single-firm analysis for each market separately.

11. a) $C(q) = 430.56q + 33.333(q - 0.1667)^3 + 50.15$ implies that $AC(q) =$

$$430.56 + \frac{33.333(q - 0.1667)^3}{q} + \frac{50.15}{q}.$$

Plotting AC reveals that AC falls until $q = 1$ and rises thereafter. $AC(1) = 500. Since the market is contestable, $p = $ minimum $AC = 500. At this price $q^D = 1,000$. Thus 1,000 carts supply the market for ice cream selling at a price $500/cart, and vendors make zero economic profits. We assume 1 vendor per cart.

b) Short-run marginal cost for an individual vendor is $MC(q) = 430.56 + 100(q - 0.1667)^2$. If there are 1,000 vendors in the market, $q^{\text{market}} = 1,000q$. $p = MC(q^{\text{market}})$ then implies that

$$p = 430.56 + 100\left(\frac{q^{\text{market}}}{1,000} - 0.1667\right)^2,$$

which gives the short-run combination of p and q^{market} on the supply curve. If demand becomes $1,600 - q^{\text{market}} = p$, demand = supply implies that

$$1,600 - q^{\text{market}} =$$
$$430.56 + 100\left(\frac{q^{\text{market}}}{1,000} - 0.1667\right)^2.$$

Solving this quadratic for q^{market} gives
$$q^{\text{market}} = 1.085 \quad \text{or} \quad p = \$514.90.$$

c) In the long run, entry will drive price back to $500, and there will be 1,100 carts supplying ice cream at this price.

Chapter 8
Review Questions

1. Apart from a government-maintained monopoly, neither can I. If you discover one, let me know. Patents, exclusive control over an essential input or territory, and other entry barriers are generally temporary.

3. Let (p_0, q_0) be the price-quantity pair in question. If $MR = MC$ at $q < q_0$, then the less elastic demand curve is preferred since price is higher at each quantity. If $MR = MC$ at $q > q_0$, the more elastic curve is preferred for the same reason. (If $MR = MC$ for one demand curve to the right of q_0 and for the other to the left, it depends.) The two graphs show both possibilities in terms of total revenues and costs.

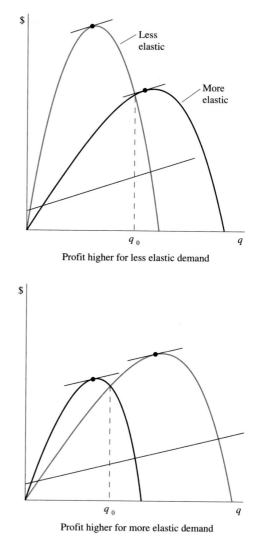

Profit higher for less elastic demand

Profit higher for more elastic demand

5. The social costs of monopoly represent lost consumer and producer surplus. Perfect competition has zero social costs since demand equals supply in equilibrium and $p = MC$ for each firm.

7. A market-segmenting firm has the option of not segmenting its market if it chooses. Thus it can do no worse by having the segmenting option.

8. If demand has elasticity -0.5 at every point,

the monopolist can raise revenue by selling a smaller quantity. Since producing the smaller quantity also costs the firm less, the firm would continue to reduce quantity to zero, an unrealistic outcome. Clearly the depiction of a demand curve with elasticity of -0.5 at *every* point must be questioned.

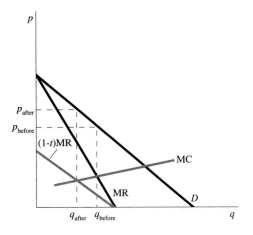

Chapter 8
Numerical and Graphing Exercises

2.

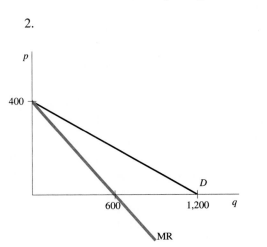

4. Set MR = MC, which implies that

$$p\left(1 + \frac{1}{\epsilon}\right) = MC \quad \text{or} \quad p\left(1 + \frac{1}{-2}\right) = 10.$$

Therefore, $p = \$20$.

5. With tax on sales t,

$$\Pi_{\text{before}} = pq - C(q) \quad \text{and}$$

$$\Pi_{\text{after}} = (1 - t)pq - C(q).$$

Thus, reaching maximum profit implies that $(1 - t)$ MR = MC.

6. The following graph shows the effect of the tax.

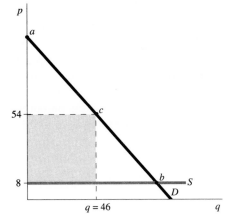

Since supply is horizontal, all of the tax is passed on. Tax revenue is therefore greatest at point c, the midpoint between points a and b, where the shaded area is greatest. For an algebraic proof, we can write

$$\text{Tax Revenue} = [(100 - q) - 8]q$$

$$= 92q - q^2.$$

Therefore

$$\frac{\Delta \text{ Tax Rev}}{\Delta q} = 92 - 2q = 0,$$

which gives us $q = 46$. That is the quantity under the tax plan. For comparison, we calculate q for the monopoly option as follows:

$$R = (100 - q)q$$
$$MR = 100 - 2q$$
$$MC = 8 = 100 - 2q.$$

Solving for q, we find that $q = 46$. The opponent is right. The tax leads to the same social costs as the monopoly would.

8. The given demand, $q^D = 400 - 8p$, implies that

$$q^D = \frac{400 - 8MR}{2} \quad \text{or} \quad MR = 50 - \frac{1}{4}q.$$

If $C(q) = 20q$, then $MC = 20$. Setting $MR = MC$, we have

$$50 - \frac{1}{4}q = 20 \quad \text{or} \quad q = 120.$$

10. $MR = (a/b) - (2q^D/b)$, where $a = 100$, $b = 2$. Neither a profit tax nor a franchise tax affects the monopolist's choice of output. Thus $MR = MC$ implies that $50 - q = 2$, or $q = 48$. The corresponding price on the demand curve is $48 = 100 - 2p$, or $p = 26$.

11. A specific import duty is like a tax on output to the foreign monopolist. It therefore raises its MC by the amount of the levy, t.

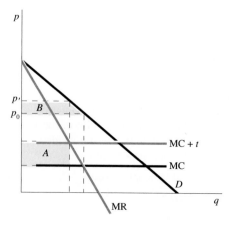

The monopolist raises price from p_0 to p', reducing domestic consumer surplus by area B. However, the domestic government collects area A in tax revenues.

A necessary condition for A to be larger than B is that price rises less than the amount of the tax.

13. The lower the sale price, and the longer the sale, the lower the average price at which the firm sells to uninformed buyers. On the other hand, a lower price on sale takes advantage of the higher marginal revenue to be had by selling to informed buyers, most of whom quickly learn of the sale and bunch their purchases into the sale period.

If x is the fraction of the month for which a sale is held, the firm sells 40 units per month to uninformed buyers at average price $60(1 - x) + 30x$. This implies revenue from uninformed buyers of $40[60(1 - x) + 30x]$. Revenue from informed buyers during the sale period is

$$(60 - p)x^{1/2}p = (60 - 30)x^{1/2}30.$$

Revenue from informed buyers during the nonsale period is

$$(60 - p)(1 - x^{1/2})p = (60 - 60)(1 - x^{1/2})60 = 0.$$

Total firm revenue is therefore

$$40[60 - (1 - x) + 30x] + 30x^{1/2}30 =$$
$$300(8 + 3\sqrt{x} - 4x).$$

Revenues for various values of x are as follows (other deciles can be found from the formula):

x	0	1/10	2/10	5/10	1
R	2,400	2,564.6	2,562.5	2,436.4	2,100

The firm is best off having a sale for 1/10 of each month on average. If the firm charges $60 uniformly throughout the month, its profits are $2,400, which corresponds to choosing $x = 0$ above.

Chapter 9
Review Questions

1. The market for personal care products, such as soap and shampoo, might come close. Brands are highly substitutable, each brand has a downward-sloping demand curve, and suppliers earn conventional profits (zero economic profits).

3. If every consumer on a beach had a vendor within a few feet, the fixed costs of so many vendors would be exorbitant. Demand would not be sufficient

to cover them. If just one location were supplied, however, there would be room for new entrants to earn economic profit by selecting product locations near major groups of buyers.

5. The costs of too many varieties are the high costs associated with many, low-volume products. The costs of too few varieties are the distance costs experienced by buyers who must consume products far away from their preferred location.

7. Sales cannibalism arises when increased sales of a firm's product come by reducing sales of another of the firm's products. Cannibalism matters to the firm's choice of variety because a firm is interested in total sales and profit, not just the sales and profit on one product line.

9. Setting the net benefit to the firm of increasing quantity sold by lowering price equal to zero,

$$\Delta q(p - MC) - (-\Delta p\, q) = 0,$$

and doing the same for the net benefit of increasing quantity sold by increased advertising,

$$\Delta q(p - MC) - \Delta A = 0,$$

leads to the advertising rule.

Chapter 9
Numerical and Graphing Exercises

1.

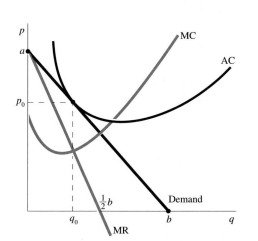

Profit maximization for a monopolistically competitive firm occurs at q_0, where AC is tangent to the demand curve. Therefore we know that MC and MR must cross at q_0. Since MR is constructed by passing a chord through point a and point $1/2b$, the result follows.

2. Since each firm is symmetrical, its share of the total market is 1 percent. Thus $q = (110 - p)/100 = 1.1 - .01p$ is the firm curve D. At price 10, quantity 1, this has elasticity $(\Delta q/\Delta p)(p/q) = (-.01)(10/1) = -0.1$.

4.

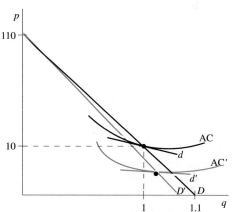

Curve d' is flatter than d as long as each remaining firm increases its output above 1 unit.

5. For each n, maximum revenue occurs where $q = (1/2)[100 - (50/n)]$ and $p = 50$ (this is the midpoint of the demand curve where $\epsilon = -1$). Maximum profit for each n is therefore $50[50 - (25/n)] - 50n = 50[50 - (25/n) - n]$. This expression reaches its highest level where $n = 5$.

8. Assume vendor 0 at location m_0 sells at price p_0, and vendor 2 at location m_2 sells at price p_2. The length of beach served by vendor 1 is $d = s_1 - s_0$, where

$$p_1 + (s_1 - m_1)g = p_2 + (m_2 - s_1)g \quad \text{and}$$
$$p_1 + (m_1 - s_0)g = p_0 + (s_0 - m_0)g.$$

Thus

$$s_1 = \frac{p_2 - p_1}{2g} + \frac{m_1 + m_2}{2}$$

$$s_0 = \frac{p_1 - p_0}{2g} + \frac{m_0 + m_1}{2}.$$

Since $q^D = 1{,}056 \times 3 \times d$, we have

$$q^D = 1{,}056 \times 3 \times \left(\frac{p_2 + p_0 - 2p_1}{2g}\right)$$

$$+ 1{,}056 \times 3 \times \left(\frac{m_2 - m_0}{2}\right)$$

$$= \frac{1{,}056 \times 3}{20}(p_2 + p_0 - 2p_1)$$

$$+ \frac{1{,}056 \times 3}{2}(m_2 - m_0)$$

$$\frac{\Delta q^D}{\Delta p_2} = \frac{\Delta q^D}{\Delta p_0} = \frac{1{,}056 \times 3}{20} = 158.4.$$

Chapter 10
Review Questions

1. Oligopolistic firms can improve their profits by raising prices in collusion with other firms or by competing more successfully against other firms. Elements of common interest and conflict of interest therefore both matter to oligopolistic competition.

3. In principle, a monopolist or group of firms operating jointly as a cartel can earn the greatest profits in a given market. A cooperative solution earning highest possible profits has only to indicate how to allocate those profits among participating firms.

5. A dominant strategy is one that is best in all circumstances. That is, its success relative to other strategies does not depend on which strategy is chosen by other firms. Very often, a dominant strategy does not exist.

7. A Nash equilibrium is one in which no firm can improve its position by changing its strategy, given the current choices of all other firms. A Nash equilibrium depends on the firm's beliefs about how other firms behave—that is, on the strategies the firm believes other firms have chosen.

9. Cournot competitors are different from Bertrand competitors in that they treat quantity as their choice variable rather than price. Also, Cournot competition frequently describes competition between firms supplying identical products or very close substitutes, whereas Bertrand competition more frequently describes competition between firms producing substitute goods. Both Bertrand and Cournot equilibria are Nash equilibria, and the two forms of competition are alike in that the firm treats the choices of competitors as fixed when it makes its choice.

11. Credibility and reputation matter to the success of certain strategic choices. A Stackelberg leader, for example, earns higher profits than a Cournot competitor, but must convince rivals that its choice of quantity will be maintained. Its choice must be credible. In the same way, a pre-emptive threat must be credible to induce the proper response by rivals. Building a reputation helps credibility.

Chapter 10
Numerical and Graphing Exercises

1.

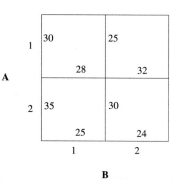

a) Player A has dominant strategy 2. Player B has no dominant strategy.
b) The Nash equilibrium is strategy 2 for player A, and strategy 1 for player B.

2.

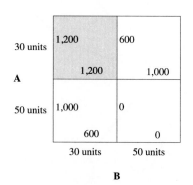

The Cournot equilibrium, which is also a Nash equilibrium, is indicated by the shaded northwest box.

4. a) If the two firms collude, they will set price at $p = 50$. Equilibrium quantity will be $q_1 + q_2 = 50$.

b) If the firms act as Cournot competitors,

$$\Pi_1 = pq_1 - C_1(q_1)$$
$$= pq_1$$
$$= (100 - q_1 - q_2)q_1$$
$$= 100q_1 - q_1^2 - q_1q_2.$$

Then

$$MR - MC = 100 - 2q_1 - q_2 = 0.$$

Firm 1's reaction curve is therefore

$$q_1 = 50 - \frac{1}{2}q_2,$$

and Firm 2's reaction curve is

$$q_2 = 50 - \frac{1}{2}q_1.$$

Solving, we have

$$q_1 = q_2 = 100/3 \quad \text{and} \quad p = 100/3.$$

c) If the firms act as pricetaking perfect competitors, then $p = 0$ and $q_1 + q_2 = 100$.

5. Using the reaction curve of Firm 2 from exercise 4, $q_2 = 50 - 1/2q_1$, we have

$$\text{Firm 1 } \Pi = pq_1 - C_1(q_1)$$
$$= pq_1$$
$$= (100 - q_1 - q_2)q_1$$
$$= \left(100 - q_1 - 50 + \frac{1}{2}q_1\right)q_1$$
$$= \left(50 - \frac{1}{2}q_1\right)q_1$$
$$= 50q_1 - \frac{1}{2}q_1^2.$$

Then

$$MR - MC = 50 - q_1 = 0.$$

Therefore

Stackelberg	Cournot, for comparison.
$q_1 = 50$	$q_1 = 100/3$
$q_2 = 25$	$q_2 = 100/3$
$p = 25$	$p = 100/3$

7. Since firm costs are $F_i + 10q_i$, we have

$$\Pi_1 = p_1q_1 - F_1 - 10q_1$$
$$= p_1(100 - 2p_1 + p_2) - F_1 - 10(100 - 2p_1 + p_2)$$
$$= 100p_1 - 2p_1 + p_2p_1 - F_1 - 1,000 + 20p_1 - 10p_2.$$

Then

$$MR - MC = 100 - 4p_1 + p_2 + 20 = 0,$$

implying that

$$p_1 = \frac{120 + p_2}{4} \quad \text{or} \quad p_1 = 30 + \frac{1}{4}p_2.$$

This is the reaction curve of Firm 1. By symmetry, the reaction curve of Firm 2 is

$$p_2 = 30 + \frac{1}{4}p_1.$$

These curves indicate that Bertrand equilibrium occurs at $p_1 = p_2 = 40$ and $q_1 = q_2 = 60$.

9. Country options are to trade freely or to engage in self-interested trade interventionism. Worldwide, the cooperative solution would be for countries to trade freely. However, national advantage can sometimes be gained by intervention if trading partners do not respond in kind. If all countries engage in interventionist behavior, all lose. The payoffs, measured in national levels of welfare, follow the classic Prisoner's Dilemma pattern.

Chapter 11
Review Questions

1. The firm's output expansion path is constructed in the short run in the same way as in the long run, except that one or more factors of production are fixed. In both cases, the output expansion path consists of the points representing the least costly combination of inputs (varying those that can be varied) for producing each level of output. We expect greater response to a change in factor prices in the long run since all, not just some, factors can be adjusted.

3. Using the information given, we see that

$$5 = pMP_K < r = 10$$
$$2 = pMP_L < w = 8,$$

implying that the firm does not satisfy the hiring condition. Both labor and capital employment should be reduced.

5. Higher w/r implies that the firm will use a technique with a higher capital-to-labor ratio for any given level of output.

7. Industry demand for a factor is likely to be less elastic because of less elastic product demand. An increase in factor price shifts product supply to the left, but the less elastic product demand means that equilibrium product quantity falls less than if demand were more elastic. The quantity of input demanded therefore falls less as well.

9. Diminishing supply of labor implies higher wage rates in the future. The presence of a close substitute with highly elastic supply suggests that labor buyers can shift to the substitute, implying greater elasticity of labor demand and lesser wage increases. Since wage increases are good for you, the labor supplier, you would rather be in the industry with no close labor substitute available, or with inelastic supply curves of substitutes when they are available.

11. A minimum wage in a monopsonistic market can raise employment and wage, as long as the minimum wage is not higher than the wage at which the labor supply curve cuts the firm's MRP_L curve. For minimum wages above this, both monopsonistic and competitive markets imply unemployment. If it is not too high, then, a minimum wage is more sensible in the monopsonistic market. Unfortunately, few labor markets are monopsonistic. The perfectly competitive model is typically a better representation of labor markets than the monopsonistic model.

Chapter 11
Numerical and Graphing Exercises

1. $p\text{MP}_L = 5(100 - 4L) = 5[100 - 4(23)] = \$40/\text{hour}$. This exceeds the wage of $\$15/\text{hour}$. Thus

the firm increases profits by hiring additional labor. The value of what the additional labor would produce exceeds the labor cost.

3. a) Since $\Delta\text{MP}_A/\Delta B = 1$ and $\Delta\text{MP}_B/\Delta A = 1$, the factors are complements in production.

b) The fact that $p\text{MP}_A = p_A$ and $p\text{MP}_B = p_B$ implies that

$$2\left(\frac{50}{A}\right) + 2B = 30$$

$$2\left(\frac{100}{B}\right) + 2A = 50$$

or $A = B = 5$. The answer $A = 50/3$, $B = 12$, would also satisfy the firm's hiring conditions, but the production function is $F(A, B) = AB + 50 \ln A + 100 \ln B$. Thus profit $= 2F(A, B) - 30A - 50B$ is higher at $A = B = 5$.

5. With labor the only input, $w = p\text{MP}_L$ determines the demand curve of labor. Using the information given, we can calculate the following values:

L	MP_L	$w = p\text{MP}_L$
0		
1	19	95
2	17	85
3	15	75
4	14	70
5	13	65
6	12	60
7	11.5	57.5
8	11	55
9	10.5	52.5
10	10	50
11	9.5	47.5
12	9	45
13	8.5	42.5
14	8	40
15	7.25	36.25
16	6.25	31.25
17	5	25
18	3.75	18.75
19	2.25	11.25
20	0	0

Plotting w on the vertical axis and L on the horizontal gives the labor demand curve.

6. Let $Q^0 = (q_0, -K_0, -L_0)$, $Q^1 = (q_1, -K_1, -L_1)$, $\Delta Q = (\Delta q, -\Delta K, -\Delta L)$, $P^0 = (p, r, w_0)$, $P^1 = (p, r, w_1)$, and $\Delta P = (0, 0, \Delta w)$, where Δx for any variable x is the final value of x minus the initial value of x.

a) $\Pi_1 = P^1 Q^1 = pq_1 - w_1 L_1 - rK_1$. Profits if the firm produces at original quantities are $P^1 Q^0 = pq_0 - w_1 L_0 - rK_0$.

b) $P^1 \Delta Q = P^1 Q^1 - P^1 Q^0 = P^1(Q^1 - Q^0) = p(q_1 - q_0) - w_1(L_1 - L_0) - r(K_1 - K_0)$.

c) Since $P^1 = P^0 + \Delta P = (p, r, w_0) + (0, 0, \Delta w)$, we have

$$P^1 \Delta Q = P^0 \Delta Q + \Delta P \Delta Q = P^0 \Delta Q - \Delta w \Delta L.$$

Thus

$$P^1 \Delta Q + \Delta w \Delta L = P^0 \Delta Q = p(q_1 - q_0) - w_0(L_1 - L_0) - r(K_1 - K_0).$$

If $P^1 \Delta Q \geq 0$, $\Delta w = w_1 - w_0 > 0$, and $\Delta L = L_1 - L_0 > 0$, then $P^0 \Delta Q > 0$. But this implies that the firm could have raised its profits initially by changing production from Q^0 to Q^1. This contradicts the assumption that the firm was originally maximizing its profits.

8.

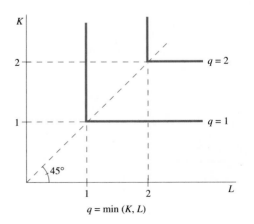

$q = \min (K, L)$

Holding output constant at 10 units, $\Delta L / \Delta w = 0$.

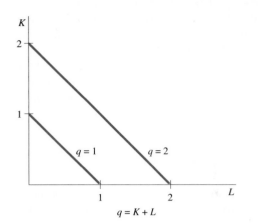

$q = K + L$

Holding output constant at 10 units, raising wages to $2 shifts demand for labor to zero.

9. $MP_L / MP_K = w/r$ implies that $k^2 = w/r$. Since w/r is fixed on an output expansion path, we have $K = L\sqrt{w/r}$ as the output expansion path.

11.

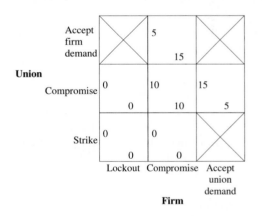

The above cells show a representative pattern of payoffs. Crossed-out cells are incompatible choices, and neither firm nor union benefits from strikes or lockouts. The Nash equilibrium is the center cell, where firm and union reach a working compromise.

If the firm has a more aggressive option (for instance, the ability to fire workers and hire low-wage replacements), it adds a column of cells to the right of the diagram with higher payoff to the firm (say, 20) and lower payoff to the union (say, 1 if the union accepts firm terms or compromises, and -5 if union members strike and are replaced). Now the center cell is no longer a Nash equilibrium. The new Nash equilibrium will involve the firm's firing union workers and hiring lower-paid nonunion replacements, and the union's accepting the firm's action or compromising.

Chapter 12
Review Questions

1. All economies must decide what to produce, how to produce it, and who will receive the output. How an economy solves these problems can vary greatly, even when the methods used to answer the different questions are not consciously recognized.

3. An individualistic approach bases the assessment of economic welfare not only on the economy's effect on people, but on how the people themselves claim their utility is affected. Other approaches might not be people-based or might not respect the preferences of constituent households.

5. No, because an economy generally has many Pareto optimal outcomes. In addition, one needs prior rules of ownership—for example, that every household owns the returns to its own labor.

7. Distributive efficiency involves tangencies between indifference curves; consumer sovereignty involves tangencies between the production possibility frontier and indifference curves; sector production-allocation efficiency involves tangencies between sectoral production possibility frontiers; and input efficiency involves tangencies between isoquants. Only full employment does not primarily relate to a tangency of some sort.

9. To answer the first part of the question, assume that an allocation is Pareto optimal but that every household strictly prefers some other household's bundle. There are eight possible patterns of preference, as shown below. In each case, there is a cycle of size two or three. (A cycle is a group of households in which each prefers the next's bundle, with the last preferring the first's). But the existence of cycles implies that we could produce a Pareto superior alloca-

tion by switching bundles. Thus the original allocation could not have been Pareto optimal.

	Strictly preferred bundle							
	A	B	B	B	B	C	C	C	C
Household	B	A	A	C	C	A	A	C	C
	C	A	B	A	B	A	B	A	B

The circled patterns are cycles of three; the others are cycles of two.

For the second part of the question, assume a Pareto optimal allocation among n households. If every household strictly prefers some other household's bundle, then there must be a cycle of size n or less. Again, a cycle implies that a Pareto superior allocation could be achieved by rotating bundles, and this contradicts the assumption that the original allocation was Pareto optimal.

Chapter 12
Numerical and Graphing Exercises

1. The heavy line indicates the Pareto optimal points.

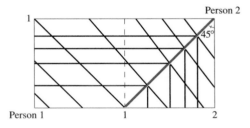

2. If $U = \min(X, Y)$ for both individuals, the Edgeworth box looks like the one below, with the shaded points Pareto optimal.

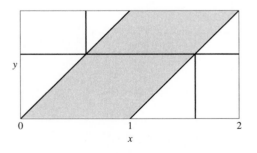

4. The heavy line shows the overall production possibility frontier.

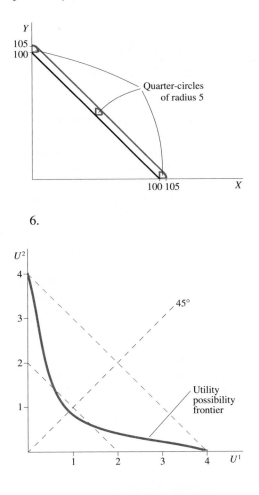

6.

Chapter 13
Review Questions

1. A market economy solves the question of what to produce by firm profit maximization, and the question of for whom the production is produced by distributing income, and hence purchasing power, according to contribution to work done. A hunter-gatherer society solves both problems by having each family decide how much to hunt and gather, with each family keeping what it produces.

3. A competitive equilibrium coordinates house-hold and firm choices by ensuring market clearing, both in goods markets and in factor markets. If markets clear, firms or households cannot use more or less of a commodity than firms or households provide.

5. Distributive efficiency is violated because the marginal rate of substitution of public transportation for income (the composite good) is lower for over-65 households than for under-65 households. In other words, there is too much transportation use by over-65s relative to under-65s.

7. Cost minimization ensures that $\text{MRTS}_{K,L} = r/w$ across firms, thus equalizing MRTSs across firms.

Chapter 13
Numerical and Graphing Exercises

1. Point a is not distributively efficient. Point b is Pareto superior to it.

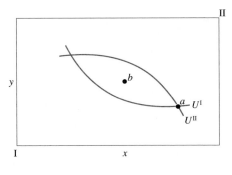

2.

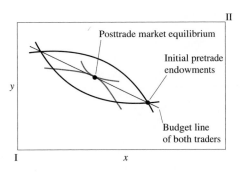

Each household's income is $p_x E_x + p_y E_y$, where (E_x, E_y) is the household's endowment of the two goods.

4. a)

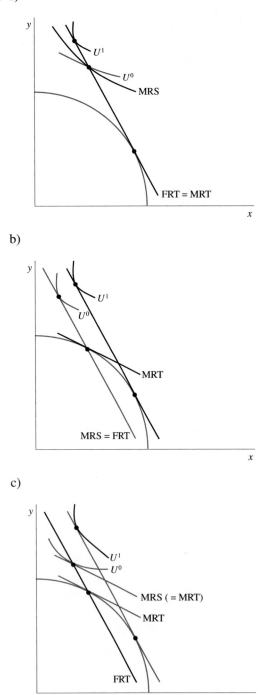

b)

c)

In each case, the equality MRS = MRT = FRT would move the utility from U_0 to U_1.

Chapter 14
Review Questions

1. Situation a) represents an externality because XYZ company does not take into account the costs implied by its using the river for waste disposal. It therefore overuses the river. Social costs equal the benefits from the river you would lose plus XYZ's out-of-pocket costs from using the river. An externality is not present in case b). Though you might prefer to pay less for use of the river, the waste-disposal use is more valuable socially than your fishing, so the river gets used in that way through the incentives of the price system.

3. Costless bargaining would eliminate all monopoly because there are net social gains to eliminating it. Coase's First Theorem implies that the economy will reach a Pareto optimum; if not, households could bargain, rearrange activities, and raise someone's utility without harming anyone.

5. A tax can be altered marginally to achieve the desired objective. In the optimum it should be set so the effective price (market price plus tax) reflects true social costs. No other direct firm or market information is needed.

7. Yes to the first part of the question. A good that is nonrival and excludable might be satellite broadcast television programming: Marginal provision cost to another viewer is zero, but signal scrambling can prevent unauthorized viewers. In contrast, purely rival and nonexcludable goods are difficult to find, since once a rival good is being used by one, it cannot be used by another.

9. Pure private goods are summed horizontally to find market demand because market demand plots total quantity demanded at each price in the usual price-quantity diagram, where quantity is on the horizontal axis. A pure public good can be consumed by many households with no diminution of benefits to other households. The total social benefit should therefore equal marginal cost for optimal provision. Since the individual demand curve plots $MRS_{G,I}$, where G is the

public good and I is income (the composite good), we need each point on the market demand curve for a public good to equal $\sum_i \text{MRS}^i_{G,I}$—in other words, vertical summation of individual demand curves for the pure public good.

11. Figure 14.10 shows that the utility frontier, given a fixed tax structure, may deviate from the Pareto optimal frontier at all but one or a subset of points. The socially preferred point may in fact not be a Pareto optimal point (the preferred point may be between $g = g^*$ and $g = g\dagger$, for example).

Chapter 14
Numerical and Graphing Exercises

1. Pedestrians ruin grass, creating both physical costs of restoration and utility costs in the form of unsightly lawns. The direct costs of grass-walking are the inconvenience costs of uneven or wet terrain (versus pavement), which corner-cutters accept because of the benefits of a shorter distance to travel.

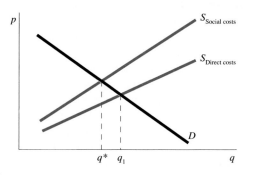

When corner-cutters see just the direct costs of grass-walking, they engage in q_1 of it. Were they made to pay the full social costs, they would engage in quantity q^*.

3. Total living costs if each woman lives separately (out-of-pocket and inconvenience costs) are $700. If they live together, each following her preferred sleep routine, the costs are $250 to Shelly and $250 + $40 to Diane (total $540). If Shelly instead conforms her sleep habits to Diane's, the total costs are $250 + $100 to Shelly and $250 to Diane (total $600).

a) The Pareto optimal outcome is for the women to room together, each pursuing her own sleep pattern.

b) This will also be the bargaining outcome, since Diane is not willing to pay enough to cause Shelly to change. Nevertheless, this is still better (or no worse) for each woman than living separately (each has total costs $\le$ $350).

c) Regardless of liability, costless bargaining implies the optimal solution. However, if Shelly is liable, she pays $40 to compensate Diane.

5.

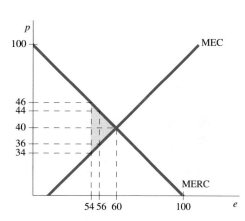

a) Since emissions are costless to the firm, it will emit at the point where it costs it a positive amount to reduce emissions further, that is, at $e = 100$. Social optimality e^* occurs at $\text{MEC}(e) = \text{MERC}(e)$ or $-20 + e = 100 - e$. Thus $e^* = 60$.

b) The tax should be set at $40 per unit of emission.

c) 10 percent below the optimal emission level of 60 is $e = 54$. MERC between 60 and 54 exceeds MEC by the shaded area in the graph, equal to $36.

d) An emission charge 10 percent too high would set $p = 44$, implying that the firm would reduce emissions to $e = 56$. Social cost is $\text{MERC}(e) - \text{MEC}(e)$ between $e = 56$ and 60, or $16.

6. a)
$$q_1^D = 100 - p_1/2 \quad \text{or} \quad p_1 = 2(100 - q_1^D)$$
$$\text{for} \quad 50 \geq p_1 \geq 0$$
$$100 \geq q_1^D \geq 0$$

$$q_2^D = 200 - 2p_2 \quad \text{or} \quad p_2 = \frac{1}{2}(200 - q_2^D)$$
$$\text{for} \quad 100 \geq p_2 \geq 0$$
$$200 \geq q_2^D \geq 0$$

$$q_3^D = 100 - 2p_3 \quad \text{or} \quad p_3 = \frac{1}{2}(100 - q_3^D)$$
$$\text{for} \quad 50 \geq p_3 \geq 0$$
$$100 \geq q_3^D \geq 0$$

Vertical summation implies that

$$p_{\text{market}} = \begin{cases} 350 - 3q & 100 \geq q_M^D \geq 0 \\ \frac{1}{2}(200 - q) & 200 \geq q_M^D \geq 100 \end{cases}$$

Setting $p_{\text{market}} = MC = \$200$ implies that $q = 50$.

b) Household 1 pays \$100 per unit; Household 2, \$75 per unit; and Household 3, \$25 per unit.

7. The households are deciding whether to provide 50 units of public good, costing 50(\$200) = \$10,000. Each household is therefore charged \$10,000/3 and asked to vote on its extra contribution. Measuring the area under each household's demand curve between $q = 0$ and $q = 50$ as the consumer surplus for the project, we find that households are better off by the following amounts.

	Public Good Value	Excess over Base Levy
Household 1	\$7,500	\$4,166.67
Household 2	\$4,375	\$1,041.67
Household 3	\$1,875	-\$1,458.33

Since each household votes its excess over the base levy, the vote total \$4,166.67 + \$1,041.67 - \$1,458.33 = \$3,750 (pennies are rounded). Total collections would therefore be \$13,750, more than enough, so the project is built. The actual excess paid by each household is the difference between the sum of everyone else's vote and zero, if the household's vote changed the outcome. Without Household 1, the vote totaled \$1,041.667 - \$1,458.33 = -\$416.667,

so Household 1 pays \$416.667. The sum of Household 1 and Household 3's votes is \$4,166.667 - \$1,458.33 = \$2,708.33, so Household 2's vote did not change the sign of the sum of all three. Household 2 pays zero additional. A similar calculation shows that Household 3 pays zero additional money. The net outcome is that the event is held, as is Pareto optimal, with the households paying the following amounts.

	Total Payments	Net Consumer Surplus
Household 1	\$3,750	\$3,750
Household 2	\$3,333.33	\$1,041.67
Household 3	\$3,333.33	-\$1,458.33
Total	\$10,416.66	\$3,333.33

Chapter 15
Review Questions

1. Yes. For risky assets 1 and 2 having identical expected returns, it is possible that investor A would prefer 1 and investor B would prefer 2. This does not conflict with the use of standard deviation as an approximate measure of risk, since the measure is understood not to represent everyone's risk preferences.

3. Standard deviation is based on the sum of squared deviations. Because they are squared, large deviations in effect become even larger with respect to smaller deviations, and therefore they contribute more than proportionately to the standard deviation.

5. The average of random variables that are less than perfectly correlated will generally have a lower standard deviation than a single such variable or a group of highly correlated variables.

7. A fair lottery would be one in which bettors were offered a fair bet, meaning that the expected return equaled the amount paid. The worth of a ticket offered in a lottery is its expected payoff less some subtraction for risk. The amount subtracted for risk depends on the individual's preferences concerning risk.

9. The rationale of insurance is that everyone in the pool pays for the benefits received, on average.

Grouping those with unequal probabilities of a claim means that those with higher claims do not pay for the benefits they receive, on average. The difference must be paid by others in the pool, who therefore pay for more than they get on average. An element of welfare transfer is then introduced, and this is not part of the basic insurance function.

Chapter 15
Numerical and Graphing Exercises

1. $EV_1 = (1/6)(1) + (1/6)(2) + (1/6)(3) + (1/6)(4) + (1/6)(5) + (1/6)(6) = 21/6.$ $\pi_{ij} = 1/36$ is the probability of outcome (V_{1i}, V_{2j}), with V_{1i}, V_{2j} the number on each die. Then

$$EV(V_1 + V_2) = \sum_{i,j} [\pi_{ij}(V_{1i} + V_{2j}]$$

$$= \sum_{i,j} \pi_{ij}V_{1i} + \sum_{i,j} \pi_{ij}V_{2i}$$

$$= \sum_{i=1}^{6}\left(\sum_{j=1}^{6}\pi_{ij}\right)V_{1i} + \sum_{j=1}^{6}\left(\sum_{i=1}^{6}\pi_{ij}\right)V_{2j}$$

$$= \sum_{i=1}^{6}\frac{1}{6}V_{1i} + \sum_{j=1}^{6}\frac{1}{6}V_{2j} = EV_1 + EV_2.$$

Therefore, the expected value of the toss of two dice is twice that of one.

3. $E[a + bV(I)] = a + bEV(I)$. Thus if $a > 0$, $b > 0$, $a + bV(I)$ is a monotonic transformation of expected utility, giving the same ranking of risky alternatives.

5. $EV = (1/2)\sqrt{400} + (1/2)\sqrt{600}$ if no insurance. $EV = (1/2)\sqrt{600 - p} + (1/2)\sqrt{600 - p}$ if full insurance at premium cost p. Therefore

$$\frac{1}{2}(\sqrt{400} + \sqrt{600}) = \frac{1}{2}(2\sqrt{600 - p})$$

$$\left(\frac{20 + 24.494897}{2}\right)^2 = 600 - p.$$

Solving for p, we find that $p = \$105.051$.

7. By the first choice we have

$$U(I + 100) < \frac{3}{4}U(I + 220) + \frac{1}{4}U(I).$$

By the second we have

$$\frac{1}{3}U(I + 100) + \frac{2}{3}U(I) > \frac{1}{4}U(I + 220) + \frac{3}{4}U(I)$$

or

$$U(I + 100) + 2U(I) > \frac{3}{4}U(I + 220) + \frac{9}{4}U(I)$$

or

$$U(I + 100) > \frac{3}{4}U(I + 220) + \frac{1}{4}U(I),$$

a contradiction.

9. If the traveler places everything in one place,

$$EV = \frac{1}{2}\sqrt{30,000 + 1,000} + \frac{1}{2}\sqrt{30,000}$$

$$= 174.6366.$$

If the traveler places money in two locations,

$$EV = \frac{1}{4}\sqrt{30,000} + \frac{1}{2}\sqrt{30,500} + \frac{1}{4}\sqrt{31,000}$$

$$= 43.30127019 + 87.32124598 + 44.01704215$$

$$= 174.63956.$$

She is better off not placing all her money in one place.

Chapter 16
Review Questions

1. The country of impatient households would have higher interest rates as long as the intertemporal frontier were convex.

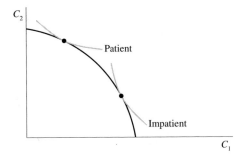

3. Less patient households, and highly productive activities left uninvested in, both imply higher interest rates. Each might accompany a society in decline.

5.

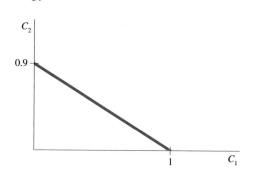

7. The real interest rate measures the purchasing power of a dollar today in terms of a future bundle of goods. It therefore equals the rate at which a bundle of goods today could be converted into bundles tomorrow. The technology is saving the currency, earning the nominal interest rate, and spending the dollar proceeds in the future period to buy bundles.

9. The faster a firm's new knowledge spreads to other firms, the harder it is for the firm to appropriate the future benefits of its invention through exercise of market power. The closer a market is to perfect competition, the more likely it is that knowledge flows are unhindered. Also, more competitors might imply quicker information transfer.

Chapter 16
Numerical and Graphing Exercises

1.

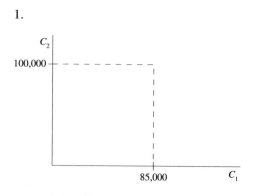

2. a) $p_1C_1 = 100 + B$ and $p_2C_2 = 85 - 1.1B$. Then

$$p_1C_1 + \frac{p_2C_2}{1.1} = 100 + \frac{85}{1.1} = I.$$

If $p_1 = p_2 = 1$, the graph looks like the following diagram.

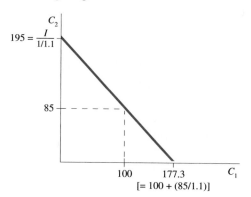

b) $p_1C_1 = 100 + B - L$ and $p_2C_2 = 85 - 1.12B + 1.05L$, where $B \geq 0$, $L \geq 0$, $BL = 0$. Then

$$p_1C_1 + \frac{p_2C_2}{1.05} = \frac{85}{1.05} + 100 \qquad \text{for } p_2C_2 > 85$$

$$p_1C_1 + \frac{p_2C_2}{1.12} = \frac{85}{1.12} + 100 \qquad \text{for } p_1C_1 > 100.$$

If $p_1 = p_2 = 1$, the graph is shown by the following diagram.

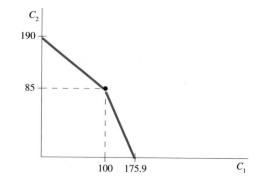

3. a)

$$\frac{C_2}{C_1} = \frac{1.1p_1}{p_2}, \quad p_1C_1 + \frac{p_2C_2}{1.1} = 100 + \frac{85}{1.1}$$

implies $p_1C_1 = 88.64$, $p_2C_2 = 97.5$.

Thus Smith saves (i.e. lends) \$11.36 in the first period.
  b) If $100 \leq p_1C_1 \leq 175.9$,

$$\frac{p_1}{p_2/1.12} = 1.12\frac{p_1}{p_2}$$

$$p_1C_1 + \frac{p_2C_2}{1.12} = 100 + \frac{85}{1.12}$$

$$\frac{p_2C_2}{p_1C_1} = 1.12.$$

This implies that $p_1C_1 = 87.95$, which is inconsistent. But if $0 \leq p_1C_1 \leq 100$,

$$\frac{p_1}{p_2/1.05} = 1.05\frac{p_1}{p_2}$$

$$p_1C_1 + \frac{p_2C_2}{1.05} = 100 + \frac{85}{1.05}$$

$$\frac{p_2C_2}{p_1C_1} = 1.05.$$

This implies that $p_1C_1 = 90.48$ and $p_2C_2 = 95$, which is the answer. Thus, Smith saves (lends) $\$100 - \$90.48 = \$8.52$ in the first period.

5.

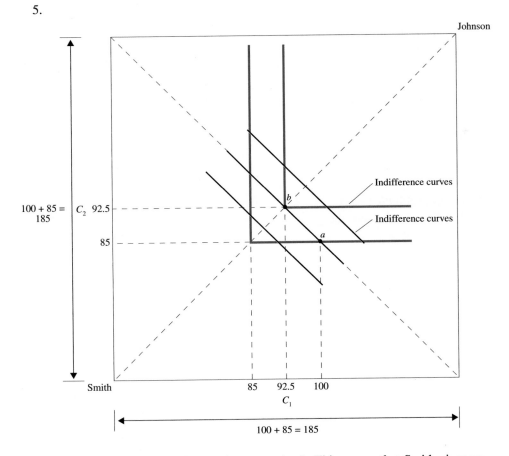

Smith and Johnson will trade from point a to point b. This means that Smith gives up 7.5 units of C_1 today in return for 7.5 units of C_2 tomorrow. The nominal interest rate is zero.

7.

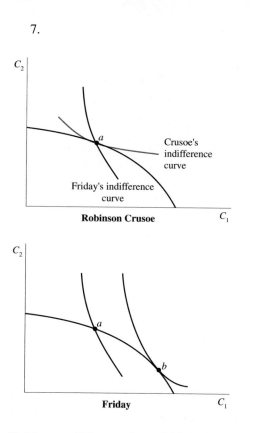

Robinson will be at point a, Friday at point b. Friday's interest rate will be higher than Robinson's since the slope, $-\Delta C_2/\Delta C_1$, is higher at b than at a.

Glossary

▼

Average cost, AC, is the cost of production per unit of output. In mathematical terms, $AC(q) = C(q)/q$. (Ch. 6)

Average fixed cost, AFC, is the fixed cost of production per unit of output. In mathematical terms, $AFC(q) = FC/q$. (Ch.6)

Average product of labor, AP_L, is the average output per unit of labor. In mathematical terms, $AP_L = q/L$. (Ch. 6)

Average variable cost, AVC, is the variable cost of production per unit of output. In mathematical terms, $AVC(q) = VC(q)/q$. (Ch. 6)

Bertrand competition Firms assume that competitors' prices are fixed and decide simultaneously what prices to charge to maximize profit (Ch. 10)

Budget set The set of bundles bounded by the budget line that the consumer can afford to purchase at market prices. For example, if there are two goods x and y, the budget set is all x and y such that $p_x x + p_y y \leq I$, where I is income. (Ch. 3)

Cartel A combination of independent producers of a common product that agree to limit competition in order to fix prices (Ch. 9)

Change in demand The quantity that consumers want to buy has changed at each possible price because of a change in other determinants of demand, such as the price of other goods, income, expectations, or taste. This leads to a shift in the location of the demand curve. (Ch. 2)

Change in quantity demanded A change in the amount consumers want to buy because of a change in the good's own price. This leads to a shift of the price-quantity point along the demand curve, which is fixed in locations. (Ch. 2)

Change in quantity supplied A change in the amount suppliers want to sell because of a change in the good's own price. This leads to a shift of the price-quantity point along the supply curve, which is fixed in location. (Ch. 2)

Change in supply The quantity suppliers want to sell has changed at each possible price because of a change in other determinants of supply, such as the price of material inputs or of other goods. This leads to a shift in the location of the supply curve. (Ch. 2)

Choice set The set of feasible bundles from which the consumer can choose (Ch. 3)

Coase's First Theorem An economy where information is perfect, where no costs are incurred for bargaining about arrangements or for enforcing them, and where property rights are clearly set will achieve an optimal assignment of resources, regardless of how property rights are assigned and without need of government intervention (Ch. 14)

Coase's Second Theorem If bargaining is costly and information is imperfect, then liability rules help achieve optimality, and the party that has the least costly way of dealing with the harmful effects of an externality should be made responsible for paying the costs associated with the externality (Ch. 14)

Commodity bundling The selling of two or more goods as a package (Ch. 8)

Comparative statics The comparison of economic variables, such as price and quantity, between two equilibrium positions (Ch. 2)

Competitive equilibrium A competitive equilibrium for an economy consists of prices P for all outputs and inputs, a production plan Y, an allocation X, and ownership by households of endowments and claims to firm profits, where the following conditions are met:
i) Firms and households take prices as given and do not act strategically
ii) Each firm's production plan is feasible, given its technology, and maximizes the firm's profits, given prices P
iii) Each household's consumption is feasible for the household and maximizes the household's utility, given its income
iv) In each market there is market clearing, meaning that consumption of goods and services by households and firm use of inputs equals the supply available (Ch. 13)

Complement Good 2 is a complement for good 1 if the cross-price elasticity of demand for good 2 with respect to the price of good 1 is negative when utility is held constant (Ch. 4)

Complements in production Two factors are complements in production if the marginal product of one factor rises when employment of the other increases. (Ch. 11)

Completeness Given any two alternatives a and b, the consumer can rank them precisely as meeting one of three possibilities: either *a* is strictly preferred to *b*, *b* is strictly preferred to *a*, or *a* and *b* are indifferent (Ch. 3)

Constant returns to scale A production process exhibits constant returns to scale if increasing all inputs proportionately increases output in equal proportion (Ch. 6)

Consumer sovereignty An economy achieves consumer sovereignty if it is impossible to change the selection of goods produced in such a way as to increase any household's utility without harming another household (Ch. 12)

Consumer surplus The difference between the amount of money the consumer would have been willing to pay for a good and the amount actually paid (Ch. 4)

Contract curve Given two households with a fixed quantity of goods between them, the contract curve is the set of Pareto optimal allocations of goods to the two households (Ch. 12)

Cost function $C(q)$, relates the level of firm output, q, to the lowest total cost of producing it. The equation is written Total cost $= C(q)$. (Ch. 6)

Cournot competition Firms assume that competitor's quantities are fixed and decide simultaneously what quantities to produce to maximize profit (Ch. 10)

Decreasing returns to scale A production process exhibits decreasing returns to scale if a proportionate increase in all inputs increases output less than proportionately (Ch. 6)

Distributive efficiency An economy satisfies the conditions of distributive efficiency if, given the available goods and services, it is impossible to redistribute them among households so as to increase the utility of one household without lowering the utility of another (Ch. 12)

Dominant strategy In a game, a dominant strategy is a choice of action that leads to the best payoff for the player regardless of the other players' choices. If the player's best choice depends on the choices other players make, the player does not have a dominant strategy. (Ch. 10)

Duopoly An oligopoly consisting of only two producers (Ch. 10)

Economic bad A commodity for which less is preferred to more (Ch. 3)

Economic good A commodity for which more is preferred to less (Ch. 3)

Economic profit The difference between total revenue and total cost, where the total cost includes the opportunity costs of inputs (Ch. 6)

Economic rent The difference between what the firm is willing to pay for an input (based on what the input can earn for the firm) and the minimum payment the firm has to make to keep the input in its present use (Ch. 5, 6)

Elasticity The percentage change in one variable caused by a 1 percent change in another (Ch. 2)

Equilibrium A state of balance between opposing or divergent influences (Ch. 1)

Expected utility The expected value of the household's utility across states of nature, U_s (Ch. 15)

Expected value The average value of a set of random numbers, where the weights used to average represent the probability that each number will occur (Ch. 15)

Expenditure function The expenditure function, $e(p_x, p_y; U)$ gives the least amount of money needed to reach utility level U, when the prices of buying goods x and y are p_x and p_y, respectively (Ch. 4)

Externality An effect on a firm or household arising from the action of another firm or household and operating directly rather than through market prices (Ch. 14)

Factor substitution effect The change in use of a factor resulting from a change in its factor price, holding output constant by adjusting the level of other factors (Ch. 11)

Fair gamble A gamble in which the expected payout equals the amount payed for playing (Ch. 15)

Fixed costs, FC, are the costs to the firm of hiring fixed factors of production, the quantities of which do not change with the quantity of output (Ch. 6)

Gamble A certain payment made in return for receiving a risky payout later (Ch. 15)

Game A set of players, a description of payoffs for each player, and a set of rules for player interaction, such that the payoff to a player depends on the choices of the player and on the choices of the other players (Ch. 10)

General equilibrium analysis An economic analysis conducted under the assumption that all markets are in equilibrium. Thus all market values and the effects of all decisions by firms and households have been accounted for in the analysis, and they are reflected in prices and quantities. (Ch. 1)

Giffen good If quantity demanded rises as price of the good rises, it is a Giffen good (Ch. 4)

Gross complement Good 2 is a gross complement for good 1 if the cross-price elasticity of demand for good 2 with respect to the price of good 1 is negative (Ch. 4)

Gross substitute Good 2 is a gross substitute for good 1 if the cross-price elasticity of demand for good 2 with respect to the price of good 1 is positive (Ch. 4)

Income consumption path For fixed prices of goods, this is the collection of bundles that the consumer buys when the consumer's income is set at different levels (Ch. 4)

Income effect The change in quantity purchased that would result from holding prices fixed at their final level and adjusting income enough to move the consumer from initial utility to final utility (Ch. 4)

Income-compensated demand The demand the consumer would have if income were adjusted in response to every price change to hold utility constant (Ch. 4)

Increasing returns to scale A production process exhibits increasing returns to scale if a proportionate increase in all inputs increases output more than proportionately (Ch. 6)

Indifference curve A collection of bundles that are indifferent to one another in the consumer's preferences (Ch. 3)

Inferior good A good whose quantity demanded falls with income (Ch. 4)

Input efficiency An economy satisfies the condition of input efficiency if, given the available supply of productive inputs, it is impossible to reassign inputs to the production of different goods so as to increase the output of one good without lowering the output of another (Ch. 12)

Interest rate The charge for borrowing money or a commodity (alternatively, the payment for loaning money or a commodity), expressed as a percentage of the quantity borrowed (Ch. 16)

Intertemporal budget constraint Constraints on the household's purchases over multiple time periods (Ch. 16)

Isocost curve All input bundles that have the same cost to the firm. If L and K are inputs with prices w and r, respectively, the equation for the isocost curve with cost C_0 is $C_0 = rK + wL$. (Ch. 6)

Isoquant The set of input bundles (K, L) that produce the same level of output, q_0. Mathematically, an isoquant is all combinations of K and L satisfying the equation $q_0 = F(K, L)$, where $F(K, L)$ is the production function. (Ch. 6)

Labor (or work) Physical or mental activity used in the production of goods or services and performed for a monetary reward such as wages or salary (Ch. 5)

Law of diminishing marginal returns As increasing amounts of an input are added to a production process with quantities of other inputs fixed, the marginal product of the factor will eventually fall (Ch. 6)

Leisure Any time not devoted to supply labor services (Ch. 5)

Long run A period of time long enough so that the firm can change all economic variables (Ch. 6)

Marginal cost, MC, is the increase in cost of production resulting from a small increase in output. In mathematical terms, $MC(q) = \Delta C / \Delta q$. (Ch. 6)

Marginal factor cost Let factor L be paid wage w. Then the change in total factor payments wL due to the employment of an additional unit of L is the marginal factor cost, $MFC = \Delta wL / \Delta L$. (Ch. 11)

Marginal product of labor, MP_L, is the increase in output for a small unit of increase in labor, holding constant the input of all other factors. This relationship is written as $MP_L = \Delta q / \Delta L$. (Ch. 6)

Marginal rate of substitution of good x for good y ($MRS_{x,y}$) The maximum amount of good y that a consumer would give up to get an additional unit of good x (Ch. 3)

Marginal rate of technical substitution of labor for capital, $MRTS_{L,K}$, is the rate at which capital must substitute for labor in production to hold output constant (Ch. 6)

Marginal rate of time preference, MRS_{c_1, c_2}, measures the number of units of period 2 that the household requires to compensate for forgoing a unit of period 1 good (Ch. 16)

Marginal rate of transformation The MRT of good x for good y is the rate at which good y must be reduced as output of good x is increased. Mathematically, $MRT_{x,y} = -\Delta y / \Delta x$. (Ch. 12)

Marginal revenue Given the market demand curve, this is the amount that total revenue changes per additional unit of good sold (Ch. 8)

Marginal revenue product of factor L, MRP_L, is the additional revenue earned by the firm from selling the output generated by an additional unit of L (Ch. 11)

Marginal utility of good x (MU_x) The increase in utility per additional small amount of good x consumed (Ch. 3)

Market A group of buyers and sellers linked together by trade in the sale or purchase of a particular commodity or service (Ch. 2)

Market demand curve A curve that shows, for each price, what quantity buyers are willing to buy (Ch. 2)

Market economy An economy characterized by significant voluntary market exchange and well-defined property rights (Ch. 12)

Market equilibrium A price p^* and a quantity q^* such that at price p^* the quantity demanded equals the quantity supplied, both of which equal q^* (Ch. 2)

Market power A seller with market power is any firm with a downward-sloping firm demand curve that has the ability to set price different from marginal cost (Ch. 8)

Market segmentation A means of dividing the market into buyer groups that pay different prices for a given product (Ch. 8)

Microeconomics The study of economics from the point of view of markets and the individual decisions of firms and households (Ch. 1)

Model Any representation of a larger reality that contains its most important features and can be more easily understood and manipulated than the object under study (Ch. 1)

Monopolistic competition A market is characterized by monopolistic competition if a large number of firms sell differentiated but highly substitutable products, and there is free entry and exit (Ch. 9)

Monopoly A market for a good without close substitutes that is supplied by a single seller (Ch. 8)

Multipart pricing Selling a product in units or blocks so that the buyer pays a different (usually higher) price for earlier blocks than for later blocks (Ch. 8)

Nash equilibrium A Nash equilibrium for a game is a choice of strategy by each player such that each player believes it cannot improve its payoff by any other choice, given the strategies of the other players (Ch. 10)

Nonsatiation For any bundle a there is another bundle b that the consumer ranks as strictly preferred to a (Ch. 3)

Normal good A good whose quantity demanded rises with income (Ch. 4)

Normative economics The study of what should be done in an economic situation. Given an objective and a set of constraints, normative economics asks what action is best to get as close to the objective as possible (Ch. 1)

Oligopoly A market situation in which each of a small number of independent, competing producers influences but does not control the market (Ch. 10)

Opportunity cost The opportunity cost of supplying a factor for a particular use is the lost benefits of supplying that factor to the next best alternative (Ch. 5, 6)

Output effect The change in use of a factor at fixed factor prices that results from the firm's change in output quantity (Ch. 11)

Output expansion path Given fixed factor prices, this is the set of least-cost input bundles corresponding to different levels of output (Ch. 6)

Pareto noncomparable Two allocations are Pareto noncomparable if neither is Pareto superior to the other (Ch. 12)

Pareto optimal/efficient An allocation is Pareto optimal or Pareto efficient if it is feasible and if there is no other feasible allocation Pareto superior to it. That is, an allocation is Pareto optimal if it is impossible to raise any household's utility without lowering the utility of another. (Ch. 12)

Pareto superior/inferior dominated Allocation A is Pareto superior to allocation B if at least one household has higher utility in allocation A than in B and no household has a lower utility. If A is Pareto superior to B, then B is also said to be Pareto inferior to A, or to be Pareto dominated by A. (Ch. 12)

Partial equilibrium analysis An economic analysis that looks only at one market, or a subset of markets, treating some or all of the variables generated in the other markets as fixed. It is not required that all market variables and the effects of all decisions by firms and households be accounted for in the analysis and reflected in the prices and quantity. (Ch. 1)

Perfect competition A market characterized by standardized product, pricetaking behavior, contestability, and perfect information (Ch. 7)

Positive economics The study of what is, how the economic system works, and what economic decision makers do. Positive economics studies existing economic conditions and explains them. (Ch. 1)

Pre-emptive threat equilibrium The dominant or pre-empting firm induces other firms to make choices favorable to itself by threatening to take harmful actions if other choices are made (Ch. 10)

Price The amount paid per unit for a good or service (Ch. 1)

Price consumption path The collection of bundles showing what the consumer will buy when the price of a good is set at varying levels, with income and prices of other goods held constant (Ch. 4)

Price theory The study of the workings of the price system, including (1) how prices are determined by the actions of buyers and sellers, and (2) how prices influence the choices of buyers and sellers (Ch. 1)

Probability The percentage of outcomes in which a particular outcome would occur in repeated trials of the identical decision (Ch. 15)

Producer surplus The economic profit of the firm plus fixed costs, or, equivalently, revenue minus variable costs (Ch. 7)

Production function, $F(K,L)$, gives the maximum amount of output, $q = F(K,L)$, that can be produced for each bundle of physical inputs, (K,L) (Ch. 6)

Pure public good A good that is nonrival and nonexcludable. Consumption by one household does not prevent other households from consuming the same unit at no additional cost of provision, and excluding others from consumption is prohibitively costly. (Ch. 14)

Quantity The amount of a good or service measured in specific numerical units such as its weight, its number, its length, its area, or its volume. (Ch. 1)

Reflexivity Given alternative a, it is always true that a is indifferent to itself (Ch. 3)

Risk The possibility of different outcomes occurring, some of which are less desirable than others and may entail loss, when the probability of different outcomes is known (Ch. 15)

Risk premium The amount by which the expected payout from a gamble exceeds the expected payout for a riskless asset or a fair gamble that costs the same (Ch. 15)

Sector Any firm or group of firms producing two or more goods, plus the fixed quantity of inputs used by those firms (Ch. 12)

Sector production-allocation efficiency An economy satisfies the conditions for sector production-allocation efficiency if, given the use of factor inputs within any two sectors, it is impossible through reassignment of sectoral output levels to increase the economy's output of one good without lowering the output of another (Ch. 12)

Security Any asset providing its owner with a claim to risky payments that vary by the state of nature (Ch. 15)

Short run A time period in which one or more economic variables are fixed because there is no way to adjust them in the available time (Ch. 6)

Shutdown point The minimum point of the firm's average variable cost curve is called the shutdown point, because at prices lower than minimum average variable cost, the firm is better off shutting down operations (producing no output) than producing positive output (Ch. 7)

Stable market equilibrium A market equilibrium is stable if, under the laws of motion that govern the market when it is out of equilibrium, the market returns to equilibrium when perturbed to a nearby position out of equilibrium (Ch. 2)

Stackelberg leader-follower competition One firm (the leader) sets its output before other firms (the followers) set their output. Follower firms treat the output of other firms as constant in deciding what quantity to produce to maximize profit. (Ch. 10)

Standard deviation Standard deviation of a set of random numbers is the square root of their variance (Ch. 15)

Strategic choice In a game, this influences the choice of the other player or players in a direction that is favorable to oneself (Ch. 10)

Strong axiom of revealed preference Given different bundles a and b, if bundle a is directly or indirectly revealed to be preferred to bundle b, then bundle b can never be directly or indirectly revealed to be preferred to bundle a (Ch. 3)

Substitutes in production Two factors are substitutes in production if the marginal product of one factor falls when employment of the other increases (Ch. 11)

Substitution effect The change in quantity purchased due to a price change when the consumer's utility is fixed at its initial level by an adjustment in income (Ch. 4)

Sunk costs Costs that can not be altered or avoided by current or future decisions of the firm. As such, they are irrelevant to the firm's decision making. (Ch. 6)

Superior good If the share of the consumer's budget spent on the good rises as income rises, the good is superior (Ch. 4)

Supply curve A curve that shows for each price, what quantity suppliers are willing to sell (Ch. 2)

Tangency Tangency between two noncrossing curves occurs where the slope of the first curve at a point is identical to the slope of the second curve at the same point (Ch. 3)

The First Fundamental Theorem of Welfare Economics If a set of prices P, a production plan Y, and an allocation X represent a competitive equilibrium, then allocation X is Pareto optimal (Ch. 13)

The Second Fundamental Theorem of Welfare Economics If Y is the feasible production plan corresponding to a Pareto optimal allocation X, then there is an assignment of property rights and a set of prices P such that P, X, and Y form a competitive equilibrium (Ch. 13)

Time endowment The total number of hours that the household has available to allocate between work and leisure (Ch. 5)

Total product of labor The total output obtained from employing L units of labor, holding constant the input of all other factors (Ch. 6)

Transitivity Given three alternatives, a, b, and c, if the consumer strictly prefers a to b and b to c, then the consumer also strictly prefers a to c. Likewise, if the consumer is indifferent between a and b, and between b and c, then the consumer is indifferent between a and c (Ch. 3)

Two-part tariff A pricing arrangement whereby buyers pay both an entrance fee and usage prices thereafter (Ch. 8)

Utility function A function that assigns a number to each consumption bundle so that if bundle a is preferred to bundle b, the number for a will then be greater than the number for b (Ch. 3)

Value The numerical representation of total worth. (Ch. 1)

Value of marginal product For factor L, this is price times marginal product: $VMP_L = pMP_L$ (Ch. 11)

Variable costs VC, are the costs to the firm of hiring variable factors of production, the quantities of which change with the quantity of output. The variable costs corresponding to a particular quantity of output are written as $VC(q)$. (Ch. 6)

Variance The variance of a set of random numbers is computed by squaring their deviations from the expected value, multiplying each by the probability and summing (Ch. 15)

Index

▼